The Encyclopedia of
Careers and Vocational Guidance

EIGHTH EDITION

The Encyclopedia of Careers and Vocational Guidance

WILLIAM E. HOPKE

Editor-in-Chief

VOLUME 4

Technicians' Careers

J.G. FERGUSON PUBLISHING COMPANY

Chicago, Illinois

Library of Congress Cataloging-in-Publication Data

The Encyclopedia of careers and vocational guidance/ William E. Hopke, editor-in-chief. 8th ed.
　　p. cm.
　　Contents: v.1 Industry profiles — v.2. Professional careers — v.3. General and special careers —v.4. Technicians' careers.
Includes indexes.
　　ISBN 0-89434-117-0 (set). —ISBN 0-89434-113-8 (v.1). —ISBN 0-89434-114-6 (v.2). —ISBN 0-89434-115-4 (V.3).
— ISBN 0-89434-116-2 (v.4)
　　1. Vocational guidance—Handbooks, manuals, etc. 2. Occupations—Handbooks, manuals, etc. I. Hopke, William E.
HF5381.E52 1990
331.7'02—dc20

　　　　　　　　　　　　　　　　　　　　　　　　　　　　　　　　　　90-3743
　　　　　　　　　　　　　　　　　　　　　　　　　　　　　　　　　　CIP

ISBN 0-89434-117-0 (set)
　　　0-89434-113-8 (volume 1)
　　　0-89434-114-6 (volume 2)
　　　0-89434-115-4 (volume 3)
　　　0-89434-116-2 (volume 4)

Copyright © 1990, 1987, 1984, 1981, 1975, 1972, 1967, by J.G. Ferguson Publishing Company

Printed in the United States of America
N-8

Editorial Staff

Editorial Director: C.J. Summerfield

Assistant Editor: Amy I. Brown

Contributing Editors: Susan Ashby, John Morse, Nancy Parsegian, Mark Toch, James Unland

Writers: Pamela Dell, Lillian Flowers, Jim Garner, Phyllis Miller, Jeanne Rattenbury, Fran Sherman

Photo Editor: Carol Parden

Indexer: Carol Nielson

Designer: Shawn M. Biner, Biner Design

Copyeditors and Proofreaders: Wordsmiths

Production Manager: Tom Myles

Contents

Volume 4: Technicians' Careers

KEY TO OCCUPATIONAL CATEGORIES

 Industry Profiles. This represents the articles that outline descriptions of industries in Volume 1.

 Professional, Administrative, and Managerial Occupations. Covering careers that involve extensive academic training or practical training, these occupations include many of the jobs that require undergraduate or graduate school education. Volume 2

 Clerical Occupations. Clerical occupations are those involved with handling the records, communications, and general office duties required in every business. Volume 3

 Sales Occupations. This section includes sales careers for goods, services, and property, and careers for sales-related business. Volume 3

 Service Occupations. Careers in service comprise occupations that assist people in various aspects of life, from protection by law enforcement to physical care. Volume 3

 Agriculture, Forestry, and Conservation Occupations. Encompassing the occupations that work with various elements of nature, this category includes skilled and technicians' work related to farm production, mining, animal care, and wildlife services. Volume 3 and 4

 Processing Occupations. These are occupations that involve the mixing, treating, and recomposition of materials, chemicals, and products, normally through the use of machinery or tools. Volume 3

 Machine Trades Occupations. Careers in machine trades are those that work with machine assembly, maintenance, and repair. They work with metals, plastics, wood, paper, and stone in construction and repair. Volume 3

 Bench Work Occupations. With an emphasis on hand tools and dexterity skills, bench workers make and repair products that require manual deftness, such as jewelry or optical equipment. Volume 3

Structural Work Occupations. This category details the occupations involved in construction and repair of all large structures from bridges to homes. Volume 3

 Emerging Technician Occupations. Falling mainly into the fields of science and technology, these technicians occupations are either not yet catalogued into one of the sections following or will not be catalogued into an existing field. Volume 4

 Engineering and Science Technician Occupations. These technicians work with scientists and engineers as part of a team trained in the technical aspects of the work performed. Volume 4

 Broadcast, Media, and Arts Technicians Occupations. The technicians who operate, maintain, and repair the equipment involved in broadcasting and the arts are trained to run electronic, electrical, and mechanical equipment. Volume 4

 Medical and Health Technician Occupations. Responsible for the technical equipment used in medical fields, these technicians run the sophisticated machinery used by medical specialists. Volume 4

 Miscellaneous Occupations. In this section are the occupations that require skilled or semi-skilled levels of training. This includes a diverse range of job categories, including graphics arts, transportation and technicians in information services as well as other fields. Volume 3 and 4

Emerging Technician Occupations

The past three decades have been a period of remarkable growth and discovery in science and technology. Travel in space; the development of computers, lasers, and robots; the introduction of commercial nuclear energy; and the spectacular growth in medical technology—all of these features of the world of today have come into existence in the past few decades. These fields are largely built around "high technology," and they are characterized by new discoveries, increasing automation and computerization in the workplace, and the development of highly specialized tasks that require special training. These factors, combined with the increasing need to use the time scientists, engineers, and other professionals more efficiently, have led to the creation of new jobs for technicians, such as those described in this section. These are recognized, well-established job categories, but they are in fast-evolving fields, and the job settings and activities of these technicians are subject to constant change brought on by major advances in materials and methods.

The technicians described in this section are mostly involved with work relating to engineering and science technology, and they mostly perform duties similar to those of the technicians described in the section on Engineering and Science Technician Occupations in this volume. Most often they work as inspectors, repairers, production supervisors, or in other positions in which they assist engineers and scientists. In many cases, they act as a communications link between the scientists and engineers who design projects and the skilled workers who perform most of the physical tasks necessary to the projects. Other technicians described in this section work in areas not traditionally associated with the employment of technicians. They may work as deep water divers, as assistants to computer systems analysts, or as nuclear reactor operators. For the most part, these other technicians perform specialized tasks that require care, attention to detail, often manual dexterity or mechanical aptitude, and an overall familiarity with the principles and concepts that are most important in the field in which they are working. This kind of knowledge is valuable to all of the technicians described in this section, for any one of them may be called upon to solve unexpected problems, evaluate unfamiliar situations, or develop new methods or procedures. As is true of most technicians described throughout this volume, however, most of the work of technicians described in this section consists of mastering a set of procedures and being able to repeat them accurately, consistently, and reliably.

Each of the technician careers described in this section has its own separate and distinct history, and no one overall statement can describe the process by which these emerging careers have come into existence. There have been instead a number of factors contributing to the emergence of the technicians described in this section, and the factors that have played an important role in one career may not have played so important a role in the history of another.

One of the most obvious and most common factors in the emergence of a new career is the emergence of a new industry. Several kinds of technicians described in this section have jobs related to the nuclear-power industry or to microelectronics. These are good examples of new career opportunities emerging for technicians because of the growth of a new industry.

Another factor that frequently leads to the emergence of a new technician career is increasing use of mechanization or instrumentation within an industry. Some of the career areas where this factor seems to be at work include biomedical equipment, diving, and telecommunications. This is not to say that mechanization and instrumentation have not always been a part of these fields, or that technically trained workers have not long participated in these industries in important ways. Rather, the reliance on and the sophistication of the equipment used in these and other fields have increased, and that increased utilization of sophisticated and complex equipment has led to a greater need for specially trained personnel to operate or oversee the operation of this equipment.

Quite often it is the recognition of this need for special training for plant, research, or operations staff members, particularly if that training is to be in an academic institution, that leads industry managers to create a job category for technicians. In some cases, a new job category means only that a worker's job title is changed; in other cases, it may involve retraining and increased responsibilities for the workers. In all cases, creation of a new job category for technicians is a recognition that the industry or activity requires special skills and special training for its technical staff.

Other factors that can lead to new jobs for technicians include stepped-up government involvement in an area, increased pressures to control costs, and heightened public demand for a service. Technicians working in the area of pollution control are often employed because governmental regulatory involvement relating to industrial pollution has increased to the point that industrial engineers can no longer do the job unassisted.

Cost is clearly a factor here. There are some jobs related to computer-aided design and computer-aided manufacturing (CAD/CAM), for example, that clearly do not require the expertise of a professional engineer. By hiring CAD/CAM technicians, the productivity of the engineer is increased, and costs involved in hiring additional engineers are kept down.

This same concern for costs and productivity has played a part in the development of careers for aeronautical technicians, plastics technicians, and robotics technicians. Of the technicians described in this section, the best example of a technician whose job developed as a response to heightened public demand for a service is the energy conservation technician.

Clearly, a broad spectrum of industries and activities can exhibit the changes and concerns that lead to the development of new technical careers. So broad is this spectrum that it is difficult to characterize the common denominator among the careers described in this section, and what it is that sets them apart from the technical careers described in other sections of this volume.

One of the ways to see what ties the technicians in this section together is to realize that almost all of the technicians in this section are performing work that not too many years ago only a scientist, engineer, or other professionally trained specialist would have understood.

Nuclear-plant operations, setting up and programming computers, maintaining and repairing robotic devices, conducting research into new kinds of plastics and plastic products—all of these activities were at one point almost exclusively conducted by engineers and scientists, by technicians in other closely related fields, and by some other skilled and semi-skilled workers.

In their infancy, each of these activities, and others described in this section, required specialists who could respond to a wide variety of circumstances, many wholly unforeseen, and who could, if needed, devise on-the-spot procedures to meet these circumstances. As the industries have matured, more knowledge and experience about their activities have been collected, and some of the activities and procedures have become sufficiently routine that technicians have been able to take over more of the tasks previously handled by professionals.

In most of the industries described in this section, this transfer of responsibilities was accompanied by a recognition that technicians involved in these areas need to be trained in the special knowledge related to the particular activity. At one point the computer industry relied on electromechanical technicians, the plastics industry on chemical engineering technicians, and the microelectronics industry on generalist electronics technicians; however, each of these industries now needs technicians with more specialized training and skills.

These specialized skills and training prepare technicians to perform different kinds of tasks, depending on the industry employing them. They may be involved in some kind of plant operation, which often means monitoring machines, calibrating instruments, and carrying out specified maintenance, repair, or emergency procedures at the direction of plant supervisors. Other technicians, sometimes referred to as service technicians, may specialize in installation, repair, and maintenance activities. They often perform the tasks that require a specialization in installation, repair, and maintenance that operations technicians lack.

Both operations and service technicians work under the supervision of engineers or other professionals, but their actual contact with the engineer may be limited. Other kinds of technicians described in this section may work much more closely with the professionals in their industry. This is especially true for technicians involved in research or new product development. However, it is also true that scientists, engineers, and other industry professionals require skilled and trained assistants to work directly with them in all kinds of tasks, including report writing, inventory control, project monitoring, mathematical calculations, and employee supervision.

Some technicians can expect to work quite independently. For example, energy conservation technicians and computer-service technicians perform tasks designed by engineers for technicians to carry out without close supervision. There are similar opportunities for other technicians described in this section.

In any of these fields, technicians must have specific knowledge and skills that can be gained only through a combination of classroom instruction and practical experience. In addition, personal characteristics that cannot be readily learned, such as strength, good eyesight, an aptitude for spatial visualization, or tolerance for extended isolation, may be necessary.

In general, the basic educational requirement for these careers is completion of a two-year post–high-school training program. Community and junior colleges, technical institutes, universities, and other schools may provide such training, which normally leads to an associate degree. In some fields, technicians may learn on the job through programs conducted by their employers. This approach, however, is usually less desirable if preparation in an academic setting is available.

Sometimes training for an emerging career field is best obtained by enrolling in a program with a more broadly defined curriculum. For example, prospective microelectronics technicians may get training in an electronics technology program, and robotics technicians may start off training as mechanical technicians.

A high-school diploma is almost always required for entrance into training programs. Because most of the careers described in this section are in engineering and science fields, prospective technicians should select as many science and mathematics courses as possible in high school, in addition to whatever shop, drafting, computer, mechanics, and other practical courses are available and appropriate, depending on their field of interest. English and other subjects that develop written and oral communications skills should also be taken in high school. In most emerging career fields, technicians deal regularly with a variety of other workers, including highly trained professionals, and they must be able to communicate easily and effectively. In many positions technicians are called on to write reports or make presentations to groups as part of the job.

College-level training programs in a given field vary somewhat from school to school. Many include both general studies courses, such as history, government, and English, and technical material in an increasingly sophisticated sequence of courses. This sequence often includes a phase in which students combine supervised on-the-job experience with classroom work.

In some fields, such as those related to nuclear energy, graduates who are hired as new employees must undergo an initial period of training and orientation to the company's operations and the procedures in their work environment. Some technicians can expect to continue their education throughout their working lives. Occasional courses may be needed to keep them up to date on technological changes affecting their job, and in some fields, continuing education is the key to advancement.

Some industries with emerging technical careers are fairly closely regulated by law. Licensure, usually at the state level, is required for anyone who engages in specified activities. For some positions, employers may prefer technicians licensed in a related area.

In some technical fields, various kinds of certification are available. Although not usually required for employment, certification is generally a recognized and desirable acknowledgment of competence that can be obtained by meeting certain requirements for education and experience that the industry has established for itself. In some fields certification is needed for advancement into jobs above an entry level. Where certification is currently an option, the trend is generally toward establishing it as part of the norm. Some emerging fields with no certification available now will probably develop certification standards in future years. Other special requirements apply in a few fields, such as security clearance or union membership.

Students in high school can begin to gauge their aptitudes and abilities by selecting courses that permit them to learn about their area of interest. Outside the classroom they may be able to develop their interests through hobbies and extracurricular activities, or they may be able to get part-time or summer employment that offers a closer look at the career field. Direct experience, however, is often not feasible. The best approach in such instances may be to visit a school that provides technical training in the area of interest, and to make an effort to talk to faculty, students, and admissions people there. Alternatively, it may be possible, especially with the help of high-school teachers or guidance counseling staff, to invite someone working in the field to speak to a science club meeting or at a career day.

Sometimes a visit to a workplace can be arranged so that students can see and perhaps talk to technicians on the job. Librarians in school and public libraries can help students to fill in details on many careers by steering them to books about careers, information pamphlets and other materials produced by industry, popular science magazines, professional journals, and other print resources.

In some fields, notably those related to nuclear energy, many technicians have first become interested in their subject through a technical training program they encountered while serving in the armed forces. This kind of experience can be an excellent introduction, but usually it needs to be followed up with further college-level training to assure good employment opportunities.

Many students in technical training programs can obtain their first employment before graduation and start work soon after. In some industries, particularly where there are fewer qualified applicants than positions, recruiters routinely visit schools to interview students in their final year. Students in programs that include a period of cooperative or work-study education may be hired on a full-time basis if their record during training is satisfactory. Sometimes employers provide financial assistance in meeting the costs of education to students who agree to work for them after graduation.

In general, the school's placement office is probably the best single source of information on job openings. Faculty members, too, may be able to suggest other possibilities because they may be in touch, formally or informally, with potential employers in the area. Specialty employment agencies, mostly located in cities, can also be helpful in placing technical workers. Many new graduates find it necessary or desirable to exploit the full range of conventional job-hunting techniques, including responding to advertisements in newspapers and professional magazines, registering with private and public employment agencies, and inquiring directly at firms that are likely to hire technicians.

In some fields, high-school graduates with no formal preparation as technicians may be able to enter a career as unskilled trainees. Working up from such a position is normally a slow and uncertain method, and, in the long run, it usually leads to lower earnings than those received by graduates of two-year degree programs.

With experience and increased expertise, many technicians can expect a series of promotions, gaining added responsibilities and correspondingly higher pay. Possible avenues of advancement may include simply taking on more complicated tasks of the same essential nature, or moving into supervisory, research and design, sales, or customer service positions, depending on the technical field and the employer. Some technicians eventually join consulting firms or organize their own independent consulting businesses after they have become familiar with their field as a whole and with the local market for their particular knowledge and skills.

In some industries, patterns of advancement seem to exist but are not well established. In general, technicians who pursue additional education and professional credentials are the ones who are most likely to advance and to respond well to the continuing developments that alter the technological climate of their jobs.

In some emerging career fields, it is already clear that opportunities for growth are limited for technicians who do not work toward obtaining a bachelor's degree. By building on their experience and prior academic training, technicians may be able to reach this goal in two years or less of full-time study, or in a longer period of part-time study while simultaneously maintaining full-time employment.

In the foreseeable future, the earnings of technicians in most of these fields will probably be competitive with, if not better than, the earnings of technicians in other engineering and science fields. As long as there is a relative shortage of qualified personnel, the pay can be expected to be good.

Salary levels vary widely according to the industry, employer, job conditions, geographical location, the individual's training and experience, and other factors. Beginning salaries for graduates of two-year programs range from around $14,000 to $27,000 and more. Potential top salaries for senior technicians are mostly in the $30,000 to $40,000 range, with some lower and many quite a bit higher.

In addition to regular salary, many of these technician jobs provide attractive fringe benefits, such as health and life insurance programs, paid vacations and holidays, and tuition and time off for job-related continuing education.

The demand for competent technicians in most of these career fields, and thus their employment outlook, will be good to excellent through the year 2000. Future directions depend on many interacting factors, among them the overall state of the economy, public tastes and opinions, and the invention of new techniques and equipment. Not only can the total employment in an industry be affected, but also the nature of the jobs, including possible paths of advancement for technicians. In some fields changes may bring an abundance of interesting opportunities in middle-level positions, such as those filled by technicians; in others, such as some areas of the computer field, the greatest growth may occur instead in either professional positions requiring much more education or in positions requiring little if any specialized training.

Conditions of work, of course, vary widely for these occupations. Some technicians work regular hours and spend most of their time in modern, clean, pleasant, office environments. Others may contend with shift work and long hours, dirt, grease, noise, temperature extremes, hazards, physical and psychological stress, living and working in cramped or isolated quarters, traveling to remote locations, and other unpleasant or irregular circumstances. Whenever possible, most employers find it in their own best interests to keep technical workers satisfied with their working conditions. As a rule, industry is very concerned with ensuring worker safety, providing instruction in safety procedures, protective equipment, and clothing, and instituting routine precautionary measures. In some of the fields described in this section, state and federal laws regulate conditions at the job site to ensure the safety of workers.

Most technicians work as part of a team, although they often have individual assignments. Therefore they must have a cooperative attitude and the ability to get along with a variety of coworkers. They must be good at following instructions systematically and accurately, yet also be resourceful problem-solvers who can confidently exercise sound independent judgment. Most of the technician careers in this section are undergoing changes, some of them substantial and rapid. Even more than technicians in established occupational areas, people employed in these emerging careers need to be professionally alert and adaptable in order to cope effectively with the evolving technology of their fields. In return they have a chance to receive significant rewards, which may include unique and varied experiences for the adventuresome, a sense of pioneering in efforts to find innovative ways of doing things, and, not least, exceptionally good pay.

Aeronautical and aerospace technicians

Definition

Aeronautical and aerospace technicians work with engineers and scientists in the design, construction, testing, operation, and maintenance of all kinds of aircraft and spacecraft, including propulsion systems, control systems, and basic structures. Many aeronautical technicians assist engineers in preparing drawings, diagrams, blueprints, and scale models of such equipment. They collect information, make computations, and perform laboratory tests. Their work may include estimating weight factors and centers of gravity, evaluating stress factors, and working on various projects involving aerodynamics, structural design, flight-test evaluation, or propulsion problems. Other aeronautical technicians are involved in the estimating of the cost of materials and labor required to manufacture the product, in serving as manufacturers' field service technicians, and in technical writing.

There are no generally accepted definitions of the terms "aeronautical technology" and "aerospace technology," and many employers use the terms interchangeably. This lack of a clear distinction is also found in education, so that many schools and institutes offer courses with similar content in aeronautical, aviation, or aerospace technology. In general, when people refer to the aerospace industry, they are referring to manufacturers of all kinds of flying vehicles, from piston and jet-powered aircraft that fly in the atmosphere to rockets, missiles, satellites, probes, and all kinds of manned and unmanned spacecraft that operate outside the earth's atmosphere. Within the aerospace industry, the term "aeronautics" is often used to refer specifically to mechanical flight in the atmosphere and especially to the design and manufacture of commercial passenger and freight aircraft, private planes, and helicopters.

On the other hand, many other publications refer to jobs connected to the engineering and developmental aspects of all kinds of flying vehicles as aeronautical technology. And in referring to technicians employed in this area these publications uses the term "aeronautical technician." Some publications also refer to these technicians as "aircraft technicians." In general, this article refers to aeronautical technicians; however, the term "aeronautical and

Aeronautical and aerospace technicians
Emerging Technician Occupations

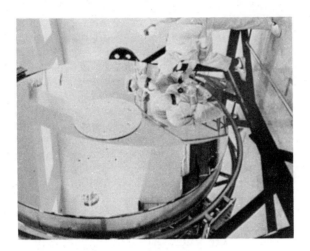

Aerospace technicians at NASA prepare a reflective device before sending it into space. They must maintain a sterile environment by covering nearly all exposed parts of their bodies.

aerospace technicians" is used periodically to remind readers that both terms are current and accurate.

History

Both aeronautical engineering and the aerospace industry had their births in the early years of the twentieth century. The very earliest powered heavier-than-air aircraft, such as the first one flown by Wilbur and Orville Wright in 1903, were crudely constructed and often the result of costly and dangerous trial-and-error experimentation.

As governments and industries came to take an interest in the possible applications of this new invention, however, increased sophistication came both to our knowledge of aircraft and to the aircraft industry. By 1908, for instance, the Wright brothers had received their first government military contract, and by 1909, the industry had expanded to include additional airplane producers, such as Glenn Curtiss in the United States and several others in France.

Aeronautical engineering and the aerospace industry have been radically transformed since those early days, mostly because of the demands of two world wars and the tremendous increases in scientific knowledge that have taken place during this century. The past three or four decades especially have brought dramatic developments: the jet engine, rocket propulsion, supersonic flight, and manned voyages outside the earth's atmosphere.

During these same recent decades, aeronautical engineers found themselves taking on

bigger and bigger projects and, hence, more and more in need of trained and knowledgeable assistants to help them in their endeavors. Over the years, these assistants have been known variously as engineering aides, engineering associates, and, most recently, as aeronautical technicians. Their task today is to take on assignments that require technical skills but do not necessarily require the scientist's or engineer's special training and education.

To meet this assignment (and unlike the aides and associates of some decades ago who usually trained on the job, often using only one type or piece of equipment), today's technicians are educated in technical institutes and junior colleges where they are taught the fundamentals of science, technology, and mathematics and how to apply these to scientific problems.

In light of the continuing shortage of professionally trained engineers and scientists, the work of aeronautical technicians has become especially crucial, as their work allows engineers and scientists to concentrate their efforts on problems and projects that only they can handle.

Nature of the work

Aeronautical and aerospace technicians are principally employed by government agencies, commercial airlines, educational institutions, and aerospace manufacturing companies. The majority of those employed by manufacturing companies are engaged in research, development, and design activities; the remainder work in production, installation and maintenance, sales engineering, technical writing and illustrating, and in other related fields. Those employed by government and educational institutions are normally assigned research and specific problem-solving tasks. Airlines employ technicians to supervise maintenance operations and the development of procedures for new equipment.

In all of these settings, aeronautical technicians work side by side with engineers and scientists in all major phases of the design, production, and operational aspects of aircraft and spacecraft technology. Typical jobs of the aeronautical technician include collecting and recording data, operating test equipment such as wind tunnels and flight simulators, devising tests to ensure quality control, modifying mathematical procedures to fit specific problems, laying out experimental circuits to test scientific theories, and evaluating experimental data for practical applications.

The following paragraphs describe jobs held by aeronautical technicians. Some of the job titles listed below are used in other industries as well, and fuller descriptions of the work associated with these titles are provided elsewhere in this volume.

Aerospace physiological technicians operate devices for training pilots and astronauts. These devices include pressure suits, pressure chambers, and ejection seats that simulate flying conditions. They also operate other kinds of flight training equipment, such as tow reels, radio equipment, and meteorological devices. They interview trainees to find out about their medical histories and to detect evidence of conditions that would disqualify pilots or astronauts from further training.

Aircraft launch and recovery technicians work on aircraft carriers. They operate, adjust, and repair launching and recovery equipment, such as catapults, barricades, and arresting nets. They disassemble the launch and recovery equipment, replace defective parts, and keep track of all maintenance activities.

Avionics technicians repair, test, install, and maintain radar and radio equipment aboard aircraft and spacecraft.

Computer technicians assist mathematicians and subject specialists in checking and refining computations and systems, such as those required for predicting and determining orbits of spacecraft.

Drafting and design technicians convert the aeronautical engineer's specifications and rough sketches of aeronautical and aerospace equipment, such as electrical and mechanical devices, into accurate drawings that are used by skilled craft workers in making parts for aircraft and spacecraft.

Electronics technicians assist engineers in the design, development, and modification of electronic and electromechanical systems. They assist in the calibration and operation of radar and photographic equipment, as well as in operating, installing, troubleshooting, and repairing electronic testing equipment.

Engineering technicians assist with review and analysis of post-flight data, structural failure, and other factors that cause failure in flight vehicles.

Industrial engineering technicians assist engineers in preparing layouts of machinery and equipment, work-flow plans, time-and-motion studies, and statistical studies and analyses of production costs to produce the most efficient use of personnel, materials, and machines.

Instrumentation technicians test, install, and maintain electronic, hydraulic, pneumatic, and optical instruments used in various aircraft systems and components, in manufacturing, and in research and development. One important responsibility of instrumentation technicians is the maintenance of the research instruments they are assigned to. As a part of this maintenance, they test the instruments, take readings and calibration curves, and calculate correction factors for the instruments.

Liaison technicians check on the production of aircraft and spacecraft as they are being built for conformance to specifications, keeping engineers informed as the manufacturing progresses and investigating any engineering production problems that arise.

Mathematical technicians assist mathematicians, engineers, and scientists by performing computations involving the use of advanced mathematics.

Mechanical technicians use metalworking machines to assist in the manufacture of one-of-a-kind parts. They also assist in rocket-fin alignment, payload mating, weight and center-of-gravity measurements, and launch-tower erection.

Metallurgical technicians work with metallurgists in processing and converting metals into finished products. They test metals and alloys to determine their physical properties and develop new ways of treating and using metals and alloys.

Target aircraft technicians repair and maintain pilotless target aircraft. They assemble, repair, or replace aircraft parts, such as cowlings, wings, and propeller assemblies, and they test aircraft engine operation.

Technical illustrators draw accurate and clear illustrations to assist in aircraft, spacecraft, and avionics maintenance and for operating manuals used by aviation mechanics, electronics technicians, flight crews, and flight instructors.

Technical sales or field representatives advise customers on installation and maintenance problems and serve as the link between the manufacturer and the customer.

Technical writers write about technical or scientific matter in various forms, including technical manuals, instruction manuals, bulletins, catalogs, and publicity releases. They also arrange for the preparation of tables, charts, illustrations, and other artwork for publication.

Tool designers develop new tools and redesign tools and devices already in use for efficient mass production.

Requirements

Aeronautical and aerospace technicians must have the ability to learn basic engineering skills. They should like and be proficient with mathematics and the physical sciences and be able to visualize size, form, and function. In addition, they should have good manipulative skills that will allow them to make, maintain, or assemble items, large or small.

Post–high-school education is required to become an aeronautical technician; therefore, students should determine the precise admissions requirements of the institutions they plan to attend as early as possible in their high-school years. A strong science and mathematics background is essential. High-school courses that will prove useful include the following: algebra through quadratics, plane and solid geometry, trigonometry, physics, chemistry, social studies, economics, history, laboratory procedures, blueprint reading, drafting, and industrial and machine shop practice. English, speech, and courses in the preparation of test reports and technical writing should also be part of a student's curriculum, as these courses are extremely helpful in developing the ability to communicate facts and ideas.

Many students will not recognize an interest in this field early enough to obtain all these courses. This should not keep them from entering this field. Many two-year post–high-school programs offer a pretechnical curriculum to fill in the missing subjects.

Specialized preparation for aeronautical technicians may be obtained in two or three years from colleges or universities, junior or community colleges, technical institutes, vocational-technical schools, through industry on-the-job training, or in work-study programs pursued while the student is on active duty with the armed forces. High-school graduation is normally a prerequisite for enrollment in any of these programs. Graduates from a junior or community college may earn an associate in engineering or associate in science degree. In selecting a school to attend, an individual should check the listings of accrediting or approval agencies, such as the Accreditation Board for Engineering Technology, the National Council of Technical Schools, and the regional accrediting associations for engineering colleges.

In general, post–high-school programs focus on strengthening the student's background in science and mathematics. Beyond that, the student's curriculum should be an interdisciplinary one, rather than one that specializes in a narrow field. Basic physics, nuclear theory, chemistry, mechanics, and computers, including data-processing equipment and procedures—all are basic to the work of the aeronautical scientist and engineer, and hence to the aeronautical technician, and should be part of a balanced program.

Special requirements

Only a small number of aeronautical technicians need to be licensed or certified; however, certificates to recognize and enhance the status of qualified engineering technicians are issued by professional organizations.

Those working with nuclear-powered engines or radioactive sources for testing usually need certification. Licensing may be required for those working on aircraft in some test programs. Some positions related to safety require certification.

Security clearances are required in those agencies carrying on work related to national defense.

Aeronautical technicians may become affiliated with professional groups. They may or may not belong to unions. If they do, requirements relating to union membership are usually determined by existing agreements between employers and unions.

Opportunities for experience and exploration

Visits to aeronautical or aerospace research or manufacturing facilities are one of the best ways to learn more about this field. The research and manufacturing facilities connected with the aerospace industry are so many and so diverse that there is sure to be some facility in nearly every area. One of the best ways to learn of such facilities is through local newspaper, radio, or television news reports, which often present special features about such facilities, especially at times such as the launching of an important spacecraft, the development of new or redesigned artificial satellites, or the introduction of a new aircraft.

Finding part-time or summer employment at such a facility is, of course, one of the best ways of gaining experience or learning more about the field.

Students should not overlook the educational aspects of a visit to local museums of science and technology, or even aircraft museums or displays, if available. Some Air Force bases or Naval Air Stations also offer tours to groups of interested students. The tours may be arranged by teachers or vocational counselors.

In addition, students should keep in mind that shop courses and science courses with lab sections not only train students for future work but also give them an opportunity to get a feel for the work they may do in the future.

Methods of entering

The best method of obtaining an aeronautical or aerospace technician's job is through the placement service of the institution one attends or has attended. Jobs may also be obtained through state employment offices, newspaper advertisements, and application for government employment. Another method is through application and acceptance by industry for work-study programs offered by many aircraft companies.

Advancement

Aeronautical and aerospace technicians learn on the job. As they gain experience in the specialized areas they have selected, their employers turn more to them as experts who can solve problems, create new techniques, devise new designs, or develop practice from theory.

Most advancement involves the taking on of additional responsibilities. For example, with experience, a technician may take on supervisory responsibilities, such as being in charge of several trainees, assistant technicians, or other technicians. Such a technician may also be assigned independent responsibility—especially on some tasks usually assigned to an engineer. Technicians who have a good working knowledge of the equipment produced by the company and who have good personalities may become company sales or technical representatives. With additional formal education, a technician may become an aeronautical or aerospace engineer.

Employment outlook

Employment levels in the aerospace industry are influenced by a number of factors: levels of defense spending, appropriations for space programs, the health of commercial airlines, and the general level of economic activity in the country. It is unlikely that all of these factors will be constantly favorable through the coming decade; however, there is reason to expect at least some growth in each of these areas through most of the 1990s.

The diversity of products created by the aerospace industry and the markets served by it contribute to its economic stability. The same company that makes components for airlines may also make parts for jet fighters or communications satellites. For the well-trained technician who is ready and willing to learn new skills, there should continue to be excellent employment opportunities in this field.

Earnings

Most aeronautical technicians earn between $20,000 and $30,000 a year, and the average is around $27,000 a year. The actual salary a person receives will depend on his or her technical specialty, educational preparation, work experience, ability, and geographical location. Technicians at the beginning of their careers usually receive starting salaries that range from $15,000 to $18,000 a year. Some senior technicians earn salaries of $37,000 a year or more.

Benefits depend on employers, but they will usually include paid vacations and holidays, sick pay, insurance, and a retirement plan.

Nearly all companies offer an educational expense refund of from one-half to full cost of tuition for related schooling. Some companies have cooperative programs with local schools in which classroom training is combined with practical experience, and student-employees are paid while they improve their skills.

Conditions of work

The aerospace industry with its strong emphasis on quality and safety is a very safe place to work. Special procedures and equipment make otherwise hazardous jobs extremely safe. The range of work covered means that the technicians can work in small teams in specialized research laboratories or in test areas that are large and "hospital" clean. Aerospace technicians are at the launch pad, involved in fueling and checkout procedures, and back in the blockhouse sitting at an electronic console. They may work in large test facilities or work in specialized shops, designing and fabricating specialized equipment. They travel to test sites or tracking stations to construct facilities or troubleshoot systems. The working conditions vary with the assignment, but the work climate is always challenging and coworkers are well-trained, competent people.

Aeronautical technicians may perform inside activities involving confined detail work, or they may work outside, or their jobs may entail a combination of inside and outside work.

Social and psychological factors

Aeronautical and aerospace technicians work in many situations, alone, in small teams, or in large groups. Commonly, technicians participate in team projects—coordinated efforts of scientists, engineers, and technicians working on specific assignments. They concentrate on the practical aspects of the project and must get along well with and interact cooperatively with the scientists who are responsible for the theoretical aspects of the project.

Aeronautical technicians must be capable of performing under the stress of time limitations, of having to meet exacting requirements and rigid specifications, and of dealing with potentially hazardous situations. To adjust to the rapidly changing technology, they must have the willingness and flexibility to acquire new knowledge and new techniques. In addition, technicians need persistence and tenacity, especially when engaged in experimental and research tasks. They must be responsible, reliable, and willing to accept greater responsibility.

Aeronautical technology is a field of endeavor that is never far from the public's attention, and aeronautical technicians have the satisfaction of knowing that they are seen by their community as being engaged in vital and fascinating work.

GOE: 05.01.01; SIC: 372, 376; SOC: 3719

◇ **SOURCES OF ADDITIONAL INFORMATION**

Aerospace Education Association
1810 Michael Faraday Drive, Suite 101
Reston, VA 22090

Students for the Exploration and Development of Space
MIT Building, W20-445
77 Massachusetts Avenue
Cambridge, MA 02139

American Institute of Aeronautics and Astronautics
370 L'Enfant Promenade, SW
Washington, DC 20024

Aerospace Industries Association of America
1250 I Street, NW
Washington, DC 20005

General Aviation Manufacturers Association
1400 K Street, NW, Suite 801
Washington, DC 20005

National Aeronautics and Space Administration
600 Independence Avenue, SW
Washington, DC 20546

◇ **RELATED ARTICLES**

Volume 1: Aviation and Aerospace
Volume 2: Engineers, aerospace; Technical writers
Volume 3: Aircraft mechanics and engine specialists; Flight engineers
Volume 4: Avionics technicians; Electronics technicians; Industrial engineering technicians; Instrumentation technicians; Mathematical technicians; Mechanical technicians; Metallurgical technicians

Biomedical equipment technicians

Definition

Biomedical equipment technicians inspect, maintain, repair, and install complex medical equipment and instrumentation used in medical therapy and diagnosis. The equipment they work with includes heart-lung machines, artificial-kidney machines, patient monitors, chemical analyzers, and other electrical, electronic, mechanical, or pneumatic devices. Working in hospitals, clinics, and research facilities, they disassemble equipment to locate malfunctioning components, repair or replace defective parts, and reassemble the equipment, adjusting and calibrating it to ensure that it operates according to manufacturers' specifications. Other duties of biomedical equipment technicians include the following: modifying equipment according to the directions of medical or supervisory personnel; arranging with equipment manufacturers for the repair of equipment, when necessary, by the manufacturer's own service personnel; and safety-testing equipment to ensure that patients, equipment operators, and other staff members are safe from electrical or mechanical hazards. Biomedical equipment technicians work with hand tools, power tools, measuring devices, and manufacturers' manuals. They may work for equipment manufacturers as salespeople or as service technicians. Working in health-care facilities, biomedical equipment technicians may specialize in the repair or maintenance of specific types of equipment such as that used in radiology, nuclear medicine, or patient monitoring.

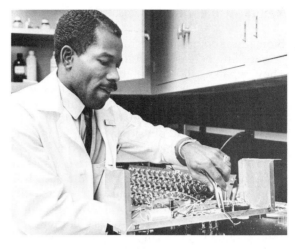

A biomedical equipment technician repairs a malfunctioning electronic monitor. In this case, he has had to expose the entire piece of equipment to replace a wire.

History

Today's complex biomedical equipment is the result of advances in three different areas of engineering and scientific research. The first, of course, is our ever-increasing knowledge of the human body and of the disease processes that afflict it. The accumulation of this medical knowledge has been going on for thousands of years; however, most of the medical discoveries that have a direct bearing on the development of medical technology have occurred during the last 300 years. During the past 100 years especially we have learned a great deal about the chemical and electrical nature of the human body.

The second area that has contributed to the development of biomedical technology is the field of instrumentation—the design and building of precision measuring devices. Throughout the history of medicine, physicians and medical researchers have tried to learn about and to monitor the workings of the human body with whatever instruments were available to them. However, it was not until the Industrial Revolution of the eighteenth and nineteenth centuries that the field of instrumentation began to develop the kind of instruments that were needed to detect the many subtle and rapid processes that are part of human physiology.

The third area is that of mechanization and automation. Biomedical equipment often relies on mechanisms such as pumps, motors, bellows, control arms, and the like. These kinds of equipment were initially developed and improved during the Industrial Revolution; however, it was not until the 1950s that the processes of automation began to be incorporated in the field of medical technology. During the 1950s, researchers developed machines for analyzing the various components of blood and for preparing tissue specimens for microscopic examination. Probably the most dramatic development of this period was the introduction of the heart-lung machine by John Haysham Gibbon of Philadelphia in 1953, a project he had been working on since 1937.

Since the 1950s, the growth of biomedical technology has been especially dramatic. Thirty years ago, even the most advanced hospitals had only a few pieces of electronic medical equipment; today such hospitals have thousands. And, to service this equipment, the biomedical equipment technician has become an important member of the health-care delivery team.

In a sense, biomedical equipment technicians represent the newest stage in the history of technicians. The first generation of technicians were skilled assistants who had learned a trade and gone to work for an engineer or scientist. The second generation learned a technology, such as electronics. The most recent generation of technicians needs integrated instruction and competence in at least two fields of science and technology. For the biomedical equipment technician, the fields may vary, but they will most often be electronics and human physiology.

Biomedical equipment technicians
Emerging Technician Occupations

Nature of the work

Biomedical equipment technicians act as an important link between technology and medicine. They repair, calibrate, maintain, and operate the biomedical equipment used in hospitals, clinics, and other health-related facilities, working under the supervision of researchers, biomedical engineers, physicians, surgeons, and other professional health-care providers.

There are thousands of different kinds of equipment that biomedical equipment technicians may work with. Some of the most frequently encountered are the following: patient monitors, heart-lung machines, kidney machines, blood-gas analyzers, spectro-photometers, X-ray units, radiation monitors, defibrillators, anesthesia apparatus, pacemakers, blood-pressure transducers, spirometers, sterilizers, diathermy equipment, patient-care computers, ultrasound machines, and diagnostic scanning machines, such as the CT (computed tomography) scan machine, PETT (positive emission transaxial tomography) scanner, and MRI (magnetic resonance imagery) machines.

Repairing faulty instruments is one of the chief functions of biomedical equipment technicians. They investigate equipment problems, determine the extent of malfunctions, make repairs on instruments that have had minor breakdowns, and assist in expediting the repair of instruments with major breakdowns, for instance, by writing an analysis of the problem for the factory. In doing this work, technicians rely on manufacturers' diagrams, maintenance manuals, and standard and specialized test instruments, such as oscilloscopes and pressure gauges.

Installation of equipment is another important function of biomedical equipment technicians. They inspect and test newly acquired equipment for compliance with purchase-order and manufacturer specifications relating to performance and safety as described in manuals and diagrams. Technicians may also be responsible for checking on proper installation of the equipment or, in some cases, for installing it themselves. To ensure safe operations, technicians need a thorough knowledge of the regulations related to the proper grounding of equipment, and they need to carry out actively all of the details of those regulations.

Maintenance is the third major area of responsibility for biomedical equipment technicians. In doing this work, technicians are trying to catch problems before they lead to more serious problems later. Towards this end, they take apart and reassemble devices, test circuits, clean and oil moving parts, and replace worn parts. They also keep complete records of all machine repairs, maintenance checks, and expenses.

In all three of these areas, a large part of the work of biomedical equipment technicians consists of consulting with physicians, administrators, engineers, and other related professionals. For instance, they may be called upon to aid hospital administrators in making decisions regarding the repair, replacement, or purchase of new equipment. As part of their maintenance and repair responsibilities, they consult with medical and research staffs to determine that equipment is functioning properly and safely. They also consult with medical and engineering staffs when called upon to modify or develop equipment. In all of these activities, they must utilize their knowledge of electronics, medical terminology, human anatomy and physiology, chemistry, and physics.

In addition to these three principal areas of responsibility, biomedical equipment technicians are also involved in a range of other related areas. For instance, some biomedical equipment technicians maintain inventories of all instruments in the hospital, their condition and location, and operator. They reorder parts and components, assist in providing people with emergency instruments, restore unsafe or defective instruments to working order, and check for compliance with safety regulations.

Other biomedical equipment technicians may assist physicians, surgeons, nurses, and researchers in conducting procedures and experiments. In addition, they should be able to explain to staff members how to operate these machines, the conditions under which certain apparatus may or may not be used, how to solve small operating problems, and how to monitor and maintain equipment.

In many hospitals, technicians are assigned to a particular service, such as pediatrics, surgery, or renal medicine. These technicians become specialists in certain types of equipment. However, unlike electrocardiograph technicians or dialysis technicians, who specialize in one kind of equipment, for the most part biomedical equipment technicians must be thoroughly familiar with a large variety of instruments. They might be called upon to prepare an artificial kidney or to work with a blood-gas analyzer, which is a millivolt meter with water circulating to keep blood at body temperature during analyses, and which requires the use of calibration gases. Biomedical equipment technicians also maintain pulmonary function machines. These machines examine and measure the patient's breathing, analyze the gases moving in and out of the lungs and the way in which they distribute themselves throughout the lung system, and measure breathing efficiency. Pulmonary function machines are used in clinics for ambulatory patients, in hospital laboratories, in departments of medicine for diagnosis and treatment, and for the rehabilitation of cardiopulmonary patients.

While most biomedical equipment technicians are trained in and involved with electronics technology, there is also a need for technicians trained in plastics to work on the development of artificial organs and for people trained in glassblowing to help make the precision parts needed for specialized equipment.

Many biomedical equipment technicians work for medical instrument manufacturers. These technicians consult and assist in the construction of new machinery and help make decisions concerning the materials and construction methods that will be utilized in the manufacture of the equipment.

Requirements

Biomedical equipment technicians should possess mechanical ability, better-than-average finger and hand dexterity, good eye-hand coordination, and they should enjoy working with tools. They should be able to work well under pressure, because health matters often demand quick decision-making and prompt repairs. They should also be extremely precise and accurate in their work, and they should have good communication skills.

Biomedical equipment technicians require post–high-school education, usually a two-year program leading to an associate degree. While still in high school, prospective technicians should take courses in chemistry, biology, and physics, as these courses will provide a helpful background for further study. Courses in English, mathematics, electronics, shop, and drafting will also help prepare students for further education and for work as technicians.

Biomedical equipment technology is a relatively new program in two-year colleges. Some schools refer to these programs as "medical electronics technology" or "biomedical engineering technology." During the course of these programs, students receive instruction in anatomy, physiology, electrical and electronic fundamentals, chemistry, physics, biomedical equipment construction and design, safety in health-care facilities, medical equipment troubleshooting, and communications skills. In addition to the classroom work, programs often provide students with practical experience in repairing and servicing equipment in a clinical or laboratory setting under the supervision of an experienced equipment technician. In this way, students learn in some detail about electrical components and circuits, the design and construction of common pieces of machinery, and computer technology as it applies to biomedical equipment.

By studying various pieces of equipment, technicians learn a problem-solving technique that is applicable not only to the equipment they have studied but also to equipment they have not yet seen and even to equipment that has not yet been invented. Part of this problem-solving technique includes learning how and where to locate sources of information.

Some biomedical equipment technicians receive their training in the military. During the course of an enlistment period of four years or less, servicemen and women can receive training that prepares them for entry-level or sometimes advanced-level positions in the civilian work force after they leave the military.

Special requirements

The Association for the Advancement of Medical Instrumentation, associated with the International Certification Commission for Clinical Engineering and Biomedical Technology, issues a certificate for biomedical equipment technicians based on a written examination and educational preparation. This program provides an opportunity for technicians to demonstrate that they have attained an overall knowledge of the field, and many employers prefer to hire technicians with this certificate. In some cases, the educational requirements for certification may be waived for technicians with appropriate employment experience.

Opportunities for experience and exploration

It is difficult for interested students to gain any direct experience on a part-time basis in biomedical equipment technology. The first opportunities for students to gain experience generally come in the clinical and laboratory phases of their training programs. Interested students, however, can explore some aspects of a career in biomedical equipment technology in a number of different ways. They can write to the sources listed at the end of this article for more reading material on biomedical equipment technology. They can visit their school or community library and seek out some of the many books written about careers in medical technology. Joining a hobby club devoted to chemistry, biology, radio equipment, or electronics could also be helpful.

Perhaps the best way to learn more about this job is to set up, with the help of teachers or guidance counselors, a visit to a workplace employing biomedical equipment technicians. It would also be highly desirable for interested students to visit a school offering a program in biomedical equipment technology to discuss career plans with an admissions counselor.

Methods of entering

Most schools offering programs in biomedical equipment technology work closely with local hospitals and industries, and school placement officers are usually informed about appropriate openings when they are available. In some cases, recruiters may visit a school during a student's final semester to conduct interviews. Also, many schools will place students in part-time jobs in hospitals as part of their instruction to help them gain practical experience. Students are often able to return to these hospitals for full-time employment after graduation.

Another effective method of finding employment is to write directly to hospitals, research institutes, or biomedical equipment manufacturers. State employment offices and newspaper want ads are other good sources of leads for job openings.

Advancement

With increased experience, biomedical equipment technicians can expect to work with less and less supervision, and in some cases they may find themselves supervising other, less experienced technicians. They may advance to positions in which they serve as instructors, assist in research, or have administrative duties. Although many supervisory positions are open to biomedical equipment technicians, some positions are not available unless the technicians gain additional education. In large metropolitan hospitals, for instance, the minimum educational requirement for biomedical engineers, who do much of the supervising of biomedical equipment technicians, is a bachelor's degree, and many engineers have a master's degree as well.

Employment outlook

Because of the increasing use of medical electronic devices and other sophisticated biomedical equipment, the demand for skilled and trained biomedical equipment technicians is growing and should continue to grow through the year 2000.

In hospitals, the need for increasing numbers of biomedical equipment technicians exists not only because of the increasing use of biomedical equipment but also because of the realization on the part of hospital administrators that biomedical equipment technicians can help hold down costs. Biomedical equipment technicians do this through their prevention and maintenance activities and by taking over some routine activities of engineers and administrators, thus releasing those professionals for activities that only they can perform. Through the coming decades, cost containment will remain a high priority for hospital administrators, and as long as biomedical equipment technicians can contribute to that effort, the demand for them should remain strong.

Many biomedical equipment technicians work for the companies that build, sell, lease, or service biomedical equipment, and employment by these companies should continue to grow also.

The federal government is also an employer of biomedical equipment technicians in its hospitals, research institutes, and the military. Employment in these areas will depend largely on levels of government spending. In the research area, spending levels may vary; however, in the health-care delivery area, spending should remain high for the foreseeable future.

Earnings

Salaries for biomedical equipment technicians vary in different institutions and localities and according to the experience, training, certification, and type of work done by the technician. In general, entry-level salaries range from $16,000 to $20,000 for technicians working in hospitals and from $20,000 to $23,000 for technicians working for manufacturers or governmental agencies. Experienced technicians earn about $19,000 to $25,000 when working in a hospital and about $25,000 to $35,000 when working for a manufacturer. Senior technicians earn about $25,000 to $35,000 in hospitals and about $35,000 to $45,000 working for a manufacturer. Experienced and senior technicians working for government agencies earn from $25,000 to $35,000 a year.

Conditions of work

Working conditions for biomedical equipment technicians vary according to employer and type of work done. Technicians working in hospitals generally work a forty-hour week; however, their schedule may sometimes include weekends, holidays, or being on call for emergencies. Technicians working for equipment manufacturers may have to do extensive traveling to install or service equipment.

The physical surroundings in which biomedical equipment technicians work may vary from day to day. Some days may find the technician working in a lab or treatment room with patients and staff; other days may be spent consulting with engineers, administrators, or other staff members; and some days may be spent at a workbench repairing equipment.

Social and psychological factors

Successful biomedical equipment technicians must possess a number of social and psychological skills. First, they must know how to give instruction to people about how to operate equipment. Some of the people these technicians may instruct include physicians, nurses, physical therapists, medical and radiological technologists, and others. Some may have some experience with similar kinds of equipment, but many may not have. More importantly, some may take instruction better than others. A biomedical equipment technician involved in instruction needs to be patient, diplomatic, and sensitive to the needs of others.

Many biomedical equipment technicians will also come in contact with patients. They cannot allow themselves to become upset at the sight of blood or critically ill patients. Just as do other health-care professionals, biomedical equipment technicians need a good bedside manner.

Biomedical equipment technicians should also be able to handle stress well. When called upon to operate or repair equipment in emergency situations, they should be able to do so calmly and competently. In such situations, tempers sometimes flare, and technicians should remember that the angry outbursts of others are often the response to stress and are not meant personally.

Finally, biomedical equipment technicians should be prepared for a lifetime of continuing education. They need to keep informed about all of the latest developments in their field. This means reading professional journals and manufacturers' literature, attending seminars, and taking classes. By continuing their education in this way, biomedical equipment technicians are best able to give good advice when it is needed, to handle their own responsibilities well, and to ensure themselves increasing responsibility and professional recognition.

GOE: 02.04.02; SIC: 384; SOC: 389, 6179

◇ SOURCES OF ADDITIONAL INFORMATION

National Association for Biomedical Research
1818 Connecticut Avenue, NW, Suite 303
Washington, DC 20006

National Society of Biomedical Equipment Technicians
3330 Washington Boulevard
Suite 400
Arlington, VA 22201

◇ RELATED ARTICLES

Volume 1: Electronics
Volume 2: Biomedical engineers
Volume 4: Cardiac monitor technicians; Dialysis technicians; Electrocardiograph technicians; Electroencephalographic technicians; Electronics technicians; Instrumentation technicians

CAD/CAM technicians

Definition

CAD/CAM technicians use computer-controlled systems to assist industrial designers and engineers in designing products and carrying out automated industrial processes. CAD is an abbreviation that stands for "computer-aided design" or "computer-aided drafting." CAM is an abbreviation that stands for "computer-aided manufacturing." Computer-aided design usually involves using computers to establish the structures and materials that will be used in a new product and to create the diagrams, drawings, and lists of specifications that are required for manufacturing the product. Computer-aided manufacturing involves using computers to determine the manufacturing processes and equipment that will be required for the product and to monitor and control the automated aspects of the actual manufacturing of the product. In some fields, such as architecture, CAD activities are separate from manufacturing activities; however, in many areas, CAD and CAM are linked parts of an automated industrial design and manufacturing process.

History

CAD/CAM technology came into being in the 1970s with the development of microprocessors, which are computer processors in the form of miniaturized integrated circuits contained on tiny silicon chips. Microprocessors opened up many new fields for computer applications by greatly reducing the size of computers while greatly increasing their power and speed. The drafters and designers working to develop these microprocessors were actually among the first to benefit from this technology. Prior to that time, designing and drafting were done with pen and paper on a drafting board. As the circuits on the chips became too complex to diagram in the conventional way, their designers began to use the chips themselves to help store information, create models, and produce diagrams for the design of new chip circuits. This was just the beginning of computer-assisted design and drafting technology. Today, there are tens of thousands of CAD workstations in industrial settings. Makers of CAD equipment expect their products to continue to sell very well in the years to come, so that by about the year 2000 nearly all drafting tasks will be done with such equipment.

The field of computer-aided manufacturing has grown just as quickly and dramatically. Before the 1970s, manufacturing processes were assisted by only a few relatively simple automated mechanisms. And until just a few years ago, CAM technology was associated almost exclusively with the use of some simple robotic devices in automobile and aircraft assembly lines. Developments in the computer field, especially in microprocessors, have opened many new applications in manufacturing. Japan led the world in introducing computers into factories on a widespread basis. More recently, a wide variety of industries in the United States has expanded the use of automated manufacturing processes.

With the fine-tuning of microprocessor applications, small companies as well as large ones have become able to benefit from the increased efficiency and versatility in design and manufacturing that computers allow. CAD/CAM technology is leading many manufacturers to enhanced productivity and more competitive positions in their product markets. In some industries, CAD/CAM has made it possible to develop and produce new products at ten to twenty times the old rate. The record of success has led some experts to suggest that this type of computer-related technology in the workplace may increase the nation's overall productivity by perhaps as much as ten times in the next few decades.

Nature of the work

CAD/CAM technicians use computers to help design, improve, modify, or produce manufactured items and manufacturing systems. CAD/CAM technicians may be involved in any aspect of the manufacturing process from start to finish; however, they usually specialize in one aspect of CAD/CAM technology, either in CAD technology or CAM technology.

Technicians specializing in CAD technology work in the design and drafting activities associated with new-product research and development. These technicians must combine drafting and computer skills. They work in any field where detailed drawings, diagrams, and layouts are important aspects of developing new-product designs—for example, in architecture, electronics, and in the manufacturing of automobiles, aircraft, computers, and missiles and other defense systems.

CAD/CAM technicians work under the direction and supervision of CAD/CAM engineers and designers, who are highly trained experts in applying computer technology to industrial design and manufacturing. These designers and engineers are involved with the conceptual planning relating to the application of CAD technology and equipment to the product-design process. They are also the ones who give assignments to the CAD technicians.

These technicians work at specially designed and equipped interactive computer graphics workstations. They call up computer data files that hold information about a new product and execute programs that convert that information into diagrams and drawings of the product. These diagrams and drawings are displayed on a video-display screen, which then acts as an electronic drawing board. Following the directions of a CAD engineer or designer, the CAD technician enters changes regarding product design and specifications into the computer. The technician then executes other programs that incorporate these changes into the data file and display revised diagrams and drawings of the product with the altered specifications. The software in CAD systems even provides suggestions and advice and points out errors to the user. The most important advantage of working with a CAD system is that the technician is saved from the lengthy tasks of producing by hand the original and then the revised drawings and diagrams of the product.

The CAD workstation is equipped to allow technicians to perform calculations, develop simulations, and manipulate and modify the displayed material. Using typed commands at a keyboard, a stylus or light pen for touching the screen display, a mouse, joystick, or other electronic methods of interacting with the display, technicians can move, rotate, zoom in on any aspect of the drawing on the screen, and project three-dimensional images from two-dimensional sketches. They can make experimental changes to the design and then run tests on the modified design to determine its qualities, such as weight, strength, flexibility, and the cost of materials that would be required. Compared to traditional drafting and design techniques, CAD offers virtually unlimited freedom to explore alternatives, and in far less time.

When the product design is completed and the necessary information is assembled in the computer files, technicians may store the data that has been developed, output it on a printer, transfer it to another computer, or send it di-

A CAD/CAM technician uses a sophisticated computer to translate his drawings onto the screen.

rectly to another step of the automated product-testing or manufacturing process.

Once the design has been approved for production, CAD technicians may use their computers to assist in making detailed drawings of parts of the design. They may also prepare designs and drawings of any tools or equipment, such as molds, cutting tools, and jigs, that must be specially made to carry out the manufacturing of the product.

Technicians specializing in CAM technology are usually involved in one of two aspects of manufacturing. They are involved either in setting up the manufacturing processes to operate with maximum efficiency and organization; or in running, maintaining, and repairing computer-controlled manufacturing devices, including all kinds of mechanisms from simple automated devices to sophisticated robots.

Technicians involved with setting up manufacturing processes use computers to gather data from various sources on the availability and location of parts and materials, conditions on the factory floor, and other similar variables in manufacturing. These pieces of data are combined in a central computer with instructions and requirements about the manufacturing process that have been specified by the management personnel. The technicians use the output information in various ways to help keep automated manufacturing equipment producing smoothly.

In a some factory settings, the computer is programmed to determine the best procedure for producing the needed products and to initiate, control, and change as necessary the automated processes of production, virtually from start to finish. This kind of sophisticated system can be very productive and highly cost effective. As the amount of product required varies and as factors relating to production needs and procedures shift, the company can easily make changes on the factory floor to use available resources most effectively.

An even more comprehensive kind of computer-controlled system is sometimes called computer-integrated manufacturing (CIM). CIM ideally involves linking all the functions related to manufacturing in one master system, including business-related activities such as accounting, purchasing, and forecasting, as well as design, drafting, and manufacturing. Because of its complexity CIM is being put into practice in only a few manufacturing industries, but because of its potential benefits, CIM promises to become much more important in the future. As more of these complex systems come into use, more CAD/CAM technicians will undoubtedly be needed to install, maintain, and repair them.

CAM technicians involved with automated and computer-controlled manufacturing equipment perform tasks that may be similar to those performed by robotics technicians, whose work is described elsewhere in the Emerging Technician Occupations section. CAM technicians may be involved in all phases of engineering related to robots and other computer-controlled manufacturing equipment, from the design and development phase, to installation, repair, and maintenance.

Many kinds of machine tools—lathes, punch presses, milling machines, and others—can be computer controlled. These machines can be made so they operate alone on the factory floor, or they can be linked in clusters. This makes such equipment relatively easy to introduce into a manufacturing process. Today, computer-controlled machine tools are used in many industries, particularly those that produce metalworking machinery, automobiles, aircraft, spacecraft and artificial satellites and construction equipment.

Technicians who are involved with the design and development of new robotic devices or automated equipment such as machine tools are part of a design team. Working closely with engineers, they carry out tests on systems and materials that have been proposed for new machines. After the initial testing is complete, they may be involved with building prototype models and with producing the blueprints and manufacturing specifications that will be used in building the machine.

Some CAM technicians are involved with assembly or testing of finished machines or components to assure that they conform to the design team's specifications.

A very common responsibility for CAM technicians is to control, monitor, and modify the operations of the robotic devices and other computer-controlled manufacturing equipment. As they monitor these operations, the data they collect is often in an electronic form that can in turn be fed back into a computer for speedy and comprehensive analysis of the manufacturing process in terms of anticipated output, materials consumption, and production efficiency. This data may then be used to further modify the operations of the automated equipment.

CAM technicians may also work as robot operators, especially in some kinds of specialized settings where the robot operation is apt to be complicated or even somewhat unpredictable in some of its aspects. CAM technicians may also work as robotics technician trainers. In this capacity, they train other employees in the installation, use, and maintenance of robots.

Finally, CAM technicians may work as maintenance technicians. These technicians make service calls to repair and maintain robots and other automated equipment. They may also be involved in installing computer-controlled machines and in establishing in-house maintenance and repair programs at new installations.

Regardless of what aspect of this work they are involved in, CAD/CAM technicians keep records of all their test procedures and results. They may be asked to present written reports, tables, or charts to document the results of their tests or other findings. If a particular system, subsystem, or material has not met a testing or production requirement—in terms either of a product being designed or produced or of the equipment being used to manufacture it—technicians may be asked to suggest a way of rearranging the components of the system or substituting alternate materials.

Requirements

CAD/CAM technicians need to have orderly minds and good analytical skills. They should be neat and methodical, accurate, and detail-oriented in all their work, and they should be able to work quietly for long periods of time in front of video-display screens. They should be able to work independently or as part of a team.

CAD/CAM technicians must receive sufficient training to give them the ability to read and understand complex engineering schematics and drawings. The minimum educational requirement for CAD/CAM technicians is graduation from high school. High-school students interested in careers as CAD/CAM technicians should take courses that provide them with a solid background in algebra, geometry, trigonometry, physics, machine-shop skills, drafting, and electronics, and they should take whatever computer courses are available to them. They should also take courses in English, especially those that improve their communications skills.

Some companies will accept technicians who have actual work experience with CAD/CAM technology instead of formal training in the field; however, acquiring that experience without training is very difficult. Therefore, most prospective CAD/CAM technicians undertake formal training beyond the high-school level, usually in a two-year associate degree program taught at a technical school or community college. Such a program should include courses in drafting and in basic engineering topics, such as hydraulics, pneumatics, and electronics. It should include courses in data processing and in computer programming, systems, and equipment, especially video-display equipment. It should also include courses in specialized topics such as computer graphics, product design, industrial and architectural drafting, and computer peripheral equipment and data storage. Some two-year programs may also require the student to complete courses in technical writing, communications, social sciences, and the humanities.

In addition, some companies have their own training programs, some lasting as long as two years, for training workers for positions as CAD/CAM technicians. Requirements for entry into these company-run training programs vary from company to company.

Students considering a career in CAD/CAM technology should realize that such a career will require taking continuing-education courses even after they have found jobs. This continuing education is necessary because technicians need to know about recent advances in technology that may result in changes in procedures, equipment, terminology, or programming concepts.

Special requirements

CAD/CAM technicians do not need to obtain a license or to join a union to get a job. Membership in a professional group is not required, but such a membership will help technicians keep current with developments in the field.

Opportunities for experience and exploration

A number of possibilities exist for the person who wishes to gain experience or first-hand knowledge about the field of CAD/CAM technology. Part-time or summer jobs involved directly with CAD/CAM technology are very hard to find; however, jobs relating to drafting can sometimes be found, and many future employers will look favorably on applicants who have had this kind of experience. In addition, jobs relating to other engineering fields, such as electronics or mechanics, may be available, and they offer the student an opportunity to become familiar with the kind of workplace in which technicians may later be employed.

In addition, high-school computer courses and courses in geometry, physics, mechanical drawing, and shop work will give a student a feel for the mental and physical activities that are part of CAD/CAM technology. Other activities that provide knowledge and skills relevant to a career in CAD/CAM technology include membership in high-school science clubs, especially computer and electronics clubs; participating in science fairs; pursuing hobbies that involve computers, electronics, drafting, mechanical equipment, and model building; and reading books and articles about technical topics.

Methods of entering

Probably the most reliable method for entering this field is through the placement office of the institution that provided the student's technical training. This is especially true for students who graduate from a two-year college or technical institute, because they can almost always receive job-placement assistance from the school's placement office. Recruiters from companies employing CAD/CAM technicians sometimes visit such schools, and placement-office personnel can help students meet with these recruiters.

Graduates of post–high-school programs who are conducting their own job search might begin with architects, building firms, manufacturers, high-technology companies, and government agencies. They can contact prospective employers by phone or with a letter stating their interest in employment, accompanied by a resume that provides details about their education and job experience. State or private employment agencies may also be of help, and want ads in newspapers and professional journals may provide additional leads.

Advancement

CAD/CAM technicians who demonstrate their ability to handle more responsibility can expect to receive promotions after just a few years on the job. They may be assigned to designing or manufacturing work that requires their special skills or experience, such as troubleshooting problems with systems they have worked with; or they may be promoted to supervisory or training positions. As trainers, they may teach courses at their workplace or at a local school or community college.

In general, as CAD/CAM technicians advance, their assignments become less and less routine, until they may actually have a hand in designing and building equipment. Technicians who continue their education and earn a bachelor's degree may become data-processing managers, engineers, or systems or manufacturing analysts.

Other routes for advancement include becoming a sales representative for a design firm or for a company selling computer-assisted manufacturing services or equipment. It may also be possible to become an independent contractor for companies using or manufacturing CAD/CAM equipment.

Employment outlook

The employment outlook for CAD/CAM technicians is excellent. Many companies in the near future will feel pressures to increase productivity in design and manufacturing activities, and CAD/CAM technology will provide some of the best opportunities to improve that productivity. By some estimates, there will be as many as a million jobs available for technically trained personnel in the field of CAD/CAM technology by the end of the century.

In the field of CAM technology, the number of industrial robots in use will increase substantially during the 1990s. Companies already using robots will probably increase their reliance on these devices, and, more importantly, companies that are not already using robots will find ways to make use of them. For prospective CAM technicians, the important part of this expansion in the use of robots is that it will require more trained technicians to design, build, install, monitor, maintain, and repair them.

Earnings

Starting salaries for CAD/CAM technicians who are graduates of two-year technical programs typically fall in the range of $18,000 to $22,000 a year; however, actual salaries will vary widely in different areas of the country for different jobs with different training requirements. With increased training and experience, technicians can earn salaries of approximately $30,000 a year, and some technicians with special skills, extensive experience, or added responsibilities may earn more.

Benefits usually include insurance, paid vacations and holidays, pension plans, and sometimes stock-purchase plans.

Conditions of work

The conditions under which CAD/CAM technicians work will vary depending on the aspect of CAD/CAM technology with which they are involved. CAD technicians almost always work in clean, quiet, well-lighted, and usually air-conditioned rooms. Most CAD technicians spend most of their days at a workstation. The work does not require great physical effort, but it does require patience and the ability to maintain concentration and attention for extended periods of time. Some technicians may find they suffer from eyestrain from working long periods in front of a video-display screen.

CAM technicians are more likely to work in a factory setting where noise levels will probably be higher, although those involved with the development and testing of CAM equipment and systems often work in fairly quiet settings. CAM technicians are also apt to be fairly active, walking, standing, stooping, lifting, or carrying equipment. Some technicians involved with CAM technology will confront potentially hazardous conditions, such as the use of laser beams, arc-welding equipment, or hazardous chemicals. Plant safety procedures will protect the attentive and cautious workers, but carelessness in such settings can be particularly dangerous.

Social and psychological factors

CAD/CAM technicians, because of their training and experience, are valuable employees. They are called upon to exercise independent judgment and to be responsible for valuable equipment. They also, of necessity, sometimes find themselves carrying out routine, uncomplicated tasks. CAD/CAM technicians must be able to respond well to both of these kinds of demands. Most CAD/CAM technicians work as part of a team. They are required to take orders, and they may well encounter situations in which their individual contributions are not fully recognized. Successful CAD/CAM technicians are those who work well as team members and who can derive satisfaction from the accomplishments of the team as a whole.

CAD/CAM technicians are working in a new and very important field. Increasing productivity in industrial design and manufacturing will play a large part in ensuring the long-term economic vitality of the country, and CAD/CAM technology is one of the most promising developments in this search for increased productivity. Knowing that they are in the forefront of this important and challenging undertaking can provide CAD/CAM technicians with a good deal of pride and satisfaction.

GOE: 05.03.02, 05.05.11; SIC: 871; SOC: 3719, 372

◇ SOURCES OF ADDITIONAL INFORMATION

American Institute for Design and Drafting
966 Hungerford Road, Suite 10-B
Rockville, MD 20854

Association for Integrated Manufacturing Technology
5411 East State Street
Rockford, IL 61108

Computer Aided Manufacturing International
1250 East Copeland Road
Suite 500
Arlington, TX 76011

Institute of Electrical and Electronics Engineers
345 East 47th Street
New York, NY 10017

Robotic Industries Association
PO Box 3724
900 Victors Way
Ann Arbor, MI 48106

Society of Manufacturing Engineers
PO Box 930
One SME Drive
Dearborn, MI 48121

◇ RELATED ARTICLES

Volume 1: Computer Hardware; Computer Software; Engineering
Volume 2: Computer programmers; Engineers; Graphics programmers; Industrial designers
Volume 3: Computer and peripheral equipment operators
Volume 4: Data-processing technicians; Drafting and design technicians; Industrial engineering technicians; Robotics technicians

Computer-service technicians

Definition

Computer-service technicians install, program, operate, maintain, and service computer systems. These technicians also diagnose problems that are caused by mechanical or electrical malfunctions both in individual computer units and in complex systems, such as local area networks (LANs). They understand the mathematics and physical sciences that are related to the installation, construction, operation, and maintenance of mainframe computers, minicomputers, and microprocessors. They also understand the electronic circuits and mechanical devices used in computer construction and installation. Computer-service technicians are also experts in the use of instruments to detect weaknesses or failures in computer systems. In addition to a thorough knowledge of computer hardware, the computer-service technician must remain current on the many software applications.

History

The computer-service technician career began to develop in the mid-1960s, during the time when computers were becoming commonly used in business, research, and government.

The first experimental versions of modern computers were built during the 1940s. Compared to present-day computers, these computers were expensive and inefficient. Some early computers used as many as 50,000 vacuum tubes and were very large and used great amounts of electric power. Moreover, they had to be kept in air-conditioned rooms to work correctly.

During the 1950s computers were improved enough that the first commercial computers became available. Their manufacturers leased them to users instead of selling them. This made the manufacturer responsible for servicing the customer's computer system. Computer-service engineers were trained by the company to keep the customer's data-processing system and computers in good working order. By the late 1950s and early 1960s the transistor was developed. It gradually took the place of vacuum tubes in computers, and computers became much smaller, more reliable, and less expensive.

In the late 1960s, the introduction of integrated circuitry made possible the development of minicomputers, which were smaller and cheaper than earlier computers but just as powerful. This was the first phase of the computer revolution. As new uses for minicomputers became evident in manufacturing, hospitals, airline ticket scheduling, and business offices, the number of computers greatly increased. New companies that produced minicomputers sprang up. These changes led to a great demand for highly skilled technicians who could keep these computers operating.

Many technical institutes, community colleges, and specialized schools started programs to prepare computer-service technicians. Some minicomputer manufacturers cooperated with schools to start such programs, and some companies opened private schools in various parts of the country.

The second phase of the computer revolution began in the early 1970s when the microprocessor became the heart of the modern computer. The discovery of how to store information on a tiny silicon chip (approximately .03 by .03 inches in size) rapidly caused new developments. The silicon chip produced a huge expansion in uses of computers. In addition, the development of the chip greatly reduced the cost of computers and caused an increase in computer applications. In turn, this increased the need for computer-service technicians, which is a need that is still growing.

Nature of the work

Computer-service technicians may work for a computer manufacturer or for a computer owner who is applying computer technology. Technicians who work for a manufacturer may help the circuit designer develop new and improved circuits for computer systems already in production. Here the technician may be required to fabricate new circuits for testing purposes or for the finished version that will be used as a model in the final production process.

The manufacturer often controls the research and development as well as the manufacturing of new electronic devices, such as integrated circuits and other solid-state devices. This creates opportunities for the technician to work alongside the physicist, the chemist, and the metallurgist, or any of the other specialists who are responsible for the final computer product.

Technicians working for the computer manufacturer may also work at the customer's or user's facilities. There they are responsible for making sure that the regular preventive maintenance of the computer systems is performed. This includes overall checking for errors in processing, instrument analysis of system or unit performance, and general troubleshooting.

At the customer's office or plant, technicians assist in site planning and system installation. The site planning helps ensure that the customer will be able to have the most trouble-free performance from the computer system after it is installed.

Installation of the system is usually the responsibility of the manufacturer, particularly if the equipment is new. The installation is performed by the technician, who can quickly communicate any problems to the manufacturer. Usually with the help of the purchaser's technicians, the computer-service technician is responsible for uncrating new computer hardware at the customer's site and carefully documenting the items. Next the equipment must be inspected for shipping damages and the major components must be placed into the unit or system according to the engineering drawings. The check-out phase is next, in which the technician runs special computer programs that certify the proper memory components, cathode-ray-tube terminals, printers, and other input and output devices. The computer-service technician usually has the resources of the manufacturer only a telephone call away if problems occur that cannot be solved at the place where the computer is being used.

An increasing number of computer users also employ computer-service technicians to assist in fully integrating the computer into the special application or task of the user. These technicians can provide valuable assistance to the owner in seeing that the newly acquired systems are properly used by the other employees at the site. They may be called on to provide special training sessions as newly installed devices are added. When the company does not purchase a service contract for system maintenance, the computer-service technician may become an operations assistant to supervise or manage the care of the system.

Computer users may choose to purchase their computer maintenance services from a contracting company that specializes in providing such services under an agreement or contract. These specialists provide the maintenance services as required and serve as the maintenance resource in some cases where manufacturer-supplied maintenance costs are considered too high by the customer. The computer-service engineering technicians working in such an environment provide the same expertise and repair service as that otherwise supplied by the manufacturer. Technicians who work for computer-service contracting companies often provide service for more than one user, and thus gain experience and expertise in several different customer's systems and uses of computers.

Some examples of entry-level jobs in the field are described in the following short paragraphs:

Electronics technicians in manufacturing assist engineers in the design and installation of computer-based systems for process and machine control. They may be required to develop the routine portions of a design and often do much of the initial installation and testing of new equipment.

Field-service technicians provide corrective and preventive maintenance for computer-based systems. Technicians may work for a computer supplier and provide special services to customers as needed. Technicians also may be assigned to the customer's site on a full-time basis.

Quality-test technicians inspect and test digital measurement systems. These technicians will often be required to use sophisticated analyzers in carrying out the testing procedures.

Traffic-signal technicians are responsible for the inspection, fabrication, and acceptance of new equipment. They provide remedial maintenance to the components of vehicle detection equipment, safety equipment, computer pe-

A computer-service technician replaces a broken element of a mainframe computer system. After the installation, he will check that the new device is running smoothly.

ripheral equipment, and communications equipment.

Terminal technicians specialize in the maintenance of computer terminals such as video-display units, keyboard data entry systems, and printers.

Laboratory technicians perform technical tasks connected with construction, installation, adjustment, maintenance, and operation of computer-controlled devices.

Requirements

Computer-service technicians must be able to function as highly skilled engineering technicians in a highly technical field. Computers and their related equipment are largely electrical and electronic devices. But they are also mechanical structures. The technicians who service and maintain them must therefore understand mechanical devices and the basic principles of mechanics.

Technicians who install, service, and maintain computers or computer systems must have a good background in the fundamentals of electronics and mechanical devices. They should have a working knowledge of basic mathematics through algebra and trigonometry. A knowledge of computer programming and microprocessors is essential. They must also be able to follow instructions, both written and spoken, and be able to communicate effectively. A high degree of manual dexterity is helpful, since technicians must also be able to assemble and disassemble parts of a computer.

The best way to prepare for this career is to attend an accredited two-year postsecondary program in a public or private technical institute, community college, or specialized technical school. These programs are designed to provide students with the basic knowledge and skills needed for computer-service and usually require about two academic years or its equivalent.

Some people with extensive electronics training and experience in the military services can, with additional study, enter the field and gradually learn the job.

Those who plan to enter postsecondary programs should take two years of high-school mathematics, including algebra; at least three years of language and communication courses; and at least one year of physics or chemistry with laboratory courses. A basic knowledge of computer programming is very desirable.

A typical college-level curriculum for these technicians in the first year might include courses in computer programming, electrical/electronic circuits, algebra and trigonometry, electronic and electrical drawing, physics of mechanics, physics of heat and light, written and spoken communication, and economic and cultural patterns. The second year might include courses in computer systems and central processors, microcomputers, computer languages and operating systems, calculus, physics of electricity, process control systems, communications, technical report writing, and political and community patterns.

Graduates from such programs may receive an associate degree or a certificate of completion, which is a valuable statement of educational accomplishment.

Normal physical health and strength is required for this career. The need for good eyesight, color vision, hand-eye coordination, and physical dexterity is also important. All who enter this exacting career must be systematic, scientific, analytical, accurate, patient, and persistent in their working methods.

Special requirements

There are no licensing requirements in most computer-service jobs. Technicians who work

in areas that come under the Federal Communications Commission's (FCC) jurisdiction may find an FCC license to be useful. If employed by companies that do a substantial amount of government work, technicians may be required to undergo a security clearance investigation before they can be hired.

Opportunities for experience and exploration

Prospective technicians should investigate the schools in their own communities to see if any offer an accredited program in computer-service. By visiting such schools in the area, prospective technicians can learn more about the programs offered at the schools and get a feel for what it might be like to be enrolled in such a program.

Students in high school or postsecondary school should talk to their guidance counselors or teachers, who may also be able to provide more information about this career.

Another good way of exploring the career is through membership in a computer club or users' group. These clubs, which have developed as the use of personal and home computers has grown, have been organized in many areas by the microcomputer or personal computer users and suppliers.

Methods of entering

Graduates of computer-service engineering programs usually find their first job through the placement center of their school. Employers regularly work with school placement officers to hire new technicians. Many employers make regular visits to schools to interview graduating students. Placement offices also keep listings of companies that have expressed interest in students.

Graduating students can also write to or visit companies that are potential employers. In addition, the classified sections of newspapers constantly advertise job openings in computer-service technology.

The well-prepared technician may enter a variety of beginning jobs where the employer provides on-the-job training to acquaint the beginner with the job. Some employers also provide further specialized training for highly specialized jobs if it is needed.

Advancement

Advancement opportunities in the computer servicing field offer a variety of possibilities because of the great growth in number and increase in variety of users in the field.

Technicians may grow to positions of increased responsibility as service technicians for a user of the equipment or for a supplier of computer systems.

They may become supervisors of technicians in large companies with extensive computer-controlled automation applications. If they work for a computer manufacturing and sales company, they may supervise crews of customer-service technicians.

Some other examples of advancement positions include owning or managing a private company that provides contract engineering service to users of computers, computer systems, and computer-controlled systems.

Computer sales managers help customers design computer systems and then supervise the delivery, installation, servicing, and monitoring of the customer's equipment.

Senior research and development technicians might design and test components of a new system, solve technical problems that may arise in the design or testing of completed systems, and supervise in the design of factory or field adaptations to existing systems.

Employment outlook

Opportunities for employment in the computer field are excellent. In the coming years, business, government, and other organizations are expected to acquire more and more computer equipment to manage information, to assist in manufacturing processes, and to be used in an ever-widening variety of other applications.

Employment of computer-service technicians will grow somewhat more slowly than it has in recent years and probably also more slowly than the amount of computer equipment is growing. The reason for this is that the newer equipment is more reliable and easier to repair. However, employment of computer-service technicians is still expected to grow faster than the average of all other occupations through the mid-1990s. In addition to job openings for computer-service technicians created by growth in the field, even more job openings will be created as employers need to replace computer-service technicians who are transferred, promoted, or retired. All of these factors taken together suggest that there will probably be thousands of job openings for computer-service technicians every year through the mid-1990s.

Earnings

In highly industrialized areas of the country, computer-service technicians will usually be in greater demand and will command a higher wage and more attractive benefits. Typical starting salaries for graduates of two-year engineering technology programs range between $16,000 and $23,000 per year, plus benefits that often include educational reimbursement.

Fully trained service technicians are paid average yearly salaries of approximately $30,000. Senior technicians with several years of experience earn from $30,000 to $40,000 per year. Those who advance to high supervisory or management positions, operate their own businesses, or enter major sales and service positions may earn upward of $48,000 per year or more.

Conditions of work

Working conditions are generally good for the computer-service technician. Computers are usually housed in air-conditioned, well-lighted, attractive environments. The most strenuous work probably is installation, because of the necessity of uncrating and positioning equipment. Under some conditions, technicians are required to work around dangerously high voltages and will need to be aware of appropriate safety measures.

The computer-service technician who works for a computer company or contractor usually will be required to drive a car from one assignment to another. In such cases, the technician is expected to see that the vehicle is cared for properly.

Very often the computer-service technician will find it necessary to work overtime to get a customer's system back into operation. How this extra time is to be accounted for may vary, ranging from compensatory time off to overtime pay.

With the rapid increase in the use of computers and computer-controlled robots, computer-service technicians may find themselves working in factory environments. There they will need to wear protective clothing and be especially aware of the hazards associated with factory work.

Social and psychological factors

Computer-service technicians deal not only with complex high-technology hardware but also with operating and management personnel. They must be able to work at peak levels of activity for extended periods of time with customers who are under pressure from top management to have their computer hardware operating. These situations require a large amount of patience and tact.

The computer-service technician's work is on the frontier of one of the most exciting technological revolutions in modern times. The service they provide is vital to the well-being of those whom they serve and to the nation's economic future. They keep the nation's most expensive and advanced machinery operating.

The career is a demanding one. It requires constant study to keep up with changes and new systems. The rewards are great, however, in job satisfaction and financial reward.

GOE: 05.05.05; SIC: Any industry; SOC: 3711

◇ SOURCES OF ADDITIONAL INFORMATION

Institute of Electrical and Electronics Engineers Computer Society
1730 Massachusetts Avenue, NW
Washington, DC 20036

Association for Computing Machinery
11 West 42nd Street
3rd Floor
New York, NY 10036

Institute for Certification of Computer Professionals
2200 East Devon Avenue
Suite 268
Des Plaines, IL 60018

◇ RELATED ARTICLES

Volume 1: Computer Hardware; Computer Software
Volume 2: Computer programmers; Graphics programmers; Numerical control tool programmers; Systems analysts
Volume 3: Computer and peripheral equipment operators; Industrial machinery mechanics; Office machine servicers; Telephone and PBX installers and repairers
Volume 4: CAD/CAM technicians; Data-processing technicians; Electromechanical technicians; Electronics technicians; Electronics test technicians; Electronics sales and services technicians; Robotics technicians

Data-processing technicians

Definition

Data-processing technicians use computers to manage and store information, organize and analyze data, make complex mathematical calculations, and provide answers to complex scientific or engineering design problems. They also help manage large quantities of office or industrial data, and provide complex and detailed information necessary to daily office operations in business and government. Data-processing technicians work with many different kinds of professionals. They include information scientists, systems analysts, information processing engineers, and engineering, scientific, and business computer programmers.

History

The field of electronic data-processing is a relatively new one. Forerunners of today's modern computers were not developed until the 1930s, and the first all-electronic general-purpose computer was not completed until 1946. This computer was called ENIAC (Electronic Numerical Integrator and Calculator). It was built at the University of Pennsylvania and used 18,000 vacuum tubes. In 1951, the first computer was used to process the U.S. census. In 1954, the first computer was used in private business. Since then, public and private industries, universities, and other research centers have developed many new different kinds of computers and have made new discoveries in information processing to solve problems faster and more accurately than ever before.

The first computer applications were in business and government operations that manage huge quantities of data. However, the use of computers and data-processing systems has now spread to almost all kinds of businesses, and typical computer applications now include payroll accounting, inventory control, customer billing, and market research.

Today, computers solve problems beyond the powers of human beings by making thousands of complex mathematical calculations in minutes. They can store information for future use and display it instantly. Computers are being applied to a rapidly growing and ever-widening range of problems as new discoveries make applied science more and more complex. Recent developments in electronics have made it possible to build miniature digital computers, minicomputers, and microprocessors. These have led to a flood of new uses in factory and office automation, scientific and medical research, robotics, aerospace engineering, and word and information processing. Perhaps no other single innovation of technology has had greater impact on the changing American scene than the computer.

Modern computer and information system advances have made it possible for large national and international systems to be put into operation. Examples include the National Crime Information Center of the Federal Bureau of Investigation, the Money Transfer System of the Federal Reserve, and the Command and Control Systems of the Department of Defense. All these are computer-based and computer-managed systems. Corporations and governments depend on computer systems for daily operations, records, and reports.

Improvements in computer design decrease the cost of computers. A computer that cost a million dollars in the 1960s costs less than a thousand dollars today. And while costs have been decreasing, the technology has been improving. In the 1970s, the largest computers performed ten million operations per second. In 1982 they performed 100 million. Now processors are being designed to perform a billion operations per second. Lower costs and greater capacity explain why computers are used in more and more ways, and why so many data-

processing technicians are needed today and in the future. In 1986, the nation's computer labor force was well over a million, including about 480,000 personnel in various levels of programming jobs. Continued significant growth is expected in this area through the mid-1990s.

Two types of data-processing occupations are now generally recognized. The daily activities of business, such as payroll and accounting, are one type. This work requires a knowledge of business administration as well as specialized training in computer operations, programming concepts, and modern management accounting techniques. The second type is scientific data processing. It requires a knowledge of mathematics, physical science, or engineering, and specialized courses in analysis techniques, computer programming concepts, and statistical analysis.

Over the years, the data-processing programmer has emerged as a key figure in the use of computers, and it is with this activity that data-processing technicians have become most involved. Two-year college programs on electronic data processing have been offered since the early 1960s. The first programs were designed to train business data-processing technicians. These were soon followed by a growing number of scientific data-processing programs. Now many schools offer two-year programs to prepare these highly specialized technicians.

Nature of the work

To understand the work of scientific and business data-processing technicians and the professionals whom they assist, it is necessary to understand computers and know how they are used to perform the complex processes of modern scientific or business data processing. These remarkable machines can do thousands of tasks and more. But they cannot do any of them without one essential thing: instructions. A computer needs to be told how to do what it does. A human being has to tell the computer how to become a word processor, a gas gauge, a speedometer, an automatic dialer, a timer, or a welder. In fact, the only thing any computer can do by itself is accept instructions and carry them out. For this reason, most of the specialized technological and scientific activities involved in using computers are associated with giving them instructions. Giving instructions to a computer is called programming. Most of the tasks performed by data-processing technicians focus on the various aspects and kinds of programming methods.

Data-processing technicians spend much of their time debugging software that they have programmed. This work often requires the attention of several technicians.

Computers that are the central data processor in large data-processing systems are called mainframe computers. They were the first types of computers to be developed. Later, smaller computers called minicomputers were developed. They were used to manage the program or list of instructions for the operation of complex programs for large mainframe computers. They also were used for relatively limited data-processing tasks.

Still more recently, the most modern and smallest computers called microcomputers or microprocessors were developed. They perform the same work as minicomputers did in large systems, and in addition are used for many small, independent computer applications in small businesses, offices, schools, or as personal computers in the home.

The personnel in large data-processing centers generally include *machine operators, data-processing technicians* (who may be called junior programmers or programmers), *senior programmers,* and *analysts.* Machine operators are not considered to be within the technician classification, although some operator positions are suitable entry-level positions for technicians. The analyst usually possesses a four-year college degree and sometimes a graduate degree and has overall responsibility for a project or system.

A computer program originates from the definition of a problem. This phase is entered upon jointly by the senior programmer and analyst who define the problem in detail and identify the relationships between all factors to be considered. In this phase, education in a noncomputer specialization is of paramount importance. It makes the difference between business data processing and scientific data processing.

For example, if the problem deals with cost accounting or large inventory control, the analyst and senior programmer must know about accounting, operational procedures, file maintenance techniques, and related subjects.

If, however, the problems deal with the design of a building, machine, or highway, or with engineering or genetics, the information analysts and senior programmers would need a strong background in engineering or science and the related mathematics. They must know about different types of computers, computer languages, and data-processing procedures.

Data-processing technicians receive the problem definition, the computer system and units to be used, and the computer language to be used as an assignment from the analyst and the senior programmer. The technicians then design the necessary flow charts and input-output forms. They collect necessary data and translate the problem definition into a set of instructions called a program.

Programs are written in systems of coding and organization called computer languages. There are many computer languages, and specific computers accept specific languages. Computers are designed to operate directly on a simple machine language, based on Boolean algebra and binary numbers, and beyond that, to process instructions and data entered by programmers in a computer language, which contains English letters and numbers.

One of the simplest languages is called BASIC. It is elementary and new computer users learn programming with it. For business data processing the most common language is CO-BOL, which means "Common Business Oriented Language." In the mid-1980s, more than half of all business programs used COBOL. Although other languages are gaining popularity, business data-processing technicians need to have a working knowledge of this language.

For scientific data processing, the technicians need to have a working knowledge of FORTRAN, whose name is derived from "Formula Translation." This language is much more useful in programming for solving mathematical equations found in engineering design analyses and other complex scientific applications.

Several other program languages are in use. RPG is used for simple business applications that do not require complex programs. It is most commonly run on minicomputers or small mainframes. PL/1 is a general purpose programming language and was designed to be an alternative to COBOL and FORTRAN. Other new languages that are gaining popularity include APL, which is a programming language developed by IBM for use on its PCs, and C, which is a programming language developed by AT&T for use with its Unix operating system.

All of these languages, when used to program a problem for a computer, must be translated to the computer's basic machine language. This is done by a compiler, which is simply a separate program that accepts the program written in COBOL, FORTRAN, or whatever language is used to solve the problem. The compiler translates it or converts it step-by-step into the computer's own machine language.

It is the responsibility of the programmer to write the program in the language most suited to the problem definition and the computer involved. These are usually specified to the technician by the systems analyst or senior programmer. In addition to writing new programs, technicians constantly modify existing programs to meet new requirements or increase operating efficiency. A technician may share an office with as many as three or four other technicians or programmers. Technicians also spend considerable time in the computer room, checking on programs to be certain they have no errors and that the answers coming from the program are correct.

Under the technician's supervision, machine operators perform the actual tasks of computer operating required to produce the desired output. Both operator and technician must know the operating characteristics of the computer and be able to identify malfunctions. The greatest part of the operator's time is spent in the computer room with the technician or other responsible programmers.

When the program has been run for the first time, the programmer analyzes the results. Often some step in the program leads to a mistake and changes or corrections need to be made. This is called debugging. After all of the debugging is done, the program provides the answer or process it was planned to perform, and the technician moves to another problem.

Scientific or business data-processing technicians spend most of their time studying data and methods of defining problems and solutions to problems involving data in the field in which they are employed. Developing programs takes much more time and effort than the computer uses in the actual running time, which may be only a few minutes or at most a few hours.

The data-processing technician, in addition to programming for problem solutions, must maintain a current and effective program library. These programs may be stored on magnetic tape, storage disks, or other machine-readable mediums. They are subject to considerable revision and modification, which requires the maintenance of appropriate records.

In specialized jobs in the scientific data-processing field, the technician may spend time in other departments where the computer programs control the final work to be done. This adds variety to the data-processing technician's work.

Similarly, the business data-processing technician may work in the accounting department with the business methods planning, study, and control managers. Here they assist in gathering data or help to plan the collection, storing, and the managing of the data in computer processing to provide the most needed and useful information for managing the business.

The following paragraphs describe some of the specific entry-level positions that are available for data-processing technicians.

Junior programmers in business or science develop computer programs to solve specified problems. The problem specification is usually given to the technician in the form of a flow chart made by a senior programmer or an experienced programmer. The junior programmer must be able to read and interpret the flow chart in order to solve the problem.

Computer operators operate the computers and load programs. They maintain surveillance of program progress and establish and maintain records of equipment use. Technicians or experienced programmers often direct the work of the operators. They also direct the work of the peripheral equipment operators.

Peripheral equipment operators operate unit records and other equipment used to support the central processing unit. This may include data-conversion units required in preparing data for computer utilization or for activities completely independent of computers.

Requirements

Advancement within the field of computer technology requires the ability to communicate and work with others. Because technicians often serve as communication channels between various people and the computer, they must be receptive to new ideas and diplomatic in resolving misunderstandings among other workers. The prospective data-processing technician should enjoy the challenge in solving problems. The ability to think clearly and logically supersedes everything else.

High-school students interested in becoming data-processing technicians should study accounting, business management, and computer technology. More and more high schools across the nation are currently offering introductory courses in computer programming. Interested students should take advantage of all opportunities to take such courses. If students wish to be scientific data-processing technicians, they should take at least one year of algebra and at least a year of physics, chemistry, or biology. For students who plan to be business data-processing technicians, subjects such as accounting, inventory control, statistical methods, and similar business subjects are recommended.

Good preparation in language is necessary. These technicians must be good readers and communicators. An elementary course in drafting or engineering drawing taken in high school will be very useful to data-processing technicians in the sciences. Drawing, diagramming, and sketching are also crucial to scientists and engineers. A course in graphic representation of business data will be very useful for data-processing technicians in business.

One of the main tasks of both scientific and business data-processing technicians is to diagram and chart data relationships and sequences in a computer program. The method of presenting data is systematic and orderly and demands preparation. A course in engineering drawing is especially useful if the technician is eventually employed in engineering or scientific research or design work.

Students who are seriously thinking of becoming data-processing technicians should be aware that their education will continue long after employment is secured. This is necessary because of advances in technology that may require changes in procedures, methods, equipment, and even computer language and programming concepts.

There are many excellent educational institutions, both private and public, that offer two-year, post–high-school programs designed to produce technicians who are employable upon graduation as junior programmers. The academic work in these institutions includes a number of specialized courses related to computer programming and system concepts. Laboratory work designed around modern equipment is a vital part of students' studies. In addition, related courses in mathematics, statistics, accounting, business principles, economics, physics, engineering science, biology, or earth science are required for graduation. The selection of these courses depends on whether the student is interested in business data processing or scientific data-processing. Many institutions offer an associate of science degree in both fields.

A two-year program in scientific data-processing technology might begin with an orientation seminar, followed by an introductory course on data processing. Other courses might include communications skills, technical mathematics, a science course (physics, electronics, chemistry, or biology), techniques of real-time and remote computation, statistics, statistical programming, life sciences, graphical representation, and technical reporting.

The second year might include courses in fundamentals of scientific computation, Boolean algebra, linear programming, industrial organization and management, programming for engineering applications, scientific programming languages, introduction to operations research, a field project of the student's choosing, and general and industrial economics.

The two-year program in business data processing technology might begin with courses in communication skills, business machines, and technical mathematics. The first year would also include introduction to business, introduction to electronic data processing, business programming languages, business statistics, and principles of accounting.

In the second year of business data processing, courses typically include economics, technical reporting, business management, systems and procedures, applied business systems, computer peripheral equipment and data storage systems, introduction to operations research, and computer language survey.

During school and after graduation, data-processing technicians in both science and business should anticipate the need for further education. Opportunities include programs offered by company schools or equipment manufacturers. In some cases, technicians work in applications so new that formal training has yet to be developed. They may need to take supplementary courses scheduled for evenings or other time outside of the regular working week. Usually the employer pays tuition and other costs for job-related outside study.

Normal good health is highly desirable for this career. Normal eyesight and hand-eye coordination are needed for writing or diagramming. The physical strength requirements, however, are minimal. Most of the work takes place indoors in comfortable conditions. Many persons with physical handicaps find this career to be very suitable.

Special requirements

There are no special requirements for licenses or certification in these careers at the present time. A special certification is available if the technician passes the examination to qualify for the Certificate in Computer Programming (CCP) conferred by the Institute for Certification of Computer Professionals. This institute is sponsored by the Data Processing Management Association, which started the program to encourage professional development within the field of data processing. The examination is offered in selected cities throughout the country each year. The CCP certificate is not formally required by employers, but it is evidence of accomplishment that is considered favorably when employers decide to hire or promote technicians. The address of the Data Processing Management Association is given at the end of this article.

Opportunities for experience and exploration

High-school students who are interested in either scientific or business data-processing technology should ask their teachers and guidance counselors about suitable courses to acquaint them with the work of data-processing technicians. Many high schools now offer computer courses where students can play computer games and learn basic programming. Science or business courses and hobbies can lead to activities involving the use of computers to solve problems in science or business activities.

Magazines and clubs are other ways for students to find out more about this career. Science magazines are available in the library; they can furnish interested students with ideas and opportunities. Similarly, joining a business or science club can open opportunities for high-school students to become acquainted with and participate in activities that may lead to a technician career.

In addition to the traditional courses, high-school students should read and study several professional journals and publications on computer technology. If it can be arranged, a visit to one or more computer installations would be most helpful. Several computer-user groups have formed professional organizations that offer opportunities for high-school students to obtain information on educational and occupational requirements.

Students can obtain valuable experience in part-time jobs. Some can be found in school or in business computer centers. These jobs provide solid experience that helps the student prepare for this demanding career.

Methods of entering

Many students in a data-processing technical program find jobs before they graduate. This can be accomplished in several ways. One is through the school's placement service, particularly those that maintain a current file on local and national job openings. Classified advertisements and employment agencies are also responsible for many placements.

Some industries and businesses send recruiters to schools that offer programs in data processing technology. Students apply directly to the recruiters of the industry or business for which they wish to work. In most instances, the personnel manager is sent to recruit.

The demand for well-qualified data-processing technicians continues to increase. However, graduates of two-year technical programs seeking entry-level programming jobs may have to compete with many other job seekers. The great interest in the programming field in recent years has spurred the development of many training programs, including programs that provide four years of college preparation. In some circumstances employers are able to pick among a large pool of applicants with varying qualifications. As the field matures, technicians with only two years of formal training may have to look harder to find satisfactory jobs.

Training on the specifics of the particular employer's data-processing system is necessary. A period of orientation at the beginning of the job, sometimes several months or even a year in length, may be required before the beginning technician is expected to have mastered the details of the employer's needs and processes.

In recent years, the trend toward computer-controlled automation in industries such as computer manufacturing and radio and television products has increased the need for scientific data-processing technicians who know the industry. Many companies have met this need by sending their experienced electronic or electromechanical technicians to school to learn computer programming and data systems management. The same kind of program is also used to train other technical workers so that they can use the computer-controlled robots now being installed in some industries.

Advancement

Advancement opportunities for skilled data-processing technicians are good. In addition to the steps from junior programmer to senior programmer, there are parallel steps in supervision and management. Technicians who are considered extremely competent in the details of problem analysis and programming generally can progress to the analyst position. Advancement can be considerably hastened by education beyond a two-year technician program. Supervision and management positions are available to technicians who show promise in managing and supervising people and projects.

Experienced scientific or business data-processing technicians who thoroughly understand programming, information acquisition, storage and retrieval systems, and equipment, are finding increased opportunities to work as consultants. There are many companies and businesses that need help in designing a custom system using a small computer, a storage and information processing system, and the programming know-how to apply computer technology to their work. Often such a system and the ability to use it will make the difference between failure and success of a business.

In a similar way, computer programming technicians and specialists in numerical process control or computer graphics can often find challenging and excellent advancement opportunities by working for consulting companies that specialize in these services.

Advancement often comes through activities and contacts in professional societies or organizations. There are many professional organizations for technicians to join. They range from organizations concerned with management of systems to special interest groups involved in research, statistical programming, and business programming.

The following professional occupations in the computer field are held by people who supervise data processing technicians and coordinate their supportive efforts.

For each of the jobs described below, technicians must obtain further education related to areas of computer application. These areas may be in the fields of physics, chemistry, genetics, statistics; the humanities; or in any one of the many fields in which computer technology is playing a vital role. For technicians in business data processing, continued study of both business and the developments in data-processing science and technology is a way of life.

Business or scientific programmers refine definitions of problems with the aid of library facilities and conferences. They determine the system and equipment that will be used in solving the problem. They also design flow charts and diagrams that express the problem and define objectives. After designing the flow chart, the programmers code the chart in an accepted computer language, compile the program, de-

bug the program where necessary, and execute the compiled program.

Computer graphics technicians may work in an engineering research or design department. They use computer graphics to prepare exploratory and developmental design concepts and final engineering drawings.

Scientific data-system programmers evaluate, design, and implement computer-based systems such as those used for processing data resulting from vehicular movement. This work could extend from passenger cars to spacecraft.

Scientific programmers analyze, program, and debug computer solutions of problems, such as those arising in missile and space-vehicle engineering, guidance and mission planning, space kinetics, spacecraft dynamics, thermodynamics and fluid dynamics, and reentry and propulsion physics.

Applications programmers in science and engineering solve problems in the design of computers, electronic components, and physical subsystems. Many of the problems involve the use of modern on-line graphics.

Numerical control programmers program automatic tool-and-die machines.

Scientific information programmers and analysts work with problems that include all phases of scientific, engineering, and medical data processing and analysis. Current areas of interest include range tracking, antisubmarine warfare, medical and educational information retrieval, statistical analysis, and total information systems for industry and government. These positions require years of experience and usually involve further formal study.

Employment outlook

Employment in the data-processing field as a whole is expected to grow faster than the average for all occupations at least through the mid-1990s. Although demand for data-processing technicians is not as strong as it was a decade or so ago, the prospects for growth in employment of technicians are also generally good. This positive outlook is related to the great variety of applications for computer technology that are constantly being devised.

The advent of minicomputers and microcomputers has allowed revolutionary changes in the ways computers are used and has greatly expanded the number of settings they are used in. The development of computer equipment, or hardware, has happened at the same time as the development of many kinds of software and software packages, which are complete sets of programs and other instructions to be used with particular types of computers. As computers, software, and programming techniques have been refined, many programming tasks for some applications have become routine or have been eliminated. This trend is slowing the growth in demand for personnel with two-year degrees in the data-processing field. In addition, competition for jobs among graduates of technical programs is increasing as more beginning programmers enter the job market with four-year degrees. As a result, technicians with only two years of formal training may find relatively fewer satisfactory jobs open to them in the future.

Although no major economic recession is forecast through the mid-1990s, the job market for data-processing technicians would be weakened if the nation experienced a period of economic recession, and entry-level positions would be most vulnerable to cutbacks.

Earnings

Entry-level technicians can expect to earn $16,000 to $20,000 per year. Experienced technicians can expect to earn an average of $26,000 per year. Beginning technicians in scientific data processing usually earn more than beginning data-processing technicians in business.

The types of benefits available to data-processing technicians will vary from employer to employer. Generally, paid vacations, holidays, and some type of insurance program are provided. In addition, many companies have a tuition refund-policy for employees who wish to pursue additional education in the evenings or on weekends.

Many employers provide liberal opportunities for technicians and other data-processing workers to study on the job or in school to keep the company up-to-date and competitive. Some employers also pay membership fees in scientific and technical societies.

Conditions of work

Both scientific and business data-processing technicians will find an excellent environment in which to work. The equipment they use normally requires minimum dust specifications and temperature control, especially if it is in a large, mainframe central computer operation. Thus, technicians will most likely be housed in a recently constructed or renovated building. However, the development of the silicon chip microprocessors and small computers makes it possible to have computer work stations wherever typewriters or business calculators would be used. These are normal office conditions and therefore are good in most cases.

The workweek for the technicians usually does not exceed forty hours, although at times they may be required to work more than forty hours. This is particularly true when the employer updates, modifies, or changes existing computer hardware. Some technicians work on a shift basis.

The data-processing technician spends considerable time working on tasks assigned by senior programmers and analysts. The technician may work somewhat independently of others on these individual assignments. Some assignments may be for the technician to write a program to solve a relatively simple problem or to revise an existing program. Other assignments may be to write and test a program that is one part of a large and complex sequence of data-processing steps. Individual or group conferences with other programmers and information analysts are a regular part of the technician's work.

Upon advancement into duties and services that require the technician to visit job sites where computer applications are in use, working conditions may vary. If the job sites are at offices or operations in rather traditional industrial, government, educational, or institutional use, conditions will be good.

Occasionally, the technician may travel to and from work in remote locations or work under unusual conditions. In these cases the persons who are in charge of the operation can advise the technician about safety, special clothing, or other matters.

Social and psychological factors

While the career of a data-processing technician is potentially exciting and attractive, it is not for everyone. Entry into the field as a technician or junior programmer must be considered as the beginning of a career in which the worker will need to study, grow, and advance in employment.

To be successful, all programmers must possess the ability to accept problem definitions as presented by information analysts. They must then refine such definitions with the aid of library facilities and conferences with other workers. In addition to these abilities, scientific data-processing technicians must have a fundamental knowledge of applied science; business data-processing technicians must have knowledge of accounting and elementary business management. Both business and scientific data processing technicians must have a practical understanding of the mathematics that supports the concepts and processes of their field of specialization.

Technicians must be able to work in a logical, analytical way to define a problem, organize data, and program a computer to solve it. They must work with patience and care, sometimes under pressure, and they must work as team members. In advanced positions, technicians will very probably be supervising other technical workers. Even as beginning technicians or junior programmers, they will work very closely with, and sometimes supervise, computer and peripheral equipment operators and other skilled workers or clerks.

Well-trained technicians who keep up with the field will find variety and challenge in this new and rapidly changing technological frontier. They can enjoy both the excellent financial rewards for a demanding job and the deep satisfaction of being part of a work force that is essential to the country's prosperity and well-being.

GOE: 11.01.01; SIC: 7374; SOC: 397

◇ **SOURCES OF ADDITIONAL INFORMATION**

American Federation of Information Processing Societies
1899 Preston White Drive
Reston, VA 22091

American Society for Information Science
1424 16th Street, NW
Suite 404
Washington, DC 20036

Association for Computing Machinery
11 West 42nd Street, 3rd Floor
New York, NY 10036

Data Processing Management Association
505 Busse Highway
Park Ridge, IL 60068

Institute for Certification of Computer Professionals
2200 East Devon Avenue
Suite 268
Des Plaines, IL 60018

◇ **RELATED ARTICLES**

Volume 1: Computer Hardware; Computer Software; Electronics; Engineering; Telecommunications
Volume 2: Computer programmers; Data base managers; Graphics programmers; Information scientists; Numerical control tool programmers
Volume 3: Computer and peripheral equipment operators
Volume 4: Computer service technicians; Integrated circuit technicians; Semi-conductor-development technicians; Software technicians

Diving technicians

Definition

Diving technicians dive in oceans or fresh water, using special underwater breathing equipment, or serve as support workers or attendants for divers. They may also serve as intermediaries between administrative, scientific, or engineering staff and other skilled workers in a wide range of marine activities. They are expected to be knowledgeable in many aspects of diving and diving equipment. They must also be competent in performing numerous skilled-worker jobs and underwater jobs.

History

Since earliest times, people have wanted to go underwater to retrieve food or valuable items or to carry out tasks such as ship building or repair. But without equipment, a diver can stay under the surface only as long as a single breath allows. Other factors that limit the unaided diver's activities include cold water temperatures, the water pressure at great depths, and strong currents.

The history of the diving technician's job dates back to the first efforts to overcome these limitations with special equipment. To bring an air supply down, early divers used sections of hollow reeds as breathing tubes. As long ago as the time of ancient Greeks, crude diving bells were in use. But it was not until the late eighteenth century that a practical diving bell was invented. It allowed one person to descend into shallow water in a container that was open at the bottom and supplied with air that was pumped by hand from above. In the nineteenth century, the first diving suit was devised. It too was connected to the surface by a tube. Even with various improvements, however, diving suits were always rather clumsy. The invention in 1943 of scuba diving equipment (self-contained underwater breathing system), allowed di- vers much more freedom of movement and helped helped to open up many new activities for divers. Since that time, diving techniques and equipment have become increasingly sophisticated.

The records of salvage from the Spanish galleon *Santa Margarita*, which sank in about twenty feet of water on the lower Florida Keys in 1622, tell something about the development of diving technology.

In 1644, an effort was made to salvage the galleon's cargo of gold and silver. Diving crews, using a bronze bell as an air source, salvaged much of the silver coins and other items of value—but not the gold, which sank into the sand and could not be found. Some divers lost their lives, swept away by the dangerous currents even in shallow water.

In 1980, 336 years later, the wreck was found again. The diving teams used scuba equipment, electronic metal detectors, and special hydraulic jets that washed away the sand covering more than $20 million worth of gold and silver coins. Ingots, gold chains, and other valuables were recovered as well. Modern equipment and techniques made all the difference.

One major problem in deep-water diving results from the additional pressure of the weight of the water. This pressure causes the nitrogen in the air breathed by the diver to dissolve in the bloodstream. Normally, the nitrogen remains in the lungs and is simply exhaled in the breathing process. When a diver returns too rapidly from deep water to the surface, bubbles of nitrogen form in the blood vessels. These bubbles can cause serious sickness and

A diving technician fastens a sunken item on to a pulley system while his colleagues observe from the boat above.

even death. This condition is called "the bends" and is a constant hazard of deep-water diving. It can be prevented by making sure the diver returns slowly enough to the surface so the nitrogen in the blood can be freed in the lungs and breathed out normally, rather than forming bubbles in the blood vessels.

Around the time of World War II, the U.S. Navy began to use new approaches to preventing the bends. A helium breathing mixture, instead of air, was shown to be safer and more efficient for deep-water divers. Divers who ascended too quickly were put in special decompression chambers. Advances such as these were very important because of the great amount of repair and salvage work in naval activities, especially in wartime. In the late 1950s and 1960s underwater exploration increased. The depths of the oceans, which cover three-fifths of the world's surface, were still the most uncharted part of the planet, presenting a challenge that many people thought was comparable to the exploration of space. The growing offshore petroleum-drilling industry added another reason for the development of diving technology. New kinds of diving bells, saturation diving systems, and a host of submersible devices now allow deeper and more effective underwater work, such as the 1985–86 exploration of the *Titanic* wreck several miles under the North Atlantic.

As diving and related activities came to involve more people and more complicated equipment, the need arose for workers who could handle many different kinds of technical tasks. Today diving technicians are employed mainly in commercial diving; a few also work in marine science and research activities. In commercial diving, numerous mechanical, engineering, and construction skills are transferred to an underwater setting. These jobs can be physically demanding and hazardous, but they can also offer adventure and excitement.

Nature of the work

The duties of diving technicians are often broad and varying. Diving technicians must be skilled in current diving methods, and in addition they should be skilled in the many jobs they may be required to perform underwater. Examples of some common underwater jobs are inspection of structures or equipment by visual, photographic, or videotape methods; mechanical construction or servicing using hand or power tools; cleaning marine growth from structures; welding or cutting in salvage, repair, or construction; and geological or biological surveying. To be a successful diving technician, diving skills alone are not enough.

The largest number of job opportunities for the diving technician is with commercial diving contractors. The work that diving contractors are called upon to perform encompasses a very wide variety of jobs in constructing foundations and other underwater features, offshore oil well piping and control systems, salvage, and repair or mechanical service for ships and structures afloat or on foundations in underwater locations. The work is frequently dirty, demanding, exhaustingly tough, and dangerous.

Sometimes diving technicians work on the surface, not in the water. Technicians may become experts in the life-support system for divers and in the management of the equipment. These technicians work with the controls that supply the proper mixture of gases for the diver to breathe. They maintain the correct pressures in the hoses leading to the underwater worker and act as the communicator and life-support partner of the diver. They monitor water depth, conditions inside diving bells and chambers,

and decompression schedules for divers. This is a highly skilled position involving many responsibilities, and it is vital to the success of all deep-water diving operations.

It is possible that the scientific and technological demands made on the life-support team may bring about the development of a group of specialists who do not dive. However, the usual practice now is for divers to work both underwater and on deck.

Other important areas of employment for diving technicians are oceanographic research and underwater military engineering. While the total number of technicians engaged in these activities is relatively small, it may increase as it becomes more desirable to extract more minerals from the ocean floor. Even during peacetime military diving crews are needed in rescue and reclamation.

Newly hired technicians are normally assigned work involving organizing the shop and caring for and maintaining all types of company equipment. Soon, they will be assigned a similar job on a diving boat or platform. When on a diving operation, technicians provide topside or surface support for the divers by assisting them with equipment, supply hoses, communications, necessary tools, and lines. They help maintain a safe and efficient operation. As a diver's tender, technicians may monitor and control diving descent and ascent rates, breathing gas supplies, and decompression schedules. They must also be able to assist in an emergency and help treat a diver injured in an accident or suffering from the bends.

As technicians gain experience in company procedures and jobs, they are given more responsibility. Technicians usually can start underwater work within a few months to two years after being hired. This depends on the technician's skills, desires, and the company's needs.

A technician's first dives are shallow and relatively easy. Subsequent dives match the technician's ability and competence. With time and experience, technicians may advance to work deep-dive bell and saturation diving systems. Saturation divers are gradually compressed in an on-deck chamber, as they would be when diving, then transferred to and from the work site inside a pressurized bell. These divers stay in a pressure-controlled environment for extended periods.

All of the personnel on a diving crew should know how to care for and use a wide variety of equipment. Some of the commonly used diving equipment includes air compressors, decompression chambers, high-pressure breathing-gas storage tanks, pressure regulators and gas regulating systems, hoses and fittings for handling air and gas, and communications equipment.

Personal diving equipment for use by the diver ranges from simple scuba, now seldom used, to full face masks, lightweight and heavy helmets for both air and helium/oxygen use, diving bells, and diving suits, from wet suits to the heavy dry suits that can be bolted to a breastplate to which the heavy helmet is attached. For cold water and deep or long duration dives, a hot-water suit may be used. This suit allows a flow of warm water supplied from the surface to be passed through a loose-fitting wet suit on the diver's body, protecting the diver from body heat loss.

The diving crew uses simple hand tools. These tools most commonly include hammers, crescent wrenches, screwdrivers, and pliers. Knowledge of arc welding equipment and underwater arc or other metal-cutting equipment is very important for many kinds of work, such as salvage, construction, or repair and modification of underwater structures. These needs are often associated with underwater petroleum explorations, well-drilling, or management of piping systems.

A well-supplied hand-tool kit is invaluable to a diver. Items such as wire cutters and volt/ohm meters are often needed. Divers should be versatile and may be expected to use all of the basic hand tools, many types of power tools, and many sophisticated and often delicate instruments. These last include video and camera equipment, measuring instruments, ultrasonic probes, metal detection devices, and other specialized equipment.

Requirements

Persons who want to become diving technicians must have diverse skills and abilities. Diving skills alone are not enough, as diving is only the process by which the technicians get to the job site.

Well-rounded diving technicians should be mechanically inclined and able to operate and maintain a wide variety of mechanical and diving equipment. They must understand drawings and simple blueprints and be familiar with piping and valves. They must know how to handle high-pressure gases, bottles, and gauges. Diving technicians also must be able to write accurate reports, keep records, and do paperwork.

Diving technicians must also become skilled divers, as well as technicians capable of working above and below the water. They must understand the physical and biological elements of the marine environment. Technicians must also be aware of the importance of teamwork, and they must be capable of working as an integral part of a team.

The best way to train for this career is to attend one of the postsecondary schools and colleges that offer an organized program, usually two years in length, to prepare such technicians. Typical basic requirements for enrollment are a high-school diploma or its equivalent, demonstrated capability to study college-level scientific subjects, completion of three to four years of language and communication subjects, at least one year of algebra, and one year of physics or chemistry with laboratory work.

Diving technicians are specialized engineering technicians. Therefore they need a basic theoretical and practical scientific background. In addition, they need to have mastered several construction-type work skills.

A typical postsecondary program consists of three types of courses. The first school program is designed to develop the skills and knowledge required of a diving technician. The second group of courses is designed to give students an understanding of the environment in which they will be working. The last consists of general education courses designed to broaden the student's knowledge and sharpen communication skills.

The first year's study includes such courses as seamanship and small-boat handling, basic diving, drafting, basic welding, technical writing, advanced diving, fundamentals of marine engines and compressors, marine welding, physical oceanography, and marine biology. Often students participate in a summer cooperative work-study program of supervised ocean dives before the second year of courses begins.

Second-year courses typically include underwater construction, biological oceanography, physics, fundamentals of electronics, machine shop operations, underwater operations, advanced diving systems, basic emergency medical technology, and speech and communications. The second year also may include fundamentals of photography, or a special project that relates specifically to diving or life-support technology.

Additional studies such as economics, American institutions, or other general studies must usually be completed. Physical requirements for the career include general good health, at least normal physical strength, sound respiratory functions, normal or better eyesight, and good hand-eye coordination and manual dexterity.

This diving technician prepares a deep-sea vehicle for launching. The vehicle will explore the ocean floor down to 20,000 feet (6,000 meters).

Special requirements

Schools that provide programs for these technicians often have special admission requirements relating to swimming ability and skills. As an example, one school's special requirements include: the completion of application, release, medical history, and waiver of liability forms for the diving technology program; an annual physical examination; and the successful performance of several tests in the presence of the school's diving officer. These tests include swimming without fins underwater for a distance of seventy-five feet without surfacing; swimming without fins underwater for a distance of 150 feet, surfacing four times; swimming without fins 1,000 feet in less than ten minutes, demonstrating swimming with snorkel and fins with and without face mask; skin diving to a depth of ten feet and recovering a ten-pound object; demonstrating the ability to rescue a swimmer and carry him or her seventy-five feet on the surface; and demonstrating the ability to tread water for ten minutes without swim aids.

When students seek employment, they usually find that many employers require completion of a recognized training program or documentation of comparable experience. A thorough physical examination may also be required. The hiring company will usually arrange for the physical with a physician of their choice. An emergency medical technician certificate is valuable and may be required by some companies.

There are no special requirements for licenses at the entry level in the United States.

The United Kingdom and some of the North Sea countries do have specific requirements for divers, however, that can be met only by training in their countries.

For specific work beyond entry level, a welding certificate may be required. Also, a certification in nondestructive testing (NDT) may enhance the technicians's opportunities. Both of these certificates are specific and beyond entry level. The employer will be able to specify the method of obtaining the special certificates desired.

Employment in areas other than commercial diving may impose more specific requirements. A specialty in photography, electronics, oceanography, biology, marine culture, or construction engineering may open other doors of opportunity for the diving technician.

Opportunities for experience and exploration

Information about training schools can be found in trade journals and sports publications. Libraries are a good place to look for program listings and descriptions. People interested in opportunities in this career would be well advised to contact several training programs and compare their offerings to their own individual needs. It would also be good to ask about employment prospects for future graduates of each program.

A visit to one or more potential employers would certainly benefit the person considering diving technician training. While observations of an offshore job would be difficult, a tour of the company shop, a look at its equipment, and a chance to talk to its technicians should be informative and worthwhile.

Anyone interested in this career should become proficient in scuba diving and outdoor swimming and diving. The experience of learning to feel at home in water and underwater not only can help the person to pass entry tests for a formal preparatory program, but also can allow students to find out if they really are suited for the career.

Methods of entering

Commercial diving contractors, where the majority of diving technicians seek employment, have in the past recruited personnel who had Navy experience, had learned skills through informal apprenticeships or by themselves, or who were friends or relatives of employees. Sometimes people were hired off the street. All personnel hired in this manner were expected to learn on the job.

As diving technology advanced and diving equipment and techniques became more sophisticated, contractors looked more and more to schools to provide qualified entry-level help. Schools upgraded their programs to meet the changing requirements of industry. Most contractors now rely on approved schools to meet their entry-level personnel needs. Some contractors will hire only graduates of diving training programs.

Schools with diving technician programs usually have of three or more staff members who have professional commercial diving experience. These instructors keep abreast of the diving industry through occasional summer work, consultation, and professional and personal contacts. Through these contacts they are able to assess industry needs and the job market, and to give help in job placement.

Major offshore contractors and other potential employers may visit schools with diving programs each year before graduation to interview prospective employees. Some employers offer summer work to students who have completed one year of a two-year program.

Some employers contact schools whenever they need additional diving technicians. The school staff then directs them to interested job seekers. While many graduates find jobs in oil-drilling operations or working for other large industries, a few graduates find positions as diving school instructors, marine culture technicians, photographer/writers, marine research technicians, and submersible pilots.

One can enter the diving technician career by joining the Navy or specialized units of the Marines, Army Corps of Engineers, or Merchant Marine Corps. Some of the military operations for salvage, recovery of sunken ships, or rescue require deep-water divers and life-support skills. Usually Navy and other diving personnel with experience can obtain civilian employment, but often they need to learn a wider range of skills for underwater construction or other work.

Advancement

A well-trained, highly motivated diving technician can expect to advance steadily, depending on personal competence and the employer's needs. Over a three- to five-year period a technician may be a shop hand, a tender (tending equipment and maintaining gear), a combina-

tion diver/tender, a diver, lead diver, and possibly supervisor of a diving crew. Or a technician may advance from surface support duties to supervisor of surface support or supervisor of a diving crew, possibly within three to five years. This nondiving life-support career, however, is much more limited in terms of employment opportunities than the combined diving and support career. Management opportunities within the company are also a possibility for a qualified technician. Those who want greater opportunities for earnings, independence, and growth may start their own business as a contractor or consultant.

Employment outlook

The world is increasingly turning to the sea to supply mineral resources, new and additional sources of food and medicine, transportation, and national defense. This growth of marine activity has resulted in a continuing demand for qualified diving technicians. A career as a diving technician offers many opportunities and challenges for the student who desires an exciting and rewarding future working in the world's last frontier.

In the past few decades, the greatest demand for skilled diving technicians has been related to the search for more petroleum and natural gas from undersea oil fields. With the production of oil and gas from the oceans, there was a virtual explosion in the amount of work and the numbers of people employed. Whether this activity will be a source of new jobs in the future is uncertain. Employment will depend on levels of drilling activity, which, in turn, depends on the levels of world oil prices. The recent history of these prices makes it impossible to predict with any confidence what will happen to employment in this field.

Hydroelectric power generating plants, dams, heavy industry, and sanitation plants that have cooling water lines or water discharges are also a source of work for divers and surface crews. Certain ship repairs, often of an emergency nature, require divers who can repair the trouble at sea or in dock, without placing the ship in dry dock to correct the problem.

While some work is being done in aquaculture, marine culture, and ocean mining, these areas are currently relatively undeveloped. The potential for these fields is great and the possibilities for technicians are exciting, but total employment in these areas is presently small.

Earnings

Earnings in this career vary widely and depend on factors such as location and nature of the job and the skills and experience of the technician. A technician working in commercial diving might work almost anyplace in the oceans, rivers, and lakes of the world. Some types of work pay the employee on an hourly or daily basis, as is the case on most union jobs.

Recent graduates of diving technician programs often start at about $16,000 to $18,000 per year, assuming they work in commercial diving six or eight months of the year. With a little experience divers may make as much as $35,000 or more a year on some jobs. A few highly experienced specialists may make up to about $100,000 a year.

Some contract jobs call for time on and time off, such as a thirty days on/thirty days off rotation, and the pay will reflect at least a certain amount of the off-time as full-time pay. An example of a rotational job would be service work on an exploratory oil-drilling vessel where diving crew members live aboard for their on-shift period and perform any work required during that time. Pay for this work includes both on and off time. Wages earned under an organized union contract are typically at higher rates, but the employee receives pay only for days worked.

Employees of diving contractors typically receive life and health insurance benefits. Some companies also provide paid vacation time.

Conditions of work

As previously stressed, diving technicians must possess numerous technical job skills. Working conditions may vary tremendously depending upon the nature of the work, the duration of the job, and the geographic location.

Some offshore sites could include boats ranging from under one-hundred-feet long to much longer ocean-going ships. Also, oil drilling vessels and many types of barges provide working and living bases for diving technicians.

Working hours or shifts offshore may only require the diving crew to be available if needed, as is common on drilling vessels. More often, however, as in construction work or jobs that are continuous and predictable in nature, the dive crew will work up to twelve hours a day and seven days a week. As might be expected, the more rigorous work provides the greater pay scale.

Living conditions on board ship or barge are usually reasonably comfortable. Rooms may accommodate from two to as many as eight people, depending on vessel size, but they are at least adequate. Food, of course, is furnished on all rigs where crews must live aboard. Quite often it is unusually good.

Diving technicians are taught to be conscious of appropriate clothing and safety practices. They must never forget them as they work in the potentially dangerous conditions encountered in deep-water diving.

Offshore work and especially construction diving is rigorous and often physically demanding. Persons entering this field should be physically fit. Companies commonly place a maximum age limit, usually thirty to thirty-two years, for entry-level employees seeking to become divers. While many divers may work well into their forties or fifties and occasionally beyond, deep and long-duration diving is considered a young person's work.

Social and psychological factors

Diving technicians are pioneers in an area of developing technology and expanding job opportunities. They must be proficient in a broad spectrum of job skills. The work of these technicians can be extremely varied, challenging, demanding, and potentially dangerous. There can be much personal satisfaction from smooth job performance.

Travel, excitement, and some amount of risk are a part of the diving technician's life. On the job, technicians should be self-starters, showing initiative and ability to work independently as well as on a team.

People who choose a career in diving technology should be ready to adapt to a life-style that seldom offers stable home and family life. Technicians must be able to follow the work. They can expect occasional changes in job locations. There is also the reality of an uncertain work schedule where a job might last for months or where the only available work may be on a short-term basis. Offshore work tends to run in a "feast or famine" pattern.

These technicians must be confident of their own ability to cope with the uncertainties and risks of deep-water diving. Their confidence must be based on a complete knowledge of procedures, gear, equipment, apparatus, support systems, and the jobs of other members of the team. They must have faith in their own ability to handle unexpected developments in a diving situation. They must be able to analyze and solve problems without panic or confusion. The real satisfactions of this career come in confidently performing their tasks as a professional in a setting that is not for the uninformed.

GOE: 05.10.01; SIC: 7389; SOC: 6179

⬦ **SOURCES OF ADDITIONAL INFORMATION**

Association of Commercial Diving Educators
c/o Marina Technology Program
Santa Barbara City College
721 Cliff Drive
Santa Barbara, CA 93109

Association of Diving Contractors
PO Box 1438
Harvey, LA 70059

National Association of Underwater Instructors
PO Box 14650
Montclair, CA 91763

Professional Association of Diving Instructors
1243 East Warner Avenue
Santa Ana, CA 92705

⬦ **RELATED ARTICLES**

Volume 1: Construction; Engineering
Volume 2: Merchant marine occupations; Oceanographers
Volume 3: Construction workers; Motorboat mechanics; Petroleum drilling occupations; Structural steel workers; Welders
Volume 4: Marine services technicians; Petroleum technicians; Welding technicians

Energy-conservation technicians

Definition

Energy-conservation technicians identify and measure quantities of energy used in heating and cooling or in operating a facility or industrial process. They assess efficiency in the use of energy and the amount of energy lost through wasteful processes or lack of insulation. They also prescribe corrective steps to conserve energy. These technicians are trained in the use and conversion of energy, techniques for improving or preventing loss of energy, and the determination of the optimum energy required in a given system or process.

History

At the start of the twentieth century, energy costs were only a small part of the expense of operating homes, offices, and factories and of providing lighting, communication, and transportation. Coal and petroleum were abundant and relatively inexpensive. These low energy prices were among the factors that contributed to the United States' becoming in this century the leading industrialized nation in the world and also the world's largest user of energy.

Because petroleum was inexpensive and easily used to produce heat, steam, electricity, and fuel, it displaced coal for many purposes. This caused the nation's coal-mining industry to decline, and the United States became dependent on foreign oil for about one-half of its energy supply.

In 1973, many foreign oil-producing nations stopped shipments of oil to the United States and other Western nations, and fuel costs suddenly became a large expense. More recently, oil prices have moderated somewhat; however, the prices are still very volatile, and the threat of oil-price increases or a cutoff of supplies in the future never quite disappears.

These events made energy conservation a new technology in the United States. This technology includes working to discover new sources of energy, finding more efficient methods and equipment to use energy, and searching out and eliminating the ways energy is

This energy-conservation technician is inspecting a home for places where heating and air-conditioning can escape outdoors. He will then suggest affordable ways to make the home energy-efficient.

wasted. This has created a large need for energy conservation technicians.

Nature of the work

Energy efficiency and conservation are major concerns in nearly all homes and workplaces that use or produce energy. This means that job settings and work assignments for energy-conservation technicians vary greatly, ranging from power plant operation to research laboratory assisting, energy audits, and equipment sales and service. The jobs these technicians perform can be divided into four major areas of energy activity: energy-related research and development, energy production, energy use, and energy conservation.

In energy-related research and development, typical employers are research and development organizations in institutions, private industry, government, and the military. Technicians in this area work under the direction of an engineer, physicist, chemist, or metallurgist. They design, build, and operate laboratory experiments that involve mechanical, electrical, chemical, pneumatic, hydraulic, thermal, or optical scientific principles, materials, and equip-

ment. Technicians also perform tests and measurements on system performance, document results in reports or laboratory notebooks, and perform periodic maintenance and repair of equipment. Test data frequently are developed and analyzed using complex measuring instruments and laboratory microcomputers. Technicians also frequently supervise other skilled research workers.

In energy production, typical employers are power plants; solar energy equipment manufacturers, installers, and users; and process plants that use high-temperature heat, steam, or hot water. Technicians in this area of the energy field work with engineers and managers to develop, install, operate, maintain, modify, and repair systems and devices used for the conversion of fuels or other resources into useful energy. Systems may be plants that produce hot water, steam, mechanical motion, or electrical power. Typical systems include furnaces, electrical power plants, and solar heating systems. They may be controlled manually, by semi-automated control panels, or by computers. Technicians in this area frequently supervise other workers.

In the field of energy use, technicians might work to improve efficiency in industrial engineering and production line equipment, building maintenance, equipment maintenance, and in the maintenance departments of hospitals, apartments, hotels, office buildings, schools, churches, shopping centers, and restaurants.

In energy conservation, typical employers include manufacturing companies, consulting engineers, energy-audit firms, and energy-audit departments of public utility companies. Technicians are also hired by municipal governments, hotels, architects, private builders, and heating, ventilating and air-conditioning equipment manufacturers.

Technicians working in energy conservation typically work on a team led by an engineer. Their work includes determining building specifications and modifications of equipment and structures. They audit energy use and efficiency of machines and systems, then recommend modifications or changes to save energy.

Requirements

Energy-conservation technicians must be broadly trained, systems-oriented technicians. They must be able to work with many types of devices and mechanisms and also must understand how the various components and devices relate to one another. Technicians can apply this knowledge in a variety of ways to develop, construct, test, sell, install, operate, modify, and maintain today's equipment in energy-related fields.

The equipment involved in the production, control, use, and conservation of energy is typical of today's most technologically complex machinery. Such equipment may contain electric motors, heaters, lamps, electronic controls, mechanical drives and linkages, thermal systems, lubricants, optical systems, microwave systems, pneumatic and hydraulic drives, pneumatic controls, and, in some instances, even radioactive samples and counters. If energy-conservation technicians are to work effectively with equipment of this kind, they must have a thorough understanding of the many underlying technical disciplines and their interrelationships.

Technicians who are successful in energy conservation have an avid interest in machines and how they operate. They not only know how machines are made, how the parts fit together and work together, but they can also figure out what is wrong if parts are not working properly. Once they identify the problem, they know how to correct it.

Students entering this field must have a practical understanding of the physical sciences, a good aptitude for math, and the ability to communicate in writing and in speaking with technical specialists and with persons not trained in the field. Work as energy-conservation technicians requires a clear and precise understanding of operational and maintenance manuals, schematics, blueprints, and computational formulas; thus the ability to communicate clearly in scientific and engineering terms is a basic requirement.

At least two years of formal technical education beyond high school is the best preparation for this career. While still in high school, however, students who are interested in this field should study algebra and geometry for at least one year each. Courses in physics, chemistry, and ecology, including laboratory work, would also form a base for the postsecondary program that follows. High-school courses in computers and mechanical or architectural drafting would also be very helpful for the prospective technician.

Postsecondary programs in energy conservation concentrate on the principles and applications of physics, energy conservation, energy economics, instrumentation, electronics, electromechanical systems, computers, heating systems, and air conditioning. A typical curriculum in a technical institute, community college, or other specialized two-year program would offer a first year of study in physics, chemistry,

mathematics, fundamentals of energy technology, energy production systems, fundamentals of electricity and electromechanical devices, and microcomputer operations.

The second year of study would include courses in mechanical and fluid systems; electrical power and illumination systems; electronic devices; blueprint reading; energy conservation; codes and regulations; heating, ventilation, and air conditioning; technical communications; instrumentation and controls; and energy economics and audits. Considerable time would be spent in laboratories, where students study devices, mechanisms, and integrated systems of machines and controls by actually assembling, disassembling, adjusting, and operating them.

In the search for a school that provides training in this field, students should remember that more and more technical colleges, community colleges, and technical institutes are providing two-year programs under the specific title of energy conservation and use technology or energy management technology. In addition, many other schools offer related programs in solar power, electric power, building maintenance, equipment maintenance, and general engineering technology.

Physical requirements for this career are not especially demanding. The normal physical strength possessed by able-bodied men or women is sufficient. Normal sight and hearing are needed and average or above-average hand-eye coordination and manual dexterity are required.

Special requirements

Currently, there are no special requirements for licensing or certifying energy-conservation and use technicians. A certificate from the National Institute for Certification in Engineering Technologies and a degree or certificate of graduation from an accredited technical program, while not required, are valuable credentials and proof of recognized preparation for work as energy-conservation technicians.

Some positions in electrical power plants require energy-conservation technicians to pass certain psychological tests to determine their behavior during crises. Security clearances, arranged by the employer, are required for employment in nuclear power plants or other workplaces designated by the government as high-security facilities.

Opportunities for experience and exploration

Persons who are considering entry into the field of energy conservation should obtain all the information they can from high-school or postsecondary school counselors and occupational information centers. School guidance programs often can arrange field trips on which students can visit industrial, commercial, and business workplaces to discuss careers in the energy efficiency field.

The electric utility company in nearly every city will have an energy analyst or a team of energy auditors in its customer service department. Consulting engineering offices are also located in major cities. Interested students may be able to talk with these energy specialists to find out about job availability and to inquire about opportunities for part-time or summer work. Other places where energy conservation specialists can be found are in large hospitals, major office buildings, and hotel chains. Frequently, universities and large manufacturing plants will have energy specialists in their plant engineering departments.

A partial understanding of the field can be gained by enrolling in seminars sometimes offered by community colleges or equipment and material suppliers on topics such as building insulation, storm windows, heat pumps, solar heaters, and the like. Useful experience can also be obtained by undertaking student projects in solar equipment, energy audits, or energy efficient equipment.

Methods of entering

Most graduates of technical programs are able to secure jobs in energy conservation before graduation with assistance from the school's placement office. The placement staff works closely with potential employers, especially with those who have employed graduates in recent years. Many large companies schedule regular recruiting visits to schools before graduation. Students may also write or visit potential employers.

It is possible to enter the field of energy conservation and use on the basis of work experience. Industrial technicians, experienced industrial equipment mechanics, and people who have extensive training in military instrumentation and systems control and maintenance may enter the field with the help of intensive study to supplement the knowledge and skills they bring to the job from previous experience.

Some jobs in energy production, such as in electrical power plants, can be obtained with only a high-school diploma. New employees, however, are expected to successfully complete company-sponsored training courses to keep their jobs and advance to positions with more responsibility.

Many positions in building or equipment maintenance are available to persons who were trained and employed in the military, particularly in the Navy. Former Navy technicians are particularly sought in the field of energy production.

Many of the jobs offered to high-school graduates in electrical power production are represented by employee unions such as the International Brotherhood of Electrical Workers or the International Association of Machinists and Aerospace Workers. Workers often start as apprentices with a planned program of work and study for three to four years.

Graduates with associate degrees in energy conservation and use, instrumentation, electronics, or electromechanical technology will normally enter employment at a higher level, with more responsibility and correspondingly higher pay, than those with less preparation. Jobs in energy research and development will almost always require an associate degree.

Because these technicians are prepared to function in all of the energy conversion fields, their adaptability to many kinds of highly technical work at the technician level makes them attractive to a variety of employers. Some employers, such as power companies, need technicians to perform energy audits. Such a job could involve assisting energy-use auditors and energy-application analysts while they make audits or analyses in businesses or homes of their customers. This provides new technicians with a period of orientation to learn about specific duties, after which they perform regular audits and analyses. The resulting data forms a base for making specific recommendations to reduce energy consumption and costs for the company or customer.

Some employers seek graduate energy technicians because of their flexibility and versatility as members of research teams. The broad understanding of different forms of energy and of the principles and devices related to them enables these technicians to function as researchers who can quickly comprehend problems and propose solutions. Their ability to make many different kinds of measurements and to gather, analyze, and interpret data makes them ideal for research and development assignments.

Other employers seek energy technicians to work in engineering departments. Their broad technical base and versatility make them promising workers in the design or modification of products. Some technicians prefer to work in engineering production activities such as process control, planning for energy-efficient production systems, and related engineering activities. Their broad technical training prepares them to be more productive as beginners than persons who have only mechanical or electrical technician preparation.

Another large and important area that energy-conservation technicians are especially prepared to enter is the management of machinery and equipment. This includes planning, selection, installation, modification, and maintenance. Energy-conservation technicians are taught to understand devices, principles, mechanisms, and systems associated with all the different kinds of energy used in modern machinery. Therefore, they can quickly understand what machines or mechanisms are, what they are supposed to do, and how they work. They usually can also find out what is wrong if the machines or devices are not working as they should and direct the work needed to correct them.

For the energy technician who is especially interested in machines and mechanical systems, attractive career opportunities in machinery engineering and management abound. Modern machines and machinery systems are rapidly becoming more technologically complex and more expensive. This means that keeping equipment in efficient working order is of increasing importance. The broad training of technicians who have graduated from energy-conservation programs provides ideal basic preparation for careers in modern machinery management as well as in energy-efficiency functions.

Finally, there are opportunities for trained energy-conservation technicians with a talent for sales. Many manufacturers of energy-efficient or energy-conservation equipment use energy-conservation technicians as salespeople who can help customers determine their needs for certain kinds of equipment and systems.

Advancement

Well-established patterns of advancement for these technicians have not yet emerged, because the career is relatively new. Nevertheless, technicians in any of the four areas of energy conservation and use can advance to higher positions. They can, for example, become senior technicians. They also can advance to supervisory positions. Formally educated technicians should expect to move into these advanced jobs. At the same time, they should realize that advancement requires diligent on-the-job study and special seminars or classes. Classes and seminars are typically sponsored or paid for by the employer.

Technicians can also advance by progressing to new, more challenging assignments. For example, hotels, restaurants, and stores hire experienced energy technicians to manage energy consumption. This often involves visits to each location, audits, and examinations of facilities or procedures for potential energy economies. Technicians in this area also provide training in energy-saving practices. Other experienced energy technicians may be employed as special sales and customer service representatives for producers of power, energy, special control systems, or equipment designed to improve energy efficiency.

Opportunities for ownership or participation in private consulting or special services are also available to technicians. Private companies already are serving government, industry, and homeowners' needs for energy audits. Technicians with experience and money to invest may start their own businesses, selling energy-saving products or providing audits, weatherizations, or energy-efficient renovations.

Employment outlook

Future employment in this career is somewhat uncertain and depends in large part on what happens to the price of oil and other energy sources. If energy costs decline, some of the economic motivation will lessen, and the demand for energy-conservation technicians will decrease. On the other hand, if costs increase, energy use will continue to constitute a major expense to industry, commerce, government, institutions, and private citizens, and the demand for technicians trained in energy conservation will remain strong. Also, if the economy slows and businesses experience financial pressures to reduce costs, energy costs may well be an area they will look to, and that could lead to a greater need for trained energy-conservation technicians.

In addition, the United States is still far from independent of foreign fuel supplies. The possibility of an interruption in foreign supplies of petroleum or an increase in its cost continues to require all energy consumers to conserve energy as a matter of economic efficiency and competitiveness.

Earnings

Earnings of energy-conservation technicians vary significantly with the amount of their formal training and experience. High-school graduates with little or no experience who begin as trainees will earn $14,000 to $18,000 per year. Technicians with military experience and three to six years of technical experience earn from $18,000 to $30,000 annually. Graduates of postsecondary technician programs earn the same.

Energy-conservation technicians with five to ten years of experience in research, engineering design, or in machinery engineering and maintenance can earn up to $36,000 annually.

Technicians typically receive paid vacations, group insurance benefits, employee retirement plans, and the like. In addition, they often have the benefit of company support for all or a part of their educational programs. These are important benefits because technicians must continually study to keep up to date with technological changes that occur in this developing field.

Conditions of work

Work assignments for energy-conservation technicians will vary from day to day and change as new innovations and equipment are introduced.

In energy research and development and also in engineering design and product planning, technicians work in laboratories or engineering departments, generally on normal daytime work schedules. In energy conservation audits and analyses and in machinery and equipment engineering, installation, and maintenance, technicians travel to customer locations or work in their employer's plant, but they usually work normal schedules.

Energy production and energy-use work frequently involves around-the-clock operations that require shifts. In these two areas technicians work either indoors or outdoors at the employer's site. Such assignments require little or no travel, but the work environments may be dirty, noisy, and sometimes hot or cold.

Appropriate work clothing must be worn in shop or factory settings and safety awareness and safe working habits must be practiced at all times. Energy production and use jobs involve

manual work that in some cases requires physical strength. Persons with orthopedic handicaps would usually be better suited for work in research and development or in energy audits.

Social and psychological factors

Jobs in energy production and energy management are in-plant jobs where the energy-conservation technician interacts with only a small group of people. Energy research and development jobs involve laboratory activities and require social interaction with engineers, scientists, and other technicians.

Energy-conservation jobs differ from the first two because they require the technician to provide special technical services to customers. This means that the technician must successfully communicate and interact with the public. In some cases, the technician may be considered a public relations representative. This responsibility implies a particular type of personality, dress, attitude, and special communication skills that create favorable impressions on those with whom technicians work.

Nearly all jobs in this field require energy-conservation technicians to communicate in a clear, concise manner, whether in the form of laboratory notebooks, reports, letters, or speech.

Job stress in this field varies. At times the pace is relaxed but businesslike, typically in engineering, planning, and design departments or in research and development. At other times, technicians respond to urgent calls and crisis situations involving unexpected breakdowns of equipment that must be diagnosed, corrected, and returned to operation as soon as possible.

Energy technicians work on a succession of highly technical problems in a wide variety of situations related to energy conservation and management. Therefore, they must be able to maintain an orderly, systematic, and objective way of approaching and solving problems. This involves defining the problem, gathering pertinent information, using appropriate methods to obtain accurate data, analyzing the facts, and arriving at a solution by using logic and judgment. Technicians must be patient, resourceful, calm, and systematic for extended periods of time in solving some problems.

Energy-conservation technicians can enjoy a deep sense of satisfaction as problem-solvers in a field that is of great economic importance. When they complete an analysis of a problem in energy use and effectiveness, they can state the results in tangible dollar costs, losses, or savings. This is a highly valuable service because it provides a basis for important decisions on using and conserving energy.

GOE: 05.03.06; SIC: Any industry; SOC: 371

◇ **SOURCES OF ADDITIONAL INFORMATION**

American Petroleum Institute
1220 L Street, NW
Washington, DC 20005

Association of Energy Engineers
4025 Pleasantdale Road, Suite 420
Atlanta, GA 30340

Energy Conservation Coalition
1525 New Hampshire Avenue, NW
Washington, DC 20036

Center for Energy Policy and Research
c/o New York Institute of Technology
Old Westbury, NY 11568

Alliance to Save Energy
1925 K Street, NW
Suite 206
Washington, DC 20006

◇ **RELATED ARTICLES**

Volume 1: Energy; Physical Sciences; Public Utilities
Volume 2: Engineers
Volume 3: Air-conditioning, refrigeration, and heating mechanics; General maintenance mechanics; Industrial machinery mechanics; Power plant occupations; Services sales representatives; Stationary engineers; Stationary firers, boiler tenders
Volume 4: Air-conditioning, heating, and refrigeration technicians; Chemical technicians; Electromechanical technicians; Industrial engineering technicians; Instrumentation technicians; Nuclear power-plant operators; Petroleum technicians; Solar collection technicians

Laser technicians

Definition

Laser technicians assemble, test, maintain, and operate different kinds of laser devices and the systems that incorporate or use lasers. Most laser technicians are involved in one or more of the following activities: assembly and production of laser devices and systems, maintenance and operation, troubleshooting and repair, research and development, and sales and service. Some laser technicians may work under the direction of engineers or physicists who conduct laboratory activities in laser research and development or design. Other technicians work alone or as members of scientific teams to operate, test, repair, and maintain laser devices and lasers.

The word "laser" comes from the first letters of the words that comprise the scientific description of the process that creates laser light, that is, light amplification by stimulated emission of radiation. The laser converts electrical power into a special beam of optical or light power. The unique character of laser light makes it different from light produced by ordinary sources and makes it useful in many different ways.

History

The technology of the laser began to develop in the early 1950s, when electrical and optical devices were combined into new types of equipment for tracking, communications, photography, and entertaining. The first laser that successfully worked was a ruby laser designed and built by Dr. Ted Maiman in 1960. This first working laser created great interest in scientific research laboratories and started intensive experimenting and development in the field of electro-optics.

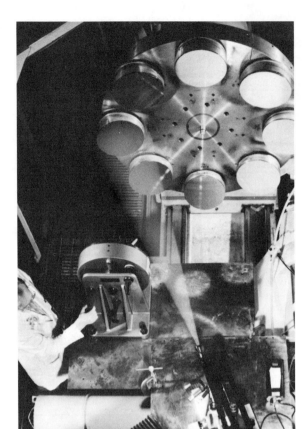

Two laser technicians operate a laser interferometer to inspect the surface finish of metal mirrors. These mirrors must be perfectly smooth for use in laser fusion experiments.

Engineers and scientists began to consider the power in a light beam in the same way as electrical power. From 1960 to 1967, new lasers and electro-optic devices and techniques were developed. Many new kinds of lasers were built, some with considerable optical power and some with only a small amount of power. It soon became clear that they could be used in a large number of ways to solve problems that previously had no practical solution.

Lasers began to be used in surgery, surveying and measuring, industrial product inspection and testing, computers, microprocessors, and manufacturing.

As lasers have moved from research laboratories to industry, the need for trained technicians has become crucial. Because of the complex technical nature of lasers, technicians in the field must be competent in a wide range of skills, yet capable of accomplishing highly spe-

cialized tasks. Since the early 1970s, laser technicians have been receiving highly specialized preparation at two-year technical institutes and community colleges.

Nature of the work

The duties of laser technicians vary greatly, depending on the application with which they are involved. To understand the wide range of possible activities in this career, one should know about three special properties of laser light known as monochromaticity (single color), directionality (light radiating very little), and coherence (light waves in step, like links of a chain).

Light may be thought of as waves traveling through space. Light occurs in different wavelengths (the distance between peaks on the light wave) just as waves on the ocean vary in length. The color of light depends on its wavelength; violet light has the shortest wavelength of all visible colors and red light has the longest. White light, such as that emitted by a light bulb, is a combination of all wavelengths.

Laser light is in a class by itself because it is made up of only one color of light. The wavelengths of this single color, while not perfectly uniform, occur within a very narrow range. The laser's property of containing only one color, monochromaticity, is one of its most important characteristics.

Laser light has a second property called directionality. The light from an ordinary source radiates away from the source in all directions. This spreading of ordinary light makes it useful for lighting homes and workplaces. By comparison, light from a laser travels in one direction. For example, a laser beam signal sent to the moon from the earth can be reflected back by a small reflector and received back at an earth receiver on a similarly small antenna area. Ordinary light would diffuse too much for such use. Thus, laser light is said to have directionality, the property of concentrating all of the laser light into a narrow beam having a single direction.

A third important characteristic of laser light is its coherence. Light waves produced by ordinary sources do not form an orderly pattern; they combine in a random fashion without producing a wave stronger or larger than any of the various single waves. Such light is said to be incoherent. The waves produced by a laser, however, travel through space in step with one another and are said to be "in phase." When all the separate waves in the beam remain in phase, the result is a signal or pulse much stronger or more powerful than that of any single wave. A very intense beam of light is generated. The property of the waves remaining in phase is known as coherence.

These three properties—monochromaticity, directionality, and coherence—are what make laser light useful in so many ways. Laser light is an intense light, containing a great deal of power within a very narrow beam that can be controlled to accomplish various tasks. Because of its directionality, laser light can travel great distances and remain intense. This characteristic makes the laser applicable to certain communication needs. The laser beam can also be focused to perform welding or to drill holes.

The monochromaticity of laser light and its consistently narrow range of wavelength make it useful in spectroscopy (analysis of chemicals based on the patterns of light each element reflects), photochemistry, and atomic isotope separation.

The behavior of coherent light is useful in measuring distances with extreme accuracy in surveying, missile tracking, and in creating three-dimensional photography.

Lasers are available in many varieties. The wavelengths of the beam generated by the laser range from ultraviolet through all of the visible colors of the spectrum to the far infrared. Some lasers produce power continuously, while others operate in short bursts. Some lasers are small enough to be held in the hand and have an output power less than that of a flashlight. Other lasers are large enough to require a 10,000-square-foot building and are powerful enough to detonate explosives and drill holes through thick metal plates. For all their variety, however, lasers have four basic elements in common.

The four elements common to nearly all lasers are the active medium, the excitation mechanism, the feedback mechanism, and the output coupler. A brief description of these elements will help the reader understand the tasks and activities performed by laser technicians.

The excitation mechanism is a source of energy, such as an electric current or a flash lamp. The source of energy is needed to pump or raise the atoms of the active medium into an excited state. Therefore, this process is known as optical pumping.

The laser beam is formed when an atom in an excited state is further excited by a photon (a tiny packet of light energy) of the proper energy and wavelength to cause it to emit a second photon identical to the first in wavelength, direction of travel, and phase. This process is known as stimulated emission.

The active medium of a laser, usually a solid or a gas, produces light by stimulated emission. If the active medium is a gas, it is usually contained in an enclosed glass tube from which air has been pumped out using a vacuum pump.

The feedback mechanism usually consists of a pair of mirrors, carefully aligned to reflect the laser light back and forth through the active medium. The feedback mechanism keeps the stimulation ongoing.

The output coupler is a partially transparent mirror that allows some of the coherent laser light to leave the laser device in the form of the output beam. Output couplers may transmit from less than 1 percent to 90 percent of the coherent light of the laser, depending on the type of laser in use. The light that is transmitted is the laser output.

Laser technicians must be able to manipulate, operate, or adjust all of the elements of the laser device to make it work. They must understand the properties of the various active media, the nature of power supplies and flash lamps, and the characteristics of mirrors and how to align them properly. The specific tasks performed by laser technicians usually include the following:

troubleshooting and repairing systems that include lasers;

performing tests and measurements using electronic devices;

performing alignment procedures on optical systems, especially those that involve lasers and laser-related optics;

preparing and reading shop drawings, diagrams, sketches, and schematics;

maintaining a laboratory notebook, gathering data, performing data calculations and displays, and preparing reports;

operating interferometers, spectrometers, monochromators, and spectrophotometers;

operating laser systems, including intracavity modulation (control) and specialized switching devices;

using and teaching basic laser and electrical safety practices in the laboratory;

performing optical inspections, cleaning, and adjustments of optical components;

operating and calibrating photodetectors, photomultipliers, optical power meters, and colorimeters;

processing photographic film and plates;

producing, reconstructing, and recording holograms (three-dimensional pictures) by using laser beam techniques;

selecting laser and optical components;

troubleshooting and repairing electro-optic devices;

fabricating or directing the fabrication and assembly of components for laser and electro-optic devices and systems; and

communicating effectively with engineers, physicians, scientists, production and sales personnel, and others through laboratory notebooks, reports, letters, oral presentations, conversations, and informal briefings.

Technicians with the skills listed above may be involved in a number of different laser applications. These applications can be grouped into ten specific areas, described below.

Machining and fabrication: The laser is used for welding, precision drilling, cutting, etching, and grinding of metals; fabric cutting in clothing manufacture; trimming and precision slicing of mechanical and electronic components and circuit elements.

Technicians in this area may be involved in establishing operating limits for lasers, determining tooling requirements, making certain that laser operation meets established quality levels, delivering finished parts on time and at specified costs. They may evaluate new products and systems and investigate new applications and uses for lasers.

Wideband and protected communications systems: The high frequency coherence of the laser permits the simultaneous transmission of a variety of signals. This fact is at the heart of fiber optics communications technology. Fiber optics systems can transmit large amounts of information—all at the same time, quickly, reliably, and cheaply.

In 1966, it was discovered that pure silica glass fibers could provide light guides for communication purposes, and the field of fiber optics was born. Technicians in the optical fiber communications industry use lasers to generate light impulses that are transmitted through optical fibers and they work on developing, manufacturing, and testing optical fiber products. Frequently, technicians use computers to perform calculations, design, set up, monitor, and maintain fiber fabrication facilities. Fiber fabrication is a highly complex technology that calls for a basic knowledge of certain chemical reactions, process control electronics, and computer programming.

Military and space projects: Lasers are frequently used for target-finding, tracking, ranging, identification, and communication. Technicians are needed both for repairing and adapting low-power lasers, which are widely used for military applications. They are also needed in the research and development of high-power lasers.

Testing and measurement: Laser holography is used for the nondestructive testing of parts from large machinery structures to tires and tiny crystals. Lasers are also used for the testing and monitoring of air and water pollution and for the dynamic balancing of rotating devices.

Data storage and retrieval: Lasers are used in storing information for large or very small applications. The uses range all the way from recording information to sequencing a read-out of stored information. The read-out might be the step-by-step moving display on large screens, such as the side of a billboard, or the tiny light-emitting device in a hand-held calculator.

Photo-optical: Lasers are used as illuminators in high-speed photography and mapping. Laser illuminators are also found in optical scanners, advanced telescopes, and specialized lighting applications.

Medical: Laser medical applications include surgical operations on delicate organs of the body, cancer operations, and burn treatment. In ophthalmology, lasers have made the repair of detached retinas a routine operation. In dermatology, they have been used to remove tattoos and skin blemishes. Lasers have become important tools for other medical research and diagnosis procedures and for the study of single cells.

Construction and excavation: The laser beam is used as a continuously visible surveying guideline in the construction of roads, highways, and airport runways. It is also used by surveyors and surveying technicians in constructing buildings and in assembling complex power plants or processing plants where structures must be placed at exact levels above "grade or floor" level. Lasers are also used in water and sewage pipe installation alignment, tunnel excavation, and in both open-pit and underground mining operations.

Research and development: Lasers are being studied as a source for producing the multi-million-degree temperatures needed to cause fusion of elements to develop controlled nuclear fusion. These studies are part of the continuing research to produce inexpensive electrical power for the nation's energy needs.

Requirements

As the activities described in the previous paragraphs show, the field of laser technology has many applications that involve a wide range of knowledge and skills. Thus, people with very different interests and skills can find work in laser technology. Some interests and abilities, however, are required for almost every application of lasers.

Prospective technicians should be genuinely interested in how devices and systems work. A reasonable degree of intelligence and a strong motivation to learn are important. Students should like mathematics, since basic mathematics is needed in this field. An interest in instruments, laboratory apparatus, and machines is highly appropriate. In addition, an interest in science and an enjoyment of high-school laboratory activities may indicate a suitability for this career. Written and spoken communications are very important in the majority of positions for laser technicians, especially those in sales, service, and research and development.

Physical strength is not usually required for laser technicians, but good manual dexterity and hand-eye and body coordination are quite important.

Careers in laser technology are demanding and are highly specialized. Those who plan to enter as technicians should expect to attend a two-year laser technician program. Such programs are offered at technical institutes, community colleges, and technical colleges.

Students who expect to prepare for this career should begin in high school. They will need four years of English, at least two years of mathematics including algebra, and at least one year of physical science, preferably physics with laboratory instruction. If available, computer programming and applications, vocational machine shop, basic electronics, and blueprint reading provide an additional useful background for studies to follow.

After high school, the prospective technician should enter a two-year technical school or community college program. The course of study they will undertake includes intensive technical and scientific study. There are usually more hours spent in laboratory study or similar work situations than hours devoted to classroom study. Laboratory study gives the students practice in the techniques and procedures related to applied theoretical physics that are necessary in this complex scientific field. These programs give the students extensive opportunities for hands-on experience with many different types of lasers, power supplies, optical devices, and vacuum systems.

Typical first-year courses in a program for laser technicians include courses in mathematics, physics, drafting or drawing, diagramming and sketching, basic electronics, electronic instrumentation and calibration, introduction to solid-state devices (including semiconductor materials, diodes, and diode circuits), electromechanical controls, introductory computer programming, and English composition.

Second-year courses typically include introduction to lasers, geometrical optics, digital circuits, microwaves, laser and electro-optic components, laser and electro-optic devices, laser and electro-optic measurements, laser applications, wave optics, glassblowing and vacuum techniques, communication skills, technical report writing, and microcomputers and computer hardware.

Often special projects related to lasers or their use are a part of the second year's study. These projects permit students to learn more about a special interest they may be developing and give them valuable experience in independent study.

Some programs may not offer the wide range of courses listed above, and yet they may be very effective in placing graduates in certain specialized areas by preparing them for further training sponsored by an employer. In general, however, the industry is most eager to hire students who have received the rigorous and extensive training in postsecondary technical programs similar to the one outlined above.

Special requirements

There are no special certification or licensing requirements for laser technicians.

In some positions, however, security clearances may be required. This is true of much work done for U.S. government agencies and for any work done under U.S. military contracts. Such clearances are usually arranged by the employer.

Opportunities for experience and exploration

For high-school students and others who are interested in a career as a laser technician, the high-school vocational guidance counselor is a valuable resource person. If a community or technical college is nearby, its occupational information center and counseling staff can also be very helpful. High-school, college, or public librarians are often able to identify ways of inquiring into a particular career field such as the laser technician.

For those still in high school, the high-school's science classes may be the best place to gain information about potential careers in laser technology. Science teachers often arrange field trips and bring speakers to the school to describe various careers. Lasers are used in so many places that a laser technician, operator, or engineer from the community can almost always be found who can share knowledge about lasers.

Opportunities to gain working experience can be found in construction, manufacturing, or mining where lasers are used in measuring, cutting and welding, and surveying. Summer or part-time work on such jobs opens the door to talking to engineers and technicians who use laser devices.

Methods of entering

The best way to enter this career is to enroll and graduate from a formal laser technician program with a curriculum such as the one described above. Graduating students of such programs are usually interviewed and recruited while still in school by representatives of companies who need laser technicians. If hired, they begin working soon after graduation.

Candidates for employment can often strengthen their position in the job market by linking their laser education with related courses such as computer hardware, computer programming, optical elements, machining operations, quality assurance and control, and instrumentation and control.

Some employers offer company-sponsored training in specialized areas, but they usually prefer to make these opportunities available to the individuals who have already received a basic education in lasers and/or electro-optics.

Another way to enter the career is to join one of the U.S. military branches under a technical training program for laser technicians. It should be noted, however, that military laser training is not equivalent to civilian training, and further study of theory and applications is needed to enter the field as a civilian.

Whatever preparatory training the beginner brings to the career, considerable training must follow under the employer's direction. This training, which involves special on-the-job study, in most cases is designed to acquaint the new technician with the employer's work.

Advancement

Opportunities for advancement in the field are excellent for technicians who keep abreast of changes in the field. In a relatively new technology such as that of the laser, changes and new developments occur very rapidly.

Technicians who investigate and adapt to new developments become more valuable to their employers and advance to greater respon-

sibilities. Technicians who rely only on their technical school education may soon find that their skills and knowledge are out of date and out of demand. On-the-job study should be viewed as the springboard to further learning and advancement.

As with many engineering technologies, employers designate various levels of employment for laser technicians. For example, research institutions often have a five-step grading system for technicians who can advance according to experience, education, and job performance. In private industry, technicians sometimes advance to supervisory or management positions if they prove themselves to be highly effective, organized, and skilled in supervisory tasks. In sales and service work, they may advance to supervisory positions.

Mature, experienced, and highly successful laser technicians may also find advancement opportunities as consultants or specialists. They may work in the broad fields of manufacturing, the military, research organizations, and even for finance companies or insurance firms, as a member of a consulting firm or as a private consultant. Some may become teachers in laser technician programs, although the latter occupation does not usually offer the financial rewards available in private consulting work.

Employment outlook

Employment opportunities for laser technicians are expected to be very good throughout the 1990s. Continued growth in this industry will almost certainly lead to continued growth in the number of technicians employed.

Many laser technicians are employed in the area of research and development. Prospective technicians interested in employment in this area of laser technology should keep in mind that growth in opportunities for jobs such as these often slows in the face of economic downturns. While few economists are currently forecasting a serious recession in coming years, some sort of slowdown of growth could well develop.

An area of laser technology in which strong growth is expected during the 1990s is that of lasers in industrial production. This includes the use of lasers for cutting, welding, drilling, scribing, marking, and trimming of many materials. The capability of laser devices to perform such tasks is now a routine matter; growth will come as more companies move to using this equipment in their plants.

Fiber-optic systems are currently experiencing one of the most dramatic increases in growth of all laser applications. Optical fiber is replacing wire cables in communication lines, and in many electronic products, and this trend is expected to continue. The demand for technicians in the fiber optics field should be especially strong in the 1990s.

Defense applications are expected to remain an area of high employment for laser technicians. As practical applications of lasers become more widespread, there should be an increased need for production technicians to construct and assemble lasers and other electro-optical devices. Other areas in which technicians will find good employment opportunities are medicine, construction, and entertainment.

Earnings

Earnings of laser technicians vary somewhat from one region of the nation to another and to some degree depend on the depth and breadth of their preparation.

The approximate overall average starting salary for laser technicians is between $19,000 and $22,000 per year. Salaries for technicians who have gained at least five years of experience average approximately $30,000 per year, depending on background, experience, and segment of the industry in which they were employed. Those who are in advanced supervisory positions, advanced sales and service, or in private consulting work earn $35,000 to $40,000 a year, or more.

In addition to salary, technicians also receive benefits such as insurance, paid holidays and vacations, and retirement plans. Many employers have liberal policies of paying for professional improvement through continued study in school or at work. Costs of activities related to the profession are also often covered.

Conditions of work

Laser technicians work in a wide variety of environments: laboratory "clean rooms," construction sites, manufacturing plants, and hospital operating rooms, to name a few.

They may work at relatively stationary jobs, assembling or operating lasers in the same environment every day; or they may be required to move around frequently, in and out of laboratory areas, production sites, or offices. Some technicians are office- or laboratory-based; others, especially those in sales and service positions, may travel the country.

Many laser technicians dress informally for work in a laboratory; others wear khakis or other work clothes. A few may wear lab coats or sterile surgical suits and caps. On the construction site and elsewhere, the laser technician will be required to observe safety rules.

Certain possible dangers are present in most areas where lasers are being used. First, the power supplies for many lasers involve high voltages. The technician must develop a careful, methodical manner of working around potentially deadly amounts of electricity. The laser beam itself is frequently a possible source of serious injury to users and bystanders, either through direct exposure to the beam or by reflected light from the laser. Technicians must wear goggles specially designed to protect against hazards from the particular type of laser with which they are working. They must also be sure that those in the area wear goggles and understand the possible dangers. Every kind and size of laser has its own special possibility for being highly dangerous.

The laser technician often works as part of a team, sometimes with scientists and engineers, sometimes as a member of a production team or supervisory group. Some technicians work alone but are usually directly responsible to an engineer, scientist, or manager.

Social and psychological factors

Laser technology calls for technicians who are dedicated to precision work that involves exact specifications. The parts used to make lasers are almost always extremely expensive. Mistakes that damage lasers or errors in applying lasers can be very costly, running into thousands of dollars. Therefore, technicians must be precise, accurate, and thorough in their work.

Laser technicians must study continually to keep up with the technology of their field. In a field that is as fast-changing as laser technology, the best and most satisfied technicians are those who are highly motivated to learn new skills and acquire knowledge.

Communication skills are extremely important in this career. Written communications in the form of laboratory notebooks, memos, technical reports, graphs, charts, and letters are required of many, if not most, technicians. Less formal communication, such as speaking in staff meetings, is equally important.

Among the greatest sources of satisfaction that laser technicians experience is the confident feeling of success whenever they see their lasers and laser systems perform correctly. This is especially true in sales and service where new users are taught to use this complicated technology and where the technician can actually see customers discovering the effectiveness of lasers. The same satisfaction is felt in research when a new development is proved to be a success.

GOE: 05.01.01; SIC: 3845; SOC: 389

For information on general science and engineering, as well as laser-related careers, contact:

Junior Engineering Technical Society (JETS)
1428 King Street
Suite 405
Alexandria, VA 22314

◇ **SOURCES OF ADDITIONAL INFORMATION**

Laser Association of America
72 Mars Street
San Francisco, CA 94114

Laser Institute of America
5151 Monroe Avenue
Suite 102W
Toledo, OH 43623

◇ **RELATED ARTICLES**

Volume 1: Electronics; Engineering; Telecommunications
Volume 2: Engineers; Physicists
Volume 3: Commercial and industrial electronic equipment repairers; Instrument repairers
Volume 4: Biomedical equipment technicians; Electromechanical technicians; Electronics technicians; Industrial engineering technicians; Instrumentation technicians; Microelectronics technicians; Telecommunications technicians

Microelectronics technicians

Definition

Microelectronics technicians work in research laboratories where they assist the engineering staff in developing and making prototype and custom-designed microchips. Microchips, often called simply chips, are tiny but extremely complex electronic devices used to control the operations of many kinds of machines and electronics equipment, from cars to toasters to VCRs. The process of manufacturing chips is often called fabrication.

Nature of the work

Microelectronics technicians operate a variety of equipment used in fabrication to process materials and to assemble and test finished chips, but they work on a small scale on making new kinds of chips, not on carrying out large-scale established production processes in a factory. In addition to operating equipment connected with fabrication, technicians may help interpret and evaluate information gathered in the laboratory, and they may help write reports and technical specifications for large-scale manufacturing.

To understand these technicians' activities, it is necessary to know something about their product. Microchips contain miniaturized electronic systems called integrated circuits. Integrated circuits include many interconnected electronic components such as transistors, capacitors, and resistors, produced on or in a single thin slice of a semiconductor material. Semiconductors are so-named because they are substances with electrical properties somewhere between those of conductors and insulators. The semiconductor used most frequently in microchips is silicon, so microchips are also sometimes called silicon chips.

Often smaller than a fingernail, chips may contain multiple layers of complex circuitry stacked on top of each other. The word "integrated" refers to the way the circuitry is "blended" into the chip during the fabrication process.

Chip fabrication involves some highly specialized tasks that must be performed in dust-free, totally controlled conditions. Microelectronics technicians must know about various kinds of processes, procedures, and equipment to assist in fabricating chips in the laboratory.

The first step in fabrication is circuit design. After a designer comes up with a detailed plan of the circuit layout, technicians operate equipment to convert the design into a working photomask, which is an outline of the circuit that can be used to reproduce the layout on a carefully prepared thin slice of silicon called a wafer. This step may involve operating a computer graphics system to generate a computer tape or disk of instructions. These instructions are loaded into other equipment that uses an electron beam to produce the circuit outlines on the wafer. Each wafer may contain many identical copies of the circuit side by side so that once the wafer is complete, it can be cut into many separate chips that will be all the same.

Technicians also carry out many different steps in preparing the wafers. They clean them, coat them with a photoresist, which is a substance that reacts to certain types of radiation, then etch, bake, cure, and otherwise treat the wafers using various kinds of processing equipment. On specified areas of the wafers they implant chemicals or deposit layers of substances that have certain desired properties. These chemicals and substances form the electronic components and pathways of the circuitry.

Once the wafers are prepared according to instructions, the technicians use test equipment, such as sensitive measuring devices, microscopes, and electrical probes, to verify that the resulting product conforms to specifications. They dice the wafers into chips and do any necessary cleaning, bonding, and packaging into electronic devices.

Requirements

Microelectronics technicians need to have received post–high-school training, preferably in a two-year program, at a community college or vocational institute. They need to have studied mathematics through algebra and geometry. They should have good enough language skills that they can easily read and understand technical manuals and instructions and write reports with correct spelling, punctuation, and grammar. While the physical demands for these technicians are light, they will have to use special procedures and devices to protect against potentially hazardous conditions on the job, such as toxic chemicals or heat from processing equipment.

GOE: 06.01.03; SIC: 367; SOC: 3711

◇ **RELATED ARTICLES**

Volume 1: Electronics; Engineering
Volume 2: Engineers; Graphics programmers
Volume 4: CAD/CAM technicians; Electronics technicians; Semiconductor-development technicians

Nuclear instrumentation technicians

Definition

Nuclear instrumentation technicians help design, assemble, install, and maintain radiation detection and control instruments inside nuclear power plants, nuclear research facilities, and other facilities involved with nuclear technology. They inspect, test, adjust, and repair the electric, electronic, mechanical, and pneumatic instruments that are used to record and control generating operations in both nonnuclear and nuclear electric-power generating plants. Among their principal concerns are to test the accuracy of and to locate defects in flow meters, pressure gauges, temperature indicators, radiation counters or detectors, and other recording or controlling instruments upon which the safe functioning of the power plant relies.

Nuclear instrumentation technicians also assemble, install, and assist in the design of the

A nuclear instrumentation technician tests the control panel of a new nuclear reactor that has recently been installed.

many kinds of instrumentation equipment that are used for testing purposes, including, among many others, laboratory instruments used for monitoring research experiments, radiation-detection devices employed in nuclear power plants and nuclear waste handling facilities, and X-ray equipment designed to examine manufactured materials, as steel or ceramics, for hidden flaws. In addition, nuclear instrumentation technicians may participate in or help coordinate the actual testing activities. They may be involved in monitoring equipment, recording data, or recommending changes in test equipment or methods to test engineers.

History

The oldest forms of instrumentation are the five senses: eyes to monitor light and movement, ears to pick up vibrations in the air, nerve endings in the skin to detect changes in temperature and pressure, and olfactory nerves and taste buds to sense the chemical composition of items in our environment.

These five senses, of course, have their limitations, and humans have always sought ways to extend or make more exact their ability to keep track of their world—at first with such primitive, yet effective, means as the sun dial, the weather vane, and the pan balance, and later with ingenious mechanical instruments such as the astrolabe, barometer, and surveyor's transit.

During the past two centuries, with the introduction of the steam engine, the automobile, and powered flight, increasingly sophisticated

forms of instrumentation have been devised. The development of nuclear energy especially has created a need for more accurate instrumentation.

Around 1900, researchers discovered that some chemical elements are radioactive, meaning that they naturally emit certain types of radiation. During this century, investigation into the nature of radiation has led to many applications of radioactivity, such as the development of nuclear weapons, the harnessing of nuclear power to generate electricity, and the use of radiation therapy in the treatment of disease.

In all of these applications, radioactive materials are unstable and the emissions they produce potentially dangerous. Thus it became clear early in the history of nuclear research and technology that accurate monitoring and controlling of nuclear radiation was crucial to all successful applications of this new form of energy. It is this monitoring and controlling that is the special concern of nuclear instrumentation technicians.

Nature of the work

The principal activities of nuclear instrumentation technicians include the design, assembly, installation, maintenance, repair, and calibrating of individual instruments and instrument systems in nuclear power plants or other nuclear-related facilities. This work is of special importance because the safety and reliability of the entire nuclear-plant operation depend on the instrumentation with which these technicians are concerned. Instruments are simply the only way nuclear reactor operators or radiation control and protection staff members can know what is going on inside the reactor and the rest of the facility, and can track the levels of radiation in the work place.

Nuclear instrumentation technicians are also sometimes referred to as *nuclear plant instrument technicians* or *instrumentation test technicians,* depending on the specific activities in which they are principally engaged. Nuclear plant instrument technicians work primarily in nuclear power plants, although some find employment in nonnuclear power plants. Working under the supervision and direction of nuclear engineers or nuclear-plant managers, they are responsible for most of the day-to-day care of plant instruments.

As part of this day-to-day care, nuclear plant instrument technicians inspect meters, indicators, and gauges to detect abnormal fluctuations in the operation of the instruments. They test the accuracy of flow meters, pressure gauges, controllers, radiation counters or detectors, and other recording, indicating, or controlling instruments. They also use these test instruments and many others, including mercury manometers, potentiometers, oscilloscopes, voltmeters, and watt meters, to locate any defective component in the system.

Nuclear plant instrument technicians are also involved in maintenance activities related to instruments. They remove from the system and replace defective instruments. They decontaminate, disassemble, reassemble, and clean instruments. When instruments require lubrication, replacement of defective wiring and tubing, or other routine maintenance or repair, nuclear plant instrument technicians often perform the tasks.

Complete and accurate record keeping is another important responsibility of nuclear plant instrument technicians. They record the calibrations they make of instruments, the names and often the numbers of all parts and components they use in their activities, and inventory levels for all parts for which they are responsible.

Nuclear plant instrument technicians also prepare schematic drawings, sketches, and reports to document changes made in instruments, circuits, or systems.

Instrumentation test technicians often work at research activities in nuclear power plants or other nuclear installations. In these settings, they assist in the design, assembly, and installation of detection and control instrumentation.

One of the principal duties of instrumentation test technicians is to test the test equipment they are helping to build or develop. They utilize principles of engineering and test technology to design, develop, and conduct the tests and record their results for engineers. As a part of these testing activities, they may coordinate or participate in the installation of the unit or system to be tested in the testing apparatus. This activity includes connecting valves, pumps, hydraulic, mechanical or electrical controls, cabling, power sources, and indicating instruments. Throughout the course of the testing, instrumentation test technicians may recommend changes in the test method or equipment to the engineers in charge.

Instrumentation test technicians often work with engineering personnel to resolve problems that arise while building new or experimental instrumentation devices. They may also confer with engineers to resolve questions about the types and cycles of tests to be performed, the conditions under which the tests should be conducted, and the duration of the tests.

Another principal area of activity for instrumentation test technicians is in the fabrication of precision parts for test apparatus. Instrumentation test technicians may use metalworking machines such as lathes, milling machines, and welding equipment, or they may interpret specifications for other workers who fabricate the parts. They use precision measuring instruments to inspect parts for conformance to specifications.

Plant safety is a paramount concern for all nuclear instrumentation technicians. Many nuclear plant instrument technicians and instrumentation test technicians work closely with radiation-protection technicians to develop strategies and equipment for monitoring personnel, the plant, and the environment for radioactive contamination; for handling nuclear materials, especially the preparing and monitoring of radioactive waste shipments; for maintaining and calibrating radiation-detection instruments; for training personnel in the proper use of monitoring equipment and safety equipment; and for making sure that radiation-protection regulations, standards, and the processes are followed and that records are kept of all regular measurements and tests of radioactivity.

Requirements

Students entering the field of nuclear instrumentation technology must have the scientific interest to study and understand radiological, electronic, and electrical theory, and they must be adept in the use of tools. The nature of nuclear instrumentation technology requires that technicians have a clear and precise understanding of written and pictorial information; hence, the ability to communicate competently in scientific and engineering terms is a necessity. Above all, they must be consciously and habitually careful, orderly, and deliberate workers, because their main task is to work at the measurement and control of the potential dangers of radioactivity.

Students who are expecting to enter this career should begin their preparation while in high school. They will need four years of language study (reading, writing, and speaking skills), at least two years of mathematics including algebra, and at least one year of physical science, preferably physics, with a laboratory section. If computer programming and applications, vocational machine shop, and blueprint reading are offered, they would provide additional useful background.

After high school, the prospective student should pursue a course of study at a two-year technical school or community college. Several public or private technical college programs are offered specifically for the nuclear instrumentation technician. Other programs called "nuclear technology" or "instrumentation technology" are also offered and can provide at least basic preparation.

A typical series of courses for the first year of a program specifically designed for the nuclear instrumentation technician might include courses in nuclear technology, radiation physics, technical mathematics, electricity and electronics, technical communications, radiation detection and measurement, inorganic chemistry, radiation protection, blueprint reading, quality assurance/quality control, principles of process instrumentation, computer applications, applied electronics, and industrial organizations and institutions.

A typical second year of study includes courses in technical writing, nuclear-systems measurement and calibration, reactor physics, advanced electronics, electromechanical controls, monitoring techniques, quality-assurance and reliability instrumentation and control, instrumentation control of reactors and plant systems, computer systems, control of heat transfer, advanced computer systems, advanced instrumentation management, and industrial economics.

Special requirements

At present there are no special requirements for licensing or certification of nuclear plant instrument technicians or instrumentation test technicians.

Federal security clearances are required for those engaged in jobs involving national security. Nuclear Regulatory Commission (NRC) clearance is valid for both government and private employees if security clearance is required. Certain projects may necessitate military clearance with or without NRC clearance. Employers usually help arrange such clearances.

Opportunities for experience and exploration

For high-school students who are interested in nuclear instrumentation technician careers, the high-school vocational guidance counselor is a useful resource. The counseling staff and the occupational-information collection at a community college or technical school can also be very valuable to a prospective technician. Li-

brarians in schools and local public libraries can usually locate various kinds of materials that may help to answer more career questions.

High-school science classes, particularly those including laboratory sections, are perhaps the best place for getting a practical taste of the careers of nuclear instrumentation technicians. Science teachers and other members of the high-school staff may be able to arrange field trips to science museums, for example, and bring speakers to the school to give first-hand accounts of their work.

For safety and security reasons, facilities such as nuclear power plants that handle radioactive materials generally cannot accommodate visitors inside the plant. They usually do have visitors' centers, however, where the public can learn more about how the plant operates. Many universities that have research reactors conduct scheduled tours of their facilities, as do some national laboratories. Some of these institutions can furnish literature or even speakers on radiation physics and safe handling of nuclear materials.

Methods of entering

Graduation from an appropriate training program is the first step to entering this field. The curriculum may be called "nuclear technology" or "nuclear radiation technology" and may be taught as a technical program at a community college, a technical institute, or a division of a four-year college. A two-year instrumentation or electromechanical technician program may also be suitable as the beginning point for this career. The U.S. Navy also provides an excellent training program for various kinds of nuclear specialists and technicians.

Representatives of companies with nuclear facilities visit some schools with training programs just before the graduation of each class of new technicians. They interview students and recruit them as prospective employees to start work soon after graduation. Technicians emerging from strong training programs may have several attractive job offers from which to choose.

Many nuclear instrumentation technicians find work with electric power utilities that operate nuclear plants. Other potential employers include the following: nuclear materials handling and processing facilities, federal and state nuclear regulatory agencies, nuclear medicine units (at larger hospitals and clinics), nondestructive testing firms, radiopharmaceutical industries, nuclear waste handling facilities, nuclear service firms, nuclear shipyards, oil-well drilling and exploration organizations, national research laboratories, and modern chemical and petrochemical companies with automatic or modern instrumentation systems for process control.

Beginning technicians can almost always look forward to further formal study and on-the-job training. Usually beginners are assigned to work with more experienced technicians or engineers in installation, servicing, troubleshooting, or calibration. As these technicians become familiar with the job, they will often find it desirable to take night school or other courses to supplement their growing practical experience.

Advancement

Regardless of the industry in which a nuclear instrumentation technician starts his or her career, there are opportunities for advancement. One avenue of growth is into sales and service, working for a company that manufactures instrumentation. Another career route might lead to designing instruments and instrument systems—a complex and challenging area with much work still to be done. Another option for a highly experienced technician may be to become a consultant, employed by a nuclear-engineering or nuclear-industry consulting firm or managing a separate and independent consulting business. For those who develop their writing skills, technical writing offers opportunities for advancement. Such technical writers often work on instructional materials, press releases, and articles for newspapers and magazines.

Some people who start as nuclear instrumentation technicians may eventually assume high-level supervisory or management positions in one of the nuclear or chemical industries whose successful operation depends on modern instrumental control and automation. Finally, some technicians return to school for the additional training to become engineers in the field of nuclear technology.

Employment outlook

Attempting to examine even the near future of the U.S. nuclear industries is quite difficult. Questions about public health and safety have continued to receive a great deal of public attention since the accidents at Three Mile Island and Chernobyl. In addition, concern about environmental effects, unresolved issues and pol-

icies for waste disposal and reprocessing, actual and proposed state and federal moratoriums on new nuclear power plant construction and operations, reductions in export sales because of concern about nuclear weapons proliferation and because of increased foreign competition, rapidly increasing construction costs, changes in required power plant design and engineering, and a reduction in forecast growth in electricity requirements all contribute to the present uncertainties and reduce potential growth in the nuclear field.

Most of the employment in the nuclear energy field for nuclear instrumentation technicians is found in three segments—reactor design and manufacture, design of nuclear facilities, and nuclear-related research and development activities. The future of the design of nuclear facilities and reactor design and manufacture is obviously related to power plant development and redesign requirements. It is now unlikely that any new nuclear power plants will be built during the next decade, and this reduction in nuclear power plant development will cause a significant decrease in activity and employment in these two segments, which employ a large number of nuclear instrumentation technicians with specialized skills.

Much of the nuclear-related research and development activity is government-funded, and the vast majority of the activity is located in government-owned, contractor-operated facilities. Obviously the future of nuclear-related research and development depends primarily on future levels and directions of government funding.

Earnings

The earnings of nuclear instrumentation technicians at the start of their careers will vary according to where they are employed: a nuclear fuel assembly plant, a nuclear power plant, a research laboratory, or some other area of the nuclear industry. They may begin as salaried staff members or be paid hourly wages, depending on the organization in which they start. If they are paid hourly wages, there are usually wage differentials for different work shifts as well as premium pay for overtime. Having been trained in both nonnuclear and nuclear instrumentation, nuclear instrumentation technicians can expect to enter their field at rates higher than ordinary instrumentation technicians.

Technician graduates entering this field can expect starting salaries of from $16,000 to $27,000 per year, and averaging close to $20,000 per year. After three to five years of experience and additional training these employees can expect to earn $28,000 to $32,000 a year or more, depending on the nature of their job advancement. Advancement to consulting work or similar services in other parts of the industry can bring incomes up to and sometimes beyond $37,000 per year.

In addition to their yearly salary or wages, nuclear instrumentation technicians usually enjoy the benefits of paid holidays and vacations, participation in insurance plans sponsored by the company, and retirement plans. Because of the rapid changes that occur in the technology and the constant need for employees to study to keep up with them, many employers in this field provide liberal reimbursement for costs of additional job-related formal study and participation in the workshops, seminars, and conferences sponsored by technical societies in the field.

Conditions of work

The working environment of nuclear instrumentation technicians depends upon the employing facility and the task being performed. The environment can vary from offices or hospital-clean control rooms to relatively cramped and cold areas of power plant plumbing. Nuclear instrumentation technicians often wear laboratory coats or regular work clothes, but they are also required sometimes to wear special radiation-resistant clothing. These technicians work under the direct supervision of nuclear engineers and scientists and often as part of a team with radiation protection technicians and operators; however, the safe and reliable function of the entire facility depends upon the quality and precision of the instruments that nuclear instrumentation technicians develop, assemble, install, or maintain.

Like all other workers in the nuclear energy field, nuclear instrumentation technicians must follow regulations limiting their exposure to radiation. They wear film badges or carry pocket monitors to determine their personal exposure. In some areas of nuclear facilities, protection from radiation is afforded through the use of hot cells, which are special areas enclosed with radiation-shielding materials. While looking through thick lead-glass windows, nuclear instrumentation technicians operate remote-controlled equipment to manipulate nuclear materials inside the area. In other areas of nuclear facilities, alarm systems are used to warn of radiation hazards.

Social and psychological factors

The work of nuclear instrumentation technicians is very demanding. They must feel confident of their knowledge and skill to measure and manage potentially dangerous radioactivity. The instrumentation for which these technicians are responsible must be trusted to provide consistently accurate information. Hence, nuclear instrumentation technicians must demonstrate a high degree of precision in their work habits.

Because nuclear instrumentation technicians are often called upon to instruct other plant staff members in the nature, workings, use, or maintenance of instrumentation, they should have good communication skills. In addition, they often work in collaboration with radiation-protection technicians, nuclear plant operators, nuclear engineers, and other nuclear personnel. In this collaborative role, nuclear instrumentation technicians must know how to listen as well as how to express themselves clearly, both orally and in writing.

Because abnormal conditions can and sometimes do develop in the nuclear power industry, nuclear instrumentation technicians must be able to withstand the stress associated with such situations. These tachnicians must be able to work long hours at such times without making mistakes and as cooperating members of a team of nuclear experts doing a demanding job.

Nuclear instrumentation technology is an ever-changing field. Technicians who want to advance and excel must expect to continue their education—either in short seminars, on-the-job training programs, outside formal instruction, or even reading and studying on their own—throughout the length of their careers.

GOE: 05.01.04, 05.05.11; **SIC:** 3825; **SOC:** 3719, 6171

◇ **SOURCES OF ADDITIONAL INFORMATION**

American Nuclear Society
555 North Kensington Avenue
La Grange Park, IL 60525

Canada Institute for Scientific and Technical Information
National Research Council of Canada
Montreal Road
Ottawa, Ontario K1A 0S2
Canada

Instrument Society of America
67 Alexander Drive
PO Box 12277
Research Triangle Park, NC 27709

National Council on Radiation Protection and Measurements
7910 Woodmont Avenue
Suite 1016
Bethesda, MD 20814

Health Physics Society
8000 Westpark Drive
Suite 400
McLean, VA 22102

Nuclear materials handling technicians

Definition

Nuclear materials handling technicians work under the direction of nuclear scientists and engineers in handling nuclear materials and in fabricating, labeling, packaging, and transporting nuclear fuel elements and radioactive wastes. Although not all nuclear materials handling technicians actually handle radioactive materials, most of them are trained in remote-control handling because such work comprises the biggest employment opportunity for these technicians. Technicians who specialize in that aspect of the work are referred to as *hot-cell technicians.* The work of hot-cell technicians is fully described in the article "Industrial radiological technicians" in the Engineering and Science Technician Occupations section elsewhere in this volume.

History

The phenomenon of natural radioactivity was first discovered in 1896 by Antoine-Henri Becquerel as part of his investigations of uranium salts. Soon afterward, and spurred in part by the discoveries of Becquerel, Marie and Pierre Curie began their investigations of radioactivity, a term first used by Marie Curie in 1898. In the same year the Curies announced the discovery of two new elements, polonium and radium, which is probably the most radioactive of the naturally occurring elements. In 1903, Becquerel and the Curies were awarded the Nobel Prize for Physics for their discoveries relating to radioactivity. In 1910, Marie Curie published a very important work on radioactivity and isolated pure radium, and in 1911, she was awarded the Nobel Prize for Chemistry for the discovery of radium and polonium and the isolation of pure radium.

The essential process in nuclear fission (atom-splitting) was first demonstrated in 1938 by Irene Curie (daughter of Marie and Pierre) and Pavle Savic and was soon interpreted by Otto Hahn and Fritz Strassmann, who are considered the discoverers of fission. The effort to develop the atomic bomb began in 1940. The development of nuclear radiation protection, nuclear materials handling, and nuclear waste management was subsequently speeded up. The work performed by nuclear materials handling technicians is the application of that technology.

During the past forty years of working with nuclear energy sources, exacting methods have been developed for handling and transporting nuclear materials. These highly complex techniques involve the use of remote-control equipment, radiation shields, and other protective devices.

Nuclear materials handling technicians
Emerging Technician Occupations

A nuclear materials handling technician operates a machine that transports barrels of nuclear waste. The barrels are so well-sealed that it is not necessary to wear protective gear.

Extensive federal regulations have been enacted in response to the hazards of radiation. The Nuclear Regulatory Commission (NRC) requires and enforces the use of specialized procedures and equipment in the handling of nuclear materials. Licensing examinations are now required for all those who work as operators in nuclear fuel processing plants. Today, nuclear materials handling technicians have an essential role in the safe delivery of nuclear power.

Because nuclear power is now a common source for electrical power generation, electric utility companies require fuel rods for their reactors and safe technologies for handling, shipping, and storing nuclear materials. Reliable disposal and recycling procedures for the used but still radioactive fuel rods have been developed and require the services of nuclear materials handling technicians.

Nature of the work

The processes of handling nuclear materials are delicate and complex. They occur at many stages, from the mining of uranium ore to radioactive waste disposal. Thus the term "nuclear materials handling technician" actually applies to a number of functions carried out in various places and at various stages of nuclear fuel element development and disposal.

Nuclear materials handling technicians perform a variety of tasks related to the milling, conversion, separation, and fabrication of nuclear materials and fuels. Materials handling and safe transportation of fuel rod assemblies to the reactor site make up their next series of

tasks. Their work also includes preparing used fuel rod assemblies and nuclear wastes for shipment to waste storage facilities.

Radioactive materials occur naturally in low concentrations of less than one percent in the mined ore. Physical and chemical methods are used to produce higher concentrations of radioactive fuel. This process is called enriching the ore. Once the materials are enriched, they are then made into small pellets. The pellets are then assembled in special alloy metal tubes. The filled tubes become a part of the fuel assemblies used in nuclear reactors.

Nuclear materials handling technicians are involved in uranium isotope enrichment and fuel fabrication, which includes manufacturing of fuel elements and fuel element assemblies; on-site storage of nuclear materials; and transportation activities relating to nuclear materials. They are also involved in fuel handling at reactors and in the manufacture of radiation sources.

Remote-control devices are often used to keep radioactive materials away from personnel. Thus, nuclear materials handling technicians are trained to use master/slave manipulators. These are mechanical devices that act as arms and hands. They are located in rooms known as hot cells, which are enclosed with radiation shields such as lead and concrete. By controlling the manipulators and observing their actions through a cell window, technicians perform handling, assembling, packaging, and the many other operations associated with radioactive materials.

Some technicians may perform chemical analysis of the cooling water needed for reactors by taking samples from the system that contains it. Some technicians operate heat exchange units, pumps, and other equipment to decontaminate or dispose of radioactive wastes. Decontamination is a process of safely disposing of radioactive material that has accidentally leaked, spilled, or rubbed off to an area where it is not wanted.

Waste is produced in all nuclear facilities. These wastes are radioactive; some only slightly so, and others are highly radioactive. They are accumulated and processed to eliminate water, reduce volume, and, in some cases, solidified with concrete or plastic. They are then packaged for storage in naturally or artificially shielded storage places. Nuclear materials handling technicians are involved in nuclear waste management. Current emphasis is on research and development efforts relating to waste management; however, in the future technicians may be involved with actual disposal of high-level fuel cycle wastes.

These technicians also understand the nature of radiation and the principles of radiation protection, including the use of instruments to detect radiation escaping during decontamination activities. Because fissionable materials are controlled by the NRC, technicians who handle nuclear materials must be competent in nuclear material inventory techniques. A great amount of scientific and processing information about nuclear systems and safety must be understood by technicians. This includes neutron physics, nuclear fission, reactor power production, nuclear criticality (the physical process that causes the release of high levels of radioactivity), and nuclear plant safeguards.

Nuclear materials handling technicians must understand the purpose and function of equipment used in the fabrication, waste handling, and transportation of all kinds of nuclear materials. They usually work under the direction of nuclear engineers, chemists, physicists, senior technicians, or senior operators. They generally work according to written procedures and have a hand in their preparation. They must be aware of nonstandard conditions and the need to record deviations from established procedures made for any reason.

Technicians operate a wide variety of chemical equipment that concentrates, decontaminates, neutralizes, and disposes of radioactive waste. They also operate remote-control equipment that performs chemical and metallurgical tests on fuel and fuel elements. This equipment includes master/slave manipulators, glove boxes, electromechanical linkages, and other specialized equipment.

Technicians operate equipment that packages and moves radioactive materials into storage systems. They also operate equipment that grinds ore and concentrates it for further processing. Technicians control concentrators, distillation towers, and related equipment.

Technicians regularly write technical reports that must be complete and highly accurate. The reports often include graphs, charts, and other means of recording and presenting data.

A most important part of the job of all nuclear materials handling technicians involves observing all specifications, such as federal regulations on packaging and handling, radiation dose rates, and exposure calculations.

Requirements

Any high-school student who enjoys operating electronic and electromechanical devices, who likes science, and who has an interest in ma-

chine operations can consider training as a nuclear materials handling technician.

Unlike many other types of materials handling, nuclear materials handling does not require great physical strength. It does require adequate eye-hand coordination, good reflexes, and the ability to be observant.

Technicians must be able to perform basic mathematical calculations and to read and understand precise instructions and detailed procedures, guidelines, regulations, charts, and directions. Writing skills are important, as technicians must write chemical laboratory reports that are based on careful observation and accurate interpretation of data.

Above all, these technicians must be consciously and consistently careful, deliberate, and orderly workers, because their main task is to work at managing potentially dangerous materials in very complex settings.

High-school students wishing to pursue a career as a nuclear materials handling technician should take basic mathematics, algebra, chemistry, physics, and English composition. Computer science, machine shop, and blueprint reading, if offered, would provide additional useful background for studies that will follow.

After high-school graduation, prospective technicians should attend a two-year technical school or community college. The course of study that they undertake should be an engineering technician program with intensive classroom study. In addition, the program should include laboratory work or simulated work situations that help students practice techniques and procedures related to applied theoretical chemistry and physics in the nuclear industry.

Typical first-year courses in a nuclear materials handling program include the following subjects or their equivalent: introduction to nuclear technology, radiation physics, mathematics, introduction to electricity and electronics, introduction to technical communications, radiation detection and measurement, inorganic chemistry, radiation protection, blueprint reading, introduction to quality assurance and quality control, principles of process instrumentation, computer applications, metrology (the science of measurement), and industrial organizations and institutions.

A typical second year of study continues with the following: technical writing, metallurgy and metals properties, applied nuclear chemistry, advanced radiation protection, basic mechanics, control of heat transfer processes, radiation monitoring techniques, computer systems and electromechanical controls, nuclear chemical processes, occupational safety and health, nuclear systems and safety, radioactive materials handling techniques, and industrial economics. In some second-year programs, special projects are assigned or may be chosen that allow students to study a particular nuclear materials handling problem.

Students who graduate from nuclear technician programs are usually hired by companies and institutions involved in the nuclear industry. These employers provide a general orientation to their operation and additional training specific to their processes and activities. When needed, they often prepare trainees for NRC licensing examinations.

Because only a very few schools offer programs that train nuclear materials handling technicians, students who want to enter this field may choose technical programs in nuclear technology, nuclear radiation protection, or chemical technology. These programs offer basic instruction that can provide entry into the industry. Further specialized training can be obtained on the job.

Special requirements

The NRC has designed licensing procedures for certain commercial nuclear fuel-cycle operations. In addition, security clearance is required for some nuclear materials handling technicians working in government settings and some private settings.

Opportunities for experience and exploration

For high-school students and others who are interested in the nuclear materials handling career, the high-school vocational guidance counselor is a valuable resource person. If a community or technical college is in the area, their occupational information center and counseling staff can also be very helpful. In addition, librarians in high school, college, or public libraries are often able to pinpoint avenues of research into a particular career field.

Universities with nuclear engineering programs may be a good source of information on several aspects of nuclear power. Representatives from such programs can be invited to speak to science clubs or career education classes.

Opportunities to visit inside operating nuclear power plants generally cannot be arranged, but most utility companies with nu-

clear reactors have representatives who can describe many important features about this career. They also usually have visitors centers where tours are available.

Methods of entering

The best way to enter this career is to enroll in and graduate from a technical program in a community college, technical institute, or division of a four-year college with a curriculum such as has been described. Another excellent way to enter the career is to join the Navy and enter their technical training program for various nuclear specialists.

Whatever background the beginner brings to the job, considerable training must follow under the employer's direction. The training of a nuclear materials handling technician is an extremely expensive endeavor for the companies and organizations with nuclear operations. Companies are unlikely to invest the high cost of training in people who have only a high-school education and no related work experience.

Those who have earned an associate degree in nuclear technology or chemical technology from a two-year, postsecondary school are far better candidates for plant training. They are usually recruited and interviewed while in school by representatives of companies with nuclear facilities and are hired to begin work after graduation. These technical school graduates normally have sufficient understanding of physics, chemistry, applied mathematics, and engineering technology to undertake company-sponsored training for licensing examinations.

Positions for entry-level technicians are available in uranium-235 enrichment facilities, nuclear power plants, nuclear research institutions, and nuclear materials equipment manufacturing firms. Many of these beginning positions do not require licensing. Their job titles may include fuel fabrication technician, hot cell technician, process supervisor, chemical technician and fuel assembler, waste disposal treatment operator, decontaminator, scientific technician, or radioactive waste dispatcher.

Advancement

Advancement opportunities may be found in the various nuclear research laboratories, nuclear mineral ore mining and processing, and with nuclear weapon producers. They are also found in nuclear power plants, with manufacturers of nuclear reactors, industrial insurance companies, and producers or users of radioactive isotopes.

These advanced positions may be as specialized professional experts in a company or laboratory, or as consultants. Consultants may be employed by nuclear engineering companies or nuclear industry consulting firms, or they may be independent consultants who manage their own consulting business. Some may enter the industrial physical radiologic business as consultants in the use of radioisotopes for a wide variety of industrial or research purposes.

Employment outlook

In 1989, more than 100 nuclear power plants were operating in the United States, and construction permits had been issued for about a dozen more; however, no orders have been placed for new nuclear plants since 1987, so the total number of plants in operation in the United States is not likely to increase by much in the foreseeable future. Because of this, the total number of nuclear materials handling technicians employed by power companies is not likely to increase either. However, new technicians will be needed to replace retiring technicians or technicians leaving their jobs for other reasons. In addition, manufacturing companies and research and development laboratories may increase the number of nuclear materials handling technicians they employ. For all of these reasons, well-trained nuclear materials handling technicians should have no trouble finding good jobs.

Earnings

The earnings of nuclear materials handling technicians who are beginning their career vary depending on where they are employed. Technicians may begin as salaried staff or may be paid hourly wages, also depending on where they work. If they are paid hourly wages, they usually work in shifts and receive pay for overtime.

Graduate technicians usually earn beginning salaries of $16,000 to $20,000 per year. After three to five years of experience and additional training, these employees can expect to earn more than $25,000 per year. Further advancement to consulting work or similar services in other parts of the industry bring potential incomes of more than $30,000 per year.

In addition to their yearly wages, technicians usually receive paid holidays and vacations, company insurance, a retirement plan, and other fringe benefits. Because of the rapid changes that occur in the technology and the constant need for employees to study, many employers provide financial support in meeting the costs of additional study and participation in formal education, workshops, seminars, and conferences.

Conditions of work

Nuclear materials handling technicians work in a variety of settings, depending on the part of the industry in which they are employed. Most technicians work in clean, orderly, dust- and gas-free environments.

Because these technicians handle and transport radioactive materials, extensive safety measures are a routine part of their jobs. Film badges are worn to detect radiation exposure. Special radiation-resistant clothing may be required in some areas. This clothing contains respiratory protection devices that reduce the level of radiation before it reaches the body.

Radiation shielding materials, such as lead and concrete, are used to enclose radioactive materials while technicians manipulate these materials from outside the contaminated area. In some areas, automatic alarm systems are used to detect radiation hazards.

Nuclear materials are handled and transported under one of the strictest inventory controls known to any industry. In all facilities where nuclear materials are fabricated or present for any reason, inventory management is required and security measures are enforced.

Social and psychological factors

The career of a nuclear materials handling technician is a very demanding one. These technicians must be confident in the use of their knowledge and skills to manage potentially dangerous materials routinely.

They must be patient and careful, and they should enjoy the challenge of understanding new ideas and changes. They must be willing to take on the responsibility of being alert and attentive during the entire workday. Only persons who are committed to performing their tasks well and thoroughly are likely to succeed in this field.

People who feel comfortable with various types of equipment, mechanical devices, and laboratory instruments are usually well-suited to nuclear materials handling. Prospective technicians should appreciate good workmanship and established procedures. In addition, technicians must understand the reasons for regulations and specified procedures. They must also recognize problems when they arise.

Graphs, charts, technical reports, and other means of written record keeping are frequently used by technicians. These technicians must take on the responsibility of writing complete and accurate reports as a regular part of their work.

Nuclear materials handling technicians, especially if they want to become senior operators, need to have the ability to work well with others, to supervise, and to communicate clearly and easily with their superiors and co-workers.

Some prospective technicians may anticipate stress from working in a highly controlled and constantly monitored environment where even a small error can expose themselves or others to potentially serious danger. However, the feeling of confidence in their ability to do an unusual and difficult job well often turns such stress into feelings of strength and satisfaction. Part of the rewarding satisfaction of the career is that these technicians are a vital part of one of the most complex modern industries, one that is essential to the nation's effectiveness and well-being.

GOE: 02.04.01, 06.01.04, 06.02.11; SIC: 2819; SOC: 3832

◇ SOURCES OF ADDITIONAL INFORMATION

American Nuclear Society
555 North Kensington Avenue
La Grange Park, IL 60525

American Society of Mechanical Engineers Education Division
345 East 47th Street
New York, NY 10017

American Society for Nondestructive Testing
4153 Arlingate Plaza
Columbus, OH 43228

Canada Institute for Scientific and Technical Information
National Research Council of Canada
Montreal Road
Ottawa, Ontario K1A 0S2
Canada

Health Physics Society
8000 Westpark Drive
Suite 400
McLean, VA 22102

Instrument Society of America
67 Alexander Drive
PO Box 12277
Research Triangle Park, NC 27709

International Test and Evaluation Association
4400 Fair Lakes Court
Fairfax, VA 22033

◇ RELATED ARTICLES

Volume 1: Energy; Nuclear Sciences; Public Utilities
Volume 2: Engineers; Nuclear medicine technologists
Volume 3: Industrial chemicals workers; Power plant occupations
Volume 4: Industrial radiological technicians; Nuclear instrumentation technicians; Nuclear power plant quality control technicians; Nuclear power plant radiation control technicians; Nuclear reactor operator technicians

Nuclear power plant quality control technicians

Definition

Nuclear power plant quality control technicians work under the direction of the quality control engineers for utilities that build and operate nuclear power plants. Almost all nuclear quality control technicians are employed in nuclear power plants. They apply the sciences of measurement, design, inspection, testing, statistical sampling, and mathematical probability to ensure that a nuclear power plant is built and operated within acceptable standards. Their work contributes much to the safe, efficient use of nuclear power.

History

Nuclear reactors have come of age in the electrical power generating industry. The first commercial nuclear-fired electrical power plant started operation at Shippingport, Pennsylvania, in 1958. By the late 1980s, more than one hundred nuclear power plants provided 17.5 percent of the nation's electrical power. By the year 2000, approximately a dozen more reactors could be operating. Outside the United States, nations on almost every continent are building nuclear power plants to produce electricity.

Producing electricity in a nuclear power plant involves an extremely complicated process. Nuclear fission consists of splitting atoms of nuclear material such as uranium into simpler chemical atoms and producing great quantities of heat.

The heat produced from the reaction is carried from the reactor in water that is used to cool the reactor core and take the heat away as steam. The steam is used to drive turbines that make electric power. All parts of this cooling system in a nuclear plant must be engineered and manufactured perfectly to specifications to prevent leaks.

For this reason, quality control technicians are needed in nuclear plants. Errors in equipment manufacture, workmanship, planning, or communications can cause extremely serious and potentially dangerous failures in nuclear plant systems. To prevent such errors, a sophisticated system of quality audits, inspections, and materials testing called quality assur-

ance and quality control is needed. Public concern over the nature of nuclear power and intense regulation under the federal Nuclear Regulatory Commission (NRC) have made quality assurance and quality control even more necessary.

Before a nuclear power plant can obtain an operating license from the government, a quality audit must be performed on every part and structure in the system, from purchase, manufacture, and construction to installation. Such a quality audit is very much like a financial audit taken by an accountant. In the nuclear power plant, written procedures, checklists, tests, and inspection records are used to prove that every detail of development and operation was carried out according to plan.

Nature of the work

At the very start of the planning and designing of a nuclear power plant, a system of records for quality assurance and quality control is set up by the chief quality assurance and quality control engineer. These records must be kept throughout the engineering, construction, installation, and operation of each part of the plant. Even when a part or a structure is repaired or replaced, the record must prove that it was done correctly.

The job of the quality control technician in a nuclear power plant is to work under the direction of quality control engineers to make certain that every detail of the plant, in its construction and in its operation, is carried out according to specifications.

The plant design specifies limits of quality and quantity for materials, equipment, workmanship, and plant processes. The technician may inspect electrical, mechanical, welding, and plumbing systems. Technicians check equipment and construction in every part of the plant, including the exterior. Reactor parts and structures that have been manufactured elsewhere are also subject to audit. Technicians may not actually inspect such items but must prove by certified records that proper inspections have been made. Building and operating a nuclear power plant requires several quality control engineers and technicians to assist

A nuclear power plant quality control technician inspects the main flange of a coolant pump that will circulate water through the reactor.

them. All must understand the system or the part of the system for which they are responsible for quality control.

In steam-driven electrical power generating plants, a fuel is used to heat water to steam. The pressure generated from the release of steam into pipes is used to rotate a turbine. The turbine drives a generator that produces the electricity. In coal-, oil-, or gas-fired plants, the fuel is burned and the steam generated in a boiler. But in nuclear plants, the boiler is replaced with a nuclear reactor where material such as uranium undergoes the atom-splitting that produces tremendous quantities of heat. Cooling water, circulated through the reactor, carries the heat away to produce steam for the turbines.

In this process, every possible precaution is taken by the design engineers and the quality control team to be certain that nuclear radiation does not contaminate the equipment or the operating personnel. The cooling water from the reactor contains high levels of radioactivity. It is transported in large stainless steel pipes that are two feet in diameter. Because the water in these pipes is at high temperatures and under extremely high pressure, special precautions must be taken to make sure that the pipes do not leak.

The steel pipes must be examined and tested all through their manufacture and installation to determine that they do not contain in-

ternal flaws that would weaken them. Each weld joint in the pipes must also be examined to determine that all the welds are perfect in every way. These examinations, performed without affecting the pipes in any way, require the use of complicated scientific techniques and equipment such as ultrasonic and X-ray devices. The quality control technician, under the direction of the quality control engineer, operates this equipment and conducts these tests. These tests are called nondestructive testing.

The structure that contains the nuclear reactor must be stable and strong. It must not crack during an earthquake or if an airplane should ever crash into it. The concrete base and dome of the building are many feet thick and contain steel reinforcing bars more than two inches in diameter. The bars are crisscrossed and welded at every intersection. The concrete must be mixed and poured according to rigorous standards. Quality control technicians check the construction procedures to see that they are carried out properly. They also examine each weld in the reinforcing bars and test the concrete that is used. This work is called civil/structural testing.

All electrical wiring and cabling in the power plant must be of the highest quality and properly installed. Alternate or backup wiring assures that the plant will operate properly even if part of the wiring is damaged. Under the supervision of the quality control engineer, quality control technicians check the quality and type of electrical materials used and examine the installations. These tests are called electrical inspections.

All mechanical equipment, such as valves and pumps, are examined by technicians for flaws upon arrival, after installation, and periodically during operation. These checks are called mechanical tests.

The quality control technician constantly works to prevent shortcomings in nuclear product reliability and to ensure plant safeguards and protection of people and the environment. Shortcomings may occur for a number of different reasons. Specifications and procedures may be incomplete. Planning may be insufficient or sloppy. Poor communications and lack of training may lead to serious problems. Tools and equipment may be inadequate. Carelessness on the part of personnel also may contribute to problems. The technician controls these factors by making planned and carefully recorded audits. These audits are generally designed by quality control engineers, scientists, and managers. A large part of the inspecting, testing, and record-keeping is done by quality control technicians.

The basic system for quality control is a complete set of written procedures and checklists that are used in performing the audits. These audits are carried out by personnel who do not have direct responsibility in the area being audited. In other words, the quality control technician works in a department of the plant separate from all others. The technician almost always works under an engineer and, in turn, may supervise the work of others.

Specific tasks performed by quality control technicians include:

keeping thorough and accurate records as required by the quality-control system;

reading and interpreting blueprints;

identifying the components and inspecting the quality of the pumps, valves, seals, and piping;

performing instrument reading and calibration techniques;

determining and verifying proper storage and handling of equipment such as may be used in heated areas, inert gas atmospheres, air-conditioned areas, and humidity-controlled areas;

writing reports, such as the results of equipment inspection, radiographs, nondestructive testing reports, survey reports, construction reports, and acceptance test reports;

understanding and applying codes and regulations, such as the American Society for Mechanical Engineers' Boiler and Pressure Vessel Code, and many others;

judging and testing the quality of weld joints for a variety of material types and weld shapes and sizes;

performing metallurgical tests, such as hardness, tensile strength, and notch ductility tests in samples of metal used in the plant or in its parts;

understanding basic metallurgical processes, such as heat treating and welding;

making accurate dimensional measurements;

understanding and interpreting criteria for passing quality control tests;

performing and verifying nondestructive testing;

following test procedures and obtaining or verifying the data needed;

measuring force, momentum, surface roughness, mass, temperature, pressure, and other factors, using the appropriate equipment;

interpreting standards for screws, bolts, pipes, and fasteners;

assisting in evaluation of customer requirements;

obtaining documents that prove that standards have been met;

providing information on previous quality problems;

evaluating the quality of work performed by possible suppliers;

reviewing purchase orders and subcontracts for quality standards;

making certain that purchased materials conform to requirements;

recommending corrective action when materials or components are below acceptable quality level;

determining the quality of manufacturing equipment, processes, testing procedures, and test equipment;

ensuring that spare units or parts and technical supplies conform to quality requirements;

ensuring that repairs and modifications are performed in accordance with approved standards; and

conducting cost-reduction studies and auditing of records and corrective actions taken when items do not meet specifications.

Nuclear power plant quality control technicians are hired to perform these various functions by utility companies, government-supported universities and national laboratories that operate research reactors, and by power plant construction contractors and consultants. They are also employed by nuclear materials handling companies and materials processing companies, by nondestructive testing firms, by architectural and engineering companies, and by manufacturers of power plant equipment.

The work done by these technicians involves a wide variety of tasks and activities. Much of the recording, reporting, and studying of tests and certification records takes place in an office. Testing and inspection tasks, however, may be performed in special laboratories or in the plant. More information about actual working conditions is given later in this article.

Requirements

Nuclear power plant quality control technicians are intensively trained in the physical sciences, engineering, and mathematics related to material-testing devices. Their studies include testing, inspection techniques, organization of systems of quality control, and management of quality in areas such as manufacturing, transportation, assembly, installation, and operations. Studies are also devoted to the assurance of maximum accuracy or quality control in all phases of nuclear materials manufacturing, and in the use of all components and parts in a nuclear power plant. These technicians, along with the quality control engineers and senior quality controllers under whose direction they work, must understand how the critical parts of nuclear reactors and power plants work. They must know how nuclear chemicals and radiation can cause failure in certain pipes, containers, and heat-exchanging parts of the system.

Special study is required to understand the operation of testing equipment (particularly nondestructive testing equipment), measuring devices, reading of specifications, design, and the measuring of tolerances to assure that a certain level of quality will be met in producing a component, unit, or system. These technicians must be able to prepare scientific or technical reports and use interpersonal skills in performing tasks as teamworkers or in supervising the work of others.

High-school students who enjoy learning about mechanical devices, basic sciences, and measuring and testing might consider pursuing a career in nuclear power plant quality assurance and quality control.

To prepare for a formal two-year college engineering technology program where they will receive the education needed for the career, interested high-school students should study algebra, geometry, and English composition. Chemistry and physics with laboratory study are basic to the training that follows. Where offered, introductory trigonometry, blueprint reading, and computer programming should be studied.

After graduating from high school, students should attend a community college or technical institute where nuclear power plant quality assurance and quality control are taught. Generally, such programs take two years to complete. During that time, more study hours are spent in laboratories or similar workplaces than in classrooms.

A typical list of first-year courses or their equivalent content includes the following: introduction to nuclear technology, radiation physics, mathematics, introduction to electricity and electronics, technical communications, radiation detection and measurements, inorganic chemistry, radiation protection, basic mechanics, introduction to quality assurance and quality control, blueprint reading, metallurgy and metals properties, metrology (scientific measurement), principles of process instrumentation, and elementary industrial economics.

The second year includes courses in technical writing, nuclear systems, mechanical component characteristics and specifications, nondestructive examination techniques, welding inspection, civil and structural inspection, mechanical inspection, electrical inspection, quality assurance practices and systems, and industrial organizations and institutions.

Currently, only a few schools offer associate degrees in nuclear quality assurance and quality control technology. More schools provide associate degrees in quality control technology. Students in such programs who wish to be nuclear power plant quality control technicians should supplement their training with courses in nuclear technology and radiation physics, either through the school or through a company-sponsored training program. A number of schools offer degree programs in nuclear technology. Students who enter these programs should supplement their training with courses in quality assurance and quality control.

Graduation from a technical program in nuclear power plant quality assurance and quality control will almost always be followed by company-sponsored training when graduates are hired and begin work. Even when a graduate's education includes courses in every aspect of nuclear power plant quality assurance and quality control, the company will need to provide training specific to the plant for which the graduate has been hired. Graduates of two-year technical schools are considered very good candidates for employment and usually enter a job immediately upon graduation if they so desire.

Physical requirements for this career include normal physical strength and the ability to move around the workplace. Good hand-eye coordination and normal sight and hearing are necessary for the testing, observation, and perceptions required on the job.

Special requirements

At present, there are no special requirements for this career. In the future it is possible that some of the special testing and measuring functions required of quality control technicians may call for proof of appropriate preparation or competence. Such a requirement would be in keeping with the recent trend toward more rigorous qualification standards for nuclear power plant technical workers.

Opportunities for experience and exploration

Among the many ways to learn about this career is to talk with high-school guidance counselors or college occupational counselors and to consult librarians for written materials. Additional information is often made available through the career classes offered in some high schools.

Nuclear reactors are in operation all across the country. Representatives from nuclear plants may be invited to speak to career classes, science classes, or science clubs. Although it is unlikely that students will be able to tour a nuclear power plant, they will probably find it easy to arrange a tour through a fossil-fuel power plant, where they can learn about procedures common to all power plants. They can also learn about quality control as it is practiced in such plants.

Methods of entering

As previously noted, graduates of two-year post–high-school programs are readily hired by utility companies that operate nuclear power generating units and by other firms involved in related activities. Recruiters from these companies visit the school, interview graduating students, and, if students qualify, make arrangements for them to begin work soon after they graduate.

In the past, much of the training needed by quality control technicians was often provided by employers. Now, since the advent of nuclear technology programs in two-year schools, employers are more likely to provide only the specialized in-plant training for graduates who have already learned much of the basic technology of the field.

Another way to enter the field is through the Navy. Nuclear technicians trained by the Navy are considered good candidates for employment in civilian nuclear power plants.

Persons who have experience in quality control may be hired by utilities and trained in the nuclear power aspects of the career. Some of the jobs for quality control technicians may be identified under the following job titles: civil and/or structural inspector, mechanical quality-control inspector, electrical quality-control inspector, nondestructive examination inspector, and welding quality-control inspector.

Advancement

As with almost all nuclear engineering technician careers, the opportunities for advancement in nuclear power plant quality control are excellent with increased experience, reliable job performance, and continued study. In a technology as new and sophisticated as nuclear power, training should never be considered complete. Technicians in this field find it necessary to participate in additional classroom training as well as in on-the-job study to keep abreast of new developments and to earn greater responsibility and a better position.

The most common pattern of advancement is found in the additional responsibility beginning technicians are given as they learn to perform more tasks in nuclear power plant quality assurance and quality control. As technicians master testing, measuring, and auditing, they become qualified to supervise other workers or new technicians.

Highly experienced nuclear power quality control technicians can find good opportunities in other industries or as consultants. These opportunities can be found in other utility companies, power plant construction companies, nuclear materials handling facilities, and manufacturers of components for nuclear facilities. Opportunities can also be found in nondestructive examination firms, chemical processing industries, architectural and engineering firms, and national laboratories.

Employment outlook

Attempting to examine even the immediate future of the U.S. nuclear industries is quite difficult. Questions about public health and safety have continued to receive a great deal of public attention since the accidents at Three Mile Island and Chernobyl. In addition, concern about environmental effects, unresolved issues and policies for waste disposal and reprocessing, actual and proposed state and federal moratoriums on new power plant construction and operations, rapidly increasing construction costs, changes in required power plant design and engineering, and a reduction in forecast growth in electricity requirements—all these contribute to the present uncertainties and reduce potential growth in the nuclear field. Because of these factors, it is unlikely that construction of any new nuclear power plants will begin before the year 2000; however, nuclear power plant quality control technicians will be needed to work in plants still under construction and those already in operation.

Even if the future course of the nuclear industry is toward moderate growth or even decline, the employment outlook for experienced technicians may still be good. New technicians will be needed to replace technicians who are retiring or leaving the field for other reasons. Some new jobs may also be provided by nuclear equipment manufacturing companies, research and development laboratories, and defense-related activities. In addition, more technicians may be needed to improve and enforce safety standards. Moreover, the skills and knowledge of nuclear power plant quality control technicians are easily transferred to industries outside the nuclear industry. Almost every major manufacturing industry employs quality control personnel to ensure product reliability.

Earnings

Salaries for technicians in this field vary based on location and to some degree educational background. The average salary for nuclear power plant technicians of all kinds is approximately $20,000 per year. Quality control technicians usually earn higher salaries than the average nuclear power plant technician because of their specialized background.

Graduates of nuclear power plant quality assurance and quality control programs earn beginning salaries of at least $18,000 per year. Nuclear power plant quality control technicians who advance beyond technician jobs may earn $28,000 to $35,000 or more per year.

In addition to a salary, technicians usually receive the benefits of insurance, paid holidays and vacations, and a retirement plan. Moreover, many employers pay for continued study and activities that are related to the profession.

Conditions of work

Working conditions for nuclear power plant quality control technicians will vary according to the employer. In a nuclear power plant, working conditions vary with the various stages of development, such as planning, building, and operating.

Technicians working at a nuclear power plant site must take the precautions required for all construction site personnel. Generally, safety shoes, helmets, safety glasses, and work clothes should be worn. Technicians on the site will probably be exposed to the hazards associated with construction work. These include falling objects, working on scaffolds, power tools, and welding. Arc welding exposes workers to light rays that are potentially hazardous to the eyes, and special lenses must be worn by everyone in the area.

When the plant is in operation, the technician usually works in an office, but performs inspections, testing, and audits in all parts of the plant. Depending on the task, the work en-

vironment could range from cold, cramped quarters to the comfortable surrounding of the plant's control room.

An important part of the technicians' work takes place in the testing and measuring laboratories of the plant. These usually are built early in the construction phase and are needed as long as the plant operates. Technicians must practice careful work habits common to all laboratory work in these laboratories. Special care must be taken in nondestructive examination laboratories, especially where X-ray machines are used.

One aspect of the work that is highly important is the precaution against radiation exposure. A relatively small proportion of employees in nuclear energy actually work in areas where radiation dangers exist. In such areas, shields, automatic alarm systems, radiation detection devices, and special clothing offer protection to workers. The Nuclear Regulatory Commission (NRC) regulates possession of radioactive materials and inspects nuclear facilities to ensure compliance with safety and health regulations.

Social and psychological factors

Nuclear power quality control technicians play a vital role in the control of one of the most complicated, technologically advanced industries. Any error can bring serious harm to people inside and outside the nuclear plant as well as involve millions of dollars of losses. The quality control technician must be constantly alert and systematic. Attention to minute detail, a good sense of personal discipline, and analytical working methods are very important. Above all, the technician must be willing to assume a great deal of responsibility on a regular basis.

As one who must sometimes monitor and verify the work of others, the technician must maintain a scientifically objective attitude. Technicians must have the courage to identify problems, even when there is pressure to do otherwise. They may also have to resist pressures that threaten to undermine an objective opinion or influence them to approve low-quality work. Honesty is important on any job, but the integrity of the quality control technician must be unquestionable.

GOE: 02.04.01, 05.01.04, 05.07.01; SIC: 491; SOC: 3719, 389, 782

⬦ **SOURCES OF ADDITIONAL INFORMATION**

American Society for Quality Control
310 West Wisconsin Avenue
Milwaukee, WI 53203

American Nuclear Society
555 North Kensington Avenue
La Grange Park, IL 60525

American Society for Nondestructive Testing
4153 Arlingate Plaza
Columbus, OH 43228

⬦ **RELATED ARTICLES**

Volume 1: Energy; Public Utilities
Volume 2: Construction inspectors, government; Engineers; Health and regulatory inspectors; Nuclear medicine technologists; Physicists
Volume 3: Power plant occupations
Volume 4: Nuclear instrumentation technicians; Nuclear materials handling technicians; Nuclear power plant radiation control technicians; Nuclear reactor operator technicians; Electrical technicians; Industrial radiological technicians; Industrial safety-and-health technicians; Quality-control technicians

Nuclear power plant radiation control technicians

Definition

Nuclear power plant radiation control technicians work under the supervision of nuclear scientists, engineers, or power plant managers to monitor radiation levels, protect workers, and decontaminate radioactive areas. These technicians are trained in the applications of nuclear and radiation physics to detect, measure, and identify different kinds of nuclear radiation. They are also familiar with federal regulations and permissible levels of radiation.

History

One of the characteristics of all forms of energy is its potential to endanger life and property if allowed to get out of control. This potential existed with the most primitive uses of fire, and it exists in the applications of nuclear power. Special care must be taken to prevent uncontrolled radiation in and around nuclear power plants. Skilled nuclear power plant technicians are among the workers who must monitor and control radiation levels.

Around 1900, scientists discovered that certain elements give off invisible rays of energy.

These elements are said to be radioactive, which means that they emit radiation. Antoine-Henri Becquerel and Marie and Pierre Curie discovered and described chemical radiation before the turn of the century. In 1910, Marie Curie isolated pure radium, the most radioactive natural element, and in 1911 she was awarded the Nobel Prize for Chemistry for her work relating to radiation.

Eventually it became understood that radiation has existed in nature since the beginning of time, not only from specific elements on earth, such as uranium, but also in the form of cosmic rays from outer space. All parts of the earth are constantly being bombarded by a certain background level of radioactivity, which is considered normal or tolerable because all forms of life have developed and flourished in an environment which has that level of radioactivity.

During the twentieth century, research into the nature of radiation has led to many kinds of controlled applications of radioactivity. These uses range from X rays to nuclear weapons. One of the most significant of these applications, in terms of widespread use in everyday life, is using nuclear fuel to produce energy. Nuclear power reactors produce heat that is used to generate electricity.

Nuclear power plant radiation control technicians
Emerging Technician Occupations

A nuclear power plant radiation control technician monitors the mechanical removal of hazardous waste from electrical transformers and capacitors.

The biological effects of radiation continue to be the subject of much research. Much has been learned about radiation exposure—from the short-term effects that include nausea, hemorrhage, and fatigue, to the long-range and more dangerous effects including cancer, lowered fertility, and possible birth defects. These factors have made it absolutely clear that if radiation energy is to be used for any purpose, the entire process must be controlled. Thus, appropriate methods of radiation protection and monitoring have been developed. These methods are highly effective when consistently and accurately used. Careful monitoring and protective control of radiation is the job of today's radiation control technician.

Nature of the work

The work of radiation control technicians is to protect workers, the general public, and the environment from overexposure to radiation. Many of their activities are highly technical in nature. Among others, they include measuring radiation and radioactivity levels in work areas and the environment and collecting samples of air, water, soil, plants, and other materials and analyzing them for radioactivity. They record test results and inform the appropriate personnel when tests reveal deviations. These technicians make certain that regulatory requirements are adequately met. They assist other power plant workers in setting up equipment that automatically monitors the processes within the plant and records deviations from established

limits. They also calibrate and maintain such instruments using hand tools.

Nuclear power plant radiation control technicians work efficiently with people of different technical backgrounds. They instruct operations personnel to make the adjustments necessary to correct excessive radiation levels, discharges of radionuclide materials above acceptable levels, or the chemical balance of the process. They also prepare reports for supervisory and regulatory agencies.

Nuclear power plant radiation control technicians are concerned with what is known as ionizing radiation. Ionization occurs when atoms are split and produce charged particles. When these particles strike the cells in the body, they cause damage by upsetting well-ordered chemical processes. They are especially concerned with three particular types of ionizing radiation, known by the Greek letters alpha, beta, and gamma.

These technicians understand not only the nature and effects of radiation, but also the principles of nuclear power plant systems. They are thoroughly familiar with the instrumentation used to monitor radiation in every part of the plant and its immediate surroundings. An important aspect of the job is educating other workers in radiation monitoring and control.

Nuclear power plant radiation control technicians work with three basic radiation concepts: time, distance from radiation source, and shielding. In terms of time, technicians know that certain radioactive materials break down into stable elements in a matter of days and even minutes. Certain other materials, however, continue to emit radioactive particles for thousands of years. Radiation becomes less intense in proportion to its distance from the source, so distance is another important concept in controlling radiation exposure. Shielding is used to protect persons from radiation exposure. Appropriate materials and specific thicknesses of materials need to be used to block emission of radioactive particles.

Because radiation generally cannot be seen, heard, or felt, radiation control technicians use special instruments to detect and measure radiation and to determine the dose of radiation that may have been received. Using devices that measure the ionizing effect of radiation on matter, technicians can determine the presence and, depending on the instrument used, the degree of radiation danger in a given situation. Among the devices used are Geiger counters and dosimeters, which measure the radiation dose received. Dosimeters are often in the form of photographic badges that are worn by personnel and visitors. They work because radioactivity shows on photographic film. Radiation control technicians calculate the amount of time that personnel may safely work in contaminated areas, considering maximum radiation exposure limits and the radiation level in the particular area. They also use specialized laboratory equipment designed to detect and analyze radiation levels and chemical imbalances.

Finally, although the radiation released into the environment surrounding a nuclear plant is generally far less than that released through background radiation sources, radiation protection technicians must be prepared to carry out monitoring techniques required during abnormal situations and emergencies.

The specific tasks of radiation protection technicians usually include the following: they monitor personnel, the plant, and the environment for radioactive contamination; they monitor radiation exposure, both internal and external, to plant workers; they train personnel in proper use of monitoring and safety equipment; they assist nuclear materials handling technicians in preparing and monitoring radioactive waste shipments; they conduct radiation surveys of the working environment; they perform basic radiation orientation training, radiation contamination surveys, air sample surveys, and radiation level surveys; they perform radiation and contamination control surveys; they maintain and calibrate radiation detection instruments using standard samples to determine accuracy; and they make sure that radiation protection regulations, standards, and procedures are followed, and that records are kept of all regular measurements and tests of radioactivity; and they carry out decontamination procedures that ensure the safety of plant workers and the continued operation of the plant.

Requirements

Radiation control technicians must possess a high standard of precision in their work. They must have an understanding of what radiation information means, both in biological terms and as it relates to nuclear plant systems.

Persons interested in careers as nuclear power plant radiation control technicians should have a solid background in basic high-school mathematics and science. They should be prepared to spend from one to two years in post–high-school technical training in chemistry, physics, laboratory procedures, and technical writing. Their language skills must be developed to the level that they can record data accurately and be able to write clear, concise technical reports.

High-school students who want to enter this career should begin their preparation while still in high school. They should take four years of high-school English, at least two years of mathematics including algebra, and at least one year of physical science, preferably physics with laboratory instruction. Computer programming and applications, vocational machine shop operations, and blueprint reading will provide a useful background for further studies.

After high school, the prospective technician should study at a two-year technical school or community college. Several public or private technical college programs are offered specifically to prepare nuclear power plant radiation control technicians. Other programs called nuclear technology or nuclear materials handling technology are offered that provide at least a basic preparation. The course of study that the prospective radiation control technician will undertake is an engineering technician–type program with intensive technical and scientific study in the classroom.

A typical first year of study for radiation control technicians includes introduction to nuclear technology, radiation physics, mathematics, introduction to electricity and electronics, introduction to technical communications, radiation detection and measurement, inorganic chemistry, radiation protection, blueprint reading, introduction to quality assurance/quality control, introduction to nuclear systems, computer applications, introduction to radiation biology, and industrial organizations and institutions.

A typical second year of study continues with technical writing, advanced radiation protection, applied nuclear chemistry, radiological emergencies, advanced chemistry, radiation shielding, radiation monitoring techniques, advanced radionuclide analysis, occupational safety and health, nuclear systems and safety, radioactive materials disposal and management, and industrial economics.

Students who graduate from nuclear technician programs are usually hired by nuclear power plants or other companies and institutions involved in nuclear-related activities. These employers provide a general orientation to their operations and further training specific to their procedures.

The work of the radiation control technician does not require great physical strength. It does, however, require adequate eye-hand coordination, good reflexes, and the ability to be observant.

Special requirements

At present there are no special requirements for licensing or certification of nuclear power plant radiation control technicians. Some graduates of radiation protection technology programs, however, may want to become nuclear materials handling technicians. In these cases, licensure may be required, but the employer usually will arrange for the special study needed to pass the licensing test.

Federal security clearances are required for those engaged in jobs that involve national security. Nuclear Regulatory Commission (NRC) clearance affects both government and private industry employees if security is required. Certain projects may necessitate military clearance with or without NRC clearance. Employers usually help arrange such clearances.

Opportunities for experience and exploration

For high-school students who are interested in this career, the high-school vocational guidance counselor is a valuable resource. If a community or technical college is in the area, their occupational information center and counseling staff can also be very helpful. Also high-school, college, and public librarians are often able to pinpoint avenues of research into a particular career field.

For those still in high school, the high-school science class may be the best place to gain familiarity with the nature of the career. Science teachers can sometimes arrange field trips and bring speakers to the school to describe various careers.

Radiation is used for medical diagnosis and treatment in hospitals all over the country. Radiology departments of local hospitals can be contacted for speakers for science or career classes. Nuclear reactor facilities are not likely to provide tours, but they may be able to furnish literature on radiation physics and radiation control. In addition, a utility company with a nuclear-fired plant may be able to offer a tour of the visitor's center at the plant, where much interesting and valuable information about nuclear power plant operation is made available. Some small reactors used for experiments, usually affiliated with universities and research centers, may give tours. Radiation control technicians employed at nuclear-related facilities may be invited to speak about their chosen field, as individuals rather than as company representatives.

Methods of entering

The best way to enter this career is to graduate from a radiation control technology program. Another excellent way to enter the career is to join the Navy and enter their technical training program for various nuclear specialists.

Graduates of radiation control technology programs are usually interviewed and recruited while in school by representatives of companies with nuclear facilities. At that time they are hired with arrangements made to begin work soon after graduation. Graduates from strong programs often have offers of several attractive jobs from which to choose.

Many graduates will find work with electric power utilities that operate nuclear plants. Other than utilities, a number of other types of firms and institutions seek technicians trained in radiation control. Some of them include nuclear materials handling and processing facilities, regulatory agencies, nondestructive testing firms, radiopharmaceutical industries, nuclear waste handling facilities, nuclear service firms, and national research laboratories.

Entry-level jobs for graduate radiation control technicians include the position of radiation monitor. This position involves working in personnel monitoring, decontamination, and area monitoring and reporting. Another entry-level job is instrument calibration technician. These technicians test instrument reliability, maintain standard sources, and adjust and calibrate instruments. Accelerator safety technicians assess accelerator operating procedures and shielding to ensure personnel safety. Radiobiology technicians test external and internal radiation effects in plants and animals, collect data on facilities where potential human exposure to radiation exists, and recommend improvement in techniques or facilities.

Hot-cell operators conduct experimental design and performance tests involving materials of very high radioactivity. Environmental survey technicians gather and prepare radioactive samples from air, water, and food specimens. They may also handle nonradioactive test specimens for test comparisons with National Environmental Policy Act standards. Reactor safety technicians study personnel safety through the analysis of reactor procedures and shielding and through analysis of radioactivity tests.

Advancement

Technicians concerned with radiation control can advance in whatever part of the nuclear power industry they may start their careers. Examples of advanced positions are described in this section.

Research technicians develop new ideas and techniques in the radiation and nuclear field. Instrument design technicians design and prepare specifications and tests for advanced radiation instrumentation. Customer service specialists work in sales, installation, modification, and maintenance of customers' equipment related to radiation control. Radiochemistry technicians prepare and analyze new and old compounds, utilizing the latest equipment and techniques. Health physics technicians train new radiation monitors, analyze existing procedures, and conduct tests of experimental design and radiation safety. Soils evaluation technicians assess soil density, radioactivity, and moisture content to determine sources of unusually high levels of radioactivity. Radioactive waste analysts develop waste disposal techniques, inventory stored waste, and prepare waste for disposal.

Some of the most attractive opportunities for advancement may be to work as specialized experts in a company or laboratory, or as consultants. Consultants may be employed by nuclear engineering or nuclear industry consulting firms, or they may become independent consultants who manage their own consulting businesses.

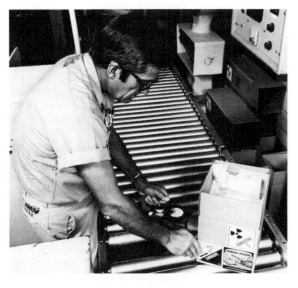

To ensure that radioactive materials meet all safety standards, a radiation control technician inspects a package before it is shipped.

Employment outlook

In 1989, there were more than 100 nuclear power plants operating in the United States, and construction permits had been issued for about a dozen more; however, no orders have been placed for new nuclear power plants since 1987, so the total number of plants in operation in the United States is not likely to increase by much in the foreseeable future.

Nonetheless, if the future course of the nuclear power industry is toward only moderate growth or even decline, the employment outlook for nuclear power plant radiation control technicians may still be good. New technicians will be needed to replace retiring technicians or technicians who are leaving for other reasons. Some new jobs for technicians may also be provided by efforts to enforce and improve safety standards. In addition, employers in related fields, such as manufacturing companies and research and development laboratories, may increase the number of radiation control technicians that they need. For all of these reasons, well-trained nuclear power plant radiation con-

trol technicians should have no trouble finding good jobs.

Earnings

The earnings of nuclear power plant radiation control technicians who are beginning their careers depend on whether they are employed in a fuel assembly plant, a nuclear power plant, a research laboratory, or some other part of the industry. They may begin as salaried staff or may be paid hourly wages. If they are paid hourly wages, technicians usually work in shifts and receive premium pay for overtime.

Graduate technicians earn annual salaries of $17,000 to $23,000 per year, averaging close to $20,000 per year. After three to five years of experience, technicians can expect to earn from $28,000 to $32,000 per year. Their earnings also depend on whether they remain in their beginning jobs as technicians or become supervisors. Consulting work brings potential incomes around $40,000 per year.

In addition to their yearly salary or wages, these technicians usually receive the benefits of paid holidays and vacations, insurance plans, and retirement plans. Because of the rapid changes that occur in the nuclear power industry, many employers pay for job-related study and participation in workshops, seminars, and conferences.

Conditions of work

Depending on the employer and the position, work conditions for radiation control technicians vary from offices and control rooms to relatively cramped and cold areas of power plants.

Radiation control technicians wear film badges or carry pocket monitors to determine their personal exposure to radiation. Of all power plant employees, the radiation control technicians are perhaps best able to evaluate and protect against the radiation hazards that are part of the occupational risk involved in this field. It is the quality and accuracy of their work on which the safety of the plant workers and themselves depends.

Like all other nuclear power plant employees, technicians must give special attention to wearing safety clothing at work. Radiation-resistant clothing may be required in some areas. This type of clothing contains materials that reduce the level of radiation before it reaches the human body.

In some of the work done by radiation protection technicians, radiation shielding materials, such as lead and concrete, are used to enclose radioactive materials while the technician manipulates these materials from outside the contaminated area. These are called hot-cell operations. In some areas, automatic alarm systems are used to warn of radiation hazards, so that proper protection can be maintained.

Social and psychological factors

The career of a nuclear power plant radiation control technician is very demanding. These technicians must have confidence in their knowledge and skill to measure and manage potentially dangerous radioactivity as their everyday duty.

Radiation control technicians play an important teaching role in the nuclear-fueled power plant. They must know the control measures required for every employee, and must be capable of explaining to other employees just how critical such measures are. A pleasantly firm manner is needed for this kind of work. Because abnormal conditions can and sometimes do develop in the nuclear power industry, radiation control technicians must be able to withstand the stress associated with such situations. They must be able to work long hours during such times without making mistakes

and participate as a cooperating member of a team of experts.

Technicians who find satisfaction in the field of radiation protection are generally individuals who can confidently accept responsibility, who communicate effectively in person and on paper, and who enjoy doing precise work. They are vital workers involved in successfully managing one of the most complex and advanced applications of modern technology.

GOE: 11.10.03; SIC: 491; SOC: 3832

◇ SOURCES OF ADDITIONAL INFORMATION

American Nuclear Society
555 North Kensington Avenue
La Grange Park, IL 60525

American Society for Nondestructive Testing
4153 Arlingate Plaza
Caller #28518
Columbus, OH 43228

Health Physics Society
8000 Westpark Drive, Suite 400
McLean, VA 22102

National Council on Radiation Protection and Measurements
7910 Woodmont Avenue, Suite 1016
Bethesda, MD 20814

◇ RELATED ARTICLES

Volume 1: Energy; Engineering; Nuclear Sciences; Public Utilities
Volume 2: Health and regulatory inspectors; Nuclear medicine technologists; Physicists
Volume 3: Occupational safety and health workers; Power plant occupations
Volume 4: Industrial radiological technicians; Industrial safety-and-health technicians; Nuclear instrumentation technicians; Nuclear materials handling technicians; Nuclear power plant quality control technicians; Nuclear reactor operator technicians

Nuclear reactor operator technicians

Definition

Nuclear reactor operator technicians are trainees who participate in formal instructional programs in nuclear science theory, its application to nuclear reactors, and nuclear power plant operations, in preparation for their becoming licensed power plant operators.

In these programs, technicians must learn about nuclear radiology, radiation detection, and reactor design, operation, and control. They must also learn about nuclear power plant materials, processes, material balances, plant operating equipment, pipe systems, electrical systems, and process control.

In addition, technicians must study and be able to perform reactor operation and control activities in strict compliance with federally required operating and safety procedures.

For at least a part of their training, nuclear reactor operator technicians work under the supervision of a licensed nuclear reactor operator; later they work as beginning operators. They will always work under the supervision of a senior operator or a more experienced operator.

History

The potential for nuclear power generation was first demonstrated in 1942, when a group of scientists led by Enrico Fermi conducted the first controlled nuclear chain reaction in a nuclear reactor located under the football stands on Stagg Field at the University of Chicago. After World War II, research was continued on peacetime uses of controlled atomic energy. In 1948, efforts were speeded up on the design of nuclear power reactors for electric generation.

By late 1963, the technology of at least two reactor systems was considered to be developed enough to allow commercial use of nuclear reactors to generate electric power. This led to the construction of the first nuclear power plants. Their successful operation and the low cost of the electric power they generated were considered very promising, and further development of nuclear power plants continued. The construction of several additional nuclear power plants was also begun.

Since then, much has been learned about the design and safe operation of nuclear-fueled electric power plants. Quality assurance and quality control procedures have been devel-

oped to ensure that every step of a plant's construction and operation is according to specifications and without mistakes. These methods have been used in the construction, operation, and maintenance of nuclear power plants.

Special procedures to protect against radiation have been developed, and special technicians have been trained and hired in each plant to make certain that there is the least possible risk of radiation exposure to workers. Studies have shown that the safest operation of nuclear plants is achieved when nuclear reactor operators are carefully selected and thoroughly trained. Since 1963, thousands of people have been trained in nuclear science theory and nuclear plant operation and have then been licensed by the federal government to be nuclear reactor operators.

Today, nuclear plant operators are highly trained specialists who bear a heavy responsibility for the safe and efficient operation of commercial reactors. The training they experience to become fully licensed nuclear reactor operators usually takes four years or more. During the training period the prospective operator is considered a nuclear reactor operator technician or trainee.

Nature of the work

The primary objective of the nuclear reactor technician is to become a licensed nuclear reactor operator. Technicians are trained to learn and perform all the duties expected of licensed operators. Almost all the skill and knowledge, however, must be learned at locations outside of the reactor control room. What the technician needs to learn can best be summarized by describing what the beginning licensed operator does.

Nuclear reactor operators are responsible for the continuous and correct operation of a reactor. From the standpoint of safety and uninterrupted operation, their job is the most critical in the plant. This is the reason for operators' licensing requirements. Training, experience, and performance under stress all are parts of the selection process under which operators are licensed by the Nuclear Regulatory Commission (NRC) and employed by an electric utility.

The importance of the operators' performance is shown by the fact that any shutdown,

Two nuclear reactor operator technicians make a final check on a new pulsed reactor. The fast-burst reactor is lowered into a shielded pit below the floor when not in use.

due to an accident or an operating error, of an average 1,000-megawatt plant can result in a loss of at least the cost of the operator's salary for ten years. This is why operators must combine good judgment with exceptional skill. The job requires a combination of learned abilities and skills that must be based on a thorough technical education and wide-ranging experience. Technicians must have expert knowledge of all the equipment and processes that occur in a nuclear power plant, both inside and outside of the reactor.

The licensed nuclear reactor operator is responsible for reading and interpreting the recording instruments and operation indicators and for starting, adjusting, and managing the controls, mechanisms, and equipment in the main control room of the reactor. This responsibility includes complete control of every function of the reactor.

Auxiliary equipment operators normally perform tasks outside the control room that promote safe and efficient operation of the entire plant. These tasks include operating auxiliary equipment, monitoring plant instruments related to machines outside the reactor and its control center, operating radiation waste systems, and housekeeping duties.

While plant operators run the machines outside of the reactor under the direction of the plant manager, reactor operators control and operate the reactor, also under the direction of the plant manager. The reactor is like an engine that provides the power—hot steam—that runs the entire plant. Reactor operators must always keep in mind that the delicate balance of the machines and systems that operate outside of the reactor must be maintained to keep the nuclear chain reaction under control.

Nuclear reactor operator technicians must be educated in nuclear science theory and power plant fundamentals as well as trained in the specific plant and specialized equipment to be operated. To understand the nature of the operator's job, one needs to have a general idea about how nuclear reactors work.

In nonnuclear electrical power plants, a fuel of some kind is used to convert water into steam in a steam boiler. The steam from the boiler flows under high pressure through pipes and into a turbine, causing it to rotate. The turbine drives an electric generator that produces the electricity.

In nuclear plants, the fuel is uranium which undergoes a fission, or atom-splitting, reaction that produces tremendous quantities of heat. Water circulated through the reactor carries the heat away in the form of steam under very high pressure through pipes to drive the turbines that produce electricity in the same way as in a conventional nonnuclear power plant.

A nuclear reactor is a structure loaded with pellets of nuclear fuel, usually uranium with about two percent of the radioactive isotope uranium-235. The pellets are lined up in thin metal tubes called fuel rods. The more fuel rods contained in a given space, the more fission reactions that take place in the reactor. When fission reactions occur, neutrons (tiny particles of radiation energy traveling at great speed) are released and cause other fission reactions to occur in what is called a chain reaction.

The reactor also includes channels through which cooling water circulates and other empty spaces where control rods can be inserted. A control rod contains material that absorbs the released neutrons and, thus, prevents some fission reactions from occurring. When control rods are inserted into the reactor they reduce the number of atoms being split, causing the reactor to cool down and generate less heat. When the control rods are withdrawn, the reaction rate speeds up and the reactor gets hot and generates more heat. Thus the power in a nuclear-fueled electrical power plant is controlled by moving the control rods in and out of the reactor.

The area of the reactor in which the fission takes place is called the core, and it is contained within the reactor vessel, which is lined by a thick inner shell of steel to keep the heat in the system and under control. This internal shield is surrounded in turn by several feet of concrete insulation that serves as a nuclear radiation shield to protect personnel and the surrounding area from radiation.

Nuclear reactor personnel must understand the control systems for all the various systems that have been already described, such as the flow of the cooling water and the position of the control rods. They must be able to monitor, record, and interpret data given by the different kinds of instruments. Nuclear reactor operator technicians must know how every aspect of activity within the reactor is affected by events outside the reactor and how to respond in an emergency. Each of the various individual instruments in the control room and all of the instruments together tell what is happening within the reactor.

The most careful operation is required in nuclear power plants to be sure that radiation does not contaminate the equipment, operating personnel, or the land and people in the vicinity of the plant. The most serious danger is the release of large amounts of atomic radiation into the atmosphere. Operating personnel are directly involved in the prevention of reactor accidents and in the containment of radioactivity in the event of an accident. For this reason, the technicians who are training to be nuclear reactor operators are carefully screened and very highly trained.

The prospective nuclear plant operator always begins employment as a trainee, gaining plant experience and technical knowledge at a functioning nuclear power plant, studying its reactor and control room, and at a special training station called a simulator. A simulator is built and equipped like an operating reactor control station. Trainees can practice operating the reactor and learn what readings the instruments in the simulator give when certain adjustments are made in the reactor control settings. This company-sponsored training is provided to help trainees attain the expertise necessary to obtain an operator's license. Even after obtaining a license, however, beginning operators work under the direction of a shift supervisor, senior operator, or other management personnel.

Requirements

The description of the work that is done by nuclear reactor operators makes it clear that technicians must be able to complete successfully a long and very demanding training program. Such a program usually requires at least four years of concentrated study and preparation.

There are two major parts to the required training. One is mastering the theoretical science and mathematics base. This base of knowledge is made up of nuclear physics, chemistry, and engineering. It must be thoroughly learned. Trainees most often learn theory in a formal nuclear technician program at a college or in a training program organized by a utility company. Learning theory usually requires two full academic years.

The second major part of training is to learn in detail all about how the power plant works. This must be learned through on-the-job experience in the nuclear power plant.

As has been stressed, the nuclear reactor operator's job requires an understanding of the plant and equipment. It is not the kind of job for which a person can simply learn which levers to pull or which buttons to push. At least a normal degree of intelligence and a high amount of motivation are required. Writing, record keeping, and basic mathematics are regularly required skills used by the technician. Physical strength is not a requirement, but keen alertness and the ability to move easily in all parts of the plant are necessary. Because of the great responsibility involved in operating a nuclear reactor, prospective technicians must be capable of remaining calm under pressure and maintaining sound judgment in emergencies.

On-the-job training must be done in the power plant itself. It consists of trainees being assigned to a series of work-learn tasks that take the trainees to all parts of the plant.

If trainees have been working in the plant as regular employees, their individual training is planned around what they already know. This kind of training usually takes two to three years and includes simulator practice.

The training of a nuclear reactor operator technician requires a substantial investment by the utility employer. Graduates of two-year programs in nuclear technology usually make the best trainees because they are already well grounded in nuclear and power plant fundamentals. The ideal approach for most persons who want to enter this occupation is to graduate from a two-year nuclear technology program in a public or private technical college, community college, or technical institute.

The best preparation for the nuclear technology program begins in high school. High-school students who wish to enter nuclear technology programs should study algebra, geometry, English composition, blueprint reading, and chemistry and physics with laboratory study. In addition to these courses, classes in computer science and beginning electronics can give students valuable preparation for the technology program that will follow high school.

A typical first-year program in a nuclear technology program may include introduction to nuclear technology, radiation physics, applied mathematics, introduction to electricity and electronics, introduction to technical communications, basic industrial economics, radiation detection and measurement, introductory inorganic chemistry, radiation protection, advanced mathematics, basic mechanics, introduction to quality assurance and quality control, principles of process instrumentation, heat transfer and fluid flow, metallurgy, and metal properties.

The second year of the technical program typically includes technical writing and reporting, introduction to nuclear systems, blueprint reading, mechanical component characteristics and specifications, reactor physics, reactor safety, power plant systems, instrumentation and control of reactors and plant systems, power plant chemistry, reactor operations, reactor auxiliary systems, and industrial organizations and institutions.

In nuclear technology programs, such as the one outlined above, there are usually more hours of laboratory or similar work-situation study than classroom hours. In some programs, students gain insight into reactor operations through visits to a functioning reactor, although such visits can sometimes be difficult to arrange.

Some reactor operator trainees are former reactor operators from the U.S. Navy. The Navy is an excellent career path for highly motivated high-school graduates desiring to enter this field without the usual expense of attending two years of technical college.

Special requirements

Nuclear reactor operators are required to be licensed, based on examinations given by the NRC. Training, experience, and performance under stress all figure into the ultimate selection process by which an operator is licensed.

Operator and senior operator examinations are divided into three parts: a written test, usually lasting one day; an oral test, usually lasting half a day; and an actual demonstration. The senior operator written test includes the written test for the operator and an additional second test. The senior oral and operating tests require the senior operator to demonstrate a higher degree of competence and knowledge than that required of an operator.

All applicants must show that they have been properly trained by the power facility, usually with a certification that lists subjects, number of subject hours, and extent of experience. Certification also states that applicants have demonstrated, to the satisfaction of the plant managing staff, the ability to operate the controls in a competent and safe manner.

Licenses are issued for a period of two years and may be renewed, subject to proof of continued competence and good health.

Utilities usually provide operating training programs for trainees with various backgrounds ranging from the untrained person with no power plant experience to engineering graduates. Naturally, trainees having the most extensive background in nuclear fundamentals and technology require a shorter period of training than do those with limited experience and education. Sometimes persons with broad and excellent experience in the plant and thorough theoretical knowledge need training only in specific power plant operations.

Utility training includes both classroom hours and work on a simulator or functioning reactor. Trainees are paid during the training period, but in some companies they may be dismissed for a failure to pass any single training examination.

Reactor operator training and licensing is always related to a specific facility. A license to operate a nuclear reactor applies to only one specific unit. If licensed operators should have reason to want to operate another unit, they would need to be examined and licensed for that specific unit.

Opportunities for experience and exploration

High-school guidance counselors and community or technical colleges are good sources of information about a career as a nuclear reactor operator. The librarians in these institutions also may be helpful in directing students to introductory literature on nuclear reactors.

Opportunities for exploring a career as a nuclear reactor operator are limited because nuclear power plants are usually located in places relatively far away from schools and have strictly limited visiting policies. Thus very few commercial or research reactors may be toured by the public. Many utility companies with nuclear power plants, however, do have visitors centers where tours are welcome. In addition, interested high-school students usually can arrange visits to nonnuclear power plants and thus can learn about the energy-conversion process common to all steam-powered electric power generation plants.

Methods of entering

In recent years, nuclear technician programs have been the best source of reactor operator technician trainees. They are usually interviewed by the nuclear power plant personnel recruiters near the end of their technical college program and are hired to start working in the power plant as trainees after they graduate.

Advancement

Normally, licensed reactor operators progress with experience and further study to the supervisory position of senior operator. This is a position of considerably more responsibility than that of operator. To meet the minimum educational and experience requirements for a senior operator's license, candidates must not only understand what is happening in the operation of a reactor but also why it happens.

A senior operator directs the activities of other licensed operators. Senior operators must be able to demonstrate a wider and more thorough knowledge of company policy and reactor controls and must know the applications of more federal regulations. They must have a greater breadth of knowledge about the entire reactor facility and power plant than is required for other operators whose license allows them only to operate a particular reactor unit. Promotion to senior operator is based on continued study, on-the-job training, reliable job performance, and the need for senior operators within the company.

Licensed nuclear reactor operators and senior operators may also move to other assignments in the industry. They may become part of a power plant's education staff or be employed in a technical college, four-year college or university, company employee training department, or an outside consulting company.

Both operators and senior operators may work for reactor manufacturers and serve as research and development consultants. They may also teach trainees to use simulators or operating models of the manufacturer's reactors. Fi-

nally, operators and senior operators may work for the NRC, which among other tasks, administers license examinations.

Employment outlook

Attempting to examine even the near-term future of the U.S. nuclear industry is quite difficult. Some estimates foresee moderate growth, and some foresee declines.

Questions about public health and safety have continued to receive a great deal of public attention since the accidents at Three Mile Island and Chernobyl. In addition, concern about environmental effects, unresolved issues and policies for waste disposal and reprocessing, actual and proposed state and federal moratoriums on new power plant construction and operations, rapidly increasing construction costs, changes in required power plant design and engineering, and a reduction in forecast growth in electricity requirements—all these contribute to the present uncertainties and reduce potential growth in the nuclear field.

Earnings

The beginning salary rate for nuclear reactor operator technicians varies with the amount of nuclear science theory and work experience the technician brings to the employer. Graduates of strong nuclear technician programs or ex-Navy nuclear technicians usually earn more than those with no such training. Salaries also vary among different electric power companies.

Reactor operator technicians whose technical training is not in nuclear technology begin their training programs at salaries ranging from $15,000 to $17,000 per year. Graduates of nuclear technology programs start at about $19,000 per year. Licensed reactor operators and senior reactor operators earn at least $30,000 to $35,000 per year, depending on their license, the particular employer, their years of service, and the amount of overtime they work.

In addition to yearly salary, benefits are usually given to salaried workers and include insurance, paid holidays, vacations, and retirement benefits.

Employers also pay for the continued formal and on-the-job study for nuclear reactor technicians and operators. Ten to 20 percent of the licensed reactor operator staff members are in formal retraining programs at any one time to renew their operator's licenses or to obtain a senior operator's license. This is all at company expense with the operators on full pay with the usual benefits.

Conditions of work

Nuclear reactor operator technicians spend their working hours in classrooms and laboratories, learning about every part of the power plant. Toward the end of their training, they work at a reactor control-room simulator or in the control room of an operational reactor unit under the direction of licensed operators.

Operators work in clean, well-lighted, but windowless control rooms. While most operators do not wear suits to work, clothing is likely to be appropriate to an office setting. Technicians, however, will spend part of their training outside the reactor area. Here, appropriate work clothing should be worn, including hard hats and safety shoes, if necessary.

Operators are shielded from radiation by the concrete outside wall of the reactor containment vessel. If leaks should occur, operators are less subject to exposure than plant personnel who are more directly involved in maintenance and inspection. In spite of this fact, monitoring by means of wearing film badges that darken upon radiation exposure is routine for all reactor personnel. In addition, radiation measurement is carried out in all areas of the plant and plant surroundings according to a regular schedule.

Nuclear operator technicians or operators usually work an eight-hour shift. Usually they rotate through each of three shifts, taking turns as required. Because nuclear reactors normally operate continuously, operators must be controlling it at all times. This means operators will work weekends as well as at night some of the time.

Social and psychological factors

A career as a nuclear reactor operator offers the opportunity to assume a high degree of responsibility and to receive a part of one's training while on a paying job. People who enjoy using precision instruments and learning about the latest technological developments are likely to find this career appealing.

The field of nuclear technology is complex and challenging. Those who enter it begin a career of lifelong learning. The operator's position is a demanding one, requiring precision,

an above-average attention span, and a commitment to excellence.

Operators must be able to shoulder a high degree of responsibility and to work well under conditions of stress. They must be emotionally stable and calm at all times, even in emergencies. The ability to make decisions and use sound judgment is needed daily. Prospective technicians should avoid thinking that the reactor is simply put into operation and then runs itself. Observing, interpreting data, and making decisions are essential skills needed to perform the operator's job.

Operators work with a team of technical experts. They must be able to communicate clearly and precisely both verbally and on paper. At various stages in their careers, operators are supervised and will supervise others.

GOE: 05.06.01; SIC: 491; SOC: 6932

 SOURCES OF ADDITIONAL INFORMATION

Professional Reactor Operator Society
PO Box 181
Mishicot, WI 54228

American Nuclear Society
555 North Kensington Avenue
La Grange Park, IL 60525

U.S. Council for Energy Awareness
1776 I Street, NW, Suite 400
Washington, DC 20006

◇ **RELATED ARTICLES**

Volume 1: Energy; Engineering; Nuclear Sciences; Public Utilities
Volume 2: Engineers; Nuclear medicine technologists; Physicists
Volume 3: Occupational safety-and-health workers
Volume 4: Electrical technicians; Industrial radiological technicians; Nuclear instrumentation technicians; Nuclear materials handling technicians; Nuclear power plant quality control technicians; Nuclear power plant radiation control technicians

Plastics technicians

Definition

Plastics technicians are skilled professionals who assist design engineers, scientists, research groups, and manufacturers in the development, manufacture, application, and marketing of plastics products. Plastics technicians perform diverse tasks in a variety of areas within the industry. Most commonly they are involved with research and development or with manufacturing. In these settings, they function at a level between the engineer or scientist in charge of a job and the production or laboratory workers who carry out most of the tasks. Other plastics technicians are involved with mold and tool making, materials and machinery, sales and services, and related technical fields.

History

The plastics industry dates back to 1869, when a printer named John Hyatt patented a mixture of cellulose nitrate and camphor. He called this mixture Celluloid, and it was used to make piano keys, billiard balls, and later, the first movie film.

In 1909, Leo Hendrik Baekeland developed phenolic plastic. This product replaced natural rubber in electrical insulation, and was used for pot handles, chemical ware, and automobile distributor caps and rotors, as it still is used today. Other plastics materials were developed steadily. The greatest variety of materials and applications, however, came during World War II, when the war effort accelerated major changes in transportation, clothing, military equipment, and consumer goods.

Today, plastics manufacturing is a major industry whose products play a vital role in many other industries and activities around the world. The electronics industry uses plastics to make computers, radar equipment, video games, televisions, and telephones. In the aerospace industry, plastics are used to make rocket nozzles, reentry heat shields, coatings, and astronauts' clothing. Modern aircraft continue to use plastics in interiors and structural parts.

The medical field relies on mass-produced plastic items that are sanitary and disposable, including syringes, plasma bags, medical tubing, and food packaging. Plastics are also used in surgical implants and prosthetic devices.

The plastics industry provides the makings for a large variety of consumer goods. Appliances, toys, dinnerware, luggage, and furniture are just a few products that require plastics.

In housing and building, plastics are used in insulation, plumbing, flooring, furniture, and countertops. Paint and adhesives are made from plastic compounds. Synthetic fibers such as nylon and polyester dominate the clothing, carpeting, and upholstery business. Fibers of glass, carbon, graphite, and boron combined with plastic resins are vital in the structure of pleasure boats, naval ships, aircraft, space vehicles, satellites, automobiles, trucks, motorcycles, large and small home appliances and building components.

Modern packaging of every kind uses billions of pounds of plastics annually.

The position of plastics technician is relatively new in the industrial work force. It was created by technological developments in the plastics industry that required people with some technical background, but not an engineering degree.

Nature of the work

Plastics technicians are employed in a wide variety of tasks that can be grouped into five general categories. These categories are research and development, mold and tool making, manufacturing, sales and service, and related technical fields. In research and development, technicians work in laboratories to create new materials or to improve existing ones. Laboratory procedures include monitoring chemical reactions, testing, evaluating test results, record keeping, and submitting reports. A wide variety of chemical apparatus is used. Testing equipment is used to conduct standardized routine tests that determine properties of materials. Technicians set up, calibrate, and operate devices to obtain test data for interpretation and comparison.

As new product designs are conceived, research and development technicians work on prototypes, assist in the design and manufacture of specialized tools and machinery, and monitor the manufacturing process. To be good at these tasks, plastics technicians must have a mechanical aptitude, thorough knowledge of a variety of materials, and the ability to solve problems.

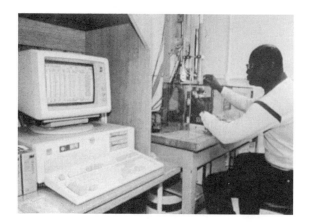

This plastics technician tests the strength and pliability of a newly designed plastic.

Mold and tool making is a specialized aspect of plastics manufacturing. Plastics technicians with drafting skills are employed as mold and tool designers or as detailers of drawings. They may also become involved in product design.

Technicians in plastics manufacturing work in molding, laminating, or fabricating. Molding involves installing molds in production machines, establishing correct molding cycles, monitoring the molding process, maintaining production schedules, testing incoming raw materials, inspecting goods in production, and ensuring that the final product meets specifications.

Technicians who work in laminating are trained in the skill of superimposing materials in a predetermined pattern. This process is used in making aircraft, aerospace and mass-transit vehicles, boats, satellites, surfboards, recreational vehicles, and furniture. Laminating entails bench work for small parts and team work for large parts. A reinforced plastic item the size of a shoe box can be built by one person, while a large motorized vehicle for a Disneyland ride requires the work of several technicians.

Technicians employed as fabricators work with plastic sheets, rods, and tubes, using equipment similar to that used in woodworking. Aircraft windshields and canopies, solariums, counter displays, computer housings, signs, and furniture are some of the products made by fabricators. Basic machine shop methods combined with heat-forming, polishing, and bonding are skills used by technicians in this area.

Sales and service work encompasses a wide variety of jobs for plastics technicians. These technicians are needed in the sales departments of materials suppliers, machinery manufacturers, molding companies, laminators, and fabricators.

Sales representatives for materials suppliers assist customers in selecting the correct grade of plastic. They provide a liaison between the customer and the company, assist in product and mold design, and solve problems that may arise in manufacturing.

Sales representatives for machinery manufacturers help customers select the proper equipment for their needs. Sales technicians are able to apply scientific training to arrive at the best selection. They are familiar with hydraulic systems and electrical circuitry in the machines they sell and are knowledgeable about the customer's manufacturing processes.

Molding companies employ technicians to contact customers who may require plastic products. Technicians help customers choose the correct plastic for the application, discuss the best product design, determine the optimum mold size for cost-effectiveness, and provide follow-up services.

Technicians employed in sales capacities by laminators call on the Air Force, Navy, Army, Coast Guard, aircraft companies, and commercial businesses. Their specialized knowledge and training must constantly be updated to keep up with the rapid technological advances in this field.

Plastics technicians are also important and valued employees in certain related fields. For example, companies that make computers, appliances, electronic devices, aircraft, and other products that incorporate plastic components rely heavily on plastics technicians to specify, design, purchase, and integrate plastics in the manufacture of the company's major product line.

Requirements

In the plastics industry, specific processes require specific knowledge. For example, injection molding skills are completely different from those required for laminating. The technician who specializes in compression molding has skills not common to other processes. Certain bodies of knowledge, however, are common to all areas of the plastics industry. The person who decides to be a technician should choose high-school subjects that are designated as college preparatory. These subjects will provide a solid foundation on which to base the specialized knowledge required of a plastics technician.

A basic understanding of mathematics, including one year each of algebra, geometry, and trigonometry, or their equivalent, is required. Mechanical drawing will also prove useful. Laboratory sciences, preferably organic chemistry and physics, are recommended. If available, courses in plastics fabrication enable future technicians to obtain skills in machine operation.

While still in high school, students should investigate the programs offered by community colleges, technical institutes, and vocational-technical schools and plan their high-school program accordingly. Some schools include plastics courses as part of mechanical or chemical technicians programs. Programs in plastics that lead to an associate degree have been designed with the advice and assistance of people in the industry.

A student who plans to enter a community college or technical school should have at least average abilities. Entrance examinations may be required at some schools to determine academic eligibility, manual dexterity, and reasoning ability.

A typical two-year curriculum for plastics technicians at a community college includes class, laboratory, and sometimes work experience. In the first year, courses typically include introduction to plastics, applied mathematics, compression molding procedures, fabrication of plastics, properties of thermoplastics, injection molding, and extrusion molding.

Second year courses typically include reinforced plastics procedures, applied chemistry of plastic materials, dies and molds, thermoforming, synthetic elastomers, foamed plastics procedures, test procedures, and basic employment information.

The hearing-impaired and those with physical handicaps can perform well in areas of research and development, testing, quality control, mold and product design, inspection, and in some production and assembly departments, as well as in sales.

No more than normal physical strength is required for most of the work in this career. Good hand-eye coordination and manual dexterity are needed to do some tasks, especially in building up laminated structures. Color blindness could be a limitation for those whose work requires color matching or keen color perception.

Special requirements

There are no special requirements for licenses or certificates for this technical career.

Opportunities for experience and exploration

For interested students, high-school counselors can arrange class visits to community colleges, vocational-technical schools, and universities that offer technical programs. Tours of laboratories, shops, and classrooms can provide first-hand information on the nature of the courses. Open house or career day exhibits are an open invitation to visit a prospective school where students and instructors can explain the program and demonstrate equipment.

Business people, guidance counselors, and successful graduates from technical programs can be invited to address interested high-school groups.

Field trips to local manufacturers or plastics users can be arranged by teachers of wood shop, machine shop, chemistry and physics, or mechanical drafting. Students can observe workers on the job and decide whether the work activities seem interesting.

Films about plastics can be obtained free of charge directly from the materials or machinery manufacturers, from lending libraries, and from professional organizations within the industry.

Where group visits are not possible, an enterprising student can contact a personnel manager of a plant and arrange a personal visit to explore opportunities and to obtain advice.

Methods of entering

Students can be employed in the plastics industry while earning a degree. Many companies operate on a three-shift basis; hours can be arranged so as not to conflict with school.

As part of the learning experience, it is possible to participate in cooperative education or work-study programs. This is a joint venture between the school and the industry where students can work a limited number of hours per month and often receive college credit.

Personnel managers maintain contact with schools that have ongoing plastics programs. Recruiting agents visit graduating technicians to acquaint them with current opportunities.

Experts in various fields are regularly invited to lecture at technical schools and colleges. The advice and information presented can provide good ideas about finding entry-level employment.

Student chapters of the Society of Plastics Engineers maintain close ties with the parent organization. Student members receive newsletters and technical journals, and they attend professional seminars. These contacts are invaluable when seeking employment.

Field trips are an important part of the technician's education. Plants and laboratories give visiting students a broad overview of the many manufacturing processes. During these tours, students can observe working conditions and discuss employment possibilities.

Students who plan to enter the military should investigate branches of service that offer training in plastics. The Air Force, Navy, Coast Guard, and Army publish procurement specifications, operate repair facilities, and carry on their own research and development. The valuable training available in the military, plus the educational benefits earned upon discharge, should not be overlooked.

Advancement

There are excellent opportunities for advancement for well-prepared technicians in the plastics industry. Some manufacturers conduct in-plant training programs to upgrade employees. Many companies provide incentives for technicians to continue their education at accredited schools. An employee with sales or customer service potential is trained in various manufacturing aspects before joining the sales or service division.

Advancement within a company is earned by demonstrating increased technical skill or supervisory ability, together with a willingness to accept added responsibility. In molding plants, technicians advance to positions as supervisors, department heads, assistant managers, and managers. Laboratory technicians advance to positions as supervisors and managers. In the field of reinforced plastics, advanced positions are shop supervisors, quality control supervisors, and training supervisors.

Some of the other positions to which technicians can advance are described below:

Plant managers formulate and execute plant policies, practices, and procedures. They direct production activities to meet sales objectives at maximum efficiency and minimum cost.

Production managers direct the work of various production departments, either directly or through subordinate supervisors. They provide information on new production methods and equipment, wage rate problems, and the need for maintenance of all plant machinery and equipment. Production managers work closely with union representatives.

General worker supervisors are responsible for the safe, efficient, and profitable operation of their work stations. They direct production activities and execute policies of the plant manager through subordinate supervisors.

Industrial engineers perform a variety of engineering tasks in planning or making the best use of plant facilities. They plan equipment layout, work flow, and accident prevention programs, and may oversee worker training programs.

Quality control supervisors are responsible for the interpretation and enforcement of established quality standards. They direct and instruct the various inspectors assigned to the processing and finishing sections.

Regional sales managers are responsible for the sale of company products in a region. They supervise one or more salespersons and head branch offices as required. They may select and develop dealers and distributors, and they may supervise warehousing and shipping.

Customer service managers work for sales representatives and managers, acting as liaisons between the customers and the company. They are primarily responsible for ensuring that customers receive the best product service possible.

Research and development department managers direct research studies in the development of new products and manufacturing methods. They are usually in charge of specialized testing and analytical services, and of test methods for evaluating conformance to national standards.

Purchasing agents are responsible for overall direction and coordination of buyers who secure raw materials, components, packaging material, office equipment, supplies, machinery, and services for a production complex.

Manufacturing engineer managers direct the activities of tooling engineers, mold designers, secondary machinery engineers, cost estimators, and workers in related disciplines. They work closely with sales and management on tooling and cost reduction requirements.

Product designers create designs for products to be produced from plastic materials. They investigate the practicability of designs in relation to the limitations of plant equipment, cost, probable selling price, and industry specifications.

Mold designers design the mold based on customer requirements. They may also be responsible for developing mold cost quotations for bids.

Estimators develop cost estimates from blueprints, samples, prototypes, or an actual mold. They select the material best suited for the application, calculate amount of material required, and determine mold capacity, type of mold, machine cycle time, and finishing operations.

Employment outlook

The plastics industry encompasses so many employment categories that employment is virtually assured for any qualified graduate of a technical program. Worldwide expansion of this industry is expected to continue through the 1990s. This expansion is expected to create a strong demand for technicians who can meet the challenges of this changing industry.

Earnings

Graduate technicians entering the industry may expect to earn starting salaries or hourly wages of about $14,000 to $20,000 per year. Skilled laminators in aerospace, aircraft, and related fields generally earn higher amounts. Promotions can lead to earnings of $4,000 to $10,000 above entry level over a period of three to seven years.

Supervisors, department heads, and plant managers with additional education, training, and experience earn from $30,000 to $40,000 or more annually.

Mold makers and tool-and-die makers earn from $30,000 to $50,000 annually after serving a five-year apprenticeship. To become eligible for a position as an apprentice, it is preferable to have a two-year machine shop education at a vocational school or community college. Apprentices usually make about half the salary of experienced workers.

Sales representatives in the industry earn about $20,000 a year and up. A company car, an expense account, and sales bonuses are usually provided by the employer. Travel both within a plastic technician's home area and to other cities and states is often necessary.

Technicians at middle management levels attend trade fairs, technical seminars, and professional society meetings, often at company expense. These functions may be local, regional, or national.

Benefits often include paid vacations, health and dental insurance, pension plans, credit union services, production bonuses, stock options, and industry-sponsored education. These benefits will vary with the size and nature of the company.

Conditions of work

Working conditions that technicians may encounter in the plastics field are varied. Research or test laboratories are clean, quiet, air-conditioned, and well lighted. Daytime working hours are usually observed, although some overtime may be necessary. Some companies operate more than one shift.

Injection-molding plants are quiet to moderately noisy. High standards of safety must be observed. Equipment is well guarded to prevent accidents to machine operators. Cleanliness in the workplace is mandatory.

Extrusion plants are quiet, clean, and efficient. Machine-heating zones are protected and product take-off or wind-up devices are guarded.

Laminating procedures range from clean to extremely messy. Catalysts, solvents, and resins present hazards unless strict precautionary measures are taken to prevent accidents.

Compression-molding shops are quiet, safe places to work. Temperatures during the summer can be uncomfortable, however, because of the 300 °F temperature of the molds.

Sales and service positions may entail travel, long hours, and some inconvenience if the sales territory covers a large area.

Social and psychological factors

Plastics technicians can be key employees in many enterprises. Such positions are rewarding from both a financial and psychological viewpoint. The work of plastics technicians benefits every type of industrial activity and has a lasting influence on society. Additionally, the wide variety of specializations available to people choosing to work in the plastics field will provide a multitude of options for advancement through the years of a career as a plastics technician.

GOE: 02.04.01, 05.05.07; SIC: 2821; SOC: 3719, 389

 SOURCES OF ADDITIONAL INFORMATION

Society of the Plastics Industry
1275 K Street, NW, Suite 400
Washington, DC 20005

Society of Plastics Engineers
14 Fairfield Drive
PO Box 0403
Brookfield Center, CT 06805

Society for the Advancement of Material and Process Engineering
Information Office
PO Box 2459
Covina, CA 91722

◇ **RELATED ARTICLES**

Pollution-control technicians

Definition

Pollution-control technicians, also known as *environmental technicians,* are principally concerned with conducting tests and field investigations to determine ways to control contamination of air, water, and soil. In the course of these tests and investigations, technicians utilize principles and methods of agriculture, chemistry, meteorology, engineering, and other disciplines, depending on their own specializations. They conduct laboratory and field procedures to determine the chemical composition or bacteriological activity of different kinds of environmental specimens. The specimens they collect may include gas samples from smokestacks and other sources; water samples from streams, lakes, liquid industrial discharges, and other processed or unprocessed waste water; and soil, silt, and mud samples. They prepare these sample substances for testing to determine their characteristics and pollutants, record the test data, and write up summaries and charts for review. In addition, they set up, operate, and maintain environmental-monitoring equipment and test instrumentation in fixed or mobile stations.

In general, pollution-control technicians do not operate on a day-to-day basis the equipment and systems designed to remove polluting materials from the environment. Rather they help to test and analyze environmental conditions and recommend the equipment and procedures to be used in removing pollutants.

Most pollution-control technicians specialize in one phase of environmental protection, such as in air pollution or in water pollution. No matter what their specialty, however, all pollution-control technicians share certain similarities in the work they do and in the preparation they require. Therefore, in discussing pollution-control technicians, this article is actually describing a cluster of similar yet distinct occupations.

History

Environmental pollution is an ancient problem. People began to affect air quality when they first began to build fires. When they began to live in cities, the problems of disposing of the wastes of daily life became serious. The sheer quantity and concentration in urban areas of refuse, garbage, sewage, smoke, and other substances became so great that they could not be readily and harmlessly dispersed in the environment. Local buildups of pollutants prompted a variety of attempted solutions. The ancient Romans, for example, had trenches outside of the city where they put their trash and occasionally human corpses, a disposal method that ensured periodic epidemic diseases. In medieval European cities, all kinds of wastes were commonly thrown out of windows into streets or dumped in waterways, despite laws forbidding these practices. Laws were also passed against fouling the air with excessive smoke. For the most part, however, efforts to restrict the dissemination of pollutants in the environment were completely unsuccessful.

With the Industrial Revolution, health problems brought on by smoke, noise, and other by-products of manufacturing became significant. By the nineteenth century, areas with high-population density and clusters of factories experienced markedly higher death and disease rates than areas with little industrial development. Some bodies of water became reservoirs of chemical wastes and virulent microorganisms from untreated sewage, thus posing a major health hazard and making living nearby all but intolerable because of the odors. The air in some cases was heavily contaminated with smoke particles and with a variety of harmful gases, both of which contributed dramatically to respiratory ailments.

The technological advances of the twentieth century added new and different pollutants to the environmental mix. Industrialization grew steadily more widespread, and for a time the marks it made on the environment were apt to be regarded as necessary signs of prosperity. As automobiles assumed a central place in the lives of Americans, automobile exhaust increasingly polluted the air. More products were manufactured and more consumed, generating more unused by-products and wastes. Not until after World War II did the public begin to see the air, water, and land as noticeably deteriorating because of the pollutants and decide that responsible action was needed to minimize the damage. New pollution-control laws and programs began to be instituted by the 1950s.

In recent years, public concern has developed about the safe disposal of hazardous wastes such as toxic chemicals and industrial by-products. Hazardous waste management has become one of the fastest growing areas of the pollution-control field.

Pollution-control technology has thus come into its own only since mid-century, combining the knowledge and approaches of several older disciplines. Today, control of environmental contamination includes a wide range of activities administered by governmental agencies, from local to federal, as well as activities of various industrial and research organizations.

Nature of the work

The two prominent specializations in pollution-control technology are air-pollution control and water-pollution control (or water and waste water technology). In addition, there are other technicians who focus, for example, on noise or light pollution or on soil quality. All are dealing with some aspect of making public resources suitable for re-use after they have been altered

A pollution-control technician tests various materials for their ability to absorb oil. In the event of an oil spill, the equipment will clean up the oil using the same basic principle.

by human activity or natural processes; however, they work in a wide variety of different settings. The variety is illustrated in the following paragraphs which describe the work of five different kinds of environmental technicians: *water pollution-control technicians, estuarine resource technicians, air technicians, noise technicians,* and *hazardous waste technicians.*

Water pollution-control technicians help to determine sources of water pollution and methods of reducing it. They collect samples from natural water bodies, industrial wastes, or other water sources, and they perform chemical and physical tests in the field to identify constituents of samples. Some set up monitoring equipment to obtain information on water flow, turbidity, temperature, pressure, and other factors, recording readings from these devices accurately and clearly. To trace flow patterns, they may introduce dyes into the water.

In the course of these tasks, they spend a good part of their time outdoors, in bad weather, aboard boats, sometimes near unpleasant smells or potentially hazardous substances. The field sites may be scattered or remote places; it may be necessary to drive a car or truck on the job or to travel, perhaps staying away from home for a long period of time.

Because sampling and monitoring are increasingly carried out with automatic equipment, technicians may analyze computer printouts of data and use computers. They often have to prepare reports, charts, graphs, or tables to display data and to aid in its analysis.

A related specialty particularly suitable for students interested in biology is estuarine resource technology. Estuaries are coastal areas where fresh water and salt water come together. These bays, salt marshes, inlets, and other tidal water bodies support a wide variety of plant and animal life with ecologically complex relationships. They are vulnerable to destructive pollution from adjoining industries, cities and towns, and other sources. Estuarine-resource technicians aid scientists in studying the resulting environmental changes. They may work in laboratories, aboard boats, and clad in diving gear in the water. They operate, maintain, and calibrate instruments; collect and analyze water samples; record observations; and perform other tasks that are part of investigating estuarine habitats and their organisms.

Air technicians collect and test air samples, record data on atmospheric conditions, and supply data to engineers in various forms. They may be involved in studying specific pollutants, such as exhaust from internal combustion engines or from the stacks and chimneys on manufacturing plants. They may observe smoke density and take samples on location, or they may recreate contaminants in the laboratory. As laboratory technicians, they may work with atomic absorption spectrophotometers, flame photometers, gas chromatographs, and other instruments for analyzing samples.

Alternatively, air technicians may focus on the quality of the open air outdoors, perhaps utilizing sampling devices on rooftops or in stationary house trailers. These trailers are sometimes equipped with elaborate, continuously operating, automatic testing systems, including some of the same devices found in laboratories. Outside air is pumped into various chambers in the trailer where it is analyzed for the presence of solid particles and certain gases. The results may be recorded by machine on thirty-day rolls of graph paper or averaged with other data and fed into a computer at regular intervals.

Air technicians are needed to drive and operate mobile monitoring units and to set up and maintain sophisticated stationary trailers. They replenish the chemicals used in tests, replace worn parts, calibrate instruments, and record results. To do these tasks they must know something of chemistry, electronics, and mathematics and have some mechanical aptitude. The job may take them into heat and cold, near fumes and chemicals, and into noisy places.

Noise technicians likewise make instrument readings and observations on rooftops or in vans that they drive to pollution areas. They may visit factories to check on the noise exposure of workers, or work at highways, airports, and similar outdoor locations. They may also test manufactured products—chain saws, construction equipment, lawn mowers, and so forth. Often working in teams of two, they may collect data for research, for environmental impact assessments, or for determining compliance with noise regulations. One of the team usually "listens" with electronic instruments while the other records the results. Noise technicians also routinely note conditions at the observation site, such as the presence of sound-absorbing or sound-reflecting materials or the distance to the sound source from the point of observation. Technicians who work for the government instead of industry may have to settle nuisance disputes and issue summonses to noise violators as part of their job.

Hazardous waste technicians are concerned with the safe disposal of toxic wastes. Among such wastes are the by-products created during the manufacture of chemicals and other industrial products. Leaks from aging underground gasoline storage tanks and even the improper disposal of household chemicals are also significant sources of hazardous materials in the environment. Hazardous waste technicians usually work for companies that are hired by public agencies or private companies to clean up landfills or other hazardous waste sites.

When working to clean up such a site, technicians may be involved with the removal of hazardous materials from a site to a processing center or safe disposal area. They may gather specimens of water and soil and perform tests on them in a laboratory to determine the kind and amount of pollutants present. At the site, technicians often use drilling equipment, pumps, and chemical-sensing devices.

In each of these areas of pollution-control technology, there are technicians who work in specialized activities or work settings. Field and laboratory technicians, for instance, collect and evaluate data in industrial, manufacturing, environmental, or laboratory settings. Working usually as members of a team along with highly trained engineers and scientific personnel, these technicians must be familiar with a variety of routine procedures and also be able to learn new techniques and methods as the situation demands. In some positions, the ability to improvise solutions to problems is important.

To obtain accurate data, field specialists often need to know about the workings of the manufacturing or energy-conversion processes that are associated with pollution sources. Similarly, they need to have some understanding of the environmental context in which they gather data, because the natural settings in which observations are made are crucial to assessing the importance of pollution factors.

Pollution-control technicians are sometimes employed as inspectors, instrument specialists, technical representatives of equipment manufacturers, or other workers in fields directly related to environmental investigation. Inspectors need to combine field and laboratory skills and also have a working knowledge of the clean-up equipment that is used in ensuring that environmental conditions meet established standards. Often a major part of the job is to judge the appropriateness of the equipment selected for performing a given control job. It may be the inspector's judgment that determines whether an operating permit should be issued to a company whose manufacturing processes produce pollution. Inspectors thus may have to know about a wide range of control equipment and manufacturing processes and be able to defend with facts their recommendations for or against issuing permits.

Some inspectors answer complaints from the public about the adequacy of existing equipment or about the need for additional pollution-control measures. Technicians in such positions must be able to work well with different kinds of people, must be perceptive enough to separate out useful information from unsubstantial accusations, and must be familiar with the applicable state, federal, or local laws.

Instrument specialists are concerned exclusively with the devices for monitoring and measuring. They install, calibrate, and maintain them, so these technicians must be good at handling tools and familiar with the chemical, electromechanical, pneumatic, and other sensing systems that the instruments involve.

Technical representatives are sometimes hired by the companies that manufacture instruments and other pollution-control equipment. Their job is to assist customers in selecting, installing, operating, and servicing the company's products. Technical representatives may also help train the customer's employees in the proper operation and maintenance of the equipment.

A pollution-control technician at a petroleum refinery collects water samples from a stabilization pond. She is checking the level of algae.

Requirements

Pollution-control technicians, regardless of specialization or type of position, need basic manual skills. They should like to work with their hands and be at home with a variety of equipment and instruments. In some jobs, pollution-control technicians need good eye-hand coordination, vision, or manual dexterity. Good overall physical conditioning is a requirement for technicians who must engage in demanding outdoor activity, such as air technicians who climb ladders to roofs or water-pollution technicians who operate small boats.

Pollution-control technicians need to be good at reading and interpreting maps, charts, diagrams, instruction manuals, and other such materials. They must be able to make accurate and objective observations, maintain clear and complete records of data, perform certain types of computations, and prepare technical reports, both written and oral, to be used in further analyses by engineers and scientists.

Some students become interested in pollution-control technology through their interest in environmental issues, others because of the essentially scientific research nature of the work. Either approach is good, but it is best

93

to begin career preparation early, in high school if possible. The prospective technician should take advantage of as many mathematics and laboratory science courses as possible. This means a minimum of two years of high-school mathematics, including algebra and geometry, and more advanced courses if the student's schedule permits. Chemistry, physics, biology, and computer courses are all highly desirable, as are any courses in conservation or ecology that the high school may offer.

Of vital importance are courses where the students can sharpen their written and oral communication skills. If courses are available in drafting or statistics, they too should be included in the high-school program.

In general, a high-school diploma and evidence of satisfactory verbal, science, and mathematics skills are required for admission to technical training programs. In some cases, however, technical schools permit students to take remedial work in certain areas after admission.

Two years of post–high-school training is the average basic requirement for starting a career in pollution-control technology. But because the field is a relatively new one among engineering technologies and because the nature of the jobs in the field varies considerably, appropriate preparation varies. The best foundation for a career may be a program specifically preparing pollution-control technologists, but a limited number of schools offer such training.

As an example, a typical two-year air technology program might include in the first year courses such as the following: introduction to atmospheric pollution, ambient atmospheric sampling and analysis, air quality management, technical mathematics, chemistry, communications skills, physics, and technical reporting. Typical second-year courses might include: air pollution instrumentation, source testing—sampling and analysis, meteorology, sources of air pollution (including manufacturing and energy conversion processes), air pollution control, biology, environmental science, and statistics.

Employers are sometimes flexible in their requirements, recognizing the value of different combinations of technical training and experience. Job applicants may need only an associate degree with emphasis in a physical science, a scientific technology, or related field. For many positions, applicants must also have practical experience in such areas as sampling techniques, or with measuring and testing equipment. Additional course work in one of the sciences, engineering, or mathematics can be substituted in some circumstances. On the other hand, a high-school diploma plus the right kind of practical experience is the normal requirement for other positions. Partly because of their diverse backgrounds, new employees often receive on-the-job instruction that helps them to relate their experience and training to their new duties.

Special requirements

Certification or licensing is required for many positions in the water pollution-control field, especially those where sanitation, public health, a public water supply, or a sewage treatment system is involved. Although such certification is not part of the curriculum of most schools offering programs of study in this area, students who have been through such programs usually have no trouble acquiring certification.

Technicians in other areas of pollution-control technology are generally not required to be licensed. The American Society of Certified Engineering Technicians, however, a professional association sponsored by the National Society of Professional Engineers, is concerned with obtaining recognition for engineering technicians. Membership in this group is recommended for professionally oriented technicians who are not required to be otherwise licensed.

Opportunities for experience and exploration

Students who want to learn about jobs in pollution-control technology can try several approaches. One is to visit a county health department or a pollution-control agency in their community. Many agencies are pleased to explain their work to visitors. In this way, it may be possible for students to get a first-hand glimpse of various pollution-control specialists at work.

Industrial or manufacturing plants that have their own air or water pollution abatement systems may offer tours of their operations to the public. A visit to such a facility would provide an excellent opportunity for students to see the equipment and conditions that technicians work with.

It is not likely that summer or part-time jobs in this field would be available to permit students hands-on experience. Insight into environmental issues, however, may be gained through organizations devoted to these concerns. School science clubs, local community groups, and naturalist clubs may help broaden students' understanding of various aspects of the natural world and perhaps may help them undertake an exploration in depth of a few specific areas of interest.

Another avenue for career investigation is to visit a large library with a good collection of technical and general interest publications in environmental science to see what topics seem to be on the minds of people working in the field.

Methods of entering

Graduates of two-year pollution-control technology or related programs are often employed during their final term by recruiters who routinely visit their schools. The demand for qualified technicians in some specialties, notably in water pollution technology, is such that it is not uncommon for new graduates to have several attractive job offers. In fact, federal, state, and municipal agencies may find it difficult to compete with private employers in hiring good personnel.

Most schools can provide job-hunting advice and assistance to new technicians in any of their training programs. Direct application to employment agencies or the personnel officers for potential employers can also be a productive approach. Students hoping to find employment outside their current geographic area may get good results through professional organizations or by advertising in the appropriate technical journals.

Advancement

In general, as pollution-control technicians gain experience they receive more responsibility and higher pay. But in many positions in this field, the greatest advancement is possible only for those who continue to pursue formal education. Many technicians with two-year degrees decide after some work experience that a bachelor of science degree provides the best tools to ensure continued challenges and promotions. In private industry and consulting firms, some technician positions are used for training newly recruited professional staff. In such cases, workers with four-year degrees in engineering or physical science are clearly more likely to be promoted.

Employees of many state and local government-operated agencies are organized under civil service–type systems that specify experience, education, and other criteria for advancement. In private industry, however, promotions are somewhat less structured, depending on a variety of factors including the supervisor's judgment of the technician's work.

With experience, technicians may become supervisors or team leaders, in charge of hiring and training new employees or overseeing quality-control operations, for example. Or they may refine their skills on the job and become expert in a particular subspeciality of their field. A technician who starts by assisting in the design and construction of water or air pollution-control systems may go on to concentrate on the instrumentation that controls these systems. A service technician who represents an equipment manufacturing company to its customers, advising them in selecting, installing, and maintaining equipment, may eventually advance to head a sales team.

Employment outlook

In general, the future looks bright for the field of pollution-control technology. The expansion and improvement of water and waste water management activities in particular should mean continued demand for technicians during the 1990s.

Other areas of the field offer more uncertain prospects. Openings are not evenly distributed throughout the country. The number of technician positions in air pollution control, for example, may vary from almost none in one region to far more than the number of available candidates in another. For this reason, technicians have a better chance for a good job if they are flexible about geographic location or have sufficient background in another phase of pollution control to qualify for another type of technical work.

Other factors influencing future opportunities are continued public awareness and pressure on government and industry; availability of funds; and levels of government enforcement of the regulations of the Environmental Protection Agency (EPA), Occupational Safety and Health Administration (OSHA), and other bodies. These factors are difficult to forecast, but the general trend toward belt-tightening in government suggests that technicians in narrower specialties ought to be prepared with a broad base of training in case they need to change specialties.

Pollution-control technicians
Emerging Technician Occupations

Earnings

Pay scales for pollution-control technicians vary widely depending on the nature of the work they do, the training and experience required for the work, the type of employer, geographic region, the demand for technicians as compared to available supply, and other factors.

In general, pollution-control technicians receive salaries roughly equivalent to those received by other engineering and science technicians. In the early 1990s, most engineering technicians earned between $18,000 and $30,000 a year, with the average being around $25,000 a year. Some technicians, however, earned as little as $14,000 a year or less, and some senior technicians earned as much as $37,000 a year or more.

Conditions of work

Conditions range from clean and pleasant indoor offices and laboratories to outdoor hot or cold, wet, bad-smelling, noisy, even hazardous situations. Anyone planning a career in pollution-control technology should realize the possibility of exposure to unpleasant conditions at least occasionally in his or her career. Employers often can minimize these negatives through special equipment and procedures. Most laboratories and manufacturing companies will have local safety committees to observe operations and oversee potentially dangerous situations.

Some jobs involve vigorous physical activity (for example, handling a small boat or climbing ladders on smokestacks for air samples). For the most part, technicians need only be able to do moderate activity. Travel may be required. It may be necessary to go to urban, industrial, or rural settings for sampling.

Social and psychological factors

The variety of specialties and functions of pollution-control technicians means that the necessary personal characteristics vary somewhat. In nearly any position, however, the characteristics that help are above-average intelligence and curiosity, an interest in environmental problems, a sense of being comfortable with mechanical devices, and perseverance.

Because the job can involve a considerable amount of repetitive work, patience and a tolerance for boring tasks are useful. On other occasions, particularly when they are working in the field, pollution-control technicians have to use their resourcefulness and ingenuity to find the best ways of responding to new situations. For example, they may have to decide how to assemble whatever equipment is available in a mobile testing unit into the most effective system for accomplishing the task at hand. In addition to having the capacity for making independent judgments, these technicians have to be able to work as team members. The ability to function smoothly in a group and to communicate well with a variety of people can be very important.

GOE: 05.03.08; SIC: Any industry; SOC: 389

◇ SOURCES OF ADDITIONAL INFORMATION

Air and Waste Management Association
PO Box 2861
Pittsburgh, PA 15230

Water Pollution Control Federation
601 Wythe Street
Alexandria, VA 22314

Environmental Protection Agency
401 M Street, SW
Washington, DC 20460

Hazardous Waste Treatment Council
1440 New York Avenue, NW
Washington, DC 20005

◇ RELATED ARTICLES

Volume 1: Waste Management
Volume 2: Biologists; Geologists; Groundwater professionals
Volume 3: Occupational safety and health workers; Agricultural scientists; Agricultural extension workers; Soil scientists; Industrial chemical workers; Wastewater treatment plant operators
Volume 4: Industrial safety and health technicians; Soil conservation technicians; Water and wastewater treatment technicians

Robotics technicians

Definition

Robotics technicians assist robotics engineers in a wide variety of tasks relating to the design, development, production, testing, operation, repair, and maintenance of robots and robotic devices.

History

Robots are devices that perform tasks ordinarily associated with humans and that operate with what seems like human intelligence. The key feature of robots is their flexibility and versatility. The instructions that control their operations can be modified, so the tasks the machines do can change as needed.

The creation of such machines is a fairly recent development; however, the history of the technology that has led to the development of robots can be traced back to the time of the ancient Greek and Egyptian civilizations. One of the early inventors whose work is known to us is Hero of Alexandria, who lived during the first century A.D. He invented a machine that would automatically open the doors of a temple when the priest lit a fire in the altar. During the later periods of the Middle Ages, Renaissance, and seventeenth and eighteenth centuries, interest in robot-like mechanisms turned mostly to automatons, which are devices that imitate human and animal appearance and activity but that perform no useful task.

During the nineteenth century, the Industrial Revolution inspired the invention of many different kinds of automatic machinery. One of the most important inventions for the development of robotics was Joseph-Marie Jacquard's invention in 1804 of a method for controlling machinery by means of a programmed set of instructions recorded on a punched paper tape that was fed into a machine to direct its movements. From this invention there eventually developed robots containing their own internal preprogrammed computers that guide and control the devices in performing specified actions in particular conditions.

The word "robot" and many of the concepts we associate with it were first introduced in the early 1920s. They made their appearance in a play titled *R.U.R.* (which stands for Rossum's Universal Robots) written by Czechoslovakian dramatist Karel Capek. The play tells the story of human-like robotic machines that were created to perform manual tasks for their human masters. Unfortunately, in the play, the robots rebel against their masters and kill them.

During the 1950s and 1960s, advances in the fields of automation and computer science led to the development of experimental robots that could imitate a wide range of human activity, including self-regulated and self-propelled movement (either on wheels or on legs), the ability to sense and manipulate objects, and the ability to select a course of action on the basis of conditions around them.

Experimental robots such as these are fascinating in their possibilities and inspire wonderful creative fantasies, such as the robots R2D2 and C3PO in the movie *Star Wars*; however, the principal economic significance of robots is in the field of industrial robotics, where robots of far more limited capabilities (such as a mechanical arm) perform complex sequences of precise movements according to a predetermined set of instructions. Today, robots such as these are used in a wide variety of industrial settings. Robots are in use in the automotive industry for welding and painting, in the textile industry for cutting cloth and tending machines, and in the computer industry for precise assembly work. In these settings, robots reduce production costs by removing the need for many of the human workers who would otherwise be required for the production tasks. In addition, robots are used in settings where it would be dangerous, uncomfortable, or even impossible for humans to work. Robots can fly into space, work in oceans, mines, or pipelines, and survive exposure to heat, chemicals, and radioactivity.

In the future, the capabilities of robots and the applications to which they are put will undoubtedly continue to expand and evolve. Where that evolution will lead will be determined in large part by robotics engineers and the robotics technicians that work with them.

Nature of the work

Robotics technicians assist in all phases of robotics engineering. Many are employed in activities related to installation, repair, and maintenance of finished robots. Others are involved

This robotics technician operates a robot with a master unit in a control room. He uses several video screens to observe the movements of the robot, which is located in another room.

in design and development of new kinds robotics equipment.

Robotics technicians who install, program, and repair robotic equipment usually work for companies that build and sell robots, and they usually work in customers' plants. They must have a knowledge of electronics, electrical circuitry, mechanics, pneumatics, hydraulics, and computer programming. They use hand and power tools, testing instruments, manuals, schematic diagrams, and blueprints.

They begin an installation by reviewing the work order and instructional information about the equipment. They verify with the customer that the intended site in the factory is correctly supplied with the necessary electrical wires, switches, circuit breakers, and other parts. They position and secure the robot in place, sometimes using a crane or other large tools and equipment. They attach various cables and hoses, such as those that connect a hydraulic power unit with the robot. After making sure that the equipment is operational, technicians program the robot for specified tasks, using their knowledge of the robot's programming language.

Once robots are in place and functioning, they may develop problems. In that case, technicians are called upon to test components and locate faulty parts. When the problem is found, they may replace or recalibrate parts. Sometimes they suggest changes in circuitry or programming. They may install different end-of-arm tools on robots to allow machines to perform new functions. They may also train the customers' employees in how to operate robots and related equipment, and they may help es-

tablish in-house basic maintenance and repair programs at new installations.

Technicians who are involved with the design and development of new robotics devices are sometimes referred to as robotics design technicians. They are part of a design team, and they work closely with robotics engineers. The robotics-design job starts as the engineers analyze the tasks and settings to which a new robotics system will be assigned, decide what kind of robotics system will best serve the necessary functions, and establish the initial design for the system. Technicians become involved in the process by first familiarizing themselves with the specifications and with any diagrams, blueprints, or sketches that have been provided. They then carry out prescribed tests on the systems and materials that have been proposed for the new robotic device. During this testing phase, they keep records of all their test procedures and results. They may be asked to present written reports, tables, or charts to document the results of their tests. If a particular system, subsystem, or material has not met testing requirements, the technician may suggest a way of rearranging the components of the system or of substituting alternate materials.

After this initial testing is completed, robotics design technicians are often involved in the building of a prototype model of the robot. Often this phase requires technicians to make sketches or drafts of components. Machine-shop workers use these sketches and drafts in making the parts. Once all of the parts and materials have been collected, the technicians assemble and test the prototype. If the prototype proves successful, the technicians help produce the formal documentation, including blueprints and manufacturing specifications sheets, that will be used by the technicians and other workers who will assemble the production robots that will actually be put in use.

Technicians involved with robot assembly, sometimes referred to as robot assemblers, commonly specialize in one aspect of robot assembly. Some technicians, for instance, specialize in materials handling. They receive requests for components or materials and locate and deliver them to the technicians doing the actual assembly or to test technicians who are performing tests on these materials or components. Mechanical assembly technicians assemble components and subsystems and install them in the robot. Electrical assembly technicians do the same work as mechanical assembly technicians but specialize in electrical components such as circuit boards and automatic switching devices. Finally, some technicians specialize in testing finished assemblies to ensure that they conform to the design team's specifications.

Other kinds of robotics technicians include *robot operators*, who operate robots in specialized settings. *Robotics trainers* are specialized robotics technicians who train other employees in the installation, use, and maintenance of robots.

Requirements

Robotics technicians need to have better-than-average mechanical aptitude and good hand-eye coordination. They should have neat and orderly work habits and the ability to think methodically. Robotics technicians should also be able to work independently or as part of a team and to maintain an attitude of patience and curiosity towards the tasks that are assigned to them.

The minimum educational requirement for a robotics technician is graduation from high school. High-school students interested in a career as a robotics technician should take courses that provide them with a solid background in mathematics, physics, machine-shop skills, drafting, and electronics.

Some service and maintenance positions in the robotics field provide on-the-job technical training and are available to people who have not attended a training program beyond high school. However, most successful robotics technicians have received formal training in a related technical field, usually in a two-year postsecondary school associate degree program taught at a vocational school or community college. These programs usually include courses in basic engineering topics, such as hydraulics, pneumatics, and electronics, and in specialized topics, such as fundamentals of robotics, robot programming, and industrial robotics. A two-year post secondary school program may also require the student to complete courses in technical writing, communications, and social sciences and the humanities.

Special requirements

Most robotics technicians do not need to obtain a license or to join a union in order to get a job. In some industrial settings or situations, however, union membership or a license may be required.

Opportunities for experience and exploration

Part-time or summer jobs involved directly with robotics are very hard to find. Jobs relating to other engineering fields, such as electronics or mechanics, are usually easier to locate, and they can offer the student a good opportunity to become familiar with a similar kind of workplace.

Other activities that will foster knowledge and skills relevant to a career in robotics include membership in high-school science clubs, participation in science fairs, and pursuing hobbies that involve electronics, mechanical equipment, model building, or reading books and articles about technical topics.

Methods of entering

Students who graduate from a two-year college or technical institute can usually receive job-placement assistance from the school's placement office. Recruiters from companies employing robotics technicians sometimes visit schools to interview and hire students who are close to graduation.

State or private employment agencies may also be able to help. Want ads in newspapers and professional journals are another source of information. In addition, students should not hesitate to contact prospective employers by phone or with a letter that states their interest in employment and describes their education and experience.

Advancement

Robotics technicians who have completed several years on the job and who have demonstrated their ability to handle more responsibility may be assigned some supervisory work or, more likely, they will become trainers or instructors for other new technicians. Experienced technicians may teach courses at their workplace, or they may find teaching opportunities at a local school or community college.

Other routes for advancement include becoming a sales representative for a robotics manufacturing or design firm or working as an independent contractor for companies using or manufacturing robots.

With additional training and education, especially a bachelor's degree, technicians can become eligible for positions as robotics technologists or robotics engineers.

Employment outlook

The employment outlook for robotics technicians is excellent. By all estimates, the number of industrial robots in use will continue to grow rapidly during the 1990s. Industry sources expect that we will see robots in wide use in automobile and farm and industrial equipment manufacturing, in mining and petroleum production, and throughout the nuclear power industry. Companies already making use of robots will probably expand their reliance on these devices. And, perhaps more importantly, companies that are not currently using robots will find ways to take advantage of this technology.

For prospective robotics technicians, the important aspect of this expansion in the use of robots is that more robots require more robotics technicians, whether it is to design and build them, install, maintain, and repair them, or to operate them.

Earnings

Earnings and benefits vary widely in different parts of the country and for different jobs with different training requirements. A typical starting salary for a graduate of a two-year technical program is estimated to be approximately $20,000 a year. With increased training and experience, technicians can earn much more. The overall salary range for technicians with a two-year degree is from about $17,000 to over $30,000 a year, although some technicians with special skills, extensive experience, or added responsibilities may earn considerably more. Of the specialized technicians mentioned in this article, those involved in design and training will be at the top of the range, sometimes earning more than $40,000 a year; those involved with maintenance and repair will earn relatively less, with some beginning at $16,000 a year or less.

Conditions of work

Most robotics technicians work in clean, well-lighted, comfortable surroundings. Some technicians will spend most of their days at a desk or work table, while others, such as those who install robots, may be more active, walking, standing, stooping, lifting, and carrying heavy weights. Technicians involved with operation, maintenance, or assembly may work in noisy factories; technicians involved with development and testing can expect to work in a quieter setting.

Some technicians will have to confront potentially hazardous conditions in the work place. Robots, after all, are often designed and used precisely because the task they will perform involves some risk to humans, such as the use of laser beams, arc-welding equipment, radioactive substances, or hazardous chemicals. In designing, testing, building, installing, and repairing robots, it is inevitable that some technicians will be exposed to these same risks. Plant safety procedures will protect the attentive and cautious worker, but carelessness in such settings can be especially dangerous.

Some maintenance technicians and robot operators may have to work extended or unusual hours.

Social and psychological factors

Most robotics technicians work as part of a team. They are required to take orders, and they may well encounter situations in which their individual contributions are not fully recognized. Successful technicians are those that can work well as team members and who can derive satisfaction from the accomplishments of the team as a whole.

The long-term economic vitality of this country will rely in large part on the increasing use of robots in military, industrial, and research activities. Robotics technicians derive a sense of satisfaction in knowing that they are taking part in this important and challenging undertaking.

GOE: 05.05.09, 05.05.11; SIC: Any industry; SOC: 3719, 6178

◇ **SOURCES OF ADDITIONAL INFORMATION**

Robotic Industries Association
PO Box 3724
900 Victors Way
Ann Arbor, MI 48106

Robotics International of SME
Society of Manufacturing Engineers
PO Box 930
One SME Drive
Dearborn, MI 48121

Robotics and Automation Council
Institute of Electrical and Electronic
Engineers (IEEE)
Education Information
345 East 47th Street
New York, NY 10017

Semiconductor-development technicians

Definition

Semiconductor-development technicians are highly
skilled workers who test new kinds of semiconductor devices that are being designed for use
in many kinds of modern electronic equipment.
They may also test samples of devices that are
already in production in order to assess production techniques. In addition, they assist in
developing and evaluating the test equipment
that is used to gather information about the
semiconductor devices. They work under the
direction of engineers in research laboratory
settings on activities related to designing and
planning for later production or on improving
production yields.

Nature of the work

To do their work, semiconductor-development
technicians must apply a thorough knowledge
of electronics theory and the operating principles of the test equipment. Beginning with instructions and specifications provided by engineers, they work on designing complex electronic circuits for new devices. To do this, they
use drafting instruments and techniques, including computer-aided design (CAD) systems.

Once devices are designed and put together, semiconductor-development technicians use various types of testing equipment to
determine whether the devices perform as expected and meet engineering requirements. In
this testing, they may operate oscilloscopes,
logic and test probes, and calibrating equipment. The technicians build or modify some
electronic components as needed, using hand
tools and power tools. If existing testing equipment does not provide the needed data, the
technicians help engineers to come up with different testing methods or to modify the equipment so the task can be accomplished. They
also carry out regular maintenance and calibration procedures on testing equipment.

Sometimes semiconductor-development
technicians serve as intermediaries between different teams of workers on a project, making
sure that information and materials flow
smoothly. They may supervise other technical
personnel.

Requirements

Semiconductor-development technicians need
at least two years of specialized training beyond
high school. Employers, however, are increasingly seeking people for these technician positions who have four or more years of
postsecondary school training in this field, and
the trend toward requiring more education will
probably continue in coming years.

Technicians need to be acquainted with algebra, calculus, and statistics. They must be
able to read and interpret scientific and techni-

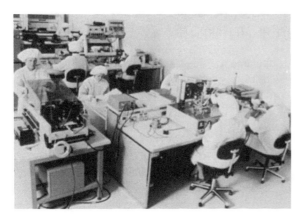

Several semiconductor-development technicians use sophisticated equipment to test new devices. Such equipment includes oscilloscopes, logic and test probes, and calibration instruments.

good vision. On the job, they may be exposed to unpleasant fumes, toxic chemicals, or the possibility of electric shock, but these negatives can be minimized by utilizing protective and safety measures.

GOE: 05.01.01; SIC: 3624; SOC: 371

◇ **RELATED ARTICLES**

Volume 1: Electronics; Engineering
Volume 2: Engineers
Volume 4: CAD/CAM technicians; Electronics technicians; Electronics test technicians; Microelectronics technicians

cal material and communicate well both orally and in writing. The work is not physically strenuous, but they need manual dexterity and

Software technicians

Definition

Software technicians plan and develop computer software programs, analyze computer program problems, enter programs into memory chips that are then installed in printed circuit boards, and test and adjust the installed programs until they function as required. They work with software used in business computer systems for word processing or record keeping, or in computer games, or in any other computer application.

Nature of the work

Technicians begin by constructing logic charts that describe the program they are developing, step by step. When the steps are complete, technicians write detailed flow charts outlining every step of the program. The program is "written" onto a computer disk memory using a keyboard and cathode-ray-tube (CRT) input device. The new program is tested and adjusted, using a computer system and input/output equipment, until it performs as desired.

The disk is then mounted in an electronic system that transfers its program onto memory chips. Technicians write instructions for operators who will use systems employing the chips. They may also install the chips into systems, using knowledge of computer circuitry and ability to read logic and wiring diagrams. Following installation, they final-test the chips in their circuits, make any final adjustments, and write data specifications describing the purpose and operation of the programs on the chips for use by the engineering department and for technical manuals for operators.

Requirements

People who are interested in careers as software technicians should have excellent mathematics skills, with high-school courses at least through solid geometry. Because writing programs requires a thorough grasp of logic, a high level of language skill is also necessary. Aspiring technicians should be prepared to pursue at least two years of post–high-school technical training in a community college or specialized computer training school. The training they receive should emphasize courses in basic computer operations and theory, programming, computer languages, and technical writing.

In general, software technicians with two-year degrees can expect tougher competition for good jobs in the coming years, as employers come to expect more versatility from programming employees. To maximize career opportunities, technicians may have to upgrade their skills to the bachelor's degree level.

Conditions of work

The work of software technicians is not physically strenuous, but it does require a high level of concentration and good visual acuity. These technicians work under pleasant indoor, air-conditioned surroundings.

GOE: 11.01.01; SIC: 7371; SOC: 3971

◇ **RELATED ARTICLES**

Volume 1: Computer Software
Volume 2: Computer programmers; Graphics programmers
Volume 4: Data-processing technicians; Microelectronics technicians

Telecommunications technicians

Definition

Telecommunications technicians install, test, maintain, troubleshoot, and repair a wide variety of telecommunications equipment, which is equipment used for transmitting voices and data across long distances. Telecommunications technicians are usually involved with communications that are not intended as entertainment and are not broadcast to the public via radio or television signals.

Telecommunications systems are typically used to link telephones, but they also involve such equipment as computers, lasers, fax machines, mobile radio telephone transmitters and receivers, and teletypes. Messages and signals can be sent using telephone or telegraph wires, undersea cables, and cable television lines via microwave transmissions, through fiber optics cables, and bounced off satellites in space. Often several kinds of equipment are linked together in a complicated system.

Nature of the work

Although their specific concerns vary according to the area of the industry where they are employed, most telecommunications technicians share some basic kinds of activities. They work with electrical measuring and testing devices and hand tools, read blueprints, circuit diagrams and electrical schematics, and consult technical manuals. The following paragraphs describe just a few of the many technicians who work in this complex industry.

Central office technicians or *switching equipment technicians* work in telephone company central offices. They install, test, repair, and maintain the equipment that automatically connects lines when customers dial telephone numbers.

PBX systems technicians work on PBXs or private branch exchanges, which are direct lines that businesses install to bypass phone company lines. PBX equipment can handle both voice and data communications and can provide specialized services like electronic mail and automatic routing of calls at the lowest possible cost.

Submarine cable equipment technicians work with machines and equipment used to send messages over underwater cables. Working in cable offices and stations, they check on and adjust transmitters and printers and repair or replace faulty parts.

Automatic-equipment technicians work for telegraph companies, maintaining and adjusting telegraphic transmitting and receiving equipment.

A telecommunications technician must be familiar with all of the complex wiring in a system before diagnosing the problem and repairing it.

Network control technicians work with electronic networks for transmitting data that use several different kinds of equipment, such as a combination of telephone lines, satellites, and computers. They electronically test the various parts of the network and monitor its performance in operation. They use computer equipment to identify problems so that other workers can do repairs.

Microwave technicians help design, test, and install various parts of microwave communications systems and radar equipment. Most of these technicians are employed by the armed forces or defense industries.

Requirements

Telecommunications employers usually prefer to hire technicians who have already learned most of the necessary skills, either through service in the military or from a post–high-school training program such as those available at community and junior colleges or vocational institutes. Programs in telecommunications technology, in electronics, electrical, or electromechanical technology, or even computer maintenance or related subjects, may be appropriate for people who want to become telecommunications technicians.

Sometimes employers, notably in the telephone industry, hire and train people who have not attended such programs. Increasing computerization in the telephone industry, however, is greatly reducing the need for technicians who provide routine maintenance and repair services. In other areas of telecommunications, such as microwave technology, the demand for qualified technicians is growing. In general, technicians should obtain the best training they can to be prepared to adapt as technology changes.

While in high school, students who are thinking about entering this field should take computer courses, mathematics at least through algebra and geometry, and physics. They should take shop courses that introduce them to principles of electricity and electronics, basic machine repair, and, if possible, engineering drawing and blueprint reading. They should also take English courses that help to develop skills needed for reading technical manuals and writing reports on their work.

The work of most telecommunications technicians is mainly indoors and involves light or medium physical demands. In some positions technicians are exposed to noise or vibration.

GOE: 05.05.05; SIC: 48; SOC: 6151

◇ **RELATED ARTICLES**

Volume 1: Electronics; Telecommunications
Volume 2: Engineers
Volume 3: Commercial and industrial electronic equipment repairers; Communications equipment mechanics; Electricians; Telephone and PBX installers and repairers
Volume 4: Cable television technicians; Computer-service technicians; Electrical technicians; Electromechanical technicians; Electronics technicians; Electronics test technicians

Engineering and Science Technician Occupations

We live in a technological world. During this century, we have moved from the era of the Industrial Revolution into the era of high technology. During the past sixty years, most of the physical labor in our farms, forests, factories, mines, transportation systems, offices, and even homes has been taken over by mass production or by mechanical devices. Worldwide instant communication has become an everyday reality. Perhaps most dramatically, computers and other kinds of electronic data-processing equipment have become faster, smaller, less expensive, more efficient, and easier to use. The engineering and science technician plays a crucial role in this world. Technicians opened the first box of rocks from the moon. Technicians are helping to develop new vaccines, new fabrics, and new pollution controls. There is virtually no area of today's engineering or scientific world in which technicians are not at work.

Engineering and science technicians are specially trained and often highly skilled assistants who work with engineers and scientists in a wide variety of capacities, including working as supervisors, inspectors, repair specialists, and in other positions of responsibility. In many settings, technicians work as part of a team composed of professionally trained engineers and scientists, technicians specially trained in the technical aspects of a particular kind of work, and practically trained craft workers. As members of such teams, they often serve in a liaison capacity; that is, they act as a communications link between the scientists and engineers who design projects and the skilled workers who perform most of the physical tasks necessary to the projects.

The work of technicians is usually more narrowly focused than that of the scientists or engineers with whom they work, as the technicians are usually principally involved with carrying out the practical applications of the theories established by scientists and engineers. For instance, they may analyze and solve engineering and scientific problems, prepare formal written reports, or conduct experiments and tests according to the directions of professional supervisors. Technicians may also assist scientists and engineers by making drawings and sketches of experimental models and equipment and by handling other aspects of design and development work.

Technicians must be able to prepare a variety of simple plans, diagrams, and codes. They often apply their knowledge of mathematics as they use complex electronic and mechanical instruments, experimental and mechanical apparatus, or drafting instruments. They also use engineering or scientific handbooks, electronic calculators, and in many cases, electronic data-processing equipment.

Historically, the evolution of the technician's occupation has paralleled the growth of the role of science and technology in our society. Scientists and engineers have long needed and long employed skilled assistants to aid them in some of the more routine aspects of their work. The need for these assistants greatly increased, however, beginning about fifty years ago, as our society found more and more industrial, commercial, and research applications for scientific and engineering principles and techniques. As these applications multiplied, there came to be a need for greater numbers of scientists and engineers and for a more efficient utilization of these professionals.

It was this drive for a more efficient use of scientists and engineers that led to the employment of assistant engineers, assistant chemists, and assistant physicists. These assistants were individuals who had a combination of manual skills and basic knowledge in a subject that enabled them to handle, under the general direction of professionals, many of the simpler, repetitive, or standardized tasks that are always a part of any scientific or technological undertaking. By taking over these tasks, these assistants were able to free the scientists and engineers to spend more of their time on those problems requiring their particular knowledge.

These assistants became known as "technicians" and emerged from the growing technological complexity of our industrial processes and from the tremendous increase in emphasis on research and development in industry. Although such assistants were engaged in scientific and technical work long before they became known as technicians, it was the growing dependence of science and industry upon such people that led to their recognition as an entirely new identifiable group in the labor force.

Although many people most readily associate technicians with the fields of chemistry, electronics, and mechanical engineering, today's technicians work in a wide variety of fields connected with engineering and science, including aeronautics; air-conditioning, heating, and refrigeration; civil engineering; industrial production; and instrumentation. They also find work in a wide variety of settings. They may work, for instance, as inspectors, assistants to civil engineers, or utility plant operators. Many technicians, attracted to the more purely scientific aspects of research, work for a college, university, or research institute. Most engineering and science technicians, however, regardless of their subject specialty or the tasks they were trained for, find employment in a company involved in or closely related to the manufacture of consumer or industrial products. Within this field, they work in nearly every area in which there is an engineering or scientific aspect, from the development of specifications for a product going into production, to the preparation of sales brochures once the product is completed and ready for distribution.

Of the technicians who find work within a manufacturing industry, a particularly large number are found in the area of research and development or in product design. Working in a research and development laboratory, these technicians conduct tests and experiments that can lead to the design and manufacture of a new product or to developing new materials or new uses for existing materials. Most commonly, they set up, calibrate, and operate many different types of laboratory instruments. In addition, they make calculations and interpret data derived from these tests, measurements, and experiments. They present their findings in reports which are used in making important technical decisions.

In the design and preproduction phases, technicians work as part of a team responsible for planning the use of workers, materials, and machines during the actual production processes. They prepare specifications for materials; make or explain engineering drawings, diagrams, and sketches; and devise tests to ensure product quality. In all of these activities, they seek ways to maximize the efficiency of the production operation.

Once a product is in production, technicians generally follow the plans and directions of engineers, but usually without close supervision. They often supervise workers and monitor the production to make sure that workers are following correct procedures and that design specifications are being followed. They will also keep engineers and scientists informed about production progress and investigate any production problems that may arise.

After the production has been completed, technicians are often called on to assist with the installation or maintenance of the product. In the case of particularly new or sophisticated products, technicians may be responsible for the complete installation or repair and maintenance of the product. In the case of less sophisticated products, technicians may only be called in for advice or troubleshooting or for handling the most difficult tasks, leaving routine installation and maintenance to other company installers, repairers, or to the customer. Technicians trained in the areas of repair, maintenance, and installation often work as instructors training customers or company personnel in the more routine aspects of these activities. They may also work as technical writers preparing installation instructions and repair manuals for a specific product.

Some technicians who are particularly knowledgeable about a product or some aspect of a product become involved with briefing sales personnel about the product, its improvements over preceding models, and other special attributes that may make it attractive to buyers.

Technicians who are good at writing may help put together sales brochures, prepare press releases, or write articles for magazines or scientific journals.

Because of this wide range of activities in which technicians are involved, the educational or personal requirements that they must meet for entry into a given field or for advancement within a field will vary from industry to industry and from company to company. In general, however, employers prefer applicants who have had some specialized technical training. Most technicians need to have the ability to apply college-level algebra, analytical geometry, trigonometry, and logarithms to their practical work; and, in general, they should be able to demonstrate some mastery of a subject in at least one specialized field.

Many types of institutions offer training of a technical nature, but high-school students should concentrate first on establishing a solid background in mathematics, science (preferably through chemistry and physics), mechanical drawing, and machine shop. They should also concentrate on developing their ability to write simply and effectively and to speak clearly.

Students preparing for training as technicians will have hundreds of different institutions from which to select in the United States, all offering technical programs. These institutions range in nature from four-year degree-granting institutions offering technical programs to the large comprehensive or technical high school. The range includes junior and community colleges, university extension divisions, technical post–high-school institutes, and on-the-job training programs offered by industries or individual companies.

Technical institute curriculums are normally less rigid and standardized than are those of four-year colleges, and admissions requirements are often less strenuous. Students are normally required to be high-school graduates and to show ability in mathematics and sciences. Some schools will admit students without a high-school diploma if they are able to pass special examinations and demonstrate an ability to perform the necessary work. The major emphasis is on the development of the student's ability to use basic scientific, mathematical, and technical concepts and principles as applied to modern design, distribution, service, and production. Such preparation usually enables the student to adjust readily to specific jobs and to respond intelligently to any on-the-job training that may be offered. Such schools normally offer programs of either one, two, or three years in length, with two years being the usual training period. Some of these technical schools offer cooperative programs whereby the students spend part of their time in school and part in employment that is related to the occupation for which they are preparing. In these schools the length of time involved for the completion of the program is extended.

Many junior and community colleges also prepare students for technician occupations. Two years of post–high-school education is usually offered by these institutions and they often award an associate of arts degree upon the successful completion of the program. Although not all junior or community colleges are prepared to offer technical training at this time, many of them are accepting this responsibility as one of the primary charges placed on them by society and, more specifically, by the residents in the community in which the school is located and by the industrial-employment needs of the locality.

Many of these junior or community colleges offer night school programs designed for those people who are employed during daylight hours. The programs enable students to take courses in their particular technical field in addition to general education courses, including English and social and natural sciences. Technical programs offered through these colleges normally combine more general education courses in their technical curricula than do the technical schools.

Some large corporations offer on-the-job training programs to develop their own technical personnel. This type of training, of course, is strictly technical and incorporates no general education courses. The instruction includes formal classroom work combined with practical on-the-job training.

There are a number of technical training programs offered by the armed forces with many thousands of technicians being trained each year in the Army, Navy, Air Force, Marine Corps, and Coast Guard.

Technicians should have an aptitude for mathematics and science and the ability to do detailed work with care and accuracy. They should have good eyesight, manual dexterity, and form perception. Perhaps most importantly, they should have the persistence and tenacity to carry on when experiments or tests they are working on end in failure, as many experiments inevitably must.

Once students have secured their required education, their best method of entering a technical occupation will vary depending on the particular field they wish to enter.

One of the most reliable and accepted methods, however, is for technicians to seek employment opportunities through the institutions that gave them their training. Most of these institutions have student placement services and are in constant touch with those industries and agencies in need of technicians.

Another method of entering is through on-the-job training programs offered by various companies. Those people who successfully complete such training programs are usually assured of finding employment as technicians with the company giving them training.

One particularly successful variation of the on-the-job training program is the work-study program. Such programs are run by schools in cooperation with local agencies and businesses and offer students the opportunity to find part-time or summer employment in jobs related to the students' studies. Very often the part-time or summer employer will become the student's full-time employer following graduation.

Advancement in the technical fields is almost unlimited. Technicians usually begin work under the direct and constant supervision of an experienced technician, scientist, or engineer. Then, as they gain experience, they are given more responsible assignments, often carrying out particular work programs under only very general supervision.

From there, technicians may move into supervisory positions, and those with exceptional ability can sometimes qualify for professional positions after receiving additional training. In general, technicians can advance by going to a higher-level technician's job, earning a supervisory post, or advancing to the professional ranks.

Promotion will usually depend upon the acquisition of additional training, as well as on-the-job performance. Those technicians who fail to obtain additional training may be limited in advancement possibilities.

Salaries for engineering and science technicians vary considerably, depending upon the individual's education, experience, area of specialization, type of employer, and the geographical location of his or her job.

In general, those technicians, such as biological technicians or mathematical technicians, who are involved principally with scientific research earn slightly less than technicians such as civil engineering technicians or industrial-engineering technicians, who are involved with industrial, engineering, or applied technologies. For example, in the late 1980s most science technicians who had graduated from two-year technical training programs earned salaries between $16,000 and $30,000 a year and averaged approximately $22,000 a year, while most engineering technicians with similar training earned between $18,000 and $30,000 per year and averaged $25,000 per year.

Starting salaries for most engineering and science technicians are about the same, ranging from around $12,000 a year to around $15,000 a year. Top salaries for senior engineering and science technicians can sometimes reach as much as $37,000 to $50,000 a year or more.

Working conditions for technicians vary according to the type of work they are engaged in. Some work in clean, well-ventilated laboratories or offices conducting scientific tests or preparing layouts. Others may work in plants on an actual production line where conditions are not as good. Some technicians are occasionally exposed to safety or health hazards from equipment or materials. The work, however, is generally performed in clean, modern surroundings.

The work of engineering and science technicians may range from uncomplicated, routine tasks to those that are highly complex and challenging. Some workers who are trained in this field may resent the more repetitive aspects of their jobs, while others may find repetition a welcome relief from their more demanding technical duties.

Technicians often serve as intermediaries between professionally trained scientists or engineers and skilled craft workers. Some technicians may feel uncomfortable in this position, but many enjoy the rewards and challenges that come with it.

The employment outlook for engineering and science technicians is generally expected to be favorable through the 1990s. As commercial and industrial products and the manufacturing methods by which they are made become more complex, an increasing number of technicians will be needed to assist engineers in such activities as production planning, maintaining liaison between production and engineering departments, and technical sales work. The trend toward further automation of industrial processes and the growing importance of environmental protection will add to the demand for technicians. In addition, many companies are developing or expanding their research and development departments. Technicians will be needed to assist the engineers and scientists in these departments.

Employment of engineering and science technicians is dependent to some degree on the general level of economic activity. During a recession, for instance, fewer technicians are hired and some are even laid off, as there is a slackening in research and development activity, in new product design, and in other engineering and scientific activities. Few economists are predicting a severe recession in the near future; however, some economic downturns are possible within an overall pattern of slow growth through the end of the century. While there may be some dislocations for some technicians, this is an economic picture that should be generally favorable for engineering and science technicians.

Looking ahead through the decade of the 1990s, some economists predict that the best employment prospects will be in the fields of computers and data processing, medical equipment, aerospace, and instrumentation; the weakest prospects may be in telecommunications, steel, and motor vehicles. Prospective technicians should be aware of such predictions but should not be overly influenced by them. These are just predictions, and they may turn out to be wrong. All industries will need to hire new technicians to replace those who are retiring or leaving their jobs for other reasons. In addition, almost all industries are facing the need to make changes and innovations either because of new technologies or changing regulations having to do with the environment or job safety, and implementing changes such as these often creates the need for more technically trained workers. Because of all these factors, well-trained engineering or science technicians—especially those who are flexible about geographical location and certain other job conditions—should be able to find employment in almost any industry that interests them.

For students interested in learning more about these fields, there are a number of possibilities for exploration of various job settings in which technicians are employed. Visits to industrial laboratories or manufacturing companies can provide perhaps one of the most vivid means of exploration. Through such visits, one is able to witness technicians actually involved in their work, and it may be possible to speak with several of these people regarding their work or with their employers about opportunities for technicians in that industry or company.

Students should also consider finding part-time or summer employment in a company or other organization that employs technicians. Even the most menial of tasks will offer opportunities to learn more about the field and will demonstrate interest to potential future employers.

Another possibility involves putting together a list of schools offering technical training and writing to a selected group of them requesting catalogs and other information regarding their programs.

Finally, taking shop courses, drafting courses, and science courses with laboratory sections opens opportunities for students to develop technical skills and to assess their own interests and aptitudes for technical work.

This overview has attempted to explain the work of engineering and science technicians in the most general terms. The capsule summaries and the longer articles that follow treat specific kinds of work that engineering and science technicians may become involved in. The capsule summaries focus mainly on the nature of the work the technicians will do. For the most part, statements in this overview section concerning requirements, methods of entering, advancement, earnings, and working conditions apply to the kinds of technicians' jobs described in the capsule summaries. In the case of technicians' jobs described in the longer articles, each of these topics is discussed separately for each kind of technician.

Air-conditioning, heating, and refrigeration technicians

Definition

Air-conditioning, heating, and refrigeration technicians work on systems that control the temperature, humidity, and air quality of enclosed environments. They participate in the design, manufacturing, installation, and maintenance of climate-control equipment. They usually assist engineering personnel and often specialize in one phase such as refrigeration, although some technicians specialize in balancing heating, cooling, and ventilating systems to meet total performance standards in building designs.

The tasks that air-conditioning, heating, and refrigeration technicians may perform include planning the requirements for the various stages of fabricating, installing, and servicing climate-control and refrigeration systems; recommending appropriate equipment to meet specified needs, based on their familiarity with supplier catalogs and technical data; and calculating heating and cooling capacities of proposed equipment units. These technicians may also work with estimating cost factors; preparing layouts and drawings for fabricating parts and assembling systems; and fabricating nonstandard parts. Air-conditioning, heating, and refrigeration technicians are also involved in installing test apparatus on the customer's premises, then analyzing and reporting test data to be used in fine-tuning the planned system; installing systems for customers; testing for compliance with codes and contract specifications; and diagnosing problems in systems under service contract so that they may be repaired by service personnel.

History

Many years ago it was considered a luxury for a home to have a mechanical refrigerator and central heating, or for a business to provide air-conditioning for its employees and customers. Now, as our expectations for comfort and convenience have changed vastly, such things are often considered necessities.

Naturally occurring ice, cut and stored for later use, was the usual source of refrigeration until the early twentieth century. The first experiments with artificial refrigeration began nearly 200 years before, but it was not until the mid-1800s that the principles on which mechanical refrigerators operate were understood. In 1842, Dr. John Gorrie invented a cold-air machine to relieve the suffering of yellow fever patients in an Apalachicola, Florida, hospital. After the Civil War a number of companies using ammonia-absorption machines established artificial ice-making plants in the southern states.

During the early part of this century, progress in mechanical refrigeration consisted largely of advances in refrigerants, the working fluids of refrigeration and air-conditioning systems. As these substances are cycled through refrigeration equipment, they change back and forth from a liquid to a gas and from a gas to a liquid. As these changes take place, the refrigerants alternately absorb and release heat. In this way they are able to transfer heat from an area to be cooled and release it elsewhere. Although commercial electric refrigerators had first appeared in the 1920s, it was not until the discovery of Freon 12, a safe refrigerant, that refrigerators became common. Today, modern equipment utilizes a wide variety of synthetic refrigerants depending on the cooling job to be done and the types of evaporators, condensers, and compressors in the system.

Since the 1960s thermoelectric refrigeration has been developed for some industrial uses. This technique relies on semiconductor materials and their unusual properties, rather than heat exchange with refrigerants or very cold substances such as dry ice or liquid nitrogen.

The ancient Greeks and Romans built buildings with central heating and ventilation systems, but the knowledge of their methods was lost during the Dark Ages in Europe. During the Industrial Revolution, piped steam heating began to appear in factories, churches, assembly halls, and other large buildings. The uncomfortable drying effect steam heat had on air quality led, around 1830, to the introduction of piped hot water heating, which does not rely on such high temperatures. Ventilation for comfort and health became a greater problem as buildings were designed to hold more people, and various arrangements were devised to combine heating with circulation of fresh air.

The scientific study of air-conditioning, including the regulation of the moisture content of the air, received a big boost in 1911 when Willis Carrier, an American inventor, published the results of years of his research. Air-conditioning was developed initially for industrial applications, particularly in textile mills. By 1930 or so, it was becoming common in stores, theaters, and other large buildings.

Initially, the equipment for air-conditioning, heating, and refrigeration systems was simple, with limited capacity to heat, cool, and regulate air quality. The skills needed to maintain such equipment were comparatively easy to learn. Most technicians and mechanics for this early equipment were trained by manufacturers and distributors. But as the field has expanded over the years and the equipment has become much more sophisticated, workers have had to acquire more and more specialized knowledge and skills. Broad instruction is now frequently provided at public and private schools and by trade associations. The activities of today's technicians are diverse, reflecting the differences among the various branches that have grown to maturity in the industry.

Nature of the work

Many industries have come to depend on carefully controlled temperature and humidity conditions during some stages of manufacturing, transporting, or storing their products. Many common foods are readily available only because of extensive refrigeration. Less obvious is the fact that numerous chemicals, drugs, explosives, oil, and other products needed by our society must be produced utilizing refrigeration processes. Some computers need to be kept in a certain temperature and humidity; spacecraft must be able to withstand great heat on the sun side and great cold on the dark side while maintaining a steady internal environment; the air in tractor trailer cabs must be regulated so that truck drivers can spend long hours behind the wheel in maximum comfort and safety. Each of these applications represents a different segment of a large and very diverse industry.

Most air-conditioning, heating, and refrigeration technicians are employed by either a manufacturer of environmental control equipment; a distributor, dealer, or contractor who markets, installs, and services equipment; or a firm concerned with air-conditioning, heating, and refrigeration among various other allied fields—for example, a consulting engineering firm, a gas or electric utility, or a building contractor.

Technicians employed by a manufacturer generally work in research or engineering departments. If they work in a research laboratory, for example, they may conduct operational tests on experimental models and efficiency tests on new units coming off the production lines. They might also investigate the causes of breakdowns reported by customers, determining reasons for failure and possible corrective measures.

Engineering-oriented technicians employed by manufacturers often work with design engineers. They may perform tests that are needed for final adjustments in designs of new equipment, or they may assist engineers in fundamental research and development, technical report writing, and application engineering. Other engineering technicians serve as liaison representatives, coordinating design engineering and production engineering in the development and manufacture of new products.

Manufacturers may also employ technicians as sales representatives who call on distributors and dealers handling the manufacturer's line of equipment. Technicians in this kind of position must have a thorough knowledge of their products. They may explain newly developed equipment, ideas, and principles, and assist dealers and distributors in layout and installation design utilizing the unfamiliar components.

Dealers and distributors, the second major category of employer, also offer opportunities for technicians to become sales workers. In general, such technicians contact prospective buyers and help them plan air-conditioning, heating, and refrigeration systems, select appropriate equipment, and estimate costs. Employed by a dealer, a technician probably would work with individual customers; employed by a distributor, he or she might usually provide information and assistance to dealers, contractors, and other quantity purchasers. Dealers sometimes hire technicians who are assigned to prepare estimates and designs for customers but who are not directly involved in selling.

Technicians may also become service representatives for dealers and distributors. For a dealer, this is likely to include installing new equipment, maintaining customers' existing units, and troubleshooting problems. Working in a distributor's service department, a technician would often be called on to assist dealers and contractors with their more difficult service problems. Finally, some technicians may work

This air-conditioning and heating technician is inspecting a system that he recently installed. The system is designed for an large apartment complex.

for contractors who only do installation and service work.

Firms with activities in allied or associated fields, the third category of employer, can furnish numerous excellent opportunities, particularly for technicians with specialized training. A consulting engineering firm, for example, may need a technician who can determine heating and cooling load requirements, select equipment, design distribution systems, draw necessary plans, and help in the preparation of specifications for varying kinds of projects. Certain types of building contractors, such as mechanical contractors, may utilize technicians to estimate costs of climate-control installations, select fittings and equipment, coordinate and help to supervise workers in various building trades, and check out the completed system.

Firms that manufacture controlling devices for climate-control systems—that is, the instruments and systems that monitor and regulate the actual heating and cooling equipment—may hire technicians to work in development and design, production, application engineering, and testing control equipment for strength and accuracy.

A final example of an allied employer is a gas or electric utility company that uses technicians as promotion representatives, working with dealers who sell air-conditioning and heating equipment to the public.

An attraction of air-conditioning, heating, and refrigeration technology since the beginnings of the industry is the possibility it offers of opening an independent business. Many technicians have drawn on their technical skills and experience, plus other qualities and resources, and successfully established themselves as entrepreneurs. Sometimes a new enterprise for selling air-conditioning, heating, and refrigeration equipment is formed as an outgrowth of a general appliance store. The service and maintenance end of the industry also provides good opportunities for a knowledgeable technician who seeks independence. Frequently such businesses develop to combine marketing parts and supplies as well as service directly to consumers.

Requirements

The requirements for becoming an air-conditioning, heating, and refrigeration technician vary with the area of the industry. In general, the successful technician must fill the gap between the skilled craft worker and the engineer, and must have some of the abilities of each. Manipulative skill and dexterity in handling equipment is needed, particularly for individuals who specialize in installation and servicing. The ability to diagnose problems by assessing indicators that the equipment presents is another requirement. Although this skill seems to come naturally to some people, it can also be fostered and developed through practice.

An acquaintance with the theoretical approaches and the principles of engineering is a necessity, especially for technicians who must explain the functioning of equipment or assist engineers in research and design activities. Some mathematical background and a tolerance for working with figures are vital, as is the ability to read blueprints, building drawings, and electrical diagrams. In many specializations within the industry, the rapid pace of change means that technicians must be able to read, comprehend, and make use of current periodicals and publications in the field. They also must be able to write reports, both formal and informal, that are concise and complete descriptions of tests, experiments, and research.

Technicians increasingly need good computer skills, as more air-conditioning, heating, and refrigeration systems and components are being installed with microcomputer controls.

In high school, a student considering air-conditioning, heating, and refrigeration technology as a career should take at least one year of physics and two years of mathematics, including two years of algebra or one year each of algebra and geometry. If possible, students should also include courses in engineering drawing, blueprint reading, and metal shop. Courses in using computers and English courses, especially those that provide composition and communication skills, are particularly important to the prospective technician.

A high-school diploma is always a prerequisite for admission to college-level programs and technical institutes. It is nearly always required for entrance into the various educational programs that manufacturers operate to train employees.

Employers of air-conditioning, heating, and refrigeration technicians generally prefer them to have graduated from a two-year applications-oriented training program. This kind of training includes a strong background in mathematical and engineering theory. However, the emphasis is on the practical uses of such theories, not on explorations of their origins and development, such as one finds in engineering programs.

In addition to technical courses, the subjects a student can expect to cover in a two-year air-conditioning, heating, and refrigeration technical program include advanced algebra, trigonometry, physics, English and technical writing, and perhaps industrial orientation.

Special requirements

For the most part, no special licensing or certification is required for air-conditioning, heating, and refrigeration technicians. In some areas of the field—for example, among technicians who work with design and research engineers—certification is increasingly the norm and viewed as a basic indicator of competence. Even where there are no firm requirements, it is generally better to be qualified for whatever license or certification is available.

In some parts of the United States there are local requirements for certification. It is possible that in the future state or federal requirements will be instituted for technicians working in certain phases of the environmental control industry.

In some jobs, technicians may be required to join a union.

Opportunities for experience and exploration

A student trying to decide on the appropriateness of a career in air-conditioning, heating, and refrigeration technology may have to base the choice on a variety of indirect evidence. Part-time or summer work in the field is usually not available to students because of their lack of necessary skills and knowledge. It may be possible, however, to arrange field trips to service shops, companies that develop and produce heating and cooling equipment, or other firms concerned with the environmental control field. Such visits can give the student a firsthand overview of the day-to-day work. A visit with a local air-conditioning, heating, and refrigeration contractor or to a school that conducts an air-conditioning, heating, and refrigeration technology training program can also be very helpful. Some individuals have been exposed to the field while serving in the armed forces and have pursued further training on returning to civilian life. Prospective technicians may also contact heating and refrigeration associations, such as those listed at the end of this article, which will send information about how to get started in this field.

An important way of testing interest in the occupation is through relevant high-school courses such as physics, mathematics, mechanical drawing, and shop work. The student who dislikes the theoretical aspects of science is likely to be at a disadvantage, because technical training programs, as well as most jobs in the field, generally require understanding of air-conditioning, heating, and refrigeration theory.

Methods of entering

Many students in two-year programs work during the summer between the first and second years at a job related to their area of training. Employers of these students may hire them on a part-time basis during the second year and may make offers of full-time employment after graduation. Even if such a job offer cannot be made, the employer may be aware of other companies that are hiring and help the student with suggestions and recommendations, provided the student's work record is good.

An air-conditioning, heating, and refrigeration technician repairs a cooling unit. Such work requires manual skill.

Some schools make on-the-job training part of the curriculum. Students can thus get practical experience in conjunction with classroom work, particularly during the latter part of their program.

It is not unusual for graduates of two-year programs to receive several offers of employment, either from contacts they have made themselves or from companies that routinely recruit new graduates. Regular interview periods are scheduled at some schools by representatives of larger companies. Other, usually smaller, prospective employers may contact faculty advisors who in turn make students aware of opportunities that arise.

In addition to utilizing the job-placement services that are made available through the technical training school, a resourceful person can independently explore other leads by responding to want ads in local papers and contacting manufacturers and contractors or the state employment service.

Finally, student membership in the local chapter of a trade association, such as one of those listed at the end of this article, will often result in good employment contacts.

Advancement

On-the-job experience is one route to increased reward and responsibility, but additional formal education, particularly at night school or trade-association training courses, helps to open up opportunities more rapidly. Technicians increase their value to their employers

113

and themselves with continued training. For example, a technician employed by a manufacturer may progress to the position of sales manager, who acts as liaison with distributors and dealers, promoting and selling the manufacturer's products, or to field service representative, who sees to it that the unusual service problems of dealers and distributors in the area are solved. Or the technician may specialize increasingly in research and development, eventually designing some components of new systems, solving complicated problems in the design or testing of existing systems, and selecting replacements for obsolete equipment.

Similar kinds of career growth and development paths are possible in most technical careers depending on the individual's inclination and the type of employer. Working for a dealer or distributor, advancement could mean promotion to a service manager position, in charge of the personnel who install and service equipment. Another possible specialization is mechanical design, which involves designing piping, duct work, controls, and the overall distribution systems for consulting engineers, mechanical contractors, distributors, or even manufacturers. And, as mentioned earlier, advancement may mean setting up a separate business to sell some combination of skills and parts directly to the consumer.

Employment outlook

Employment in the air-conditioning, heating, and refrigeration field is expected to increase about as fast as or faster than the average for all occupations through the 1990s. Some openings will occur because of experienced workers retiring or transferring to other work. Other openings will be generated as more climate-control systems are installed in new and existing buildings and as old applications for the technology are expanded and new ones developed.

Comfort is only one of the major reasons for environmental control. Conditioned atmosphere is a necessity in any precision industry where temperature and humidity can affect fine tolerances. As products and processes become more complex and more highly automated, the need for closely controlled conditions becomes increasingly important. For example, electronics manufacturers must keep the air bone-dry for many parts of their production processes to prevent damage to parts and to maintain nonconductivity. Pharmaceutical and food manufacturers rely on pure, dirt-free air. High-speed multicolor printing requires temperature

control of rollers and moisture control of the paper racing through the presses. There is every reason to expect that these and other sophisticated industries will rely more and more in the coming years on precision control of production conditions. The actual amount of growth of such industries and thus demand for technicians will be generally related to the overall health of the nation's economy.

Employment levels for technicians involved with service and repair of climate-control equipment is generally less sensitive to economic downturns, because the need to service and repair equipment already in place is independent of economic conditions.

Despite recent moderation in the cost of some energy sources, a general interest in energy conservation does appear to persist in this country. Because of this, installation of more energy-efficient air-conditioning and heating systems in existing buildings should be a spur to future growth in the industry.

Earnings

The earnings of air-conditioning, heating, and refrigeration technicians vary widely according to the level of training and experience, the nature of their work, type of employer, region of the country, and other factors. In private industry the average beginning salary for air-conditioning, heating, and refrigeration technicians who have completed a two-year post-secondary–school program is around $14,000. Salaries for all air-conditioning, heating, and refrigeration technicians, including those with several years' experience, usually fall between $20,000 and $30,000 and average around $25,000 a year.

Conditions of work

The nature of the working conditions for air-conditioning, heating, and refrigeration technicians varies considerably depending on the area of the industry in which they work. For the most part, the hours are regular, although certain jobs in production may involve shift work, and service technicians may have to be on call some evenings and weekends to handle emergency repairs. In laboratories or industrial plants and at construction sites, training in safety aspects of the work minimizes any dangers associated with the mechanical and electrical equipment that is part of the job. Those technicians employed by distributors, dealers, and consulting engineers usually work in an office or similar surroundings and are subject to the same benefits and conditions as other office workers. Some types of technicians—sales representatives or service managers, for example—usually go out periodically to visit customers or to installation and service sites.

Technicians performing maintenance and repair work in the field may encounter extremes of temperature, when servicing outdoor or rooftop equipment, and cramped quarters, when servicing indoor commercial or industrial equipment.

Social and psychological factors

The social and psychological factors involved in a career in air-conditioning, heating, and refrigeration technology vary according to the area of the industry in which the technician is employed. Technicians who spend most of their time at a desk preparing drawings or estimates must be able to tolerate a great deal of detailed paperwork, a quality not required in so great a degree by technicians who work for mechanical contractors, coordinating and helping to supervise workers in various trades. A technician in a research laboratory will need to feel much more at home with sophisticated testing equipment than will a technician working for the sales department of the same company.

Regardless of the area, the successful technician should be prepared to continue his or her education throughout the career span. Technicians in the newest and most advanced areas of the industry are often skilled people already employed in other branches of the industry who are offered positions that allow them to build on their backgrounds through learning new but related concepts.

GOE: 05.03.07, 05.05.09; SIC: 1711; SOC: 3713, 616

◇ SOURCES OF ADDITIONAL INFORMATION

Air-Conditioning and Refrigeration Institute
1501 Wilson Boulevard
Arlington, VA 22209

Air Conditioning Contractors of America
1513 16th Street, NW
Washington, DC 20036

Refrigerating Engineers and Technicians Association
111 East Wacker Drive, Suite 600
Chicago, IL 60601

American Society of Heating Refrigeration and Air-conditioning Engineers
1791 Tullie Circle, NE
Atlanta, GA 30329

Refrigeration Service Engineers Society
1666 Rand Road
Des Plaines, IL 60016

◇ RELATED ARTICLES

Volume 1: Construction; Engineering
Volume 2: Engineers
Volume 3: Air-conditioning, refrigeration, and heating mechanics; Appliance repairers; Construction workers; Service sales representatives
Volume 4: Architectural and building construction technicians; Energy-conservation technicians; Mechanical technicians; Solar collector technicians

Architectural and building construction technicians

Definition

Architectural and building construction technicians assist architects and engineers in planning and designing structures. Their work includes testing materials, building and inspecting structures, constructing models, transporting, storing, inspecting, and using construction materials, and dealing with contracts and specifications.

History

Historians often judge societies of the past by the beauty, permanence, and usefulness of their buildings. The architecture and construction of different times in history reflect the goals and ideals of the civilization itself. Time after time, the architectural forms and the buildings of the past have influenced what people built in eras that followed.

People working in the fields of architecture and construction have always begun with the basic human needs for housing and shelter. They provide homes, churches, schools, theaters, public buildings, industrial plants, and other needed buildings. These buildings are designed to be utilized by people for work, domestic life, recreation, worship, education, and government.

The building methods of modern architecture use hundreds of kinds of materials and many special construction procedures. They require highly trained technicians to assist the architects and the construction engineers. These technicians attend to many details of the work and help to ensure that no mistakes are made in the complex activities and processes involved in building safe, beautiful, and useful buildings.

Nature of the work

Architectural and building construction technicians help turn the architect's designs into the client's reality. Architectural technicians help architects design buildings. Building construction technicians help plan and control the de-

tails of building the structure. They inspect job sites and supervise construction crews; they check every step of construction with the blueprints and specifications. Building construction technicians make sure the materials are right, the dimensions correct, and that every feature of the structure is located correctly. They use surveying transits and laser beam devices to be sure floors are level and at the correct height. Building construction technicians also inspect construction progress and help appraise buildings. They may investigate for casualty insurance companies.

In general, architectural technology concerns the application of engineering principles to the design and planning of structures. Construction technology involves construction work itself. Thus, architectural technicians may perform more of their work inside the office at a desk or a drawing board. Construction technicians may expect to spend more of their time at the construction site.

Architectural and building construction technicians—like most skilled technicians—are members of a team working on a particular objective. Their activities vary greatly, and there is plenty of variety for an individual technician's talents. The buildings they are concerned with range from single-family compact homes, to factories, high-rise apartments, and tall office buildings with more than forty acres under a single roof. Architecture and construction also involve a challenging variety of materials, from conventional pine and hardwood lumber to plastics, fiberboards, ceramics, glass, cloth, and metals.

Architectural and building construction technicians work in many types of jobs. In very broad terms, architectural and building construction technicians work in five kinds of situations: architectural and engineering offices; construction companies and government agencies related to construction; building supply companies; plant engineering and operations departments; and government agencies engaged in building inspection, appraisal, and planning.

In architectural and engineering offices the technician assists professional staff members. For instance, in an architect's office the technician may help complete presentation drawings, calculate excavation cuts and fills, complete the architect's sketches, transform these sketches into working prints, and help prepare specifications.

Because the architect represents the owner of the building, an architectural technician may assist the architect in inspecting phases of construction, estimating percentages of completion, and making sure the construction is on schedule. Near the end of the work, the technician may assist in inspecting the structure for "sign-off" (acceptance by the owner), making certain that required corrections have been made and, for certain types of contracts, helping check the costs. In general, architectural technicians perform whatever tasks the architect can pass on to them.

The building construction technician employed by a construction company may work both in the office and at the job site, depending on what tasks need to be done. Large construction companies accept jobs within a radius of several hundred miles of their home office. A few very large construction companies contract for work overseas. The construction technician in such a company may expect to move from one job site to another as each job is completed.

The technician's duties in a construction company may range from entry-level jobs, such as materials checker or timekeeper, to construction supervisor for the entire job. The construction technician who acts as an inspector or supervisor carries heavy responsibilities requiring experience beyond schooling. The pay for such positions reflects the heavy responsibilities.

Some architectural and building construction technicians work in sales for building supply companies. As construction materials and methods become more complex and varied, only trained personnel can effectively sell such products. The construction supply salesperson should know product uses and limitations, building codes, deliveries, and methods of fitting deliveries into construction schedules. The salesperson should know permissible substitutions of materials and must understand construction methods.

Large manufacturing plant engineering and operations departments hire some technicians. Many large plants cannot afford to depend on outside companies for maintenance. These plants employ their own maintenance, renovation, and even new construction personnel in a department most often called plant engineering. Maintaining the wiring, plumbing, heating, and ventilating systems, as well as the building itself, calls for trained construction technicians to plan, supervise, and inspect. These technicians hold well-paid, responsible jobs.

An architectural and building construction technician confers with the supervisor of a construction site. The technician must make sure that the specified materials are being used and that the building is being constructed as planned.

Various levels of government also engage in architectural and construction work. Government agencies often regulate construction. The most common of government regulatory duties is developing and enforcing zoning and building codes. Cities and counties often employ either architectural or construction technicians as building inspectors and appraisers.

Architectural and building construction technicians may work in businesses quite different from those described above. For instance, some work as inspectors and adjustors for fire insurance companies. Some work for savings institutions and insurance companies that lend money to builders. Others work with real estate developers. Still others become purchasing agents. The variety of opportunities is large.

Other typical jobs suitable for architectural and building construction technicians are described in the following paragraphs:

Architect's assistants or *junior engineers* assist architects or engineers with writing specifica-

117

tions and making calculations for quantity estimates or with completing drawings.

Architectural drafters draw, sketch, and make models. A position like this is the most common starting position for architectural or building construction technicians.

Structural drafters or *detail checkers* perform the same duties as architectural drafters, except with more emphasis on concrete, steel, glass, or precast parts of buildings. They check architectural prints for dimensions, section views, and mechanical equipment lines. This position is best suited for an architectural technician.

Assistant plant engineers or *building supervisors* supervise personnel in plant maintenance, renovation, and minor new construction.

Architectural sales representatives, building supplies salespeople, or *manufacturer's representatives* call on architects and engineers to explain the use of materials and products. They may furnish specifications and shop drawings, materials take-offs (estimates of kinds and quantities of materials needed), and prices of materials.

Estimators or *assistant estimators* make or help make materials take-offs and estimates.

Requirements

The well-prepared technician should have a background broad enough for any of the five general areas listed in the preceding section. In order to obtain this background, technicians need to train in a formal post–high-school program in architectural or building construction technology. Vocational schools and technical institutes offer the best programs. Typically, such programs last two school years of full-time classes. Upon graduation, a student receives a certificate, a diploma, or an associate degree. A few technical colleges offer four-year degrees in architectural engineering technology. Graduates receive bachelor's degrees, and are sometimes called technologists to distinguish them from the two-year graduates.

Prospective technicians may wonder which of the two fields—architecture or construction—they should enter. In general, a person who enjoys mathematical calculations, drawing, and sketching buildings should prepare for architectural technology. The person who enjoys working in the open and watching structures take shape should consider building construction technology. Architecture deals more with computation, calculation, and abstract creation. Construction deals more with actual building and operation.

For most positions, architectural and building construction technicians should be in good health with no serious physical disabilities. For indoor work in architectural technology, technicians do not need to meet any physical requirements. But on many construction projects technicians must be physically able to visit the job site, ride construction hoists, and walk on scaffolding that might be several stories above the ground.

Like almost anyone planning a technical career, prospective architectural and building construction technicians should plan for the future while in high school. Skill in arithmetic and basic algebra is essential in architecture and in construction. Some skill in geometry and trigonometry is almost as essential. Courses in drawing will be useful even though the student must later take more drawing courses. Writing courses are also important, because technicians must make written and oral reports. To become technicians in this field, students must continue their education after graduation from high school.

Almost all schools that train architectural and building construction technicians require applicants to have one to two years of high-school algebra. Many require two years of algebra, a year of trigonometry or geometry, and one or two years of physical science, preferably physics with laboratory work. Schools may require applicants to have four years of high-school English and language skills courses.

During the last year of high school, students should take the standard college entrance examinations and aptitude tests required to enter the school of their choice.

If students wait too long to prepare to enter a technical school program, they may not meet the entrance requirements. These students must then find a school that offers noncredit remedial courses.

Programs in architectural and construction technology vary with the schools offering the programs; however, all such programs share one basic approach—a blend of theory presented in classroom lectures and outside reading with applied studies in labs and at field sites. All such programs have a clear purpose: to train a student in practical application of theoretical concepts. Programs in architectural technology usually include courses in architectural design and mathematics through calculus. Programs in construction technology usually include more courses in building practices and construction methods.

Typical courses offered in the first year of architectural and building construction technology include introductory architectural drawing, technical mathematics, applied physics, building materials and construction methods, communication skills, construction planning and control, and architectural history.

Second-year courses include architectural drawing and model building, elementary surveying, advanced architectural drawing, technical reporting, building service systems, contracts, codes, specifications and office practices, computer applications, general and industrial economics, and construction cost estimating.

The theoretical courses are especially important because they prepare the students with an understanding of the scientific principles underlying their work and the mathematics that support it. This base of understanding makes the technician able to understand changes in year-to-year practice on the job, and thus remain up to date.

Special requirements

Architectural and building construction technicians do not usually need any type of license. These technicians, however, often work and consult with licensed craft workers, such as plumbers and electricians. Construction technicians often must supervise skilled, licensed craft workers.

Even though licenses are not required, some technicians work toward licenses. For instance, some technicians take additional training, acquire the specified work experience, and pass the examination for licensed architects or land surveyors. Other technicians become certified engineering technicians. Such certification, even if not required on a job, represents professional achievement.

Architectural and building construction technicians may also, upon completion of the required years of service, take an examination for licensing as a licensed land surveyor. Successful completion of this examination enables technicians to operate their own surveying business.

Opportunities for experience and exploration

High-school students who are exploring their interest in becoming architectural and building construction technicians should talk to their counselors and teachers. Whenever possible, students should visit construction sites. If such visits can be in a school program, the teacher in charge can usually get someone on the job to explain his or her work. Sometimes high-school students can get summer work on construction jobs. This is one of the very best ways to learn what the work is all about.

Some post–high-school technical schools include cooperative programs where the student studies a few months and then works for pay with an architectural firm or construction company. This helps the student to learn the job and see why the theory taught in school is important. These programs often lead to a job with one of the employers upon graduation.

Methods of entering

Some people work their way into architectural or building construction technology by starting with no special education or training. They go from high school to an hourly routine architectural or construction job, such as a carpenter's helper. Eventually, they either work their way up in a skilled trade or they become technicians. This is the long hard way to become a technician, and often the study needed to learn the relevant science and theory never gets done.

The ideal way to find a job in architectural or building construction technology is to graduate from a recognized technical school, community college, or vocational program. These can be public or private. Employment managers and other recruiters regularly visit schools that offer programs in architectural or building technology. Graduates can usually choose from several job offers. Many students accept jobs weeks before they graduate and go to work soon after graduating.

Every good technical school offers placement help and counseling. Some schools continue to offer placement service to alumni who wish to change jobs. Graduating students may seek their own openings in addition to those offered through their school's placement office. These students apply directly to the employment offices of the companies for which they wish to work. Other students will have attended school under cooperative education programs. Such programs help the students pay their school expenses and give students valuable practical experience. Students who have worked in a cooperative program will often continue working with the same company after graduation.

Completion of a formal program in architectural or building construction technology qualifies a person for many beginning jobs as a technician. Some persons trained in architectural technology find work in construction.

Conversely, some persons originally trained in construction technology work in architectural offices. Students also should not limit their job searches to architectural firms and construction companies. As mentioned earlier in this article, building supply companies, industrial plant engineering departments, and some federal government agencies need well-trained technical personnel.

Advancement

New career possibilities open up as architectural and building construction technicians gain practical experience. A few technicians will eventually own their own contracting businesses; the very successful contractor or developer can become wealthy. Technicians who would rather work for someone else also advance with experience.

A few examples of the jobs held by experienced architectural and, particularly, building construction technicians are described in the following paragraphs:

Chief drafters or *job captains* supervise and plan the work of architectural or structural drafters. They also draft the more important projects.

Contractors operate their own construction businesses and may eventually become developers of houses, larger buildings, or other types of construction. This position requires financial resources as well as skill, ingenuity, and experience. *Field inspectors* represent contractors, clients, architects, or owners in checking construction work at various stages. They ensure compliance with the contract, working prints, specifications, and approved construction practices.

Building inspectors inspect buildings, proposed sites, property line placements, setbacks, and construction progress for a county or municipality.

Plant engineers assume responsibility for maintenance, repair, rehabilitation, or new construction of plant utility services. They may also have responsibility for large heating systems or boilers used in industrial processing. They supervise personnel in carrying out duties within their responsibility.

Surveyors set up corner stakes, batter boards, utility line stakes, and other markers for construction crews. This job is sometimes an entry-level job. Large construction projects, however, require very well-trained and experienced surveyors.

Employment outlook

Several factors ensure the future of architectural and building construction technicians. The population continues to increase and people still desire to own their own homes. There is a constant need to renovate and modernize offices and commercial buildings. People must have buildings in which to work and schools for their children. Older buildings must be replaced. Many cities, aided by state, federal, or private funds, are rebuilding whole sections.

Architectural and building construction technicians should become increasingly important employees for several reasons. First, the architectural and construction industry is adapting existing products, finding new products to use in building projects, and developing new ways to increase efficiency. Much of this work calls for the use of computers and other new approaches that require technicians' skills. Untrained or even semiskilled labor cannot contribute much to adoption of new techniques; a trained technician can. Second, many buildings must be made more energy-efficient and fireproof; many will be rebuilt entirely in years to come. This effort too will require the skills of trained technicians. Third, the development of new industries and the movement of companies from old plants in one part of the country to new plants in another is causing whole new communities to be built. This will increase the need for all kinds of architectural and building construction personnel, including technicians.

Earnings

Architectural and building construction technicians earn salaries comparable to those of most engineering technicians. They are usually salaried workers, not hourly wage earners. Beginning salaries for graduates of two-year technical programs range from approximately $12,000 to $18,000 a year and average around $14,000 to $15,000 a year. Graduates with more experience usually earn $20,000 to $30,000 a year and average around $25,000 a year. Some senior technicians earn as much as $37,000 a year or more. Technicians who start their own businesses or who take overseas jobs can often expect even higher pay.

Job benefits other than salary vary with the individual company. In general, large companies offer more benefits but less opportunity. Typical benefits for the construction industry include sick leave, paid vacations and holidays, and insurance. Some companies pay part or all of a technician's cost of additional schooling. In higher job levels, technicians may qualify for bonuses. Technicians do not usually receive extra pay for overtime; they often do receive compensatory time off to make up for overtime.

Employment in construction fluctuates with the season, the availability of mortgage money, labor problems, and other factors. Work fluctuation, however, affects hourly laborers much more than it affects technicians. Generally, a technician can expect steady career-type work, with less fear of layoffs than an hourly worker.

Conditions of work

Working conditions vary for these workers. The architectural technician who works inside an architectural or engineering office can expect working conditions as safe and comfortable as conditions in business and industry can be. Architectural offices are almost always clean, comfortable, and well lighted. An architectural technician can do much of the work seated at a desk or on a drawing stool.

Technicians' jobs on construction sites are generally as safe as the technicians make them. If safety precautions are followed, care is exercised on job sites, and a hard hat is worn on the job, the technician should be safer at work than at home. On the other hand, construction work is dangerous for the careless person. Probably the three greatest dangers are being struck by falling objects, working at heights, and failing to step carefully. Minor hazards also exist from snagging oneself on nails or other projections. Certain construction equipment is dangerous if improperly used. Technicians ordinarily will not actually operate these pieces of equipment, but they must pay attention when working near them. The careful technician should work a lifetime without injury. Working in a construction office away from the job site is of course as comfortable and safe as working in an architectural office.

On the job site, the architectural or building construction technician must dress for the weather. Until all walls are up, the work may go on in hot weather or cold, rain or shine. Generally, the materials being used will determine whether a crew works during certain weather conditions. For example, construction crews try to avoid pouring concrete in freezing weather or finishing roofing in rainy weather. But unless the work is in a warm climate, technicians on site must accept unpleasant weather. They must also wear work clothing for all weather conditions and often potentially dirty conditions.

Construction sites are usually cluttered in the early stages of the job. Construction technicians must cope with mud, dust, and trash. As the structure nears completion and cleanup, the site itself will be cleaner. Because of these job site conditions, architectural and building construction technicians usually dress less formally than do many other technicians. In fact, on many job sites, engineers, architects, technicians, and job supervisors may all be wearing khaki or blue work clothes. Technicians who always work inside will normally wear standard office attire.

Responsible companies furnish safety clothing or equipment such as hard hats. Sometimes companies furnish rubber boots, prescription-ground safety glasses, steel-toed shoes, and gloves. Technicians will almost always furnish their own regular clothing.

Technicians are not usually considered hourly laborers, but rather as members of a support team. They will ordinarily not be affiliated with a craft union.

Social and psychological factors

People who wish to become architectural or building construction technicians should enjoy seeing buildings being built. Every step of building, from initial sketches to turning the key in the front door, should fascinate them. Moreover, they should understand the social importance of architecture and building construction. Technicians who succeed see their career as more than a good living for themselves; they know that it fills one of society's most pressing needs.

In addition to appreciating the importance of construction as an activity, the successful technician must recognize and constantly strive for good workmanship. Architecture and construction should produce structures that meet the owners' or users' requirements, are properly designed and structurally sound, and are pleasing to look at and comfortable to occupy. Good workmanship provides all three of these specifications.

Good workmanship is especially important in architecture and building construction because of the product's life span. A typical homeowner, for instance, expects a house to last a lifetime. An industrial company will usually expect its plant to last at least thirty-five years. Thus, architectural or building construction technicians must uphold craftsmanship in both their work and the work of other employees that they supervise.

The architectural and the building construction technician also needs patience. An architectural technician may spend hours on a detailed estimate or days in aiding an architect in preparing working drawings. Such tasks demand a willingness to pay attention to details, to verify dimensions, or to check such apparently minor matters as window schedules and wiring plans. At the construction site, construction technicians must patiently make sure that every bit of work they do or supervise is according to specifications. They must watch for errors that would later be hard to correct—errors such as a course of brick off level or a joist with too much sag.

Both architectural and building construction technicians must have the ability to organize work. Most construction jobs require a planned or even computerized sequence. Technicians must visualize how the various stages fit with one another. Computers and planning will help in scheduling many large jobs. The architect, the contractor, and their technicians, however, must organize the work sequence and must constantly check it as the plan is carried out.

This technician career and jobs to which it leads bring the challenge of change. New methods, new materials, and new projects all bring an interesting variety of activities. Constant study to keep up with these changes is a necessary part of the career.

GOE: 05.01.07, 05.01.08; SIC: 8712; SOC: 3719, 6479

◇ **SOURCES OF ADDITIONAL INFORMATION**

Alliance of Women in Architecture
PO Box 5136
FDR Station
New York, NY 10022

American Institute of Building Design
1412 19th Street
Sacramento, CA 95814

American Society of Certified Engineering Technicians
PO Box 371474
El Paso, TX 79937

Associated General Contractors of America
1957 E Street, NW
Washington, DC 20006

National Architectural Accrediting Board
1735 New York Avenue, NW
Washington, DC 20006

National Institute for Architectural Education
30 West 22nd Street
New York, NY 10010

◇ **RELATED ARTICLES**

Volume 1: Engineers; Construction
Volume 2: Architects; Assessors and appraisers; Construction inspectors, government; Drafters; Engineers; Health and regulatory inspectors; Industrial designers; Labor union business agents
Volume 3: Boilermaking occupations; Bricklayers and stonemasons; Carpenters; Cement masons; Construction workers; Drywall installers and finishers; Electrical repairers; Electricians; Elevator installers and repairers; Glaziers; Lathers; Layout workers; Marble setters, tile setters, and terrazza workers; Painters and paperhangers; Plasterers; Plumbers; Roofers; Sheetmetal workers; Structural-steel workers; Welders
Volume 4: Air-conditioning, heating, and refrigeration techicians; CAD/CAM technicians; Civil engineering technicians; Drafting and design technicians; Industrial engineering technicians; Poured-concrete technicians; Welding technicians

Automotive cooling system technicians

Definition

Automotive cooling system technicians inspect and test automotive cooling systems, analyze system malfunctions, and estimate repair or replacement costs.

Nature of the work

Automotive cooling system technicians work with vacuum and pressure testing equipment to check hoses and radiators, and with electrical testing equipment such as voltmeters and ammeters to check electrical components. On the basis of their examination, they prepare estimates of repair costs for customers and may make recommendations about repair versus replacement on the basis of their experience and their examination of the system. Occasionally, especially in smaller repair facilities, they may also help perform the repairs using appropriate hand tools. They compile charges and, when the work has been completed and approved, send them to the billing department.

Requirements

Students who are interested in becoming cooling system technicians should take specialized automotive service training for at least two years past high school. This training is offered by many community colleges and technical schools and by some automotive manufacturers. Beyond basic study of automotive technology, the most useful courses will be in cooling systems and electrical systems. They should also receive training in mathematics through al-gebra and geometry and language training that allows them to read technical manuals and write reports with correct spelling, grammar, and punctuation. People who contemplate going into business for themselves eventually should also take courses in business management and accounting.

Conditions of work

The physical demands of this work are medium, involving occasional lifting of up to fifty pounds and frequent bending and reaching. Technicians need good manual dexterity, visual acuity, and hearing. They should be able to talk comfortably with strangers, as they will need to gather information from customers about their cars and explain test results and required repairs to them. Technicians work indoors in garage facilities and they usually work alone.

GOE: 05.05.09; SIC: 753; SOC: 6111

◇ **RELATED ARTICLES**

Volume 1: Automotives
Volume 2: Engineers
Volume 3: Air-conditioning, refrigeration, and heating mechanics; Automobile mechanics; Automobile-repair-service estimators; Diesel mechanics; Farm-equipment mechanics
Volume 4: Automotive, diesel, and gas turbine technicians; Automotive exhaust technicians

Automotive, diesel, and gas turbine technicians

Definition

Automotive, diesel, and gas turbine technicians help automotive engineers design, develop, maintain, and repair automotive equipment. They also maintain and repair all kinds of vehicles and equipment powered by gasoline, diesel, or turbine engines. These technicians also use and calibrate diagnostic and testing equipment.

History

The events leading to the development of combustion engines began when human beings discovered mechanical devices that made work, such as moving objects and people, easier or faster. Wheels and axles were used for vehicles such as carts, wagons, and carriages for thousands of years before the first century B.C., when the Romans discovered ball bearings and how to hitch a front axle to a wagon to provide flexible steering. Another milestone was reached by Hero of Alexandria, who developed the first crude steam engine in the first century A.D. However, it was only about 400 years ago that Leonardo da Vinci and other European machine designers discovered how to modify wheels into gears. Da Vinci envisioned an automobile powered by an engine and foresaw the principles of transmissions with gear ratios that would control power speeds. He also saw the need to use bearings to overcome friction.

In 1769, James Watt and Nicolas-Joseph Cugnot both built usable steam engines that were subsequently refined and applied to transportation, manufacturing, and other industrial uses. In England, France, and Germany, steam buses for transporting people became fairly common. One of the first buses was built in England by Sir Goldsworthy Gurney in 1829 and could carry eighteen people on a regular schedule from London to Bath, a distance of 170 kilometers. In time, the steam automobile evolved from such buses.

By the 1880s the basic principles of electricity were discovered and electric-motor-driven automobiles were developed and on the market. They were quiet and comfortable but never very important, because the batteries that drove the motors were too heavy and had to be recharged too often to be widely accepted.

By the early 1880s, engineers in Europe and the United States had learned enough about wheels, shafts, gears, steam cylinders, hydraulic pumps, and elementary electrical sparking devices to attempt to combine them into an automobile. Experience with steam-driven buses and other machines had taught them much that would apply to automobiles. Gasoline, kerosene, alcohol, and benzene were also available as cheap fuels for internal combustion engines.

The first successful high-compression engines grew out of the research of Daimler and Benz in Germany and Peugeot and Renault in France. Between 1885 and 1889 all produced engines and built automobiles. In the United States, Henry Ford, Eli Olds, and Frank Duryea were working on gasoline engines and automobile development. Wagons with engines were also developed, and the way was made clear for modern trucks to become the hauling vehicles of the twentieth century.

By the 1890s, the western world saw a need for better land transportation. The newly created automobiles promised unprecedented personal mobility if they could be made more powerful, less noisy, safer, more comfortable, and more dependable to operate. In the United States, there were thousands of people who lived on farms and in small cities. They needed a cheap way to travel from home to town or to larger cities; they needed trucks for hauling, especially for taking farm and forest products to market.

The jobs of automotive engineers and automotive technicians both came into being in the period between 1880 and 1910. In Europe and the United States, the fierce competition to develop faster, fancier, and cheaper automobiles caused many small companies to develop and produce successful automobiles.

The challenge to build automobiles that pleased the public and that could be sold at a price many people could afford brought to light the special genius of Henry Ford. He, along with engineers and technicians, designed, built, and marketed thousands of his first "Model A" Fords beginning in 1903. From 1903 until 1908, they designed and built 18 different models ("B" through "S") and finally their Model T, which was enormously successful. It was the first mass market car: simple, roomy, dependable, and very affordable. More than 15 million were built during the next two decades.

Worldwide automobile racing began in 1898, only a few years after the first autos were built. The competition to set records for the fastest automobile became a way for auto makers to prove the quality of their machines. Henry Ford personally drove his Model 999 to win the 1903 fastest car record at a speed of 147 kilometers per hour.

Their success in races popularized Ford cars and helped to sell them to a growing market. It also helped Ford designers and technicians to develop important new technology, such as use of alcohol fuel for racing cars.

The most important development Henry Ford brought to the auto industry was an efficient assembly-line production method for making his automobiles. His engineers and production technicians designed a carefully timed system for bringing parts together at assembly stations. These stations divided the work of assembling the car into separate simple steps. The system reduced the cost of the Model T Ford from $850 in 1908 to $380 in 1926. On October 31, 1925, more than 9,000 Model T's were completely assembled—a production record that stood for many years.

European and U.S. manufacturers continued to build more refined and more technologically complicated automobiles in the 1920s and 1930s. They developed better and more powerful engines, more sophisticated muffling designs, automatic gear-shifting transmissions, self-starters, electrical ignition, automatic speed controllers, supercharged engines, large luxury autos, and small sports cars. All were produced by higher and higher precision manufacturing and assembling technology.

In recent years, important changes have occurred that greatly affect the work of automotive technicians and the engineers and managers they support. In 1973, the Arab oil-producing nations stopped exporting petroleum to the West, then raised oil prices. This forced the U.S. auto industry to completely redesign for greater fuel efficiency.

Meanwhile, the Japanese and Western European automobiles had already been designed to be smaller, more fuel-efficient, and less air-polluting; large numbers of them were imported into the United States, causing serious unemployment among U.S. automobile workers. Both Japan and West Germany improved their automobile manufacturing and assembly operations by using modern robots and computer-aided manufacturing processes. Thus, for the first time, they became more efficient than U.S. automobile manufacturers.

The changes that forced U.S. automotive engineers, managers, and their technicians to redesign their automobiles and to develop computer-aided manufacturing processes have made important changes in the skills and knowledge automotive technicians must acquire. They have also sharply increased the demand for well-prepared technicians in the field.

Nature of the work

Automotive, diesel, and gas turbine technicians work in a great variety of industries and positions. They may be broadly grouped into five general categories: research and product development technicians, service and sales representatives, technicians in related fields, service or operator technicians, and manufacturing technicians.

Research and development technicians prepare engines or related equipment for testing. Most tests are standardized procedures that have been developed by engineers, and technicians are chiefly responsible for preparing the engine or unit for the tests. This often involves calibration and installation of various electronic, mechanical, and hydraulic instrumentation devices. The technician then conducts the test, records data, and reports the results.

Technicians who work as *service representatives* try to ensure that the customer receives the maximum performance from an engine. Service representatives employed in a tractor manufacturing company might diagnose poor performance in a tractor. Then they correct the problem and test the tractor to see that it is working properly. Finally, they report the problem to the research and development division. Service representatives also tell owners and dealers about new products, service techniques, and developments in maintenance.

Sales representatives use their understanding of engineering and their knowledge of the product to advise customers in buying the best kind of unit for their needs. A thorough understanding of the company's products plus the ability to apply mathematics and science principles to analyzing customer requirements are necessary in establishing confidence and rapport with the customer.

Automotive, diesel, and gas turbine technicians may serve a variety of industries in related technical positions. Some of these positions include *drafting and design technicians* in transportation and power companies, *safety engineers, service* and *sales engineers* for oil companies, and *insurance claims adjusters* with transportation insurance companies. In these

After completing an annual check up, an automotive technician tightens the bolts on a vehicle's engine.

positions the technician's practical understanding of automotive, diesel, or gas turbines provides the necessary background for the related type of technical work.

Automotive, diesel, and gas turbine technicians who work in service or operator capacities are mainly found in dealerships or wholesale distributors. They may be *service managers* for automotive, tractor, or engine dealers. This position requires technically competent personnel who can plan facilities and equipment, organize shop management, select and train personnel, develop a strong product sales program, and build good public relations. In addition, the service manager is often required to diagnose difficult problems related to the customer's automobile, truck, tractor, or heavy equipment. The service manager must be broadly prepared in electromechanical engineering principles and also must rely on a practical understanding of the equipment.

The demand for *high-performance-engine technicians* is primarily in automotive dealerships located in medium or large cities. These technicians are responsible for the maintenance and replacement of special components according to customer requirements. Frequently, this specialist may be requested to modify compression and horsepower ratios, injection or carburetor systems, fuels and lubricants, cam systems, computer control adjustments, and the like.

Present trends indicate that the *high-performance-engine technician* may become the most important staff member of the automotive service department. This specialist may advance into one of the many auto racing fields. The high-performance-engine technician is responsible for the reliable operation of the most sophisticated power plants in the automotive business. Critical analysis, dynamometer and balance testing, design, and retrofitting are the main responsibilities of this specialist. Generally, this technician guides the major operations of the racing team.

In the manufacturing plant, numerous jobs are available to technicians. They can work as *machine maintenance employees, machine operators, quality control personnel,* and *production supervisors.* Many firms will hire these technicians and start them in such positions, advancing them when they become more experienced or when openings become available.

Within these five broad areas, many automotive, diesel, and gas turbine technicians work principally at one specialized activity or with one specific kind of product. The following paragraphs describe some of these jobs, all of them open to entry-level technicians.

Utility technicians compare fuels by ratings on laboratory test engines. They determine the knock characteristics of motor fuels and compare diesel fuel on the basis of ignition delay. They also assist in tests to determine characteristics of lubricant deposits on engine parts.

Engineering testers in diesel engine manufacturing firms assist test engineers in recording data obtained from diesel engines running with different lubricating oils to determine performance and wear characteristics. They also learn to operate electric dynamometers and related instrumentation.

Safety and maintenance supervisors inspect trucks and tractor-trailers for safety equipment. They also control and keep individual maintenance records, expense reports, and special fuel reports.

Automotive field-test technicians work in manufacturing research and development. They prepare vehicles for road tests in field proving grounds. They also install various test instruments, operate the vehicle according to the test procedure, and record test data.

Associate research technicians prepare automotive and diesel test engines and related instruments for conducting fuel and fuel additive tests in the laboratory section of a petroleum company.

Engine test cell technicians prepare gas turbine and jet engines for operation in a test cell. They also install various test instruments to record certain information requested on the test request form and record the data obtained.

Lubrication sales technicians prepare lubricant and maintenance procedures and schedules for truck fleet operators, heavy construction equipment, road-building concerns, and manufacturing companies. They evaluate failures in equipment resulting from wear, improper lubrication, corrosion, and other problems. These technicians also test oils and grease and recommend changes in types of lubricants and maintenance procedures.

High-performance-engine technicians who work at dealerships analyze, test, and maintain new high-performance engines that are available to the public. Those who work in car-racing design, test, analyze, and maintain high-performance engines in the various auto racing fields. They also redesign and make special parts for better design and performance.

Requirements

To be successful in this field, technicians must be intensely interested in automotive, diesel, and gas turbine equipment. The ability to read well is an important requirement for a successful technician, because it is often necessary to refer to manuals and other instructions and to read to keep up with technological changes in automotive equipment. A sincere interest in the safety of others is a highly desirable trait that promotes efficiency, reliability, and pride of workmanship.

Above all, technicians must understand the science and mathematics that support their work. Although principles remain the same, materials and designs change. Technicians cannot keep up with changes in their field if they do not understand the underlying science and mathematics.

The best way for interested persons to prepare to be technicians in this field is to complete a formal postsecondary program. Most such programs take two years, although there are several four-year programs. It is possible to start as an unskilled worker with a high-school or equivalent education, but it is very difficult to get the necessary science background without a formal program. Certain branches of the Army, Navy, and Marines offer this type of training. In addition, a few apprenticeship programs are available, but most will not provide thorough preparation.

High-school students interested in working as automotive, diesel, and gas turbine technicians should prepare themselves for rigorous college-level programs. Students should gain as many language skills as possible in high school, but they should also expect to continue their language-skills training in the college-level program.

The student entering a technician training program should have completed at least two years of mathematics, preferably one year of algebra and one year of plane geometry. Completion of third-year mathematics is advisable. The student should have taken at least one year of a laboratory science, preferably physics or chemistry. Basic drafting, automotive, electrical, and metals courses are also very helpful. It is also necessary that the student develop the ability to work as a productive member of a team.

Because the real value of technicians to industry is their ability to apply an integrated science-math background, specialized skills, and technical knowledge to a practical situation, the aims of a technician training program are specific. Students are taught basic skills with hand and machine tools, diagnostic test equipment, measuring instruments, and recording devices. They learn the chemistry and physics that pertain to internal combustion engines used in the transportation and power-generation fields. They develop the ability to use mathematics in solving problems relating to testing, selection, and design. They master the technical knowledge and skills concerned with automotive, diesel, and gas turbine equipment.

First-year courses in a postsecondary program often include mathematics, English composition, engineering drawing, hydraulic and power brakes, basics of internal combustion engines, physics, instruments, measurement, basic electricity and electronics, alignment, balance and control, and gears and transmissions.

The second-year courses may include physics, sociology, circuit analysis and instrumentation, generators, alternators and regulators, internal combustion engines, economics, political science, engine technology, fuel systems, and digital or other computer controls. Some schools offer cooperative programs where students work for pay at an employer's place of business. These are excellent and realistic programs that provide valuable experience.

Physical requirements include good physical health, better than average hand-eye coordination, freedom from color blindness, good hearing, and the ability to work in a wide variety of conditions.

Special requirements

In most settings, automotive, diesel, and gas turbine technicians are not required by law to be licensed or certified; however, for some kinds of work, especially when it involves public vehicles, certification is required. In addition, dealerships often give preference to personnel who have certificates of special training from industry educational centers. Similarly, employers do not require employees to hold college degrees, but these are recognized as valuable records of educational preparation.

Opportunities for experience and exploration

High-school libraries and guidance offices, technical institutes, community colleges, and vocational schools can be good sources of information about this career. It is helpful to visit schools that offer technician training and to talk with students who are enrolled in the program. Visiting workplaces where these technicians are employed also helps interested students form an opinion about how suitable their own talents are for the work involved in this career.

Methods of entering

Many graduates of technical programs secure jobs during the last semester of school. Recruiters from automotive and diesel factories and automotive equipment dealers usually visit schools where these programs are offered. Although the more varied types of industries do not regularly recruit, students can still learn about job openings from their department heads, teachers, or placement officers. Graduating students may also apply directly to the personnel office of any auto, truck, or tractor dealership or to the many related industries.

Advancement

As automotive, diesel, and gas turbine technicians gain experience, they become more valuable to their employers. Some advance from associate or junior laboratory technicians to senior engineering technicians. Others are promoted from district representatives to supervisory positions at the regional or manufacturing level. Some examples of advanced technical positions are described in the following paragraphs.

Service managers in a dealership plan the automotive service department, select equipment, organize and manage the shop, select and train personnel, assist in diagnosing customer problems, and develop an effective service department.

Lubrication sales engineering supervisors supervise the work of a number of lubrication sales and service technicians. They also select and train new personnel.

Branch managers in a carburetor company estimate liquid petroleum gas conversion costs, compute fuel requirements for engines, and match carburetors and accessories to meet effi-

ciency requirements. They also take charge of all business records and the selection and training of sales and service personnel.

Design engineering technicians design specific engine parts for automotive and diesel trucks. Working under the direction of a design engineer, they calculate sizes, determine locations, select materials, and determine tolerances.

District sales engineering technicians promote new sales, conduct analyses of fuel and lubricant information for use in the field, and develop customer relations. They organize and teach short-term lubrication and maintenance schools for manufacturing and heavy equipment service and maintenance personnel.

Regional service managers in manufacturing service divisions call on automotive and truck dealerships. They assist them with customer complaints, warranties, company policy, and all problems concerned with service.

Factory service manager instructors organize and teach all phases of service procedures and new-product information to field service representatives. They also assist in the development of service bulletins and other service literature.

Senior product development technicians supervise diesel engine testing that is being conducted in engine dynamometer test cells. They check the accuracy of all data collected and make sure proper procedures are used in running the tests. They also gather data that pertains to the test and write reports.

Supervisors of field testing supervise the testing of new farm tractors and equipment under actual ranch or farm conditions. They supervise test procedures, installation and accuracy of instrumentation, and data recording.

Employment outlook

Modern industry, agriculture, and the military have all come to depend on flexible, efficient, and mobile-powered equipment. This equipment is used to help build highways, extract minerals from the earth, irrigate farms, propel tanks and weapons, and in hundreds of other ways. This continuing demand has created a need for technicians who can maintain, operate, and repair such equipment.

The worldwide competition for the automobile, truck, and light industrial automotive product markets is creating many opportunities for highly qualified technicians in the design of better, more fuel-efficient automotive machinery and for more cost-efficient production of the machines themselves.

Despite these favorable factors, persons interested in a career in automotive, diesel, and gas turbine technology should keep in mind that most jobs in this field are involved with manufacturing, and the outlook for many manufacturing industries in this country is somewhat uncertain. The employment figures in the automobile industry, for instance, have fallen from the levels reached during the 1970s and are not expected to return to those levels. On the other hand, one of the factors driving down employment in manufacturing is the movement toward more automation and greater productivity per employee. Technicians involved with this aspect of the industry should find a continuing demand for their skills.

Earnings

Graduates of automotive, diesel, and gas turbine programs in technical schools enter employment at salaries ranging around $15,000 to $20,000 per year; the average beginner's salary is often about $18,000. With three to five years of work and study on the job, the technician's earnings may increase to a range of $25,000 to over $30,000 per year. Further advancements often allow technicians with seven to ten years' experience to earn from $30,000 to more than $40,000 per year. This is especially true of technicians entering sales engineering positions who have increased their knowledge through additional specialized courses.

Technicians who are graduates of a two-year high-performance-engine technician curriculum, which is available in some new vocational and technical programs, have an earning potential of $25,000 to $30,000 per year to start. Top-rated technicians in the speedway racing circuit earn approximately $40,000 per year. Chief technicians on winning teams may earn $60,000 per year.

Benefits often include paid vacations and health and life insurance. Some employers will pay for additional education.

Conditions of work

The workplaces in the automotive field are so varied that technicians usually can find working conditions to suit their preferences. Design, test, and research and development technicians often work in engineering design departments or in laboratories. These working conditions are usually clean, comfortable, and well lighted, with regular working hours. Sometimes testing may require senior technicians who are supervising or managing the tests to put in longer hours, for which they may be paid extra or given time off.

The research and development laboratories of transportation and power industries normally maintain very high standards for cleanliness and safety. Equipment is usually well guarded to prevent accidents, and safety engineering staff are continually working to improve safety practices.

Field work in servicing or testing various kinds of equipment may be outdoors in all kinds of weather, for which special clothes may be needed. Field repair may involve physical labor when technicians must rig their own lifts. Resourcefulness and careful judgment must be exercised to make the work safe.

Social and psychological factors

Technicians in the automotive industry are key members of one of the largest industries in the world. They can feel lasting satisfaction in their careers. Their work directly benefits every industrial activity in the country and influences the lives of everyone. To do well in their jobs, these technicians must be disciplined, systematic, and analytical, and have careful work habits. They must understand every detail of every part, how all the parts work together, and what happens if parts are not assembled or working correctly. This requires constant study to keep up with new models of machines.

Technicians must be able to perform as team members. As they sometimes work alone, they also must be capable of working without supervision. Often their work includes supervising others, so they must be able to understand and work with people. These technicians perform important services and must be comfortable with assuming responsibility.

GOE: 05.05.09; SIC: 753; SOC: 6111

◇ **SOURCES OF ADDITIONAL INFORMATION**

Automotive Service Association
1901 Airport Freeway, Suite 100
PO Box 929
Bedford, TX 76095

Automotive Service Industry Association
444 North Michigan Avenue
Chicago, IL 60611

Motor and Equipment Manufacturers Association
PO Box 1638
300 Sylvan Avenue
Englewood Cliffs, NJ 07632

Motor Vehicle Manufacturers Association of the United States
7430 Second Avenue
Suite 300
Detroit, MI 48202

◇ **RELATED ARTICLES**

Volume 1: Automotives
Volume 3: Automobile mechanics; Automobile-repair-service estimators; Diesel mechanics; Farm-equipment mechanics; Mobile heavy equipment mechanics
Volume 4: Agricultural equipment technicians; Automotive cooling system technicians; Automotive exhaust technicians

Automotive exhaust technicians

Definition

This automotive exhaust technician inserts a testing probe into the exhaust pipe of a car. The probe will measure the amount of pollution that the car emits.

Automotive exhaust technicians conduct tests on automotive vehicles to check exhaust emissions. There are a variety of tests that an exhaust technician can administer. Thus, they must inspect the emissions systems in accordance with instructions relating to the particular tests to be performed.

Nature of the work

Typically, automotive exhaust technicians attach an emissions-testing machine to the exhaust system. They then start and run the engine according to the instructions, read the results that are displayed on the emissions-testing equipment, and compare them with the standards that the vehicle is supposed to meet. In this way, they test the effectiveness of the vehicle's emissions-control device, which may be a catalytic converter, exhaust-gas recirculation system, or fuel-injection system.

Automotive exhaust technicians are also responsible for maintaining the emissions testing equipment. In some cases, they diagnose and repair vehicle malfunctions relating to exhaust emissions. To do this, they drive the car onto a dynamometer, which measures the mechanical power produced by the engine, and they perform tests on the engine's timing and idle speeds, making adjustments as necessary. They also install or repair emissions control devices on the vehicles being tested.

Requirements

Automotive exhaust technicians need to have good manual dexterity and good vision. For the most part, they work indoors and should be able to tolerate the noisy working conditions that are sometimes created in engine shops. They need to be high-school graduates, and, in addition, they usually need to have graduated from a two-year training program after high school. They should be able to perform basic mathematical operations and calculate ratios and percentages with ease, and they should be able to read instruction manuals, fill in forms, write reports, and speak with the public. While in high school, students interested in this career should be sure to take science courses, especially those that include training in physics and chemistry. In addition, they should take courses in mathematics and shop, especially automobile shop and electrical shop. Courses that include training on computers and that increase reading skills are also valuable. The two-year training program after high school should include courses in gasoline-engine systems, automotive chemistry, and engine diagnosis and tune-up, as well as courses in language skills, mathematics, and general chemistry.

GOE: 05.05.09; SIC: 7533; SOC: 6681

◇ **RELATED ARTICLES**

Volume 1: Automotives
Volume 2: Engineers
Volume 3: Automobile mechanics; Automobile-repair-service estimators; Farm-equipment mechanics
Volume 4: Agricultural equipment technicians; Automotive cooling system technicians; Automotive, diesel, and gas turbine technicians

Avionics technicians

Definition

Avionics technicians inspect, test, adjust, and repair the electronic devices that are components of aircraft communication, navigation, and flight control systems. Avionics (a term formed by combining the words "aviation" and "electronics") is the application of electronics to the operation of aircraft, spacecraft, and missiles.

Avionics technicians also complete maintenance-and-overhaul documentation for the equipment they work on. They calibrate and adjust the frequencies of communications equipment when it is installed, and perform periodic checks on those frequency settings.

History

The field of avionics grew out of World War II applications of electronic equipment to the operation of military aircraft. As aircraft rapidly grew more complicated, the amount of electronic equipment needed for navigation and for monitoring equipment performance greatly increased. The World War II B-29 bomber carried several thousand avionic components; the B-52 of the Vietnam era carried 50,000; the B-58 supersonic bomber required more than 95,000 such components.

The development of large ballistic missiles during and after World War II and the rapid growth of the U.S. space program after 1958 resulted in even greater development of avionics technology. Large missiles and spacecraft require many more electronic components than even the largest and most sophisticated aircraft. Computerized guidance systems became especially important with the advent of manned space flights.

Avionics continues to be an important branch of aeronautical and astronautical engineering. The aerospace industry places great emphasis on research and development, assigning a much higher percentage of its trained technical personnel to this effort than is usual in industry. In addition, stringent safety regulations require constant surveillance of in-service equipment. For these reasons there is high demand for trained and experienced avionics technicians and engineers to help in the development of new satellites, spacecraft, aircraft, and their component electronic systems, and to maintain those in service.

Nature of the work

Avionics technicians assist avionics engineers in developing new electronic systems and components for aerospace use. They also adapt existing systems and components for application in new equipment. Most of their work, however, involves installing, testing, repairing, and maintaining navigation, communication, and control equipment in existing aircraft and spacecraft.

Using testing equipment, such as circuit analyzers and oscilloscopes, technicians test and replace such sophisticated equipment as transceivers and Doppler radar systems, as well as microphones, headsets, and other standard electronic communication equipment.

New equipment, once installed, must be tested and calibrated to prescribed specifications. Technicians also adjust the frequencies of radio sets and other communication equipment by signaling ground stations and then adjusting setscrews until the desired frequency has been achieved. Periodic maintenance checks and readjustments enable avionics technicians to keep equipment operating on proper frequencies. The technicians also complete and sign maintenance-and-overhaul documents recording the history of various equipment.

Avionics technicians involved in the design and testing of new equipment must take into account all the conditions under which the equipment will have to operate, determining its weight limitations, resistance to physical shock, atmospheric conditions it will have to withstand, and other factors. For some sophisticated projects, technicians will have to design and make their tools first, and then use them to construct and test new avionic components.

The range of equipment in the avionics field is so broad that technicians usually specialize in one area, such as radio equipment, radar, computerized guidance, or flight-control systems. New specializations are constantly opening up as new developments occur in avionics. The development of these new specializations requires avionics technicians to keep informed about their special fields, through reading technical articles and books and through attending seminars and taking courses in new developments, often sponsored and offered by manufacturers.

Avionics technicians usually work as part of a team, especially if involved in research and testing and the development of new products. They are often required to keep notes and records of their work and to write detailed reports.

Requirements

Avionics technicians must have completed a course of training at a post–high-school techni-

cal institute or community college that includes at least one year of electronics technician training. If not trained specifically in avionics, they should obtain a solid background in electronics theory and practice. Further training in specialty areas will be received on the job, where technicians will work with engineers and senior technicians until they are competent to work without direct supervision.

Larger corporations in the aerospace industry operate their own schools and training institutes. Such training rarely includes theoretical or general studies but concentrates on areas important to the company's functions. The armed forces also conduct excellent electronics and avionics training schools. Persons graduating from these schools are in high demand in industry after they leave the service.

Persons interested in pursuing a career in avionics should take high-school mathematics courses at least through solid geometry and preferably through calculus. They should develop language skills sufficient to enable them to read complex and detailed technical articles, books, and reports; to write technical reports; and to present those reports to groups of people when required.

Students who are thinking about this kind of work should also have an aptitude for science and mathematics. They will need to have good manual dexterity and mechanical aptitude and the temperament for exacting work.

Special requirements

Federal Communications Commission (FCC) regulations require that anyone who works with radio transmitting equipment has a restricted radiotelephone operator's license. Such a license is issued upon application to the FCC and is issued for life.

Opportunities for experience and exploration

It is possible to visit factories and test facilities where avionics technicians work as part of teams designing and testing new equipment. It is also possible to visit a large airfield where there are repair facilities in which avionics technicians inspect, maintain, and calibrate communications and control apparatus.

Useful information about avionics training

programs and career opportunities is available from trade and technical schools that offer such programs and from the armed forces. These organizations are always pleased to answer inquiries from prospective students or service personnel.

Methods of entering

No one should consider entering the field of avionics without first obtaining the necessary training in electronics. Following that training, the placement officer at your school can be of great help in locating prospective employers, arranging interviews, and advising about an employment search. Other possibilities are to contact an employment agency (many specialize in technical placement) or to approach a prospective employer directly.

Advancement

Avionics technicians usually begin their careers in trainee positions, until they are thoroughly familiar with the requirements and routines of their work. Having completed their "apprenticeships," they are usually assigned to work independently, with only minimal supervision, testing and repairing avionic equipment. The most experienced and able technicians go on to install new equipment and to work in research and development operations. Many senior technicians move into training, supervisory, and sales and customer relations positions.

Employment outlook

The aerospace industry as a whole is closely tied to government spending and to political change, as well as to downturns in the economy. The economy also affects the aircraft and airline industries strongly. The cancellation of one spacecraft program or a fall in airline travel that leads to employee cutbacks may throw a large number of avionics technicians out of work, making competition for the remaining jobs very keen.

On the positive side, avionics is an important and developing field for which there will be need through the foreseeable future, and for which more and more trained technicians will be required.

An avionics technician uses a microcircuit television microscope that enables him to make minute adjustments on miniaturized electronic circuits.

Earnings

Beginning avionics technicians earn about $15,000 to $18,000 a year. Experienced senior avionics technicians earn salaries that range from $20,000 to $30,000 a year. Average salaries for these experienced technicians are around $27,000, and sometimes go as high as $37,000 a year. Federal government employees (not including Armed Forces personnel) on the average earn slightly less than avionics technicians employed by private aerospace firms. Their jobs, on the other hand, have greater security.

Conditions of work

Avionics technicians work under pleasant indoor conditions. Their work requires little lifting or carrying of heavy objects but does require bending, kneeling, and manual dexterity. It also requires the ability to speak clearly, especially when testing communications equipment.

Social and psychological factors

The work of avionics technicians is very precise and requires a personality suited to meeting exact standards and to working within small tolerances. Technicians sometimes work in teams, cooperating closely with engineers and other technicians, and should have the ability to work with a team spirit of coordinated of effort.

GOE: 05.05.10; SIC: 4581; SOC: 6151

◇ **SOURCES OF ADDITIONAL INFORMATION**

Aerospace Education Association
1810 Michael Faraday Drive, Suite 101
Reston, VA 22090

Aerospace Industries Association of America
1250 I Street, NW
Washington, DC 20005

American Institute of Aeronautics and Astronautics
370 L'Enfant Promenade, SW
Washington, DC 20024

General Aviation Manufacturers Association
1400 K Street, NW, Suite 801
Washington, DC 20005

◇ **RELATED ARTICLES**

Volume 1: Aviation and Aerospace; Engineering
Volume 2: Astronauts; Pilots
Volume 3: Aircraft mechanics and engine specialists; Flight engineers
Volume 4: Aeronautical and aerospace technicians

Biological technicians

Definition

Biological technicians assist biologists by performing laboratory experiments on biological substances (blood, tissue, and the like) and living organisms (molds, fungi, and microscopic organisms). They gather and record data during experiments that enable biologists to draw conclusions about the functioning of organisms and to develop new products such as medications, food additives, insecticides, and fertilizers.

Nature of the work

Biological technicians may work with laboratory animals, insects, or microscopic organisms. They utilize a variety of laboratory techniques and equipment such as microscopes, chemical scales, and centrifuges. They ensure the integrity of experiments by carefully controlling the conditions under which they are performed. They record instrument readings and may analyze their data to indicate overall trends.

Some biological technicians are involved in the still small but exciting new area of biotechnology research. Biotechnology encompasses a number of different fields having to do with modifying organisms to meet some need, particularly in medicine, agriculture, or energy management. Genetic engineering is one such field. Biological technicians in this field help research scientists to transfer genetic material from one kind of animal, plant, or microorganism to another in order to create a slightly different organism. By transplanting specific genes, scientists can produce, for example, a breed of crop plant with better yields or improved resistance to insect infestations or to freezing temperatures.

Another field of biotechnology that may involve technicians is monoclonal antibody research. Technicians in this field work in laboratories where new kinds of antibodies are being created by cloning them from a single hybrid cell. Some biological technicians may also be involved with helping to set up the processes necessary to manufacture these new products for market.

Requirements

People interested in careers as biological technicians should take as many high-school science courses as possible, including biology, chemistry, and physiology. They should also have mathematics training through at least solid geometry and be familiar with and be able to use the elements of statistics. They should have at least an additional year of post–high-school training in biology, laboratory procedures, microbiology, and organic chemistry. They should have language skills developed sufficiently to enable them to read technical literature related to their work and to write detailed reports on their laboratory experiments and the resulting data.

In addition to biological training, technicians who work with animals should feel comfortable with the common laboratory animals, such as mice, rats, and guinea pigs.

Conditions of work

Biological technicians work primarily under pleasant laboratory conditions of controlled temperature and humidity. Some technicians, working with larger animals, may spend time in barns or other housing facilities. Some biological technicians work with live animal experimentation. This has come under some controversy in the past and may continue to be argued about for some time to come. Technicians need to reconcile themselves with the gains made in experimentation on animals to the protection of animals from harm.

The work of biological technicians is not very strenuous but does require lifting and

This biological technician is a member of an immunology research team. She is studying the effect of certain antibodies on various types of cancerous tumors in mice.

bending. It often also requires long hours at the microscope, which can lead to eyestrain.

GOE: 02.04.02; SIC: 8071; SOC: 382

◇ **RELATED ARTICLES**

Volume 1: Biological Sciences
Volume 2: Biochemists; Biologists; Biomedical engineers; Medical technologists
Volume 3: Agricultural scientists; Pharmaceutical industry workers
Volume 4: Animal health technicians; Animal production technicians; Biological specimen technicians; Biomedical equipment technicians; Chemical technicians; Farm crop production technicians; Medical laboratory technicians; Pharmacy technicians

Biological specimen technicians

Definition

Biological specimen technicians prepare specimens of plant and animal life for use as educational aids.

Nature of the work

Specimen technicians select the plant or animal specimen, which is usually in a preserved state; dissect the specimen, cleaning away all matter from skeletal or organ structures; and prepare slices or cross sections of small animals, embryos, or animal organs. They trim and stain flowers, leaves, and stalks to show plant structures and systems. They also select proper stains to indicate the supportive structures, circulatory systems, and other features of plants and animals.

As part of their work, biological specimen technicians may embed the plant or animal specimens in plastic. They assemble and position the components of the specimen in a plastic mold, mix the plastic or other material, and complete the embedding by various molding techniques. Biology specimen technicians are sometimes also involved in growing or raising the plant or animal life used for the specimens.

Requirements

Biological specimen technicians should plan on receiving two to four years of post–high-school training. During the course of their instruction, they should receive training in algebra and geometry. They should be able to read magazines, encyclopedias, and instructional materials for training in the use of tools and other equipment. They should also be able to write reports with proper spelling and punctuation, speak before small audiences, and understand mechanical drawings.

A biological specimen technician inspects a channel catfish for disease at the U.S. Fish and Wildlife Service's Catfish Farming Experimental Station.

Conditions of work

The work of biological specimen technicians is seldom physically strenuous and the working environment is usually safe and comfortable.

GOE: 02.04.02; SIC: 8071; SOC: 382

◇ **RELATED ARTICLES**

Volume 1: Biological Sciences
Volume 2: Biologists
Volume 4: Biological technicians; Medical laboratory technicians; Museum technicians

Calibration technicians

Definition

Calibration technicians, also known as *standards laboratory technicians,* work in the electronics industry and in aircraft and aerospace manufacturing. They test, calibrate, and repair electrical, mechanical, and electronic instruments used to measure and record voltage, heat, magnetic resonance, and other factors.

Nature of the work

Calibration technicians set up standardized laboratory equipment to test and measure the accuracy of instruments, and they plan the sequence of procedures for testing and calibrating instruments, using blueprints, schematic drawings, and other data. As part of their inspection of recording systems and measuring instruments, they measure parts for conformity to specifications, using micrometers, calipers, and other precision instruments, and they repair or replace parts, using jeweler's lathes, files, soldering irons, and other tools. They also assist engineering personnel in developing calibration standards, in devising formulas to solve problems in measurement and calibration, and in writing procedures and practical guides for other calibration technicians. Calibration tools are now so refined that surfaces can be measured to one-thousandth of an inch.

Requirements

Calibration technicians should be high-school graduates and should have attended a two-year post–high-school training program. During the course of their training, they should receive instruction in algebra, calculus, and statistics. They should develop their language skills to the point that they can read newspapers, manuals, and encyclopedias; write letters and re-

A calibration technician measures the strength of elastomer rubber by stretching it to its breaking point. He is testing the rubber to determine its practical use.

ports with proper spelling and punctuation; and express themselves clearly in informal conversation and in formal discussions.

Conditions of work

Calibration technicians work both indoors and outdoors and the physical demands connected with their work are generally light.

GOE: 02.04.01; SIC: 36; SOC: 3711

◇ RELATED ARTICLES

Volume 1: Aviation and Aerospace; Electronics; Engineering
Volume 2: Engineers
Volume 4: Aeronautical and aerospace technicians; Avionics technicians; Electronics technicians; Electronics test technicians

---

Chemical technicians

Definition

Chemical technicians assist chemists and chemical engineers in the development, testing, and manufacture of chemical products. Most chemical technicians are designated as being *chemical-laboratory technicians* or *chemical-engineering technicians*. In general, the distinction between these two careers is that the chemical-laboratory technician is more concerned with the laboratory testing that goes on during both the development and the manufacturing of chemical products. The chemical-engineering technician is more concerned with the actual manufacturing aspects of the product.

More specifically, chemical-laboratory technicians conduct tests to determine the chemical content, strength, stability, purity, and other characteristics of a wide range of materials, including ores, minerals, pollutants, and consumer products such as foods, drugs, plastics, dyes, paints, detergents, paper, and petroleum. Often this testing is done as part of a research and development program for new products and materials. The testing, however, may also be involved with a variety of other fields: establishing process and production methods; quality control; maintenance of health and safety standards; environmental testing; and other fields involving experimental, theoretical, or practical applications of chemistry and related sciences.

Chemical-engineering technicians work closely with chemical engineers to assist in developing and improving the processes and equipment used in chemical plants. They test experimental and operating equipment and instruments used in the manufacturing of chemicals and chemical products. They observe and record the performance and operating characteristics of the equipment and the processes involved to establish standard operating procedures and to recommend changes or modifications in the equipment or processes. To communicate their findings, they prepare tables, charts, sketches, diagrams, and flow charts that record and summarize the engineering data they have collected. Chemical-engineering technicians are also involved in building, installing, modifying, and maintaining chemical-processing equipment. Some chemical-engineering technicians observe, instruct, confer with, and direct the activities of equipment operators and other technical personnel.

While the chemical-laboratory technician is chiefly concerned with the characteristics of a product and the chemical-engineering technician chiefly concerned with the manufacture of the product, there are areas where their activities overlap. For instance, both chemical-laboratory and chemical-engineering technicians are concerned with new-product development and both must be aware of the goals and constraints of the other. In addition, both technicians often perform similar tasks, such as setting up testing apparatus and preparing chemical solutions for use in manufacturing or processing materials. Both chemical-laboratory and chemical-engineering technicians may also become involved with technical writing or selling chemicals or chemical products.

History

The modern science of chemistry has roots going back thousands of years to the earliest human efforts to extract medicinal juices from plants and to shape metals into tools and utensils for daily life. As late as the Middle Ages in Europe, chemistry (or alchemy, as it was then called) was concerned chiefly with the study of metals and the search for cures for diseases. Alchemy was a mixture of science and superstition and was a colorful chapter in the history of chemistry.

In the late eighteenth century, chemistry became established as a scientific discipline through the great discoveries of scientists such as Antoine Lavoisier, Henry Cavendish, and Amedeo Avogadro. Also during that century, the range of products in which chemistry and chemical processes were involved began to expand, chiefly due to the demands and discoveries created by the Industrial Revolution.

During the twentieth century, and especially following World War I, the pace of expansion in the application of chemical principles to human needs and problems rapidly increased to include the entire range of manufactured goods and consumer products such as gasoline, antifreeze, weed killers, water repellents, furniture polishes, and meat tenderizers.

This rapid expansion resulted in an increased need for professionally trained chemists and for assistant chemists who, with their combination of basic knowledge and manual skills, were able to handle many of the tasks and problems that did not require the special training of the professional chemist or chemical engineer. By handling these simpler tasks and problems, the assistant chemists increased the productivity of the chemist and chemical engineer, allowing them to concentrate their efforts on those problems requiring their special skills.

In time, these assistants became known as "technicians," and today the growing complexity of our industrial processes and the increase in emphasis on research and development in industry has led to a growing dependence upon these people in the chemical and chemical-related industries.

Nature of the work

Most chemical technicians are employed by the chemical industry, one of the largest industries in the United States. Many others work in the petroleum, aerospace, metals, electronics, automotive, and construction industries. Other chemical technicians are employed by educational institutions and government agencies.

The majority of chemical technicians perform work connected with one of four areas: research and development; design and production; quality control; and customer service. The first of these areas requires mostly the services of chemical-laboratory technicians; the second mostly requires chemical-engineering technicians. The third and fourth areas offer opportunities for both kinds of chemical technicians.

In research and development, chemical technicians help to create new chemical products and find new ways to make chemicals from different starting materials. They set up and conduct tests on chemical processes and products that are being developed or improved. Those helping with experiments take measurements, make computations, and tabulate and analyze the results. They may have to vary the conditions of the experiment—for instance, the concentration of a chemical solution, the temperature, or the pressure—until a satisfactory result is obtained. They may then analyze the product or yield of the experimental reaction to determine the quantities of each component by using both simple and quite complex equipment and procedures.

Chemical technicians in the design and production area, mostly chemical-engineering technicians, are concerned with planning the processes and designing and operating the equipment used to manufacture the product that has been developed in the research laboratories. They work with pipelines, valves,

This chemical technician is performing routine laboratory tasks so that scientists may turn their full attention to research.

pumps, and metal and glass tanks. They assist chemical engineers in answering manufacturing-related questions, such as how to transfer materials or heat from one point to another. The work may require them to work at drawing boards, to operate small-scale equipment for designing or evaluating manufacturing processes or equipment, or to use computers to design new plants or to maintain operations of a production facility. They also assist in installing equipment and training and supervising operators on the production line.

Chemical technicians in the quality-control area test raw materials received by the company to determine if they are of a good enough quality to use. They keep a close watch on every step in the chemical process and test the final product to assure that the product meets all required specifications. An error by the chemical technician in this area can result in the loss of huge amounts of money and material. Many technicians in this area work with computers to obtain the fast and accurate information they need. Technicians trained in quality control are often called upon to help establish quality-control standards and to design quality-assurance techniques.

Chemical technicians in the customer-service field work at keeping old customers for their company and at gaining new ones. Changes in the needs of customers and in the nature of a company's competition create new demands for chemicals and give chemical technicians many opportunities to handle customer problems. As many companies sell their products to other manufacturing companies, chemical technicians in this area need to understand the nature of their customers' products and

139

manufacturing processes as well as their own products and processes.

Within these four broad areas, many chemical technicians work principally at one specialized activity or with one specific kind of product. The following short paragraphs describe some of these jobs, all of them open to entry-level chemical technicians.

Food-product technicians enforce quality-control standards for food by analyzing sugar and vitamin content, shelf life, and microorganism counts.

Fuel technicians determine viscosity of oils and fuels, measure flash points and pour points, and evaluate the heat productivity of fuels.

Pilot-plant operators make erosion and corrosion tests on new construction materials in small-scale or pilot plants. They evaluate new pumps, make new chemicals for field testing, and report on the effectiveness of new design concepts.

Chemical-design technicians work with data from operating plants and pilot plants. They prepare drawings of chemical processing units and make cost estimates for products, processes, and equipment.

Applied-research technicians usually work as part of an applied research team and use their knowledge of basic chemical concepts to help design new manufacturing or research equipment.

Nuclear-laboratory technicians determine rates of nuclear disintegration, prepare complex chemical compounds, evaluate shielding materials, and calibrate measuring equipment.

Chemical technicians in most of these areas share certain routine activities. They are often responsible for maintaining and repairing the equipment they work with. They install new equipment or supervise those doing the installation. Chemical technicians in all of these areas may also move into related activities: technical writing, technical sales, and employee supervision.

Requirements

Successful chemical technicians need to have a strong desire and ability to use both mental and manual skills. Prospective chemical technicians should have a good supply of patience because experiments must frequently be repeated several times. They should feel at ease doing close detail work and be able to follow directions closely when dealing with unfamiliar equipment or processes. Chemical technicians also need good communications skills and the abil-

ity to keep clear, accurate, and complete records.

Most employers of chemical technicians prefer to hire graduates of two-year college programs specifically designed for training technicians. To meet the entrance requirements of these programs, prospective chemical technicians should begin their educational preparations while in high school and should plan on earning a high-school diploma. They should take at least one year of algebra and at least one year of a science, preferably chemistry, that includes laboratory experience. Several colleges offering programs for preparing chemical technicians require as much as three years of mathematics, including algebra, geometry, and trigonometry; two years of physical sciences, including chemistry; and four years of English and language skills.

Students are advised to take one or more of the standard college entrance examinations, such as the ACT or SAT, that are given during high school.

Realizing that many students become aware of technical career possibilities too late to satisfy college requirements, many community and technical colleges that offer a program to prepare chemical technicians have also developed a schedule of noncredit courses that allow students to meet the requirements.

Once enrolled in a two-year college program designed for chemical technicians, students should expect to take a number of chemistry courses with strong emphasis on laboratory work and the presentation of data. These courses will include basic concepts of modern chemistry, such as atomic structure, descriptive chemistry of both organic and inorganic substances, analytical methods including instrumental analysis, and physical properties of substances.

Students should also expect to take courses in mathematics, physics, psychology, industrial safety, and management techniques. Of special importance are courses that improve the student's ability to write technical reports and to communicate orally.

It may be possible for a student to take courses for a specific area of employment. These may include biology, chemical engineering, metallurgy, or electronics.

Special requirements

Only a small number of chemical technicians need to be licensed or certified. Those who work with food products, especially milk or dairy products, may be required to have state or local licenses. Chemical technicians working with radioactive isotopes may need a license or certification for certain types of work.

Opportunities for experience and exploration

Because part-time and summer employment for young people is difficult to secure in specialized fields such as chemistry and chemical engineering, students must test their interest and abilities in different ways. For example, the junior-high-school student who has enjoyed science as a hobby through the use of a chemistry set at home or who has performed simple experiments in school science courses has had experience with chemistry and thus an opportunity to test his or her interest in the field. High-school students can best explore the strength of their interests in science by assessing the quality of their experiences in high-school science classes.

In addition, chemistry teachers or high-school guidance counselors may be able to arrange field trips to industrial laboratories or manufacturing companies. Through such visits students are able to observe technicians involved in the field, and it may be possible to speak with several of these people regarding their work or with their employers about possibilities for technicians in that industry or company.

Methods of entering

Most graduates of chemical technology programs find jobs during the last term of their two-year programs. Company recruiters regularly visit most colleges where chemical technology programs are offered. The placement staff and the teachers at the school are frequently able to give useful advice about employment opportunities.

If a student does not find a job while still in school or desires to work for a particular employer, he or she may apply directly to personnel officers at companies of interest. In addition, many opportunities are listed in the classified ads of newspapers or through private and public employment offices.

Some schools have a cooperative education program that permits regularly enrolled students to work as chemical technicians while still in school. Students in such programs develop a good knowledge of the employment possibilities and frequently stay with the cooperative employers.

Advancement

Chemical technicians become more valuable to their employers as they gain experience. Those who take additional courses or show that they can accept responsibilities are often given promotions. Many technicians prefer promotions that allow them to continue working in the laboratory, plant, or office where they started their careers. Others prefer to use their experience as background for a different type of work. The following paragraphs describe some of the different types of work available to chemical technicians who have gained the required experience.

Chemical-process analysts work to prevent failure of chemical-processing equipment. They compare new equipment with older equipment and try to find the least expensive ways to do a given job.

Chemical-process supervisors maintain schedules, prevent downtime, point out problems to design and engineering staffs, and supervise small groups of workers.

Quality-control specialists train inexperienced chemical technicians, test new procedures, and supervise routine quality-control operations.

Chemical-research associates suggest and evaluate procedures for making new compounds, modify instruments, prepare patent reports, and make literature searches.

Customer-service specialists work with customers' processing units, suggest design changes, locate spare components, and correspond with customers.

Chemical-design specialists supervise drafters, incorporate new control instruments into existing processing units, determine construction materials, and evaluate bids.

Air- and water-pollution technologists use precision measurement equipment, survey geographical areas, design sampling systems, and identify pollution sources.

Chemical-instrumentation technicians determine instrument accuracy, troubleshoot erratic equipment, modify equipment, and design new auxiliary apparatus.

Product-evaluation technicians design and construct test apparatus, make commercial compounds, and suggest changes and improvements in chemical products.

Employment outlook

The employment outlook for chemical technicians varies according to the industry in which they are employed. The pharmaceutical industry offers the best opportunities. A variety of factors, including the growing number of older people in our society with their need for more medical services, has created an increased demand for pharmaceutical products. This increased demand has led to a need for more chemical technicians in both the research and development area and in production operations.

Employment levels for chemical technicians involved with either research or manufacture of consumer and industrial chemical products are more dependent on general economic conditions. Most economists predict only modest growth for the economy throughout the mid-1990s, and this slow growth will limit the growth of employment in this area. Regardless of economic conditions, however, the chemical and chemical-related industries will continue to become increasingly sophisticated in both their products and their manufacturing techniques. There will always be a demand for technicians who can contribute to the development of successful new products and to finding more efficient and economical ways to produce these products. Because of this, employment levels for chemical technicians in general are expected to rise faster than the average of all occupations through the mid-1990s.

Earnings

Chemical technicians on their first job who have completed a two-year post–high-school training program earn approximately $17,000 a year in private industry. Experienced technicians with similar post–high-school training earn salaries ranging from $20,000 to $30,000 a year and averaging approximately $25,000 a year. Some senior technicians earn as much as $37,000 a year or more.

Benefits depend on the employer, but they usually include paid vacations and holidays, insurance, and tuition refund plans. If the technician belongs to a union, wages and benefits depend on the union agreement.

Conditions of work

The chemical industry is noted as one of the safest industries in which to work. Laboratories and plants normally have safety committees and safety engineers who closely observe equipment and practices to prevent hazards. Chemical technicians usually receive safety training in school, as well as at work, so that potential hazards are recognized and appropriate measures are taken.

Most chemical laboratories are maintained in a clean and well-lighted condition. Most companies avoid crowding so that chemical technicians usually have a very few people working in the immediate area. Chemical plants are usually as clean as other types of manufacturing operations. The number of operating personnel is usually very low for the space involved. Processing equipment may be either inside a building or out in the open, depending upon the characteristics of the manufacturing unit.

Social and psychological factors

Chemical technicians are involved in work that may range from uncomplicated, routine tasks to those that are highly complex and challenging. Although prospective technicians should have a tolerance for both kinds of work, it is possible to find jobs that focus on one or the other of these kinds of work.

Many chemical technicians act as intermediaries between professionally trained scientists and engineers and skilled laboratory or production workers. Some technicians may feel awkward in this position. Technicians who do best in this role enjoy the challenge of being able both to carry out carefully and to issue clearly the instructions and directions required in chemical laboratory or production technology.

GOE: 02.04.01; 05.01.08; SIC: 8731; SOC: 3719; 3831

◇ **SOURCES OF ADDITIONAL INFORMATION**

American Chemical Society
Educational Activities Department
1155 16th Street, NW
Washington, DC 20036

American Institute of Chemical Engineers
345 East 47th Street
New York, NY 10017

Chemical Industry for Minorities in Engineering
PO Box 2558
Midland, MI 48640

Chemical Manufacturers Association
2501 M Street, NW
Washington, DC 20037

Junior Engineering Technical Society (JETS)
1428 King Street, Suite 405
Alexandria, VA 22314

◇ **RELATED ARTICLES**

Volume 1: Chemicals and Drugs; Chemistry; Engineering
Volume 2: Chemists; Pharmacologists
Volume 3: Industrial chemicals workers; Paint and coatings industry workers; Petroleum refining workers; Pharmaceutical industry workers; Plastics products manufacturing workers
Volume 4: Industrial engineering technicians; Medical laboratory technicians; Petroleum technicians; Pharmaceutical technicians; Plastics technicians

Civil engineering technicians

Definition

Civil engineering technicians assist civil engineers in the design, planning, and building of highways, railroads, subways, airports, dams, bridges, tunnels, and waterway systems. Civil engineering technicians working in the planning stages of a construction project estimate costs, prepare specifications for materials, or carry out surveying, drafting, or designing assignments. Other civil engineering technicians, working in the actual construction phases, assist the contractor or superintendent in scheduling construction activities or in inspecting work to assure that it conforms to blueprints and specifications. Technicians are frequently involved in community planning, urban renewal, or other kinds of development projects. They may also work inallied fields, such as building-materials manufacturing.

History

Engineering, including both military and civil engineering, is one of the oldest of professions. The pyramids of ancient Egypt and the bridges, roads, and aqueducts of the Roman Empire, some of which are still in use, are all examples of ancient engineering feats.

Although from earliest times engineers have been at work building locks and dams, public buildings, cathedrals, and highways, until the nineteenth century most of the highly trained and knowledgeable engineers were military engineers. It was not until the eighteenth century in France and England that civil engineers began to organize themselves into professional societies for the exchange of information or the planning of projects. At that time most civil engineers were still self-taught, skilled craft workers. Thomas Telford, for instance, Britain's leading road builder and first president of the Institution of Civil Engineers, started his career as a stonemason. And John Rennie, the builder of the new London Bridge, began as a millwright's apprentice.

The first major educational programs intended for civil engineers were offered by the Ecole Polytechnique, founded in Paris in 1794. It was followed by courses at the *Bauakadamie*, founded in Berlin in 1799, and at University College, London, founded in 1826. In the United States, the first courses in civil engineering were taught at Rensselaer Polytechnic Institute, founded in 1824.

From the beginning, civil engineers have required the help of skilled assistants to handle the many details that are a part of all phases of civil engineering. Traditionally, these assistants have always had to possess a combination of basic knowledge and good manual skills. As construction techniques have become more and more sophisticated, however, the need has increased for these assistants to be technically trained in special fields of knowledge relevant to civil engineering.

Three civil engineering technicians refer to blueprints before they approve of the installation of pipelines.

These technically trained assistants are known today as civil engineering technicians, and just as educational programs and a separate professional identity developed for the civil engineer in the eighteenth and nineteenth centuries, so are programs and an identity developing for the civil engineering technician in this century. Today, the civil engineering technician is a respected member of the civil engineering team comprising scientists, engineers, technicians, and craft workers.

Nature of the work

Civil engineering technicians engage in varied activities. State highway departments utilize their services to collect data, to design and draw plans, and to supervise the construction and maintenance of roadways. Railroad and airport facilities require similar services. Cities and counties have transportation systems, drainage systems, and water and sewage facilities that must be planned, built, and maintained with the assistance of civil engineering technicians.

Civil engineering technicians participate in all stages of the construction process. During the planning stages, they help engineers prepare lists of materials needed and help estimate costs of projects. One of the most important positions held by civil engineering technicians at this stage is that of the structural engineering technician. Structural engineering technicians calculate size, number, and composition of beams and columns needed and investigate allowable soil pressures that are developed because of the weight of such structures. They design special piers, rafts, pilings, or footings if the pressures are such that they will cause excessive settling or other failure.

During the planning stages, civil engineering technicians also assist engineers in drafting and in preparing drawings, maps, and charts.

During the actual construction phase, construction technicians assist building contractors and site supervisors in work scheduling, cost estimating, and work inspection. One of the most important duties of these technicians is ensuring that each step of construction is completed before workers arrive to begin the next stage.

Some technicians specialize in specific kinds of construction projects. Highway technicians, for example, perform surveys and cost estimates and plan and supervise the construction and maintenance of highways. Rail and waterway technicians survey, make specifications and cost estimates, and help plan and construct railway and waterway facilities. Assistant city engineers coordinate the planning and construction of city streets, sewers, drainage systems, refuse facilities, and other major civil projects.

Other technicians specialize in specific phases of the construction process. Materials technicians sample and run tests on rock, soil, cement, asphalt, wood, steel, concrete, and other materials. *Photogrammetric technicians* use aerial photographs to prepare maps, plans, and profiles. *Party chiefs* for licensed land surveyors survey land for boundary-line locations and plan subdivisions and other large-area land developments.

Other specialized positions for civil engineering technicians include *research engineering technicians* who test and develop new products and equipment; *sales engineering technicians* who sell building materials, construction equipment, and engineering services; and *water resources technicians* who gather data, make computations and drawings for water projects, and prepare economic studies.

Requirements

A student contemplating a career in civil engineering technology should have a desire to be a builder or planner, an understanding of the basics of mathematics and sciences, the ability to get along with other people, an aptitude for learning, and the ability to think and plan ahead.

Prospective civil engineering technicians should take all the mathematics, sciences, and communications subjects that they can in high school. In general, they should follow the course for admission to a four-year engineering college.

Mathematics, including at least two years of algebra, is necessary. Plane and solid geometry and trigonometry are other recommended mathematics courses. Physics, with laboratory experience, is an important requirement. Chemistry and biology are desirable science courses. General science courses are also helpful.

The ability to read and interpret swiftly what has been read is very important, so four years of high-school English and language skills courses are basic requirements. Reports and letters are an essential part of the technician's work, so a firm grasp of English grammar is important.

Mechanical drawing and any available shop courses should also be taken. Civil engineering technicians often make use of mechanical drawings to convey their ideas to others, and neat, well-executed drawings are important for creating an impression of accuracy and competence.

Finally, courses in history, world cultures, and current events will help develop and broaden thinking and attitudes necessary to produce mature minds that are better equipped to deal with the complexities of today's ever-changing world.

Prospective civil engineering technology students should be careful to choose a technical institute that offers an accredited program in civil engineering technology. In such programs, more mathematics and science subjects, including physics, will be studied to prepare the student for subsequent technical specialty courses, such as surveying, materials, hydraulics, highway and bridge construction and design, structures, railway and water systems, heavy construction, soils, steel and concrete construction, cost and estimates, and courses in management and construction technology. Students can also take courses in computer programming and photogrammetry.

A great deal of the student's time will be spent in laboratory and field study of the above-mentioned technical specialties. It is this type of hands-on experience that prepares technicians for their special role in the civil engineering team.

In addition, drafting procedures and techniques will be developed and polished in intermediate and advanced-level courses. Courses in law, human relations, economics, and professional ethics are available and recommended. Most important of the nontechnical subjects is English, which will help technicians to convey their thoughts to others. Courses in public speaking and report writing are also a good idea.

Special requirements

To advance his or her professional standing, a civil engineering technician should try to become a Certified Engineering Technician. Civil engineering technicians may also, upon completion of the required years of service, take an examination for licensing as a Licensed Land Surveyor. Successful completion of this examination enables technicians to operate their own surveying businesses.

Opportunities for experience and exploration

One of the best methods for acquiring first-hand experience in the field of civil engineering is through part-time or summer work with a construction company. Even if the job is the most menial, young people can still have the opportunity to see surveying teams, site supervisors, building inspectors, skilled craft workers, and civil engineering technicians at work at their jobs. If such employment is not possible, students can organize field trips to various construction sites or to facilities where building materials are manufactured.

Shop courses and drafting courses will also provide future technicians with excellent opportunities to sample some of the work they may be doing later.

Methods of entering

Most civil engineering technicians receive assistance from their school in finding jobs upon graduation. Most schools maintain placement offices, and many prospective employers will contact such placement offices when they have job openings. The placement offices, in turn, help the student or graduate prepare a resume of relevant school and work experiences and usually arrange personal interviews with prospective employers.

Many schools also have cooperative programs with particular companies and government agencies that provide students with actual work experience while they study. Under such a program, the company or government agency often becomes the new technician's place of full-time employment after graduation.

Some students make use of state and private employment services that have listings in the field. Others consult want ads or write directly to possible future employers. Students should also take every opportunity to meet and get to know people in the field. Such people often know about present and future job openings and can pass the word along to interested newcomers.

Advancement

Civil engineering technicians must keep studying and learning throughout their careers. They must learn new techniques, master the operation of new equipment, and study to give themselves greater depth in their chosen fields and to keep themselves abreast of the latest developments. If they do all this, their value to their employer will rise, and they can advance to positions of greater responsibility. Some technicians may move on to supervisory positions. Other technicians will get additional education and become civil engineers. A few of the opportunities for technicians with advanced skills and experience follow.

Associate municipal designers direct their workers in the preparation of design drawings and feasibility studies for dams and municipal water and sewage plants.

Associate structures designers direct workers in the preparation of design drawings and cost estimates of structural features, such as foundations, columns, piers, and beams.

City or county building inspectors review and approve or reject plans for construction of large buildings.

City and county engineers operate, plan, and direct city or county engineering or public works departments.

Licensed land surveyors operate land surveying businesses as owners or partners.

Photogrammetrists direct the preparation of maps and charts from aerial photography.

Project engineers or *resident engineers* supervise numbers of projects and field parties for city, county, or state highway departments.

Finally, some technicians go on to become *construction superintendents* or even *owners* of their own construction company, supply company, or laboratory testing company.

Employment outlook

The employment outlook for civil engineering technicians is good. Although the total amount of civil construction may be affected by general economic conditions and levels of government spending, there will remain a need for more technicians to assist civil engineers and to re-

lieve them of duties that may be delegated to technically trained personnel. And despite short-term or even protracted periods of economic dislocation, there will remain pressing needs for construction projects that address the problems of urban redevelopment, water shortages, transportation systems, industrial waste pollution, and traffic congestion. All of this points to a continuing and expanding demand for civil engineering technicians.

Earnings

Civil engineering technicians usually begin their first jobs at a salary range of about $14,000 to $15,000 a year. Most experienced technicians earn around $18,000 to $30,000 a year, and the average is about $25,000 a year. Some senior technicians earn as much as $37,000 a year or more.

The incomes of many civil engineering technicians who operate their own construction, surveying, or equipment businesses are quite attractive. Some of these companies can do a gross business of millions of dollars each year.

As is the case for all industries, paid vacations, pension plans, and insurance are normal parts of the benefits paid to civil engineering technicians. Many companies pay the superintendent a bonus if a job is completed ahead of schedule or if the job is completed for less than the estimated cost. These bonuses are sometimes more than the employee's regular annual salary.

Conditions of work

Working conditions vary from job to job. A technician who enjoys being outdoors may choose a job in construction or surveying. Those who prefer working indoors may choose to work in a consulting engineer's office on computations, drafting, or design, or they may work inside on map plotting, materials testing, or making various calculations from field notes and tests. In either site, the work done by civil engineering technicians is usually cleaner than the work done by most other construction trades workers.

Civil engineering technicians usually work forty hours a week with extra pay for overtime work.

Social and psychological factors

Civil engineering technicians occupy a position between the professionally trained scientist or engineer and the skilled trade worker. They feel the special pride that comes from being a member of a team that constructs major buildings or important bridges and dams. Such projects become monuments, so to speak, to the efforts of each member of the team. And there is the accompanying satisfaction that comes from knowing that the project one has been working on has improved, if only in a modest way, the quality of life in a community.

The work of civil engineering technicians may vary from the uncomplicated and routine to the highly complex and personally challenging. A successful civil engineering technician needs a high tolerance for both kinds of activities.

As stated earlier, successful civil engineering technicians keep their minds sharp by continued studying and learning throughout their careers.

GOE: 05.01.07; SIC: 8711; SOC: 3719

◇ **SOURCES OF ADDITIONAL INFORMATION**

American Congress on Surveying and Mapping
210 Little Falls Street
Falls Church, VA 22046

American Society for Engineering Education
11 Dupont Circle, Suite 200
Washington, DC 20036

American Society of Certified Engineering Technicians
PO Box 371474
El Paso, TX 79937

American Society of Civil Engineers
345 East 47th Street
New York, NY 10017

◇ **RELATED ARTICLES**

Volume 1: Construction; Engineering
Volume 2: Cartographers; Geographers; Surveyors; Urban and regional planners
Volume 4: Architectural and building construction technicians; Drafting and design technicians; Laboratory technicians; Traffic technicians

Coal mining technicians

Definition

Coal mining technicians are involved in a wide variety of coal mining activities. They assist in the extraction, preparation, and transportation of coal. Their training enables them to assist coal mining engineers or managers or to assume independent responsibilities for tasks relating to surveying, mapping, and planning the mining of a coal field or for directing the drilling of test holes and analyzing test samples. Their training covers the methods, equipment,

techniques, and procedures used in underground coal mining, surface mining, and coal beneficiation, which is the cleaning, purification, and conditioning of coal for market.

Their work also includes managing safe mining operations and training other workers in mine safety practices. They help manage the disposal of mine waste and the reclamation of strip-mine areas after coal has been removed, and they prepare required environmental-impact reports on the mining operation. They test and analyze the quality of coal as it is

A coal mining technician measures the viscosity of a coal-oil mixture fuel sample.

mined and measure and test the levels of air impurities in mines. They assemble, operate, and maintain specialized machinery and equipment, and they plan for maximum recovery of salable product from each deposit of coal by the most economical methods.

History

When coal was first discovered and used for fuel is unknown. Ancient peoples in several areas of the globe seem to have known about it. There is evidence that coal was burned in Wales during the Bronze Age about 3,000 to 4,000 years ago, and by the early Romans in Britain. The first industrial use of coal was in the Middle Ages in England. Consequently, the English were far more advanced in mining methods than other nations for many years.

The first Americans to produce coal were the Hopi Indians around the eleventh century. In the seventeenth century a Jesuit missionary found the Algonquin Indians "making fire with coal from the earth," and later in that century the French explorers Jacques Marquette and Louis Joliet reported coal use in what is now Illinois.

Commercial mining started in the United States around 1750, near Richmond, Virginia, with the first recorded commercial shipment of American coal—thirty-two tons from Virginia to New York. Most of the coal produced was used to manufacture shells and shot for the Revolutionary War.

At first, the use of coal as a fuel source in the United States lagged far behind that in England because of the readily available supply of timber from the vast and plentiful North American woodlands. It was easier to fell a tree than to dig for coal. Wood was the major source of fuel for industry, home heating, and charcoal for metallurgical production from early colonial times until 1885.

Around 1760, the soldiers of Fort Pitt, Pennsylvania, were using bituminous coal mined nearby for fuel. This mine was located in one of the most valuable coal deposits in the United States, which today is known as the Great Appalachian Field. It extends nearly 900 miles from Pennsylvania to Alabama.

Coal fired the furnaces and fed the steam engines that began the Industrial Revolution in this country. Coal superseded wood as the nation's main fuel around 1885 and continued as the chief source of commercial energy until petroleum replaced it in the 1950s.

The earliest method of coal production was strip mining, which is the gathering of deposits near the earth's surface. Early strip mining did not produce large amounts of coal, because methods of removing soil that lay over the coal were crude and slow. Beginning in 1910, strip, or surface, mining became more practical as powered machinery came into use.

Early underground mining was also crude and very difficult at best, based on hand use of the pick, shovel, and crowbar. The coal, once broken from the ground, was removed from the mine in wheelbarrows. People provided all of the power in both the mining and removal of coal. Eventually, horses or mules were used to haul the coal out of the mine. Blasting powder was also used to break coal loose, but the rest of the work was still done by hand.

Beginning about 1830, many new machines for coal mining were invented. Most of them used steam power fueled by wood or coal. This made underground coal mining more profitable.

During the last 150 years, the advances in mechanical devices for easier and more efficient underground coal production have been staggering. Early important inventions included punching and cutting machines, chain cutters for undermining coal, compressed air and steam drills, locomotives for hauling waste rock and coal out of mines, and hoisting machines.

Modern technology and improved management have revolutionized coal mining in the last half century. Specialized machinery has been developed that replaces human effort with electric, pneumatic, hydraulic, and mechanical power—remotely controlled in some applications by electronic computers. This means that highly skilled technicians and workers are needed to direct, operate, maintain, modify, and control the work performed by very expensive machinery. For the past two decades, about twenty schools have been providing successful two-year postsecondary programs for coal mining technicians. Using this education, coal mining technicians have become an essential part of the support staff to the skilled workers, engineers, and managers of mining operations.

Nature of the work

Coal mining is an extractive industry, one that removes from the earth a nonrenewable natural resource that fills a need at the time it is mined.

The depth where coal can be found varies from a few feet below the earth's surface in the West to approximately 800 feet in the Midwest and much deeper in some of Appalachia. It is located and mined in approximately twenty-seven of the fifty states. Mining methods include strip mining and underground mining. The coal mining technician performs a wide variety of duties throughout the industry.

Those who work in surface mines work outdoors all kinds of weather to expose the seam of coal. By the time the mining actually starts, coal mining technicians have already assisted the managers, engineers, and scientists in surveying, test drilling, and analyzing the coal deposit for depth and quality. They have also mapped the surface and helped plan the drilling and blasting to break up the rock and soil that cover the coal. The coal mining technicians have also helped in preparing permits that must be filed with federal and state governments before mining may begin. Information must be provided on how the land will be mined and reclaimed, on its soil, water conditions, and vegetation, on wildlife conservation, and on how archaeological resources will be protected.

The coal mining technicians also have assisted the mining engineers and superintendents in selecting the machinery to be used in mining. Such a plan must include selecting machines of a correct size and capacity to match other machinery and planning the sequences for efficient use of machines. The plan also includes mapping roads out of the mine pit, planning machine and road maintenance, and above all, using safety methods for the whole operation.

Various methods may be used to remove the coal from an underground coal mine. They each require the professional use of complex specialized equipment. The same kind of sur-

veying, drilling, testing, mapping, and planning needed in surface mining is also needed in underground mining. In some ways, however, the planning, machinery, and selection of mining methods are more complex in underground mining.

Underground mining is done in areas where it is too expensive to remove the soil and extract the coal as done in surface mining. Usually, underground mines are 100 to 1,000 feet below the surface.

Underground mines are found in most of the coal-producing states. They are classified as shaft, slope, or drift mines, depending on the angle at which the tunnel between the surface opening and the coal seam is cut. A shaft mine is entered through a vertical tunnel known as a shaft. Usually shaft mines are used to mine a coal bed that is 100 feet or more below the surface, but some of the deepest go to 2,000 feet and below.

When the coal seam is nearer to the surface, a sloping tunnel is cut from the surface on a downward slant to the coal seam. Drift mines are simple mining tunnels that cut directly from the surface opening to the seam on a horizontal path. They are used in hilly areas where underground mining is necessary, but where the coal is easily approached on a relatively level tunnel pathway.

In the underground mines, a variety of jobs is performed by many specialized workers. Workers use mining machinery to cut the coal from the face and load it onto shuttle cars. The shuttle cars transport the coal onto a conveyor belt or mine car for removal from the mine. As coal is removed, pillars of coal, wooden or steel supports, and steel roof bolts and roof plates are used to hold up the mine roof to prevent it from collapsing.

In addition, large quantities of air—at least 3,000 cubic feet of air per minute—must be supplied to each underground working face. This air is circulated through the active working areas of the mine. It removes the poisonous or explosive gases and dust produced during mining. Rock dust is sprayed on the side walls and roof to prevent the formation of explosive dust mixtures.

Some specific entry-level jobs for coal mining technicians are described in the paragraphs that follow:

Survey helpers, surveyors, or *survey drafters* operate surveying instruments to gather numerical data. They calculate tonnage broken and incentive pay, map mine development, and provide precise directions and locations to the work force. They also conduct studies on operations and equipment to improve methods and to reduce costs.

A coal mining technician at a research center monitors an experimental installation that produces gas from coal.

Ventilation technicians operate dust counting, gas quantity, and air volume measuring instruments. They record or plot this data, and plan or assist in planning the direction of air flow through mine workings. Ventilation technicians also help in prescribing the fan installations required to accomplish the desired air flow.

Industrial engineering assistants observe work practices and obtain related time and process measurements; they also assist in the planning of more efficient materials handling and work methods.

Geology assistants gather geological data as mining activities progress. They identify rocks and minerals, record and map structural changes, locate drill holes, and identify rocks, coal, and minerals in drill cores. Their work also includes mapping geological information from drill core data, gathering samples, and mapping results on mine plans.

Mill technicians in coal cleaning and beneficiation regularly determine and control mill feed density. They also analyze mill solutions for correct chemistry and routinely check the quality of the final product. In the laboratory, these technicians conduct ore beneficiation tests, using flotation, gravity, or magnetic concentration methods.

Chemical analysts analyze mine and mill samples and coal exploration samples, using volumetric or instrumental methods of analysis. They also write reports on all analyses.

Requirements

The coal mining industry requires educated, ambitious employees who want to make a lasting career for themselves. To keep their skills sharp and knowledge up to date, coal mining technicians should expect to study throughout their careers by enrolling in courses offered through professional associations, junior colleges, and technical colleges. Continuing education credits may also be available.

Preparation for a career as a mining technician is best begun in high school. Students should take mathematics and science courses that provide an educational base for a two-year training program at one of the schools that offer mining technology programs. High-school students who plan to be technicians should complete at least two years of mathematics, including algebra and geometry, and four years of English and language skills courses, with emphasis on reading, writing, and communication training.

Students should also complete a strong course in physics, and, if possible, chemistry with laboratory study. These courses, combined with mathematics, provide the necessary foundation for the study of electronics, advanced physics, and other engineering-type technical courses in the postsecondary school program. They also prepare students for assignments in surveying and mapping, preparation of coal, equipment maintenance, blasting, crushing, coal cleaning, and other specialized coursework.

High-school students who are considering this career should learn to use computers and particularly computer-aided drafting and design software programs. A course in mechanical drawing or drafting in high school is useful experience for the surveying and mapping tasks the technician may perform.

It is possible to start a coal mining career as an unskilled worker with a high-school diploma. But it is difficult to advance within the coal mining industry without the foundation skills. In general, companies prefer employees who bring formally acquired technical knowledge and skills to the job.

The real value of technicians to the coal mining industry is their ability to apply an integrated scientific and mathematical background, specialized skills, and technical knowledge to a practical situation in the field. A technical college education is geared to preparing coal mining technicians to be able to function this way.

The first year of study in a typical two-year coal mining technician program in a technical or community college includes courses in the basics of coal mining, applied mathematics, mining law, coal mining ventilation and atmospheric control, communications skills, technical reporting, fundamentals of electricity, mining machinery, physical geology, surveying and graphics, mine safety and accident prevention, roof and rib control, and industrial economics and financing.

A typical second year in a program continues to build a solid technical base with courses in mine instrumentation and electrical systems, mine electrical maintenance, mine hydraulic machinery, machine transmissions and drive trains, basic welding, coal mine environmental impacts and control, coal and coal mine atmosphere sampling and analysis, mine machinery and systems automation and control, application of computers to coal mining operations, first aid and mine rescue, and institutions and organizations.

In some programs, students spend the summer working as interns at coal mining companies. Internships are especially advantageous to students. They provide a clear picture of the field and help students choose the work area that best fits their abilities. Students gain experience using charts, graphs, blueprints, maps, and machinery. They also develop job confidence through an approach to the real operation of the industry.

Certain personal qualifications are also needed for success in this career. The ability to work with others and to accept supervision is most important. Technicians must also learn to work independently and accept responsibility. Coal mining technicians must be accurate and careful workers. Mistakes can prove expensive or hazardous to the technician and to other workers.

Special requirements

Laws governing the coal industry vary from state to state, and so do the requirements for certification of mine workers. Typically, a state may require that any person engaged at the face of the mine, as a *coal loader, loading machine operator, cutting machine operator, driller, shooter, timberman,* or *roof bolter,* first obtain a certificate of competency as a miner. This certificate is often obtained from the state's miner's examining board. In some cases, a miner may obtain a certificate of competency after completing one year of underground work. A miner who has an associate degree in coal mine technology may, however, be able to obtain the certificate after completing six months of underground experience.

A state may also require coal mining technicians seeking a certificate of competency as a mine examiner or a certificate of competency as a mine manager, to have at least four years of underground experience. Graduates of a program offering an associate degree in coal mining technology may be able to obtain certification after only three years of underground experience.

Coal mining technician students usually can meet the criteria for employment in the various coal-producing states while they are in their technician preparatory program. It is important to be familiar with these criteria if technicians plan to work in a state other than the one where they begin their education and work experience.

Opportunities for experience and exploration

Local high schools, community colleges, and technical institutes can provide considerable information on coal mining technician careers. If it can be arranged, a visit to a producing coal mine makes it possible to observe the machinery and the work. Workers on the job can also supply information about the career. One of the best opportunities for experience is a summer job with a coal mining company, preferably in an activity closely related to the actual mining operation.

Methods of entering

Coal mining technicians are usually hired by recruiters from the major employers in the field before they complete their last year of technical school. Industry recruiters regularly visit the campuses of schools with coal mining technician programs and work with the school's placement officers.

Many two-year graduates take jobs that emphasize basic operational functions. Technicians are then in a position to compete for higher positions in most cases through the system of job bidding, which considers such factors as formal education, experience, and seniority.

In some cases, graduates may already have jobs because their employers have sent them to school so they could obtain the needed preparation. Graduates usually have special interests that make them qualified for technical positions in one or more of the following areas: production, planning and control, maintenance, repair, electrical, welding, support services, surveying and mapping, or environmental control and management.

Most companies will provide orientation sessions that familiarize the newcomer to company operations. Orientation may include a review of state and federal laws that pertain to coal mining and health and safety training. After that, continuous study, careful work, and on-the-job learning are a way of life for the technician.

Advancement

For the coal mining technician who works steadily and keeps up to date on new technological developments, opportunities for advancement are excellent. Some technicians may advance to management positions such as section supervisors, production superintendents, or mine managers. The possibilities are attractive for knowledgeable, dependable individuals.

After a period of on-the-job experience, coal mining technicians may become supervisors, sales representatives, or possibly even private consultants or special service contractors. A few examples of such advancement patterns and jobs are listed below:

Shift bosses are responsible for the efficient operation of a mine area. They train new workers and enforce strict safety practices. *Mine superintendents* or *captains* are responsible for the total mining area. They supervise the work of all shift bosses.

Technical sales representatives work for a manufacturer of mining equipment and supplies and sell such products as explosives, flotation chemicals, rock drills, hoists, crushers, grinding mills, classifiers, materials handling equipment, and safety equipment.

Special services consultants provide consulting services, either independently or as a partner in a consulting business. This work is also a route to advancement for the experienced technician with an excellent record of scientific and field success.

Employment outlook

Employment levels for all mining occupations are expected to remain about the same or to decline through the year 2000, because of low growth in the demand for coal. In the long run,

demand for coal may well increase; however, this will depend largely on the availability and price of other sources of energy, such as oil, natural gas, and nuclear energy, as well as coal from other countries.

Even if national employment levels do not improve, there will continue to be a need for well-trained coal technicians. First, some new coal mining technicians will be required in order to replace those technicians who are retiring or leaving their jobs for other reasons. Also, more efficient and more technologically sophisticated coal mining systems and further enforcement of health, safety, and environmental regulations may increase the need for coal mining technicians.

Earnings

Establishing a scale of earnings for coal mining technicians is difficult because of the many different work situations in which they may be involved and the great variation in their working conditions. Normally, the Bituminous Coal Operators' Association and the labor unions that represent the workers contract for a set scale of pay for the industry.

According to the best information available at this time, graduates of two-year coal mining technology programs are hired as beginning technicians in the early 1990s at approximately $18,000 to $24,000 per year. This assumes that the coal mining technician works a year when there are no labor strikes, which would close the mine where the technician was employed.

Benefits for workers within the coal mining industry are progressive and competitive with those of most energy industries today, and they may include education benefits, health and life insurance, work schedules, paid holidays, and health benefits.

Many coal companies now provide tuition payment plans so that their employees can take college courses related to their jobs. This is an incentive to continue the education process and thus ensure a better employee. The arrangement is especially beneficial for technicians who need to keep up with new technology and to learn new skills.

Within five years, coal mining technicians whose pay started near $20,000 may be earning $32,000 to $40,000 if they are effective, competent workers and demonstrate the ability and desire to assume greater responsibilities. Those who become highly successful technical sales directors, managers, or specialized consultants after several years may earn considerably more than $40,000 per year.

Conditions of work

Coal mining takes place in a hazardous environment. There is a danger of mine explosions, roof falls, and a wide variety of other mine-related accidents. In the past, working conditions have varied from mine to mine and state to state. State and federal regulations, however, have been established over the years, and working conditions have improved greatly, although coal mining is still considered dangerous.

Coal mining machine operators, supervisors, engineers, and their supporting technicians work under unusual and often harsh conditions. At surface mines, operators work outside and may be exposed to bad weather. In underground mines, operators work in tunnels that may be cramped, dark, dusty, wet, and cold. At times, several inches of water may be on the tunnel floor. In both surface and underground mines, operators and other crew members are exposed to loud noise from the loud and continuous operation of large machinery. And, although much of the work is done by machines, most of the mining jobs are physically demanding and almost always involve coal mining technicians' getting dirty from dust, the processing of coal, waste, mud, and from atmospheric contamination.

Because of the variety of activities in mine and mill development and in actual mining operations, coal mining technicians must always be alert to avoid accidents and hazards as they work. Employers supply safety instruction, certain items of safety equipment, and health care services to the best of their ability. The safety and health of a coal mining technician must depend, however, on the intelligence, alertness, and judgment that the workers themselves exercise in the potentially dangerous work situations of the industry.

Since the passage of the Coal Mine Health and Safety Act in 1969, the coal mining industry has taken many steps to improve ventilation and lighting in underground mines and to eliminate the many inherent safety hazards. Nevertheless, mining machine operators and other coal mining workers, including supervisors and technicians, must constantly be alert. They must recognize and correct safety hazards, acting quickly and correctly to get the crew to safety in dangerous situations.

In both surface and underground mines, workers may be injured or killed in accidents involving mining machinery. In underground mines, all workers face the additional hazards of roof cave-ins, accumulation of poisonous and explosive gases, and exposure to coal dust. Coal mining workers exposed to coal dust over a period of many years may develop pneumonoconiosis (black lung), a disabling and sometimes fatal disease.

Social and psychological factors

Much of the personal satisfaction and reward in this career depends on becoming accustomed to doing difficult work in dark, potentially dangerous places. Underground mining requires workers to wear battery-operated hat lights. Usually no other lights are used except on the machines and at the entrance and the face of the mine. Under such conditions, teamwork is essential, as is a tolerance for being enclosed and underground. The ability of coal mining workers to get along well with and communicate with coworkers is essential, because fellow workers' safety is dependent upon their concern for one another.

Coal mining technicians must be patient, systematic, accurate, and objective in their work. They must have the urge and the ability to keep learning. They must be able to work cooperatively and especially to work in a subordinate role under experienced managers, professional engineers, and scientists. They must be able to plan ahead. These qualities, along with integrity, will determine the success of the technician in this field.

GOE: 05.01.08, 05.02.05, 05.11.02; SIC: 124; SOC: 3719

◇ **SOURCES OF ADDITIONAL INFORMATION**

American Institute of Mining, Metallurgical and Petroleum Engineers
345 East 47th Street
New York, NY 10017

American Mining Congress
1920 N Street, NW
Suite 300
Washington, DC 20036

Bituminous Coal Operators' Association
303 World Center Building
918 16th Street, NW
Washington, DC 20006

International Union United Mine Workers of America
900 15th Street, NW
Washington, DC 20005

National Coal Association
1130 17th Street, NW
Washington, DC 20036

Society of Mining Engineers, Inc.
900 15th Street, NW
Washington, DC 20005

Drafting and design technicians

Definition

Drafting and design technicians convert ideas for engineering or architectural designs into detailed drawings and precise working specifications from which products can be made. They assist architects and mechanical, electrical, civil, and other engineers in designing and drawing up plans for machines, electrical circuits, buildings, and many other structures and manufactured devices. They prepare layouts, detailed drawings, charts, graphs, diagrams, and models, and they may work either on paper or on computers.

History

The original and natural method of describing the forms of objects is with drawings. Drawings are usually much easier to use than written or spoken language in describing complicated shapes and structures. Drafting, also called engineering drawing, has long allowed architects to develop and record their design ideas and to transmit those ideas to the people who construct their buildings. Certainly as early as Babylonian times, engineering drawings were used in planning buildings. A surviving example is a stone engraving of a fortress plan done by a Babylonian engineer about 4,000 years ago. By about 2,000 years later the Romans were designing and building excellent structures, many of which survive today. The Romans understood well the importance of drafting; in fact, the earliest known textbook on engineering

drawing was done by the architect Vitruvius around 27 B.C. Another important figure in the history of drafting was Leonardo da Vinci, who made many technical drawings and also wrote the first book explaining projection drawing.

The principles of modern engineering drawing were first organized around 1800 by the French mathematician Gaspard Monge, whose treatises developed methods of applying geometry to the problems of construction and thus revolutionized engineering design. His contributions formed the basis of orthographic projection, which is the most common form of engineering drawing today. In orthographic projection, any object, no matter how complex, can be seen from any direction. Objects are drawn as if projected onto three perpendicular planes, such as the front, side, and top of a box, then revolved into the positions of the other planes. This approach provided engineers and architects with a much more effective way of organizing their design ideas than they had previously.

Leonardo da Vinci wrote, "All of our knowledge has its origin in our perceptions." Perception is the key to the work of modern drafting and design technicians. They have cultivated their perceptions as well as their ability to think in three dimensions and draw in two, to visualize objects and then present their visualization in a way that another person understands quickly and clearly.

Drafting is presently in the midst of a revolution that has made visualizing objects much easier. Drafters are very rapidly coming to rely on computer-aided drafting (CAD) systems. By the end of the 1990s most drafters will sit not at traditional drawing boards, but at computer work stations, drawing on video screens. Drafters will still need the same knowledge as they have traditionally, along with some additional skills, but they will be able to be much more productive.

Today drafting work in many workplaces is still done using the traditional drawing board and tools like compasses, protractors, dividers, and triangles to make drawings on paper. Although CAD technology has been available for some years, it takes time to shift procedures in many offices, and the cost of new computer systems is not insignificant. The cost is dropping, however, and within a decade the transition to CAD as the main method of drafting should be largely complete.

Nature of the work

Drafting and design technicians illustrate designers' ideas in graphic form. They produce detailed drawings from notes, rough sketches, verbal instructions, and specifications, and they assemble the drawings into working plans. The final drawings they make show the product or structure from all sides, specify materials that the product will be made from, procedures for making it, and other information needed to carry out the process. They work as members of a team, primarily as intermediaries between architects, engineers, and scientists, who design products, and craft workers, who make products. In some settings, their drawings are entered into computers that control machines that make products.

Whether the technicians work on paper or on a computer, they use technical handbooks, tables, and calculators to help them in their work. A finished drawing consists of lines that represent contours, edges, and surfaces together with symbols, dimensions, and notes. The drawings may be of just about any object, large or small, that is manufactured or constructed, including machinery, buildings, consumer products, vehicles, and electrical systems. Drafting technicians usually specialize in a particular field, such as architectural, mechanical, electrical, civil, or aeronautical drafting, and get to know the special problems and methods of their field.

Beginning drafting and design technicians devote most of their time to the drawing board or computer work station. At this stage, their work may involve drawing detailed minor parts of a project based on engineering design sketches, design directives, and preliminary data; working with designers and engineers in

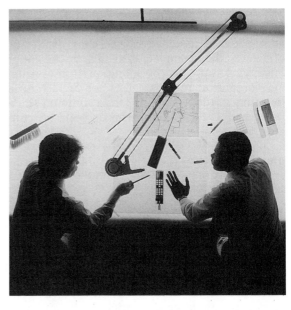

Two drafting and design technicians discuss the rough draft of a project. Often, technicians must make several revisions of a design before the final version is approved.

the design and operation of production systems; making preliminary drawings and sketches of a proposed design in sufficient detail to resolve project problems; and investigating pertinent design factors such as ease of manufacture, interchangeability, replaceability, and efficiency of machine and tool designs.

Most of the jobs held by these workers are usually designated as particular kinds of drafters rather than as technicians.

On their first job, drafting and design technicians frequently hold the position of detail drafter. Detailers start with layout drawings and make complete detailed drawings in preparation for manufacturing, showing exact dimensions, tolerances, finish, material, number and all other necessary information for production. They may make simple decisions but they generally receive explicit instructions from an engineer or designer. Detailers must know about dimensioning practices and the fundamentals of depicting designs most advantageously.

The following short paragraphs describe other typical positions held by drafting and design technicians.

Aeronautical drafters specialize in drawing developmental and production airplanes, missiles, and ancillary equipment.

Architects' assistants assist architects or structural engineers in assembling specifications, performing routine calculations for quantity estimates, and completing drawings.

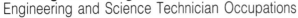

Architectural drafters carry out drafting tasks on architectural drawings, sketches, and presentations, as assigned by the chief drafter or architect. They complete drawings by detailing, "heavying up" or correcting existing prints, and preparing materials lists for architectural drawings. This position is also a common starting position for architectural or building construction technicians.

Cartographic drafters draw maps of geographical areas showing natural and constructed features, political boundaries, and other features.

Civil drafters detail construction drawings and maps for use in planning and building highways, river and harbor improvements, flood control, drainage, and other civil engineering projects.

Electrical drafters draw up plans for electrical systems such as those in electrical power generation plants, large industrial plants, and municipal lighting systems.

Electromechanisms design drafters draft designs of equipment such as rocket engine control systems, biomedical equipment, and automatic materials-handling machinery.

Engineering specifications technicians analyze plans and drawings to determine material specifications. They prepare lists of materials specifying quality, size and strength, and compare requirements to company, government, or other contract requirements.

Heating and ventilating drafters specialize in drawing plans for installing heating, air-conditioning, and ventilating equipment in buildings.

Landscape drafters prepare drawings and tracings of landscape site plans, including grading and drainage, irrigation, plantings, and garden structures.

Marine drafters draw the structural and mechanical features of ships, docks, and other marine structures and equipment.

Mechanical drafters work from engineering sketches to develop mechanical drawings for manufacturing equipment such as tools and machinery.

Patent drafting technicians prepare mechanical drawings of various devices for use by patent attorneys in obtaining and recording patents.

Quality-control technicians test and inspect components at various stages of manufacture, ensuring final quality of products as specified by engineering drawings.

Structural drafters draw plans and details for structures that employ reinforcing steel, concrete, masonry, wood, and other building materials. They develop plans for foundations, framing, and other major structural elements.

Technical illustrators draw pictures and diagrams for sales literature and owner's handbooks. They illustrate equipment to help equipment buyers assemble, install, operate, and repair the equipment on their own.

About a third of all drafters work for engineering and architectural firms. Another third work in industries that manufacture durable goods such as machinery, fabricated metals, and electrical equipment.

Requirements

Drafting and design technicians need to be able to think in three dimensions. Technicians must be comfortable with construction projects, laboratories, and scientific instruments. They should be good team members and listeners who can take as well as receive directions. They need to be able to do very detailed work accurately and neatly. Good eyesight and manual dexterity are important, and artistic ability can be very helpful in many fields.

The best way to become a drafting and design technician is to attend a two-year postsecondary training program, such as is offered at many community and junior colleges, technical schools, divisions of universities, and vocational institutes. Some technical training programs are shorter than two years. Programs that are a year or even less in length can enable graduates to find jobs performing basic drafting functions. Employers increasingly prefer applicants, however, who have the more complete preparation that a two-year program provides. Depending on the program length, graduates receive a certificate or associate degree in their major field.

In high-school, students who are interested in drafting and design should consult their guidance counselor to find out about the specific admission requirements of schools that they might attend later. Requirements are likely to include two years of mathematics, including algebra, geometry, and trigonometry; one year of physical science, preferably physics with laboratory work; four years of English and related courses that teach communications skills; and a year of mechanical or architectural drawing.

People who have not obtained a solid preparation in high school and who develop an interest later should not be discouraged. Many technical training programs can provide extra courses to help students fill gaps in their background.

In a two-year program, the first year may include courses in mathematics, mechanics, engineering design and drawing, production processes, introduction to CAD, and English composition. Second-year classes may cover engineering materials, tool and machine design, machining or other manufacturing practice, architectural drawing, advanced CAD, and technical report writing.

These programs involve demanding college-level study and are designed to provide the student with a strong base of science and mathematics. They also provide experience and practice in using modern drafting methods and equipment.

Some people enter the drafting field through an apprenticeship program. These programs usually take three to four years to complete and combine learning on the job with attending classes on a part-time basis.

Training in specific industrial specialties can also be gotten through cooperative programs. In these, people who are already familiar with the fundamentals of drafting receive training in the practical and theoretical aspects of a particular craft, enabling them to perform specialized drafting duties associated with the craft.

Specialized training in the use of one manufacturer's CAD equipment may not be easily transferred to another kind of CAD equipment. Because the various CAD systems now in use are so different from each other, new employees may have to undergo a period of on-the-job training to acquaint them with the employer's system.

Special requirements

There are no requirements for licenses or certificates for this career. However, employers are favorably impressed by technicians who earn voluntary certification from the National Institute for Certification in Engineering Technologies. Certification is generally regarded as evidence that the technician is competent on the job and is interested in advancement.

Opportunities for experience and exploration

High-school students who are interested in drafting and design should ask their guidance counselors for as much information about the field as they can provide. If there is a vocational education or drafting and design program being taught in the high school, students should consider taking such courses, or at least talk to the instructors and students in the program to learn what the classes are like.

A visit to a nearby school that offers drafting courses could be very informative, as would be trips to workplaces where drafting and design work is done. At the offices of a business that involves drafting, students could see drafters at work and perhaps get them to talk about what they do and how they see the career field.

Part-time work can also be helpful. Prospective technicians may be able to get jobs as beginning clerks or assistants in an engineering and design department of a manufacturing company, architect's office, or other employer of drafters. Such part-time work or summer work provides a good understanding of what the work is all about.

Methods of entering

Technical schools and colleges help graduates find employment through their own student placement services and in cooperation with public and private employment agencies. Sometimes corporate recruiters visit schools to interview and hire students who are close to graduating. Job offers like this are usually the best, because they mean jobs are waiting for students when they graduate from the program.

Newspaper classified advertisements and direct inquiries to employers of drafting and design technicians are other important ways of finding employment in the field.

Advancement

After several years of experience, technicians who start as detailers may advance to the position of layout drafter. Layout drafters transform sketches, models, or verbal instructions into assembly drawings that will be filled in by the detailer. Layout drafters must have a two-year technical school education with a good background in tolerances, algebra, geometry, and trigonometry. Previous experience as a detailer is almost always needed so the technician can work more closely with detailers as members of the engineering team.

Several years of experience in layout drafting can permit one to advance to senior drafter. Senior drafters are sometimes referred to as designers, because they contribute to the initial development of the product rather than being concerned solely with the expression of an idea in graphic form. This job requires a combination of experience in the drafting and design area and specific technical know-how.

With further education, experienced technicians may advance to technical jobs in research, quality control, sales, management, product development, manufacturing, and perhaps ownership. The following paragraphs list some of the advancement possibilities, along with descriptions of job duties.

Assistant production managers manage production through involvement with receiving, manufacturing, and shipping operations. They also supervise other employees.

Customer relations engineers travel as company representatives to service equipment wherever it may be installed. They make necessary repairs and provide the technical know-how to do repair jobs.

Process engineers or *work simplification engineers* study engineering drawings and convert them to simpler process schedules showing a number of operations to be performed by semi-skilled machine operators.

Quality-control engineers promote precision in manufacturing through constant surveillance of the quality of finished products and of incoming raw materials and parts received from suppliers or subcontractors. Technicians in this position may supervise other workers.

Research designers develop new and better products through research and development procedures in laboratories.

Technical sales representatives show and demonstrate the company's products to possible consumers and provide any necessary advisory services.

Tool designers design tools such as milling machine cutters, fixtures, or jigs that are used to produce manufactured products. They modify tool designs for new models, making changes necessary to improve the product.

Tool engineers or *machine designers* design special machines and equipment used in manufacturing and supervise other drafters and detailers.

Time-and-motion study engineers are responsible for a time-and-motion study department, promoting more efficient work rates and use of time and materials in manufacturing.

Experienced drafters may also become teachers in schools and colleges that offer technical training.

Employment outlook

During the 1990s, employment in the drafting and design field will probably grow about as fast as the average for other occupations. While growth in the manufacturing sector and the expanding use of sophisticated computer technology will probably create more demand for drafting services, CAD systems will increase each worker's productivity, with the likely effect of little net change in employment in this field. Many openings that do occur will be related to the need to replace workers who have retired or moved to other areas of the labor force. Increasingly, employers will be seeking workers who have solid training that prepares them to do more than basic routine tasks.

Most drafters work in industries that would experience setbacks if the national economy went into a recession. Most economists foresee no such serious problems with the economy during the coming years. Drafters could, however, have more difficulty finding jobs or staying employed during an economic downturn, because employers would have to cut back on manufacturing and building activities that require drafting services.

Earnings

Salaries vary according to area of the country, the type of work, and other factors. Graduates of technical training programs who are entering their first jobs in the early 1990s can expect to start around $15,000 or more a year. After several years of experience they can be making salaries in the range of $17,000 to $27,000. Drafters who have considerable experience, especially in a specialized field, can earn $33,000 or more a year. Benefits depend on the employer and may include paid vacation days, holidays, insurance, pension plans, profit-sharing, and tuition refund plans.

Conditions of work

Most drafting duties confine technicians to indoor work, usually in an engineering department. Usually the work station is in a modern, adequately lighted, temperature-controlled office building. Safety and comfort are probably among the highest of any industrial job.

Some related tasks, however, may take technicians to a research laboratory, machine shop, or some manufacturing department. These tasks might be inspection or simple liaison duties between the engineering and design department and the producing or developing department. While on these shop or laboratory assignments, technicians need to be aware of safety in the area where they are working and may need to wear protective clothing or other gear.

Social and psychological factors

Drafting and design technicians are highly skilled workers who work individually. However, most of what they do reflects research results and ideas originally developed as sketches and data by an architect, engineer, or other professional. This means that technicians must be good team workers. They must be good at understanding and communicating in writing, sketching, and speaking. They must be analytical, careful, neat, and accurate in all they do because mistakes cause wasted time, material, and effort.

Often drafting and design technicians supervise other workers in drafting or in the production of the products. In this role they need to know how to get along well with people and how to encourage people that they supervise to work efficiently.

GOE: 05.03.02; SIC: 7389; SOC: 372

◇ **SOURCES OF ADDITIONAL INFORMATION**

National Architectural Accrediting Board
1735 New York Avenue, NW
Washington, DC 20006

American Institute for Design and Drafting
966 Hungerford Road, Suite 10-B
Rockville, MD 20854

Industrial Designers Society of America
1142-E Walker Road
Great Falls, VA 22066

Accreditation Board for Engineering and Technology
345 East 47th Street
New York, NY 10017

◇ **RELATED ARTICLES**

Volume 1: Construction; Design; Engineering; Machining and Machinery
Volume 2: Architects; Cartographers; Designers; Drafters; Engineers; Graphics programmers
Volume 4: Architectural and building construction technicians; CAD/CAM technicians; Surveying and mapping technicians

Electrical technicians

Definition

Electrical technicians work in support of and under the direction of electrical engineers. They work in nearly all phases and areas of the electric power industry. In general, their task is to apply their knowledge of electrical theory and related subjects to the design, assembly, testing, and modification of electrical circuits, devices, machines, and systems, both operational and experimental, in laboratories and industrial plants. Examples of equipment that electrical technicians might work on include motor-control devices, switch panels, transformers, generator windings, and solenoids.

As part of their work, electrical technicians may diagnose the causes of electrical or mechanical malfunctions and perform preventive or corrective maintenance. They develop wiring diagrams, layout drawings, and engineering specifications for system or equipment modification. They plan, direct, and record the results of periodic testing of electrical equipment and recommend or initiate modification or replace-

An electrical technician installs a switch near the doorway of a house that is being renovated.

ment of equipment that fails to meet acceptable operating standards. Electrical technicians also direct personnel performing routine installation and maintenance duties.

Electrical technicians use precise electrical measuring devices as well as a variety of hand tools, such as screwdrivers, pliers, and soldering irons. They also read blueprints and consult electrical and engineering handbooks.

History

The modern electrical utility industry was born on September 4, 1882, in Thomas Edison's central generating station, a small brick building on Pearl Street near New York City's business district. On that day, a switch was thrown and immediately incandescent lamps began to glow in homes and offices in the surrounding neighborhood.

Edison first became interested in the possibilities of electrical lighting in 1878. In the following year he demonstrated the first practical incandescent lamp designed to give a soft, even glow instead of the hard, flickering light of gas jets. Then he turned his attention to developing the machinery and equipment necessary to distribute electrical power—including generators, sockets, fuses, and devices to measure and regulate the flow of current.

No special training was needed by workers in the early days of the electrical power business. Workers needed only to be handy with tools and have good common sense. The growing complexity of the industry, however, called for more and more professionally trained scientists and engineers and for trained assistants,

now known as electrical technicians, to work with them. Today automation and advanced technology, including developments in microcircuitry and the laser, have made their work much more sophisticated than it was in the days of the first incandescent bulb.

Nature of the work

Electrical technicians are employed in many different settings—power plants, manufacturing facilities, research laboratories—and in many different capacities—research, maintenance, repair, sales, employee supervision. One of the most commonly held positions for an electrical technician is that of the *power system technician* who operates and maintains power generation and distribution equipment. These technicians are employed by public utility companies and other institutions such as hospitals, colleges, military bases, and large industries that generate their own electricity. These technicians monitor control panels, diagnose equipment problems, carry out inspections, order repairs, and supervise crews of electrical workers who do routine work in the plant.

Another commonly held position for electrical technicians working for electric power companies is that of *relay technician.* Relay technicians test and repair equipment and circuits used in the transmission and distribution of electric power. They also perform tests to locate defects such as poor insulation and malfunctioning relays.

Electrical research technicians, electrical laboratory technicians, and *engineering aides* are other positions for electrical technicians. These technicians often work with electrical engineers in commercial manufacturing companies or in engineering consulting firms in the design of electrical equipment, from small household appliances to huge power generating stations. They prepare layout drawings, wiring diagrams, and engineering specifications for new equipment. They also assemble, test, modify, and supervise the installation of new circuits, devices, and equipment.

Commercial manufacturing plants also provide job settings for electrical technicians. Here they repair, modify, and maintain electrically controlled or electrically powered manufacturing equipment. Automation and the growing number of computer-controlled machine tools have today made the electrical technician an increasingly important member of the production team. An electrical technician on the scene can solve production bottlenecks and devise miniaturized backup power sources. A technician's skills may make his or her contribution an important one in managerial decision-making, such as in determining the positioning of electrically powered machinery on the assembly line.

Possibly the most exciting opportunities for electrical technicians are in the field of communications. Telephone lines, for example, are used for more than spoken messages. Pictures, video signals, and computer data are all capable of being converted into digital form and transmitted through a cable system alongside thousands of ordinary telephone calls traveling on the same cable. Satellites, cable television, and low-power television are all areas in the communications field that offer opportunities for the electrical technician who is eager for the challenges that are attendant in developing new technologies.

Requirements

Electrical technicians should have good manual dexterity, the ability to learn new concepts and adapt to changing demands, well-developed skills in both spoken and written communication, and the ability to get along with others.

Preparation for a career as an electrical technician should begin early in a student's high-school program. The more thorough a background a student receives in mathematics and the physical sciences, the easier his or her future training and career path will be.

Students should look into the entrance requirements of postsecondary schools in which they are interested as early in their high-school programs as possible. In this way they will be certain that they meet all the entrance requirements. They should work closely with their guidance departments and carefully follow the department's advice.

Students planning careers as electrical technicians should consider attending a two-year technical institute in the field of electrical technology. Primary emphasis in such a program will be on specialized subjects in the student's chosen field. These programs will include such courses as basic electricity, electrical machinery, electrical power and control systems, and electronics.

Students may also take technical courses in mathematics, physics, and drafting. Courses will be provided that will improve the student's ability in written and spoken communications. Courses will also be required in the humanities

to help round out the student's sense of self and of the outside world.

Special requirements

Licenses and certification are usually not required for positions available to electrical technicians. They are, however, a recognition of education, experience, and ability. Because of this, many employers and technicians feel that a license or certificate is well worth earning.

Some electrical technicians are required to belong to unions.

Opportunities for experience and exploration

Visits to electrical power plants, industrial laboratories, or manufacturing facilities can provide a vivid means of career exploration. Through such visits a student can watch technicians actually involved in their work. It may be possible to speak with them about what they do on the job or talk with their employers about possibilities for future employment.

Electrical shop courses in high school offer a good opportunity for getting the feel of working with electrical appliances and devices and for beginning to learn some of the basic principles of their operation.

Students can also learn much about this career and the training required for it by writing to schools providing the training and requesting information about their programs.

Methods of entering

Private companies often send lists of job openings or, in some cases, their recruiters to schools offering programs in electrical technology. Most graduating students have their choice of a number of offers.

Some students may seek employment opportunities other than those offered on campus. These contacts can result in excellent opportunities. State employment agencies, school placement directors, and newspaper want ads may also provide openings. Students may also write directly to utility companies and other companies that hire technicians.

Advancement

As electrical technicians gain experience, they are generally given more responsible assignments and generally work with less and less supervision. Some technicians acquire advanced and specialized training and move into research activities and other areas of electrical technology that require more sophisticated skills. Other technicians move into supervisory positions, and those with exceptional ability can sometimes qualify for professional positions after receiving additional training.

The following is a list of some of the positions that electrical technicians commonly advance to:

Electrical construction supervisors do production scheduling, estimating, and coordinating.

Product-development technicians develop and research new products, including their market possibilities.

Electrical-laboratory associates handle complex testing and measuring on laboratory equipment and systems.

Field-service technicians handle technical sales, maintenance, service, and product adaptations to meet customer needs.

Senior technical writers develop complex instruction manuals involving operation, maintenance, and repair of electrical equipment and systems.

Electrical-instrumentation supervisors calibrate and design various kinds of instruments, as measuring and control devices, and supervise maintenance and repair procedures affecting them.

Electrical-research associates do research into electrical current phenomena, such as the behavior of electrical current at low temperatures or under other specialized circumstances.

Employment outlook

The field of electrical technology is one of continuing growth as new electrical products and services are constantly being developed for military, industrial, and consumer markets. It appears that the employment levels in this area will grow faster than the average of all other occupations through the 1990s. Technicians who graduate from a two-year technical school will probably be able to find work most easily.

Jobs that have recently come into being include overseeing the operation of cable television networks that use their own cable system or share a cable with another transmission company. Newspapers and magazines are also now requiring the services of technicians to work with equipment for electronically transmitting typeset material from typesetting plants, via microwave frequencies, to presses hundreds of miles away.

As advanced forms of microcircuitry become more important, so will the electrical technician. Technicians interested in research and development may find themselves devising miniature power systems for space capsules and communications systems for orbiting satellites. An understanding of microcircuitry may even take them into such medical fields as heart transplant surgery.

Employment levels for electrical technicians working in defense-related industries could fall somewhat if the government decreases its rate of military spending.

Earnings

Most electrical technicians receive salaries that range from $18,000 to $30,000 a year, with the average roughly $25,000. Some electrical technicians, especially those at the beginning of their careers, earn as little as $10,000 to $14,000 a year. However, some senior technicians earn as much as $37,000 to $50,000 a year or more.

Other benefits that a company may offer will vary. Tuition refunds, paid holidays and vacations, health and life insurance, and profit-sharing may be included.

Conditions of work

Electrical technology is generally considered to be an excellent employment area in which to work. Facilities are usually quite new, and every attempt is made to keep the equipment and working areas in excellent condition.

Electrical current can be dangerous; however, the electrical safety practices that are in effect reduce problems to a level where they need not be a serious factor in considering employment in this field. Some electrical technicians working in generating plants or on production lines will be exposed to a high noise level. Hours may vary, and some technicians may be required to perform overtime work, especially in the case of equipment failure.

Social and psychological factors

Electrical technicians must be adaptable and willing to learn. The rapidly changing nature of electrical technology requires individuals who can continue to keep abreast of the advances in the field.

The days of inventors working alone in attics are gone. Technicians must be able to get along well with others, both with the skilled trade worker whose work they may direct and supervise and with the professionally trained scientists and engineers who hold final responsibility for a project or installation.

Electrical technicians are asked to handle a wide range of duties, from the uncomplicated and routine to the highly complex and challenging. Technicians need to have the personal flexibility to handle all of these duties with attention and precision.

GOE: 05.01.01; SIC: Any industry; SOC: 3711

◇ SOURCES OF ADDITIONAL INFORMATION

American Society for Engineering Education
11 Dupont Circle, Suite 200
Washington, DC 20036

Institute of Electrical and Electronic Engineers
345 East 47th Street
New York, NY 10017

Junior Engineering Technical Society (JETS)
1428 King Street
Suite 405
Alexandria, VA 22314

National Action Council for Minorities in Engineering
3 West 35th Street
New York, NY 10001

◇ RELATED ARTICLES

Volume 1: Electronics; Energy; Engineering; Public Utilities
Volume 2: Engineers
Volume 3: Communications equipment mechanics; Electrical repairers; Electricians; Power plant occupations; Telephone and PBX installers and repairers
Volume 4: Cable television technicians; Electromechanical technicians; Electronics sales and service technicians; Electronics technicians; Electronics test technicians; Industrial engineering technicians; Nuclear reactor operator technicians; Telecommunications technicians; Transmitter technicians

Electromechanical technicians

Definition

Electromechanical technicians build, test, adjust, and repair automated equipment that incorporates electronic sensing devices for monitoring, controlling, or activating mechanical operations. They assist mechanical engineers in the design and development of such equipment, analyze test results, and write reports. An electromechanical technician may follow blueprints, operate metalworking machines, and use hand tools and precision measuring and testing devices to build instrument housings, install electrical equipment, and calibrate instruments and machinery. Some electromechanical technicians specialize in the assembly of prototype instruments and are known as development technicians. Electromechanical technicians who specialize in the assembly of production instruments are known as *fabrication technicians*.

History

Electromechanical technology is a relatively new field that is concerned with the interaction of electrical, electronic, and mechanical devices. It has its roots in the late eighteenth and early

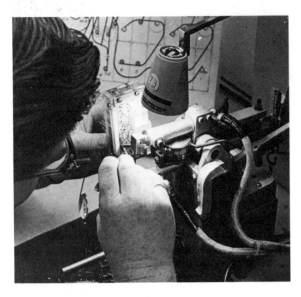

An electromechanical technician repairs a control device that maintains the quality of a product during its manufacture. Such work requires patience and manual skill.

Nature of the work

Electromechanical technicians work in many different aspects of the building, testing, installation, and repair of electromechanical devices and systems such as plant automation equipment, automated environmental control systems, elevator controls, missile controls, computer tape drives, and other auxiliary computer equipment.

Electromechanical technicians working in the manufacturing and product-development side of the computer industry develop and test precision mechanical devices such as magnetic tape drives and readers and high-speed printing machines. In the continuing search for means of increasing speed and reliability, these technicians make laboratory studies in experimental applied physics, vibration analysis, and environmental testing, in addition to researching problems in assembly and manufacturing techniques.

The computer and office equipment industries also offer opportunities in the areas of preventive maintenance and repair of existing equipment, both in-factory and on-site.

In addition to performing jobs directly related to computers, electromechanical technicians also work in a broad range of manufacturing, research, and repair occupations, including operating electronic control systems in factories; ensuring proper quality control in the manufacturing of electromechanical devices; providing maintenance services for electromechanical devices, both those returned to the factory and those still on the customer's premises; and working in the new-product field.

The technician employed in the operation of electronic manufacturing-control systems is usually a specialist in the calibration and repair of specialized control devices that electronically sense the temperature, thickness, color, or other characteristic of some product or material, and automatically maintain the continuing manufacture within accepted standards. In the manufacture of paper, for instance, electromechanical technicians maintain the devices that determine the texture of fibers and the thickness of the final product. Similar controls, designed to fit the specific requirements of their field, are adapted to steel rolling mills, the manufacture of ball bearings, and the manufacture of plastics.

The nature, purpose, and complexity of electromechanical devices will vary according to the manufacturing processes to which they have been applied. In cases where manufacturing processes require especially sophisticated control, there is sometimes a need for specially

nineteenth centuries, when engineers developed countless machines designed to do the work previously done by human workers. Many of these mechanical devices, however, could not be considered fully automated, for they still required alert and sharp-eyed human attendants to operate, monitor, and control all of the machine's activities.

During the first half of the twentieth century, electronic devices were invented that could sense various aspects of their environment. These devices included photocells that sense the presence or absence of an object between itself and a light source; thermocouples and resistance thermometers that electronically measure and reveal changes in temperature; stress and strain sensors that convert mechanical stresses into measurable electrical currents; and proximity sensors that can measure the distance between two electrical conductors or any two objects to which the conductors are attached. It was the wedding of these electrical and electronic devices with various kinds of automated machinery that gave birth to the field of electromechanical technology.

Today, many electromechanical technicians work in the computer and office equipment industries; however, electromechanical devices are also employed in many other industries. Among the many uses are automatic guidance systems in rockets, missiles, and satellites, in quality control systems in manufacturing, and in oil and gas exploration.

trained operations technicians, who work in conjunction with the technicians who perform repairs and recalibration. These operations technicians control the day-to-day functioning of equipment used in manufacturing and in other fields whose workings are too complex for ordinary operating personnel to handle.

Technicians employed in the quality control of the manufactured electromechanical product will usually be required to adjust, interpret, and calibrate complex equipment. Upon acquiring further knowledge of the product, the technician may test completed assemblies that interact with other units that are required for a larger system, whether that system be a radar station, a computer network, or a communications system.

Electromechanical technicians working in the field of maintenance may function at many levels of experience and knowledge. For instance, the theory required for maintaining a dictating machine will not be as extensive as that required for the maintenance of a missile guidance system. The opportunities in the maintenance field are wide, including the opportunity for travel for technicians who are so inclined. The maintenance of especially complex products, such as the probes used in oil and gas exploration and drilling and the electrical control or detection devices used in military and industrial security, may call for travel to any part of the world where the installation has been made, if that is where the maintenance must be conducted.

Electromechanical technicians working in maintenance may also be employed at the manufacturing plant or branch facilities, where they maintain electromechanical equipment that has been removed from the installation and returned for overhaul, recalibration, or repair. These technicians will be expected to have special skills for maintaining the product but need not be as skilled at customer relations as the traveling technician must be.

Technicians employed in product development need the ability to conceive new ideas and to imagine the results that come from modifying designs or principles or from introducing entirely new ones. Because new products are meant to be better products, technicians should be able to analyze how new or modified techniques will work in place of established concepts. These technicians will operate under the supervision of development engineers and be required to understand their language to translate into functioning products the principles originated by the engineers.

Research technicians frequently work with no direct supervision. They may work on their own or as part of a team doing research and design of an entirely new product. Successful research technicians frequently advance to engineering work or are classified as engineers for the work they do.

Requirements

The requirements for a successful career as an electromechanical technician will vary according to the specific area of electromechanical technology in which a person chooses to become involved. In general, however, electromechanical technicians should have an aptitude for mathematics and science, good eyesight and finger dexterity, and the ability to pursue complex questions patiently and methodically. A tolerance for following prescribed procedures is essential, especially in undertaking assignments that require an undeviating system of problem-solving, such as troubleshooting a complex computer. All electromechanical technicians need to feel the kind of motivation for their work that will help sustain interest, patience, and steady habits even in the face of repetitive tasks.

Electromechanical technicians involved in the on-site repair of customer's equipment should have the ability to maintain good customer relations. For those involved in repairing electronic manufacturing-control systems, the ability to remain calm under pressure is especially important. Because the equipment on which they work is essential to continuing production, delays can cost tens of thousands of dollars. Successful technicians are able to provide solutions quickly and accurately even in this kind of stressful situation.

Manufacturing control technicians and operations technicians need to have a strong background in basic electrical, electronic, and mechanical principles, as well as a broad understanding of the system, machinery, or equipment to which the electromechanical controls are being applied. In addition, operations technicians especially should have a thorough understanding of all of the functions of the electromechanical equipment with which they are working and with its purpose and end product.

Despite the need for accuracy and a willingness to follow precise approaches to problems, the electromechanical technician's abilities must not be limited to rigid performance of duties. Electromechanical technicians are something like physicians in that they must diagnose the ailment before applying treatment. Also like physicians, they must be ready and able to find new and original answers when a prescribed treatment does not work. Many improvements result from the experience of technicians who discover that a theory does not always work and that a practical approach sometimes can solve problems that were not anticipated by the original designers.

Because of the possibilities for advancement in the field, a technician's ability to accept change and the ambition to keep abreast of new products and scientific discoveries are important personal qualifications.

The personal qualifications of those involved only in the assembly of electromechanical devices are not as varied as those mentioned above. In such capacities, the manufacturer is likely to place more emphasis on the study of related subject matter than on the ability to improvise solutions or work with other team members or customers.

High-school students interested in a career in electromechanical technology should learn all of the mathematics and science possible. Courses designed for students preparing for engineering education are appropriate for the technician. Minimum requirements for most programs that prepare the student for training beyond high school usually include one year of geometry and one year of algebra (or two years of algebra), a year of physics, and another year of a laboratory science. English courses are a basic requirement in all high-school programs, and potential technicians should look especially for English courses that stress speech and composition skills.

Students who lack this kind of well-balanced foundation should not be discouraged. Most schools of higher education provide courses or intensive-study programs designed to overcome a lack of preparation in various subjects.

For those who expect to make electromechanical technology a lifetime career, education beyond high school is essential. Many colleges and training institutes have training programs in electromechanical technology. Others offer programs in related areas such as electronics or electrical or mechanical engineering technology. Such programs usually take two years to complete. Typical courses during the first year include electricity and electronics, principles of physics, mathematics, technical graphics, English composition, introduction to data processing, and mechanisms. Typical courses for the second year include digital computer fundamentals, electromechanical components, control systems, digital computing systems, input-output devices, storage principles and devices, psychology and human relations, and hydraulics and pneumatics.

Companies employing technicians in the business equipment field usually provide training programs to supplement the background of employees recruited from technical institutes and colleges. All new employees receive training in an introductory course that may extend eight to fifteen weeks. Upon graduation from the basic program, those who are selected for technical training are then sent to a special school where all the techniques required by the company are taught. The time spent in both schools may last nearly one year, during which the technician receives a weekly salary and living expenses.

Special requirements

Electromechanical technicians still in school may become members of the Institute of Electrical and Electronic Engineers or the American Society of Certified Engineering Technicians, provided they are in an engineering technology program. Membership in either of these associations is voluntary.

Some of the organizations listed at the end of this article offer certification programs available to electromechanical technicians. Such certification is seldom a requirement for employment, but it is a way of demonstrating interest and accomplishment in the field.

Some technicians are required to belong to a union.

Opportunities for exploration and experience

There are a number of possibilities for the exploration of the various fields in which electromechanical technicians are employed. In towns where equipment manufacturers maintain manufacturing facilities, repair shops, or industrial laboratories, school counselors may plan field trips. It may be possible for a student to get a summer or weekend job at such a facility or to arrange to accompany a technician on service rounds. Repair and installation of data-processing and other office machines may be observed in the student's own school if the school uses such equipment. Visits to major industrial installations, such as steel mills, automobile factories, or petroleum refineries, offer an excellent opportunity to see electronic manufacturing-control devices in operation.

Methods of entering

The most reliable and accepted method of entering into this field is through the institution that provided the student's technical training. Most of these institutions have a student placement service and are in constant touch with those industries in need of technicians.

People not enrolled in a technical institute or college should visit companies where they hope eventually to find employment. In the course of such a visit they should inquire about employment opportunities and about what courses of study will be most helpful.

Advancement

Advancement in this field is quite regular for those who continue studying during employment. Technicians usually begin work under the direct supervision of an experienced technician, scientist, or engineer, and then, as they gain experience, they are given more responsible assignments, often carrying out particular work programs under only very general supervision.

From there, technicians may move into supervisory positions and those with exceptional ability can sometimes qualify for professional positions after receiving additional training. Some technicians advance by becoming technical writers, sales representatives, or instructors.

Employment outlook

The computer and business equipment industries are major employers of electromechanical technicians, and the long-term outlook for these industries is favorable. In addition, the ongoing movement toward more automation in manufacturing industries will call for more technicians with a combined knowledge of electronic, electrical, and mechanical principles. Because of these factors, the demand for electromechanical technicians should remain strong through the year 2000. However, all of these industries are vulnerable to downturns in the economy, and some mild or temporary downturn has been predicted by some economists for the 1990s. Because of this there may be periods when the demand for electromechanical technicians slackens and competition for good jobs increases. In periods like this, technicians with less training and motivation may find good jobs hard to find.

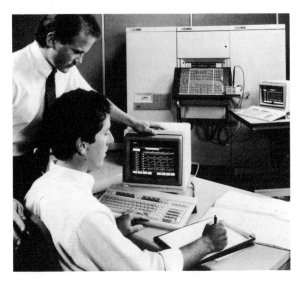

An electromechanical technician operates a combinational board-test system that performs both in-circuit component tests and functional tests.

Earnings

Salaries for electromechanical technicians vary considerably depending on the extent of the individual's education, experience, area of specialization, the type of firm in which the technician is employed, and the geographical location of the job.

In general, however, starting salaries for those who are graduates of post–high-school technical programs average from about $15,000 to $19,000 per year in industry. Those with less formal training earn somewhat less. Most experienced electromechanical technicians earn between $20,000 and $30,000 a year, and some successful technicians earn between $30,000 and $40,000 a year or more.

Conditions of work

Because the work of electromechanical technicians is connected with and serves other industries, the conditions vary greatly from place to place. In general, however, electromechanical equipment will only work well in temperature- and humidity-controlled environments. Therefore most electromechanical technicians can be assured of a safe and comfortable working environment. Most technicians work regular thirty-five to forty-hour weeks, although some service technicians may be required to work overtime on short notice or to be away from home for several days in a row traveling on a service call. Some technicians do elect to work for extended periods of time on equipment in rugged or out-of-doors environments; however, such technicians are compensated financially for the hardships involved.

The work of the electromechanical technician rarely requires great strength or strenuous exertion, although it may require the technician to spend hours in an awkward position, standing, sitting, or crouched beside a machine.

Social and psychological factors

Electromechanical technicians may work alone, in pairs, or as part of a small team. Almost all technicians need the ability to get along well with and work cooperatively with other people—both customers and coworkers. In some cases electromechanical technicians need to be able to work well under pressure. Most will also need a healthy tolerance for routine, uncomplicated, and sometimes repetitive tasks.

Electromechanical technology is a field that is constantly changing. These changes bring both the opportunities for advancement and the risks of being left behind by an advancing technology. Successful technicians have a sense of ambition that helps them pursue both formal and informal continuing education so that they are well poised to take advantage of changes.

GOE: 05.05.11; SIC: Any industry; SOC: 6171

◇ SOURCES OF ADDITIONAL INFORMATION

International Society of Certified Electronics Technicians
2708 West Berry Street, Suite 8
Fort Worth, TX 76109

Institute of Electrical and Electronic Engineers
345 East 47th Street
New York, NY 10017

American Society of Mechanical Engineers
345 East 47th Street
New York, NY 10017

Computer and Business Equipment Manufacturers Association
311 First Street, NW
5th Floor
Washington, DC 20001

American Society for Engineering Education
11 Dupont Circle
Suite 200
Washington, DC 20036

◇ RELATED ARTICLES

Volume 1: Engineering; Machining and Machinery
Volume 2: Engineers
Volume 3: Computer and peripheral equipment operators; Industrial machinery mechanics
Volume 4: CAD/CAM technicians; Computer-service technicians; Electronics technicians; Industrial engineering technicians; Instrumentation technicians; Mechanical technicians; Robotics technicians

Electronics sales and service technicians

Definition

Electronics sales and service technicians work with customers interested in acquiring electronics equipment for use in their homes or businesses. This equipment typically includes televisions, audio and video equipment, microwave ovens, and other kinds of home electronic devices. Technicians meet with potential customers and discuss their requirements and the various kinds of equipment that are available to meet those requirements. In order to meet special needs, they may recommend how existing equipment can be modified or combined with other equipment in some new way to provide what the customer wants. Once equipment has been selected, the technician supervises its installation and maintains the equipment in good working order. Technicians also make repairs when necessary and advise customers regarding the replacement of equipment that is no longer practical to maintain. Some electronics sales and service technicians may work with electronic office equipment, such as photocopy machines, dictating machines, and facsimile, or fax, machines.

History

Most of the electronics products that we use today were developed during the twentieth century; however, most of these products are based on principles of electronics that were discovered in the nineteenth century. Modern television, for instance, is based on principles that were first demonstrated in the 1850s by Heinrich Geissler, whose experiments showed that electricity discharged in a vacuum tube causes small amounts of rare gases in the tube to glow. Later investigations showed that the glow is caused by the freeing of electrons. Experimenters in the late 1800s and early 1900s worked further with vacuum tubes until Karl Braun, in 1898, made the first cathode ray tube that could control the electron flow. In 1907 Lee De Forest developed the first amplifying tube, used to strengthen electronic signals.

At this point, the basic elements of modern television transmission existed, but they had not yet been combined into a system. In 1922, a sixteen-year-old named Philo Farnsworth developed a practical electronic scanning system. Shortly afterwards, in 1923, Vladimir Zworykin developed the iconoscope and the kinescope, the basic elements of, respectively, the television camera and the television receiver. Zworykin's first practical, all-electronic, television system was demonstrated for the first time publicly in 1929.

Radio followed a similar path of development. But though the roots of television and radio lie in the 1800s, neither medium had developed to the point of needing a sales and service industry until regular commercial broadcasting began and people began to purchase receivers. For radio, commercial broadcasting began in 1920, when KDKA, Pittsburgh, and WWJ, Detroit, went on the air. For television, regular broadcasting began in 1946, when six stations went on the air. By 1950 there were 6 million television sets in the United States; by 1989 there were more than 100 million. Almost every household now has at least one television, and almost two-thirds of U.S. households have more than one television set.

Owners of early radios made most of their own repairs. Sets were simple, and the range of possible solutions to problems was small. As the broadcasting industry grew and new improvements resulted in more complicated sets, trade and technical institutes were established to train technicians. Correspondence schools were started and became popular during the Great Depression of the 1930s, when many people were seeking new careers or ways to supplement their incomes.

The explosive growth of television broadcasting after World War II created an almost instant demand for trained television service technicians. Trade and technical schools again boomed, aided this time by the GI Bill's educational benefits, which enabled many veterans to study television servicing. The field was especially attractive to those ex-servicemen who had been communications or electronics technicians in the armed forces. The subsequent development of the transistor, stereophonic sound, and color television resulted in television sets, radios, and other home electronics equipment that could only be serviced by trained technicians with adequate testing equipment and repair tools.

An electronics sales and service technician must know how to install and repair electronic business equipment.

The 1970s and 1980s saw a tremendous growth in the number and variety of electronic devices introduced into homes and businesses. Miniature and super screen projection televisions, video cameras and videocassette recorders (VCRs), microcomputers and printers, microwave ovens, telephone answering machines—all became common household items, and fax machines, desktop photocopiers, and electronic securities systems became common in offices. The growth in this field has led to a continuing and expanding need for trained technicians to assist in the sales, installation, maintenance, and repairing of home and office electronics equipment.

Nature of the work

The primary work of electronics sales and service technicians who are involved with service and repair is to diagnose and repair malfunctions in electronic home-entertainment equipment, including television sets and video recording equipment, radios and audio recording equipment, personal computer peripheral equipment, and such related electronic equipment as garage door openers, microwave ovens, electronic organs, and amplifying equipment for other electrified musical instruments. Their work usually begins with gathering information from customers about the problems they are having with their equipment. A preliminary inspection may reveal a loose connection or other simple problem, and the technician may be able to complete repairs quickly. In other cases a problem may be more complicated and may require that the equipment be taken to a shop for more thorough testing and the installation of new components.

Electronics sales and service technicians are classified as inside or outside technicians. The outside technicians make service calls on customers, gather information, and make preliminary examinations of malfunctioning equipment. Inside, or bench, technicians work in shops where they make more thorough examinations of problems using testing equipment and hand tools such as pliers and socket wrenches to dismantle sets and make repairs. Testing equipment used includes voltmeters, oscilloscopes, and signal generators. Both inside and outside technicians need manual dexterity, mechanical aptitude, and a solid knowledge of practical electronics.

The servicing of other kinds of electronic equipment, such as audio and videocassette recorders, requires special knowledge of their components. Electronics technicians gain knowledge about such special areas and keep up with new developments in electronics by attending short courses given by manufacturers at their factory or by a factory technician at local shops.

Electronics sales and service technicians involved with the sale of electronics equipment meet with potential customers and discuss and explain the kinds of equipment that are available to meet the specific needs of the customer. They describe the features of the equipment, explain the manufacturer's specifications, and demonstrate the use of the equipment. For customers with special needs, they may recommend ways in which existing equipment can be modified or combined with other equipment in some new way to provide what the customer wants. Once equipment has been selected, the technician may also be involved, often in a supervisory capacity, with the installation and maintenance of the equipment. These technicians also make repairs when necessary, and they advise customers regarding replacement of equipment that is no longer practical to maintain.

Requirements

Persons interested in careers as electronics sales and service technicians should take mathematics courses at least through algebra and plane geometry in high school, and should have a good working knowledge of shop math. They should develop their language skills so they can read electronics texts and manuals comfortably and express themselves well when making spoken and written proposals. People interested in electronics should have at least two years of training beyond high school in a technical institute or community college, studying electronics theory and repair of televisions, radios, and other electronic equipment.

Electronics sales and service technicians need manual dexterity and mechanical ability to perform their duties. They should be familiar with and able to use electrician's hand tools and basic electronic and electrical testing equipment. Precision and accuracy are often required in adjusting electronic equipment. The physical requirements of their work are moderate, sometimes involving lifting and carrying television sets and other equipment. Technicians are often required to stand and bend for extended periods while working.

Technicians often work in customer's homes; therefore, they should be able to meet and communicate clearly with strangers. The ability to extract useful information from customers about their equipment can be a great time-saver.

Special requirements

Some states require some electronics sales and service technicians to be licensed. Such licenses are obtained by passing tests in electronics and demonstrating proficiency with testing equipment. Prospective technicians should check with a training institution in their state to determine whether licensing is required.

Only a few technicians belong to labor unions. Most of those who belong are members of the International Brotherhood of Electrical Workers.

Opportunities for experience and exploration

Local electronics sales and service technicians are usually willing to share their experience and knowledge with interested young people. Owners of stores or repair shops may be especially helpful with the business aspects of a career in the field. Summer employment as a helper or a delivery person can provide an opportunity to observe the day-to-day activities of technicians.

Schools that offer training in radio, television, and other related technology fields are usually glad to supply information about their programs to prospective students. Local chapters of the International Brotherhood of Electrical Workers and local offices of the state employment service can also supply information about training opportunities and about the employment outlook in your area.

Methods of entering

Entry into this field may be through graduation from a technical school, through an apprenticeship program, or through on-the-job training.

By far the majority of persons entering the television and radio service technician field do so by graduating from an accredited technical training program and beginning work as a trained technician. These technicians either apply directly to a prospective employer for a position or look for work with the help of their school placement officer. Most of them require a further year of shop supervision before they are able to work independently without the supervision of a more experienced eletronics technician.

Apprenticeship programs stress practical experience over theory. In a typical four-year postsecondary school program comprising about 8,000 hours, approximately 550 are devoted to classroom work and the remainder to supervised shop work.

On-the-job training is becoming much less common. Where shops formerly provided complete on-the-job instruction for untrained employees, they are now usually limiting such training to current employees—delivery drivers, antenna installers, and so forth—who show a basic understanding of electronics, a flair for careful work, and an interest in learning. Such opportunities usually occur in shops that place a higher value on practical experience than on theory. Even so, individuals in such programs will have to supplement their practical training with evening school or home-study courses.

Advancement

Advancement in this field depends to a large extent on the size and character of the technician's place of employment. Early advancement usually comes in the form of increased salary and less supervision as a recognition of the technician's increasing skill. In a small shop, the only other advancement possibility may be for the technician to go into business alone, if the community can support another retail store or repair shop.

In a larger store or shop, the electronics technician usually advances to a supervisory position, as a *crew chief, sales supervisor, senior technician,* or *service or sales manager.* This may involve not only scheduling and assigning work, but also training new employees and arranging refresher courses and factory training in new products for experienced electronics technicians.

Technicians with strong theoretical training in electronics may go on to become technical school instructors. They may also become service representatives for manufacturers. Those employed in stores or shops that handle a wide variety of electronics sales and service work may become involved in working on the more complicated equipment, from radio-frequency heating equipment to electron microscopes. This work may also lead to working with engineers in designing and testing new electronic equipment.

Employment outlook

Employment of electronics sales and service technicians is expected to increase about as fast as the average of other occupations through the year 2000. The increased demand will stem from an increased number of television and radio receivers in service, and from the rapid growth of other home electronics equipment such as VCRs and computer video games operated through television sets. On the other hand, continuing improvements in electronics technology and the increasing use of modular components will limit somewhat the demand for service technicians and will keep employment levels from rising as fast as might otherwise be expected.

Earnings

As trainees, electronics sales and service technicians earn between $8,000 and $17,500 a year. More experienced technicians earn between $14,000 and $50,000 a year, with the average being about $27,000 a year. Self-employed technicians earn higher than average salaries, generally, but they also work longer hours. For employed technicians, forty-hour weeks are normal, with time-and-a-half for overtime and an increment for night work.

Conditions of work

The work of electronics technicians is performed indoors, in homes and shops, under generally comfortable conditions. Outside technicians may spend considerable time driving from call to call. All technicians risk occasional electrical shock.

Social and psychological factors

Once they have completed their training, electronics sales and service technicians work with a minimum of supervision. They must be able to work carefully and accurately. Because the result of their work is often immediately evident to the owner of the equipment, service technicians especially must be able to take criticism when they are not completely successful.

Because of the constantly changing technology of electronic devices, electronics sales and service technicians must be willing to keep growing and learning in their trade skills if they are to be successful.

GOE: 05.05.05, 05.10.03; SIC: 367; SOC: 6153, 6155

◇ SOURCES OF ADDITIONAL INFORMATION

American Electronics Association
5201 Great American Parkway
Suite 520
Santa Clara, CA 95054

Electronics Industries Association
1722 I Street, NW
Suite 300
Washington, DC 20006

Electronic Industries Foundation
1901 Pensylvania Avenue, NW
Suite 700
Washington, DC 20006

Electronics Technicians Association
604 North Jackson
Greencastle, IN 46135

International Society of Certified Electronics Technicians
2708 West Berry Street
Suite 8
Fort Worth, TX 76109

National Electronics Sales and Service Dealers Association
2708 West Berry Street
Ft. Worth, TX 76109

Semiconductor Industry Association
10201 Torro Avenue
Suite 275
Cupertino, CA 95014

American Society of Certified Engineering Technicians
PO Box 7789
Shawnee Mission, KS 66207

◇ **RELATED ARTICLES**

Volume 1: Electronics
Volume 2: Engineers; Retail business owners; Retail managers
Volume 3: Commercial and industrial electronic equipment repairers; Electronic home entertainment equipment repairers; Office machine servicers; Retail sales workers
Volume 4: Audiovisual technicians; Electro-mechanical technicians; Electronic organ technicians; Electronics technicians; Electronics test technicians

Electronics technicians

Definition

Electronics technicians assemble, install, repair, maintain, calibrate, and modify electronic circuitry, components, and systems. Electronics technicians involved with the development of new electronic equipment work closely with electronics engineers and help to determine changes or modifications in circuitry or other design elements.

Other electronics technicians are concerned principally with checking out newly installed equipment or with instructing and supervising lower-grade technicians in installation, assembly, or repair activities.

All technicians working in the field of electronics technology may be called upon to set up test apparatus, conduct tests, analyze test results, and prepare reports, sketches, graphs, and schematic drawings to describe electronics systems and their characteristics.

Electronics technicians operate bench lathes, drills, and other machine and hand tools. The work of electronics technicians requires high levels of manual dexterity, patience to handle small electronic parts, and excellent eye sight.

Depending on their area of specialization, electronics technicians may be designated *computer-laboratory technicians*, *development-instrumentation technicians*, *electronic-communications technicians*, *nuclear-reactor electronics technicians*, *engineering-development technicians*, or *systems-testing laboratory technicians*.

History

Electronics is a field of technology concerned with the behavior of electrons as they pass through gases, liquids, solids, and vacuums. Historically, electronics can be seen as an outgrowth of electrical engineering, which is concerned chiefly with the movement of electrons along conductors. As the field of electronics has expanded in scope, however, so has its definition, and today the term is often used to describe all areas of technology, including electrical engineering, that are concerned with the behavior of electrons in electronic devices and equipment. Examples of electronic equipment include consumer products such as radios, televisions, stereos, and calculators and industrial and office equipment such as computers and radio and television broadcasting equipment.

Although the field of electronics has had its most spectacular growth and development during the twentieth century, it is actually the product of more than 200 years of study and experiment. One of the important early experimenters in this field was Benjamin Franklin. His experiments with lightning and his theory that electrical charges are present in all matter influenced the thinking and established much of the vocabulary of the researchers who came after him.

The invention of the electric battery, or voltaic pile, by the Italian scientist Alessandro Volta in 1800 ushered in a century of significant discoveries in the field of electricity and magnetism. Researchers working throughout Europe and the United States made important breakthroughs in understanding how to strengthen, control, and measure the flow of electrons moving through vacuums. These experiments culminated around the turn of the century in the description and measurement by Sir Joseph John Thomson of the particle we call the electron.

During the early years of the twentieth century, further discoveries concerning the flow of electrons in vacuums were made by experimenters such as Lee De Forest and Vladimir Zworykin. These discoveries led the way to developing equipment and techniques for long-distance broadcasting of radio and television signals. It was the outbreak of World War II, however, with its needs for long-distance communications equipment, and ultimately missile-guidance systems, that brought about the rapid expansion of electronics technology and the creation of the electronics industry.

As the field of electronics technology turned to the creation of consumer and industrial products following the end of the war, its growth was spurred by two new technological developments. The first was the completion in 1946 of the first all-purpose, all-electronic digital computer. This machine, crude as it was, could handle mathematical calculations a thousand times faster than the electromechanical calculating machines of its day. Since 1946, there has been a steady growth in the speed, sophistication, and versatility of computers.

The second important development was the invention of the transistor in 1948. The transistor provided an inexpensive and compact replacement for the vacuum tubes used in nearly all electronic equipment up until then. Transistors allowed for the miniaturization of electronic circuits and were especially crucial in the development of the computer and in opening new possibilities in industrial automation.

Discoveries during the 1960s in the fields of microcircuitry and integrated circuitry led to the development of microminiaturized and more sophisticated electronic equipment, from pocket calculators, digital watches, and microwave ovens to high-speed computers and the long-range guidance systems used in space flights.

By the 1970s, electronics had become one of the largest industries and most important areas of technology in the industrialized world, a world which has, in turn, come to rely on the instantaneous worldwide communications, the computer-controlled or computer-assisted industrial operations, and the wide-ranging forms of electronic data processing that are made possible by electronics technology.

Throughout the growth and development of electronics theory and its commercial and industrial application there has been a need for skilled assistants in the laboratory, on the factory floor, and in a wide variety of settings where electronic equipment is used. As the technology has become more sophisticated, the need has increased for these assistants to be specially trained and educated. Working in partnership with scientists and engineers, today's electronics technicians belong to one of the fastest-growing occupational groups in the United States. Their importance, already widely acknowledged, will continue to be increasingly recognized in coming years.

Nature of the work

Most electronics technicians work in one of three broad areas of electronics: product development; manufacturing and production; and service and maintenance. Technicians involved with service and maintenance are included among *electronics sales and service technicians* and are described elsewhere in this volume. The work of technicians involved in the other two broad areas, as well as some related areas, is described in the following paragraphs.

In the product-development area, electronics technicians work directly with engineers and scientists. They build, test, and modify prototype or experimental models of new electronics products. As part of their work they use hand tools and small machine tools; make complex parts, components, and subassemblies; conduct physical and electrical tests, using complicated instruments and test equipment; and make complete reports of their observations.

Electronics technicians in the product-development field may make suggestions for improvements in the design of a device. They may also have to construct, install, modify, or repair laboratory test equipment.

Electronics drafting is a field of electronics technology closely related to product development. Electronics drafters convert rough sketches and written or verbal information provided by the engineers and scientists into easily understandable schematic, layout, or wiring diagrams that are used in manufacturing the product. These electronics drafters may also prepare lists of parts and bills of materials of the component parts of the equipment needed for producing the final product.

Another field of electronics technology closely related to product development is cost estimating. Electronics technicians working in this area prepare estimates of the costs of manufacturing a new product with sufficient accuracy to allow the sales department to determine in advance the price at which a product can be sold. After the engineers have prepared drawings, engineering specifications, and other information on the new product, cost estimators will use this engineering data to estimate all labor and material costs involved in assembling the product, lay out the assembly processes, plan the type of tools required and the cost of such tools, and determine whether the component parts should be manufactured or purchased. They may even find it advisable to review the design with the engineering department and suggest changes to lower costs or facilitate manufacture.

In the manufacturing and production phase, electronics technicians work in a wide variety of capacities. In general, they are involved with the day-to-day handling of production problems, schedules, and costs. Some supervise and train production teams in methods of testing or building new products as they proceed from the development to the production phase. Others maintain the complex automated machines used to build the electronics product.

Those involved in the quality-control aspect of production inspect and test the products at various stages of completion. They also maintain and calibrate the test equipment used in all phases of the manufacturing. They determine the causes for rejection of parts or equipment by assembly-line inspectors, and they analyze field and manufacturing reports of product failures.

Electronics technicians in the quality-control area may make specific recommendations and submit reports to their supervisor for elimination of causes of rejects, and may even suggest design, manufacturing, and process changes, and establish quality-acceptance levels. They may interpret quality-control standards to the manufacturing supervisors. And they may establish and maintain quality limits on items purchased from other manufacturers, thus insuring the quality of parts used in the equipment being assembled.

One other area of electronics technology worth mentioning is that of technical writing and editing. Technicians in this area compile, write, and edit a wide variety of technical information. This includes instructional leaflets, operating manuals, books, and installation and service manuals having to do with the products of the company. To do this, they must confer with design and development engineers, production personnel, salespeople, drafters, and others to obtain the necessary information to prepare the text, drawings, diagrams, parts,

When assembling circuit boards, electronics technicians must have steady hands, keen eyesight, and patience.

lists, and illustrations. They must understand thoroughly how and why the equipment works to be able to tell the customer how to use it and the service technician how to install and service the equipment.

At times, they may participate in the preparation of reports and proposals of a technical nature and in writing technical articles for engineering societies, management, and other publications. Their job is to produce the means (through printed word and pictures) by which the customer can get the most value out of the purchased equipment.

Requirements

Prospective electronics technicians should have an interest in and an aptitude for mathematics and science. They should have good manual skills and enjoy using tools and scientific equipment. They should be patient, methodical, persistent, and able to get along with a variety of different kinds of people.

While still in high school, a student interested in a career as an electronics technician should take two years of mathematics including algebra and geometry, and one year of physical science, preferably physics, or an introductory electricity or electronics course. Four years of English or other communications-skills courses are usually required for graduation. Shop courses and courses in mechanical drawing are also desirable.

Most employers of electronics technicians prefer to hire graduates of two-year post–high-school training programs. These programs are designed to develop proficiency in electronics and to supply enough general background in science as well as other career-related fields such as business and economics to aid the student in advancing to positions of greater responsibility.

Typical first-year courses include physics for electronics; technical mathematics; electronic devices; communications; circuit analysis—AC and DC; electronic amplifiers; and instruments and measurements.

Typical second-year courses include communications circuits; introduction to digital electronics; technical reporting; drawing, sketching, and diagramming; control circuits and systems; communications systems; electronic design and fabrication; introduction to new electronic devices; and industrial organizations and institutions.

If after high school a student is not able to attend a post–high-school technical training program, but still desires technical training, he or she should not overlook the training programs offered to active-duty members of the armed forces and to members of reserve organizations.

Special requirements

Most jobs involving radio and television transmission equipment require certification from the International Society of Certified Electronics Technicians (ISCET). Usually the certification may be earned before graduation in a post–high-school program or through home study.

Some employers require that an electronics technician be a certified technician. This certification is issued by the Institute for the Certification of Engineering Technicians or by ISCET.

The majority of jobs available to electronics technicians require neither licenses nor certification.

Opportunities for experience and exploration

Anyone considering a career as an electronics technician should take every opportunity to discuss the field with people working in it. It is advisable to visit a variety of different kinds of electronics facilities—service shops, manufacturing plants, and research laboratories—either through individual visits or through field trips organized by teachers or guidance counselors. These visits will provide a realistic idea of the opportunities in the different areas of the electronics industry. It is also suggested that students take an introductory course in basic electricity or electronics to test their aptitude, skills, and interest.

Students can also gain relevant experience by taking shop courses, by belonging to electronics or radio clubs in school, and by assembling electronic equipment with commercial kits.

Methods of entering

Before completing their technical training, students may be hired through on-campus interviews by a company representative. Most schools have excellent placement programs and have a high rate of placement of their graduates by the time they graduate.

Another method of obtaining employment is direct contact with a particular company. It is best to write to the personnel department and to include a resume summarizing one's education and experience. If the company has an appropriate opening, a company representative will schedule an interview for the prospective employee. There are also many excellent public and commercial employment organizations that can aid in obtaining a job appropriate to the training and experience of the graduate. Most metropolitan Sunday newspapers devote several pages to advertising job opportunities with companies in the area.

Advancement

Advancement possibilities in the field of electronics can be almost unlimited. Technicians usually begin work under the direct and constant supervision of an experienced technician, scientist, or engineer. As they gain experience or additional education, they are given more responsible assignments, often carrying out particular work programs under only very general supervision.

From there technicians may move into supervisory positions, and those with exceptional ability can sometimes qualify for professional positions after receiving additional academic training.

The following short paragraphs describe some of the positions to which electronics technicians can advance.

Engineering technicians are senior technicians or engineering assistants who work as part of a team of engineers and technicians developing new products.

Production-test supervisors determine what tests should be performed on equipment as it progresses down an assembly line. They may be responsible for designing the equipment setup used in production testing.

Quality-assurance supervisors determine the scope of a product-sampling and the kinds of tests to be run on production units. They translate specifications into testing procedures.

Employment outlook

There is good reason to believe that the electronics industry will be one of the most important industries, if not the most important industry, in the United States through the year 2000. It is involved in new and exciting consumer products such as videocassette recorders, compact-disc players, home computers, and home appliances with solid-state controls. Increasing automation and computer-assisted manufacturing processes rely on advanced electronic technology. Computers, in general, are the biggest growth area for electronics. Schools, offices, libraries, warehouses, hospitals—all are settings where computers are becoming a more and more common sight.

All of these new uses for electronics should continue to stimulate growth in the electronics industry. Hence, the job outlook for electronics technicians is favorable through at least the end of the 1990s. Foreign competition, general economic conditions, and levels of government spending may have an impact on some areas of the field to some degree. This is an industry, however, that is becoming so central to all our lives and for which there is still such growth potential that it seems unlikely that any single factor could substantially curb its growth and its need for specially trained personnel.

Earnings

Electronics technicians who have completed a two-year post–high-school training program and are working in private industry earn starting salaries of about $14,000 to $18,000 a year.

The average yearly earnings of all electronics technicians is approximately $25,000, with many technicians earning $30,000 a year or more. Some technicians who have been particularly successful earn $50,000 a year or more.

Electronics technicians generally receive premium pay for overtime work on Sundays and holidays and for evening and night-shift work. Many workers in electronics manufacturing plants receive two to four weeks vacation with pay, depending on their length of service. In almost all cases, electronics technicians are covered by pension plans and other fringe benefits, including financial aid and released time to obtain more education.

Conditions of work

Because electronics equipment usually must be manufactured in a dust-free, climate-controlled environment, electronics technicians can expect to work in modern, comfortable, well-lighted surroundings. Many electronics plants have been built in industrial parks with ample parking and little traffic congestion. Frequency of injuries in the electronics industry is far less than it is in most other industries, and any injury that does occur is usually not serious.

Many workers in electronics manufacturing are covered by union agreements. The principal unions involved are the International Union of Electrical, Radio and Machine Workers; International Brotherhood of Electrical Workers; International Association of Machinists and Aerospace Workers; and the United Electrical, Radio and Machine Workers of America.

Social and psychological factors

The work of electronics technicians is varied and so are the social and psychological factors associated with the work. For electronics technicians working in the product-development area, there is a minimum of supervision. Teamwork and the ability to get along well with others, however, are very important for these technicians. They may also be called upon to supervise or direct other personnel. Technicians in this area often feel that they are acting as assistant engineers or assistant scientists. There are great personal rewards that come with this situation, but there are also great demands and pressures. Some technicians, for instance, may feel awkward serving as an intermediary between the scientists and engineers who design projects and the craft workers who carry them out.

For other electronics technicians, the work may be more monotonous and repetitious. Some technicians resent this aspect of the work; others find it a welcome relief.

Electronics technicians who wish to advance in their careers should be willing and able to continue their education, either formally or informally, in order to keep up with new developments in the field.

GOE: 05.01.01; SIC: 36; SOC: 3711

⬦ SOURCES OF ADDITIONAL INFORMATION

Electronic Industries Association
1722 I Street, NW, Suite 300
Washington, DC 20006

International Society of Certified Electronics Technicians
2708 West Berry, Suite 8
Fort Worth, TX 76109

Electronics Technicians Association
604 North Jackson
Greencastle, IN 46135

Junior Engineering Technical Society (JETS)
1420 King Street, Suite 405
Alexandria, VA 22314

⬦ RELATED ARTICLES

Volume 1: Electronics; Engineering
Volume 2: Engineers
Volume 3: Commercial and industrial electronic equipment repairers
Volume 4: Computer-service technicians; Electromechanical technicians; Electronics sales and service technicians; Electronics test technicians; Instrumentation technicians; Microelectronics technicians; Semiconductor-development technicians; Telecommunications technicians

---

Electronics test technicians

Definition

Electronics test technicians perform electronic, mechanical, and electromechanical tests on electronic products, systems, and components such as those that go into television sets and computers. They carry out these tests in factories to make sure that new parts and systems are working properly and in repair shops to find out what is wrong with a customer's malfunctioning system.

Nature of the work

For almost any job they do, electronics test technicians must first learn all about the part or system they are testing. They do this by studying wiring diagrams, technical manuals, and other instructional material. They also learn about the various tests they can perform on the part or system from the manuals or through special instructions they receive from engineers or other supervisors.

When they do the testing, they often begin by connecting the part or unit to a special testing device. The device is usually a piece of electronic equipment such as a signal generator, frequency meter, or spectrum analyzer. They may do the test under specified environmental conditions, such as at a controlled temperature, pressure, humidity, or vibrational level. The technician reads dials on the testing device that indicate electronic characteristics such as the amount of voltage that is going through the unit, distortion, inductance, or capacitance. The technician then compares the results with the correct level specified in manuals. In this way, the technician can locate a problem such as a short circuit or a defective component. If a problem becomes apparent, the technician replaces the wiring or component or sends instructions to a repair or production department to fix it.

Some electronics test technicians may write short programs to test computer components. Others physically examine switches or measure pins, shafts, or other mechanical parts, and some may use X-ray machines to examine internal parts and assemblies.

Electronics test technicians are also responsible for calibrating their test equipment and sometimes are called on to design the setup of test equipment to evaluate nonstandard pieces of equipment.

Two electronics test technicians perform routine checks on newly-manufactured equipment. They must ensure that the parts are working properly before they are sold.

Requirements

Most employers of electronics test technicians prefer to hire graduates of two-year post–high-school training programs offered by community and technical colleges. These programs provide training in electronics, basic science, and other subjects relating to the workplace, such as economics and business administration. Graduates of such programs should have received training in mathematics through algebra and geometry and should be familiar with quadratic equations, exponential notation, and logarithmic functions. They also should be able to read instruction manuals and other reference books with ease and be able to write reports with proper spelling, grammar, and punctuation.

While in high school, students interested in this career should take courses in mathematics and in a physical science, preferably physics, and, if possible, electrical shop and introductory electronics.

The physical demands of this job are light, requiring only walking, standing, and some light lifting. Electronics test technicians need good manual dexterity, hearing, and vision.

GOE: 06.01.05; SIC: 36; SOC: 6881

◇ RELATED ARTICLES

Volume 1: Electronics; Engineering
Volume 2: Engineers
Volume 4: Computer service technicians; Electronics sales and service technicians; Electronics technicians; Instrumentation technicians; Quality-control technicians

---

Fire safety technicians

Definition

Fire safety technicians recognize fire hazards, apply technical knowledge, and perform services to control and prevent fires. The major emphasis of the work of fire safety technicians is the prevention of fires. Typical services they perform include conducting safety inspections and planning fire protection systems.

History

Every year thousands of people in the United States die due to fires. Property destroyed by fire costs billions of dollars each year. In some states, grass or brush fires periodically rage uncontrolled and advance at the speed of the wind. Buildings are destroyed and livestock is lost. Forest fires consume millions of feet of lumber every year. Some fires increase the problems of wildlife conservation and flood control, requiring that considerable sums be spent on reforestation programs. Fires in homes and at workplaces are the greatest destroyers of human life and property.

In the early days of the United States, fire protection was usually left to a few volunteers in a community. This group formed a fire brigade and had simple fire fighting devices. Later, fire departments were established and fire fighting equipment became more sophisticated. Even so, fire protection was still mostly left to a small group. As cities grew and large industrial plants were built, it became apparent that fire prevention was as important, and probably more important, than fire fighting skills and techniques.

Today, business and industrial firms realize that fire protection is one of the most important considerations in the construction and operation of their plants. Fire insurance rates are determined by fire probability factors, such as the type of construction, ease of transporting personnel, and the quality and quantity of fire protection equipment available. Managers realize that payments from claims on fire insurance will not cover the total loss caused by fire. The loss of production or sales during a shutdown can represent a tremendous, unrecoverable loss.

In addition, all property owners and workers expect adequate protection for their homes, property, and for themselves at the workplace.

The public expects fire departments to be well staffed with competent specialists and fire fighters who can minimize property damage and save lives by rescuing people from fire, giving safety education courses, and conducting inspections. Employees expect that their employers will have warning and fire extinguishing devices. They also look for the inspection of exits, corridors, and stairways designed to carry traffic in an emergency.

The need for carefully planned, well-organized fire protection has created a demand for highly trained personnel. Specialists are needed who are skilled in the newest methods of fire prevention and fire fighting. Such specialists are also familiar with new synthetic materials used in building construction, decorative drapes, floor coverings, furnishings, and even clothing. These materials have made fire protection more complicated because of the dangerously toxic fumes they produce when burned.

Because of all of these factors, more and more well-trained fire safety technicians and engineers are being hired by business, industry, and other employers to prevent loss of property and life from fires while people are on the job, in school, in recreational or entertainment places, or traveling.

Nature of the work

Fire safety technicians are employed in local fire departments, fire insurance companies, industrial organizations, government agencies, and business firms that deal with fire protection equipment and consulting services.

The range of duties performed by fire fighters varies with the size of the fire department and the population of the city in which they are employed. Within the fire department, however, each worker's responsibilities are clearly defined. For example, when their department goes into action, fire fighters know their exact duties. Duties may include trying to rescue persons caught in fires, raising ladders, connecting hoses to hydrants, or attempting to break down doors, windows, or walls with fire axes.

While fire fighters are on station duty between alarm calls, they perform varied but regular duties. They must keep all fire fighting equipment in top condition. They must hold practice drills for timing and procedure, verify and record fire alarms, and stand watch at fire alarm instrument stations.

Workers in fire departments are mostly highly skilled workers. In the early 1990s there were more than 200,000 fire department workers. However, only a small percentage of these were technically prepared inspectors, supervisors, or technical workers.

In large public fire departments, experience gained by mastering the various duties that fire department personnel must perform, plus study on the job or in a part-time program, can lead to good technician-level jobs in inspection, public information services, or supervision.

Fire science specialists employed by insurance companies make recommendations for fire protection and safety measures in specific buildings. They may help set insurance rates, examine water supply and sprinkler facilities, and make suggestions to correct hazardous conditions. They may be part of an arson investigation squad, or they may work with adjusters to determine the amount of personal injury or property loss caused by fire.

In industry, fire safety technicians and engineers are often part of an industrial safety team. They inspect areas for possible fire hazards and formulate company procedures in case of fire. They make periodic inspections of fire fighting equipment such as extinguishers, hoses and hydrants, fire doors, automatic alarms, and sprinkler systems. An important part of their duties is to hold fire prevention seminars to keep department heads and key workers aware and alert to potential fire hazards in their particular areas. Technicians also teach these employees what to do in case of fire or other emergencies.

Many restaurants, large hotels, and entertainment or recreational centers employ fire safety technicians. There is a great hazard of fire from food cooking in kitchens, lint in laundries, and sparks that fall on draperies and bedding. The possible loss of life from fire makes it necessary to have the best possible fire protection program.

Many government agencies employ fire safety technicians. They are largely responsible for inspecting government buildings, property and storage, or handling systems for reducing fire hazards. They arrange for installation of adequate alarm systems and fire protection devices. They may be required to organize a fire fighting unit in a government agency or assist with designing sprinkler systems in buildings.

Many technicians are employed by companies that manufacture fire protection devices and alarm systems. Their training enables them to explain technical functions to customers and to give advice on installation and use. They also

A fire safety technician inspects an automatic fire and explosion system that detects fires and suppresses them. Such equipment must be tested periodically.

help to place smoke detectors and other fire prevention or extinguishing devices in the correct locations to give the greatest protection from fire.

Public education is also an important area of activity for fire control and safety technicians. Working with the public through schools, businesses, and service clubs and organizations, they can expand the level of understanding about the dangers of fire and teach people about methods of fire protection and fire prevention.

Newly hired technicians generally receive on-the-job orientation before they are given full responsibility in an entry-level position. Examples of entry-level positions are described in the following paragraphs.

Fire insurance inspectors inspect buildings and offices and make recommendations for fire protection and general safety conditions.

Fire insurance underwriters help set rates to conform with company policies and building codes.

Fire insurance adjusters determine losses due to fire and compute rates for adjustment and settling claims.

Fire protection engineering technicians design and draw up plans for the installation of fire protection systems for buildings and structures. Using their knowledge of drafting, physical sciences, engineering principles, and fire protection codes, they analyze architectural blueprints and specifications to determine the kind and size of fire-protection system needed to meet fire protection codes, and they estimate the cost of the system. During building construction, they work with the construction superintendent to ensure the proper installation of the system. They may inspect fire-damaged buildings to look for malfunctioning systems, and they may specialize in one kind of fire protection system, such as foam, water, dry chemicals, or gas.

Fire inspectors check fire fighting equipment and report any potential fire hazards. They recommend changes in equipment, practice, materials, or methods to reduce fire hazards.

Plant protection inspectors inspect industrial plants for fire hazards, report findings, and recommend action. *Fire alarm superintendents* inspect alarm systems in government buildings and institutions.

Fire service field instructors hold training sessions throughout a state to keep fire fighters up to date on methods and techniques of fire fighting. They may also inspect small fire departments and report on personnel and equipment.

Requirements

The requirements for becoming a fire safety technician are similar to those for industrial engineering technicians. Both kinds of technicians need much of the same educational preparation. They need to master the chemistry and related science of how things burn, and what makes some things more likely to catch fire and generate fumes, heat, and smoke. They are scientific technicians, and they must learn the fundamentals of the science and mathematics that support their field.

These technicians must also learn about materials, combustion, structures, and devices and equipment that prevent or extinguish fires. They must be able to communicate well and to read and write with ease so they can study technical information and give good written or oral reports.

Technicians do not have to qualify in all cases to enter fire departments because an increasing number of these technicians are being employed by industries. Those who seek technician jobs in fire departments, however, usually must meet rigorous physical requirements. They frequently start as fire fighters and are promoted to positions as supervisors or fire inspectors.

High-school students who plan to attend a two-year, postsecondary program in fire technology should study the physical sciences. They should take either physics or chemistry courses that include laboratory work. Fire science demands some knowledge of hydraulics, physics, and chemistry. Laying out sprinkler systems requires skills that are introduced in high-school mechanical drawing courses. Algebra and geometry are also recommended, as well as English and writing courses.

Two-year, postsecondary fire technology programs are now available at more than one hundred technical institutes and community colleges. These programs provide educational depth in the fire science specialization to persons who want to work for industries, institutions, or government as fire safety technicians. These programs are also available to members of fire departments or related fire science specialists.

Courses in these programs include physics and hydraulics as they apply to pump and nozzle pressures. Fundamentals of chemistry are taught to provide an understanding of chemical methods of extinguishing fires and the chemistry of materials and combustion. Skill in communications is also emphasized.

Typical courses in the first year of a two-year program are fire fighting tactics and strategy, fire protection equipment and alarm systems, fundamentals of fire suppression, introductory fire technology, chemistry (especially combustion and chemistry of materials), college mathematics, and communications skills.

Second-year courses may include building construction for fire protection, hazardous materials, fire administration, industrial fire protection, applied physics, introduction to fire prevention, and applied economics.

Like most professional workers in high-technology careers, fire safety technicians will have to continue to study during their careers in order to keep up with new developments in their field. Improved fire detection and prevention instruments, equipment, and methods for making materials fireproof or fire-suppressing are being developed all the time.

Those who wish to work in fire science technology in fire departments may train as technicians and apply for specialist jobs in large fire departments. Others may choose to enter the fire department as untrained fire fighters. For the latter group, very rigid physical examinations are usually required. Also required are physical performance tests that may include running, climbing, and jumping. Fire fighters must keep themselves physically fit and conditioned since they may be required to do hard work in all types of weather and sometimes for long hours. These examinations are clearly defined by local civil service regulations but may vary from one community to another.

In most cases, prospective fire fighters must be at least 21 but not over 31 years of age. They must also meet height and weight requirements. Applicants must have good vision

(20/20 vision is required in some departments), no hindering physical impairments, and strong stamina. Some fire departments require that applicants be nonsmokers.

Fire fighters must be able to follow orders and to accept the discipline that is necessary for effective teamwork. While on active call, fire fighters usually work under the close supervision of commanding officers such as battalion chiefs or assistant fire chiefs. Their work requires highly organized team efforts to be effective, since there is usually a great deal of excitement and confusion at fires in large structures or fires that threaten to be very dangerous or damaging.

Fire science technicians who do not work as fire fighters but as industrial or government inspectors, consultants, or fire preventers do not need unusual physical strength. They do need normal dexterity, health, eyesight, coordination, and stamina to do their work.

Special requirements

For fire safety technicians in industry or government, but not in fire departments, no licenses are usually required. Good records of study in educational programs and an appropriate two-year degree or certificate are given special consideration by most employers. Becoming a member of the Society of Fire Protection Engineers is a valuable mark of achievement of which employers take note.

For those who want to enter fire departments as fire fighters and work toward technician-level tasks, civil service examinations are required in most cases.

Other than mental and physical examinations, physical ability and stamina, and the height and weight requirements already discussed, no special license or certificate is required. It should be understood, however, that fire fighters are a highly organized occupational group, and many fire fighters do belong to the International Association of Fire Fighters.

Opportunities for experience and exploration

Students in high school and high-school graduates who are especially interested in fire science can obtain valuable information from their school guidance departments. Science teachers can also provide information about the various careers in fire protection, safety, and preven-

tion. Students who live in a large town or city can visit the fire department, look at the equipment, and talk with the fire fighters and their commanding officers. In some departments, students may be able to gain experience by working as volunteer fire fighters. Courses in lifesaving and first aid also offer helpful experience. Summer jobs as aides with the government park and forest service are available as well. In these jobs, students may learn about fire prevention, control, and detection in forest and grassland conservation work.

It is usually possible for students to arrange a visit with an insurance company to learn about the huge economic losses caused by fire. Large insurance offices often have agents or officers who can describe fire technician jobs or services in inspection, fire insurance, rate setting or claim settlement, and fire prevention services.

Methods of entering

Graduates of two-year programs in technical colleges, community colleges, or technical institutes usually secure jobs before they graduate. They are hired by employers who send recruiters to the school placement offices, which arrange interviews for graduating students. The placement officers or fire science instructors usually are aware of potential employers. They keep contacts open to help place their current graduates.

Some schools have cooperative work-study programs where students study part-time and work part-time for pay. Employers who participate in cooperative programs provide experience in different tasks so the student learns about various aspects of the job. Often students in such programs are hired permanently by the cooperating employer.

Some students may find jobs in fire departments that are large enough to need special technicians outside the ranks of regular fire fighters. Others may choose to become fire fighters and advance to technical positions.

Some fire departments place new employees on probation, a period during which they are intensively trained. After training is completed, they may be assigned to specific duties.

Students with a high-school diploma or its equivalent can enter a fire department apprenticeship program. These programs run from three to four years. They combine intensive on-the-job training with active fire fighting service, and include related study in the science and theory of fire fighting. These apprenticeship programs may or may not be union-sponsored.

183

Even after completing an apprenticeship program, fire fighters who want to advance to the level of supervisor or inspector must continue to study. Part-time courses are available in community colleges or technical institutes.

In some small communities, applicants may enter through on-the-job training as volunteer fire fighters or by direct application for such an appointment.

Advancement

Examples of advanced positions are described below.

Fire prevention analysts analyze overall fire prevention systems in an organization and confer with fire inspectors to obtain detailed information and recommend policies and programs for fire prevention. Safety directors are responsible for general safety throughout a plant as well as fire safety.

Deputy fire marshals inspect possible fire hazards and analyze the amount of loss because of fire. They have the authority to condemn buildings, and they report cases of arson and work with district attorneys to prosecute arsonists. This is an appointed position, although those holding the position usually have considerable fire experience.

Fire captains work under the supervision of a fire chief on a military base or in a municipal area. They are responsible for fire protection in a specific location. *Fire chiefs* are responsible for all fire fighting units in a municipal area. Several fire captains may report to and support the activities of this administrator.

Owners of fire equipment or consulting businesses employ *fire prevention and control technicians and specialists*. Their employees contract for, deliver, and install equipment and provide training and other services in fire prevention.

Employment outlook

Technical careers in fire prevention and control are predicted to grow more rapidly than the average for all other occupations. In coming years, these technicians will probably be needed in more places and industries than ever before.

The greatest increase in employment will be in industry. More and more industries are finding that the cost of replacing buildings and property destroyed by fire is greater than the yearly cost of fire protection and control expertise and equipment.

New products are being developed and used in almost all areas of modern living. Many have different characteristics that relate to fire hazards. As new products appear, new fire prevention and control techniques must be developed. The ever-changing techniques of fire prevention and protection make this a most challenging field with unlimited opportunities for the person with ambition and imagination.

Earnings

Beginning salaries for fire safety technicians who qualify for technical jobs tend to be higher than those of other technicians. This is partly due to the shortage of qualified personnel in the field.

Starting salaries are approximately $14,000 to $17,000. Experienced technicians earn salaries that average around $29,000 to $32,000 per year. Those who advance to positions of great responsibility in the various industrial or fire department careers may earn up to $57,000 per year or more.

Benefits for these employees usually include compensatory time off or overtime pay for hours worked beyond the regular work schedule. Other benefits include liberal pension plans, disability benefits, and early retirement options. Also included are paid vacations, paid sick leave, and in some cases, paid holidays or compensatory time off for holidays worked.

Conditions of work

Working conditions for fire safety technicians may involve danger when they observe fires, assist in fire fighting, or inspect and analyze structures damaged or destroyed by fire. Floors, walls, or entire buildings can collapse on fire fighters as they work to save lives and property. Exposure to smoke, fumes, chemicals, and gases can injure or kill them. Most of the duties of technicians, however, are performed in offices where the surroundings are typically well-lighted, clean, and comfortable.

The work of fire safety technicians often involves inspecting factories, buildings, manufacturing methods, and any place where fires may occur. These workers must therefore follow safety regulations and wear protective clothing when appropriate. They must be confident and comfortable in the environments they visit, inspect, and analyze.

Social and psychological factors

Fire safety technicians are applied science personnel. They must have a natural curiosity about everything that relates to fire and the property for which they are responsible.

They must be patient and willing to study the physics and chemistry of fire and fire prevention and control. They must also be able to think systematically and objectively as they analyze fire hazards, damages, and prevention.

These technicians must be observant and they must understand how human factors of carelessness, thoughtlessness, fatigue, or haste may cause fires. One of the great challenges of the career is to learn how to teach people to avoid the mistakes that cause fires and to establish safety procedures and controls that prevent fires.

Fire is one of the most feared and most destructive hazards. Fire science technicians can find continuing satisfaction and challenge in saving lives and property by preventing fires.

GOE: 05.01.02, 05.03.06, 11.10.03; SIC: 6411; SOC: 1472, 1473, 1634, 5122

◇ **SOURCES OF ADDITIONAL INFORMATION**

Society of Fire Protection Technicians
c/o John Fannin
2106 Silver Side Road
Wilmington, DE 19810

Society of Fire Protection Engineers
60 Batterymarch Street
Boston, MA 02110

American Society of Safety Engineers
1800 East Oakton Street
Des Plaines, IL 60016

National Fire Protection Association
Batterymarch Park
Quincy, MA 02269

Board of Certified Safety Professionals
208 Burwash Avenue
Savory, IL 61874

◇ **RELATED ARTICLES**

Volume 1: Civil Service; Engineering
Volume 2: Engineers; Health and regulatory inspectors
Volume 3: Fire fighters; Occupational safety and health workers
Volume 4: Industrial engineering technicians; Industrial safety-and-health technicians; Nuclear power plant quality control technicians; Nuclear power plant radiation control technicians

Fluid power technicians

Definition

Fluid power technicians work with equipment that utilizes the pressure of a liquid or gas in a closed container to transmit, multiply, or control power. They work under the supervision of engineers. Fluid power technicians fabricate, assemble, service, maintain, and test fluid power equipment, which is used in a variety of fluids. Among those are hundreds of applications that affect the daily lives of all Americans.

Nature of the work

Many different machines involve some kind of fluid power system. These include equipment used in industry, agriculture, defense, transportation, and in our daily lives, in such applications as automatic door closers, tire inflators, the brakes, steering, and transmissions of cars and other vehicles, and many others.

There are two types of fluid power machines. Hydraulic machines use water, oil, or another liquid in a closed system to transmit

A fluid power technician operates a machine that prepares aluminum housings for tank lubrications and scavenge pumps.

the energy needed to do work. For example, a hydraulic jack, which can be used to lift heavy loads, is like a cylinder with a piston fitted inside it. When a liquid is pumped into the bottom of the cylinder, the piston is forced upward, lifting the weight on the jack. To lower the weight, the liquid is released through a valve, returning the pressure in the system to normal.

Pneumatic machines, the other type of fluid power machines, are activated by the pressure of air or another gas in a closed system. Pavement-breaking jackhammers and compressed-air paint sprayers are common examples of pneumatic machines.

Fluid power systems are a part of most machines used in industry. Fluid power technicians therefore work in many different settings. Typically, they work in factories where fluid power systems are used in manufacturing. In factories, they may, for example, maintain and service pneumatic machines that bolt together products on an automated assembly line.

In their work, fluid power technicians analyze blueprints, drawings, and specifications. They set up various milling, shaping, grinding, and drilling machines and make precision parts. They use sensitive measuring instruments to make sure the parts are exactly the required size. They use hand and power tools to put together components of the fluid power system they are assembling or repairing. These components may include pumps, cylinders, valves, motors, filters, and control devices. To determine whether a piece of equipment is working properly, technicians connect the unit to test equipment that measures such factors as fluid pressure, flow rates, and power loss because of friction or wear. Based on their anal-

ysis of the test results they may recommend changes in the equipment setup or instrumentation.

Some technicians work in laboratories as part of research and development teams in companies that are looking for ways to make better use of fluid power systems. Other technicians work as sales and service representatives for companies that make and sell fluid power equipment to industrial plants. These technicians travel from one plant to another, providing customers with specialized information and assistance with their equipment. Some technicians repair and maintain fluid power components of heavy equipment used in construction, on farms, or in mining. Because fluid power technology is important in the flight controls, landing gear, and brakes of airplanes, many technicians are employed in the aircraft industry.

Requirements

Most employers prefer to hire fluid power technicians who have at least two years of post–high-school training, such as that offered by community and technical colleges. There are relatively few technical training programs that are primarily concerned with fluid power technology, but, depending on the job, training in a related field, such as mechanical or electrical technology can be adequate preparation for employment.

A good high-school background for students interested in this field would include as many courses as possible in mathematics, especially geometry and algebra, a physical science, preferably physics, as well as shop, computers, and courses in language skills.

The work of these technicians is not strenuous and is usually performed indoors.

GOE: 05.05.07; SIC: 3593; SOC: 613

◇ **RELATED ARTICLES**

Volume 1: Engineering; Machining and Machinery
Volume 2: Engineers
Volume 3: Industrial machinery mechanics; Machinists
Volume 4: Mechanical technicians

Geological technicians

Definition

Geological technicians assist geologists in their studies of earth phenomena. Modern geology is particularly concerned with the study of seismic activity and the exploration for mineral and petroleum deposits in the earth.

Nature of the work

Technicians set up seismic recording apparatus and record its measurements for later analysis by geologists. They also conduct field analyses of earthquake effects, recording visual observations and measurements. Technicians involved in exploration for minerals and petroleum deposits analyze soil core samples obtained from drillings. They use radiation detection equipment to obtain data that will help geologists evaluate possible mining locations. They conduct tests on potential drilling sites by detonating explosions and recording resulting sound wave patterns.

Requirements

Aspiring geological technicians should have a good mathematical background, with as many high-school math courses as possible. They should have a year or more of a laboratory science, preferably chemistry or physics, as well as courses in computers. They should have several years of post–high-school training, including geology and mineralogy and the use of laboratory instruments and the recording of data. They should have language skills sufficient for reading technical information in journals and manuals, and they should be able to write concise, detailed reports on the results of their tests and analyses. They should also continue training in mathematics, including calculus.

Their work will be performed both in- and out-of-doors and may require carrying testing equipment into primitive locations.

GOE: 02.04.01; SIC: 8999; SOC: 389

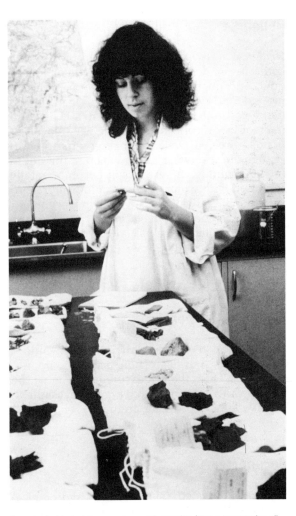

A geological technician examines rock samples from a prospective oil field. Through various tests, she will be able to determine the presence or absence of oil.

◇ **RELATED ARTICLES**

Volume 1: Mining; Physical Sciences
Volume 2: Geologists; Geophysicists; Oceanographers; Petrologists
Volume 3: Petroleum drilling operations
Volume 4: Hydrological technicians; Petroleum technicians

Hydrological technicians

Definition

Hydrological technicians assist hydrologists by gathering and recording data on water levels, flow, and quality. They place and periodically monitor and record the readings of instruments that record rate of flow of water in streams and rivers. They record the changing water levels of ponds, streams, wells, and reservoirs to chart changes in the water table, which is the depth in the ground where the soil becomes totally saturated with water. They examine and record water quality through physical inspection for color and amount of sediment present and through chemical analysis. Recorded data are analyzed to monitor long-term changes, and trends are noted.

Nature of the work

Hydrological technicians work in both indoor and outdoor settings. Their activities are not strenuous, but their measurements must be precise, and they must have good eyesight to observe and record data accurately.

Requirements

Persons interested in careers as hydrological technicians should take courses in high-school chemistry and physics, mathematics at least through plane geometry, and have language skills developed sufficiently to enable them to read technical manuals and to write analytical reports on their findings. Additional preparation by taking post–high-school technical courses is almost always necessary, especially courses in geology, physics, and laboratory practice.

GOE: 02.04.01; SIC: 1781; SOC: 389

◇ **RELATED ARTICLES**

Volume 1: Physical Sciences
Volume 2: Geologists; Groundwater professionals; Oceanographers
Volume 3: Soil scientists
Volume 4: Geological technicians; Pollution-control technicians; Soil conservation technicians; Water and wastewater treatment technicians

---

Industrial engineering technicians

Definition

Industrial engineering technicians collect and analyze data and make recommendations concerning the efficient use of personnel, materials, and machines to produce goods or to provide services. Working usually in support of industrial engineers, industrial-engineering technicians conduct studies of the time, movements, and methods a worker uses to accomplish production, maintenance, clerical, or other kinds of tasks.

Industrial engineering technicians prepare charts, graphs, and diagrams to illustrate work flow, floor layouts, materials handling, and machine utilization. They make statistical studies; analyze production costs; prepare layouts of machinery and equipment; aid in the planning of work flow and work assignments; and recommend revision of methods of operation, materials handling, or equipment layout in order to improve production methods or improve standards.

As part of their job, industrial engineering technicians often use timers, motion-picture cameras, videotape recorders, and similar equipment.

History

Industrial engineering is a direct outgrowth of the Industrial Revolution, which began in England in the eighteenth century and soon spread to the United States. By linking a power source, such as a steam engine, to simple mechanical devices, early mechanical and industrial engineers were able to design and build factories to produce textiles, clothing, and other materials rapidly and at lower costs.

Today, factories in the United States and around the world produce almost all of the consumer products that we rely on, everything from paper clips and ballpoint pens to cars, clothes, food, and books. This growth in the importance of industrial production led to a greater need for industrial engineers. They are the people who have been concerned not only with the machines that go into the factory (as is the mechanical engineer) but also with the materials that the machines process, the people who run the machines, the costs and efficiency of operations, and other factors that determine the success of an industrial operation.

Industrial engineering as a separate specialty emerged only during the twentieth century. For as long as there have been industrial engineers, however, there have been skilled assistants working with them to handle those tasks that do not require the engineer's direct involvement. Today's industrial engineering technicians are the direct descendants of these assistants. As the years have gone by, the number, variety, and complexity of the responsibilities falling to industrial engineering technicians have increased greatly. And, whereas in the past assistants could rely purely on common sense and on-the-job experience, today's industrial engineering technicians are specially trained and educated before entering the workplace.

Our modern industrial society relies more and more on industrial engineering to provide us with the goods and services we need. The industrial engineering technician is a recognized and respected team member in this effort.

Nature of the work

The type of work done by an industrial engineering technician depends on the location, size, and products of the company he or she works for. Usually a technician's duties fall in one or more of the following areas: methods engineering, work measurement, control determination, wage and job evaluation, and plant facilities and design.

Industrial engineering technicians involved in methods engineering analyze new and existing products to determine the best fabricating and assembly processes with the lowest costs. In these analyses, methods-engineering technicians make recommendations concerning the best kinds of processing equipment to be used. They determine how fast materials can be processed, develop flow charts, and consider all materials-handling, movement, and storage aspects of the production.

The technician most responsible for materials handling is the *materials-handling technician.* This technician studies present methods of handling material; compares and evaluates alternative methods; and suggests changes that will reduce physical effort, make handling safer, and reduce handling costs and damage to products.

Work measurement is a method of measuring the production rate of a given product and of establishing the amount of time required for all individual activities. *Work-measurement technicians* determine the output rates of industrial processes and establish operation times by any of a number of methods available, including timing the motions necessary for a complete operation, analyzing films of workers' motions, and consulting previously accumulated statistics collected in the factory.

One special kind of work-measurement technician is the *time-study technician,* who analyzes and determines elements of work, their order, and the time required to produce a product component.

Control determination is the area of industrial engineering that includes production control, inventory control, quality control, cost control, and budget control. Technicians in the production-control area often work in scheduling departments where they coordinate the many complex details to ensure product delivery to the customer on the requested date. To do this, production-control technicians must know the products and the assemblies to be made, the routes to be used through the plant, and the time required for the process. These technicians also issue orders to produce products, check machine loads, and maintain constant surveillance of the master schedules.

An industrial engineering technician uses a computer to analyze the flow of materials from one work station to another. His conclusions will aid in finding a more efficient system of production.

Production-control technicians also work in dispatching offices where they issue orders to the production areas, watch department machine loads, report progress of products, and expedite necessary parts to avoid delays.

Inventory-control technicians maintain inventories of raw materials, semifinished products, completed products, packaging materials, and supplies. They ensure an adequate supply of raw materials, watch for obsolete parts, and prevent damage or loss to products.

In quality control, technicians work with inspection departments to uphold the quality standards set by production engineers by checking all incoming materials and forecasting the quality of obtainable materials. *Quality-control technicians* use various techniques to carry out their work and perform other duties that include part-drawing surveillance, checking of parts with inspection tools, identifying trouble, and providing corrective procedures. The work of quality-control technicians is described in more detail elsewhere in the Engineering and Science section elsewhere in this volume.

Cost-control technicians measure actual product costs and compare them with budgeted allowances. These technicians investigate cost discrepancies, offer corrective measures, and analyze results.

Budget technicians gather figures and facts, compile these, and make graphs to determine break-even points. They present budgets to management and report on the effects of production schedules on profitability.

Technicians working in the area of wage and job evaluation gather and organize material pertaining to the skill, manual effort, education, and other factors involved in the jobs of all hourly employees. They collect this information to help set salary ranges and establish job descriptions.

The technician most involved with plant facilities and design is the *plant-layout technician*. This technician works with materials-handling personnel, supervisors, and management to assist in making alterations in manufacturing facilities. Plant-layout technicians study old layouts, consider all present and future aspects of operations, revise, consult, and then propose layouts suitable to production and management personnel.

Requirements

Industrial engineering technicians should enjoy and be good at compiling and organizing data, and they should be able to express themselves clearly and persuasively.

Most employers prefer to hire graduates of two-year post–high-school programs; therefore, prospective technicians should see that their high-school education prepares them adequately for further schooling. Specific subjects that students should study include algebra, geometry, trigonometry, mechanical drawing, metal shop, and English and communications. Additional skills that students should try to acquire include computer skills, shop sketching, blueprint reading, graph making, and model making.

"Industrial technology" is the term usually used to refer to post–high-school programs designed for prospective industrial engineering technicians. Most of these are two-year programs. Typical first-year courses include mathematics, orthographic and isometric sketching, blueprint reading, manufacturing processes, communications, technical reporting, introduction to numerical control, and introduction to computer-aided design (CAD). Typical second-year courses include methods and operations analyses, industrial materials, statistics, quality control, computer control of industrial processes, plant layout and materials handling, process planning and manufacturing costs, production problems, psychology and human relations, and industrial organization and institutions.

Special requirements

There is no special license required for industrial engineering technicians. To give recognition and encouragement to technicians, the National Society of Professional Engineers has established a certification program that some industrial engineering technicians may wish to participate in.

Government clearance may be required for certain high level and security positions within industries that perform defense and other sensitive work for the federal government.

Opportunities for experience and exploration

Opportunities to gain experience in high school are somewhat limited. Students, however, can obtain part-time work or summer jobs in industrial settings even if not specifically in the industrial engineering area. This type of work may consist of the most menial tasks, but it offers first-hand experience and it demonstrates interest to future employers.

Insights into the field can also be gained in less direct ways. Industrial firms frequently advertise or publish articles in professional journals or business or general-interest magazines that discuss new innovations in plant layout, cost control, and plans for improved productivity. By finding and perhaps collecting these articles or advertisements, prospective technicians can become acquainted with and keep abreast of developments in industrial engineering technology.

Methods of entering

Many industrial engineering technicians find their first jobs through interviews with company recruiters who usually visit campuses during the last semester of a student's program. In many cases, the student is invited to visit the prospective employer's plant for further consultation and to become better acquainted with the area, the product, and the facilities. Some students find job opportunities through ads in local newspapers, local employment services, and leads provided by friends, relatives, or teachers.

Advancement

As industrial engineering technicians gain additional experience, and especially if they pursue related advanced education, they become likely candidates for various advanced positions in this field. Some examples of advanced positions and their duties follow.

Production-control managers supervise all production-control employees, train new technicians, and coordinate manufacturing departments.

Production supervisors supervise production department personnel, check departmental records of production, scrap, and expenditures, and compare these records with departmental allowances.

Plant-layout engineers supervise all plant-layout department personnel, estimate all plant-layout costs, and confer directly with all other department heads to obtain information needed by the layout department.

Managers of quality control supervise all inspection and quality-control employees, select techniques used, teach employees new techniques, and meet with toolroom and production people when manufacturing tolerances and amount of scrap become a problem.

Chief industrial engineers supervise all industrial engineering employees, consult with all department heads, direct all departmental projects, set departmental budgets, estimate annual savings from their department's efforts, and submit annual reports of their group's activities and accomplishments.

Employment outlook

The vast majority of industrial engineering technicians are employed in the manufacturing sector of the economy. Most economists foresee declines in employment levels in this sector of the economy through the 1990s. Not all areas of manufacturing, however, will be similarly affected, and some areas, such as computer equipment, medical instruments and supplies, and many plastics products, will experience growth. In addition, continuing financial pressures will lead to a greater demand for increased industrial efficiency and hence for more well-trained industrial engineering technicians to assist in this drive to reduce and control manufacturing waste and inefficiency. Also, new environmental and safety regulations may lead companies to change some of their procedures and practices, and new technicians may be needed to assist in these changeovers.

Prospective technicians should remember that advances in technology and management techniques make industrial engineering a constantly changing field. Technicians will only be able to take best advantage of the increased need for their services if they are willing to continue their training and education throughout their careers.

Earnings

The salary range for entry-level industrial-engineering technicians varies according to the product being manufactured, geographical location, and the education and skills of the technician. Most industrial engineering technicians earn between $20,000 and $30,000 a year. Some technicians, however, especially those at the very beginning of their careers, earn $18,000 a year or less, while some senior technicians with special skills and experience earn as much as $37,000 a year or more. In addition to salary, most employers offer paid vacation time, holidays, insurance and pension plans, and tuition assistance for work-related courses.

Conditions of work

Industrial engineering technicians generally work in pleasant indoor areas. Depending on their jobs, they may work in the shop or office areas only, or in both. The type of plant facilities depends on the product. For example, an electronics plant producing small electronic products, requiring very exacting tolerances, has very clean working conditions.

Industrial engineering technicians can expect to do some traveling, as they may accompany company engineers to technical conventions or on visits to other companies to gain insight on new methods, components, and procedures.

Social and psychological factors

In terms of both training and responsibility, industrial engineering technicians occupy a position between the professionally trained manag-ers or engineers and the hourly workers or other employees who actually produce the product or provide the service. Some people may find this an awkward position to occupy, and some may find themselves associating more, both socially and psychologically, with one or the other of these groups. However, most technicians realize that their role is an important one, and they take pride in the part they play in today's industrial team.

GOE: 05.03.06; SIC: 8711; SOC: 3712

◇ **SOURCES OF ADDITIONAL INFORMATION**

Institute of Industrial Engineers
25 Technology Park/Atlanta
Norcross, CA 30092

American Society of Certified Engineering Technicians
PO Box 371474
El Paso, TX 79937

American Society for Engineering Education
11 Dupont Circle
Suite 200
Washington, DC 20036

Junior Engineering Technical Society (JETS)
1420 King Street
Suite 405
Alexandria, VA 22314

◇ **RELATED ARTICLES**

Volume 1: Engineering; Machining and Machinery
Volume 2: Engineers; Industrial designers
Volume 3: Industrial machinery mechanics;
Volume 4: CAD/CAM technicians; Electromechanical technicians; Fluid power technicians; Mechanical technicians; Robotics technicians

Industrial radiological technicians

Definition

Industrial radiological technicians are employed in industrial settings to work with materials that emit radiation. The three most common types of industrial radiological technicians are *radiographers*, known also as *X-ray technicians; isotope-production technicians;* and *hot-cell technicians.* These three career fields are all concerned with the practical applications of our understanding of radiation in its various forms.

There are two major kinds of radiation: nonionizing or electromagnetic radiation, which is energy that takes the form of wavelike emissions such as radio waves, microwaves, visible light, X rays, and gamma rays; and ionizing radiation, which is usually the emission of subatomic particles plus energy. The unprotected human body can tolerate only small amounts of certain types of either kind of radiation, yet some of these same types have become very important in modern life. All industrial radiological technicians share the necessity of taking various special precautions in their work, including the use of thick shielding, protective clothing, and so forth.

Radiographers conduct X-ray examinations of materials such as metals, plastics, and concrete and of specific products such as metal castings, pipes, and tubing. For the most part, they are looking for flaws, cracks, or the presence of foreign materials.

Isotope-production technicians help produce and prepare radioisotopes and other radioactive materials for use in biological, biomedical, and industrial applications.

Hot-cell technicians operate remote-controlled equipment that functions inside a hot cell (an area enclosed with radiation-shielding materials, such as lead or concrete). Working from outside of the cell, they move metal or chemical materials in and out of shielded containers inside the hot cell and perform standard chemical or metallurgical tests on radioactive materials.

History

During the 1880s and 1890s, scientists conducting research into naturally occurring chemical elements began to suspect that there were special forms of energy radiating from certain elements, either spontaneously or under the influence of specific stimuli. Early investigators in the field of radioactivity and X rays included Wilhelm Roentgen, who discovered X rays in 1895; Henri Becquerel, who discovered radioactivity in uranium in 1896; and Pierre and Marie Curie, who discovered polonium and radium.

During the twentieth century, investigation into the nature of radiation has led to various successful applications in many fields of human activity. Almost as soon as X rays were discovered, medical researchers began exploring their usefulness as a diagnostic tool, and as early as World War I this new technology was widely used for locating bullets in wounded soldiers.

The most dramatic outgrowth of the work came in the 1940s with the development of nuclear weaponry. In the years following World War II, another significant step was achieved: the harnessing of nuclear energy to produce electric power on a large-scale basis for both home and industry.

During the 1970s the nuclear energy field matured as research and development activities led to profitable commercial enterprises. In addition, the fields of radiography and other nuclear-related activities continued to grow. These nuclear-related activities now include such industries as nuclear-plant maintenance, the manufacture of protective clothing, transportation and shipping of nuclear materials, and environmental-monitoring equipment services.

From its earliest years, radiological technology has relied on skilled assistants both in the research and development field and in the area of practical applications. In recent years especially, the increasing use and rapid development of more radiation applications has led to a demand for more and better trained, qualified industrial radiological technicians. Today's radiological technician is a highly trained and trusted individual working in important areas of radiological technology.

Nature of the work

In addition to the three specific technical careers described at length in this article, there is also a wide variety of other types of work performed by industrial radiological technicians, ranging from health and safety work to sales and personnel supervision.

Some industrial radiological technicians are responsible for the collection of data concerning radiation exposure levels in radioisotope laboratories, nuclear-fuel processing facilities, particle accelerator complexes, nuclear reactor installations, or in other locations where potential human exposure exists.

Industrial radiological technicians are also involved in research pertaining to the limitation and evaluation of human exposure as well as to the effects of radiation on the plants and animals of a region, and upon other physical objects.

Design, testing, application, manufacture, sales, and maintenance of nuclear instrumentation and radioisotope or X-ray quality-control equipment are other common activities for industrial radiological technicians.

Radiographers take X rays (often called "radiographs") of a wide variety of objects and materials including welds, metal castings and tubing, poured concrete structural members, and molded plastics. Radiographs are taken by placing the object to be examined in front of a photographic plate and exposing the plate to a source of radiation. Radiographers select the proper type of radiation source, film, and exposure distance and time. They process the film, examine it for the presence of cracks, points of weakness, foreign objects, and other flaws, and otherwise assist in the analysis of the X-ray plates and readings.

An important part of the X-ray procedure is the preparation of the object to be examined. As part of this preparation, radiographers align the object between the source of X rays or gamma rays and the film or plate. Sometimes this can be done manually; other times it requires electric trucks, chain hoists, or cranes. Other preparation often includes masking peripheral areas (areas that are not to be examined) with lead shields.

Other activities of radiographers include monitoring working areas, usually with the use of survey meters, to protect personnel; replacing radioactive isotope sources in containers with manipulating tongs; and maintaining the radiographic equipment (for instance, verifying the radiation intensity coming out of the X-ray or gamma-ray source).

Isotope-production technicians work in nuclear laboratories where they produce the radioactive materials, including radioisotopes (the unstable form of an element that emits radiation), which are used for a wide variety of purposes, including medical, biological, and industrial applications.

Most radioisotopes are produced by enclosing a naturally occurring element within a specially designed container and then bombarding the substance with neutrons in a process known as irradiation. One of the many responsibilities of the isotope-production technician is to place specified amounts of chemicals into such containers to be irradiated at a nuclear reactor or with other irradiation equipment. To prepare such containers for shipping to the irradiation facility, isotope-production technicians secure vacuum pumps to the special containers and replace the air in the container with inert gas.

Isotope-production technicians are also responsible for receiving back the irradiated chemicals delivered inside shielded cells. They operate manipulators to open the containers and transfer the irradiated contents into glass vessels. Again using manipulators, they add specified types and quantities of chemical reagents into the glass vessels to produce the desired radioactive product.

In addition, isotope-production technicians control manipulators to perform standard chemical analyses of the radioactive materials. They may also extract radioactive samples that are transported to chemical laboratories for analysis. Once approval of the sample has been received, they fill shipping containers with specified quantities of radioisotope material for shipment to users of the product.

Hot-cell technicians are the technicians who specialize in the use of "slave manipulators," the remote-controlled mechanical devices that act like a pair of arms and hands inside an area enclosed with radiation-shielding materials. While looking through thick lead-glass windows, these technicians operate the manipulators to test chemical or metallurgical properties according to standardized procedures. They also set up and operate machines to cut, fold, stack, polish, and chemically treat test samples, following blueprints, sketches, and X-ray negatives.

In performing the various tests, hot-cell technicians utilize a wide variety of equipment including tensile testers, hardness testers, metallographic units, and micrometers and gauges. Hot cell technicians also use special environmental chambers to test the reaction of irradiated nuclear fuels to temperature changes.

Other responsibilities of hot-cell technicians include recording results of tests for further analysis by engineers, scientists, or customers; placing specimens in shielded containers for removal from the cell, using manipulators; devising adapters and fixtures for use in hot-cell operations; and participating in cleaning and decontaminating the cell during maintenance shutdowns.

Requirements

To be a successful industrial radiological technician, one must be capable of performing well both manually and mentally. A cooperative attitude and good communications skills are also important assets.

The first measure of skill for a technician is laboratory technique. This involves the ability to follow directions, to operate familiar and unfamiliar equipment with finesse, and to transmit clearly facts and observations associated with such operations.

Mentally, the technician must be able to understand, as well as to prepare, a wide variety of charts and graphs. Since these preparations will invariably involve mathematical calculations, competence in this area is also necessary.

Limited physical impairment will not hinder a good technician's advancement in this field. Performance and attitude are the criteria for success, regardless of the position or individual involved.

Since the foundation of radiological technology lies in physical and mathematical principles, prospective technicians are well advised to build strong backgrounds in these disciplines while in high school. English, chemistry, physics, and at least three years of mathematics, including one year each of algebra and plane geometry, are basic prerequisites.

For people who have not yet met these requirements, most institutions that offer programs in radiological technology make available noncredit, remedial courses to make up deficiencies. These courses are also appropriate for those who have fulfilled the requirements but whose grades indicate that refresher material is warranted.

Entrance requirements at most institutions offering a radiological or nuclear technician program state that a prospective student must have graduated from an accredited high school or have the equivalent training from the General Equivalency Diploma program.

A wide variety of programs is available for the training of industrial radiological technicians. These programs vary from eight-week short courses, to two-, three-, or four-year curricula, through five years of academic work. These programs go by such names as radiation and nuclear technology or physical radiologic technology.

Most of these programs begin with an introduction to the fundamentals of radiation, followed by courses in specialized areas of the profession. The specialized courses may include radiation biology, radiation measurements, and environmental radiation fundamentals.

Concurrently, students take supporting courses such as physics, chemistry, technical report writing, mathematics, and electronics. When put into a well-organized curriculum, these courses are designed to give graduates a well-rounded view of the field and to enable them to perform their functions as technicians in any specialty of the profession with a minimum of on-the-job training.

After successful completion of such a program, students may graduate with a certificate, an associate degree, or a bachelor's degree in radiation technology. Employers are generally satisfied with students who have graduated from two-year a two-year program, but four-year college graduates are becoming increasingly important in the eyes of some potential employers.

Special requirements

Certification or licensing is required of few, if any, industrial radiological technicians. The National Institute for Certification in Engineering Technologies does offer general certification if an individual desires.

Security clearances provided through the Nuclear Regulatory Commission are mandatory for both government and private industry employees engaged in jobs involving national security. Certain projects may necessitate military clearance with or without Nuclear Regulatory Commission clearance.

Opportunities for experience and exploration

The work done by industrial radiological technicians requires such extensive preparation that summer or part-time jobs in the field are not possible. However, there are a number of other ways to become familiar with the duties of such technicians.

For students in high school, their high-school science classes may be the best place to gain a familiarity with the nature of and potential careers in industrial radiological technology.

Most nuclear or radiation-related facilities are not likely to provide tours of their operations, but they may be able to furnish literature on radiation physics and radiation control. Some facilities that handle radioactive materials, such as nuclear power plants, have visitors' centers where the public can see educational exhibits about their operations. Science teachers, working with high school counselors, may be able to bring speakers to the school or to invite industrial radiological technicians to the school to speak about their fields.

Methods of entering

The best way to enter this field is to graduate from a technical school or institute, a community college, or a division of a four-year college with an industrial radiological technology program such as has been described above. Students who are about to complete an associate degree in radiological technology at a two-year, postsecondary program are usually interviewed and recruited near the end of the program by representatives of companies with nuclear or X-ray facilities. Graduates from strong programs often have several attractive offers to choose from.

Graduates will find work in a variety of fields including the following: nuclear materials handling and processing facilities, nondestructive testing firms, nuclear waste handling facilities, nuclear service firms, nuclear shipyards, chemical and petrochemical companies, and radiopharmaceutical companies.

Whatever preparatory training the beginner brings to the job, study and training will probably continue under the employer's direction. Beginning industrial radiological technicians usually work with more experienced technicians or engineers.

Advancement

There are opportunities for advancement for industrial radiological technicians in whatever industries they choose to start their careers. The following short paragraphs describe jobs to which technicians may advance with additional experience and training.

Research technicians develop new ideas and techniques in the radiation and nuclear field.

Quality-control specialists do product evaluation and testing to ensure strict adherence to product specifications.

X-ray calibration technicians test X-ray calibration, equipment reliability, safety, and evaluate field and filter performance.

Instrument-design technicians design and prepare specifications and testing of advanced radiation instrumentation.

Customer service specialists work in sales, installation, modification, and maintenance of customers' apparatus.

Radiochemistry technicians prepare and analyze compounds utilizing the latest in equipment and techniques.

Radioactive waste analysts develop new waste disposal techniques, inventory present waste on hand, and prepare waste for disposal.

Employment outlook

Attempting to examine even the near-term future of the U.S. nuclear and radiation-related industries is quite difficult. By some estimates, employment in this field will grow faster than the average for all industries through the 1990s. Other estimates foresee more moderate growth, and some foresee actual declines.

Questions about public health and safety have continued to receive a great deal of public attention since the accidents at Three Mile Island and Chernobyl. In addition, concern about environmental effects, unresolved issues and policies for waste disposal and reprocessing, actual and proposed state and federal moratoriums on new nuclear power plant construction and operations, reductions in export sales because of concern about nuclear weapon proliferation and because of increased foreign competition, rapidly increasing construction costs, changes in required power plant design and engineering, and a reduction in forecast growth in electricity requirements—all contribute to the present uncertainties and reduce growth in the nuclear energy field.

Much of the nuclear-related research and development activities are government-funded, and the vast majority of the activity is located in government-owned, contractor-operated facilities. Obviously the future of nuclear-related research and development depends primarily on future levels and directions of government funding.

The outlook for radiographers is slightly less complicated than it is for isotope-production technicians and hot-cell technicians, as radiographers are dependent on X-ray, rather than nuclear technology. During the coming years, many industries will be looking for ways to exploit the advantages of nondestructive testing provided by X-ray technology. However, many of these same industries—steel, construction, manufacturing—are expected to experience only modest growth in the coming years.

Earnings

Starting pay for industrial radiological technicians depends on the employer and on the academic background and work experience of the employee. Average annual starting salaries range from $16,000 to $20,000 in industry and slightly less in government. Experienced technicians usually earn salaries that fall approximately in the $22,000 to $30,000 a year range. Maximum earnings can range from about $37,000 to $50,000 a year and depend primarily on the value of technicians to their employers as based on performance, ability, and acceptance of responsibility.

Most employers offer fringe benefits such as paid vacation and holidays, insurance, and financial help in educational advancement as incentives.

Conditions of work

The need for cleanliness while working with radioisotopes and the cost involved in equipping a radiation laboratory usually ensure excellent working conditions for the industrial radiological technician. Delicate equipment usually requires year-round, dust-free, conditioned air, which also adds to laboratory employee satisfaction. As the job descriptions imply, some responsibilities involve working in welding shops, shipyards, and construction sites where conditions are extremely variable.

The radiation and nuclear industry has accumulated one of the best safety records of any industry in America. Full attention and effort are being given to keep this outstanding record intact.

Social and psychological factors

The careers of all industrial radiological technicians are very demanding. They must have confidence in their knowledge and skill to measure and manage potentially dangerous materials routinely. They must possess a high standard of precision in their work and maintain the instruments they work with so that they can be trusted to provide consistently accurate information.

Because abnormal conditions can and sometimes do develop in the job settings described in this article, industrial radiological technicians must be able to withstand the stress associated with such situations. They must be able to work long hours at such times without making mistakes and as a cooperating member of a team of experts doing a demanding job.

GOE: 02.04.01, 05.03.05; SIC: 3844; SOC: 3832, 399

◇ **SOURCES OF ADDITIONAL INFORMATION**

American Nuclear Society
555 North Kensington Avenue
La Grange Park, IL 60525

U.S. Council for Energy Awareness
1776 I Street, NW, Suite 400
Washington, DC 20006

American Society for Nondestructive Testing
4153 Arlingate Plaza
Caller #28518
Columbus, OH 43228

◇ **RELATED ARTICLES**

Industrial safety-and-health technicians

Definition

Industrial safety-and-health technicians work in industrial plants, where they are involved with evaluating and designing controls to reduce potential health and safety hazards. Using precision measuring instruments, they measure noise levels and air quality in industrial environments and administer hearing tests to workers. Technicians also give lectures and demonstrations, sometimes using audiovisual aids, to instruct employees and supervisors on safety regulations and to encourage compliance with them. They develop, implement, and monitor emergency action plans. They investigate industrial accidents and prepare detailed written reports. Technicians also help plant managers prepare safety and health program plans and budgets, and they recommend changes in plant policies or procedures to prevent accidents.

History

In the eighteenth century when the Industrial Revolution began, water power and steam-driven machines made mass production possible. The primary objective then was to achieve high production rates. Safety on the job was often considered the responsibility of the worker—not the employer.

By the beginning of the twentieth century, working conditions had vastly improved. Both workers and employers found that the cost of injuries and the loss of production and wages from industrial accidents were an expensive loss to everybody. Industry owners and leaders began to try to prevent industrial accidents and diseases by using safety-engineering methods.

The combined efforts of business, government, and labor organizations have resulted in increased safety awareness and much safer and more healthful working environments. Industrial-safety engineers and industrial hygienists have learned more about ways to make workplaces safe for employees. They have led the development of industrial-safety standards and practices.

With the passage of the Occupational Safety and Health Act (OSHA) in 1970, highly developed and well-accepted standards for safety and health in the workplace became the legal responsibility of employers. Many large industrial companies with established safety programs hired safety-and-health technicians to make sure that their programs met OSHA requirements.

Many companies, large and small, that had no formal safety programs started them to be sure of OSHA compliance. Insurance companies expanded their loss-control consulting staffs, and the number of independent safety consulting firms increased because many small businesses needed reliable help to make their workplaces safe.

The demand for trained safety-and-health personnel increased accordingly. The work performed by industrial safety-and-health technicians had always been important, and it became even more necessary. In the 1980s, continued public support and concern for occupational safety and health made it clear that there was a need for broadly educated, specially trained, and highly skilled industrial safety-and-health technicians.

A growing number of technical colleges, community colleges, technical institutes, and even a few four-year colleges have developed excellent two-year, college-level industrial safety-and-health technician programs. These programs award an associate degree or a certificate to their graduates and are the largest source of these technicians.

The work of industrial safety-and-health technicians is directly related to the work done by industrial safety-and-health engineers who design safety equipment and procedures. More and more, the industrial safety-and-health technicians are becoming the workers who implement the details of the safety and health program.

Nature of the work

Industrial safety-and-health technicians are the on-the-job members of the industrial safety staff whose objective is to reduce industrial worker accidents or work-related sickness to the lowest possible level.

Industrial work has become much more mechanized in about the past fifty years and therefore more complex and potentially danger-ous. The use of power machinery in factories, forests, transportation, mines, farms, offices, and hospitals makes the work physically easier to do. But modern machines also create more opportunities for people to get hurt or become ill.

Each year there are over six million cases of work-related sickness or injury in the United States. About half of these cases are serious enough to cause at least one lost workday. Many cases involve far more time lost from work, or death.

Employers are required by law to provide Workers' Compensation and Liability Insurance to protect workers and others against the finan-cial hardships and losses caused by job-related accidents. No insurance, however, really pays the costs of an accidental injury or death. No insurance can relieve all the pain and suffering, the inconvenience, and the personal hardships caused by accidents. Only the prevention of ac-cidents and disease in the workplace can cir-cumvent the cost and suffering that they cause. It is the task of the industrial safety and health staff, including technicians, to prevent on-the-job accidents and illness from occurring.

Industrial safety-and-health technicians are employed by many kinds of employers. These include large and small manufacturing indus-tries and businesses, construction or drilling companies, transportation, mining, and most other industrial or commercial employers. They also include medical, educational, and scientific institutions. Experienced industrial safety-and-health technicians may be employed as instruc-tors in programs for training safety personnel; in federal, state, and local government agen-cies; in insurance firms; and in safety-con-sulting firms.

These technicians usually work as members of a team directed by a safety engineer or in-dustrial hygienist. They may also work under the supervision of the head of the engineering department or a general manager. The team fol-lows a safety plan that may have been drawn up by safety engineers or outside consultants. In such cases, technicians may be expected to work more independently and to assume more individual responsibility for safety. Depending on their backgrounds and experience or the na-ture of the workplace and its organization, in-dustrial safety-and-health technicians may be asked to assume responsibility for safety within a given department, a single site, or several lo-cations.

The work of these technicians is typically a combination of three general activities. The first activity is communicating safety consciousness and teaching safety practices to employees.

Their second duty is performing on-the-job in-spections and analyzing potential safety and health hazards in the workplace. The third ac-tivity consists of writing reports, keeping records, working with engineers to design safe-guards, studying ways to improve safety, and communicating suggestions to supervisors.

Because the majority of job-related acci-dents involve workers who are within their first six months of employment, many company safety plans call for intensive safety instruction sessions for all newly hired workers. Industrial safety-and-health technicians usually are ex-pected to work with the personnel department to organize, schedule, and conduct these ses-sions. Sessions vary for different categories of workers. The basic plan for each session is usu-ally worked out with the safety engineer and other supervisors.

Most of the instruction sessions for new employees involve orientation and tours through the areas where the new employees will work. The tours include explanations of the safeguards, safety rules, and protection sys-tems, and explanations of job hazards, safety signs, and warnings. They also include a de-scription of the work rules regarding safety shoes, clothing, glasses, hard hats, or other special safety regulations.

These instructional duties are among the technician's most important activities. They are the beginning of a process that is most effective in preventing accidents—that of developing a work-safety attitude in every worker, based on understanding and avoiding actions that cause accidents.

Potential hazards in the workplace moni-tored by technicians include airborne health hazards such as dusts, mists, fumes, and gases; physical hazards such as noise, vibration, tem-perature, and pressure; and mechanical and electrical hazards such as unguarded machin-ery or improperly grounded or insulated equip-ment. Technicians also review facilities, includ-ing walking and working surfaces, fire protection systems, sanitation facilities, and utilities.

Specific tasks performed by industrial safety-and-health technicians cover many ar-eas. They conduct periodic investigations, sur-veys, and specific monitoring programs for dis-covering and defining substances, conditions, and activities that contribute to contamination of the working environment or to potentially harmful exposure to workers. Technicians re-view safety evaluation and inspection reports by outside consultants such as state or insur-ance inspectors or by worker committees or management, and they coordinate or assist in coordinating the actions taken to correct haz-

An industrial safety-and-health technician works with a health inspector to test for toxic substances in or near industrial and nuclear work sites.

ards. Technicians also inspect safety equipment, arrange for necessary repairs, and maintain inspection records on safety equipment.

Other duties are reviewing operating, maintenance, and emergency instructions to be sure that they are adequate and up-to-date. Technicians also conduct or assist in accident and injury investigations and maintain follow-up records to make sure that corrective actions were actually taken.

They recommend to their supervisors ways to improve the company's safety and health performance record and work with management to create a more effective safety policy. This may involve reading current safety reports and attending industrial safety-and-health conferences.

Technicians also maintain records of the company workers' compensation program and OSHA illness or injury reports. These duties are coordinated with the company's personnel and accounting departments.

Requirements

Industrial safety-and-health technicians must be thoroughly trained in safety engineering and industrial health. Because the main objective of their work is preventing industrial accidents and illness, their basic education must include learning how to communicate ideas clearly and quickly to workers with various levels of education, using written signs, bulletins, or verbal instructions.

Technicians must be able to make careful, systematic, step-by-step analyses of possible industrial accidents or illness in many different kinds of work stations and work activities. These may be in factories, offices, or wherever people work. Safety and health hazard inspections must be thorough. They are based on systematic observation and knowledge of potential dangers to workers, as well as methods and systems that are commonly used to make job sites and workplaces as safe as possible.

To prepare for this technical career, formal study is required. This study should include courses in physics, chemistry, and mathematics as they are applied to safety engineering and industrial health. Other requirements include a knowledge of industrial organization; the functions of personnel departments, accounting departments, and industrial insurance; and the organization of industrial engineering departments.

The most common way to become an industrial safety-and-health technician is to graduate from a two-year industrial-safety-and-health program at a technical or community college. High-school students who plan to enter this career should take classes that will prepare them for such a program. They should complete four years of courses in English and language skills, with special emphasis on reading, writing, and speaking. Two years of mathematics, including algebra, and physics or chemistry with laboratory study will provide a basic science background.

Other valuable courses include computer science, photography, and mechanical drawing. Not all high schools offer these courses, nor are they required for students to enter the field. If available, however, they are useful and should be studied. Mechanical drawing, for instance, is helpful because drawing and sketching are the second language of engineers and many factory workers, and they are therefore very useful in industrial communications.

A typical two-year program for industrial safety-and-health technicians involves intensive classroom study with more hours of laboratory or similar kinds of study than classroom hours.

A typical first-year program would include the following courses: fundamentals of fire protection; safety-and-health regulations and codes; advanced first aid; human relations; basic algebra; applied physics; introduction to technical communications; safety-planning layout and arrangement; power sources and hazards; principles of traffic safety; record-keeping and accident investigation; noise control and acoustical engineering; workers' compensation and industrial insurance; preventive maintenance; industrial economics; and applied chemistry.

The second year would typically cover the following subjects: industrial chemical hazards; materials handling and storage; environmental health; sanitation and public health; preventing and combating drug abuse in industry; construction safety and health; occupational safety engineering systems and techniques; radiation safety; industrial fire prevention; oral communication; industrial organizations and institutions; disaster preparedness; instrumentation and analysis; occupational safety and health management; special field work; technical reporting; and charting, diagramming, and sketching.

Physical requirements for this career include general good health, good eyesight, and at least normal physical strength and coordination. Color blindness can be a limiting factor, because most factories or industrial plants have color-coded wiring and piping systems. Normal hearing is needed to communicate in offices and in the plant and to interpret normal and abnormal sounds in the workplace that might indicate potential health or safety hazards.

Two industrial safety-and-health technicians conduct tests that monitor radiation levels in master/slave manipulator operations. These tests ensure the maximum safety for the workers at the plant.

Special requirements

There are no special licensing or certification requirements that must be met to enter this career. A few states may have requirements for the safety engineers or industrial hygienists for whom technicians work. There are, however, recognized marks of achievement that technicians can earn. One is the designation of Certified Safety Professional. Another is the title Member of Fire Protection Engineers, conferred by the Board of Certified Safety Professionals.

The Occupational Safety and Health Administration provides safety training programs to corporate employees and to the general public several times each year. After course completion, each student receives an official OSHA certificate.

Opportunities for experience and exploration

Students who are interested in the career of an industrial safety-and-health technician should obtain information from their high-school guidance counselors. In addition, students who live near a community college with an industrial health-and-safety program should visit the college occupational information center, library, and counseling staff to learn about the career. The public library may also have information.

A person who is interested in safety can learn much about safety by simply observing work being done in public, such as the use of safety signs, danger markers, and lights. One can also observe construction, highway work, utility crews, and fire fighters.

Most manufacturing companies have a safety officer, an industrial hygienist, or a safety engineer. In addition, many insurance companies have safety-and-health specialists on their staffs. Interested students or their guidance counselors can contact these specialists to find out about job opportunities and the type of activities associated with specific job titles. State OSHA offices and local chapters of the National Safety Council can also provide excellent information about this career.

Safety journals, such as *National Safety News*, *Professional Safety*, and *Job Safety and Health*, also provide information about occupational safety and health.

Any kind of summer or part-time work can introduce potential safety technicians to the workplace, where there are always potential hazards. Work experiences usually include learning on-the-job safety and health rules.

Methods of entering

Graduates of industrial safety-and-health technology programs usually have found their first jobs before graduation. Recruiters regularly visit schools with such programs. They learn from the school's placement officers who the graduating students are, interview them, and arrange for their employment. Work-study arrangements may also result in placements for students.

Another method of entering the career is to advance to the position by first working as an assistant to a safety engineer or a member of the industrial safety-and-health staff of a large company.

Sometimes the people who join a safety-and-health staff are experienced in specialized work such as arc welding, machining, foundry work, or metal forming, all of which can be especially hazardous. These experienced workers have already learned safety-and-health principles. With study, they can become industrial safety-and-health technicians in their special field.

Entry-level jobs for industrial safety-and-health technicians may have different names in different companies. One of the most commonly used titles is safety technician. Others are safety engineering assistant, safety inspector, fire inspector, accident investigator, hazardous waste disposal technician, safety compliance officer, staff safety and health specialist, and safety officer.

In companies with large safety-and-health staffs, the technician's job can be specialized. For example, a technician may only conduct inspections, or design safeguards to prevent accidents, or train employees in safety practices. In smaller companies, the beginning technician may simply be called the "safety engineer" and work under the direction of the engineering department or the plant manager. In such a case, the technician would be responsible for an entire safety program that may have been prepared by an outside consultant.

Advancement

Advancement for industrial safety-and-health technicians usually results from formal training and continued study as well as job experience. Keeping abreast of new developments and safety practices is very important for industrial safety-and-health technicians, as it helps them in their efforts to reduce costs, increase productivity, and improve worker morale, and company image. Such measurable service usually leads to higher status and salary for technicians who help make such improvements.

Advancement for safety technicians who work in large organizations with specialized departments allows technicians to learn all phases of the safety program by working at various assignments. Eventually they can advance to a supervisory position with higher pay and greater responsibilities.

After several years of experience and a good record of success, technicians can become specialized safety consultants or government inspectors. In the same way, they can also become private consultants to insurance companies or small businesses. Many small companies cannot afford a full-time safety engineer and hire consultants to set up an industrial safety-and-health plan. In such cases, the consultant who drew up the plan usually returns to make sure the plan is working and suggests changes where needed. All of these advanced positions represent independence, responsibility, and financial rewards for successful industrial safety-and-health technicians.

Employment outlook

The future employment picture for industrial safety-and-health technicians is not easy to foresee. While much of the demand for these technicians is created by industrial employers themselves and their insurers, the overall level of demand is affected by the level of government regulation and enforcement regarding safety and health. During the 1980s there was a general pullback in governmental regulation and spending on industrial safety and health. If this trend continues in the 1990s, employment levels will probably grow only slowly, and the demand for new industrial safety-and-health technicians will not be great. However, there are indications that the federal government is prepared to increase its involvement in this area in the 1990s, both in terms of new legislation and increased spending. If this were to happen, employment levels for industrial safety-and-health technicians could rise substantially.

Earnings

The national average earnings of industrial safety-and-health technicians is difficult to determine. The salaries of the various inspectors, safety officers, and assistants to safety engineers vary with the industry and with the education and experience of the individual safety worker.

In general, industrial safety-and-health technicians earn salaries that are equivalent to other engineering technicians. As a group, technicians usually earn between $20,000 and $30,000 a year and average around $25,000 a year. Some technicians, especially those at the beginning of their careers, may make between $10,000 and $14,000 a year, while some senior technicians who have acquired special skills and experience may earn $40,000 a year or more. Men and women in this career can expect benefits such as paid vacation, insurance, and paid holidays to be as good as those for other salaried employees in the organization.

Some employers provide a special plan for the industrial safety-and-health staff so that each may receive a yearly bonus for measurably improving the company's safety record. In addition, technicians and other safety workers often find that employers provide liberal support for job-related study and professional programs. This may include paid memberships in professional organizations, travel, and costs of attending meetings or conferences.

Conditions of work

Industrial safety-and-health technicians may work in an office or in the part of the plant for which they are responsible. In the plant, they may perform inspections, study possible dangers for workers, take samples, and talk with workers. Technicians must therefore be able to move around the workplace and be in good physical condition. Technicians' tasks, however, do not generally involve manual work or require greater than normal physical strength.

Whether they work in an office, in an employee safety training program, or in the plant, technicians must always set an example of safety. When required, they must wear safety clothes, hats, shoes, glasses, or other protective clothing and follow good safety practices at all times.

Technicians usually work during the day, but in plants that operate three shifts a day, some evening and night hours may be necessary. Jobs in mining and oil drilling may require safety technicians to be present around the clock, with "on-and-off" work shifts. Rates of pay for such situations are usually higher than for regular eight- or ten-hour shifts.

Office work usually involves reading government regulations, filing reports, maintaining records, and studying planned changes in

safety procedures. Such work is likely to be fairly routine.

Social and psychological factors

Industrial safety-and-health technicians have special responsibilities as team workers. They are members of a safety program team whose first responsibility is to prevent work-related illnesses and accidents. They are also a part of the management of the organization in which they work. They must work with people in all of the organization's major departments. This means that technicians must be able to get along with employees on every level.

Constant study is an important part of their work. Technicians need to keep up with changes in safety practices so that they can recommend changes that should be made to prevent accidents and hazards.

Psychologically, the duties of industrial safety-and-health technicians are complicated. This is because almost all workers at some time become careless about their safety. Safety technicians are constantly trying to help all workers, especially newly hired employees, to develop and maintain habits of working safely. Technicians therefore must be informed about all job activities and work stations in their area of responsibility. They must be recognized by the employees as persons who are concerned for their safety and who represent the company management in working to promote the well-being of employees.

Technicians must communicate effectively with coworkers, union representatives, and supervisors. They must also be effective teachers, able to impart information and instill a "safety first" attitude in others. Sometimes technicians must remind other employees about safety rules and regulations, persuading them that the rules are truly for their own good.

Industrial accidents and work-related illnesses are personal hardships and sometimes physical and psychological disasters for the worker who suffers them. Every accident or case of industrial illness that safety technicians prevent is a special service to their fellow workers. In addition, technicians may save time and money for both employer and worker.

Safe working habits are not acquired naturally. Industrial safety-and-health technicians who help their fellow employees to work safely at their best rate of productivity can derive great satisfaction from their work.

GOE: 11.10.03; SIC: 7389; SOC: 1473

Instrumentation technicians

Definition

Instrumentation technicians test, install, repair, inspect and maintain, and help to develop complex instruments that sense, measure, and record changes in industrial environments. Examples of such instruments include altimeters, pressure gauges, and radiation detection devices. Some instrumentation technicians operate the laboratory equipment that produces or records the effects on test instruments of actual or simulated conditions, such as vibration, stress, temperature, humidity, pressure, altitude, and acceleration. Other technicians sketch, build, and modify electronic and mechanical fixtures, instruments, and related apparatus. Other specific duties include verifying the dimensions and functions of devices assembled by other technicians and craft workers, planning test programs, and directing technical personnel in carrying out these tests. Instrumentation technicians also often perform mathematical calculations on instrument readings and test results to put them in usable form for preparing graphs and written reports.

History

The use of instruments as a means for people to monitor and control their environment and to guide their activities is as old as the sun dial, the weather vane, and the stick plunged in a river to determine its depth. As modern technology has progressed, however, we have found ourselves in need of information that must be quite precise and that often presents physical obstacles to our obtaining it.

For instance, with the advent of the steam engine in the nineteenth century it became necessary to know how much pressure there was inside a boiler. Humans cannot step inside a boiler to find out, and even if they could, none of our five senses, unaided by instruments, can tell us what we need to know about boiler pressure.

The early twentieth century saw the development of the internal combustion engine and powered flight. With these developments came the need for more instrumentation: speedometers, altimeters, and tachometers (to measure how fast an engine is turning).

Since World War II instrumentation technology has become a fast-growing field, responding to needs in the fields of space exploration, oceanographic research, biomedical studies, and nuclear technology.

Today instrumentation technology is actually both measurement and control. Inside a nuclear reactor, devices measure heat, pressure, and radiation, and their rates of change. If any of these factors are not at their desired levels, other instruments can make the necessary adjustments.

Traditionally the field of instrumentation has been associated with electronics, pneumatics, hydraulics, heating, and mechanics. The development of the laser, however, has widened the scope of possible measurements. The laser, in various forms, is being used as a precision drilling device, as a replacement for the surveyor's transit, and as a surgical knife in operations so delicate they were previously untried.

Nature of the work

The work that instrumentation technicians carry out varies according to their education, personal qualities, and the kind of apparatus they are assigned to.

There are three major categories of apparatus. Pneumatic and electropneumatic instrumentation equipment includes temperature and flow transmitters and receivers and other devices that start or are started by such things as pressure springs, diaphragms, and bellows, which receive or transmit pneumatic or electropneumatic signals. Hydraulic instrumentation equipment includes hydraulic valves, hydraulic valve operators, and electrohydraulic equipment. Electrical and electronic instrumentation equipment includes electrical sensing elements and transducers, electronic recorders, electronic telemetering systems, and electronic computers.

Instrumentation technicians may find themselves employed in any of many industrial groups, including aeronautics, chemistry, petroleum, foods, metals, ceramics, pulp and paper, power, and textiles, as well as space exploration, oceanography, air and water pollution, biomedical instrumentation, and national defense systems.

Technicians can advance, through experience and further study, from routine mechanical functions to repair, troubleshooting, and assisting in design. Each of these goals is achieved by combining the technician's general background with specific knowledge about the system apparatus.

The work of *mechanical-instrumentation technicians* consists principally of routine mechanical functions but also requires the ability to visualize functions or malfunctions of various mechanisms. The work includes checking out equipment prior to operation, calibrating equipment in operation, rebuilding equipment using standard replacement parts, mounting interconnecting equipment from blueprints, and performing regular mechanical functions requiring the use of simple tools (screwdriver, wrench, pliers, electrical drill, soldering iron and other similar tools). Ability to read both instrumentation and electronic schematic diagrams is necessary.

The primary functions of *instrumentation-repair technicians* are determining the causes of malfunctions and carrying out the needed repairs. Such repairs usually involve individual pieces of equipment, as distinguished from entire systems, and would include mechanisms, components, and circuits contained in the individual instruments. This type of job requires preparation, primarily laboratory-oriented, beyond that of mechanical-instrument technicians. General education, including physics and a good knowledge of both spoken and written English, is also desirable.

The *troubleshooting instrumentation technician* diagnoses malfunctions in instrumentation and control systems, adjusting instruments to meet requirements of specific processes and correcting troubles in individual instruments. Troubleshooters calibrate equipment either at the onsite installation or using bench facilities. They make suitable test set-ups, diagnose malfunctions, and revise existing systems. Background knowledge beyond that of the instrumentation-repair technician is required. This knowledge includes a fundamental knowledge of graphics, mathematics, and physics becomes important at this level of work.

Assistant instrumentation-design technicians usually work under the supervision of design engineers. Technicians in this type of job duplicate or modify instrumentation or control systems, individual pieces of apparatus, or the components or circuits within this element. They also assist in the planning and construction of such systems and mechanisms, building models and prototypes and preparing freehand sketches, working drawings, and diagrams of interconnecting equipment, and frequently using tools.

Instrumentation-design technicians contribute to the final design of equipment, basing their decisions on knowledge of standard practices and empirical judgments. These technicians are not involved with a high level of mathematics and their duties are not primarily dependent on creative thought. They will, however, "breadboard," or make mockups of new instrument systems, test out new system designs, order parts, and make sketches and electronic schematic diagrams.

In most industries, design functions performed by instrumentation technicians include analyzing and troubleshooting malfunctions of newly designed equipment, designing and fabricating various items of hardware, and preparing sketches to be used in mounting or interconnecting equipment, as well as preparing original schematic electronic diagrams.

Instrumentation-maintenance technicians perform standard calibrations for production purposes. They may be employed to work on pneumatic, hydraulic, electrical, or electronic equipment. This work requires using hand

This instrumentation technician demonstrates a new portable system that is controlled by electronic computers. Such a system makes it easier to repair and test instruments.

and have enough interest in science to study and understand electrical and electronic theory. The work requires clear and precise understanding of written and pictorial information; hence, the ability to communicate competently in scientific and engineering terms is a necessity. A broad knowledge of English and general subjects is desirable, particularly if the student enjoys working with others and is considering a career in technical sales, selling equipment, or instrument services.

While in high school, prospective instrumentation technicians should study mathematics for at least two years, becoming acquainted with algebraic and geometric functions. Depending on the person's goals, general or college-preparatory physics should be included, as well as some study in a laboratory science that may or may not be part of the physics requirement.

Courses that students take in their technical training programs are likely to include both theoretical background and some laboratory instruction. In some institutions, instrumentation is not offered as a separate discipline. Since instrumentation technicians use knowledge and techniques drawn from mathematics and physics, these subjects and learning experiences are part of a solid foundation in any program. Courses in the fundamentals of electronics, electrical theory, graphics, and digital computers are also important. Industrial economics, applied psychology, and plant management are courses that will be very useful to instrumentation technicians who advance in the field as customer service representatives or as design technicians.

Many public and private technical schools offer two-year programs specifically designed to train instrumentation technicians. These programs frequently lead to an associate degree of applied science. Such courses of study have in general a practical approach, with the technician expected to develop hands-on and laboratory skills, as well as learn the background theory. Because of the interdependence in instrumentation of electronic, electrical, and mechanical functions, students must have some theoretical understanding of electrical and electronic circuitry and digital and microprocessing computers. Students in these programs should also take English courses that develop their skills in technical report writing.

tools, including a soldering iron, electric drills, wrenches, and pliers.

Instrument-sales technicians work for equipment manufacturing companies. They analyze customer needs for specific control instruments, outline specifications for cost and functions of equipment, and need to be capable of doing emergency, goodwill troubleshooting.

Biomedical-instrument technicians receive special education in the biomedical area in which their instruments are used. They must understand the calibration and repair of those instruments. Biomedical-instrument technicians are concerned with the safety and welfare of both the patient and the medical technician using the equipment. These technicians must be constantly alert for the problems of electrical interference of one device on another as the number and variety of such equipment expands.

Instrumentation-systems sales representatives, after company training, work on preliminary specifications and designs of relatively standard installations and develop understanding and goodwill with their customers.

Requirements

Students entering the field of instrumentation technology must be adept in the use of tools

Special requirements

Instrumentation technicians who are graduates of qualified technical institutes may become certified by the Institute for the Certification of Engineering Technicians. Technicians may also become members of the Instrument Society of America and similar professional societies. Membership in such organizations is optional but encouraged as a means of keeping abreast of advancing technology.

Opportunities for experience and exploration

There are numerous possibilities for the exploration of the various fields in which instrumentation technicians are employed. Visits to industrial laboratories, instrument shops, research laboratories, power installations, and manufacturing companies, especially those that rely on automated processes, can provide a glimpse of the working environment and activities of these technicians. During such visits one is able to see technicians actually on the job, and it may be possible to speak with several of these people regarding their work or with employers about possibilities for instrumentation technicians in their company, industry, or institution.

In addition, it is possible, while still in high school, to obtain summer or part-time employment as a helper on an industrial maintenance crew. This helps students evaluate their own mechanical and technical aptitude and manual dexterity and to observe working conditions in a particular industry.

Students may also gain some experience and understanding of their ability by repairing household appliances, by building and maintaining ham radio sets or stereo sets in their spare time, and by taking high-school courses in machine shop, electrical shop, and mechanical drawing.

Methods of entering

Many companies send recruiters to technical schools where students who are about to graduate may be seeking jobs as instrumentation technicians. Chemical and medical research companies especially need maintenance and operations technicians and usually recruit at schools where training in these areas is strong. Similarly, many industries in search of design technicians recruit at technical institutes and community colleges where the program is likely to meet their technician needs. In gen-

Testing is done with highly-sophisticated instrumentation equipment. These technicians are using electrical sensing elements, computers, and special recorders to diagnose a problem.

eral, well-qualified graduates often find that the search for employment is not difficult; rather, employment will seek them.

Advancement

At their first job upon completion of their education many technicians begin by doing instrument maintenance and adjustment tasks to develop their skills with their employer's equipment. Technicians whose school record indicates appropriate training may, upon completion of an employer's basic program, start at an advanced level in sales or another area where a general understanding of the field is more important than specific laboratory skills.

With increased experience and sometimes with additional training, technicians who have demonstrated their proficiency in instrumentation may advance to supervisory positions or specialized positions that require knowledge of a particular aspect of instrumentation.

Employment outlook

Employment opportunities for instrumentation technicians are expected to be favorable through the 1990s. Opportunities will be best for graduates of postsecondary technical training programs.

Anyone who watches television cannot help noticing the tremendous future for instrumentation. When new surgical procedures are reported, instrumentation is often seen to be crucially important. Likewise, most new developments in automated manufacturing techniques, including robotics and computer-controlled machinery, rely heavily on instrumentation devices.

The emerging fields of air and water pollution control are other areas of growth. Scientists and technicians measure the amount of toxic substances in the air or test water with the use of instrumentation. Additionally, instrumentation is required to quickly evaluate toxic waste in land.

Oceanography, including the search for undersea deposits of oil and minerals, is another quickly expanding field for instrumentation technology, as is the field of medical diagnosis, including long-distance diagnosis by physicians through the use of sensors, computers, and telephone lines.

One important aspect of technology often overlooked is the teaching profession. As instrumentation continues to expand and the need for skilled technicians increases, the shortage of qualified instructors having combined knowledge of theory and application will become more acute. Opportunities already exist, not only in educational institutions but also increasingly in those industries that have internal training programs.

Earnings

Earnings and benefits for instrumentation technicians vary in different parts of the country. Most instrumentation technicians earn between $20,000 and $30,000 a year, and the average salary is around $25,000 a year.

Some instrumentation technicians, especially those at the beginning of their careers, earn less than $18,000 a year during the early 1990s, while some senior technicians with special skills and experience earn as much as $50,000 a year or more.

Conditions of work

Working conditions vary widely for instrumentation technicians. An oil-refinery plant job is as different from space-mission instrumentation work as a nuclear-reactor instrumentation job is different from work in the surgical room of a hospital. All employment for these workers use similar principles, however, and instrumentation technicians can master new areas of application by applying what they have learned previously. For technicians who would like to travel, the petroleum industry, in particular, provides employment in foreign lands.

Social and psychological factors

Instrumentation technicians' tasks may range from the uncomplicated and routine to the highly complex and challenging. Some workers who are trained in this field may resent the more repetitive aspect of their jobs. Others may find it a welcome relief from their highly technical duties, or they may prefer doing this type of work on a full-time basis.

A calm, well-controlled approach to work is essential. Calibration and adjustment require the dexterity and control of a watchmaker. Consequently the person who is easily excited or impatient is not well suited to this kind of employment.

In general, the most pleasant surroundings are industries where the instrument work has become routinized; the greatest opportunity for advancement is likely to be where the work must be accomplished under trying circumstances and away from home. Students entering the field will find the greatest satisfaction and reward in this field if they are free to move from place to place and are able to work with people of different and unusual backgrounds.

GOE: 05.01.01; SIC: Any industry; SOC: 3711

◇ **SOURCES OF ADDITIONAL INFORMATION**

American Society for Engineering Education
11 Dupont Circle
Suite 200
Washington, DC 20036

Association for the Advancement of Medical Instrumentation
1901 North Meyer Drive
Suite 602
Arlington, VA 22209

IEEE Instrumentation and Measurement Society
c/o Institute of Electrical and Electronics Engineers
345 East 47th Street
New York, NY 10017

Instrument Society of America
PO Box 12277
67 Alexander Drive
Research Triangle Park, NC 27709

Junior Engineering Technical Society (JETS)
1420 King Street, Suite 405
Alexandria, VA 22314

Scientific Apparatus Makers Association
1101 16th Street, NW
Washington, DC 20036

◇ **RELATED ARTICLES**

Volume 1: Engineering
Volume 2: Engineers
Volume 3: Appliance repairers; Instrument makers; Instrument repairers; Watch repairers
Volume 4: Aeronautical and aerospace technicians; Calibration technicians; Electronics technicians; Fluid power technicians; Nuclear instrumentation technicians; Robotics technicians

Laboratory technicians

Definition

The term "laboratory technicians" is used in many industries to designate technicians who perform a variety of tasks relating to the measurement, testing, and preparation of materials in laboratories. There are laboratory technicians designated in this way in the auto industry; the chemicals and plastics industry; the pharmaceutical industry; the glass manufacturing industry; the light, heat, and power industry; the petroleum refining industry; and veterinary medicine. For a general description of the kind of work these technicians do, see the article titled "Chemical technicians" in this section. As many of these technicians perform laboratory tests relating to the quality of raw materials and manufactured products, readers might also want to see the article titled "Quality-control technicians" also in this section. Laboratory technicians specifically involved with the artificial breeding of animals are described in the article entitled "Animal production technicians" in the Agriculture, Forestry, and Conservation Technician Occupations section of this volume. *Clinical laboratory technicians* and *medical technicians* are described in Volume 2 under the title "Medical technicians."

Layout technicians

Definition

Layout technicians lay out and specify work that is to be done by optical lens finishers. According to their specific assignments, they may be designated as bench-layout technicians or surface-layout technicians.

Layout technicians work on precision optical elements such as the lenses in eyeglasses, binoculars, and microscopes. These workers, however, are not responsible for preparing lenses for eye glasses. These workers are called opticians and optical mechanics.

Nature of the work

Technicians first inspect lens blanks for defects and ensure that they are the correct size and power. They read specifications provided in work orders and, using a protractor, mark centers, axes, and terminal points on the blanks. They write out specifications and instructions in detail to guide lens finishers. They mount the lens blanks to be finished in optical testing equipment and check their focus, power, and axis specifications. They reject defective blanks. Using a marking device on the optical equipment, they mark the optical center of the lens blanks, and their horizontal axes.

Requirements

Persons interested in careers as layout technicians should be high-school graduates and should have at least one additional year of specialized vocational training. They should take mathematics courses at least through plane geometry, and they should have sufficient language skills to be able to read technical manuals and to understand and communicate instructions. Layout technicians' work is not strenuous, but it demands precision and patience. In addition, they need to have clear, readable handwriting when they write out instructions for lens finishers to follow.

Conditions of work

Layout technicians work in pleasant indoor surroundings. They spend a considerable amount of their workday on their feet, and the equipment they work near operates with a steady whining sound that may become irritating.

GOE: 06.01.04; SIC: 3229; SOC: 6824

◇ **RELATED ARTICLES**

Volume 1: Glass; Machining and Machinery
Volume 2: Dispensing opticians
Volume 3: Contact lens manufacturing workers; Layout workers; Opticians and optical mechanics
Volume 4: Optics technicians; Ophthalmic laboratory technicians

Mathematical technicians

Definition

Mathematical technicians, also known as *data-reduction technicians,* work in a variety of industrial and research settings. In these settings, they apply standardized mathematical formulas, principles, and methods to solve technological problems in engineering and the physical sciences. These problems usually concern specific industrial and research objectives, processes, equipment, or products.

Nature of the work

Mathematical technicians analyze raw data and confer with scientists and engineering personnel to plan projects. They select the most practical and accurate combination and sequence of computational methods, using algebra, trigonometry, geometry, vector analysis, and calculus to reduce the raw data to useful and manageable terms. They also select the most economical and reliable combination of me-

chanical and computerized data-processing methods and equipment; modify standard formulas to conform with the data-processing methods selected; analyze the processed data; and, in some cases, operate the data-processing equipment. Finally, they transcribe data into equations, flow charts, graphs, or other media.

Requirements

Mathematical technicians should receive two to four years of post–high-school training. During the course of their training, they should receive instruction in algebra, calculus, statistics, and the use of computers. They should develop their language skills to the point that they can read scientific and technical journals; write reports and instructions; and express themselves clearly in informal conversations and in more formal oral presentations. The work of mathematical technicians is seldom physically strenuous, and the working environment is usually safe and comfortable.

GOE: 11.01.02; SIC: None; SOC: 384

Mathematical Association of America
1529 18th Street, NW
Washington, DC 20036

◇ **SOURCES OF ADDITIONAL INFORMATION**

American Mathematical Society
PO Box 6248
Providence, RI 02940

Industrial Mathematical Society
PO Box 159
Roseville, MI 48066

◇ **RELATED ARTICLES**

Volume 1: Mathematics
Volume 2: Mathematicians; Statisticians
Volume 3: Statistical clerks
Volume 4: Data-processing technicians

Mechanical technicians

Definition

Mechanical technicians assist mechanical engineers in a broad range of functions involving the design, building, maintenance, and modification of many kinds of machines, mechanical devices, and tools. In general, mechanical technicians apply their knowledge of mechanical engineering technology to the problems of manufacturing industries, including the automotive and aerospace industries, the industrial-equipment industry, and the whole range of consumer-product manufacturers.

The work of mechanical technicians includes reviewing blueprints and project instructions, analyzing costs and practical values of design plans, sketching rough layouts of proposed machines or machine parts, assembling new or modified devices or components, setting up and conducting tests of completed assemblies or components, analyzing test results, and writing reports. In their work, mechanical technicians use complex instruments, test equipment, and gauges. Mechanical technicians may also supervise the actual manufacturing process as it is carried out by skilled craft workers.

History

Mechanical-engineering technology, being principally concerned with applications of machines to the manufacturing process, is as old as the Industrial Revolution itself. This revolution began in England in the late eighteenth century as inventors found ways of linking James Watts's steam engine first to simple mechanical devices, as spinning and weaving machines, and later to precision machine tools such as lathes and boring machines.

One of the most important figures in this revolution was Eli Whitney. Having received a government contract in 1798 to produce 15,000 muskets, he hired not gunsmiths, but mechanics. In those days all articles, including muskets, were built one by one by individual craft workers. A musket, for instance, was built by grinding, filing, and drilling the parts, fitting them together as the gunsmith went along. No two muskets were ever alike.

Whitney took a different approach. For two years after receiving the contract, he did nothing but invent and build machines and train mechanics to specialize in making separate parts of the gun.

In the course of this project, Whitney invented new machine tools and attachments such as the milling machine and jig, made a reality of the concept of interchangeable parts, and paved the way for the modern manufacturing assembly line.

This manufacturing process inevitably required not only ingenious inventors and skilled mechanics to operate the machines; it also required skilled assistants to help the inventors in developing new machines, in setting or resetting tolerances, in maintaining and repairing operational equipment, and in directing, supervising, and instructing workers. These assistants have become today's mechanical technicians, and they are a crucial part of today's manufacturing team.

Nature of the work

Mechanical technicians are involved in the manufacturing process from start to finish. The first stage in manufacturing a product is research and development. In this area of work, the mechanical technician may work as an assistant to an engineer or scientist in the design and development of products from ball-point pens to space shuttles. These technicians prepare drawings of the project being developed. In the design of an automobile engine, for instance, they make detailed drawings of each screw, nut, bolt, and gear to be used in the engine. They estimate cost and operational qualities of each part, taking into account friction, stress, strain, and vibration. In doing these tasks, they free the engineer to accomplish other research assignments.

When a product has been accepted for production, preparations must be made for manufacture. In this effort, mechanical technicians assist in the design by making design layouts and detailed drawings of parts to be manufactured and of any special manufacturing equipment that will be needed.

These technicians, known as *drafting technicians,* usually work as *tracers, detailers,* or sometimes as *patent-drafting technicians.* Tracers copy plans and drawings, usually by tracing with ink or pencil on a transparent material in preparation for blueprinting. They may also make some simple drawings under close supervision. Detailers make detailed drawings from layout drawings, showing exact dimension, tolerances, finish, material, and other information necessary for production. Patent drafting technicians prepare mechanical drawings of many varieties of devices for use by patent attorneys in obtaining and recording patents.

Another specially trained mechanical technician who comes into play in the manufacturing process at this point is the *tool designer.* Tool designers prepare sketches of designs for cutting tools, jigs, special fixtures, and other devices used in mass production. Frequently they redesign existing tools to improve their efficiency. They also make drawings of tools and fixtures or supervise other workers who are making similar drawings.

Other mechanical technicians, working as *cost-estimating technicians,* conduct studies to determine costs of required materials, necessary labor, and plant space required for production. For efficient management, a product analysis must be completed before the product advances to the manufacturing stage. As a new product approaches this stage, mechanical technicians observe and direct the setup of machinery and production lines as well as check arrival and storage of raw materials.

After the production of a product begins, the mechanical technicians work toward perfecting the manufacturing process to make the product a more profitable one. This is accomplished by *time-and-motion study technicians* who observe and record time and motions involved in the manufacture of parts, comparing these time-and-motion values to accepted standards. They may also revise methods of manufacture to promote efficiency.

After the product is manufactured, mechanical technicians may assist with storage and shipping problems, while other mechanical technicians may assist in customer relations where servicing or installation of the product is required.

As a result of the technician's education, personal interests, or employer needs, many technicians are employed in very specialized positions within the manufacturing process. The following is a list of some of these specialized positions, all of them open to the properly trained entry-level technician:

Mechanical-design technicians develop mechanical drawings from engineering sketches and notes into complete, accurate working plans to be used for manufacturing a product. They also make necessary changes in drawings as requested by engineers.

Quality-control technicians test and inspect components at various stages of manufacture, thus ensuring final quality of products as specified by engineering drawings and records.

Standards-laboratory technicians test and calibrate measuring instruments used in manufacturing to assure precision accuracy and performance of these measuring tools. They also establish laboratory maintenance procedures to assure the accuracy of their measuring equipment.

Standards-practice technicians draw up sets of standards on the basis of information obtained from the production department as to the specifications of the materials needed. They also make changes in existing specifications and standardize records and descriptions of processes.

Test technicians evaluate characteristics and check operations of newly manufactured products or equipment and compile records of observed characteristics.

Programmer technicians work from parts drawings to prepare programs for numerically controlled and computer-operated machine tools.

Engineering-safety technicians promote safety through the study of accident records and by organizing safety committees. They also plan for fire prevention and check on the use of safety equipment.

Engineering-specifications technicians examine plans and drawings to determine material specifications. They also prepare lists of materials specifying quality, size, and strength and compare these specifications to company, government, or other requirements.

Computer programmers convert engineering problems to a language that a computer can process. They operate the computer, review results, and develop new subroutines for specific new computer uses.

Production-planning technicians plan production schedules for the manufacture of industrial products, coordinating supply of the product with demand for the product and forecasting needs for production.

Process-planning technicians plan the manufacturing sequence for a given part, including production, assembly, and shipping. They check daily manufacturing output of parts, expedite operations that cause delay, and prepare reports that analyze production and raw material needs.

Order-analyst technicians analyze the needs for parts and raw materials, preparing in advance for the manufacturing needs of a plant and organizing and modifying requests for supplies.

Plant-layout technicians work with engineers to develop an efficient plant layout to promote smooth flowing manufacturing processes from raw-material intake to product shipment.

Requirements

Mechanical technicians must be good with both their hands and their minds. They must be interested in people and machines and have the ability to become involved in carrying out detailed work. They must be able to analyze sketches and drawings and to apply scientific principles to problems in the shop or laboratory, in either the design or the manufacturing process. They must have patience, perseverance, resourcefulness, and integrity.

Prospective mechanical technicians should have an aptitude for mathematics. Clear understanding of written directions and the ability to communicate in both spoken and written reports is an absolute necessity.

Young people who plan on undertaking training in mechanical technology should begin their preparation in high school. Although schools offering training in this field vary somewhat in their entrance requirements, one year of algebra and one year of geometry are gen-

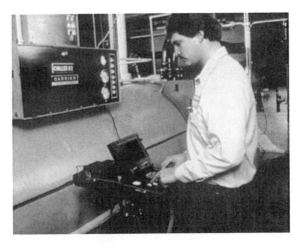

A mechanical technician uses a portable computerized device to test the control panel of a pressurized tank.

erally required for this career. Other desirable courses would include computers, mechanical drawing, shop, and language skills. It is wise to check the entrance requirements of specific mechanical technician training programs to assure that all high-school course requirements are being met.

High-school diplomas are required for entrance to most mechanical-technician training programs. High-school counselors can advise which entrance examinations should be taken.

Associate degree or two-year mechanical technician programs are designed to prepare students for entry-level positions. Most programs offer one year of a basic program with a chance to specialize in the second year. The first year of the program generally consists of courses in mathematics, science, and communications skills. Other courses introduce the student to the manufacturing processes, drafting, and the language of the industry.

Many schools offer several majors in the second year of the program, each of which provides training for a specific area of work in the manufacturing industry. Perhaps the best known and most popular major is design. This major includes courses on properties of metals, tool design, machine motions, and the design of machine elements. It also includes several courses in drafting, taking the student from basic procedures used in drafting to courses in the design and development of intricate mechanisms. After this training a student should be able to take a manufactured product, draw it in three dimensions, and carefully describe, through specifications, how it should be manufactured.

Many other mechanical technicians follow a curriculum that is known variously as a manufacturing major, production major, or industrial major. The second year of such a program offers instruction in acceptable manufacturing processes and practices. It includes courses in process planning, production control, quality control, manufacturing costs, and time-and-motion study. Also included may be courses in psychology, business administration, and industrial relations.

Special requirements

Some training programs, such as tool design, require a formal apprenticeship of from two to four years of combined classroom instruction and on-the-job training.

Mechanical technicians can be certified under in administered by a variety of professional or technical societies. Such certification is not required for many mechanical technician positions; however, certification always works in the favor of the applicant who has taken the trouble to earn it.

Mechanical technicians are encouraged to become affiliated with professional groups that organize continuing education sessions for members. Some mechanical technicians may be required to belong to unions.

Opportunities for experience and exploration

There are several avenues that lie open to the young person who wishes to gain experience or first-hand knowledge of the field of mechanical technology. High-school courses in geometry, physics, mechanical drawing, and shop work will give a student a feel for the mental and physical activities involved in mechanical technology.

Field trips to industrial laboratories, drafting studios, or manufacturing facilities can offer overall views of the type of work done in this field. Hobbies like automobile tinkering, model making, and electronic kit assembling can also be helpful. Repairing home appliances for friends and family can also be good experience.

It may be possible to obtain part-time or summer work in a machine shop or factory. This type of work usually consists of sweeping floors and clearing out machine tools, but it offers first-hand experience and it demonstrates interest to future employers.

Methods of entering

Schools offering mechanical technician education usually assist their graduates in finding employment. At most colleges, company recruiters interview prospective graduates during their final semester of training. Many students receive job offers as a result of these interviews.

Other graduates may prefer to apply directly to employers, use newspaper classified advertisements, or apply through public or private employment services. At most colleges, placement personnel or teachers are ready to give employment advice and counseling.

Advancement

As mechanical technicians remain with a company, they become more valuable to the employer. Opportunities for advancement will be available to those who are willing to accept greater responsibilities, either by taking on more technically complex assignments or by assuming supervisory duties. Some technicians advance by moving into technical writing or technical sales. Mechanical engineering technicians who get more education may become mechanical engineers.

The following paragraphs describe positions to which mechanical technicians might reasonably expect to advance:

Tool designers design and modify the tools, such as milling machine cutters, broaches, fixtures, and jigs, that are used to produce the manufactured products.

Tool engineers (also called *machine designers*) design special machines and equipment used for manufacturing purposes and supervise drafters, detailers, and tracers.

Technical sales representatives show manufactured products to potential customers, providing the necessary advisory services and selling the product.

Customer-relations engineers travel as company representatives to service equipment wherever it may be installed, making necessary repairs or offering technical advice to others performing repairs.

Research designers develop new and better products through research and development procedures in laboratories.

Assistant production managers manage production through receiving, manufacturing, and shipping operations, including supervision of other employees.

Technical writers write reports, bulletins, and descriptive literature of all kinds, including specification sheets. They also write technical manuals required for manufactured products.

Production supervisors oversee specific production areas, assigning duties, interpreting engineering drawings, and checking for quality and quantity of production.

Production coordinators supervise a product's manufacture to expedite movement of supplies and finished parts and are responsible for completion of a product at a specified date.

Time-and-motion study engineers are responsible for time-and-motion study departments. They provide recommendations concerning work rates, efficient use of time, and materials used in manufacture.

Quality-control technicians promote precision in manufacturing through constant surveillance of quality of work produced as well as of incoming parts received from suppliers or subcontractors. They control this area of work through supervision of others and through their own personal inspections.

Methods engineers work from engineering drawings to route raw materials to proper locations in the plant and select proper and efficient work methods of manufacture for each part.

Production engineers study engineering drawings of jobs to be done and produce schedules and work plans showing the sequence of simpler operations to be performed, thus making it possible for skilled and semi-skilled machine operators to perform their tasks properly.

Employment outlook

Employment opportunities for mechanical technicians depend, to some degree, on general economic conditions. The slow economic growth that many economists forecast for the early and mid-1990s should lead to at least modest growth in the need for industrial machinery and tools and for skilled technicians to help create them.

In addition, there should be continuing efforts in the research and development field in search of new products, processes, and equipment. Manufacturing companies will be looking for more and more ways to apply the advances in mechanical technology to their operations. New concepts in manufacturing, new materials, new designs, new consumer demands—all of these factors should provide more work for the well-trained mechanical technician.

Earnings

Salaries for mechanical technicians will vary depending on the nature and location of the job, the employer, the amount of training the technician has received, and number of years of experience.

In general, mechanical technicians earn salaries similar to other engineering technicians. Most earn between $20,000 and $30,000 a year, and the average is around $25,000. Some mechanical technicians, especially those at the beginning of their careers, may make around $18,000 a year or less, while some senior technicians with special skills and experience may make from $30,000 to $50,000 a year or more.

These salaries are, of course, for the standard workweek. Overtime or premium time may be paid for work outside the regular workweek or regular daytime hours.

Other benefits that mechanical technicians may receive, such as vacation, insurance, pension plans, profit sharing, and tuition-refund plans, depend upon the company and sometimes upon company-union agreements.

Conditions of work

Mechanical technicians may find a variety of working conditions, depending on their field of specialization. Technicians who specialize in design may find that they spend most of their time at the drafting board. Those who specialize in manufacturing may spend some time at a desk, but they also spend considerable time in manufacturing areas or shops.

Conditions also vary according to industry. Different industries require technicians to work, variously, in foundries, die-casting rooms, machine shops, assembly areas, or punch-press areas. Most of these areas, however, are well lighted, heated, and ventilated. Moreover, most industries employing mechanical technicians have fine safety programs.

Social and psychological factors

Mechanical technicians, because of their training and experience, are valuable employees. They are called upon to exercise independent judgment, to be responsible for valuable equipment, and to act as effective leaders. They also, of necessity, sometimes find themselves carrying out routine, uncomplicated tasks. Technicians must be able to respond well to both of these kinds of demands. Similarly, they must respond well to supervising and being supervised. In return for this flexibility and versatility, mechanical technicians are usually accorded considerable respect and recognition by their employers and by their coworkers in the industry.

GOE: 05.01.01; SIC: Any industry; SOC: 3713

◇ **SOURCES OF ADDITIONAL INFORMATION**

American Society for Engineering Education
11 Dupont Circle, Suite 200
Washington, DC 20036

American Society of Mechanical Engineers
345 East 47th Street
New York, NY 10017

Junior Engineering Technical Society (JETS)
1420 King Street, Suite 405
Alexandria, VA 22314

Metallurgical technicians

Definition

Metallurgical technicians work in support of metallurgical engineers, metallurgists, or materials scientists in the production, quality control, and experimental study of metals. Metallurgical technicians conduct tests on the properties of metals, develop and modify test procedures and equipment, analyze data, and prepare reports. Specific activities of metallurgical technicians include photographing metal samples with a photomicroscope; taking, developing, and mounting photomicrographs; examining samples with X-ray, gamma-ray, and other inspection equipment to detect internal fractures, impurities, and other defects; and testing samples in pressure devices, hot-acid baths, and other apparatus to determine hardness, elasticity, toughness, and other properties of metals.

History

Metallurgy as an art and as a craft is thousands of years old. It includes both the processes by which metallic elements and compounds are extracted from the ores in which they naturally occur and the processes by which useful metals are made from those extracts.

Copper was probably one of the first metals to be crafted into useful objects. Weapons made from readily available bits of copper were being forged (heated and pounded into shape) in the Near East 6,000 years ago. Copper, along with lead, was probably also among the earliest metals to be smelted (separated from its ore by means of heating). The smelting of iron dates back in Egypt to at least 2,000 B.C.

Down through the centuries metallurgy remained, for the most part, an art and a craft, relying heavily on trial and error and inspired guesswork. Medieval alchemists added to our store of knowledge about metals as they carefully studied the behavior, properties, and uses of metals. As years went by, and especially during the nineteenth and twentieth centuries, metallurgy developed into a combination of art and science, involving knowledge of the chemical and physical principles that underlie the properties and behavior of metals. Many natural metals and alloys (special metals made by fusing together metals or a metal and other elements) that were rare or unknown just a few decades ago are now economically produced in large quantities. Tantalum, zirconium, uranium, and molybdenum are just a few of the elements now commonly used in alloys.

In more recent years, scientists interested in metallurgy have extended their research into nonmetallic materials, such as ceramics, glass, plastics, and semiconductors. The field of study has become so broad that it is now often referred to as materials science to emphasize that it deals with both metallic and nonmetallic substances.

Nature of the work

The conversion of rocky ore into finished metal products requires a wide variety of activities. After the ore has been mined and the metals extracted from it, the metals need to be further refined into purer forms and fashioned into usable shapes, such as rolls, slabs, ingots, or tubing. Throughout these processes technicians carry out laboratory and on-the-spot testing to ensure proper production flow and to monitor the condition of the equipment and the quality of the product. Other technicians work in laboratories to test and develop new alloys or new methods or equipment to produce existing products. In the metallurgy industry, these activities are seen as falling into three areas—production, quality control, and research and development.

Modern metal-production techniques involve advanced equipment and require trained supervisory personnel. Such personnel may be involved in checking production instruments, acting as observers, calculating furnace charges, taking samples for the production laboratory, and consulting with the laboratory concerning the quality of heats (batches of material that have been through the smelting or refining process). In some settings, metallurgical technicians may assist in the supervision of production employees, including the crews that operate the furnaces and other smelting equipment and the people that work the machinery

Using a special microscope, this metallurgical technician can view the magnified image of a metal microstructure on a small television screen.

that converts metal into industrial or commercial products.

Quality control of both incoming materials and finished parts is the responsibility of the metallurgical laboratory. As metals undergo processes such as forging, welding, extruding, drawing, and heat treating, their properties may be altered. In the laboratory, metallurgical technicians use a variety of equipment, such as spectrographs and X-ray diffraction and carbon-analysis equipment, to perform tests that determine grain structure, soundness, consistency, and other physical properties of metal materials and products, including forgings, castings, and tubing.

In metallurgical and materials-science research technicians work as part of a scientific research team. They build and test a variety of furnaces to develop new methods of producing existing metals and they help in the development of new alloys. They conduct tests to determine heat and corrosion resistance, machinability, workability, and other qualities of newly developed alloys. Metallurgical technicians keep accurate records, maintain equipment, and monitor stocks and inventories.

These three general areas of activity are, of course, interrelated. They share many concerns and often require similar skills. As the following list of representative entry-level jobs makes clear, technicians employed in metallurgy will often find themselves involved in more than one of these general areas.

Metallurgical laboratory technicians set up equipment, gather and record test results, prepare and mount metal specimens, and polish specimens for microscopic study.

Metallographers study and photograph metal samples under microscopes and metallographs to determine grain structure and other properties and develop photographic techniques to make adequate photomicrographs.

Materials-testing technicians prepare samples for and perform tests of the sheerness, hardness, tensile strength, impact resistance, compression, and fatigue life of specimens. They operate a variety of equipment and record data.

Foundry-laboratory technicians conduct tests on foundry sands to determine moisture, permeability, clay content, and bond strength. They use and maintain testing equipment, record data, and report to the foundry superintendent.

X-ray technicians examine metal and alloy samples by taking X-ray or gamma-ray photographs to detect the presence of cracks, foreign substances, or other internal defects. They process film and check radiation levels.

Metallurgical observers take samples and record temperatures of molten metal or rolling-mill products in steel-plant operations.

Spectrographic technicians analyze metal and alloy specimens for chemical content, using spectrographic procedures and carbon analyzers.

Heat-treatment technicians supervise furnace operations, monitor quality control of metals and alloys undergoing heat treatment, and check pyrometer calibration, immersion baths, and other heat-treatment equipment.

Metallurgical-research technicians participate in research for production of metals, development of protective finishes, and development of new alloys to withstand specified conditions. They also build and operate special laboratory furnaces for specific needs.

Metallurgical-sales technicians maintain inventories at sales facilities and draw up detailed specifications for alloys and metals from warehouses and metal-producing plants, using requirements established by the customer and the company's technical sales representative.

Requirements

Metallurgical technicians should have an interest in science and have at least an average ability in mathematics. Prospective technicians should be interested in and willing to participate in a wide variety of laboratory work, from operating heavy melting furnaces to handling extremely sensitive instruments. They should be willing to learn proper techniques in handling equipment and to assume the responsibility for its care. Because of the range of op-

portunities, from direct contact with people as in supervision or sales, to independent laboratory work, a wide variety of personality types are needed. Students should develop the ability to communicate well, both orally and in writing, to gather and interpret data, and to present facts graphically, as these skills will be essential in any metallurgical technician's career.

While in high school, prospective metallurgical technicians should take at least two years of mathematics, and two of science, including a physical science, preferably chemistry. Laboratory work in the science courses is a most important requirement for metallurgical technicians. Although requirements for entrance into for technical training programs vary, high school students should take at least several years of English courses to develop language and communications skills. Shop courses of any kind will also be helpful.

In all cases, students should expect to get a high-school diploma and should consider taking College Entrance Examination Board tests, as they are sometimes required by post–high-school educational institutions that provide technical training.

Students who go on to attend a two-year metallurgical or materials-science technology program at a community college, technical institute, or junior college can expect to take courses in the following subjects: general and analytical chemistry, physics, mathematics, communication skills or English, and social science. An effective program will also include courses in physical metallurgy and metallography (the study of the internal structure of metals and alloys), foundry and metal casting, nondestructive inspection, strength-of-materials and physical testing, and process metallurgy, with sufficient laboratory exposure in each area to allow the student to become familiar with the equipment and to develop skill in its use. Additional courses that are useful include industrial instrumentation, analytical spectroscopy, mechanical drawing, and machine tools.

Special requirements

The American Society of Metals has instituted three recognized registration and certification programs for metallurgical and materials science technicians. These levels of certification are determined by the amount of experience, education, and recognized skill the person has accumulated.

In some cases, technicians may be required to join a production, office, or technician's union.

Opportunities for experience and exploration

The specific type of experience or opportunity for exploration that a person should seek out depends on the aspect of metallurgy that he or she is most attracted to. If the production aspect is most appealing, students should try to arrange for individual or group visits to a foundry, steel mill, or other plant. Part-time or summer job opportunities in such settings may be restricted to the most menial tasks. This should not, however, be a discouragement. Having held even the most menial job is often seen by employers as a sign of interest and can work in an applicant's favor in a future job application.

Students interested in the laboratory or research side of metallurgy should consider visits to industrial laboratories. Ideally, these would be metallurgical or materials-science laboratories, but visits to industrial laboratories in related industries would also be useful. Through such visits students are able to see technicians actually go about their work and perhaps to speak with them about what they do.

Methods of entering

Students who graduate from an intensive program of metallurgical and materials-science technology are often recruited while still in school by companies that employ technicians. They then begin work as soon as possible after graduation. If they don't find good employment in this way, students can make application to any company of their choice directly through its personnel office. They can also go to a private employment agency or the local state employment security office or watch the want ads to see where openings exist. The administration and teaching staff at a college or school can also be a valuable source of information when looking for employment.

Advancement

After some years of on-the-job experience, metallurgical technicians who have proved their

A metallurgical technician uses a specially designed polisher to prepare microsections of metal for examination.

ability to handle more responsibility and who have developed technical competence are able to move on to advanced positions. Research or quality-control technicians, for examples, may be assigned to more complex and advanced equipment, or they may be put in charge of other technicians. In general, technicians can advance by going to a higher-level technician's job, earning a supervisory post, or advancing (usually through further education as well as experience) to the professional rank of metallurgist or metallurgical engineer.

Some representative jobs for technicians that usually come through advancement follow.

Metallurgical laboratory supervisors interpret results from metallographic investigations, recommend production procedures and heat-treat cycles, and direct other laboratory functions.

Physical-testing laboratory supervisors develop specifications for physical-testing procedures, interpret results of tests performed, and conduct specialty tests.

Foundry melters calculate charges to foundry furnaces to make alloys that meet specifications, sample heats for chemical content, and direct furnace operating crews.

Metallurgical troubleshooters perform a variety of tests on parts that have failed in service to determine liability and ways to improve manufacturing techniques.

Nondestructive inspection specialists determine the presence of internal or external flaws or discontinuities in all types of metals by using X-ray, ultrasonic, electromagnetic, and other types of inspection equipment.

Production supervisors oversee and coordinate various aspects of the manufacture of the finished product. They must be familiar with all aspects of metal production and with the equipment involved.

Analytical specialists use X-ray diffraction equipment, spectrographs, microprobes, and other equipment to determine the chemical content and structure of metals and alloys.

Pilot-plant supervisors operate pilot plants under the direction of research metallurgists who are working on developing new alloys and developing new manufacturing procedures for existing alloys.

Technical sales representatives call on engineers and purchasing agents to determine specifications of metals and alloys for particular applications.

Research assistants act as members of scientific teams in the metallurgical investigation of new products. They devise new procedures and equipment under direction of a research manager.

Employment outlook

The employment opportunities for metallurgical and materials-science technicians in foundries and in metals production should remain good through the 1990s. Better and more efficient processes for the production of metals from their ores are constantly being sought, and many metals are being produced in large tonnages by established methods. Searching for new processes and running ongoing production processes both involve technicians, and there continue to be fewer technicians available than there are openings for them.

Continued growth in new product development also assures an increasing need for research and development technicians to help explore physical factors affecting how metals can be used in particular products.

Earnings

Most metallurgical technicians earn salaries that range from $20,000 to $30,000 a year and average around $26,500 a year. Some technicians, especially those at the beginning of their careers, may earn as little as $18,000 a year or less, while some senior technicians with special skills and experience earn between $30,000 and $50,000 a year or more.

Benefits depend on the employer but generally include paid vacations, insurance, stock option plans, and tuition refund programs for further education. If technicians belong to a union, wages and benefits depend on the union agreement.

Conditions of work

Metallurgical technicians in research or laboratory activities work in clean, well-equipped laboratories. The equipment at their disposal varies from uncomplicated furnaces and machines to highly sophisticated and sensitive optical and electronic devices.

Metallurgical technicians engaged in production activities spend a good deal of time in mills or foundries. Such jobs frequently involve strenuous or possibly unpleasant conditions. The plants can be hot or wet, and there may be sparks, fumes, and gases.

Technicians involved in sales may work from an office or in a wide variety of plant environments.

Social and psychological factors

The metallurgical technician's work may range from simple, routine tasks to those that are highly complex and challenging. Some workers who are highly trained in this field may resent the more repetitive aspects of the jobs. Others may find these aspects a welcome relief from their more demanding duties and may even prefer routine-type work on a full-time basis.

Metallurgical technicians occupy a middle ground between the professionally trained scientist or engineer and the skilled trade worker. Some people may find this an awkward position to occupy, but most technicians take great pride in being part of this team.

Technicians in the professional areas are often encouraged to join professional societies associated with their coworkers in a particular plant. In some cases they are required to join a production, office, or technicians' union.

GOE: 02.04.01; SIC: 34; SOC: 3719

◇ **SOURCES OF ADDITIONAL INFORMATION**

American Foundrymen's Society
Golf and Wolf Roads
Des Plaines, IL 60016

American Society for Engineering Education
11 Dupont Circle, Suite 200
Washington, DC 20036

Junior Engineering Technical Society (JETS)
1420 King Street, Suite 405
Alexandria, VA 22314-2715

Minerals, Metals, and Materials Society
420 Commonwealth Drive
Warrendale, PA 15086

◇ **RELATED ARTICLES**

Volume 1: Ceramics; Engineering; Metals; Physical Sciences
Volume 2: Engineers
Volume 3: Coremakers; Forge shop occupations; Heat treaters; Iron and steel industry workers; Molders; Scrap metal processing workers
Volume 4: Geological technicians; Industrial engineering technicians; Quality-control technicians

Meteorological technicians

Definition

Meteorological technicians, also known as *weather observers*, observe and record weather conditions for use in weather forecasting. They observe sky conditions visually, and they utilize thermometers, barometers, hygrometers, and other specialized instruments to determine and record specific conditions such as temperature, relative humidity, barometric pressure, wind velocity, and precipitation.

Nature of the work

Technicians use computer links, telephones, fax machines, and other communications equipment to exchange weather information with other weather reporting facilities. They may utilize weather balloons and radiosonde equipment to determine upper atmosphere conditions. Technicians may also be called upon to give pilot briefings on prevailing atmospheric conditions.In order to assist meteorologists in studying atmospheric conditions, technicians not only observe and record weather conditions, but they also help to analyze and evaluate the data that has been gathered. They carry out regular calibration procedures on instruments and specific experiments as directed. They may also help in the development of new scientific instruments.

A meteorological technician observes storm activity on several color display screens at a facility in Montana.

Requirements

Technicians need good visual acuity, especially for distance viewing. Students interested in careers as meteorological technicians should take high-school mathematics courses at least through algebra and solid geometry. They should develop their language skills to enable them to understand technical manuals and articles and to communicate detailed technical information both orally and in writing. They should plan to spend at least one year beyond high school in a training program in meteorology, either at a technical institute or a community college. The armed forces offer excellent training in meteorological technician skills.

Conditions of work

The work of meteorological technicians is not strenuous and is usually conducted under pleasant, indoor conditions.

GOE: 02.04.01; SIC: 8999; SOC: 389

◇ **RELATED ARTICLES**

Volume 1: Physical Sciences
Volume 2: Meteorologists
Volume 4: Geological technicians; Hydrological technicians

Mortuary science technicians

Definition

Mortuary science technicians work under the direction of morticians or funeral home managers to perform embalming and related funeral services. Most mortuary science technicians are trainees who are working to become licensed embalmers and funeral directors. These technicians apply a practical knowledge of physiology, anatomy, chemistry, and the human circulatory system, as well as the techniques, procedures, and methods for using various embalming products. They use special techniques to maintain sanitation and avoid potential dangers of disease-carrying organisms, and they know how to use the materials and techniques of cosmetology in preparing a body for interring. Technicians are also skilled communicators. Writing technical reports and keeping official records are important aspects of their jobs. Most important, these technicians excel in the interpersonal relationships that are so essential in the funeral service and mortuary industry.

History

Since the beginning of civilization, funeral ceremonies have been held both to honor the dead and to help mourners return to normal activity. In all cultures, people have dealt with the awesomeness and inevitability of death by means of rituals and ceremonies. Early peoples often buried weapons and household utensils with their dead, as if to aid the dead person in an afterlife.

Embalming was practiced by the Egyptians as early as 4,000 B.C. Bodies were first soaked in a soda solution, then rubbed with oil, spices, and sometimes tar and pitch, and finally wrapped carefully in linen. Mummies preserved in this way have been discovered intact by archaeologists in this century.

Modern methods of embalming were developed in Europe during the eighteenth century. Today, precise anatomical knowledge, standardized chemical preparations, and synthetic materials enable the embalmer to restore the appearance of the deceased to a condition approximating appearance in life.

Funerals, like all ceremonies, are intimately related to the society that fosters them, and as society has changed, so have funerals. Emphasis in funeral customs in the United States has recently shifted from a preoccupation with the dead to a concern for the living. Today, men and women in the funeral service industry are concerned with the emotional and physical well-being of the survivors. This change in emphasis points up the most necessary quality for any person employed in this field: sensitivity to the needs of others at a time when they are under considerable strain. Sensitivity, tact, discretion, and compassion are essential on the part of the entire staff of the funeral home.

Nature of the work

Mortuary science technicians are highly specialized technicians who assist and work under the supervision of practicing morticians, who are usually funeral home owners, managers, or directors. After mortuary science technicians have gained experience under the guidance of these professionals, they often advance to professional status.

Most mortuary science technicians find employment in funeral homes. There are more than 20,000 funeral homes in the United States. They include many small, family-owned establishments that conduct fewer than one hundred services each year and where the funeral director is often the owner. In some cases, the director may also be the embalmer and may employ one or more mortuary science technicians and other workers to assist in various tasks.

In larger establishments, there may be twenty or more professional funeral directors and licensed embalmers. Additional staff members include mortuary science technicians, embalmer apprentices, funeral attendants, and drivers. In these larger organizations, technicians have opportunities to specialize. Mortuary science technicians can become skilled embalmers and devote almost all of their efforts to that activity for their entire careers. In such cases, they may supervise other technician embalmers and train apprentice embalmers.

The area of work in a funeral home that requires the most specialized scientific and technical knowledge is that of caring for the bodies of the deceased. The work begins with a telephoned request for services. Under the direction of the funeral director, the staff transports the body of the deceased in a hearse or ambulance to the funeral home. The mortuary science technician may or may not take part in this task, depending on the size of the funeral home and on other day-to-day circumstances. Technicians, however, are usually able to assist in this function.

When the body is brought to the funeral home, the technical work of the embalmer begins. The embalmer may be assisted by embalming apprentices. First the body is thoroughly washed with a germicidal soap and then dried. This step is required by law, and it is one of many strict sanitation practices to protect the health of the funeral home workers and the public.

The embalming process follows. The embalmer makes a surgical incision in the deceased's arm or leg and inserts and securely fastens a tube in a large artery. A pump is then attached to the tube and embalming fluid is pumped through the entire circulatory system.

It pushes the blood ahead of it and out of the open end of the artery. Thus the embalming fluid completely replaces the blood.

Embalming fluid serves several purposes. It is strongly antiseptic and makes the transmittal of contagious disease impossible. It retards the body's decomposition process. It provides a normal degree of firmness and fullness to the body and therefore helps in the cosmetic application that follows. Embalming fluids are carefully and scientifically formulated. Several kinds are available, each with a different chemical content and color tint. Learning the differences in the various types of embalming fluids is an important part of the technician's work.

After the body is embalmed, the embalmers apply cosmetics to the body to create a natural, lifelike appearance. This process is one of the most challenging activities in embalming. A variety of cosmetic materials is used, and the techniques of applying them must be carefully studied and practiced. The result must satisfy and comfort the people who view the body during the funeral service. Tactful discussion with a member or representative of the deceased's family can provide valuable guidelines in cosmetic application.

In cases where disease or an accident has disfigured the body, the damaged parts must be restored and cosmetically repaired. Each restoration job is different. Use of clay, cotton, plaster of paris, special plastic materials, and cosmetics is always a challenge. These skills and techniques can be learned by the technician embalmer only by experience, observation, study, and finally by practice applications under the supervision of the embalmer.

After the cosmetic application is complete, the body is dressed in clothes that have been provided by the funeral home or the family. The body is then placed in a casket of the family's choice and transported to a temperature-controlled room. The deceased may be viewed or funeral services may take place immediately. Services may take place at the funeral home or the deceased may be transported in a hearse to a church or temple.

Lastly, the embalming staff cleans the embalming area and equipment in accordance with required standards of sanitation. All supplies and equipment are put back in place, ready for the next time they must be used.

Mortuary or funeral service technicians may also perform duties related to the actual funeral service. They may prepare the casket for the service, under the direction of the funeral director. They also may transport the casket to the cemetery. Technicians may assist in receiving and ushering mourners to their seats at the funeral service, organizing and managing

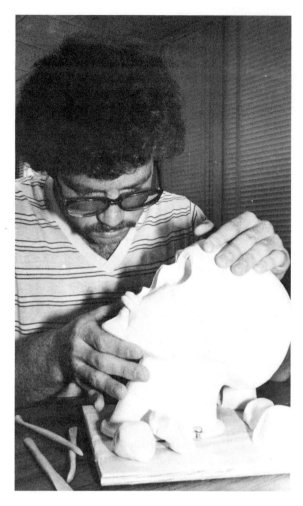

In order to understand the basic concepts of cosmetology and learn human bone structure, this mortuary science technician is sculpting a skull. Much of a mortuary science technician's works involves reconstructing a deceased person's appearance.

the funeral procession, and whatever other tasks are necessary for the occasion.

This work involves ability to use tact and discretion in all contacts with the bereaved family and friends. Technicians must always be compassionate, courteous, and sympathetic. But, at the same time, they must be confident, knowledgeable, and emotionally stable.

Requirements

A mortuary science technician must be able to learn and apply the scientific and technical knowledge required to prepare bodies for funeral services and burial. Most mortuary science technicians are in the process of preparing to be a fully licensed funeral service director or

mortician. This includes earning a required license to be an embalmer.

As previously stated, technicians must be able to work under the supervision of a funeral director. They also must always be sensitive to the emotional needs of bereaved people. The family and friends of the deceased are under considerable strain. They may be confused and bewildered in the face of events and details that they may not fully comprehend but which require their response.

The ability to communicate effectively with bereaved people is of critical importance. Grief-stricken people are hardly able to handle with ease the details of a funeral. When details such as cosmetic application and clothing are discussed, technicians must be especially attentive to the client's wishes.

Physical requirements for the career include at least average physical strength, as the work sometimes includes lifting the deceased or their caskets. Good to excellent hand-eye coordination is needed to perform the exacting procedures used in embalming, restoration, and cosmetology.

Persons interested in becoming mortuary science technicians should take high-school courses in algebra and in chemistry, biology, physics, and any other laboratory science courses that are available. They should study English all through high school and learn to type and use computers. Keyboard skills are needed for operating the computers that funeral homes frequently use for bookkeeping. A high-school diploma or its equivalent is required by all accredited funeral service schools. State licensing authorities also require a diploma prior to admission to a technician curriculum.

The funeral home industry is carefully regulated at both the state and federal level. Thus, all mortuary science schools and community colleges or divisions of colleges and universities that teach funeral service education must be accredited. Their programs lead to the licensing of graduates after successful completion of state-required job internships and enable students to become licensed embalmers or funeral service directors. In 1988, there were forty such programs in public and private community colleges, technical institutes, divisions of four-year colleges or universities, or specialized schools. All these schools are accredited by the Committee on Accreditation of the American Board of Funeral Service Education. These schools are also approved or accredited by the state board of funeral directors or embalmers in the state where the school is located. In recent years, the number and quality of graduates from these recognized schools have made it almost impossible to enter the career in any other way but through formal education. The accredited programs offer a variety of course sequences leading to a one-year diploma, a two-year associate degree or a four-year bachelor's degree.

Technicians who wish to become embalmers or funeral home directors must have a state license. Because each state has its own licensing law, prospective mortuary science technology students should make early contact with the licensing authority in the state in which they expect to practice to learn the educational specifications of that state.

Graduates may work as apprentice embalmers, funeral service directors, or both. Apprenticeships, also called internships, range from one to three years and are required for licensing.

A typical first year of a two-year postsecondary program in mortuary science technology includes courses in introduction to funeral service, funeral service sanitation, funeral law, basic chemistry, human physiology, human anatomy, communications skills, public relations, social environment, and health analysis and improvement.

A typical second year would include classes in principles of funeral service, funeral service cosmetology, embalming, restorative art, pathology, microbiology, funeral home operation, advanced embalming, funeral service psychology, public health laws and regulations, embalming chemistry, accounting, and business.

Laboratory study is essential in many of the courses, especially in anatomy, pathology, microbiology, embalming, cosmetology, and restorative art. Laboratory work can account for up to a quarter of the program.

Completion of a program such as the one described above usually leads to a degree such as an Associate in Science in Funeral Service Education. Graduate technicians who want to obtain a license in either embalming or funeral directing (most graduates have that desire) must work as apprentices or interns in an established funeral home for at least a year to become officially licensed.

Some programs take less time and result in the granting of a certificate. Technicians who receive certificates must serve a longer apprenticeship to become licensed; otherwise they work as unlicensed technicians with much less potential for advancement.

Special requirements

The funeral service industry is closely regulated by federal and state laws. Technicians can work without a license in embalming or other funeral services only under the close supervision of an embalmer or a funeral service director who is licensed to work in the particular state where the work is done.

Those who wish to advance in the field need to plan to become licensed in either embalming or funeral service directing, or both. Each state has different laws regulating licenses. Most states require that students enrolling in a funeral service program preregister with their state boards of funeral directing. They can then obtain information concerning licensing requirements in their home state. Students are responsible for becoming familiar with licensing requirements of other states in which they may eventually seek a license. Some states issue a single license for morticians, which covers both embalming and funeral service directing.

After completing their apprenticeships, prospective embalmers or funeral directors must pass a state board examination consisting of written and oral tests and demonstration of skills. Then they receive a license to practice in the state. If they wish to practice in another state, they may have to pass that state's examination as well, although some states have reciprocal courtesy arrangements to waive this requirement.

Opportunities for experience and exploration

High-school guidance counselors and occupational information center personnel can supply information to those who are exploring this career. Public librarians and school librarians can also provide useful books, magazines, and pamphlets.

The best sources of information, however, are local funeral homes, where interested persons can visit with the funeral directors and embalming staff. Here they can learn about the nature of the work and gain an understanding of the importance and intricacies of funeral services.

After they have become acquainted with local funeral homes, prospective mortuary science technicians may arrange to work part-time in clerical or custodial jobs. State licensing requirements make it difficult for these technicians to perform more specialized duties. The experience of working in a funeral home, however, even at simple tasks, gives a clearer insight into the career.

Methods of entering

About the only way to enter the funeral service career is to attend an accredited school of mortuary science after obtaining a high-school diploma, and then to enter the field as a mortuary science technician.

Most mortuary science schools provide a free placement service for graduates. Placement services receive many requests from funeral homes for qualified specialists. Many schools conduct internship programs where students work in funeral homes as part of their formal education. After graduation, students frequently obtain permanent jobs with the funeral home where they interned. School organizations, professional associations, funeral director associations, and funeral service supply salespeople are also good sources of information on employment.

Entry-level jobs for graduates of mortuary science technology programs tend to be limited because graduate technicians are not licensed and must therefore work as interns, apprentices, or technical assistants. This is why most graduate technicians continue their study to gain the experience and qualifications that will permit them to take the required examinations for a license.

Job titles vary and often depend on the size of the funeral establishment. The first job for the graduate technician usually carries the title of embalming and funeral director trainee. Regulations pertaining to this position vary according to the state in which the trainee is working. Usually, however, this trainee works under the direct supervision of a licensed funeral director or embalmer. The trainee position lasts for one or two years and is a necessary condition of licensure in most states. Trainees participate in all phases of funeral home operation, including embalming, setting up, and directing funeral arrangements. Unless they become licensed, trainees will be confined to such tasks indefinitely, with little opportunity for advancement.

Advancement

With licensure, there are numerous opportunities for advancement. The newly licensed technician can advance by gaining further education, acquiring additional work experience, and participating in professional organizations. The prospective funeral director or embalmer should always bear in mind that advancement opportunities after licensure depend on keeping up to date in the applications and advances in mortuary science and on always conforming to the legal requirements of the career.

While most people who enter this career as technicians may aspire to eventually owning a funeral home, others prefer employment in related positions. For example, technicians may become licensed embalmers and funeral directors. They oversee the preparation and care of the dead, starting with providing services at the place of death and continuing through final interment. Funeral home managers manage employees and assume general responsibility for the total operation of a funeral home. They also maintain records and order supplies. Another advanced specialty is that of trade embalmers, who embalm under contract for funeral homes. Their work usually includes restorative art treatment.

The percentage of mortuary science technology graduates who pursue employment in related fields is small, but many opportunities are nonetheless available. Funeral supply organizations frequently employ licensed funeral service personnel because of their familiarity with the products and their ability to deal with and explain technical problems. People employed in this area are responsible for customer relations, the sale of products, and the demonstration of new products at funeral homes and professional conventions.

Major hospitals, especially teaching or research hospitals, need licensed funeral service personnel. These institutions perform many autopsies. Licensed technicians are trained in the treatment and care of the dead, and experience with pathological examinations equips them for employment as a pathologist's assistant. This work includes preparing the deceased for autopsy, assisting the pathologist during a pathological examination, keeping records, and preparing reports. This practitioner works closely with the hospital laboratory technician and is occasionally asked to serve as liaison between the hospital and the funeral home.

Another category of employers of licensed funeral service personnel is medical schools. Work in this setting includes cadaver preparation, care of cadavers undergoing dissection, supervision of final disposition, recordkeeping, and report writing.

Employment outlook

Little change in the employment of funeral service personnel is expected through the 1990s. Demand for funeral services will rise as the population grows and deaths increase. Most funeral homes, however, will be able to meet the demand without adding new employees. The average funeral home conducts only one or two funerals each week and is capable of handling several more without hiring additional professional personnel.

In recent years, the number of funeral-service college graduates has approximately equaled the number of jobs available. Because there are a limited number of employers in any geographical area, many students should secure a promise of employment before entering a program. Barring any significant growth in enrollments during the early and mid-1990s, future mortuary science graduates should find job opportunities available. Persons who expect to make a career in the industry would be more assured of employment if they made at least tentative arrangements with some established funeral home to employ them after they graduate from school and perhaps for work during vacation periods during school.

Earnings

Salaries received by technician-level workers who are not yet licensed as either embalmers or funeral directors vary widely and a national average is difficult to determine. One reasonable estimate is that the average is approximately $12,000 a year.

The average annual salary for newly licensed personnel who have served an internship or apprenticeship is around $16,000 to $18,000. Those with licenses and about five years of experience earn about $24,000 per year; and those who have advanced to supervisory positions in large organizations but who are not owners earn from $25,000 to $30,000 per year. Many of the owners and the highest paid officers of funeral homes make from $40,000 to $60,000 a year or more.

Benefits beyond salary vary widely and may include residency allowances in some cases, as well as participation in health, life, or retirement insurance plans, paid holidays, and paid vacations. Clothing allowances are often included. Some establishments pay part or all of the cost of membership and participation in professional or technical society activities and programs that are educational and developmental in nature.

In large funeral homes, employees usually have a regular schedule. They generally work a normal eight-hour day, five or six days a week. Occasionally, however, overtime may be necessary.

Conditions of work

Working conditions vary with the tasks being performed by the technician. In large funeral establishments, it is possible for some workers to specialize in one major function, such as embalming. This is not, however, the common pattern for most funeral homes. In most places, those who enter as technicians help with all or most phases of the work.

In smaller funeral homes, technicians, together with their supervisors, often work long hours at odd times. They may need to be on call and within a short distance of the funeral home. Some may work in shifts, for example, nights one week and days the next. They must be prepared to work indoors or outdoors and in all kinds of weather, because removal of the deceased cannot wait.

The clothing that mortuary science technicians wear varies depending on their activities. Sometimes the work takes them outdoors in bad weather. Laboratory-like uniforms or aprons usually are worn in the embalming process. For activities related to funerals, clothing should always fit the dignity of the occasion.

Occasionally embalmers may come into contact with contagious diseases, but the possibility of their becoming ill is remote, even less likely than for a physician or nurse because funeral establishments are required to meet such strict standards of cleanliness and sanitation.

Social and psychological factors

Mortuary science technicians are beginners who later usually advance to embalming and preparing human bodies for funeral services and burial or other disposition, or to conducting and managing funeral services. These technicians must know the theory and the practical applications of mortuary science. They must be orderly, systematic, and exacting as they serve as capable assistants to a licensed embalmer or licensed funeral director.

Some technicians find that they have a special interest in embalming, restoration, and cosmetic arts. This interest can be very rewarding because the effect the technician creates may help the family and friends of the deceased to adjust at a time when they are greatly stressed by grief and bereavement.

Above all, technicians must learn special psychological and interpersonal skills. They must always be tactful, discreet, and compassionate with the families and friends of those whose funeral services they help to arrange and direct. They must remain emotionally stable and quietly confident. They help to provide an essential social service and one that, when well done, brings comfort and satisfaction to all who are involved in it.

GOE: 02.04.02, 11.11.04; **SIC:** 7261; **SOC:** 399, 1359

◇ **SOURCES OF ADDITIONAL INFORMATION**

Associated Funeral Directors Service International
PO Box 23023
St. Petersburg, FL 33742

National Funeral Directors Association
11121 West Oklahoma Avenue
Milwaukee, WI 53227

National Funeral Directors and Morticians Association
PO Box 377993
Chicago, IL 60637

◇ **RELATED ARTICLES**

Volume 1: Biological Sciences; Personal and Consulting Services; Religious Ministries; Social Services
Volume 2: Biologists; Funeral directors and embalmers; Guidance counselors; Human services workers; Physician assistants; Psychologists; Taxidermists
Volume 3: Cosmetologists; Nursing and psychiatric aides
Volume 4: Biological technicians; Biological specimen technicians; Medical laboratory technicians; Orthotic and prosthetic technicians; Psychiatric technicians; Surgical technicians

Optics technicians

Definition

Optics technicians work at a variety of different jobs relating to the design, fabrication, assembly, or installation of optical instruments, such as telescopes, microscopes, aerial cameras, and eyeglasses. The four most common types of optical technicians are *optomechanical technicians, precision-lens technicians, precision-lens grinders,* sometimes called *optical technicians,* and *photo-optics technicians.* (For a description of careers specifically concerned with eyeglasses and other prescription vision aids, readers should see the article titled "Ophthalmic laboratory technicians" in the Medicine and Health Technician Occupations section elsewhere in this volume.)

In general these four careers may be distinguished one from the other in the following ways: Optomechanical technicians are con-

cerned with the building and testing of complete optical and optomechanical devices. Precision-lens technicians are concerned with the whole range of manufacturing activities related to the fabrication of the lenses that go into optical and optomechanical devices. Precision-lens grinders are concerned specifically with the grinding, polishing, cementing, and inspecting of the lens. Photo-optics technicians are the technicians who install, maintain, or actually use the optical or optomechanical devices for scientific and engineering measurements and projects. More detailed definitions are presented in the following paragraphs.

Optomechanical technicians, working under the direction of an engineering staff, review project instructions and preliminary specifications. They draw up requirements for the fabrication, purchase, assembly, and testing of parts, write work orders, and prepare purchase requests for items and services that are to be furnished by others. They design, build, and modify the fixtures that will be used to assemble the parts. They supervise the testing of the parts, including, in some cases, computing the test data or operating the controls of the test apparatus or of the device being tested. They meet with technical and engineering staff members to recommend design and materials changes and may be assigned as group leaders of technicians, model-makers, or other skilled craft workers.

Precision-lens technicians study blueprints, work orders, and sketches to formulate machining plans and sequences used in the fabrication of optical parts, including lenses, prisms, and mirrors, and of optical systems. They select and prepare the compounds and mixes used in grinding, polishing, and cementing of lenses. They use a variety of machines, such as saws, lathes, grinders, milling machines, polishers, and edgers to fabricate optical parts, fixtures, tools, and mountings. They develop specifications and drawings for optical parts, conduct tests and measurements, and may perform experimental research to develop new production procedures.

Precision-lens grinders set up and operate the grinding and polishing machines used to make lenses and other optical parts. They operate machines to rough-grind blanks of optical glass to approximate size and shape and to fine-grind optical elements to final size and shape. As part of this work, they also inspect and measure elements for accuracy and degree of completion. They also polish, cement, and mount optical elements in holders for use in instruments.

Photo-optics technicians set up and operate optical devices that are usually used in conjunction with photographic equipment to measure and record data for scientific and engineering projects. They install and calibrate optical and photographic equipment in missiles, aircraft, weaponry, weather or communications satellites, and underwater devices. They also operate the equipment that tests the accuracy of these devices, and they perform analyses of their test results. In addition, they evaluate the data that is collected by the photo-optical devices, they may make modifications to the devices, and they participate in planning and testing new equipment and procedures.

History

Humans have been using simple lenses for magnification for more than a thousand years,

An optics technician makes final adjustments on a segmented mirror that was designed for a research program in optics technology.

and eyeglasses have been in use since the fourteenth century. More complex optical instruments, however, such as the microscope and telescope, were not developed until the seventeenth century. These first microscopes and telescopes were crude by modern standards, as the first lenses of moderately good quality for these instruments were not developed until the nineteenth century.

During the nineteenth century, many of the basic principles used for making the calculations necessary for lens design were expounded, first in a book by Karl Friedrich Gauss published in 1841 and later in other studies based on Gauss's work during the 1850s. These principles remained the basis for making the calculations needed for lens design until around 1960, when computer modeling became the predominant way of designing lenses.

Up until the early part of the twentieth century, engineering problems associated with designing optical instruments were handled by mechanical engineers, physicists, and mathematicians. During World War I, however, because of the increasingly important applications of optical instruments, optical engineering emerged as a separate discipline, and today it is taught in a separate department in many universities.

And just as the field of optical engineering has emerged as a field separate from other forms of engineering, so too have the optics technicians described in this article emerged as distinct from all other engineering and science technicians. They have their own instructional programs, their own professional societies, and, when necessary, their own licensing procedures.

Nature of the work

The optical manufacturing industry offers many different kinds of jobs for the skilled and well-trained technician. There are jobs, especially for optomechanical technicians, that are mostly involved with scientific and theoretical concerns. There are other jobs, such as those that precision-lens grinders often perform, that focus on craft working skills. Precision-lens technicians most of all, but many other optics technicians as well, are involved with work that combines both of these kinds of activities. Finally, there are many jobs for optics technicians, but especially for photo-optics technicians, that require the mechanical skills and ingenuity of a repairer and troubleshooter.

In general, optics technicians are employed in one of the following areas: research and development; product manufacture; maintenance and operations; and lens fabrication.

Technicians working in the research and development area are involved with creating new optical instruments or with new applications for existing instruments. They are often called upon to invent new techniques for conducting experiments, for obtaining measurements, or for carrying out fabrication procedures requested by engineers or scientists.

Among the products that research-and-development technicians may be involved with are night-vision instruments for surveillance and security, ultraprecise distance-measuring devices, and instruments for analysis of medical and clinical specimens, for monitoring patients, and for routine inspection of materials including industrial wastes.

Technicians in the product-manufacturing area work mostly at the assembly, alignment, calibration, and testing of common optical instruments, such as microscopes, telescopes, binoculars, and cameras. They may also help produce less common devices, such as transits and levels for surveying or spectrographs and spectrophotometers used in medical research and diagnosis.

A relatively new field that can give both research-and-development technicians and product-development technicians opportunities to combine their interests in optics and photography is the development and production of integrated electronic circuits. These highly complex, tiny devices are widely used in calculators, computers, television equipment, and in control devices for electronic systems, whether in the cockpit of a jet airliner or the control room of an electric generating plant. The manufacture of these electronic circuits requires a wide variety of skills, from the production of large patterns and plans, called art work, to the alignment and operation of the microcameras that produce the extraordinarily small printing negatives used to make the final circuits on the tiny metallic chips that are the bases of the integrated circuits.

In the field of maintenance and operations, technicians are involved with the on-site use of optical instruments, such as technical and scientific cameras, large observatory telescopes and auxiliary instruments, light-measuring equipment, and spectrophotometers, some of which operate with invisible or ultraviolet radiation.

Operations and maintenance technicians (usually photo-optics technicians) may find themselves working at a rocket or missile test range or at a missile or satellite tracking station where they may be assembling, adjusting, aligning, and operating telescopic cameras that produce some of the most important information about missiles in flight. These cameras are often as big as the telescopes used by astronomers, and they weigh up to fifteen tons. Large powerful motors enable the camera to rotate and, thus, to follow a rocket in flight until it comes down. The picture information gathered by these long-range tracking cameras is often the only clue to missile flight errors or failure, as there is often virtually nothing left of a missile after it lands.

In the lens-fabrication area there are many different kinds of jobs for optics technicians. The following short paragraphs describe some of these jobs, all of them open to entry-level technicians.

Lens molders work with partially melted glass. Their principal task usually is to press the partially melted glass into rough lens blanks.

Lens blockers assist senior lens makers in setting lens blanks into holders in preparation for curve generating, grinding, and polishing.

Lens generators, using special grinding machines, give the glass blanks the correct curvature as they are held in the holders.

Lens grinders work with cup-shaped tools and fine grinding powders. They bring the blanks in the holders to the required curve within close tolerances.

Lens polishers use ultrafine powders and special tools made of pitch or beeswax to bring the surfaces of the fine-ground blank to bright, clear polish.

Lens centerers or *lens edgers* make true, or perfect, the various optical elements with finished spherical surfaces.

Optical-coating technicians carefully clean finished lenses and install them inside a vacuum chamber. Special mineral materials are then boiled in small, electrically heated crucibles in the vacuum, and the vapor condenses on the lenses to form extremely thin layers that reduce glass surface reflections.

Quality inspectors examine the finished lenses for tiny scratches, discolorations of the coating, and other faults or errors that may require rejection of the finished element before it is assembled into an instrument.

Requirements

Optics technicians should have a strong interest in and a good aptitude for mathematics and physics. Patience, care, and good manual skills are important in the design of precision telescopic lenses, in the grinding and polishing of the glass elements, and in the assembly and alignment of the instrument.

High-school students considering careers as optics technicians should take courses that will give them a strong general background and that will prepare them for further study in technical fields. These should include courses in mathematics, science, technical reading and writing, as well as some shop courses. Courses in photography, particularly those involving darkroom work, are also valuable, as photography plays an important role in many of the fields where optics technicians are at work.

There are only a few schools that offer training for optics technicians specifically. A good alternate way to obtain advanced education is to attend a technical institute or community college where two- or three-year engineering or science programs are available and to pick out those courses best suited for a career as an optics technician.

During the first year of a two-year program students should take courses in geometrical optics, trigonometry, lens polishing, technical writing, optical instruments, analytical geometry, and specifications writing. During the second year the student may take courses in physics, optical shop practices, manual preparation, mechanical drawing, and report preparation.

Prospective optics technicians should be aware that some large corporations have training programs for beginning technicians. These programs are not always publicized and may take some searching out to find. There are also some commercially run technical schools that

Two optics technicians at a convention demonstrate how a segmented mirror helps solar telescopes to "see" more clearly despite the earth's obstructive atmosphere.

can provide training; however, they are often costly and should be investigated carefully, preferably by talking to former students, before one undertakes such a course.

Special requirements

Except for optics technicians who are involved in making and dispensing eyeglasses, there are no licensing requirements. However, in some areas of optics technology it is necessary to be familiar with governmental requirements for safety, and to obtain safety certificates. In a few cases, the correct function of an instrument to be used in a governmental application or for medical or clinical purposes must be legally certified by the technician. In these instances, technicians should discuss the certification requirements with their employer or supervisor.

231

Opportunities for experience and exploration

One of the proven ways for students to gain experience in and exposure to various aspects of the field of optics is through membership in hobby clubs, student societies, or groups with scientific interests, such as organizations for amateur astronomers, amateur radio builders and operators, and amateur telescope makers. School clubs in photography, especially those involving activities with film processing, print and enlargement making, and with camera operations, also provide valuable experience.

Visits to industrial laboratories or manufacturing companies can also provide a vivid means of exploration. Through such visits one is able to witness technicians actually involved in their work, and it may be possible to speak with several of these people regarding their work or with employers about possibilities for technicians in that particular industry or company.

Methods of entering

Many students enrolled in two-year training programs can find jobs through interviews with company recruiters conducted on campus during the second year of their program. Other students find employment through participating in work-study programs while enrolled in school. In many cases, the student's part-time employer will offer the student full-time work after graduation.

For students who do not find suitable employment in one of these ways, there are some employment agencies that specialize in placing personnel in the optics industry. There are also very active societies in the optical, photographic, physical science, and engineering fields that can be sources of worthwhile job leads. The optics technician should contact technical societies for advice and help in job hunting. The primary purpose of a technical society is to aid the industry it represents, and there is no better way the society can do this than to attract interested personnel into the field and help them find their best job.

Advancement

As technicians gain experience and additional skills, new and more demanding jobs are offered to them. The following paragraphs describe some of the jobs to which experienced technicians may advance.

Hand lens figurers shape some lenses and optical elements, using hand-operated grinding and polishing methods. These shapes are called "aspheric," as they cannot be made by the normal mass-production grinding and generating machines. Special highly sensitive test machines are used to aid these advanced polishing technicians.

Photographic technicians use the camera in many important research and engineering projects, as well as in the production of optical items such as reticles, optical test targets, and integrated electronic circuits. These technicians will be involved in the operation of cameras and with photographic laboratory work, sometimes leading a team of technicians in these tasks.

Instrument assemblers and testers direct the assembly of various parts into the final instrument, performing certain critical assembly tasks themselves. When the instrument is complete, they, or other technicians under their direction, check the instruments' alignment, functioning, appearance, and readiness for the customer.

Optical model-makers work with specially made, or purchased, components to assemble a prototype or first model of a new instrument, under the direction of the engineer in charge. These technicians must be able to keep the prototype in operation, so that the engineer may develop knowledge and understanding of production problems.

Research and development technicians help to make and assemble new instruments and apparatus in close cooperation with scientists and engineers. The opportunities for self-expression and innovation are highest in this area.

Employment outlook

The fields of optics technology and manufacturing should continue their pattern of sustained growth through at least the 1990s. This growth should create an increasing number of jobs for optics technicians in both the research and development and the manufacturing areas.

Traditionally, the space program and weapons-development programs run by the military have been employers of large numbers of optics technicians. Employment in this field is determined by levels of government spending and hence is difficult to predict. Even if there are cutbacks in this spending, however, the public demand for modern complex cameras, binoculars, and telescopes and the need for advanced medical equipment should sustain employment levels for most kinds of optics technicians.

Earnings

Salaries and wages vary according to the industry and the type of work the technician is doing. In general, starting salaries for technicians who have completed a two-year post–high-school training program range from around $14,000 to $18,000 a year. Technicians involved in apprenticeship training may receive reduced wages during the early stages of their apprenticeships. Technicians who have not completed a two-year training program receive starting salaries several hundred dollars a year less than technicians in the same industry who have completed such a program.

Most technicians who are graduates of these programs and who have advanced beyond the entry level earn salaries that range from $20,000 to $30,000 a year and average around $25,000 a year. Senior technicians receive average salaries ranging from $30,000 to $50,000 a year, or more, depending on their employers and type of work done.

Conditions of work

Optical grinding and polishing shops are generally clean, ventilated, and temperature-controlled. In some polishing and hand-figuring rooms, and in the first assembly rooms, it is sometimes necessary to provide special dust, humidity, and temperature controls. The technicians are required to wear clean, lint-free garments, and to use caps and overshoe covers. These rooms are widely used whenever the work requires the most meticulous cleanliness, since a single piece of lint might cause the loss of an entire component or assembly.

On the other hand, technicians working with large astronomical telescopes, with missile-tracking cameras on a military test range, or with instrument cameras for recording outdoor activities will have to work in a variety of conditions.

Very often optics technicians, particularly those associated with the assembly, alignment, and testing of complete instruments, will find themselves working in the dark or at night. In very few cases is the work apt to be grimy or dangerous.

Social and psychological factors

Part of the discipline of optics is concentrated in the scientific and technical world, another in the world of the skilled artisan working with hands and eyes. For prospective optics technicians who feel an interest in and an aptitude for both of these kinds of activity, optics technology provides many opportunities to make personal contributions to the advancement and development of optical science and the optical industry.

Because optics technology is involved in creating the instruments and equipment necessary in ever-expanding and complex fields such as medical research, space exploration, communications systems, and microcircuitry design and manufacture, optics technicians can feel some satisfaction in knowing that they are working in some of today's most exciting fields of scientific and technological research. The work that optics technicians perform directly affects the lives of most Americans.

As with all technicians in the engineering and science field, optics technicians are often called upon to perform both very challenging and very routine and repetitive work. Optics technology offers technicians a spectrum of jobs, so that prospective technicians can choose jobs that fit their temperaments. However, almost all technicians should expect some mixture of the routine and the challenging in their jobs.

Optics technicians almost always work as part of a group effort. Often they serve as intermediaries between scientists and engineers who run projects and skilled craft workers who carry out much of the work. In such positions, technicians must be able to give and to take orders well. Oral and written communications skills, therefore, are extremely important.

GOE: 02.04.01, 05.01.01, 05.05.11, 06.02.08; SIC: 3229; SOC: 3713, 389, 6864, 7477

◇ **SOURCES OF ADDITIONAL INFORMATION**

Junior Engineering Technical Society
1420 King Street, Suite 405
Alexandria, VA 22314

Optical Society of America
1816 Jefferson Place, NW
Washington, DC 20036

Society of Photo-Optical Instrumentation Engineers
1022 19th Street
Bellingham, WA 98227

For information on training programs for precision optical manufacturing technicians, contact:

American Precision Optics Manufacturers Association
2020 K Street, NW, Suite 800
Washington, DC 20006

◇ **RELATED ARTICLES**

Volume 1: Engineering; Physical Sciences
Volume 2: Dispensing opticians; Engineers; Optometrists; Physicists
Volume 3: Contact lens manufacturing workers; Glass manufacturing workers; Instrument makers; Opticians and optical mechanics
Volume 4: Instrumentation technicians; Ophthalmic laboratory technicians; Optometric technicians

Packaging and paper products technicians

Definition

Packaging and paper products technicians work at various jobs related to designing and manufacturing paper products, especially those used in packaging, such as cardboard boxes, and in advertising displays. Some of these technicians are concerned chiefly with the machinery used to make paper products, and they are sometimes referred to as *automated equipment technicians.* Others are involved with designing packages and products and with assembling and testing sample products, and they are sometimes referred to as *packaging technicians.*

Nature of the work

Automated equipment technicians install, test, modify, and maintain the machines and equipment that are used in the making of cardboard boxes, advertising displays, and similar die-cut, scored, folded, and embossed paper products. These technicians are usually employed by the manufacturers of the equipment, but they do most of their work at plants where the paper products are made. They confer with paper-products manufacturers to decide how best to arrange the equipment and to anticipate and avoid any problems that might occur during construction and assembly of the equipment. They arrange the equipment to make best use of floor space and to make operations most ef-

ficient. During installation, they direct the positioning of the equipment, following the floor plan previously agreed upon. They install the electrical and electromechanical parts of the system using electrician's hand tools and following engineering drawings and wiring diagrams. Following installation, technicians test-run the equipment and make necessary adjustments to enable the system to function as designed.

When a system is installed, technicians adjust controls and the setup of machinery for the size, thickness, and type of stock to be processed, and establish the proper sequence of processing stages. They instruct the operating personnel in the proper operating and maintenance procedures. Technicians service and repair equipment at the clients' request and perform regular preventive maintenance. At times they may also be called on to modify equipment already in operation, to achieve higher efficiency or to provide additional safety features.

Packaging technicians assemble, test, and help design samples of paperboard containers used for shipping, protecting, or displaying products. They make sketches and scale drawings of containers or aspects of them. The drawings normally include descriptions and measurements of the package and the materials it will be make from. These technicians also assemble prototype containers using knives, saws, adhesives, and staples, and they test the samples using strain, strength, and stress test equipment.

Requirements

Persons interested in careers in this field should take high-school mathematics courses through solid geometry, have a good working knowledge of shop procedures, and be able to read technical instruction manuals and technical articles. They should be prepared to complete at least a two-year course past high school at a technical institute or community college. Courses in electrical and electromechanical theory and practice and in blueprint and wiring diagram reading are appropriate for students who want to be involved with the machinery for manufacturing paper products. For those who are interested in the design and testing of paper containers, the requirements are more flexible. In general they should try to take courses that help them develop their skills in mechanical drawing, using hand tools, and operating test equipment.

A packaging and paper products technician oversees the manufacture of cardboard boxes.

Conditions of work

Packaging and paper products technicians work in an indoor environment that includes no unusual hazards. Their work is not strenuous, although it does involve carrying small components and hand tools, and some bending and stretching. Dust from paper fibers may be a problem during mass production of paper products.

GOE: 05.05.05, 06.01.04; SIC: 3565; SOC: 6178, 6862

◇ **RELATED ARTICLES**

Volume 1: Packaging
Volume 2: Designers; Engineers; Industrial designers; Packaging engineers
Volume 3: General maintenance mechanics; Industrial machinery mechanics
Volume 4: Drafting and design technicians; Electrical technicians; Electromechanical technicians; Mechanical technicians; Product test technicians

Parking engineering technicians

Definition

Parking engineering technicians develop plans for the building and use both single and multi-story parking of parking lots and garages. They carry out land and traffic surveys and studies to determine the best locations for new facilities.

Parking engineering technicians also study the factors that will influence decisions about whether or not to build facilities on new sites.

Nature of the work

To develop a parking site, the parking engineering technician must consider such factors including the total parking capacity needed, rate of turnover of vehicles, probable parking fees and revenue that can be generated, and property changes that will be necessitated by the new facility. Much of their work concerns the environmental impact on the location and the appearance of new facilities. Technicians

This parking engineering technician is designing city parking locations for a new segment of a roadway. The blueprints will be used during construction.

and represent their department at meetings and hearings concerning their work.

Requirements

People interested in careers in this field should obtain a basic high-school background in mathematics (at least through plane geometry) and should be competent in basic statistics. They should be prepared to take at least two years of schooling past high school, probably at a community college or university, concentrating on the study of statistics, methods of conducting surveys, oral communications, technical writing, and economics.

Their language skills should be developed to the point that they can read and prepare detailed technical reports. Technicians should be comfortable working with both documents and people and addressing large meetings and making oral presentations.

Their work is not physically demanding and is performed both in offices and at prospective sites.

GOE: 05.03.06; SIC: 1771; SOC: 399

consider alternative sites and varying proposals for the design of each facility. They gather technical environmental information from experienced groups such as engineering firms, environmental scientists, and park district officers. They also control budgets for the gathering, analysis, and dissemination of this information,

◇ **RELATED ARTICLES**

Volume 1: Engineering
Volume 2: Engineers
Volume 4: Industrial engineering technicians

Petroleum technicians

Definition

Petroleum technicians assist in the exploration of petroleum fields and the production of oil and gas. They may work on land or offshore. Technicians may assist geologists, earth scientists, seismologists, petroleum engineers, or oil and gas field managers. Projects that can involve petroleum technicians include seismic testing of promising geological formations, drilling test wells, improving drilling technology, analyzing cores from drilling, logging drilling cores, col-

lecting petroleum from producing wells, delivering oil to holding points or pipelines for transport to refineries, or capturing gas and retaining it at holding points for marketing.

History

For the past 4,000 years, crude oil has been dipped up and used as a fuel, lubricant, and medicine by those who could find it. The oil industry as it is known today began in Pennsylvania about 130 years ago when the first productive well was drilled. In 1859, an exploratory oil drilling operation, led by Edwin L. Drake, a retired railroad conductor, began in an area where oil seepage was common. Drake and his workers thought that there might be an underground pool enclosed in rock. After several months of drilling, they discovered oil when their steam-driven drill reached a depth of about seventy feet. The well was not a large producer by today's standards, but it started a new industry of exploring and drilling for oil and refining it, because of oil's potential use as a cheap and abundant fuel.

Thousands of wells were drilled in the years that followed the first oil well, first in the original field, then in other areas in Pennsylvania and adjoining states, and later in Kansas, Oklahoma, and Texas. It soon became evident that petroleum was a much more abundant mineral resource than was first thought and was a great potential source of mineral wealth, as well as personal wealth.

Several new fields of technology were brought into being by this new source of energy. Geologists began to study systematically how to predict where oil could be found. Soon they developed a new area of earth science to improve the accuracy of determining where to drill for oil. Engineers began to develop better drilling machinery. Chemists and chemical engineers analyzed crude oil and discovered how to separate it into useful products and how to refine it commercially. Universities and colleges developed new programs to educate petroleum engineers in the new technologies related to petroleum.

One of the first important products to be produced was kerosene, which was found to be a good substitute for whale oil and other animal fats that for centuries had been used for oil lamps and heating fuel. Whale oil was expensive and in limited supply; kerosene was cheap, and it soon became an important product in both national and international trade.

It soon became evident that liquid fuels— kerosene, naphtha, and gasoline—could be used in the internal combustion engines that were being developed for mechanical power. These engines were more practical than steam engines that burned wood or coal. The heavier oils were a cheap and easy substitute for coal in electric power plants and other steam generating boilers.

From 1880 to 1910, the automobile engine was invented and developed. It was found that gasoline was by far the cheapest and best available fuel for these new engines and the automobiles, trucks, and other machines they

would make possible. The business world recognized the value of petroleum. Large corporations were formed to discover, produce, refine, and market petroleum products. This mineral resource became known as "liquid gold" by those who benefitted from owning oil reserves.

Great improvements were soon made in drilling equipment and in the predictions of geologists about where to find oil deposits. A worldwide search for oil led to the development of oil fields in several areas of the United States, Canada, and South America. The growth of settlers in states like Arkansas and Texas was spurred by oil discovery. Later, oil fields were developed in Iran, Saudi Arabia, Russia, North Africa, Mexico, the North Sea, and Indonesia.

In the search for petroleum deposits, large quantities of natural gas were found along with the oil in some fields. Other fields produced large quantities of gas but little oil. At first the gas was simply burned to eliminate it. The developing petroleum technology soon found uses for the gas in home heating and cooking, industrial heating, and even running large engines. Gas thus became another valuable petroleum commodity. Storage and pipeline distribution systems were built for both oil and gas. More recently natural gas has become the major raw material for the plastics and synthetic fiber industry, thus creating what is called the petrochemical industry.

By 1970, the United States and most of the other highly industrialized nations in the world had turned to oil as their main energy source. They became dependent on oil-rich nations such as Saudi Arabia, Libya, Iran, Venezuela, and several other countries for a large percentage of their energy needs. The United States had allowed its coal mining industry to become weak because oil was cheap and plentiful. The United States was one of the world's largest producers of oil but was also the largest buyer of foreign oil.

It soon became obvious to oil-producing countries that the world supply of petroleum would be almost all used up in twenty to forty years, with no known way of replacing it to meet the industrial energy needs of the future. In 1973, foreign petroleum producers changed their price policy for selling oil, because they were afraid all of their oil and its wealth-producing value would soon be used up. They also believed that much oil was wasted by inefficient use. Led by the Organization of Petroleum Exporting Countries (OPEC), many foreign producers suddenly stopped sales to their customers and raised the price of oil from two dollars a barrel to more than twelve dollars a

A petroleum technician consults the charts from a seismograph before continuing with the drilling operation.

barrel. This historic action became known as the oil embargo of 1973. In successive raises after 1973, the price of oil rose to approximately $36 per barrel in 1980. By the mid-1980s, the price of oil was back to approximately the $12-per-barrel level; however, by the beginning of the 1990s the price had risen again to approximately $20 per barrel.

The events of the 1970s and 1980s significantly altered the nation's attitude toward the price and availability of petroleum products. Domestic oil companies came to realize that foreign sources of oil could easily be lost through regional conflicts or international tensions. The drop in prices during the mid-1980s, however, reinforced the point that domestic producers would have to continue to find economical methods of producing oil to remain competitive with foreign-produced oil.

These developments have fostered great changes in the technology of oil drilling, in the science related to oil exploration, and in the management of existing oil fields. In many old abandoned fields, scientists found that they still had nearly as much oil as had been produced from them by older methods. New technology is being developed and used to find ways of extracting more of this remaining oil in an economical way from old and new fields alike.

The occupation of petroleum technician was created to help the industry meet such challenges. Technological changes make it necessary to have scientifically competent technical workers on seismic exploration crews, well-drilling crews, and on oil field management crews. A major problem, however, in oil and gas well drilling is that the work conditions cause many crew members to change jobs so often that it is often very difficult to keep drilling rigs working with a full crew. For about thirty years, there have been technical insti-

tutes and community colleges where these specialized technicians can be trained. Well-prepared, loyal, regularly working crew members, especially at the technician level, are an essential requirement of the business today and will continue to be in the future.

Nature of the work

Petroleum exploration, drilling, and oil field production management have always been outdoor, all-weather, rugged activities. Worldwide exploration has revealed many fields, but new oil fields are often found in more and more remote, rugged, and inaccessible places. Offshore exploration and drilling in recent years has opened up underwater areas that could not be drilled a few years ago because of lack of equipment to drill offshore in water hundreds of feet deep. But now offshore oil fields are operating from arctic oceans to tropical seas.

A second major characteristic of careers in the industry is that the work is rapidly becoming more scientifically and technically complicated. Special instruments and electronic equipment, often involving built-in computer components, are used in exploration and drilling for both oil and gas fields. This equipment keeps records of the progress and kinds of stone, clay, or mineral layers the drill passes through. This is called "logging." In recent years, special instruments have been developed to measure hole diameter and the different kinds of mineral layers or deposits, their radioactivity, and their depth and thickness. They are lowered on a cable to the bottom of the hole. Electronic messages are sent back up the cable to electronic instruments that automatically record the information on a digital tape. This equipment provides a more reliable map of the geological deposits the drill goes through. It also requires technicians who know how to operate it and to help interpret the information it provides.

The oil well drilling crews who are developing a newly discovered and proven field usually use several drill rigs, all under the supervision of a *tool pusher*. A tool pusher serves as a general planner and supervisor of the whole operation. Each individual well-drilling rig is first transported by trucks to the well site. The parts—engine, pumps, derrick, pipe and tool racks—are bolted together by rig builders and their helpers. Permanent rigs are often built for very deep wells.

When the rig is ready to begin drilling, the crew usually includes a *rotary driller*, who supervises and manages the actual drilling operation. Also included is a *derrick operator,* who works on a platform high up on the derrick. The derrick operator mixes the special drilling muds that are pumped down through the drilling unit to lubricate and cool the cutting tools and to help control the flow of oil and gas when the well strikes oil. The derrick operator also helps disconnect and store lengths of drill rod and pipe when the drill tools are brought to the surface. This operator also helps in the reverse process when the tools are lowered again. Four or five helpers, called *roustabouts,* help on the drilling platform.

The well-prepared technician may work as the assistant to the driller or to the derrick operator, assistant to the tool pusher, or as a technical worker and general assistant taking technical measurements and mud analyses, but filling in as a regular worker when needed.

One very specialized position held by some petroleum technicians is that of *oil well fishing-tool technician.* These technicians analyze conditions at oil or gas wells where some object or material, such lost equipment, liners, or broken casings, screens, or drill pipes, has obstructed the borehole. They plan techniques and direct the work of removing the obstacle, which may include taking soundings, drilling around the obstacle, and applying circulating fluids under pressure into the borehole.

Offshore operations are organized along the same general plan. In most cases the crew lives in special quarters on the rig and generally works longer hours. Various arrangements are made, but working one week offshore and having two weeks off work is a common arrangement. The workers may be transported from the drilling platform to a ship or flown to shore by helicopter.

Living quarters on offshore platforms are usually small, like those on a ship. They are adequate and comfortable. The pay is designed to compensate for the isolation, hard work, limited recreation opportunities, and the safety hazards of offshore drilling.

Offshore drilling platforms are very large and complex. They are moderately self-sufficient units. They house crews, paramedical specialists, heating, lighting, mess halls, communications, helicopter landing pads, and all sorts of related facilities as well as the drilling machinery. More types of technical jobs are potentially available on offshore platforms than on land because of the greater variety and quantity of electronic, mechanical, and technologically complex equipment on board.

Another important and growing area of employment for petroleum technicians is in the management of the oil field after the drilling operations have been largely completed. There have been many technological developments in oil production in recent years. Efficient production methods are increasingly necessary. Today it is no longer a simple matter of drilling a hole and taking whatever oil can be pumped out. Although they appear some distance apart, most wells in a field are probably drawing from the same underground reservoir. The producer who is more efficient gets more oil.

One technique of modern production is referred to as "shooting" oil and gas wells. This involves using a nitroglycerine explosive charge to open a crack in the underground sandstone, allowing oil to be brought to the surface more readily. Shooting is also done directly through the casing wall into more layers of oil, using steel bullets like those fired from high-powered rifles.

Another technique is "fracturing," in which white sand suspended in a thick fluid is forced under pressure into cracks in a layer of rock holding oil. As the fluid runs away, this process increases the flow of oil through the layer.

A third technique is called "acidizing." A solution of hydrochloric acid and water is pumped under pressure into oil-bearing limestone. The acid dissolves cavities in the rock and speeds up oil movement. Other techniques include directional drilling and the pumping of very deep wells with special equipment. Another technique is the deliberate flooding of nearby wells with water to increase the flow of oil into the one well that is to be pumped. This is referred to as "secondary recovery" and can be done successfully if the project is correctly engineered. All of these techniques, and other ones that are being experimented with and developed by petroleum engineers and earth scientists, make it necessary for the petroleum technicians to be familiar with the science and technology associated with the techniques.

Another area of work for which a petroleum technician needs special education is the exploration for new oil or gas fields using the techniques of seismology. In this activity, the technician works with geologists, earth scientists, and seismologists in petroleum exploration to determine the location of oil in the subsurface structure. One method involves using a seismograph and measuring the transmission of sound waves from explosions. Other techniques include one which uses a special vibrator on the surface to produce shock waves instead of explosions. Sound or shock waves reflect differently from oil- and gas-bearing geological formations than from other more solid rock layers, thus indicating to seismic crews where oil or gas might be found.

Remote-sensing exploration techniques use airborne infrared (heat-sensitive) color photography and highly sensitive magnetometers to locate petroleum. Subsurface maps are made that show what the best available information suggests is below. To assist in mapping, relatively shallow test holes may be drilled; core samples may be taken and data collected with electronic or other devices lowered in the hole.

The technicians' work in seismological exploration includes taking care of scientific instruments and shock-processing equipment, assisting in making measurements, logging test drill holes, and logging cores showing the different strata thicknesses and depth. If technicians are trained to use surveying and mapping instruments and techniques, they can assist in accurately locating and mapping test holes or results of seismic tests. They also assist with the underground mapping tasks necessary in the analysis of test results and with recording important locations as scientists identify them in the course of exploring an area.

Sometimes technicians work in offices and laboratories where planning and analysis of existing geological data are conducted before field exploration begins. Or the work may be done after the field tests, so that data and geological samples may be analyzed as reports and records are being completed.

In seismic or drilling operations, technicians' workplaces and conditions vary as widely as their duties. The workplace is often outdoors. Oil producing may require working in swamps, plains, deserts, offshore, or in the mountains. Less frequently, work is done indoors in laboratories, computer centers, or on offshore drilling rigs. Oil and gas exploration and production take place all year, sometimes during severe weather.

Petroleum technician must be flexible and adaptable about their working conditions. They should not mind getting dirty on the job. They seldom have routine daytime forty-hour workweeks. Workers must make personal sacrifices to fulfill their job responsibilities. Long hours and extended work, both days and nights, are not unusual. The worker on an offshore rig must be able to deal with a restricted environment for several weeks at a time. An exploration or drilling crew may be away from its home base for several days at a time. It is not unusual to be moved around frequently from one location to another.

Much of the work in petroleum exploration and drilling involves physical labor and is potentially dangerous. Petroleum technicians must be strong and healthy, and should enjoy the outdoors in all weather. They must like working with heavy off-the-road trucks and machinery. They must also understand and appreciate how modern scientific equipment and instruments work and how they apply to the petroleum industry.

Requirements

Preparation for the career of petroleum technician should begin in high school. The student should plan a program of study that will provide an educational base leading to a two-year petroleum technician program in a technical or community college.

In high school, the prospective technician should complete at least two years of mathematics, including algebra and geometry, and four years of language skills courses that emphasize reading and writing. The student should learn to use computers and become familiar with typewriter or computer keyboards while in high school, because keyboard skills are needed to use the computers that are increasingly important in this field.

The high-school student should complete a solid course in physics with laboratory study. Combined with mathematics, this course provides the necessary foundation for the study of electronics, advanced physics, and various engineering-type technical courses in the post–high-school program. Courses like these are required for technicians who want to enter seismic exploration or well drilling and oil field production careers.

Students who have a desire to be technicians in oil and gas refining or petrochemical processing should plan to become chemical technicians. Their study should emphasize organic chemistry and chemical production.

High-school courses in drafting, mechanics, or auto shop would be excellent preparation to include if possible. These courses, however, should not prevent fulfilling the physics and mathematics requirements.

The most important value of technicians is their ability to apply a background that combines scientific and mathematical training, specialized skills, and technical knowledge. The courses they take in technical colleges are aimed at developing this background.

Graduates are trained to be able to interpret and understand common exploration methods and problems and to use the major tools of subsurface exploration. Students gain a working knowledge of the physics involved in the drilling process, and they learn how to operate computers to obtain or to analyze data and how to communicate effectively. They learn how to correct common oil field production breakdowns, supervise production crews, and apply physics, chemistry, and math to oil field management.

The first year of study in a typical technical college program for petroleum technicians includes courses in general chemistry, petroleum chemistry, introduction to the petroleum industry, applied mathematics, graphic presentation, introduction to data processing, petroleum geology, communication skills, introduction to surveying, petroleum services and supplies, and industrial economics and financing. These courses are taught in classrooms and laboratories, and, where possible, in work situations.

In some programs, students spend the summer between the first and second years in an internship program, working as a summer employee of a company. Such a program is very helpful to the student. It provides a clear picture of work in the field and helps the student choose an area of specialization. Internships make students more receptive to classroom instruction and also teach specific technical skills needed in the field. These skills include the use of charts and graphs, map reading, and communication and supervisory techniques. The student develops job confidence because of having experienced a practical approach to the industry. The student learns to read and digest technical information from trade journals and professional papers as examples of how to continue to learn after leaving school.

In the second year of the program the student may take courses in physics, petroleum drilling technology, petroleum electronics, advanced applied mathematics, petroleum, well completion techniques and processes, human relations in business and industry, elementary refining methods, industrial electronics, salesmanship and distribution, and industrial water pollution and wastewater treatment.

In addition to the technical qualifications provided by education, certain personal qualifications are needed to be successful in this career. The ability to work with others and accept supervision is most important. Technicians must also learn to work independently. They must be accurate and careful workers. Mistakes can prove to be either expensive or hazardous to the technician and to others in the workplace.

Petroleum technicians must be physically able, have good eyesight and hearing, and have excellent hand, eye, and body coordination. They need the ability to work with delicate instruments and to do heavy physical work.

Technicians must be able to operate off-the-road vehicles needed to transport people, supplies, and equipment to exploration sites or drilling and production sites. Much of this must be learned on the job after they finish their formal training. Technicians must be able to learn and to cope resourcefully with the demands of the work without being defeated by its demands, surprises, hazards, rigors, and at times, isolation.

Special requirements

There is very little licensing or certification required for a job as a petroleum technician. Some positions in the offshore industry require additional safety training. First-aid training and, in some cases, special physical examinations are required throughout the industry for certain positions. Both of these requirements are generally met by technicians after they are hired.

Opportunities for experience and exploration

People considering entry into this career can obtain considerable information from high schools, community colleges, or technical institutes. School catalogs describing petroleum technician programs are also helpful.

If it is possible, prospective technicians should visit a producing oil field, especially when active drilling is being done. They can observe the work and talk to workers and thus find out about the career firsthand. One of the best opportunities for experience is a summer job with a drilling or oil-field-production managing company.

Methods of entering

High-school graduates without advanced technical study can enter petroleum exploration or production as unskilled workers. They can work up to highly skilled technical jobs, responsibilities, and rewards. However, anyone who wants to become a technician after working on the job for a few months or years should seriously consider attending a technical college program full-time. It is very difficult for a person to gain access to the theoretical scientific and technical subject matter that must be learned while working long hours in remote parts of the world. Because of the rigors of the career, the average worker does not have enough time to study on the job to become a well-qualified petroleum technician.

The well-prepared graduate technician has the basic knowledge to work in the petroleum industry, but field work such as seismic exploring or working on a drilling rig is indispensable. It may be that the first job many two-year graduates will take will be in one of these basic operations.

Graduate technicians are usually hired by recruiters from the major companies and employers in the field before they finish their last year of technical school. Industry recruiters regularly visit the placement offices of schools with petroleum technician programs.

Graduates usually have special interests that make them qualified for technician-level positions in one or more of the following career subdivisions: exploration, drilling, production, refining, storage, or sales and service.

People trained as electronics technicians with a good computer and electronic communications background may also be very attractive to oil exploration and production company recruiters.

Typical entry-level job titles for petroleum technicians who have graduated from associate degree programs are exploration technician, engineering aide, log technician, mud test technician, production technician, oil field well-servicing technician, oil and gas storage technician, service and supply technician, and petroleum industry supply sales representative.

The beginning technician gains field experience in an area of the employer's choice. Generally, beginning technicians are assigned where they are most needed. Most often these orientation assignments are field operations such as seismic exploration or in well drilling operations.

Because many graduates have not had much experience, if any, at either seismic or well drilling operations, new technicians work as assistants to the leaders of the operations. They also may be expected to help with the semiskilled or skilled work of exploration or drilling rig work so that they become familiar with the skills and techniques of the work and can do the tasks themselves if necessary.

It is not uncommon, however, for employers to hire newly graduated technicians and immediately send them to a specialized training program. These programs are designed for oil company employees and usually are offered by the suppliers of the special materials, equipment, or services. After the training period, technicians may be sent anywhere in the world where the company has exploratory drilling or production operations.

Advancement

For the technician who works steadily and keeps up to date on the new technological developments in the field, opportunities for advancement are excellent.

In the exploration field, a technician may be promoted to assistant field exploration seismologist. The assistant seismologist directs the other crew members in taking measurements and gathering seismic data, plotting it, and assisting the chief seismologist, geologists, and earth scientists in interpreting the data.

Excellent opportunities may be found for experienced and highly competent exploration technicians in the sales and servicing of geological and mineralogical exploration or detecting instruments. Some of these opportunities may also involve research and development of new equipment, and teaching customers how to use it in the field.

In oil drilling and production, there are excellent opportunities to advance to the position of head driller or chief assistant to the tool pusher. The tool pusher is in charge of major field drilling. Often these positions lead to promotions to oil production management. Managers who begin as technicians have experience that gives them special skills and judgment.

For technicians who want to get into business for themselves, this career offers interesting opportunities because of the excellent pay they provide. For example, technicians can become independent owners and operators of drilling rigs. Many drilling rigs are owned by small private owners. The rewards for successfully operating an independent drill can be very great, especially if the owner discovers new fields and then shares in the royalties for production.

Working as a consultant or a technical salesperson is also a route to advancement in the petroleum industry. To succeed in either endeavor, a technician must have an excellent record of field success in oil and gas drilling and production.

Employment outlook

Although oil prices increased in the late 1980s and early 1990s from their depressed levels in the mid-1980s, they are still well below their peaks of the early 1980s. Levels of employment are also well below the highs of the early 1980s and are not expected to rise rapidly in the near future. However, in time, oil prices will certainly rise as demand for oil remains constant or grows and supplies of readily available oil are drawn down. It is uncertain when this will happen, but when it does, drilling activity will increase and employment levels will rise. In the meantime, growth in employment opportunities will be slow, and most job openings will result from the need to replace technicians who retire or leave their jobs for other reasons.

Earnings

It is difficult to establish a precise scale of earnings for petroleum technicians because of their many work situations and conditions. In general, technicians working in remote areas and under severe weather conditions usually receive high rates of pay. Graduates of two-year petroleum technology programs are usually hired as beginning technicians in a salary range from $16,000 to $27,000 per year.

These figures reflect the earnings of technicians who are employed in moderately accessible oil field work on land and also some who are in such remote places as offshore drilling rigs in the North Sea or the Gulf of Mexico.

Pay increases come with experience gained on the job and perhaps with changes of work location to more remote places. Within five years, technicians whose average pay started near $20,000 may well be earning $30,000 to $35,000 if their job performances show that they are increasing their effectiveness and ability to assume important responsibilities.

Fringe benefits in the petroleum industry are as progressive and competitive as any industry today, especially in terms of education benefits, insurance, and work schedules for faraway places.

Conditions of work

Work in exploration activities, well drilling, and production is likely to involve frequent moving. This exposes technicians to a wide variety of climate, geography, and weather. Technicians may also come in contact with workers from various foreign countries.

Because of the variety of conditions, petroleum technicians must always be alert to avoid accidents and hazards as they work. Employers supply safety instruction, appropriate clothing, and health care services to the best of their ability, but the safety and health of a petroleum technician must, in the last analysis, depend most on the intelligence, alertness, and judgment of the workers themselves.

Living conditions on offshore drilling platforms are usually reasonably comfortable. Rooms may accommodate from two to eight people, depending on the rig's size. Housekeeping service to clean and make beds and change linens is also usually adequate. Food is, of course, furnished on all rigs where crews must live aboard.

Social and psychological factors

Much of the potential for deep satisfaction and great rewards in this career depends upon the flexibility, stability, and adaptability of the individuals as they respond to the heavy work, long hours, and isolated or primitive living conditions. In many ways, petroleum technicians are pioneers. They are pioneers in faraway and difficult work places, and at the same time they are pioneers in the use of modern technology.

Petroleum technicians must be patient, orderly, systematic, accurate, and objective in their work. They must have the urge and the ability to learn. It is important that they know how to get along with people and sometimes how to work in a subordinate role. They must be willing to work cooperatively and they must have the ability to think and to plan ahead.

This career can be exciting and highly rewarding. It has the potential for satisfactions that can come from applying modern technology in faraway and remote places, with the aim of helping to keep vital energy supplies available to support civilization.

GOE: 02.04.01, 05.02.01, 05.03.04, 05.11.03; SIC: 131; SOC: 3833

◇ SOURCES OF ADDITIONAL INFORMATION

American Petroleum Institute
1220 L Street, NW
Washington, DC 20005

American Gas Association
1515 Wilson Boulevard
Arlington, VA 22209

Society of Exploration Geophysicists
Box 702740
Tulsa, OK 74170

Society of Petroleum Engineers
PO Box 833836
Richardson, TX 75083

**American Institute of Mining,
Metallurgical, and Petroleum Engineers**
345 East 47th Street, 14th Floor
New York, NY 10017

U.S. Geological Survey
U.S. Department of the Interior
National Center
12201 Sunrise Valley Drive
Reston VA 22092

◇ **RELATED ARTICLES**

Volume 1: Energy; Engineering
Volume 2: Engineers; Geologists
Volume 3: Petroleum drilling occupations; Petroleum refining workers; Roustabouts
Volume 4: Chemical technicians; Civil engineering technicians; Coal mining technicians; Geological technicians

Pharmaceutical technicians

A pharmaceutical technician creates new drugs in a specially equipped laboratory. It takes years to develop new drugs, test their effectiveness, and obtain approval from the government to issue them.

Definition

Pharmaceutical technicians work for drug companies where they assist scientists and engineers in developing and manufacturing pharmaceutical products. These products include the medicines that doctors prescribe, such as antibiotics, tranquilizers, and vaccines; medicines and other health products that do not require a prescription, such as aspirin, cold remedies, and vitamin pills; and other chemical compounds used in the manufacture of pharmaceutical products.

Nature of the work

Most pharmaceutical technicians work in either research and development activities or in manufacturing and production. Those who are involved in research and development usually work in laboratories where they help chemists, biologists, physicians, or veterinarians carry out tasks that are necessary to the development of new or improved drugs. Drugs can be synthesized from chemicals, or they may be derived from plant or animal sources. Before they can be given to human beings, newly developed drugs must be analyzed, purified, modified, studied, and tested. Many of these routine tasks are performed by technicians. Most commonly technicians are working to learn more about the chemical structure, content, or behavior of particular substances or compounds. To do this, they carry out experiments using standard laboratory equipment such as microscopes, scales, and culture dishes, reference books and materials such as the *U.S. Pharmacopoeia*, and electronic equipment such as spectrophotometers. Some technicians are responsible for operating machines that grind, mix, heat, or filter the ingredients of new drugs. Other prepare drugs to be given to test animals. Pharmaceutical technicians keep records of the work they do, record the results of their experiments, and do mathematical calculations to help to analyze those results.

Once a drug is proven to be effective and safe to use, it can be manufactured and sold to the public. Pharmaceutical technicians who work in manufacturing usually assist the engineering staff in designing, constructing, running, and supervising the production process. Some pharmaceutical technicians work on improving the methods and efficiency of the production process. They may devise schedules, write reports, work up cost estimates, and make charts and drawings that help explain their findings and recommendations. Other technicians are involved in quality control. They operate machines and do tests that check on the concentration and purity of drug ingredients and on how well the finished product measures up to company standards.

Requirements

A few people who are hired by pharmaceutical companies to do routine technical jobs have only a high-school education but they gradually learn the necessary skills through on-the-job training. For most kinds of positions, however, employers prefer technicians who are graduates of two-year post–high-school training programs, such as those available at community and junior colleges. Programs that would be suitable for people who plan to become pharmaceutical technicians include chemical, biological, industrial, and mechanical technology.

High-school students who are thinking about this field should take courses in mathematics, computers, and physical and biological sciences, including courses with laboratory sections.

GOE: 02.04.01, 05.01.08; SIC: 2834; SOC: 3719, 5831, 389

◇ **RELATED ARTICLES**

Volume 1: Biological Sciences; Chemicals and Drugs
Volume 2: Biochemists; Biologists, Chemists; Engineers; Medical technologists; Pharmacists; Pharmacologists; Toxicologists
Volume 3: Pharmaceutical industry workers
Volume 4: Biological technicians; Biological specimen technicians; Chemical technicians; Pharmacy technicians

Poured concrete technicians

Definition

Poured concrete technicians survey and mark construction sites for excavation, set up and true up concrete forms, and direct the pouring of concrete to form the walls of buildings made of poured-concrete construction. Technicians use various hand tools and surveying instruments such as transits and theodolites (such as surveying instruments).

Nature of the work

Poured concrete technicians begin by reading blueprints and site-layout plans and surveying the construction site. When wall plans have been laid out, they set up and bolt together metal or wooden concrete forms, then survey the assembled forms to ensure true angles and corners. These technicians measure distances to established points and record the distances and elevations in the site log book for later reference. Poured concrete technicians also measure out and mark the site to guide bulldozer operators in excavating the site to proper depth. These technicians guide the concrete trucks' chutes in pouring formed walls, and remove forms after the concrete has cured. Finally, they waterproof lower walls by spraying asphalt on them, and excavate and lay drainage tile to promote adequate drainage away from walls toward sewers.

Two poured concrete technicians add wet concrete to a wooden form that they previously measured and constructed.

Requirements

Following a basic high-school education, including shop courses and mathematics through geometry, prospective technicians should have at least two years of additional training, including courses in surveying and construction methods. They should become familiar with common construction site procedures and equipment.

Conditions of work

The work of poured concrete technicians is strenuous; they commonly lift and carry up to fifty pounds and may have to lift one hundred pounds. There is also a great deal of bending and stretching in this work. All work is performed out-of-doors, which makes it seasonal work in many climates. They face the usual construction-site hazards of working with and near power machinery, on uneven footing, and near overhead construction activities.

GOE: 05.10.01; SIC: 3241; SOC: 6479

◇ **RELATED ARTICLES**

Volume 1: Construction; Engineering
Volume 2: Construction inspectors, government; Engineers; Surveyors
Volume 3: Cement masons; Construction workers; Plasterers
Volume 4: Architectural and building construction technicians; Civil engineering technicians; Surveying and mapping technicians

Product test technicians

Definition

Product test technicians are involved with the testing of all kinds of experimental or prototype mechanical, electrical, and electromechanical products. Working in consultation with and under the supervision of engineers and other engineering personnel, they build and install testing equipment, conduct tests, and record test results regarding product design.

Nature of the work

They review test plans with engineers, sometimes discussing the types of tests to be run and the conditions under which the tests should be conducted. In building testing apparatus and components, some test technicians use milling machines, lathes, and welding equipment; other technicians may be involved with giving direction and instruction to the technicians doing the building. Other activities of test technicians include installing units to be tested in test fixtures and connecting valves, pumps, and hydraulic, mechanical, or electrical controls, cables, and tubes. In addition, test technicians may be asked to recommend changes in test methods or equipment.

Requirements

Technicians also need good eyesight, including good color vision, depth perception, and peripheral vision. To qualify for this kind of job, product test technicians usually need to have received two years of vocational training beyond high school. This training should include engineering courses and instruction in both mathematics and language skills. The mathematics instruction should include courses in algebra, geometry, and shop math. The

language-skills instruction should prepare technicians to read magazine articles, textbooks, manuals, and other reference books, to write business letters and reports with standard grammar, punctuation, and style, and to speak publicly in discussions and before small groups.

Conditions of work

Most technicians work inside, and the physical demands of their jobs are light, involving good manual dexterity and eye-hand coordination and the ability to move about normally.

GOE: 05.01.04; SIC: Any industry; SOC: 3719

◇ RELATED ARTICLES

Volume 1: Engineering
Volume 2: Engineers
Volume 4: Electromechanical technicians; Electronics test technicians; Mechanical technicians

Quality-control technicians

Definition

Quality-control technicians test and inspect industrial products, parts of products, and materials that go into products in order to maintain the quality and reliability of products and to determine their mechanical, electrical, chemical, or other material characteristics. They also record, compile, and evaluate statistical data.

History

Quality-control technology is an outgrowth of the Industrial Revolution. One of the principal

features of the Industrial Revolution as it began in England in the eighteenth century was that each person involved in the manufacturing process was responsible for a particular part of the process. The worker's responsibility was further specialized by the introduction of the concept of interchangeable parts by Eli Whitney in the late eighteenth and early nineteenth centuries. In a manufacturing process using the concept of interchangeable parts, a worker could concentrate on making just one component, while other workers concentrated on creating other components. Such specialization led to increased production efficiency, especially as manufacturing processes became increasingly mechanized during the early part of the twen-

A quality-control technician compliments the employees on correcting a problem with the packaging of tablets.

tieth century. It also meant, however, that no one worker was responsible for the overall quality of the product. This situation led to the need for another kind of specialized production worker, a worker whose primary concern was not in a particular aspect of assembling the product but rather in assuring overall quality of the product.

At first, this kind of responsibility belonged to the mechanical engineers and mechanical technicians who developed the manufacturing systems, equipment, and procedures. However, with the increasing sophistication of the instruments, techniques, and theories invoked in quality-control activities, the field has emerged as a separate kind of industrial technology.

As the field of quality-control technology has become more complex, so too has the work of quality-control technicians. No longer is their job simply periodically to remove finished or semifinished products from the assembly line for visual inspection and testing to see if the item works as it should.

Today's quality-control technician operates sophisticated instrumentation devices, helps develop testing programs according to advanced statistical sampling theories, and confers with engineering personnel regarding materials, equipment, and procedures. While there is still some room today for the conscientious and intelligent technician who lacks advanced educational training, more and more quality-control technicians are graduates of specialized two-year or sometimes even four-year

training programs in community and technical colleges.

Nature of the work

There is a wide variety of activities involved with quality-control technology in addition to the basic inspecting and testing of products and components. For example, to arrive at the quality and reliability standards used in testing programs, quality-control technicians interpret drawings, schematic diagrams, and chemical, mathematical, and physical formulas. They select products for testing at specified stages of production and set up and perform destructive and nondestructive tests on materials, parts, and products. (In destructive tests, the part being tested is effectively destroyed as part of the testing; in nondestructive testing, the object of the testing is left intact.)

Another important area of quality-control technology involves the recording and evaluation of test data. Using statistical quality-control procedures, technicians prepare data in chart form and write summaries about a product's conformance to or departure from existing standards. Most importantly, they offer suggestions in written or oral form to engineering personnel regarding ways of modifying existing quality standards and manufacturing procedures to achieve the optimum product quality from existing or proposed new equipment.

Quality-control technicians may specialize in any of the following areas of quality-control engineering: product design, incoming materials, process control, product evaluation, inventory control, product reliability, research and development, and administrative applications.

Quality-control technicians are at work in nearly all industries, and it would be nearly impossible to describe all of the kinds of work they do. However, the following descriptions of the work done by quality-control technicians in some selected settings should provide a good idea of what this kind of work is like.

One industry that relies heavily on quality-control technicians is the food and beverage industry, where quality-control technicians work in a wide range of activities. Some are mostly concerned with canned and bottled beverages. They perform a variety of physical-measuring and chemical-analysis tests of the beverages and of the materials used in packaging. They select samples of crowns, cans, lids, bottles, labels, and cartons from the packaging lines, following established procedures concerning the time, place, and frequency of sampling. They measure the dimensions of the crowns, cans, bottles, lids, and labels, and they conduct abrasion tests on these items with an abrasion machine. They also measure the hardness of these items using a hardness tester and the bursting strength of bottles using an hydraulic bursting machine. They test the wet and dry tearing strength of labels and cartons, and they weigh filled cans and bottles to measure the volume of beer. Finally, they record the results of all of these tests and, when necessary, prepare graphs and charts to explain or present their findings.

Other technicians are concerned with taste-testing. They compile taste-preference data on foods and beverages for use by laboratory personnel in developing improved methods of production. As a first step in compiling this data, they request samples of food or beverages from warehouses or from production workers for both tasting and laboratory analysis, specifying the brand of the product and the serial numbers of the batches from which the samples are to be taken. Technicians also schedule designated persons to taste the various products and assist in various ways during the tasting sessions. Following the tasting session, they prepare reports about the tastings, including the date of the tasting, the name of the product, and the serial numbers of the batches from which the samples were taken. They forward these reports to laboratory personnel.

Finally, some quality-control technicians in the food-processing industry inspect incoming foodstuffs and outgoing finished food products. They also test and adjust the packaging equipment used during the processing of the foods. They determine oil, salt, and moisture content of both raw foods and finished products, using measuring devices such as thermometers, scales, pyrometers, and conductivity testers, and they adjust and calibrate the devices as needed. They also record inspection data and write reports about product conformance or deviation from established standards.

Another industry that relies on quality control technicians is the glass-manufacturing industry, where quality-control technicians inspect flat glass and compile data on defects based on samples to determine variance from quality standards. They remove samples of glass containers or other glass objects from shipping cases and examine the containers for defects such as chips, cracks, and other imperfections. They inspect the packed cases for irregularities in packing, sealing, and printing. They mark rejected cases and case lots. They also record their findings on work sheets and compile data on product and packaging defects

for use by other production, packaging, and supervisory personnel.

There are also quality-control technicians who are concerned with fiberglass products. They test fiberglass yarn, fibers, and binder solutions at various stages of the manufacturing process to determine if quality standards are being met. They weigh samples of fibers and binder solutions before and after key manufacturing processes in both experimental and operational settings. Quality-control technicians examine and test goods returned by customers or at the customer's establishment to detect manufacturing defects or damage incurred in transit. They also record and compile their findings for use by quality-control and production supervisors.

In the building-materials industry, there are quality-control technicians who are involved with the testing and inspecting of gypsum wallboard. They collect, measure, and weigh samples of chemical additives and minerals such as gypsum and vermiculite that will be used in the wallboard. Quality-control technicians perform tests on the samples to determine purity, particle size, and hardness. They also test finished panels for strength and edge hardness. Sometimes they inspect wallboard at a job site to verify a customer's claim about a defect, and they may propose compensation offers to resolve claims.

Quality-control technicians concerned with delivering developed photographic film to customers have two basic kinds of responsibilities: product and equipment inspection and customer relations. In the area of product and equipment inspection, they examine photographic prints, processed film, cameras, and other photographic equipment to identify defects or faulty operations. They spread negatives and prints on illuminated worktables and use magnifying glasses to detect defects, such as incorrect coloring, shading, or cutting. They determine the cause of the defect and the type of correction required.

In the customer-relations area, quality-control technicians review unresolved requests for satisfaction of complaints, read customer comments to determine the basis of customer complaints, and plan courses of action needed to resolve the complaints. In some cases, they meet with customers to explain defects and the course of action being recommended. They also prepare reports for forwarding to processing departments and quality-control supervisors suggesting remedies to prevent future errors in processing. Quality-control technicians also confer with sales-service personnel to resolve technical questions and to demonstrate correct ways of using photographic equipment.

Quality-control technicians
Engineering and Science Technician Occupations

Requirements

Quality-control technicians should have an aptitude for and an interest in mathematics, science, and other technical subjects and should feel comfortable using the language and symbols of mathematics and science. They should have good eyesight and good manual skills, including the ability to use hand tools. They should be able to follow technical instructions and to make sound judgments about technical matters. Finally, they should have orderly minds and be able to maintain records, to conduct inventories, and to estimate quantities.

Educational requirements for quality-control technicians will vary from industry to industry. For some prospective technicians, employers may require only that beginning technicians possess basic arithmetic skills and the ability to read simple instructions so that they can complete short on-the-job training programs. Most employers of quality-control technicians, however, require more advanced levels of training. Certainly all students who want to assure themselves the greatest range of employment opportunities should plan on finishing high school and completing a two-year post–high-school training program.

While in high school, prospective technicians should concentrate on courses in English, composition, mathematics (including algebra and geometry), and science. They should also take some shop and computer courses and at least one course in mechanical drawing. Students should especially seek those English courses that will develop their reading skills, their ability to write short reports with correct spelling and punctuation, and their ability to speak comfortably and effectively in front of a group of people.

In two-year, post–high-school training programs, students are required to take courses in the physical sciences, in mathematical subjects related to materials testing, and in engineering-related subjects. In these courses, students learn about the devices, components, and organizational principles used in quality-control systems. They learn about design, production and inspection, testing (both destructive and nondestructive), statistical sampling, mathematical probability, reading of specifications, and designing and measuring tolerances to assure levels of quality in manufactured units, components, and systems. Such a post-secondary program should also include instruction in the preparation of scientific or technical reports and in the development of interpersonal skills required in working with or in supervising other workers.

Special requirements

There are no licensing or certification requirements designed specifically for quality-control technicians. As quality-control technicians work in a variety of industries, however, some may find that they have to meet special requirements that apply only within the industry employing them.

Opportunities for experience and exploration

Quality-control technicians work in a wide variety of settings, so prospective technicians who want to learn more about quality-control technology can consider a range of possibilities for experiencing or further exploring such work. Because quality-control activities are so often directly involved with manufacturing processes, one might try to obtain part-time or summer jobs in manufacturing settings, even if not specifically in the quality-control area. This type of work may consist of the most menial tasks, but it offers first-hand experience and it demonstrates interest to future employers.

Much of the work of quality-control technicians consists of working with scientific instruments; therefore, students can gain relevant experience in academic or industrial-arts courses that introduce them to different kinds of scientific or technical equipment. Electrical and machine shop courses, mechanical drawing courses, and chemistry courses with lab sections all offer useful experience. Joining a radio or computer club or school science club is also a good way to gain experience.

Methods of entering

Students who attend a two-year, post–high-school training program usually find their first jobs through job interviews conducted at the school by company recruiters during the second year of the program.

Students at both the high school and the post–high-school level should take advantage of any work-study program that is available to them. These programs often lead to full-time employment after graduation.

Students should also remember that guidance counselors and faculty members will have valuable advice to offer in this effort.

Other proven methods of finding employment include reading and responding to newspaper want ads, writing directly to companies employing quality-control technicians, and using the services of state and private employment services.

Advancement

In general, quality-control technicians advance by going to higher-level technicians' jobs, earning a supervisory post, or by advancing to the professional ranks of quality-control engineers. Quality-control technicians usually begin their work under the direct and constant supervision of an experienced technician or engineer. As they gain experience or additional education, they are given more responsible assignments. From there, technicians may move into supervisory positions, and those with exceptional ability can sometimes qualify for professional positions after receiving additional academic training.

Promotion usually depends upon getting additional training, as well as performance on the job. Those technicians who fail to obtain additional training may be limited in advancement possibilities.

Employment outlook

The vast majority of quality-control technicians are employed in the manufacturing sector of the economy. Employment levels in this sector will depend, to some degree, on general economic conditions. The modest economic growth that many economists forecast through the year 2000 should lead to at least modest growth in manufacturing operations and in the quality-control activities associated with them.

In addition, the decade of the 1990s should see vigorous efforts on the part of industry to make their manufacturing processes more efficient, and these efforts will undoubtedly include upgrading quality-control activities. This will be especially true for those quality-control activities directed at evaluating product defects and formulating recommendations on how to avoid future defects, thus increasing manufacturing efficiency and productivity. It will also be true for those activities directed at inspecting, accepting, or rejecting incoming materials. Technicians interested in these areas of quality-control technology should anticipate a strong employment picture regardless of other economic conditions.

Earnings

Earnings for quality-control technicians vary according to the type of work they do, the industry in which they are employed, and the part of the country in which they are working. Most beginning quality-control technicians with two years of post–high-school training who are entering jobs that require such training earn salaries that range from around $14,000 to $18,000 a year. Most experienced technicians with a two-year degree earn salaries that range from $18,000 to $30,000 a year, and some senior technicians with special skills or experience may earn much more. However, some technicians without such training may earn no more than the minimum wage, or about $9,000 a year on their first job. In general, the more formal training a technician has, the better paying a job he or she is likely to find.

No matter what their educational level, quality-control technicians employed on a full-time basis can expect to receive standard benefits such as health insurance, paid holidays and vacations, and a pension plan. Some companies employing quality-control technicians also offer profit-sharing plans and tuition-reimbursement programs.

Conditions of work

Quality-control technicians work in a variety of different settings, and their conditions of work vary accordingly. Some quality-control technicians work on the factory floor along with other production workers, and they should expect to encounter some noise and dirt in their workplace. Technicians involved with testing and product analysis can expect to work in more comfortable surroundings, in a laboratory or workshop for instance. Even in these settings, however, they may be exposed to unpleasant fumes and toxic chemicals. In general, all quality-control technicians work inside and are expected to do some light lifting and carrying (usually not more than twenty pounds) in their work.

Social and psychological factors

In their positions as inspectors and evaluators of products, quality-control technicians often have to bring information that amounts to or can be construed as criticism to other workers, including some workers who may occupy more advanced positions in manufacturing, production, or purchasing departments. For technicians with good personalities and easy dispositions, this aspect of the work will not prove troublesome; for others it may be the source of some unpleasantness. All quality-control technicians, however, should expect that their role will sometimes make them unpopular. Nevertheless, the job they do is an important one, and most quality-control technicians feel a sense of pride and satisfaction in the work they do. In addition, most employers recognize the importance of good quality control, and they make efforts to communicate their appreciation to the people involved in the activity.

As with most engineering and science technicians, quality-control technicians should expect their work to present a combination of some intellectually challenging or otherwise highly skilled work and some repetitious, even tedious tasks. Quality-control technicians can usually seek out a position in which the combination of such qualities is to their liking; however, most technicians should expect to encounter at least some of both kinds of tasks in their work.

GOE: 02.04.01, 06.03.01; SIC: Any industry; SOC: 389, 783

◇ **RELATED ARTICLES**

Solar collector technicians

Definition

Solar collector technicians fabricate and assemble metal solar collectors, using shop tools and equipment and following written specifications.

Nature of the work

Beginning with metal sheets and tubing, they lay out and mark reference points according to specifications, using rules and scribers. They then bend, cut, and drill sections of pipe and copper sheeting to form absorber units, which they then assemble and paint. They form enclosures for the solar absorbers and assemble them using hand and power tools. Technicians caulk and insulate finished units and pack them for shipment. In their work, solar collector technicians use a wide variety of shop tools including power brakes, which are machines for forming sheet metal, rivet guns, drills, paint sprayers, and hand tools such as screwdrivers, hammers, wrenches, and crimpers.

Requirements

People who are interested in working as solar collector technicians should be prepared to take at least three months of specialized training beyond high school. They should take as many shop courses as possible in high school, along with shop math and blueprint reading. The minimum should be a basic technician course offered by a technical school or community college, emphasizing reading blueprints and understanding written specifications, using hand tools and bench tools, and following safe working procedures. Their reading ability should be good enough that they can easily read and understand instructions for such projects as assembling model airplanes and cars.

Conditions of work

The work of these technicians involves frequent lifting of weights to fifty pounds, and occasional loads to one hundred pounds. Working with power tools involves some hazards, and safety rules must be followed on the job.

GOE: 06.02.24; SIC: 3435; SOC: 6829

◇ **RELATED ARTICLES**

Volume 1: Machining and Machinery
Volume 2: Engineers
Volume 3: Machinists; Pipe fitters and steam fitters; Sheet-metal workers
Volume 4: Air-conditioning, heating, and refrigeration technicians; Energy-conservation technicians

Surveying and mapping technicians

Definition

Surveying and mapping technicians help civil engineers, professional surveyors, and mapmakers determine, describe, and record geographic areas or features. They know how to use modern surveying and mapping instruments and understand the scientific principles and mathematics that relate to each method of measurement and recording. They are prepared to participate in photogrammetric surveying and mapping operations. Surveying and mapping technicians also have a basic knowledge of the current practices and legal implications of surveys to establish and record property size, shape, topography, and boundaries. They often supervise assistants during routine surveying conducted within bounds established by a professional surveyor.

History

From ancient times, people have needed to define their property boundaries. Marking established areas of individual or group ownership was a basis for the development of early civilizations. Landholding became important in ancient Egypt, and with the development of hieroglyphics people were able to keep a record of their holdings. Eventually, nations found it necessary not only to mark property boundaries but also to lay out and record principal routes of commerce and transportation. For example, records of the Babylonians tell of their canals and irrigation ditches. The Romans surveyed and mapped the principal roads of their empire.

The process of making surveys by using instruments traditionally required at least two people. A scientist who had mastered the technology of the times was the leader, the professional surveyor. Helpers made measurements with chains, tapes, and wheel rotations, where each rotation accounted for a known length of distance. The helpers held rods with measured marks for location and drove stakes or placed other markers to define important points. As the measuring instruments became more complex, the speed, scope, and accuracy of the surveying process increased. As a result, the surveyor's assistants needed to know more about the equipment and the process to be able to work on the surveying team. For most modern surveying operations of any size a surveying technician is the leading helper to the professional surveyor. The technician's tasks therefore are usually closely associated with those of the professional surveyor.

As the United States expanded, surveyors and their technical helpers were among the first and most needed workers. It was they who established new land ownership by surveying and filing claims. Since then, precise and accurate geographical measurements have always been needed, whether for the location of a highway; the site of a building; the right-of-way

While one surveying technician measures the parameters of a construction site, the other records the measurements.

must be able to use specialized techniques as they assist surveyors or scientists in charge of surveys. For example, every missile fired from the Kennedy Space Center is tracked electronically to determine if it is on course. Mapmakers have recently used photogrammetry to map the moon. The technological complexity of such undertakings allows professional surveyors to delegate more tasks to technicians than ever before.

Nature of the work

As essential assistants to civil engineers or surveyors, surveying and mapping technicians are usually the first to be involved in any job that requires precise plotting. Many projects demand such work. They include highways, airports, housing developments, mines, dams, bridges, monuments, and buildings of all kinds.

The surveying and mapping technician is a key worker in field parties or major surveying projects. The technician is often assigned the task of being chief instrument worker under the surveyor's supervision. In this capacity, technicians use a variety of surveying instruments including the theodolite, transit, level, and different types of electronic equipment to measure distance or locate a position. As a transit worker, the technician uses many of these instruments, assembling, adjusting, sighting, and reading them. A rod worker, using a level rod or range pole, assists in making elevation and distance measurements. A chain worker measures shorter distances and uses the surveyor's chain or a metal tape. In the course of a survey, it is important to accurately record all readings and keep orderly field notes so that the survey can be checked for accuracy.

Surveying and mapping technicians may specialize if they join a surveying firm that focuses on one or more particular types of surveying. In a firm that specializes in land surveying, technicians are highly skilled in technical measuring and tasks related to establishing township, property, and other tract-of-land boundary lines. They assist the professional surveyor in using maps, notes, or actual land title deeds. They help survey the land, check the accuracy of existing records, and prepare legal documents such as deeds and leases.

Similarly, technicians who work for highway, pipeline, railway, or power line surveying firms help to establish points, grades, lines, and other points of reference for construction projects. This survey information provides the

for drainage ditches, telephone, or power lines; or for the charting of unexplored land, bodies of water, or underground mines. Through the years, measuring science has improved our ability to establish exact locations and to determine distances. In these processes, most of the actual measuring work is done by surveying technicians and other helpers under the direction of professional surveyors.

Developments in surveying and mapping technology have made great changes in theplanning and construction of highway systems and in the design and building of stationary structures of all kinds. In surveying for roadway route selection and design, surveying and mapping technicians increasingly use photogrammetry. With this method, automatic plotting machines are used to scribe routes from aerial photographs of rural or urban areas. Route data obtained by photogrammetry may then be processed through computers to calculate land acquisition, grading, and construction costs. Photogrammetry is far more accurate and faster than former methods. New electronic distance-measuring devices have elevated surveying to a higher level of technology. Technicians can measure distance more accurately and much more quickly and economically than it was possible with tapes or rod and chain. This requires better educated technicians to serve as chief assistants in complex surveying operations.

New technological discoveries, advances in measuring distances, and the use of computers in data processing have made surveying and mapping technical careers more complex and challenging than they were just a few decades ago. These changes have further increased the accuracy of surveying and mapping and extended its use beyond the surface of the land to making detailed maps of ocean floors and the moon. Surveying and mapping technicians exact locations for engineering design and construction work.

Technicians who work for a geodetic surveyor help take measurements of large masses of land, sea, or space that must take into account the curvature of the earth and its geophysical characteristics. This information sets major points of reference for smaller land surveys, for determining national boundaries, and for preparing maps.

Technicians also specialize in helping to take measurements for hydrographic surveyors. Hydrographic surveyors make surveys of harbors, rivers, and other bodies of water. These surveys are needed in designing navigation systems; planning and building breakwaters, levees, dams, locks, piers, and bridges; preparing nautical maps and charts; and establishing property boundaries. Technicians are key workers in making these surveys. They often supervise other workers as they make measurements and record data.

In mining companies, the technician is usually a member of the engineering, scientific, or management team. Working from the survey or engineering office, technicians take part in regular mine surveying. They set up the instructions and limits of the work team. In the office, technicians make survey calculations, develop maps, and calculate the tonnage of ore and broken rock.

In recent years, costly new surveying instruments have changed the way mining survey technicians do their jobs. These technicians work on the geological staffs of operating mining companies or on the staffs of exploration companies. At operating mines, technicians may be engaged in mapping underground geology, sampling, locating diamond drill holes, logging drill cores, and mapping geological data derived from boreholes. Their work may include mapping data on mine plans and diagrams and assisting the geologist in determining ore reserves.

In the search for new mines, mining survey technicians operate delicate instruments to obtain data on variations in the earth's magnetic field, the earth's conductivity, or the earth's gravity. They use the data to map the boundaries of potential areas for further exploration.

Surveying and mapping technicians may find interesting and challenging work helping to make topographical surveys. These surveys determine the contours of the land. They indicate such features as mountains, lakes, rivers, forests, roads, farms, buildings, and other distinguishable landmarks.

In topographical surveying, technicians often help take aerial or land photographs. These photographs are taken with special photographic equipment installed in an airplane or ground station that permits pictures of large areas to be made. This is called photogrammetry. From these pictures accurate measurements of the terrain and of surface features can be made. These surveys are helpful in highway planning and in the preparation of topographical maps. Photogrammetry is particularly helpful in charting areas that are inaccessible or difficult to travel. The method is widely used to measure farm land planted in certain crops and to verify crop average allotments under government production planning quotas.

By far the largest number of survey technicians are employed in construction work. Technicians are needed from start to finish of any construction job. They keep the structure's progress from foundation to finish within engineering specifications of size, height, depth, level, and geometric form.

Several entry-level technician positions available in the fields of drafting, mapping, geodetic surveying, and geological exploration are described in the following paragraphs.

Survey helpers, surveyors, or *survey drafters* operate surveying instruments to gather numerical data. They calculate tonnage broken and incentive pay, map mine development, and provide precise directions and locations to the work force. Under direction, they conduct studies on operations and equipment to improve methods and to reduce costs.

Assistant field or exploration geologists operate a variety of geophysical instruments on a grid pattern to obtain data on variations in the earth's magnetism, conductivity, and gravity. They map the data, and they analyze stream waters, soils, and rocks from known locations in the search for ore occurrences. Such technicians often work in remote areas.

Highway technicians, under the direction of a surveyor, make surveys and estimate costs. They also help plan, lay out, and supervise the construction and maintenance of highways. *Party chiefs* for licensed land surveyors survey land for boundary line locations and plan subdivisions and additions to cities.

Photogrammetric technicians use aerial photographs to prepare maps, mosaics, plans, and profiles. Surveying technicians locate the critical construction points on the job site as specified on design plans within the bounds of the property. They locate corners of buildings, foundation detail points, center points for columns, walls, and other features, height of floor or ceiling levels, and other points requiring precise measurements and location.

Rail or waterway surveying technicians make surveys, specifications, and cost estimates to help plan and construct railway or waterway facilities. Instruments surveyor assistants use a variety of surveying instruments to obtain measurements used in construction. They compile notes and sketches, record work performed, and supervise work of subordinate members of the surveying team.

Topographical drafters or *photocartographers* draw and correct topographical maps from source data such as surveying notes, old maps, or photographs. They may be part of a surveying crew in the field to compile original measurement data.

Requirements

Graduation from high school or the equivalent is a basic requirement for most opportunities in a surveying technician career.

Future surveying and mapping technicians should take all the mathematics, science, and communications subjects available in their high school. They should also take other courses that are part of the school's general college-preparatory program.

Mathematics, including at least two years of algebra, should be part of such a program, as should plane and solid geometry and trigonometry. If available, mechanical drawing and computer courses should be taken. Physics, including laboratory experience, is very valuable. Chemistry and biology are also desirable science courses.

Reading, writing, and comprehension skills are vital in surveying and mapping. Four years of high-school English and language skills courses are highly recommended. Reports and letters are an essential part of the technician's work, so a firm grasp of English grammar and spelling is important.

It is sometimes possible to enter the field of surveying immediately after high school by securing a position where on-the-job training is provided. To advance to a better position the prospective technician can expect to supplement the work experience by taking courses in surveying. However, this way of becoming a technician can take a long time. It involves several years of intensive part-time formal study to master the basic science and technical knowledge of the field.

Graduates of accredited post–high-school training programs who have a strong background in surveying, photogrammetry, and mapping are in the best position to enter the field as beginning surveying and mapping technicians.

Opportunities for this kind of training are available in postsecondary programs at junior colleges, technical institutes, and specialized schools. These are demanding technical programs, usually two academic years long and sometimes with field study in the summer. Typical courses in the first year include English, composition, drafting, applied mathematics, surveying and measurements, construction materials and methods, applied physics, statistics, and computer applications. The second year courses continue with technical physics, advanced surveying, photogrammetry and mapping, soils and foundations, technical reporting, legal practices and problems, industrial organizations and institutions, and transportation and environmental engineering.

A program such as the above can form a base for employment; later, with additional part-time study, the technician can specialize in geodesy, topography, hydrography, or photogrammetry.

Because surveying and mapping technicians may spend considerable time in field surveys, candidates should have an interest in working outdoors. Technicians must work with other people and often direct or supervise them. They must, therefore, have strong leadership qualities.

The ability to work with numbers and to perform mathematical computations accurately and quickly is very important to a surveying and mapping career. Equally important is the ability to understand and effectively use words and ideas. Other abilities that are helpful in the work of these technicians include the ability to visualize and understand objects in two or three dimensions and the ability to discriminate among and compare shapes, sizes, lines, shadings, and other aspects of objects and pictures of objects.

To function as members of a survey party in the field, technicians are usually required to be in good physical condition. They must be able to negotiate all types of terrain. Surveying technicians are on their feet a great deal of the time. Often they must carry the surveying instruments and equipment.

Surveying and mapping technicians need excellent eyesight to read precision optical instruments used in modern surveying. Their hearing ability must also be good because members of surveying teams sometimes have to shout over intermediate distances. Radio communication, however, is now becoming the common way to communicate. In either case, the surveying and mapping technician must give instructions clearly and precisely. Endurance, coordination, and lack of physical impairment are important physical assets for the surveying technician.

Special requirements

Unlike professional land surveyors, there are no special requirements for registration or licensing for surveying and mapping technicians. Technicians who seek government employment must pass a civil service examination.

To advance their professional standing and become more attractive to a wider variety of employers, surveying and mapping technicians should try to become certified engineering technicians. This certification is similar to the licensing of engineers, but the requirements are based on and consistent with the tasks, skills, and responsibilities that are expected of these technicians.

Surveying and mapping technicians may also, upon completion of the required years of service, take an examination for licensing as a Licensed Land Surveyor. Successful completion of this examination enables technicians to operate their own surveying businesses.

Opportunities for experience and exploration

Persons considering entry into this career can obtain information from high schools, community colleges, and technical institutes. Visiting construction sites is one way of observing how surveying technicians work.

One of the best opportunities for experience is a summer job with a construction firm or a company involved in survey work. Even if the job does not involve direct contact with survey crews, it will provide an opportunity to observe them at work and discover more about the surveying technician's activities.

Methods of entering

A few high-school graduates without formal surveying training are hired as rod workers or chain workers with a surveying firm and may eventually become qualified technicians by combining experience with part-time course work.

Graduates of a technical institute or a four-year college will find the placement service of their institution to be very helpful in arranging examinations or interviews. Regular employers of surveying technicians often send recruiters to schools before graduation and arrange to employ promising graduates. In many cities, there are employment agencies that specialize in placing technical workers in positions in surveying, mapping, construction, mining, and related fields.

Graduates of junior college and technical institute programs can enter the field immediately as instrument workers. Later, they can secure positions as surveyor aides, instrument operators, computers, observers, recorders, or plane-table operators.

Some community or technical colleges have work-study programs that provide cooperative part-time or summer work for pay. Employers involved with these programs will often offer full-time jobs to students after graduation.

Advancement

Possibilities for advancement are linked to the level of the technician's formal education and experience. As they gain experience and technical knowledge, technicians can advance to positions of greater responsibility and eventually to surveyor or chief of a surveying party. The latter, however, is almost impossible without formal education beyond high school.

Steps are being taken by some of the professional engineering and surveying associations to increase the requirements needed to become a registered or licensed land surveyor. One requirement being considered is a bachelor's degree in engineering. If this action is taken, it will be nearly impossible for the high-school graduate to advance to higher levels or professional positions. Accordingly, advancement will be more difficult for the technicians who graduated from formal two-year technical programs in surveying technology. Graduates of two- and three-year programs can usually transfer at least a part of their college-level credits to degree-granting engineering programs if they decide they want to obtain a professional degree and become a registered professional surveyor. Some survey workers choose to work for a year or two before continuing with their formal education. Others make the transfer immediately upon completion of their two- or three-year degree program.

The surveying technician must continue studying to keep up with the technological developments in surveying, measuring, and mapping. Computers, lasers, and microcomputers will continue to change the job. Studying to keep up with changes, combined with experience gained on the job, increases the value of technicians to their employers. Some examples of advancement that technicians may attain in this way are described as follows.

Licensed land surveyors operate a land survey business as owner or partner. This almost always requires further study to qualify for a state license. Some technicians become owners of companies that have franchises for the distribution and sales of surveying and measuring equipment, supplies, and related products and services. *Photogrammetrists* direct the preparation of maps and charts from aerial photographs. Technicians in large construction or mining and exploration companies can be promoted to senior surveying technicians. These senior technicians supervise surveying operations on large jobs or a number of small or medium-sized jobs. This position often requires the knowledge and experience to do all of the work expected of professional surveyors except to certify boundaries or locations.

Field-map editors identify features on aerial photographs and verify information used in mapmaking. They travel over the land that the map is supposed to cover and record features needed in the completed map. They obtain information about boundary lines and other official information from county records.

Employment outlook

The employment outlook in the surveying field is expected to be good through 1990s. This outlook applies to those who have at least two years of junior college or technical institute preparation as surveying or civil engineering technicians.

One of the factors that is expected to increase the demand for surveying services—and therefore surveying technicians—is growth in urban and suburban areas. New streets, homes, shopping centers, schools, and gas and water lines will require property and boundary line surveys. Other factors are the continuing state and federal highway improvement programs and the increasing number of urban redevelopment programs. The expansion of industrial and business firms and the relocation of some firms in large undeveloped tracts is also expected to create a need for surveying services.

The continuing search for new petroleum fields and mineral deposits involves increasingly complex measurements and surveying techniques. Exploring for oil and gas will require the services of many technicians on surveying teams.

Although new electronic equipment is reducing the time necessary to complete land surveys, it is not expected that it will reduce the number of job opportunities. The new equipment and technology being introduced into the surveying field will continue to require additional educational preparation at the technician or instrument worker level.

Earnings

Most surveying and mapping technicians earn between $16,000 and $26,000 a year, and the average is around $20,000 a year. Some technicians, especially those at the very beginning of their careers, may earn as little as $11,000 a year, while some senior technicians with special skills and experience may earn as much as $36,000 a year or more. In the early 1990s, surveying and mapping technicians with two-year degrees working for the federal government received starting salaries of around $13,000 a year, and the overall average salary for surveying technicians working for the government was around $18,000 a year.

Conditions of work

Surveying and mapping technicians usually work about forty hours a week except when overtime work is necessary. The peak work period for many kinds of surveying work is during the summer months when weather conditions are most favorable. It is not uncommon, however, for surveying crews to be exposed to all types of weather conditions. Surveying technicians on construction jobs who, with their helpers, take daily point-to-point and step-by-step measurements on construction jobs must work in all kinds of weather.

Some survey projects involve a certain amount of hazard depending upon the region and the climate as well as local plant and animal life. Field survey crews encounter snakes and poison ivy. They are subject to heat exhaustion, sunburn, and frostbite. Some survey projects, particularly those being conducted near construction projects or busy highways, impose the dangers of injury from cars and flying debris. Unless survey technicians are employed for office assignments, where working conditions are similar to those of other office workers, their work location quite likely will change from survey to survey. Some assignments may require technicians to be away from home for varying periods of time.

While on the job, surveying crews and especially technicians who often supervise other workers must take special care to observe good safety practices. Construction and mining workplaces are usually "hard-hat" areas where special clothing and protective hats and shoes are required.

Social and psychological factors

Surveying and mapping technicians must be patient, orderly, systematic, accurate, and objective in their work. They must be able to work in a subordinate role as an assistant to the surveyor or cartographer. They must be willing to work cooperatively, and must have the ability to think and plan ahead. Probably one of the most important qualities is a willingness to work long hours for extended periods of time as is sometimes required in the work of all technicians.

These technicians' careers offer great potential for job satisfaction. As technicians perform the supportive functions to professional surveyors, they share the opportunity for travel and exploration. Well-prepared and experienced technicians can secure positions that require extensive travel and exposure to varied conditions of living, from field campsites to hotel accommodations. As the survey party moves from one location to another, these technicians will find that each assignment is unique. Each new assignment represents an opportunity to open new areas to develop. In this sense, the technician becomes a part of an exploration team. In the more routine, and perhaps less adventuresome tasks, the surveying technician performs an essential and especially valuable social and commercial service.

GOE: 05.03.01, 05.03.02; SIC: 8713; SOC: 1649, 3734

SOURCES OF ADDITIONAL INFORMATION

American Congress on Surveying and Mapping
210 Little Falls Street
Falls Church, VA 22046

American Institute of Mining, Metallurgical, and Petroleum Engineers
345 East 47th Street
New York, NY 10017

Accreditation Board for Engineering and Technology
345 East 47th Street
New York, NY 10017

RELATED ARTICLES

Volume 1: Construction; Energy; Engineering; Mining
Volume 2: Architects; Cartographers; Engineers; Surveyors
Volume 3: Coal mining operatives; Construction workers
Volume 4: Architectural and building construction technicians; Coal mining technicians; Drafting and design technicians

Tap-and-die maker technicians

Definition

Tap-and-die maker technicians set up and operate machinery to make taps, dies, and precision cutting tools from such materials as tungsten-carbide and high speed steel. These technicians are involved in making the cutting tools used in many manufacturing industries.

Nature of the work

Tap-and-die maker technicians work from blueprints and specifications that describe the metal piece, such as a master tap, that they are to make. They plan and lay out the work and set up the equipment they will need, and they utilize a variety of precision measuring instru-

These tap-and-die maker technicians are adjusting their machines and replacing parts in preparation for new materials that they will be manufacturing.

ments to check the set-up of the equipment and the progress of their work as they proceed. They grind the part, often working to tolerances of 0.00001 inch, by adjusting machine controls to move the work against lathes, tap grinders, or emery- or diamond-faced grinding wheels. The master tap is the piece that sets the markings or shape on the die. The die is used as a reverse image which the final shapes will be created from. After the master tap is made, it is often used to thread a master die. Tap-and-die maker technicians use the master taps and dies and other machine tools to make working taps and dies. They also heat-treat and anneal the finished parts to harden them. After the job, or as needed, technicians remove, dress (clear and refurbish), and then install emery-charged, diamond-charged, and diamond-impregnated cast-iron grinding wheels.

Requirements

Tap-and-die maker technicians are very specialized craft workers. People interested in such a career need to have from one to four years of post–high-school technical training to qualify for this work. They need to have mathematical skills at least through algebra and plane geometry, as well as an excellent working knowledge of shop math. Their language skills should enable them to read technical manuals and operating instructions, and they should be able to read and follow specifications and blueprints.

Conditions of work

The work of tap-and-die maker technicians is performed indoors in generally pleasant surroundings, although fumes generated by the heat of the grinding process may be irritating at times. Little lifting or carrying is required. Good visual acuity and steady hands are needed, especially for close work.

GOE: 05.05.07; SIC: 354; SOC: 6811, 7322

◇ **RELATED ARTICLES**

Volume 1: Machining and Machinery
Volume 2: Numerical control tool programmers
Volume 3: Heat treaters; Job and die setters; Machine tool operators; Patternmakers; Tool makers and die makers; Watch repairers
Volume 4: Industrial engineering technicians

Textile technicians

Definition

Textile technicians assist in producing textiles and making apparel goods and other products. They may work in textile research, design, development, production, or service.

Textile technicians work in either of two broad areas: textile manufacturing or apparel manufacturing. *Textile manufacturing technicians* specialize in the nature and character of textile fibers and their processing into yarn and fabrics. They understand the steps in spinning, weaving, knitting, bonding, dyeing, and finishing, and they are experienced in testing fibers and textiles for tensile strength, heat resistance, crease resiliency, and laundering durability. Textile manufacturing technicians are familiar with textile production machines and the methods for making, marking, packaging, storing, and shipping textiles.

Apparel manufacturing technicians specialize in clothing design and production. They are familiar with the production methods used to make apparel and other textile goods. These include computer-controlled production, pattern analysis, machine evaluation, work measurement, heat setting, and warehouse and inventory control. They have an expert knowledge of fabrics—how each must be laid out, marked, cut, sewn, formed, finished, inspected, packaged, stored, and shipped. They are knowledgeable in computer-controlled automatic knitting-machine production of sweaters and other knit goods. Garment-size grading, which is the way the proportions of a garment must be graded during a size change, is a difficult and important part of their work.

History

The growth of the textile industry started with the primitive collection and processing of natural fibers into yarn, and the hand weaving or knitting of clothing and other products. When the Industrial Revolution began, textiles manufacturing was one of the first areas of manufacturing to be affected by the development of new machines. Everybody needed clothes and fabrics. But the earlier processes of making them by hand had taken so much time and effort that even a little mechanization made a great difference in cost.

Two hundred years ago, almost no cloth was manufactured in the United States; most was imported from England. The textile industry was so important to England by that time that neither drawings of textile machines nor the mechanics who operated them were allowed to leave the country. In 1789, however, an English textile mechanic named Samuel Slater disguised himself as a farmer and sailed to the United States. He carried the details of the machinery in his head. A few years later, he opened a spinning mill in Pawtucket, Rhode Island. His efforts helped lay the groundwork for America's industrial revolution.

The first synthetic fibers were developed more than seventy-five years ago. Since then, synthetics have improved the function and versatility of textiles, changed how people lived,

and helped to improve the quality of life. New fibers and finishes have made caring for clothes less time-consuming and less costly. Stretch fabrics have kept pace with active sports and leisure interests. Durable, soil-resistant carpets cover the floors of U.S. homes, schools, offices, and hospitals. The car industry uses textiles in seat belts, upholstery and carpeting, and reinforcement of tires, belts, and hoses.

New properties have been engineered into fibers and fabrics so that textiles now are used in medical dressings and bacteria-resistant hospital gowns, in artificial veins and arteries, in space suits and in flame-resistant coats for fire fighters. They are also used in cables for deep-sea oil-drilling rigs and in reinforced boat hulls, in road building and industrial plant filters. The military uses textiles in a myriad of items, from rifle slings and body armor to parachutes and uniforms that resist infrared rays.

Production of this wide variety of goods creates employment for approximately two million people in the United States. The textile industry is one of the largest employers of women and minorities. It has also long been an entry-level employer and training ground for unskilled men and women entering industry.

The textile industry is located in nearly every state. Fiber, either natural or man-made, is produced in forty-five states; textile mill products are made in thirty-three states; and apparel is made in forty-four states. The industry began in New England, where water power was abundant and workers were available. In the past five decades, however, the textile industry has grown rapidly in the southern states. Today, companies in three states—North Carolina, South Carolina, and Georgia—employ more than half of all U.S. textile workers.

During the past decade or so, the U.S. textile industry has been forced by intense foreign competition to improve its already highly developed technology and processing methods. Because the textile market in this country is so large, it has attracted textile and apparel imports from Japan, Hong Kong, Korea, Taiwan, China, and other countries. In response to this competition, the industry has undergone the most revolutionary changes in its history.

Open-end spinning, for instance, is a new technique that boosts the rate of production of yarn four times over the older spinning technique. It has also reduced the steps in manufacturing yarn from as many as fifteen to as few as three.

Until recently, fabric was woven with a wooden shuttle moving back and forth across a loom. Now yarns are propelled by air or water jets that yield three times the speed and can

A textile technician in the apparel industry must be familiar with all aspects of the industry from fabric selection to cutting, sewing, and shipping.

through the use of thousands of tiny dye jets individually controlled by computer.

Better utilization of human effort in the industry through better management is also a part of the modernization of the textile industry. "Quality circles," which are groups of workers, technicians, and managers, meet regularly to discuss and plan how to improve the quality and efficiency in their department. All of these efforts to improve methods and efficiency and to better compete in the world markets have produced a need for highly qualified technicians to assist scientists and engineers and act as links with production workers.

Nature of the work

Textile technicians can work in three major areas: research and development, quality control and production, and customer service and sales.

In research and development, technicians help to develop new techniques to process standard fibers, find new uses for standard fibers, or adapt new fibers to new products. Although technicians may devote some time to basic research under the direction of scientists, engineers and managers, they usually work on finding new applications.

To carry on their work, textile technicians need a thorough knowledge of the textile processes. They may have to analyze a fabric for fiber type, construction, color, ease of weaving, or mildew resistance, and then improve it.

Technicians in quality control and production must measure every major characteristic of the raw fiber material: fiber strength, elongation, chemical resistance, length and length distribution, diameter, condition, and character. Similarly, yarn properties such as evenness, elongation, and grade must be determined. There are about 130 million cotton fibers per pound, for instance, and making that number of fibers into a pound of yarn ten, twenty, or thirty miles long must be performed under strict quality control. Further, the finished fabrics must meet exacting standards of strength, weight, thickness, water and/or air permeability, color abrasion resistance, wrinkle resistance, and tear strength. Similarly, apparel manufacturing technicians must check every step of garment production.

Production technicians supervise the output of a department section, an entire department, or more than one department. Such technicians are well trained in quality control. Their job also requires a special talent for directing

produce seven to eight times the fabric. They are also safer and quieter.

In the other major fabric area, knitting, recent developments have been made in electronic knitting machines. This technology may be the most important development in sweater production in decades. With electronic machines, a sweater design is transferred to a computer tape that operates the machine automatically. The present generation of electronic knitting machines can produce a newly designed sweater in two to three hours. With the previous generation of knitting machines, the process took as long as a week and was not nearly as accurate.

In the apparel industry, where labor is a major part of the cost, technology is also advancing. Because of the intricacies of working with a limp, flexible fabric, the process of automation has been much harder.

The traditional art of marking a clothing pattern on fabric and cutting it to form the pieces of a garment has undergone technological change. A computerized marker-maker and cutting system has been developed that has brought the apparel industry into present-day high technology.

Other types of research and development have occurred. One leading textile company has developed a machine that applies complex colors and patterns to carpets and other fabrics the people who carry out all the operations that are required to make the end product.

Textile technicians who specialize in quality control help by making regular tests of the product at various stages. They determine the cause of variations in quality and correct them before the product falls below standards.

Both production and quality control technicians need to understand the details of the scientific principles underlying the making of textile products. They must also know how the manufacturing and testing equipment operates and on occasions operate the machinery or perform the tests themselves. They also teach new operators.

In customer sales and service, textile technicians may work in direct selling or in customer service. Both areas require an intimate knowledge of production and quality control, as well as considerable traveling and an outgoing personality.

Within these three broad areas of activity of textile technicians, specific jobs will have titles that vary somewhat from plant to plant. However, the following descriptions of entry-level positions are representative of those generally available to textile technicians.

General laboratory technicians test cloth samples and chemically analyze fiber blends. Evenness tester technicians operate electronic testers, analyze the results, and report needed changes in machine settings to the appropriate department. This is a critical quality-control task requiring a high order of skill, intelligence, and reliability.

Dye-lab technicians use sample dyeing equipment to dye sample cloth according to dye formulas in order to verify that products meet company specifications. They calculate the amount of dye required for machines of different capacities, and they weigh and mix dyes and other chemicals, using scales, graduated cylinders, and titration cylinders.

Production control technicians who work in either textile production or apparel production gather data and make the calculations necessary to keep materials flowing smoothly through the various production departments. *Job study technicians* conduct time and motion studies, establish fair job loads and piece rates, and make recommendations to management on work sequence, layout, and processes such as cutting and automation.

While the above job titles do represent basic areas in which technicians may begin their career in textiles, prospective technicians must bear in mind that large plants subdivide such duties among several technicians to accommodate the volume of production. Technicians in smaller plants may have a modest amount of work to do in each of many areas.

Requirements

Textile technicians must be broadly prepared, systems-oriented technicians. They must be able to work with a wide variety of textile fibers and fabrics. Their work also involves equipment for producing textiles and apparel. Recent refinements and use of computers have made this equipment some of today's most technologically complex machinery. Textile technicians must have an understanding of the technical disciplines that support this kind of machinery.

Prospective technicians must have a practical understanding of physics, chemistry, and mathematics. They must also be able to communicate in written and spoken presentations to both technical specialists and persons not trained in the field.

At least two years of formal education beyond high school in a technical institute, technical college, or community college is the best preparation for this career. High-school students who plan to enter a technical program in textiles should take four years of English and at least two years of mathematics, including algebra and geometry. Courses in physics and chemistry that include laboratory work are also very important preparation. High-school courses in computers and mechanical drafting and design are most valuable.

The first year of a typical two-year associate degree program for textile manufacturing technicians includes courses in current fabric manufacture, natural and synthetic fibers, English composition, industrial organization and management, public speaking, applied physics, yarn manufacturing, apparel and home furnishings, algebra, trigonometry, advanced English composition, advanced yarn manufacturing, industrial safety, textile testing, and textile cost analysis.

Second-year courses for textile manufacturing technicians might include textile quality control, general psychology, textile merchandising, engineering graphics, computer programming, fundamentals of supervision, economics, weaving and fabric analysis, managerial communications, finishing mill operations, and chemistry.

A typical two-year associate degree program for apparel manufacturing technicians begins with textile processes, employee selection and training, algebra, trigonometry, English composition, business composition, technical

A textile technician operates a machine that winds strands of yarn onto spools for weaving.

writing, engineering drawing, pattern analysis and drafting, analytical geometry, industrial organization and management, apparel manufacture, and cutting-room analysis.

For apparel manufacturing technicians, second-year courses include mechanics, electricity, and magnetism; physics, including heat, sound, and light; computer programming; machine evaluation and selection; apparel production planning; pressing and finishing; industrial statistics; managerial accounting; methods of work analysis; work management; textile testing and control; and plant engineering.

In some programs, the summer between the first and second years is devoted to an internship or cooperative education session which is spent working as a paid employee of a textile company.

In addition to educational requirements, certain personal qualifications are needed to be successful in this career. The ability to work with others and to accept supervision is most important. Textile technicians must also learn to work independently and accept responsibility for their work. They must be accurate and careful workers.

Physical requirements for this career are not especially demanding. The normal physical strength possessed by most men and women is sufficient. Normal sight and hearing are needed, and average or better hand-eye coordination and manual dexterity are required. Color blindness can be a serious disadvantage for textile technicians.

Special requirements

There are no special certificates, licenses, or other requirements that need to be met by textile technicians.

Opportunities for experience and exploration

Persons considering entry into this career can obtain considerable information from guidance centers in high schools, community colleges, or technical institutions. Occupational information centers and catalogs of schools that offer programs for textile technicians are also good sources of information.

Guidance counselors can obtain excellent descriptive materials and audiovisual presentations on the textile industry from the American Textile Manufacturer's Institute. If it is possible, a visit to a producing textile factory makes it possible to observe the machinery and work and gives prospective technicians an opportunity to talk to workers and to get an idea about the work. One of the best opportunities for experience is a summer job with a textile company, preferably in some activity closely related to the actual production operations.

Methods of entering

Graduate textile technicians are often hired by recruiters from the major employers in the field. Recruiters regularly visit schools with textile technician programs and arrange interviews with graduating students through the school's placement center.

Some students, however, attend school under the sponsorship of a textile company and usually go to work for their sponsor after graduation. Some are cooperative students who attend school with the understanding that they will return to their sponsor plant. Some companies, however, do not place any restriction on their co-op students and leave them free to find the best job they can find. Students may also write to or visit potential employers that are of special interest.

The two-year college curriculum condenses the traditional four-year textile engineering program, yet it includes the basics that industry needs. Many employers have a strong preference for graduates of the two-year program, and give such graduates a short, intensive in-plant orientation and training program so that they can be placed where their skills can be used immediately. Many graduate technicians who participated in a cooperative program are given responsible positions immediately upon graduation. Some in-plant training programs are designed to train new technicians to work as supervisors.

Advancement

Opportunities for advancement are excellent for textile technicians. They may become section supervisors, production superintendents, or plant managers. Not all technicians, however, are suited for the production floor. Those persons can advance to responsible positions in industrial engineering, quality control, production control, or specialized technical areas.

One advanced position is that of fabric development specialist. Technicians in this position help translate the designer's ideas into a new fabric. This work requires an expert knowledge of textile manufacturing processes and machinery. Fabric development specialists are employed by textile fiber producers or textile knitting or weaving firms. They may further advance to the position of fabric development stylist and finally to the management level.

Other advanced positions include *textile converter*, who decides the ways textile materials are to be dyed or printed; *textile dyeing and finishing specialist*; *quality-control analyst*; *textile purchasing agent*; and *technical service representative*.

Some technicians may become *plant training specialists* or *plant safety experts and directors*. Safety training on the job is important in textile and apparel manufacturing and is an attractive and satisfying career.

With the recent technological improvements in the textile industry, the opportunities have increased for technical specialists to work as self-employed consultants or to start their own businesses.

Employment outlook

For the foreseeable total textile employment is expected to grow more slowly than the industry's output. Labor-saving machinery and synthetic fibers have increased worker productivity, and management will probably rely more and more on computers to control production.

Although this advanced equipment will limit the number of machinery operators, the demand for professional and managerial personnel will continue to grow. Skilled craft workers, such as knitter machine mechanics and dyers, will become more essential as textile machines become more complex. New technologies, such as computer-controlled processing and instrumentation, will require more textile technicians and computer specialists. The industry's demand for engineers, managers, and chemists also will grow, responding to federal safety and health regulations as well as the need for continuing scientific research and development. More technicians will probably be needed to assist them.

Earnings

Graduates of two-year postsecondary textile manufacturing technician programs with little or no previous textile experience earn beginning yearly salaries ranging from $14,000 to $20,000. Graduates of apparel manufacturing technician programs earn salaries ranging from $14,000 to $25,000.

After four to six years of experience, textile manufacturing technicians usually advance to salaries of $20,000 to $25,000 per year. Apparel manufacturing technicians advance to salaries that are equivalent or slightly higher.

After ten to twenty years of advancement to top-level positions, persons who started as technicians can earn annual salaries up to and above $40,000.

Textile technicians usually receive the benefits of salaried staff such as paid holidays, vacations, group insurance benefits, and employee retirement plans. In addition, they often have the benefit of company support for all or a part of educational programs. This is an important benefit because these technicians must continually study to keep up to date with technological changes in this rapidly developing field.

Conditions of work

The textile industry of today is a comparatively safe industry and one that grows more comfortable every year. Textile plants have temperature and humidity controls that outdo those in most homes and apartments. Heavy lifting is now handled by machines. The new plant is typically a one-story building, clean, well-lighted, smaller than its counterpart a few years ago, and vastly more efficient. The industry places great emphasis on safety, cleanliness, and orderliness.

Social and psychological factors

The work of textile technicians, whether they work in textile manufacturing or apparel manufacturing, involves a succession of problems that are highly technical in nature in a wide variety of situations. Technicians must define each problem, gather pertinent information, use the appropriate measurements and methods to obtain accurate data, analyze the facts, and arrive at a solution to the problem through logic and judgment. This process may involve consultation with scientists, engineers, or managers. All of this requires patience, resourcefulness, and the ability to work calmly and systematically for extended periods of time. It also requires constant study of the new developments in the field.

These technicians can enjoy a deep sense of satisfaction as problem solvers in an industry that provides cloth, fabrics, and garments. The textiles they produce for many applications have qualities and characteristics that are not understood by the user but that add immeasurably to their quality of life.

GOE: 02.04.01, 05.01.08; SIC: 22; SOC: 3719, 3831, 389

◇ **SOURCES OF ADDITIONAL INFORMATION**

American Association for Textile Technology
295 Fifth Avenue, Room 621
New York, NY 10016

American Apparel Manufacturers Association
2500 Wilson Boulevard, Suite 301
Arlington, VA 22201

American Textile Manufacturers Institute
1801 K Street, NW, Suite 900
Washington, DC 20006

National Council for Textile Education
PO Box 391
Charlottesville, VA 22902

◇ **RELATED ARTICLES**

Volume 1: Engineering; Textiles
Volume 2: Engineers
Volume 3: Knit goods industry workers; Textile manufacturing occupations
Volume 4: Chemical technicians; Industrial engineering technicians; Quality-control technicians

Traffic technicians

Definition

Traffic technicians conduct field studies to determine what factors influence traffic conditions on roads and streets and to what extent they do so.

Nature of the work

Traffic technicians interview motorists at intersections where traffic is often congested, or where an unusual number of accidents has occurred. They use radar equipment or timing devices to determine the speed of passing vehicles at certain locations, and they use stopwatches to time traffic signals and other delays to traffic.

Technicians also observe such general traffic influences as street lighting, visibility of signs, the angle of entrances to and exits from traffic flow, signal locations, and other factors that may affect how well traffic moves. They apply standardized mathematical formulas to certain measurements to compute traffic signal duration and speed limits, and they prepare drawings showing the location of new signals or other traffic control devices. They may perform statistical studies of traffic conditions, flow, and volume, and may—on the basis of such studies—recommend changes in traffic controls and regulations.

Requirements

Persons interested in careers as traffic technicians should have mathematical skills through training in algebra, logic and geometry, and a good working, knowledge of statistics. They should have language skills that will enable them to write extensive reports making use of statistical data, and they should be able to present such reports before groups of people. To begin such a career, applicants should have at least two years of vocational preparation beyond high school.

Conditions of work

Traffic technicians perform their duties both indoors and outdoors, under a variety of conditions. They are subject to the noise of heavy traffic while gathering data for some of their studies, but their calculations and analyses are performed in the quiet of an office.

GOE: 05.03.06; SIC: 8748; SOC: 399

Water and wastewater treatment technicians

Definition

Water and wastewater treatment technicians inspect, study, and survey water and wastewater treatment systems to ensure that pollution control requirements are met. They evaluate both existing structures that are being repaired or modified and new construction projects that are in progress or just completed.

Nature of the work

Technicians review plans and specifications to check details and review general specifications such as size and location of units, capacities, strength of reinforcing materials, and length of piping to ensure conformity to construction requirements. To monitor water supplies, they set up and maintain equipment that obtains samples and gathers flow measurements and other data. They survey streams and perform studies of basin areas to determine water availability. As part of their work assisting engineers, technicians prepare graphs, tables, sketches, and diagrams to illustrate survey data. They file plans and documents, answer public inquiries, assist in training new personnel, and perform various other support duties.

Requirements

People interested in careers as water and wastewater treatment technicians should obtain a

A water and wastewater technician checks water samples from units at a water treatment plant. The water must meet certain standards before it is released into the environment.

statistics. They should be able to read scientific material comfortably and be able to prepare reports containing statistics and other supporting documentation. Water and wastewater treatment technicians should also have some physical science education that includes studies of the properties of water and the environmental influence on water paths and composition.

After high school, they should plan to obtain at least two years of specialized training at a technical institute or community college. The training should include courses in engineering drawing, technical writing, environmental studies, and water-treatment systems.

The work of these technicians is not strenuous, but it does require manual dexterity and good visual acuity, especially when reading detailed statistics and drawings.

GOE: 05.03.08; SIC: 4952; SOC: 3719

◇ **RELATED ARTICLES**

Volume 1: Engineering; Waste Management
Volume 2: Health and regulatory inspectors
Volume 3: Wastewater treatment plant operators
Volume 4: Civil engineering technicians; Pollution-control technicians

---

solid high-school background in mathematics and communications skills. They should be able to work basic algebra problems and be familiar with the mathematics of probability and

Weapons and ammunition technicians

Definition

Weapons and ammunition technicians test and evaluate the performance of firearms and ammunition (including explosives) under controlled conditions. The work requires precise measurements and observations, and adherence to established safety and testing procedures. Performance of a weapon or explosive under varying conditions determines its effectiveness.

Nature of the work

They experiment with new types of ammunition, firearms, and methods of firing ammunition and explosives, working under the direction of engineers and ordnance experts. They set up heavy weapons and connect electrical apparatus that controls the test-firing of weapons. They mount small weapons in bench devices and rig remote trigger-pulling equipment. They load, aim, and fire weapons, measuring gun-barrel pressures, muzzle velocities, and accuracy, using special laboratory equipment and high-speed photography. They heat, refrigerate, and soak ammunition in water before test-firing it, to test performance under adverse conditions.

Technicians also prepare and detonate bombs and mines, both on land and underwater. They load aerial bombs into airplanes that will test-drop them. Firing and evaluation of weapons and explosives is done remotely by electronic sensors and photographic recording equipment. Technicians also are responsible for recording test findings and reporting them to supervising engineers and scientists.

Requirements

Prospective technicians should be prepared to take as many mathematics and science courses as possible in high school—at least through solid geometry and basic physics—and to spend one to two years in post–high-school studies in engineering technology, physics, mechanics, and mathematics. They should be

skilled enough in language to read technical manuals and articles and to write technical reports on their tests.

Conditions of work

The work of weapons and ammunition technicians is not strenuous, but they are subject to loud sounds and strong vibrations during test-firings.

GOE: 02.04.01; SIC: 3484; SOC: 399

◇ **RELATED ARTICLES**

Volume 1: Military Services
Volume 2: Engineers
Volume 3: Gunsmiths
Volume 4: Product test technicians; Quality-control technicians

---

Welding technicians

Definition

Welding technicians supervise, inspect, and help develop and find applications for a wide variety of welding processes. Some welding technicians work in research facilities and assist engineers in testing and evaluating newly developed welding equipment, metals, and alloys. These technicians conduct experiments and evaluate data concerning applications of new equipment or improved techniques and make recommendations to engineering personnel regarding their findings. Other welding technicians, working in the field, inspect welded joints and conduct tests to ensure that welds meet company standards, national code requirements, and customer job specifications. These technicians record inspection and test results, prepare and submit reports to welding engineers, and conduct certification tests for the qualification of welding personnel according to national code requirements.

History

The origins of modern welding reach back thousands of years. Archaeological evidence suggests that primitive forms of welding were known even in prehistoric times. Ancient Egyptians practiced a form of welding similar to our gas welding in which they employed a blowpipe and a flame from burning alcohol to heat the metal surfaces to be welded.

During the nineteenth century, new methods for joining two pieces of metal were developed and existing methods were refined. Resistance welding was developed in the laboratory of James Prescott Joule in 1857. In this method, the metal parts to be joined are pressed together, and a surge of electrical current is sent through the metal at the point of contact. The combination of pressure and heat formed by electrical resistance results in the formation of a solid welded nugget that holds together the pieces of metal.

This method was not perfected until 1886 because of the lack of sufficient electrical power.

Thermite welding, which fuses two pieces of metal by means of thermite (a mixture of aluminum and iron oxide), was first used in 1898.

Arc welding, a process of fusing metal by means of heat generated from an electrical arc, was developed experimentally in 1881 and was used commercially in 1889.

Gas welding uses the heat of burning gas, such as acetylene or natural gas, and oxygen. Although oxygen was identified in 1774 and acetylene in 1836, the effect of joining the two gases was not discovered until 1895, when improved methods of commercial production of acetylene and oxygen were developed. The year 1903 marks the beginning of the commercial use of the oxyacetylene process in welding and cutting.

During the twentieth century these methods were further improved and dozens of new methods developed. In addition to the methods already mentioned, two other methods in common use are brazing and induction welding. In brazing, a filler metal is heated along with the metal surfaces and flows into a specially prepared joint. Induction welding uses an induction coil that generates heat and is very efficient for certain shapes such as small-diameter, thin-walled steel tubing.

Nature of the work

The welding technician is the link between the welder and the engineer or production manager. Welding technicians fill positions as supervisors, inspectors, experimental technicians, sales technicians, assistants to welding engineers, and welding analysts.

Some beginning welding technicians are employed as welding operators. They perform manual, automatic, or semi-automatic welding jobs. They set up work, read blueprints and welding-control symbols, and follow specifications set up for a welded product.

As welding inspectors, welding technicians judge the quality of incoming materials, such as electrodes, and of welding work being done. They accept or reject pieces of work according to required standards set forth in codes and specifications. A welding inspector must be able to read blueprints, interpret requirements, and have a knowledge of testing equipment and methods. Closely related to this work is that of the welding qualification technician. This person keeps records of certified welders and supervises tests for qualification of welding operators.

Other welding technicians work as welding process-control technicians. These technicians set up the procedures for welders to follow in various production jobs. They specify welding techniques, types of filler wire to be used, ranges for welding electrodes, and time estimates. Welding technicians also provide instructions concerning welding-control symbols on blueprints, use of jigs and fixtures, and inspection of products.

Equipment maintenance and sales technicians work out of welding supply houses. They troubleshoot equipment for customers, set up equipment sold by their companies, and train welding operators to use the new equipment.

Welding technicians also work as technical writers. In this position, they work closely with professional staff members to prepare reports and to develop articles for the technical or professional press. They may also work for house organs or for technical or professional magazines.

After more years of experience, welding technicians may be employed as welding analysts and estimators, welding engineering assistants, or welding equipment or product salespeople. Welding analysts and estimators analyze all factors involved in a job such as labor, material, and overhead to determine the cost of the job. Welding engineering assistants test welded metal parts, analyze differences in designs for a variety of welded structures, and determine the effect of welding on a variety of metals. Welding equipment or product salespeople are responsible for selling and servicing welded products, for distributing welding materials or equipment, and for all phases of customer relations.

Some senior welding technicians may eventually advance to positions as welding supervisors, welding instructors, and welding production managers.

Requirements

Welding technicians should enjoy working with their hands as well as doing research work. They must be able to use drawing instruments and gauges, perform laboratory tests, and supervise and control machinery and test equipment. Additionally, they are required to collect data and assemble it into written reports. Because welding technicians work with management as well as with production personnel, they must have a sense of responsibility and the ability to get along with people.

High-school students who are interested in welding technology should have a good background in English, mathematics, and science, preferably physics or chemistry, or both. Courses that teach composition and communications skills are particularly important to the prospective technician. Shop courses will also prove helpful.

Most prospective welding technicians should plan to complete a two-year, post–high-school, associate degree program. Generally, the minimum requirements for such a program are one year of algebra, one year of geometry, and a year of physics or chemistry with laboratory experience. The Armed Forces also provide a welding technician training program.

Students who concentrate on welding technology in a technical institute or community college should take comprehensive courses in welding practice or theory. Students should also take at least one course in applied physics, covering mechanics, heat, light, and elementary electricity. They need to learn the technical knowledge and laboratory skills in materials and metallurgy, so that they understand metals common in industry, basic metal production and fabrication techniques, and structures, physical and chemical properties, and uses of metals.

Welding technicians should understand lattice structure, alloy systems, mechanical tests, and characteristics of strength, elasticity, ductility, malleability, and heat treatment. Elementary chemistry, which relates to metallurgy, is usually covered in metallurgical class and laboratory study.

Another area of training helpful to the welding technician is a course in metal shaping, forming, and machine-shop practice. Knowledge of drilling, tapping, reaming, shaping, and lathe and mill operation is useful. In addition, welding technicians should have some training in electronics. They may be called upon to read an electrical wiring diagram for a particular piece of equipment or to check the voltage on a machine. Courses in nondestructive testing could also be helpful for the prospective welding technicians.

Special requirements

Welding technicians may qualify for certification as engineering technicians. In addition, they may be certified under any of the many certification programs conducted for welders; however, certification is usually not required for technicians who do not perform actual production welding.

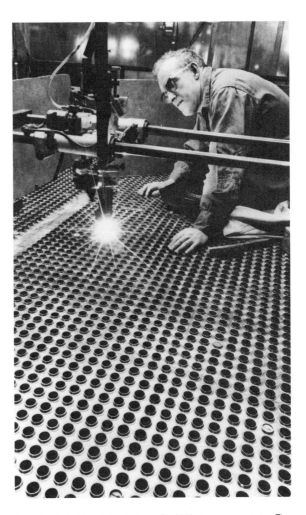

A welding technician makes leak-proof welds in a steam generator. The generator, containing about thirty-nine miles of tubing, is used in a nuclear power plant.

Opportunities for experience and exploration

In high school, a student has several ways of exploring the welding occupations. Shop courses often offer some welding, as well as instruction in basic principles of electricity, drafting, and blueprint reading.

To observe welders or welding technicians at work, students may arrange to take field trips to manufacturing companies that use various welding processes to get an overall view of working conditions and the type of work performed.

Methods of entering

Students who graduate from schools with accredited programs in engineering technology

A welding technician performs an ultrasonic examination on a piece of tubing to ensure uniformity in the welding of the product.

ance and see that operations are performed correctly and economically. Other technicians become welding instructors and teach the theory of welding as well as the techniques of welding and related processes. Finally, some technicians advance to the position of welding production manager and are responsible for all aspects of welding production, including equipment, materials, process control, inspection, and cost control.

Employment outlook

The variety of jobs open to welding technicians in industry is increasing because of the great number of new inventions and technical processes using an even wider variety of metals, alloys, and nonmetallic materials that can be joined by welding processes.

Most welding technicians work in industrial production settings, and as such the actual number of welding technicians employed will be influenced by economic conditions. However, anticipated modest industrial expansion through the 1990s and the increasing complexity of modern technology suggest an increased need for all kinds of engineering technicians, including welding technicians, especially for those capable of assisting in the search for and development of new and technically advanced products, equipment, and procedures.

Employment can be found in practically any industry: aircraft, appliances, automobiles, food processing plants, guided missiles, nuclear energy, radio, railroads, shipbuilding, structural engineering, and television. This diversity of industries in which welding technicians are employed helps cushion the welding technician against possible threats to employment caused by economic downturns for a particular industry. If economic conditions, and hence employment opportunities, turn unfavorable in one industry in which a welding technician is employed or is seeking employment, there remain other industries to turn to that require the welding technician's training and experience.

seldom have problems in finding employment. Employers usually keep in close contact with such schools and often hire able students before graduation.

The transition from school to industry can be a challenging one. Most graduates of two-year welding technician programs enter industry as welding operators or as assistants to welding engineers or welding production managers. This experience can be the foundation for future problem-solving and growth on the job, and it gives the graduate technician a chance to apply both practice and theory. Welding technology programs, by providing a broad theoretical and practical base, enable the prospective technician to adapt to specialized and diverse positions with different companies and to adjust to technological changes as they occur.

Advancement

As welding technicians gain in experience they become eligible for higher-paying jobs. Advancement is most likely to go to those who have displayed a sense of personal initiative, especially in attending courses, seminars, and technical meetings that help broaden their knowledge and prepare them for more responsible positions.

With higher-paying jobs comes greater responsibility. Some welding technicians, for instance, become welding supervisors and take on the responsibility for assigning jobs to workers and showing them how the tasks should be performed. They must supervise job perform-

Earnings

The salary range for welding technicians will vary according to job function, geographical location, and level of education. In general, however, starting salaries for those who are graduates of post–high-school technical programs average $16,000 to $18,000 per year in industry.

Salaries will increase with experience. Most graduates of technical or other recognized institutions offering technical training earn salaries that range from $20,000 to $30,000 per year after five years on the job.

Conditions of work

Welding technicians are employed by a variety of industries, ranging from aircraft manufacturers to heavy-equipment plants. Working conditions vary from clean, well-lighted research and testing laboratories to laying pipeline in the extreme heat of the desert or the extreme cold of Alaska.

Social and psychological factors

In terms of both training and responsibility technicians occupy a position between the professionally trained scientist or engineer and the skilled trade worker. Although no position carries with it the promise of complete happiness, many welding technicians have found that this position offers them status and security, steady employment, and the opportunity to travel.

GOE: 05.01.01; SIC: 1799; SOC: 3719

◇ **SOURCES OF ADDITIONAL INFORMATION**

American Welding Society
PO Box 351040
550 LeJeune Road, NW
Miami, FL 33135

American Welding Institute
10628 Dutchtown Road
Knoxville, TN 37932

Edison Welding Institute
110 Kinnear Road
Columbus, OH 43212

◇ **RELATED ARTICLES**

Volume 1: Construction; Metals
Volume 3: Construction workers; Sheet-metal workers; Structural-steel workers; Welders
Volume 4: Architectural and building construction technicians; Industrial engineering technicians; Metallurgical technicians; Nuclear power plant quality control technicians; Quality-control technicians

Agriculture, Forestry, and Conservation Technician Occupations

Agriculture, forestry, and conservation activities have always occupied a central position in human affairs. From very ancient times, humankind has sought ways to cooperate with and control the natural world to meet human needs. Long ago, people learned to foster the growth of living things to provide food and other products, and they began to understand how to conserve or change natural resources, including plants and animals, to assure that future needs could be met. After many centuries of relatively slow evolution, these basic human activities have been radically transformed in the last hundred years or so. Scientific research into improved products, materials, and methods; increasing mechanization; and the adoption of better business techniques by farmers, foresters, and conservationists and by those who buy and sell goods and services to and from them—all of these have contributed to creating an unprecedented level of productivity in agriculture and forestry. Today fewer workers produce more food and forest products for more people than ever before; however, they are supported by a widening array of people in related fields and activities, such as equipment manufacturers, seed and fertilizer companies, food-processing firms, and agricultural extension agencies. In all of these areas, trained technicians play a crucial role in the ongoing effort to produce more products at less cost than ever before.

Agriculture, forestry, and conservation technicians are specially trained assistants who work with farmers, agricultural scientists, government agencies, equipment manufacturers, and many kinds of companies that buy, sell, distribute, or process agricultural and forestry products. Their usual role is to provide some kind of specialized service to their employer. Often this service involves the application of a new or well-established form of technology or the application of the results of scientific research to some aspect of agriculture, forestry,

or conservation work. Many technicians, for instance, work in the area of measurement and testing. This area includes laboratory work for agricultural, forestry, or conservation scientists, design testing for agriculture equipment manufacturers, and inspecting agricultural and forest products for government agencies and food-processing companies.

Other technicians may be involved in the repair and maintenance or in the selling of agricultural or forestry equipment. Some technicians work as supervisors of other farm or forest workers, or as liaison people between food-processing companies or other large purchasers of agricultural or forest products and the independent farm or forest operators who produce those products. Technicians also work for state and county agricultural extension agencies offering advice and information to farmers.

In all of these settings, agriculture, forestry, and conservation technicians need to be able to evaluate situations, to call upon a fund of specialized information, and to carry out appropriate tasks. For the most part, these responsibilities require that agricultural, forestry, and conservation technicians receive training beyond the high school level, usually in a program offered by a two-year vocational, agricultural, or community college and leading to an associate degree in an area of specialization.

The need for such specially trained technicians in the fields of agriculture, forestry, and conservation is the result of the very same developments that have served to transform agriculture, forestry and conservation into the sophisticated endeavors that they are today, namely more mechanization, more scientific research, and better business practices. The history of all three of these developments can probably be traced back more than 10,000 years to the birth of agriculture; however, the history of these developments as they relate to technicians really begins in the nineteenth century.

As late as the beginning of the nineteenth century, 70 percent of the U.S. labor force worked on farms. For the most part they did their farming on the basis of traditional or local customs, without the benefit of agricultural equipment or supply companies, and without any well-developed national or even regional distribution networks. Most food that was produced on the farm was consumed on the farm, with only a little left over to sell to bring in enough cash to buy those essentials that could not be made on the farm. And most of what was used on the farm, in terms of equipment and supplies, was also made on the farm, since the small amounts of cash that farmers did have did not go very far. In short, the farm of this period was, in many respects, a self-contained unit.

In many respects it was the Industrial Revolution of the late eighteenth century that contributed most to the great changes that would affect agriculture. At a very basic level, the Industrial Revolution encouraged people to think about the jobs they were doing and to consider finding better ways of doing them. Thomas Jefferson, a farmer as well as a politician and statesman, is an example of someone who felt this urge. His inventiveness led him to devise a new kind of seed drill, a threshing machine, a brake for separating the fibers of hemp, a sidehill plow, and an improved plow blade for moving soil more efficiently.

The best-known invention from this period was the cotton gin created by Eli Whitney to separate cotton seeds from fibers that cling to them. An equally important invention dating from the early part of the nineteenth century was the mechanical reaper. Several inventors had a hand in developing the mechanical reaper; however, it was Cyrus McCormick who was most successful in this effort. By 1851, McCormick was producing approximately 1,000 reapers a year. The success of this reaper and other horse-powered devices encouraged a trend toward machines that do not depend on human muscle power. A corn cultivator and a hay and grain rake, both drawn by horses, were also developed during the first half of the nineteenth century.

The same drive towards increased mechanization also had its effects on forestry. Early settlers in this country relied on forests that they had cleared to make room for homes and farms to provide the wood they needed. As machines were developed that could cut logs into usable lumber and other wood products more easily and for less cost, more forests were cut down and the demand for forest products increased. This increase in production and de-

mand led to the development of the forest-products industry in this country.

Labor shortages during the Civil War encouraged farmers to invest in these and other forms of mechanization. It was the introduction of the self-propelled tractor in the late nineteenth and early twentieth centuries, however, that led the way to the widespread mechanization of farms and to the need first for mechanics and later for technicians to work for equipment manufacturers, for equipment sales and service agencies, and for farmers using such equipment.

Another significant way in which the Industrial Revolution influenced the development of agriculture and forestry was in its tendency to draw workers away from rural areas and into cities to work in factories. This movement of workers meant that there were fewer workers available for agricultural work and in this way encouraged the adoption of equipment and techniques that would allow crops to be produced more efficiently. The movement also meant that there was a greater market for farm and forest products, as more people became consumers rather than producers of agricultural products. As more and more cities grew in size, new ways for getting farm and forest to markets had to be created. Processing companies grew up, and networks for distribution were created.

By the late nineteenth century, this trend toward giving farmers and foresters the means to produce greater amounts of their products and the markets to sell them in had progressed to the point that other scientific discoveries began to look attractive. By 1910, commercial fertilizer had been demonstrated, although farmers at first resisted adopting it because of its high price. Commercially produced seeds and feeds also came on the market in the early part of the century. It was not until after World War II, however, that their use led to a successful feed and seed industry and to the need for trained technicians to help in the development of new hybrids and other seed, feed, or fertilizer products.

By the early 1900s, it had become apparent that most of the prime timber land available for producing lumber had been cut down. Foresters in this country realized that they needed to follow the conservation and management techniques that were already in use in Europe. This realization led to the development of professional careers in tree genetics, forest-culture research, and forest management.

The concentration of more people in urban areas and the understanding that more and more of the wilderness areas of this country were being given over to agriculture, forestry, or some other kind of economic development led to an increased interest in parks where people could enjoy contact with the natural world. In the 1850s, city planners in New York City created Central Park, the first large landscaped area within a city in the United States. In 1872, President Ulysses S. Grant signed an act of Congress establishing Yellowstone National Park, and in the years that followed, many other areas were set aside for public enjoyment. In 1916, the National Park Service was established to manage the country's national parks, monuments, and historic sites.

Another change occurring in the early part of the twentieth century was an increasing awareness of the need to preserve the natural resources of the land. In 1908, President Theodore Roosevelt created the National Conservation Commission, and many state and local organizations were formed soon thereafter. One aspect of conservation that became important in this period was soil conservation. During World War I and in the years that followed, overcultivation of farmlands, especially in the Midwest, led to depletion of the soil and destruction of much natural ground cover. It was these conditions that led in large part to the disastrous dust storms of the mid-1930s. In 1935, Congress established the Soil Conservation Service, but by that time, more than 800 million tons of topsoil had been blown away.

Since World War II the progress in the areas of agriculture, forestry, and conservation has been especially dramatic. The number of people living and working on farms has continued to drop until now a little more than one percent of the nation's population work as farmers or farm laborers. During the same period, the population of the country has continued to grow. All of this means that fewer workers must produce more farm and forest products. It also means that farmers and business people have had to find new and better ways to transport, process, store, sell, and market farm and forest products. These developments have led us to the point where banks, businesses, government agencies, universities, research institutes, as well as small independent and large corporate farms, all share responsibilities for managing the production of the nation's agricultural and forest products and for conserving the resources required for this production.

Today's technicians may work for any of these institutions or organizations. Technicians interested in the growing or raising of agricultural products usually work for independent or corporate farm operators. Many of these technicians are, of course, interested in someday owning or operating their own farms or ranches or other agricultural or forestry operations. Individual ownership or operation of a farm or ranch, however, often requires considerable financial resources and is always best undertaken by people who have had training and gained extensive experience, often while working for someone else. Employment of this sort allows technicians to earn money, gain a reputation for reliability in their area, establish credit, and develop expertise—all important qualities if one is to become an independent farm operator.

Technicians whose interests in agriculture are not as firmly focused on production operations often find employment in related businesses that buy or sell goods and services to and from farmers. These include companies that manufacture and sell seed, fertilizer, chemicals, farm supplies, and tractors, combines, and other forms of agricultural equipment to farmers and foresters, as well as the companies that buy, process, distribute, and market agricultural and forest products.

Many agriculture, forestry, and conservation technicians work in laboratories doing scientific research for government and industry. This research may be used to provide new or improved food and fibers at lower costs or to improve or conserve species of plants or animals or a natural resource such as soil or water.

Finally, many agriculture, forestry, and conservation technicians work for local, state, or federal government agencies. They may work as produce inspectors or for fish and wildlife commissions. Many technicians work for government agencies involved in managing parks, forests, and other state and national lands set aside for recreation or conservation purposes.

To prepare themselves properly for employment in any of these areas most technicians need to have continued their education beyond the high-school level, usually through a two-year specialized training program in a community, technical, or junior college or in a special division of a four-year college or university.

There are two-year post–high-school training programs designed for students interested in courses in agriculture, forestry, or conservation in every state of the nation. Students interested in a directory of such institutions should write to the United States Department of Education's Office of Vocational and Adult Education at the address listed at the end of this article.

The entrance requirements for these programs vary, so students should investigate the requirements of programs they might be interested in early in their high-school years to assure that they can meet these requirements.

Each of the articles in this section includes information about the kinds of educational preparation technicians should get to be successful in a career in agriculture, forestry, or conservation. What technicians must learn will vary for each career area, and even within a given career area there will be slight differences in sequence and emphasis from school to school. In general, however, students should expect to undertake a full-time, two-year educational program of classroom instruction and supervised practical experience.

The supervised experience usually takes place in the summer between a student's first and second year. The experience allows students to find out firsthand what their chosen work is like on a day-to-day basis. Employers involved in such programs generally make special arrangements to ensure that the students gain the fullest possible understanding of the employer's entire operation. Sometimes a student engaged in this relatively brief supervised occupational experience works at many jobs with the same employer in a preplanned rotation system, thus gaining the broadest possible picture of the occupational area.

One variation on this relatively informal supervised occupational experience is the cooperative work-study plan. In a work-study plan students combine going to school with working for an employer. The program not only helps students meet their financial needs; many students also find that the work helps them in their courses, just as their courses help them in their work. One thing to keep in mind, of course, is that programs involving work-study plans may take longer than two years to complete, depending on whether any academic credit is given for the work experience.

The completion of a two-year post–high-school training program is the basic educational requirement for agriculture, forestry, and conservation technicians. In addition, there are personal characteristics which, even if not required, are certainly shared by most technicians in these fields. Nearly every technician's job in agriculture, forestry, or conservation has something to do with life and living things. It is not surprising then that most technicians in this area, as children, cared for pets, grew plants, or in some active way showed an interest in and curiosity about plants or animals. Through such activities they were able to develop their powers of observation and their abilities to analyze situations. And these skills can lead to the one characteristic that all technicians must have—the ability to apply scientific principles and methods to a given area of interest.

Although there are many indoor jobs performed by agriculture, forestry, and conservation technicians, most technicians share a love of the outdoors. As young people, they may have gone hunting, fishing, or hiking; they may have caught butterflies, been bird-watchers, or simply have been avid readers of magazines and books about outdoor life, earth science, or soil or water conservation.

Many aspects of today's agricultural and forestry operations are highly mechanized. Prospective technicians interested in any of these operations usually have an interest in machines and a fair degree of mechanical aptitude. They know how to use tools and they have an interest in engines, tractors, automobiles, trucks, airplanes, and the like. They enjoy working on them, and they like to watch them working properly.

Agribusiness technicians

Definition

Agribusiness technicians apply their background and training both in business and economics and in agriculture to matters relating to the organization, operation, and management of farms and agricultural businesses. Agribusiness technicians, also called *agricultural business technicians,* work in a wide variety of businesses concerned with the production and propagation of plants and animals, with agricultural supplies and services, and with the processing and marketing of agricultural products.

Agribusiness technicians may also be involved with providing farmers with financial credit, power, fuel, transportation services, and other farm supplies and services. These technicians may also help farmers arrange contracts for the marketing, delivery, and processing of their products.

History

Agribusiness technology is a fairly recent outgrowth of the application of science, technology, and business management techniques to the field of agriculture. As late as the early nineteenth century, there were virtually no agricultural businesses providing farms with goods or services or marketing their products. The typical family farm raised its own horses and oxen, grew its own seed, made its own implements, and built its own buildings, usually from materials at hand. In addition, most of what it produced was consumed by the family itself.

Agricultural businesses began to appear in the middle of the nineteenth century, with the introduction of the reaper and moldboard; however, it was not until the introduction of the self-propelled gasoline tractor in the late nineteenth and early twentieth centuries that supplying farmers with machinery and equipment began to lead the way to the development of agribusiness.

The systematic application of scientific knowledge to the problems of agriculture began to reach significant levels by the late nineteenth century. By 1910, the value of commercial fertilizer had been demonstrated. Farmers still resisted using it because of its high price, but continued research found ways to lower the cost and to improve methods of application—all of this leading to its popular and widespread use today.

Similarly, developments in feed and seed started out slowly in the early part of this century. It was not until after World War II that the scientific feeding of livestock led to a successful commercial feed industry. Genetic developments in creating varieties of seeds, especially for corn, caught on more quickly, and today the seed industry produces seeds for a wide variety of crops.

The business side of agribusiness has profited from the shift by farmers from consuming the goods they grew to selling those products. This shift has created needs for transportation, processing, storing, selling, and marketing. This shift was already well on its way during the nineteenth century; however, new forms of technology and new business strategies have expanded possibilities and continue to create new opportunities and new markets for people involved in the processing, distribution, and selling of farm products.

Thus, because of developments in science, technology, and business techniques during the course of this century, the agricultural business industry has grown from a business supplying farmers with a narrow range of manufactured items, such as tools and harnesses, to a thriving enterprise supplying a wide variety of goods and services needed on the farm. This whole field has grown so rapidly that it is virtually a new area of endeavor for each generation. In fact, the development of this field has been so rapid that the profession of agribusiness technician is still relatively unknown outside of the agricultural community.

Nature of the work

Agribusiness technicians are trained to perform in several very different capacities. The three main areas of employment are the following: management of an agricultural business or of a business closely related to agriculture; sales, services, and distribution; and record keeping.

In the area of business management, technicians can find employment with large farms or farm-service businesses. For instance, they may work as part of a personnel-management office for a large corporate farm or dairy. In such a position, they may be responsible for hiring and firing employees, for coordinating work plans with farm managers, and for the entire structure of salaries for farm or other production workers.

Agribusiness technicians may also be employed by credit institutions to solicit the business of farmers and agricultural business people, to make appraisals of real estate and personal property, to organize and present loan requests, to close loans, and to service those loans with periodic reviews of the borrower's management performance and financial status.

Another employment opportunity is to work in a field capacity for a food company or other business that buys farm products. Two kinds of technicians working in this field are the *dairy production field-contact technician* and the *poultry field-service technician*.

Dairy production field-contact technicians serve as contact people between dairy companies and the farmers who produce the milk the companies buy. They negotiate long- or short-term contracts for purchasing milk and milk products according to agreed specifications. They meet with farmers to test milk for butterfat content, sediment, and bacteria and to discuss methods for solving milk-production problems and for improving milk production. They may, for instance, suggest methods of feeding, housing, and milking to improve production or to comply with sanitary regulations. They may set up truck routes to haul milk to the dairy; solicit membership in cooperative associations; or even sell items such as dairy-farm equipment, chemicals, and feed to the farmers they contact.

Poultry field-service technicians, usually representing food-processing companies or cooperative associations, inspect farms for compliance with contract and cooperative agreements regarding facilities, equipment, sanitation, and efficiency and to advise farmers regarding programs to improve the quality of their products. These technicians may examine chickens for evidence of disease and growth rate to determine the effectiveness of medication and feeding programs, and they may recommend changes in equipment or procedures to improve production. They inform farmers of new techniques, government regulations, and company or association production standards to enable them to upgrade their farms and to meet requirements. They may recommend laboratory testing of feeds, diseased chickens, and diet supplements. In these cases, they often gather samples and take them to a laboratory for analysis. They report their findings regarding farm conditions, laboratory tests, their own recommendations, and farmers' reactions to the company or association employing them.

The second area in which agribusiness technicians are employed is in sales and services. One of the services often sold is aerial crop spraying. Working in this field, technicians contact farmers and offer cost estimates based on acreage involved, crops grown, insecticide needed, and other factors, including physical hazards involved. Other services include the distribution of farm produce on both a national and international level, advisory and support services from food-processing companies, and insurance coverage against fire or liability.

The third area of employment for agribusiness technicians is in record keeping. The records that farmers and other agricultural business people must keep are becoming more detailed and varied every year. Agribusiness technicians may set up complete record-keeping systems. They analyze records and help farmers make management decisions based on the facts they accumulate. Computerized record keeping is common now, so there is a tremendous need for agricultural records technicians who can facilitate the use of this equipment and who can help farmers get maximum benefit from the output. Technicians are also needed to gather information for specific enterprises, sometimes deciding also what data is necessary and in what form the problem can best be presented to the computer. Further, they may analyze the output and be responsible for making practical applications of the information analyzed.

A cotton researcher from a southern university brings many agribusiness technicians together to discuss the latest development in cotton production.

The following paragraphs describe some of the specific jobs that agribusiness technicians may hold. Each of these positions is appropriate for entry-level agribusiness technicians.

Beginning agribusiness technicians often work as *sales representatives* for any of a number of agricultural products or services, including grease and oils, farm record systems, or farm machinery.

Agribusiness technicians may also work as *farm sales representatives,* finding the best markets for the produce of farms on a country, state, or national level. They do a good deal of traveling and work closely with records technicians or other personnel of the farm or farms they represent.

Farm representatives work for banks, cooperatives, or federal lending institutions. They sell the services of their organizations to farmers or agricultural business people, make appraisals, and do the paperwork involved in the lending of money.

Purchasing agents do all the buying for a large farm or farm-service business, buying large quantities at lower per-unit costs.

Food-processing field-service technicians, sometimes called *field-contact technicians,* furnish advice to farmers and sell the services of the food-processing company to the farms.

279

Requirements

Three qualities are especially necessary for successful agribusiness technicians. First, they must be able to work well with other people. This includes the ability to delegate responsibility and to establish friendly relations with farmers, laborers, and other people with whom they come in contact. Second, agribusiness technicians must be able to analyze problems of management and make sound decisions based on existing data. And, third, they must be able to communicate well with others. They should be able to present written and oral reports, to offer comments and advice clearly, and, when necessary, to train other workers for a particular job.

A high-school diploma is an absolute necessity for anyone interested in becoming an agribusiness technician. While in high school, interested students should take the broadest possible selection of courses. Specifically, courses should include social studies, laboratory science (biology, chemistry, or physics), mathematics, and, if possible, courses in agriculture and business. English literature and composition will be particularly helpful as oral and written communications are central to the work of the agribusiness technician.

After completion of high school, it is necessary to train in a two-year agricultural or technical college. A technical or agricultural college program will provide basic economic theory, training in analyzing and solving practical problems, and intensive training in all phases of communications, such as public speaking and report writing.

Typical first-year courses in an agricultural or technical college include English, biology, health and physical education, introductory animal husbandry, principles of accounting, agricultural economics, microbiology, botany, introductory data processing, soil science, and principles of business.

Typical second-year courses include marketing agricultural commodities, farm management, social science, agricultural finance, agricultural marketing institutions, forage and seed crops, personnel management, and agricultural records and taxation.

Special requirements

Aside from a two-year technical college degree, there are no other special requirements for this profession.

Opportunities for experience and exploration

High-school students interested in exploring this field should look for summer or part-time employment in the area in which they might like to specialize—for example, a clerical job in a farm insurance agency, or a laborer in a feed and grain company. Because many technical colleges offer evening courses, it might be possible to obtain permission during senior year to audit a course or even to take it for future college credit.

Once enrolled in junior college, supervised occupational experience is generally an integral part of the educational program, further helping the student to decide upon an area on which to focus.

Methods of entering

Summer employment often leads to an offer of a permanent job with the same employer if the person has made a favorable impression. College faculty members are often another good source of job leads; they have personal contacts outside the campus and many employers get in touch with them directly.

In addition, employers carry on recruitment programs by the use of flyers on college bulletin boards or by using college enrollment lists for direct mail approaches to prospective employees.

Agribusiness technicians need only to be interested in their vocation and have the initiative to look around them. There are usually employers seeking their services.

Advancement

The ultimate aim of many technicians is certainly to own a business. Technicians can start their own businesses in any agricultural business area, or act as independent agents under independent contract to a group of firms to perform specific services. For example, an experienced agribusiness technician may purchase data-processing equipment time, set up necessary programs, collect data, and return an analysis of data to firms contracting for the service.

Other technicians develop careers as consultants or market researchers. In the field of farm insurance, they may progress from the writing of insurance policies to claims adjuster or underwriter for their company.

The following short paragraphs describe some other positions that experienced agribusiness technicians might hold.

Farm managers oversee all operations of a farm. They work closely with owners and other management, with customers, and with all farm departments on larger farms.

Regional farm credit managers are in charge of several of a bank's farm representatives. They suggest training that their farm representatives may need, recommend changes in lending procedures, and conduct personal audits of randomly selected farm accounts.

Sales managers act as liaisons between company sales representatives and individual dealers, distributors, or farmers.

Employment outlook

The employment outlook for this profession is moderately good. As small farms continue to give way to large corporate farms, the technician's services will be in increasing demand. The large corporate farm, as never before, requires people who are highly trained in very specific areas to handle the vast and diversified management operations. Since the demand for such people so far exceeds the supply, it is expected that numerous employment opportunities will be available for the foreseeable future.

Earnings

Annual starting salaries for agribusiness technicians with a two-year college degree range approximately from $14,000 to $18,000, with reasonable advances to be expected with growing experience, especially in the sales area. Senior technicians may earn $25,000 a year or more.

Fringe benefits vary widely, depending upon the employer. Some amount to as much as one-third of the base salary. More and more employers are providing such benefits as pension plans, paid vacations, company insurance, and tuition refunds for further education. For those working in relatively remote or isolated areas, recreational facilities and programs are often provided.

Conditions of work

Because the field of the agribusiness technician is so large, working conditions vary greatly.

Those who work in the area of sales are likely to travel a good deal. The job may require a few nights spent on the road or a few weeks spent out of the country. Technicians who work for banks or data-processing services usually work in clean, pleasant surroundings. The technician who goes into farm management or who owns a farm needs to work outdoors in all kinds of weather.

Social and psychological factors

When working with other people, technicians must be able to delegate responsibility and authority and be able to follow up on these assignments to see that a project is completed satisfactorily. They should be able to show someone else how to do a particular job physically as well as theoretically; in short, they must be willing to get their hands dirty when necessary. They must be able to establish rapport with both the professional staffs or owners they work with and with the laborers who work for them. They must be well informed on their specialties, and they must keep this information current.

Agribusiness technicians will often be confronted with problems requiring careful thought and decision. As a consequence, they must be able to remain calm when things get hectic, to make sound decisions, and then to stand by their decisions in the face of possible disagreement. It is a profession that requires initiative, self-reliance, and the ability to accept responsibilities which may bring blame at times of failure as well as substantial rewards for successful performance. For those technicians with the qualities of leadership and a strong interest in agricultural business, it can be a challenging, exciting, and highly satisfying profession.

GOE: 03.01.01, 08.01.03; SIC: 8748; SOC: 1449, 5627

◇ **SOURCES OF ADDITIONAL INFORMATION**

Future Farmers of America
National FFA Center
PO Box 15160
Alexandria, VA 22309

Agribusiness Council
2550 M Street, NW
Suite 300
Washington, DC 20037

Agriculture Council of America
1250 I Street, NW
Suite 601
Washington, DC 20005

Agricultural and Industrial Manufacturers Representatives Association
5818 Reeds Road
Mission, KS 66202

U.S. Department of Agriculture
Department of Public Information
Washington, DC 20250

Agricultural equipment technicians

Definition

Agricultural equipment technicians assemble, adjust, operate, maintain, modify, test, and help design a whole array of modern farm machinery. Such machinery includes computer-controlled automatic animal feeding systems; milking machine systems; and tilling, planting, harvesting, irrigating, drying, and handling equipment of all kinds. Agricultural equipment technicians work with various kinds of electrical, hydraulic, pneumatic, thermal, and gas- or diesel-powered machines and mechanisms involved in this sophisticated equipment. Agricultural equipment technicians often supervise skilled mechanics and related workers who keep machines and systems operating at maximum efficiency.

History

When primitive people ceased to be nomadic hunters and started to plant grains and fiber-producing crops, they began slowly to develop tools for planting, tilling, harvesting, and processing farm products. First, hand tools were developed. Then, over the centuries, tools using the power of oxen and horses gradually developed, increasing the farmer's productivity.

The Industrial Revolution, which brought great advances in the design and use of specialized machinery for strenuous and repetitive work, quickly spread to agricultural production. Cyrus McCormick's reaper appeared in 1831 and was the forerunner of the development of modern agricultural equipment.

The combined efforts of governmental experiment stations, which developed high-yielding, standardized varieties of farm crops, and the agricultural equipment-producing companies brought rapid development in farm machinery during the first half of the twentieth century.

In the late 1930s, the abundance of inexpensive petroleum fuels made gasoline and diesel engines economical for farm machinery. During the early 1940s, the resulting explosion in complex and powerful farm machinery multiplied production and replaced most of the horses and mules used on farms in the United States.

In part because of these advances in mechanization, today's farmer in the United States can produce, on average, enough agricultural output to feed and clothe more than fifty people, whereas the average production of farmers in other countries serves the needs of fewer than ten people. Agricultural products are now among the most important export commodities for our nation.

Modern farming is heavily dependent upon very complex and expensive machinery. It therefore requires highly trained and skilled technicians and farm mechanics to install, operate, maintain, and modify the machinery that ensures the nation's farm productivity.

Recent developments in agricultural mechanization and automation make the position of the agricultural equipment technician both challenging and rewarding. Sophisticated machines are being used to plant, cultivate, harvest, and process food; to contour, drain, and renovate land; and to clear land and harvest forest products in the process. Qualified agricultural equipment technicians are needed to service and sell this equipment and to manage this equipment on the farm.

Farming is big business and is becoming increasingly competitive. The successful farmer may have very large amounts of money invested in land and machinery, perhaps hundreds of thousands or millions of dollars. For this investment to pay off, it is vital that the machinery be kept in good operating condition and that it be ready to go when needed. Thus prompt, reliable service from the farm equipment manufacturer and dealer is necessary for the success of both farmer and dealer. Interruptions or delays because of poor service are costly for everyone involved. To provide this, service manufacturers and dealers need technicians and specialists who possess agricultural and engineering knowledge in addition to technical skills.

Nature of the work

Agricultural equipment technicians work in a wide variety of capacities both on and off the farm. In general, most agricultural equipment technicians find employment in one of three areas: in equipment manufacturing, in equipment sales and services, and in on-farm equipment management.

Agricultural equipment technicians employed by equipment manufacturing firms are involved principally with design and testing of agricultural equipment such as farm machinery; irrigation, power, and electrification systems; soil and water conservation equipment; and agricultural harvesting and processing equipment. The following paragraphs describe two kinds of agricultural equipment technicians working in this field: the *agricultural engineering technician* and the *agricultural equipment test technician*.

Agricultural engineering technicians usually work directly under the supervision of design engineers. They prepare original layouts and complete detailed drawings of agricultural equipment. They also review plans, diagrams, and blueprints, utilizing their own knowledge of biological, engineering, and design principles, to ensure that new products comply with company standards and design specifications. They also maintain a working knowledge of functions, operations, and maintenance of various types of equipment and materials used in the industry to assure appropriate utilization.

Agricultural equipment test technicians test experimental and production agricultural machinery and equipment such as motors, tractors, and accessories to evaluate their performance. In particular, they test the equipment for conformance with operating requirements, such as horsepower, resistance to vibration, and strength and hardness of parts. They conduct their tests under actual field conditions on company-operated research farms and under more controlled conditions using test equipment and recording instruments such as bend-fatigue machines, dynamometers, strength testers, hardness meters, analytical balances, and electronic recorders.

Test technicians are also responsible for recording the data gathered during the course of these tests. They also compute values such as horsepower and tensile strength using algebraic formulas. They report their findings by making graphs and tables, drawing sketches, and describing test procedures and results in test data logs.

Some test technicians work with attachments for agricultural equipment to evaluate, for instance, depth of tillage or harvesting capabilities for different types of crops.

After the design and testing phases are complete, other agricultural equipment technicians work with engineers in performing any necessary adjustments to the design of the equipment. By performing these functions under the general supervision of the design engineer, technicians do the engineers' "detective work" and thus enable them to give more time to research and development.

Agricultural equipment technicians involved with equipment manufacturing may also be employed by large agricultural machinery companies to supervise production, assembly, and plant operations.

In the sales area, most manufacturers of agricultural equipment market their products through regional sales organizations to individual dealers. Technicians may serve as sales rep-

Three agricultural equipment technicians inspect a new tractor. Given the expense of such large tractors, it is important that the tractors remain in excellent condition. Thus, the technicians service them on a regular basis.

resentatives of regional sales offices. In this position, they are assigned a number of dealers in a given territory and sell agricultural equipment directly to them. They may also conduct sales-training programs for dealers to help them demonstrate and sell equipment to farmers.

These technicians are also qualified for sales work within dealerships, either as equipment sales workers or as parts clerks. These technicians should be able to demonstrate various features of the equipment and be able to appraise the value of used equipment for trade-in allowances. Technicians in these positions may advance to being sales managers or parts managers.

Some technicians in the sales area become *systems specialists.* They work for equipment dealerships where they assist farmers in the planning and installation of various kinds of mechanized systems, such as irrigation or materials-handling systems, grain bins, or drying systems.

In the service area, technicians may be employed as *field service representatives* working as a liaison between the companies they represent and the dealers, assisting the dealers in product warranty work, diagnosing service problems, and keeping dealer service personnel informed about new service information and techniques.

Some technicians in this area specialize in public relations work or in holding dealer service training sessions.

Technicians working in the service area may begin as specialists in certain kinds of repairs. *Hydraulic specialists,* for instance, specialize in maintaining and repairing the component parts of hydraulic systems in tractors and other agricultural machines. Another kind of specialist is the *diesel specialist* who specializes in rebuilding, calibrating, and testing diesel pumps, injectors, and other components of diesel engines.

Many service technicians have as their goal the position of *service manager* or *parts department manager.* Service managers assign work to repair workers, diagnose tractor and machinery problems, estimate repair costs for customers, and are directly responsible for efficient shop management.

Parts department managers working in equipment dealerships are responsible for maintaining proper inventories of all the parts that may be requested either by customers or by the service departments of the dealership. They deal directly with customers, parts suppliers, and dealership managers. They must be effective at both sales and purchasing as well as at being good business managers.

Technicians working on the farm are involved in a varied set of activities largely centered on keeping machinery in as nearly perfect working condition as possible during the growing season. During off-season periods they may be involved with overhauling or modifying equipment, or simply with keeping the machinery in good working order for the next season.

Some technicians find employment as *on-farm machinery managers*. These technicians usually work on large farms and are responsible for servicing or supervising the servicing of all automated equipment. They are also responsible for monitoring the field operation of all machines and for keeping complete records regarding the costs, utilization, and repair procedures relating to the maintenance of each piece of mechanical equipment.

Requirements

Normal physical strength and health are required for this career. Good eyesight, hearing, and hand-eye coordination are needed.

Agricultural equipment technicians must often function as engineering-type technicians. They must have a knowledge of physical science and engineering principles, as well as the mathematical techniques that support these principles. They must have a working knowledge of farm crops and the machinery and related products used with them.

A high-school diploma is a necessity for anyone planning further education in the field of agricultural equipment technology. The high-school curriculum should include as much mathematics as is available and four years of English and language skills, as well as courses in the social sciences, natural sciences (especially those with laboratory sections), mechanical drawing, shop work, and any other pre-engineering or practical mechanics courses that the school offers.

Vocational agriculture courses, where available, are usually extremely useful in helping prospective technicians understand the needs and problems of the farmers with whom they will be working. These courses, however, are not absolutely necessary. Many people who have been educated in urban areas without access to such programs at the high-school level have graduated from two-year agricultural technician programs in community or technical colleges, technical institutes, or four-year colleges and found highly successful careers in this field.

Because agricultural equipment technicians may work in either a sales or an engineering position, their curriculum at both the high-

school and the postsecondary level should be oriented toward both of those fields.

The postsecondary curriculum for the agricultural equipment technician should include courses in general agriculture, agricultural power and equipment, practical engineering, hydraulics, agricultural-equipment business methods, electrical equipment, engineering problems, social science, economics, and sales techniques. On-the-job experience during the summer is invaluable. This is frequently included as part of the regular curriculum. Students are placed on a farm to function as technicians-in-training. They may also work in an approved farm equipment dealership where their time is divided among the parts, sales, and service departments. Occupational experience can be one of the most important phases of the postsecondary training program. It gives students an opportunity to discover the field for which they are best suited and the phase of the business they prefer. Upon completion of this program, most technical and community colleges award an associate degree.

Typical courses offered in agricultural equipment technology during the first year of a two-year program include communication skills; drawing, sketching, and diagramming; agricultural machinery; technical physics and mathematics; diesel and gasoline engines; hydraulics; technical reporting; and business organizations.

Second-year courses may include equipment selling, distributing, and servicing; hydraulic equipment and air conditioning; principles of farm mechanization, computers, and automatic controls; materials handling; power unit testing and diagnosis; advanced agricultural equipment; and agricultural business management and accounting.

It is still possible to enter this career by starting as an inexperienced worker in a machinery manufacturer's plant or on a farm with considerable mechanized equipment. This approach to the career, however, is becoming more and more difficult because of the complexity of the machinery. Because of this complexity, some formal classroom training is necessary, and many people find it difficult to complete even part-time study of the field's theory and science while also working a full-time job.

Special requirements

There are no special requirements for this career. Agricultural equipment technicians are not required to be licensed or certified. Some manufacturers of diesel pumps require certification of personnel in service departments that repair and service fuel pumps.

Opportunities for exploration

Possibilities for exploring the career of agricultural equipment technician are more plentiful for persons who live in farming areas. They are naturally best for those who actually live and work on farms. However, even for those who live in towns or cities away from farm work, there are ways to explore and become acquainted with the career.

Vocational agriculture education programs in high schools may be found in most rural and many suburban settings and in some schools in urban areas. The teaching staff and counselors in these schools can provide considerable information about the career.

Light industrial machinery is used for so many purposes in both the country and the city that it is always possible for those with an interest in modern machinery to watch it being used and to talk with people who own, operate, and repair it.

Summer and part-time work on a farm, in an agricultural equipment manufacturing plant, or in an equipment sales and service business offers opportunities to work on or near agricultural and light industrial machinery. Such a job may provide a clearer idea about the various activities, challenges, rewards, and possible limitations of this career.

Methods of entering

The demand for qualified agricultural equipment technicians exceeds the supply. Operators and managers of large, well-equipped farms and farm equipment companies in need of employees keep in touch with colleges offering agricultural equipment programs. Students who do well during their occupational experience period usually have an excellent chance of going to work for the same employer after graduation. Many colleges have an interview day on which personnel representatives of manufacturers, distributors, farm owners and managers, and dealers are invited to recruit students who are completing technician programs. In general, any student who does well in a training program can expect employment immediately upon graduation.

A moderate percentage of students in agricultural technician programs are sons, daughters, or other close relatives of farm owners and operators. They are often assured of immediate employment and by returning full-time to the farm in which they may have an ownership interest. They have prepared themselves to be future owners and operators of farms in the best way they can to assure success.

Advancement

Opportunities for advancement and self-employment are excellent for those who have the initiative to keep abreast of developments in the farm equipment field. Technicians will often have the opportunity to attend company schools in sales and service or to take advanced evening courses in colleges.

Employment outlook

Agricultural equipment businesses are now demanding more know-how than ever before. A variety of complex specialized machines and mechanical devices are steadily being produced and improved to aid farmers in improving the quality and productivity of their labor. These machines require trained technical workers to design, produce, test, sell, and service them. Trained workers are also needed to instruct the final users in their proper use, repair, and maintenance.

The demand for agricultural equipment technicians is great and should increase as our growing population catches up with our ability to produce food, fiber, and shelter. Additionally, the need will grow as we expand export of agricultural products to foreign markets in exchange for raw materials, oil, and other goods.

As agriculture becomes more and more technical, the agricultural equipment technician assumes an increasingly vital role in helping farmers solve problems that interfere with efficient production. These opportunities exist not only in the United States but also worldwide, as agricultural economies everywhere become mechanized. Inventive technicians with training in modern business principles will find expanding employment opportunities abroad.

Technological advances in power and equipment offer many new employment opportunities. Automated forest products machines, light industrial equipment, and automated lawn and garden equipment are only a few allied fields that are undergoing change and growth.

Earnings

Starting salaries for agricultural equipment technicians range from approximately $11,000 to more than $18,000 per year for those who have graduated from a two-year technical or community college. Technicians may earn a much larger salary (often ranging from $20,000 to $30,000) after more training and experience. Technicians working on farms often receive room and board as a supplement to and incentive above their annual salary. The salary that technicians eventually receive depends, as do most salaries, on individual ability, initiative, and the supply of skilled technicians in the field of work or locality.

In addition to their salaries, most technicians receive fringe benefits such as health and retirement benefits, paid vacations, and other benefits usually received by engineering technicians.

Technicians employed in sales usually are paid on an incentive basis. They may receive a bonus from farm equipment sales in addition to their basic salary.

Conditions of work

Working conditions vary according to the type of work the agricultural equipment technician chooses to do: farm machinery applications, care, and management; research, development, and manufacturing; sales; or customer equipment servicing and maintenance.

The technician who is a part of a large farming operation might work either indoors or outdoors depending on the season and the tasks that need to be done. Planning schedules of machine overhaul and the directing of such work usually are done in roofed workplaces equipped for such work. Field servicing and repair are done in the field.

Some agricultural equipment sales representatives work in their own or in nearby communities; others must travel widely. Work hours vary according to the distances between customers and their accessibility.

In agricultural equipment research, development, and production, technicians usually work under typical factory conditions: some in an office or laboratory, some in a manufacturing area. In some cases, field testing and demonstration must be performed where the machinery is to be used.

For those technicians who assemble, adjust, modify, or test equipment and for those who provide customer service, application studies, and maintenance services, the surroundings may be similar to large automobile service centers.

In all cases, safety precautions must be a constant concern. Appropriate clothing, cleaning up oil spills and other dirt in workplaces, and careful lifting or hoisting of heavy machinery elements must be a way of life. The surroundings may be noisy and grimy. Some of the work is performed in cramped or awkward positions. Gasoline fumes and odors from oil products are a constant factor. While the safety practices have improved greatly over the years, certain risks do exist. Heavy lifting may cause injury, and burns and cuts are always possible. The technician ordinarily works a forty-hour week, but emergency repairs may require working overtime.

Social and psychological factors

Successful agricultural equipment technicians must have a good scientific and engineering background combined with technical skills. They must be reliable, healthy, and willing to work outdoors. A farm background is desirable, but not essential.

The challenge of constant change in agricultural equipment and in farming methods is a part of this career. The technician can expect new types of farming procedures, new hybrids and strains of crops and livestock, and new techniques for soil conservation and use. In the next several decades new methods must be found to turn marginal crop production land into economically efficient acreage. This becomes increasingly important as millions of acres of prime crop production land are covered by buildings, cities, and roads or are eroded away and lost to productive farm use.

Skilled agricultural equipment technicians can find work suited to their personal desires. They can work independently or with others, indoors or outdoors, and they can travel or work in one place. They are important to the community's and nation's well-being because they are essential to producing needed food and fiber commodities.

GOE: 05.01.07, 05.03.07; SIC: 7699; SOC: 3719, 389

⬦ **SOURCES OF ADDITIONAL INFORMATION**

U.S. Department of Agriculture
Washington, DC 20250

Accreditation Board for Engineering and Technology
345 East 47th Street
New York, NY 10017

Future Farmers of America
PO Box 15160
Alexandria, VA 22309

Agricultural and Industrial Manufacturers Representatives Association
5818 Reeds Road
Mission, KS 66202

Farm and Industrial Equipment Institute
410 North Michigan Avenue
Chicago, IL 60611

◇ **RELATED ARTICLES**

Volume 1: Agriculture; Engineering; Machining and Machinery
Volume 2: Engineers
Volume 3: Farm equipment mechanics; Farmers; Farm operators and managers; Industrial machinery mechanics; Manufacturers' sales workers; Mobile heavy equipment mechanics
Volume 4: Agribusiness technicians; Automotive, diesel, and gas turbine technicians

Animal production technicians

Definition

Animal production technicians assist in the breeding, raising, and marketing of a variety of farm animals, including cattle, sheep, swine, horses, mules, chickens, turkeys, geese, and ducks. These technicians, especially when they are principally involved with the breeding and feeding of animals, are sometimes referred to as animal husbandry technicians. Although not specifically discussed in this article, technicians trained in this area might find employment in such specialized enterprises as mink or fox farming, pheasant or quail farming, or earthworm farming.

In general, animal production technicians are concerned with the propagation, feeding, housing, health and diseases, and economics of production and marketing animals and animal products. Animal production technicians work in many different settings and in many different capacities. For example, they may work on farms supervising unskilled workers or serving as field representatives who assist in the sales of animals or animal products to customers, for farm-product or farm-services vendors as sales representatives, or for food-processing and packaging firms as purchasing agents, assistants to purchasing agents, or in other technical capacities. The diversity of employment situations for the well-trained and well-qualified animal production technician makes this career one of substantial flexibility. As science advances, the areas into which these technicians will move will become even wider.

History

Raising cattle, hogs, sheep, and poultry is apparently one of the oldest of human occupations. In the United States, the production of beef cattle and sheep became a large-scale operation during the nineteenth century as the population of cities increased and the great grazing areas of the Great Plains regions were opened. The famous Texas Longhorn cattle, superseded in the twentieth century by the Hereford, Aberdeen-Angus, and Shorthorn breeds, were descended from cattle brought to the West Indies by Columbus. Cattle ranching requires large areas of grassland, and until the 1880s, the open range of government-owned land in the West served as "free" pasturage for cattle and sheep. A hundred years later, cattle and sheep ranches in the Southwest tend to be tens of thousands of acres in size, privately owned, with hundreds or thousands of animals on each ranch, representing huge investments for their owners.

Animal production farming is the leading agricultural enterprise in the nation. Food supplies must keep pace with population growth. The demand for animal products continually increases as new products are developed and old products improved.

The methods, techniques, and business management principles involved in profitable production today are far different and more complex than they were just a few decades ago. The application of science and technology to animal production has caused a marked change in the type of resources used by the farm owner. As the amount of human labor needed has dropped, the amount of capital represented by feed, machinery, and fertilizers has increased.

As farm owners rely more and more on technological advancement to sustain and increase their production, the demand for a higher level of technical competence increases. Each year better-educated men and women are needed to supply the materials of production and to raise, distribute, and market the products of animal production agriculture.

Nature of the work

Most animal production technicians are employed either as *livestock production technicians,* meaning they work with cattle, sheep, swine, or horses, or as poultry production technicians, meaning they work with chickens, turkeys, geese, or ducks.

Most livestock production technicians find employment either on livestock farms or ranches or with the businesses that service these farms and ranches. Working on a farm or ranch, they might be involved in the area of animal feed preparation. A typical entry-level job in this area is that of the *scale and bin tender* who weighs and records all feed grain entering, leaving, or being used in the feeding yards. This person also arranges for proper storage of the grain and must keep an accurate inventory of all animals and types of feed on hand.

Another entry-level position in this field is that of the *feed-mixing technician* who weighs, mixes, and blends animal feed according to the recommendations made by the ration technician.

The *ration technician* is an experienced livestock production technician who selects the feed and feed supplements that are most desirable for keeping animals healthy and growing rapidly and to produce the best return for the dollar invested.

Experienced livestock production technicians interested in animal feeding may also be employed as *feed buyers* or as *feed lot managers.* Feed buyers are responsible for supplying the feed needed for all of a farm's operations. They must buy the kinds of feed that are most suitable and economical for each operation.

Feed lot managers supervise the entire feed lot operation. They must be familiar with shipping, receiving, mixing of feeds, buying and selling of livestock, and the work of each employee.

Another on-farm occupation of livestock production technicians is that of the *disease prevention technician.* This technician protects animals from disease and parasites, administers disease prevention treatments such as dipping and vaccination, conducts frequent examinations, and treats livestock for cuts, wounds, and minor diseases.

Livestock production technicians working off the farm are employed in a variety of different capacities. Once again, they may be involved with feed preparation. Small producers of cattle, sheep, and hogs often do not have facilities for storing, mixing, or grinding feed, and hence must rely on feed companies. Those companies, in turn, hire technicians to perform the various feed-related activities already described.

Livestock production technicians are also employed in selling, servicing, and sometimes installing the mechanical equipment used in livestock production, such as trucks and tractors, mechanized feed mixers and feed carriers, and manure-turning machines.

Another off-farm area of employment for livestock production technicians is in judging and purchasing livestock. Technicians working in this area are usually employed by slaughterhouses or meat-packing companies. They inspect, grade, and weigh livestock to determine value and yield. They may also be responsible for arranging for the transportation and sale of the livestock.

Some livestock production technicians working off the farm are employed as *veterinarians' assistants.* They assist in the care of animals under treatment, sterilize equipment, and administer medication under the direction of the veterinarian.

The work of *poultry production technicians* can be divided into seven areas. In the area of breeding-flock production, poultry technicians may work as *farm managers,* directing the operation of one or several farms. They may be *flock supervisors* with five or six assistants working directly with farmers under contract to produce hatching eggs. On pedigree breeding farms, poultry technicians may be in charge of all of the people who transport, feed, and care for the poultry. Technicians involved in breeding-flock production are concerned with efficiency in the use of time, materials, and labor and with making effective use of data-processing equipment.

In the area of hatchery management, technicians operate and maintain the incubators and hatchers in which eggs develop as embryos. Poultry technicians working in this area must be trained in incubation, sexing, grading,

This animal production technician is supervising a group of calves. These calves were part of a reproduction program that enhances the number of calves born in a year. Embryos from registered cows with high production records were transplanted into surrogate mothers who then produced small herds of genetically uniform animals.

scheduling, and making effective use of available technology.

The production and marketing of table eggs requires poultry technicians for handling birds on pullet-growing farms and egg farms. Experienced poultry technicians often work as supervisors of flocks and dictate management procedures for those who provide the actual care of the flocks. Poultry technicians may also work in or supervise the work of smaller, specialized production units, such as those that clean, grade, or package eggs for wholesale or retail trade.

The egg processing phase begins when the eggs leave the farm. *Egg processing technicians* are involved in egg pickup, trucking, delivery, and quality control. With experience, technicians in this area work as *supervisors* and *plant managers*. These technicians need training in egg processing machinery and in refrigeration equipment.

In the area of poultry meat production, technicians supervise the production, management, and inspection of birds bred specifically for consumption as poultry meat. Technicians may work directly with flocks or in supervisory positions.

Poultry meat processing and sales require technicians who supervise or carry out the task of picking up meat birds at the farms on schedule to keep processing plants operating efficiently. Technicians working as supervisors at the plant are involved with all phases of processing, including inspection for quality, grading, packaging, and marketing. They are also involved with machinery operation and maintaining and managing plant personnel.

Finally, poultry technicians are employed in the sales and service of poultry equipment, feed, and supplies.

Within these seven broad areas, there are a number of specific kinds of jobs commonly performed by poultry technicians. The following short paragraphs describe some of these, each appropriate for entry-level technicians.

Poultry graders certify the grade of dressed or ready-to-cook poultry in processing plants according to government standards.

Poultry husbandry technicians conduct research in breeding, feeding, and management of poultry. They examine selection and breeding practices to increase efficiency of production and to improve the quality of poultry products.

Poultry inspectors examine poultry to certify wholesomeness and acceptability of condition of live, dressed, and ready-to-cook poultry in processing plants.

Egg candlers inspect eggs to ascertain quality and fitness for consumption or incubation, according to prescribed standards.

Egg graders inspect, sort, and grade eggs according to size, shape, color, and weight.

Some poultry technicians also work as *field-contact technicians*, inspecting poultry farms for food processing companies to ensure that growers are maintaining contract standards for feeding and housing birds and controlling disease. They tour barns, incubation units, and related facilities to observe procedures for sanitation and protection from weather. Field-contact technicians make sure that specified kinds of grain are being administered according to prescribed schedules, inspect birds for evidence of disease, and weigh them to determine rates of growth. This occupation is described in more detail in the article titled "Agribusiness technicians."

One area of animal production technology that merits special mention is that of artificial breeding. Three kinds of technicians working in this specialized area of animal production are the *artificial-breeding technician,* the *artificial-breeding laboratory technician,* and the *poultry inseminator,* sometimes called an *artificial insemination technician.*

Artificial-breeding technicians collect and package bull semen for artificial insemination of cows. They examine the semen under a microscope to determine density and motility of sperm cells, and they dilute the semen according to standard formulas. They transfer the semen to shipping and storage containers with identifying data such as the source, the date taken, and the quality. They also keep records related to all of their activities. In some cases they may also be responsible for inseminating the cows.

Artificial-breeding laboratory technicians are involved with the artificial breeding of all kinds of animals, but most often these technicians specialize in the laboratory aspects of the activity. They measure purity, potency, and density of animal semen and add extenders and antibiotics to the semen. They keep records, clean and sterilize laboratory equipment, and perform experimental tests to develop improved methods of processing and preserving semen.

Poultry inseminators collect semen from roosters and fertilize hens and eggs. They examine the roosters' semen for quality and density, measure specified amounts of semen for loading into inseminating guns, inject semen into hens, and keep accurate records of all aspects of the operation. This area of animal production should have a good future as poultry production expands.

Requirements

Animal production technicians must be strong and healthy, as much of the work they do is physical labor, often done outdoors, in all kinds of weather conditions.

High-school students who wish to enter the field of animal production technology will find that the more background pertaining to agriculture they acquire while in high school, the better prepared they will be. In addition, courses in mathematics, business, communications, chemistry, and mechanics will be valuable. A high-school diploma is nearly always necessary for entrance into any technical education program beyond the high-school level.

There are many colleges with two-year programs in animal science or animal husbandry where additional knowledge, skills, and specialized training may be acquired. Typical first-year courses include agricultural mechanics, agricultural structures and equipment I, introduction to soil science, introduction to animal husbandry, beef production, feeds and feeding, and animal husbandry techniques.

Typical second-year courses include meat products, farm management, introduction to agricultural machinery, agricultural structures and equipment II, forage and seed crops, animal husbandry techniques, meat animal management, livestock breeding, and animal health.

Animal production technicians also need the ability to speak well, to conduct meetings, and to work cooperatively with individuals and with groups of people.

Special requirements

There are no special requirements in this field at the present time.

Opportunities for experience and exploration

Children of farm families have, of course, the greatest opportunity for deciding whether this is a field that will appeal to them. For those who have not grown up on a farm, however, there are often summer jobs available on livestock farms that will enable them to decide whether this type of work is what they want. In addition, organizations such as 4-H Clubs and Future Farmers of America offer good opportunities for hearing about, visiting, and participating in farm activities.

Methods of entering

Most of the programs now available in animal production technology are relatively new and many of the job placement procedures have not been developed to the fullest degree. However, many avenues are open and employers have recognized the importance of education at the technical level. Many junior colleges participate in a "learn-and-earn" program, in which the college and prospective employer jointly share the responsibility of training the student in the classroom and in actual on-the-job work with livestock and other animals. Most technical programs have placement services for graduates, and the demand for qualified people often exceeds the supply.

Advancement

Even when a good training or technical program is completed, the graduate may be required to begin work at a lower level before advancing to a more responsible job. But the graduate of a technical program will advance much more rapidly to positions of major responsibility and greater financial reward than the untrained worker.

Those graduates who are willing to work hard and keep informed of changes in their field may advance to such positions as livestock breeder, feedlot manager, supervisor, or artificial breeding distributor. If they can raise the money, they can own their own livestock ranches.

Employment outlook

Continuing changes can be expected in the next few years, both in the production and the marketing phases of the animal production industry. Because of the costs now involved, it is almost impossible for a one-person operation to stay in business. As a result, cooperatives and corporations will become more prevalent in the future, and greater emphasis will be placed on specialization. This, in turn, will increase the demand for the graduates of technical programs. Other factors such as small profit margins, the demand for more uniform products, and an increasing foreign market will result in a need for more specialized trained personnel. This era of specialization in the animal production industry is new, and graduates of the program in animal production technology have an interesting and rewarding future ahead of them.

Earnings

Salaries of animal production technicians vary widely depending on the kind of employer, the technicians' educational and agricultural background, the kind of animal the technicians work with, and the geographical areas in which they work. In general, the salaries of all agricultural technicians tend to be lower in the northeast part of the nation and higher in California and some parts of the Midwest, such as Minnesota and Iowa. Currently, the range for starting salaries for animal production technicians runs from approximately $12,000 a year, or sometimes less, to $16,000 a year or more. In addition, many animal production technicians receive food and housing benefits that can be the equivalent of several thousand dollars a year. Other fringe benefits vary according to type of employer but can include paid vacation time, health insurance, and pension benefits.

Conditions of work

Working conditions, of course, vary from operation to operation, but certain factors always exist in varying degrees. Much of the work is done outside in all types of weather. It is often necessary to put in long, irregular hours and to work on Sundays and holidays. Salaries are usually commensurate with the hours worked, and there are usually slack seasons when time off is given for any extra hours worked.

Social and psychological factors

Animal production technicians are often their own bosses and hence have their own decisions to make. While this can be considered an asset to those who value independence, prospective animal production technicians must be aware of the fact that self-discipline is a most valuable trait to possess if they wish to be successful.

Probably the most important factor is the satisfaction one gets from watching animals grow. Animal production technicians must know which of the different methods to use on each type of animal to produce the best possible product for the customer. The effort involved is, in itself, an exciting experience, and being able to produce a successful product brings great satisfaction and rewards.

GOE: 02.04.02, 03.02.04, 03.04.05; SIC: 021; SOC: 382

◇ **RELATED ARTICLES**

Volume 1: Agriculture; Food Processing
Volume 2: Biologists; Buyers, wholesale and retail; Medical technologists; Purchasing agents; Veterinarians
Volume 3: Agricultural scientists; Agricultural extension service workers; Dairy farmers; Dairy products manufacturing workers; Farmers; Farm operatives and managers
Volume 4: Agribusiness technicians; Animal health technicians; Biological technicians; Biological specimen technicians

Farm crop production technicians

Definition

Farm crop production technicians assist farmers and agricultural businesses in the planning, planting, cultivating, caring for, harvesting, and marketing of field crops, such as grain and cotton, and of orchard and vineyard crops, such as fruits, nuts, and berries. Technicians who specialize in orchard and vineyard crops are often referred to as *orchard and vineyard technicians*. Technicians who specialize in testing and doing experiments related to improving the yield or quality of crops or to increasing the plants' resistance to disease, insects, and other hazards are referred to as plant technicians. Farm crop production technicians work in a variety of places from laboratories to farms. Although not specifically discussed in this article, technicians trained in farm crop production technology might also find employment in specialized enterprises such as mushroom or mustard farming. Some work for farm-product or farm-service vendors as researchers in new-product development, as production technicians in the manufacturing process, or as sales representatives. Others work on farms as farm workers supervising unskilled workers or as field representatives assisting in the sale of crops to customers. Finally, some farm crop production technicians work for food processing and packaging firms as purchasing agents, assistants to purchasing agents, or in other technical capacities.

History

Food is a need of everyone every day, a more basic need even than clothing or shelter. One of the most important discoveries in history was that plants could be grown from seeds. With the discovery that food supplies could be controlled, humans gave up their nomadic existence and established permanent fields and orchards to raise their own food. Through experimentation and trial and error, the early farmers slowly learned when and where to produce certain crops. With every increase in the world's population comes an increase in the need for greater and more efficient food production.

To spur production, imaginative research programs are being carried on in the scientific laboratories of public and private firms. As a result, new crops and new methods of production that currently seem impossible will most probably be developed in the future. Even now, large mainframe computers and delicate recording instruments help with some of the difficult decisions farmers had to make without aid in the past.

The farming of today and of the future requires that knowledge of both natural and physical sciences be applied directly to production. The increasing complexity of farm crop production has created a vital role for the farm crop production technician involved in the production, processing, or marketing of farm products.

293

Nature of the work

Farm crop production technicians are usually employed in one of three broad areas of food production: servicing and supplying the farmer, farm product production, and processing and distribution of farm products.

Nearly everything used in a farm is now purchased away from the farm: seed, fertilizer, pesticides, machinery, fuels, and general supplies. Companies selling these products need farm-trained and farm-oriented technicians who can understand the buyer's farm problems and needs.

Farm supply companies also need technicians to assist in research. Scientists in feed or chemical companies work with technicians to carry out the details of the testing program under their supervision. The farm-machinery technician tests and recommends improvements or adaptations in machinery designed by company engineers.

Farm crop production technicians specializing in sales and services to orchards and vineyards usually work with the firms or agencies that sell or provide fruit growers with the supplies they need: nursery stock, fertilizer, pesticides, herbicides, and machinery. Examples of these firms or agencies include nurseries, agricultural chemical companies, pest control firms, irrigation equipment companies, farm machine companies, petroleum companies, and private or public service agencies.

In addition, technicians working for service and supply firms try to help fruit growers who are interested in the results of research, who need help with production problems, or who are looking for the latest and best rootstocks or pest controls. Technicians in this area may assist in the research, participate in the problem-solving, or help produce the new products. They inform fruit growers about the latest developments and help sell their company's products or services. To serve these needs, technicians in this area must be well trained in the area of fruit production.

The production phase of crop technology involves making soil or tissue tests to determine the efficiency of fertilizer programs. Another technician may be responsible for certain kinds of farm machinery. Some experienced farm crop production technicians may even find themselves charged with the complete management of a farm, including personnel, machinery, and finances.

In the fruit industry, some of the larger production firms hire technicians to run soil and tissue tests for fertilizer programs. Technicians are also needed for machinery and labor management. Orchard management for resident or absentee owners is a common occupation in the industry. Technicians who take on management responsibilities need to be able to make decisions regarding new equipment, production techniques, and weed and frost control.

Practically all agricultural products need some processing before they reach the consumer. Processing involves testing, grading, packaging, and transporting. Some of the technicians in this area work closely with farmers and need to know a great deal about crop production. For example, *field-contact technicians* working for food-processing companies monitor various aspects of crop production on farms from which their companies buy products. In some processing companies, they supervise the whole crop operation; in other cases, they act as buyers or are responsible for determining when crops will be harvested for processing and shipping. They often do public relations work with the farmers for the food-processing company.

Other technicians may work in a laboratory doing quality-control work or nutrition research. Others work as inspectors or in any of a number of phases of processing.

Processing and distributing technicians in the fruit industry work either in the laboratory or with the grower in the field. A laboratory technician works with a scientist in processing, quality control, testing, grading, measuring, and record keeping. The field technician supervises seed selection and planting, weed and pest control, irrigation, harvesting, and on-the-spot testing to ensure harvesting at precisely the right state of maturity. Other technicians work as inspectors to see that product quality and grade standards are maintained. Still other technicians are involved in sales and distribution of the products. Processing and distribution technicians may find jobs with canneries, freezing and packing plants, cooperatives, distributors, or with public or private agencies.

Within these three broad areas there are a number of specific occupations in which farm crop production technicians are frequently employed. The following short paragraphs describe some of these positions, each of them appropriate for entry-level technicians.

Farm-and-orchard supply sales workers call on farmers to sell their products. They must understand the production problems of farmers so that they can show how their products will be most useful.

Seed production field supervisors help coordinate activities of farmers engaged in producing seed stocks for commercial seed companies. They inspect and analyze soil and water supplies of farms and study wind currents, land contours, and wind breaks to plan production for effective utilization of planted crops. They distribute seed stock to farmers, specify areas and numbers of acres to be planted, and give instructions to workers engaged in cultivation procedures, such as fertilization, tilling, and detasselling. They may also determine dates and methods for harvesting, storing, and shipping of seed crops.

Biological aides assist research workers in biology, bacteriology, plant pathology, mycology, and related agricultural sciences. They set up laboratory and field equipment, perform routine tests, and clean up and maintain field and laboratory equipment. They also keep records of plant growth, experimental plots, greenhouse activity, use of insecticides, and other agricultural experimentation.

Soil conservation aides work with professional soil scientists in the collection of information through examination and recording of data in field notes and soil maps. They help prepare conservation plans, help present information to farmers, and help farmers with selecting appropriate soil conservation plans. This occupation is described in more detail in the article on soil conservation technicians.

Farm technicians have various duties depending on the farm. They may take soil samples to determine fertilizer needs, read tensiometers for determining irrigation schedules, or run maturity tests to determine harvesting schedules.

Rodent-control assistants usually work for state departments of agriculture. They aid in rodent counts, estimate rodent damage, and help inspectors perform various rodent-control measures.

Agricultural inspectors work for state, county, and federal departments of agriculture. They inspect grain, vegetables, or seed, working in the field, at a packing shed or shipping station, or at a terminal market. They must know grades and standards and be able to recognize common pests and disease damage.

Disease and insect control field inspectors, working under the supervision of insect and disease inspection supervisors, inspect fields, applying their knowledge of identifying characteristics of insects and diseases to detect the presence of harmful insects and plant diseases. They walk through fields and examine plants at periodic intervals. They count numbers of insects on examined plants or numbers of diseased plants within a sample area. They record the results of their counts on field work sheets. They also collect samples of unidentifiable insects or diseased plants for identification by a supervisor.

Picking-crew or *packing-house supervisors* schedule jobs to be done, supervise crews, and

Two farm crop production technicians take samples of wheat to study the DNA structure of plants. Such research will help develop methods to prevent diseases, increase crop yield, and enhance seed quality.

keep records. They must know grades and standards used for maturity tests on crops ready for picking.

Plant propagators work for nurseries. They propagate new plants by various methods to produce new rootstocks of trees and vines. They select the best hybrid seeds or cuttings to start young plants and bud them over to other trees.

Spray equipment operators work for pest-control companies. They select proper herbicides or pesticides for particular jobs and apply them selectively. They formulate mixtures and operate various types of spraying and dusting equipment. A specialized technician within this occupation is the *aircraft crop duster* or *sprayer.* The person who goes into this activity must have a current license to operate a plane or helicopter.

A farm crop production technician adjusts the track mechanism on a mobile canopy that measures the effect of acid rain on soil quality and crop yield.

Requirements

Farm crop production technicians need manual skills and mechanical ability to operate various kinds of equipment and machinery. They must also have the knowledge to apply scientific principles to the processing procedures, techniques, materials, and measuring and control devices found in the modern laboratory or on the farm. They must be able to communicate to others what needs to be done and to interpret orders given to them.

A career as a farm crop production technician requires a rigorous, two-year technical or agricultural college program in order to understand fully the principles of crop production. To prepare for this, students should have a good high-school background in mathematics and science. They should complete as much vocational agriculture work as possible, including agricultural mechanics. In addition, English is very important, because much of the work requires good communications skills.

Once enrolled in a two-year post–high-school training program, prospective farm crop production technicians can expect to take a broad range of courses relating to agriculture in general and farm crop production in particular, as well as some general education courses. Typical first-year courses include the following: in-troduction to agricultural machinery, introduction to animal husbandry, introduction to soil science, entomology, English, physical education, and science and mathematics.

Typical second-year courses include agricultural economics, soil fertility, plant pathology, forage and seed crops, and social science.

Technicians who wish to specialize in vegetable or fruit production can sometimes modify their programs to place concentration in these areas. They may add courses such as vegetable and fruit production in the first year and fruit and vegetable marketing in the second.

Special requirements

The majority of technicians in the field of farm crop production technology are not required to have a license or certification. However, those technicians involved in grading or inspecting for local, state, or federal government units must pass examinations to be qualified. Some other government jobs, such as that of research assistant, may also require taking a competitive examination.

Opportunities for experience and exploration

Traditionally, those students who have grown up on farms will have the best opportunity for deciding whether to specialize in this area. But a farm background is no longer essential because 4-H Clubs and the Future Farmers of America are open to anyone with a genuine interest. It is also relatively easy to obtain work experience during the summer when extra labor is always required for planting and harvesting. During post–high-school training, heavy emphasis is placed on supervised occupational experience, so that one gains a familiarity with job requirements.

Methods of entering

Students should decide as early as possible in their school programs which phase of crop technology they prefer to enter, because contacts made while in school can be helpful in obtaining a job after completion of the program. One of the common ways of finding employment is by being hired by the same firm where a student worked during a work-study program. If that firm does not have a position open, a recommendation from the employer will be of help with other firms.

Most faculty members in a technical program have contact with prospective employers and can aid in placing qualified students. Many schools also maintain a placement service and arrange interviews between students and prospective employers. For those students who complete the technical program and are willing to work to advance on the job, employment possibilities are very good.

Advancement

Technicians in the field of farm crop production have many opportunities for advancement. Those who combine a technical education in school with work experience will find early advancement easier. Those who have had several jobs in the industry will probably advance to managerial levels more rapidly than those who have not. As more post–high-school institutions are established in local communities, it becomes more possible for employed persons to continue their education through evening classes while they work.

The following short paragraphs describe some employment possibilities that are appropriate for experienced technicians.

Farm managers and *farm owners* perform or supervise all farm activities, including buying and selling, keeping records and accounts, and hiring and supervising employees.

Managers of cooperatives supervise and schedule crop planting and harvesting, handle buying and selling, and supervise employees.

Sales managers supervise company sales forces. They help train new salespeople, set up sales territories, and make studies of product demand and selling techniques.

Secretary-managers of growers' or dealers' associations do public relations work. They keep the membership informed of important legal and other matters affecting their business; they collect dues and maintain membership lists; and they represent the group at various meetings and on legislative matters.

Employment outlook

The student exploring a career in crop production technology should not be misled by the fact that the number of farms is decreasing. Although the part of the population living on farms has decreased over the last century from 85 percent to just a few percent, farming has not decreased in importance. Farmers today are farming more acres, are more mechanized, and are outproducing the farmers of one hundred years ago. But as the number of farmers decreases, there is a proportionately greater gain in the number of workers in service and supply or processing and distribution. In addition to jobs within the United States, such agencies as the Peace Corps and other organizations can use greater numbers of agricultural technicians in the underdeveloped nations of the world.

Because of all of these factors, food production in all of its facets should continue to provide good employment opportunities throughout the coming years.

For technicians interested specifically in orchard and vineyard production, the future is also good. Those technicians looking forward to owning or operating their own orchards or vineyards should remember, of course, that not all crops are necessarily good investments at all times. Local conditions, business cycles, and supply and demand must be considered when making decisions on the planting of a certain kind of orchard, grove, or vineyard. However, a person who can obtain good land in the right location and who can grow efficiently will find fruit-growing offers great rewards.

Employment opportunities for those who do not wish to own their own orchard, but to specialize in one of the many aspects of this profession, should find an increasing demand for their services. The orchard and vineyard industry needs technicians both here and abroad. Technical help in fruit-growing and processing is in demand in many foreign countries. Such careers offer a chance to travel and see the world, as well as to help other people.

Earnings

Salaries of farm crop production technicians will vary widely depending on a number of factors. For instance, technicians employed in off-farm jobs often receive higher salaries than technicians working on a farm. Technicians working on a farm, however, often receive food and housing benefits that can be the equivalent of several thousand dollars a year. Salaries will also vary according to the geographical area in which the technician is working, with jobs in the northeast region being at the lower end of the scale and jobs in California, Minnesota, and Iowa being at the upper end of the scale.

Salaries also vary according to the technician's educational background, agricultural experience, and the type of crop involved.

In general, most farm crop production technicians receive starting salaries in the range of $12,000 to $16,000 a year; however, some technicians may receive salaries that are significantly above or below this range.

Conditions of work

Many of the technicians in this field will be required to work outdoors a great deal of the time. They should like outdoor work and be able to adapt to extreme weather conditions. There may be certain seasons of the year when they are required to work long hours under considerable pressure to get a crop harvested or processed at the right time.

The work of laboratory technicians in this field involves exacting systematic procedures in facilities that are generally clean and well lit. Inspection technicians may work long hours during harvest season. Those involved in sales may spend considerable time in travel. Work in the processing phase is usually indoors, except for the field-service or field-contact personnel who must spend much of their time outdoors.

Social and psychological factors

Planting a new field, orchard, or vineyard, then watching it grow and develop, can be extremely satisfying work. But the continual uncertainties of weather conditions, possible blight, premature frost, and the wiping out of one's labor and investment call for a stable temperament and the ability to withstand setbacks.

For technicians who feel they may lack some of these characteristics, employment in the sales, services, or other off-farm area may be better. Here too there is the satisfaction of knowing that one is playing a vital role in producing humanity's most basic need.

GOE: 02.04.02, 03.02.01, 03.02.04; SIC: 01; SOC: 382, 5611

◇ **SOURCES OF ADDITIONAL INFORMATION**

American Society of Agronomy
677 South Segoe Road
Madison, WI 53711

Future Farmers of America
National FFA Center
PO Box 15160
Alexandria, VA 22309

U.S. Department of Agriculture
Washington, DC 20250

◇ **RELATED ARTICLES**

Volume 1: Agriculture
Volume 2: Biologists; Buyers, wholesale and retail; Food technologists; Purchasing agents
Volume 3: Agricultural scientists; Agricultural extension service workers; Farmers; Farm operatives and managers; Grain merchants; Pest control workers; Soil scientists
Volume 4: Biological technicians; Agribusiness technicians; Soil conservation technicians

Forestry technicians

Definition

Forestry technicians work under the direction of a professional forest scientist or a manager of a forest. As members of a forest management team, forestry technicians help plan, supervise, and conduct the operations necessary to modern forest growth: protection, harvesting, re-

planting, and marketing of forest products. Forestry technicians are knowledgeable in the science and technology of producing wood fiber and forest products. They help manage forests and wildlife areas, control fires, insects, and disease, and limit the depletion of forest resources. Land surveying and forest product measurement are part of the work of forestry technicians, as are operating logging and log-handling equipment.

History

Forests have served as sources of wood and timber for shelter and fuel since before civilization began. By the time of the Roman Empire, vast amounts of wood were being cut in many forested areas of Europe. But most of these forests grew back fast enough and were large enough to supply the needs of the Romans as well as those who succeeded them.

Several hundred years ago, however, with the development of machines that reduced the cost and increased the speed of cutting logs, forests were cut down faster than they could grow. Realizing this, the Europeans began to conserve and manage their forests. This marked the beginning of the science of forestry.

Forests covered huge areas in North America when the Pilgrims first arrived. Early settlers first cleared the forests so they could build shelters and farm the land. As colonial expansion moved westward, much of the forested area in North America was cleared, and most of the trees suitable for prime lumber were cut down by the beginning of this century.

In the early 1900s, it became evident that the United States needed to follow the methods of forest management and conservation already in use in Europe. Professional foresters, tree genetics experts, forest-culture research scientists, and forest management scientists were trained to work in government and private industry. By about 1960, these professional foresters saw a need for technical workers to do the jobs between the manually skilled forest worker and the professional levels. The forestry technician occupation came into being, and the demand for technicians grew rapidly.

Forestry technicians now work in year-round forest management and related industries. Forests are regarded as a resource to be farmed, harvested, and replanted. Technicians have become an essential part of the management team in this total process.

Nature of the work

A forestry career is a tough, demanding, outdoor job. Good health, a willingness to work and to study, an active interest in specialized machinery and equipment, and a desire for challenge are essential for success in the forestry technician's job.

Forestry technicians carry out duties that require scientific training and skill. Technicians frequently do work that professional foresters once did. They must be capable of working closely with forest scientists, foresters, and other professionals. They must be able to supervise and coordinate the efforts of skilled laborers and field workers. Their training and supervisory abilities make forestry technicians important members of a team whose work is to plan, organize, and operate various forest enterprises for government or private industry.

Most forestry technicians are employed in forest land management and administration. Technicians working in this area may be involved in timber production, recreation, wildlife forage, water regulation, preservation for scientific studies and special uses, or a combination of these.

The day-to-day work of the forestry technician is based on a cycle of activities for managing and harvesting a forest. The first major step in the cycle is planting trees to replace those that have been cut down, harvested, or lost to disease or fire. Next comes caring for the trees, which includes thinning them if necessary to obtain the best growth, and protecting them from fire, disease, or damage. Periodic measuring or scaling of trees to find the amount of lumber they would provide is done to plan for harvesting and marketing. Harvesting and marketing the trees is the last step, after which the cycle begins again with reconditioning the area and planting new trees.

Technicians, working under the direction of professional foresters or managers, play an active part in each step of the cycle. In addition, each forest area is managed with a particular objective. If the plan is to produce large saw-logs, the planting, thinning, and care are different from the plan used to produce pulp wood. A plan to produce timber as a habitat for deer and grouse results in trees that are short enough for deer to feed on and full enough to provide cover.

To prepare for harvesting, access roads for logging machinery and trucks must be planned, surveyed, and built. Aerial photography surveys may have to be made to determine topography and the condition of the forest. Technicians must know about these surveys and be able to interpret aerial photographs.

The work of a forestry technician is more complicated than it was just a few decades years ago. Equipment and methods used to detect, prevent, or fight tree diseases and parasites have developed rapidly. Harvest machinery has changed too. Powerful log handlers and loaders are now commonly used.

A forestry technician checks for the presence of beetles. Beetle infestation can threaten the livelihood of trees and destroy an entire forest preserve.

Forestry technicians usually work far from cities and thickly populated areas. At times, the work can be lonely. Those who choose the career must be self-sufficient, resourceful, and prepared to live in sparsely settled areas.

In spite of the remoteness of most forestry work, personal communication with others is an important part of the work of forestry technicians. They must deal with other workers, members of the public who use the forest for recreation, and conservationists who protect fish, game, and plant life. They must also make written and oral reports as a regular part of their work.

A forestry technician's work includes many different kinds of activities. Most forestry technicians are employed by private industry, where they cruise timber (measure the volume of standing trees), scale logs to find their lumber content, survey logging roads, prepare maps and charts, and mark trees for cutting or thinning.

The following paragraphs describe some positions open to forestry technicians. These positions may be found with federal or state agencies or private forestry concerns. Each requires a different mix of skills and abilities. These skills and abilities may be improved by study on the job.

Information and education technicians write news releases and act as public relations specialists in nature centers.

Survey assistants locate and mark boundary lines. These technicians also locate positions for dams and impoundments, prepare maps of surveys, and work on land appraisal and acquisition problems for private, state, and federal employers.

Biological aides work in forest insect and disease reconnaissance and control. They record and analyze data, run experiments under supervision, and prepare maps.

Technical research assistants assist scientists in basic and applied research problems that relate to timber, watershed, and wildlife management. These specialized technicians gather and analyze field data and operate research equipment.

Buyers for sawmills purchase high-grade logs for milling and furniture manufacture.

Pulp buyers for paper mills purchase pulp logs for pulp and paper companies.

Lumber inspectors and/or graders grade and calculate the volume of hardwood and softwood lumber at mills, or in retail and wholesale yards.

Tree-nursery management assistants help operate and manage tree nurseries. They keep records, hire temporary personnel, and supervise tree production during planting season. These technicians may also run seed tests and analyze data, operate and maintain equipment, and help supervise forest planting-stock production.

Wildlife technicians conduct field work for the various game commissions and federal agencies engaged in fish and game management. They catch and tag animals with radio collars to establish territories and animal survival records. They conduct experiments under supervision. Wildlife technicians also repair and operate various kinds of machinery, help take wildlife censuses, and maintain daily crew records.

Forestry technicians employed by the federal government may specialize from the beginning and progress through the ranks in a limited scope of activities. More often, they work as an assistant to a professional forester in research connected with watershed management, timber management, wildlife management, forest genetics, fire control, disease and insect control, recreational development, and other important matters.

Many state forest agencies have revised their personnel classification systems to recognize the forest technician as a vital link between the professional forester and the forest laborer. Many communities now employ forestry technicians in the management of their municipal watersheds and in their parks and recreation development programs.

Requirements

Forestry technicians must have special abilities and characteristics. They must have a genuine enthusiasm for outdoor work. They must be logical and observant. Above all, they must be able to work without supervision. This characteristic is perhaps the most important, as supervision is minimal in forestry. A technician's duties often require being separated from a supervisor and from other workers for days or weeks at a time. The job must be accomplished without constant supervision. To many people, the fact that the technician is without supervision for a great part of the time is one of the most attractive characteristics of the work.

Forestry technicians must be able to apply both theoretical knowledge and specialized occupational skills. They must be familiar with certain principles of engineering, biology, mathematics, and statistics, and they should have a working knowledge of how to use a computer.

It is extremely important for technicians to communicate effectively. Much of their work will result in written reports. These reports may include charts, diagrams, and sometimes maps.

The best way to become a forest technician is to graduate from a formal training program after high school. Before doing this, it is necessary to get the right high-school preparation. Almost all of the technical forestry programs require a high-school diploma. Two courses in college-preparatory mathematics and one course in physics are necessary to enter most technical programs. It is very important for students to read and write well. Courses in technical reporting, college study techniques, and biology are also recommended.

The companies and agencies who hire forestry technicians are looking for people who have a scientific knowledge of forestry and who have also mastered the "how-to" part of forestry. In other words, one is not so much required to know how a formula was obtained as how it works under a given set of circumstances. Of course, enough theory must be learned so that technicians will understand why a job must be done. Such knowledge will, in turn, assist them in determining how to do a job. Technicians must communicate with professionals and scientists; therefore, they must think along the same lines and speak the same language.

Whether prospective technicians attend a technical institute or a junior or community college, they will probably take a two-year program leading to an associate degree. More than eighty schools offer such programs, and thirty-six of these programs have been recognized by the Society of American Foresters as meeting their standards.

Students in forestry technician programs take mathematics appropriate to forestry, communications, botany, engineering, and technical forestry courses. The type of forestry courses given varies depending upon the seasons in a given locale and the nature of local forestry practice.

Since forestry technicians must learn both scientific theory and applied science activities, the technical program is a demanding one. It requires organized classroom study and considerable time in laboratory or field work.

Technicians must learn about forests, the kinds of trees and plants that grow in a forest, and how they relate to or affect other plants. Two formal fields of study in this area are silvics and dendrology. When this knowledge is directed to managing forests, it is called silviculture. Technicians must also learn about measuring and calculating the amount of lumber in a tree. This is called mensuration, or forest measurements.

A typical first year's study in a two-year forestry program includes the following courses or their equivalent: elementary forest surveying, communication skills, technical mathematics, dendrology (tree identification), botany of forests, forest orientation seminar, technical reporting, elementary forest measurements, applied silviculture, forest soils, technical drawing, computer applications, and elementary business management.

A typical second year's courses include the following or their equivalent: personnel management, forest business methods, timber harvesting, advanced forest surveying and map drafting, outdoor recreation and environmental control, wildlife ecology, elements of social science, forest products utilization, forest protection, forest insect and disease control, forest fire control, advanced forest measurements, and aerial photographic interpretation.

Almost all forestry technician programs include work in forest areas. Some schools arrange summer jobs for students between the first- and second-year courses. Student technicians need the experience provided by working in the forest to learn the duties and tasks associated with forest care. Many forestry technician programs own or use a small sawmill where students can learn the basic elements of sawmill operation.

A special feature of some forestry technician programs is a second-year seminar that includes visits to tree nurseries, sawmills, paper mills, veneer mills, wallboard manufacturing plants, and furniture factories. These visits help students understand how forest products are processed and used, measured, and classified according to quality. It also gives them a better understanding of possible employment areas.

Physical requirements include moderate physical strength, and normal eyesight and hearing. Technicians also need average or better-than-average physical coordination.

Special requirements

For some duties, forestry technicians must be licensed in some states. Those who work with pesticides or chemicals may need to be licensed. Also forestry technicians who specialize in surveying may have to be licensed if they make surveys of property for legal public property records.

Opportunities for experience and exploration

High schools, colleges, and forests are all sources of information for people interested in a forestry technician career. High-school counselors can provide materials and information on forestry. Community and technical colleges usually have career information centers or other services that can provide information about this career. People who live near forest areas may be able to visit a park or public land area and talk with forestry technicians who can explain the features of their careers. People who live near forest areas may also obtain summer work in forest-related work, especially when forest fires occur and when unskilled workers are needed for timber harvesting, clearing, or planting operations.

Methods of entering

The best way to enter this career is to graduate from a community college or technical college program for forestry technicians. The qualifications that graduates of such programs have been bringing to the job market in recent years have made it very difficult to enter the career in any other way. A high-school diploma and a willingness to work hard are generally not enough to encourage an employer to hire a person who wants to become a technician.

Students who have worked during the summer are frequently hired on a permanent basis. Personal contacts with company repre-

sentatives and forestry instructors' contacts can provide excellent leads in finding a desirable permanent position.

The graduate technician may be employed by a private firm or a government agency. Government agencies where forestry technicians can be hired include the Forest Service, Bureau of Land Management, Soil Conservation Service, National Park Service, and many others. More municipal governments and city managers have been hiring forestry technicians. Most forestry technicians, however, work in private industry.

Advancement

Forestry technicians can advance to a number of positions. Some are within private companies; others involve working on a consulting basis. Many forestry technicians find advanced positions in research work.

Timber cruisers supervise crews in the measurement of trees for volume computations. They keep records and run statistical analyses of volumes, and mark timber for sale. They recommend logging methods and use aerial photographs to locate future timber harvesting areas.

Forest-fire control technicians maintain fire control supplies in a central area and report fires by radio-telephone. They help dispatch fire crews and serve as fire-crew leaders in fire suppression. They also conduct investigations into the causes of fires. An important aspect of their job is educating communities in fire prevention. They also recruit, train, and supervise forest-fire wardens and crews.

Refuge managers supervise work crews in game and fish management. They help plant food plots for wildlife and other plants for habitat improvement. They also patrol restricted areas, conduct census studies, and make maps.

Sawmill managers manage and supervise sawmills, control crew and production schedules, and keep payroll records.

Fish and game preserve managers supervise controlled hunting and fishing. They stock, raise, and feed fish and game species, and improve habitats. They also keep hunting and fishing census accounts and records.

Kiln operators supervise and control the kiln schedules for correct drying of lumber. They run drying tests and submit reports on loads of drying lumber.

Forest recreation technicians supervise the operation and maintenance of outdoor recreation facilities. They are responsible for tactful enforcement of the rules and fire watches.

Assistant logging superintendents control harvesting and loading operations for timber sales. They help maintain safety, keep payroll and supply records, and write technical reports for superintendents.

Forestry consultants play an increasingly important role in forestry by providing forestry services to people whose property or business does not require a permanent full-time forester. Technicians who work for consulting firms perform various tasks that increase the consultant's work capacity and hence the annual earnings of the firm. Experienced technicians can also start their own consulting business.

Forestry technicians may also build rewarding careers in research. *Research technicians* may be called upon to obtain data for computer analysis. They may help develop new chemical fire retardants or new machines to prepare forest soils for planting. Research technicians may work for private industry, for a large city, or for a state or federal government agency.

Other forestry technicians are finding employment with wood-using firms, such as logging and sawmill operations. Still others go into business for themselves as *surveyors* or *consultants*.

Employment outlook

Forestry-related employment is expected to grow only moderately through the 1990s. This means that there will be keen competition in the field. Technicians with good preparation in forestry technology and machinery management will have an advantage in the job market.

One promising aspect of the employment picture for forestry technicians is in the area of forest recreation, including hunting and fishing. Ever-increasing numbers of people are enjoying the forests. These resources must be managed for the protection of the users, as well as of the resource itself. Such management requires equipment and services that can be coordinated and supplied by forestry technicians.

Land owned by private timber companies has traditionally been open to limited and controlled public use. The amount of land available for this practice is increasing. Greater public use of private forest land requires technicians to make sure the land's resources are appropriately used.

The production of water from forest areas is of major importance in all parts of the United States. Activities related to finding adequate water sources and bringing them into use increasingly provides both practical and research jobs for forestry technicians.

New uses for wood and wood products are being found all the time. Meeting this growing demand requires a growing supply of timber and pulp. Forestry technicians who specialize in land management and the various aspects of logging and sawmill work play a valuable role in assuring this supply. Research technicians who help find ways to improve methods of planting, growing, and timber and pulp production are also needed.

Overseas employment with oil, rubber, and timber companies is also a possible outlet for the talents of technicians who like to travel. Compensation for work of this nature has been quite good in the past and should continue to be so.

Earnings

Most forestry technicians begin their careers as hourly paid workers if they work in private industry. If they start their career in a government agency, they probably will be paid a monthly or annual salary. Forestry technicians who have graduated from a two-year technical program usually start their first job at roughly $13,500 to $16,000 per year.

Graduates with three to five years of experience in private industry earn salaries ranging from about $15,000 to $19,000. Salaries of persons who started as technicians and advanced to supervisory positions or special consulting positions may be around $25,000 or more, depending on their specialization, the quality of their work, and their employer.

Salaries for beginning forestry technicians who work for government agencies usually start at slightly lower levels than those paid by private industry. However, they soon become comparable to salaries in industry. In recent years most of the graduates of two-year forestry technician programs have been employed by private industry.

In addition to their yearly salary, forestry technicians usually receive paid holidays and vacations, sick days, and insurance and retirement plan benefits. Benefits vary according to the employer. Some employers pay part or all of the cost of job-related schooling to help the technician keep up with developments and changes that occur in the field.

Conditions of work

The forestry technician's work is concerned with managing forests. This involves working in forest settings that may be primitive and re-mote. Many forest areas do not have paved roads and large areas have only a few roads or trails that are passable. Because of this, forestry technicians must feel at home in forest sur-roundings and be adaptable to the kinds of ve-hicles and other equipment used to do their work.

Forestry technicians must always use good safety practices. Forest fires are always danger-ous and fire fighting must be done as safely as possible. There is always a possibility of acci-dents and injury in logging and harvesting jobs and in sawmill operations. Appropriate safety shoes, hard hats, and suitable clothing should be worn.

Some forestry technicians spend most of their working day outdoors. They may be re-quired to do their jobs in unpleasant weather. Those technicians whose jobs are centered in an office or laboratory generally work in clean, well-lighted surroundings.

Working hours are usually reasonably nor-mal. In case of fires or other unusual situations, longer hours may sometimes be necessary.

Social and psychological factors

Forestry technicians play an important part in carrying out scientific, long-range plans for for-est management. Forests must be carefully farmed so they will produce the best and larg-est possible amount of forest products. At the same time, they should provide as much rec-reational opportunity as possible for an ever-increasing number of people.

The twin purposes of forestry present great challenges to forest technicians. If both pur-poses are carried out successfully, the forestry technician will feel a deep satisfaction in having conserved and improved the forests and pro-vided an essential public service.

GOE: 03.01.04; SIC: 085; SOC: 572

◇ **SOURCES OF ADDITIONAL INFORMATION**

American Forest Council
1250 Connecticut Avenue, NW, Suite 320
Washington, DC 20036

American Forestry Association
1516 P Street, NW
Washington, DC 20005

American Pulpwood Association
1025 Vermont Avenue, NW, Suite 1020
Washington, DC 20005

Forest Products Research Society
2801 Marshall Court
Madison, WI 53705

National Recreation and Park Association
3101 Park Center Drive, 12th Floor
Alexandria, VA 22302

Society of American Foresters
5400 Grosvenor Lane
Bethesda, MD 20814

Society of Wood Science and Technology
PO Box 5062
Madison, WI 53705

TAPPI—Technical Association of the Pulp and Paper Industry
Technology Park/Atlanta
PO Box 105113
Atlanta, GA 30348

U.S. Forest Service
Department of Agriculture
Washington, DC 20250

◇ **RELATED ARTICLES**

Volume 1: Pulp and Paper; Wood
Volume 2: Wood science and technology ca-reers
Volume 3: Agricultural extension service workers; Agricultural scientists; Farm operatives and managers; Foresters; Landscapers and grounds managers; Logging industry workers; Park rangers; Paper processing operations; Range managers; Sawmill workers; Soil scien-tists
Volume 4: Agribusiness technicians; Farm crop production technicians; Ornamental horti-cultural technicians; Park technicians; Soil con-servation technicians

Ornamental horticulture technicians

Definition

Ornamental horticulture technicians grow, arrange, market, and care for flowers, shrubs, trees, and grass for the beautification of human surroundings. They raise and propagate flowers, hedges, shrubs, and related crops for commercial purposes; they plant and care for ground cover and trees in parks, playgrounds, along public highways, and in other special areas; and they landscape public and private areas. The skills of ornamental horticulture technicians include knowing how to raise and care for decorative flowers, shrubs, and trees in greenhouses and out-of-doors; how to display their products advantageously; and how to market them successfully.

History

The landscaping of formal gardens and the cultivation of flowers are ancient and honorable arts. The famed Gardens of Babylon, the vast landscaped areas of Persia and India, the smaller formal gardens of Athens, and the terraces and geometric gardens of Italy are early examples of this art. Gradually the practice spread to the northern European countries. Holland established its preeminence in growing dozens of varieties of tulips by the middle of the seventeenth century. The gardens of the kings of France were often exercises in formal fantasy. In the eighteenth century, gardens became more informal and natural, typified by the plantings around George Washington's home, Mount Vernon. In the United States the first large landscaped area was New York City's Central Park, which was created in the 1850s. While flowers, parks, and gardens have not been as dominant in the United States as in other countries, a growing enthusiasm is creating a new and large demand for trained ornamental horticulture technicians.

Nature of the work

Ornamental horticulture technicians usually specialize in one or more of the following areas: floriculture (dealing with flowers), nursery operation (dealing with bushes, hedges, and shrubs), turfgrass, arboriculture (dealing with trees), and landscape development.

The activities of *floriculture technicians* and of *nursery-operation technicians* are closely related in that both kinds of technicians are involved in raising and selling plants. Even the distinction between them that floriculture technicians raise and sell flowers while nursery-operation technicians raise and sell bushes, hedges, and shrubs, is not always valid. Nursery operators may well want to include flowers among their products for sale, and floriculture technicians need to know something about the bushes that produce ornamental flowers. In general, both floriculture and nursery-operation technicians must be able to determine correct soil conditions for specific plants, the proper rooting material for cuttings, and the best fertilizer for promoting growth. Both kinds of technicians may also be involved with the merchandising aspects of growing plants.

Technicians working in floriculture or nursery operations may become *horticultural-specialty growers*. Horticultural-specialty growers propagate and raise specialty products and crops, such as flowers, ornamental plants, bulbs, rootstocks, sod, and vegetables, both in fields and under environmentally controlled conditions such as in greenhouses and in growing sheds. Working either inside or outside, they plan growing schedules, quantities to grow, and utilization schemes for field acreage or space within structures. Some of their duties include planting seeds; transplanting seedlings; inspecting crops for nutrient deficiencies, insects, diseases, and unwanted plant growth; removing substandard plants; and pruning other plants.

In greenhouses and growing sheds, horticultural-specialty growers monitor timing and metering devices that control frequency, amount, and type of nutrient applications. They also regulate humidity, ventilation, and carbon dioxide conditions; dispense herbicides, fungicides, and pesticides; and explain and demonstrate growing techniques and procedures to other workers. When working with field crops they may drive tractors or harvesters, attach implements, or adjust and repair equipment.

Horticultural-specialty growers may also become involved with hiring personnel, working with vendors and customers, and with record-keeping of all sorts.

An ornamental horticulture technician measures mums that have been treated with a growth retardant. He is trying to produce a shorter and more desirable stem length without affecting the size or shape of the blossoms.

Another position that both floriculture and nursery-operation technicians may hold is that of *plant propagator*. Plant propagators work with greenhouse or nursery management in initiating new kinds of plant growth. After conferring with management to determine the types of new plants or varieties to be propagated, they develop and revise nutrient formulas to use with the new plants, select growth media and other kinds of materials to be used, and prepare the growing containers. Following these preparations, they initiate the new growth using any of a number of different techniques, including planting seeds; taking cuttings of leaves, stems, or rhizomes and placing them in a growth medium; and breaking apart rootstocks to create several different root systems that will each grow into separate plants. Plant propagators also monitor temperature and humidity conditions and regulate systems of heaters, fans, and sprayers. They also train and supervise coworkers, keep records, and prepare reports to supervisors.

The following short paragraphs describe some jobs which floriculture technicians in particular may hold. In each case, these are entry-level positions.

Floral designers design all kinds of floral settings, such as funeral pieces, corsages, bouquets, wreathes, and decorations for weddings.

Wholesale florist assistants help in the preparation and marketing of cut flowers and potted plants, grown either indoors or outdoors, for sale to customers who buy wholesale.

Flower salespeople sell fresh flowers, potted plants, floral arrangements, ferns, greenery, and other flower products at the retail level.

Most entry-level technicians work as growers, propagators, or as retail or wholesale salespeople. One specialty job that nursery-operation technicians may hold is that of *storage manager*. Storage managers work only in large nurseries and are responsible for putting plants into and taking them out of temporary storage with minimum loss of plants.

Some of the jobs that more experienced floriculture and nursery-operation technicians may hold include *garden center manager, greenhouse manager, flower shop manager,* and *nursery manager.* In each case, these managers are responsible for all of the duties necessary to the operation of a retail or wholesale outlet. They maintain inventories; deal with customers and suppliers; hire, train, and supervise employees; direct advertising and promotion activities; and keep all kinds of records and accounts. Often they are aided by assistant managers who may also be trained technicians but who have less experience.

Another kind of work done by experienced floriculture or nursery-operation technicians is that of *horticultural inspector*. These people usually work for state or federal government agencies. They inspect plants, especially those that may be transported across state lines or those that are about to come into the United States. They look for insects and diseases, quarantine the plants when necessary, and see that forbidden plants are not brought across state or national borders.

With additional experience and education (usually a degree from a four-year institution), some floriculture and nursery-operation technicians go on to become *horticulturists*. Horticulturists conduct experiments and investigations into problems of breeding, production, storage, processing, and transit of fruits, nuts, berries, vegetables, flowers, bushes, and trees. They develop new varieties of plants and determine methods of planting, spraying, cultivating, and harvesting plants.

Ornamental horticulture technicians working in the area of turfgrass management are usually employed in one of three major areas: in commercial lawn maintenance and construction; in planning and maintaining public lands, such as parks, highways, and playing fields; and in allied areas such as sod production, seed production, irrigation, transportation, and sales of other products and services.

In the private sector, *turfgrass technicians* may run their own businesses or work in someone else's business. In general, these businesses provide lawn care services to homeowners, corporations, colleges, and other large institutions with extensive grounds. These services include mowing; fertilization; insect, disease, and weed control; irrigation; installing new lawns; and renovating old lawns. They may provide tree and snow removal services. Sometimes these businesses work with engineering and architectural firms who need help in planning turfgrass areas and in preparing specifications.

In the public sector, turfgrass technicians usually work for local, county, state, or federal government agencies. They may be involved in planning turfgrass areas sturdy enough to stand up to hard use in parks or playing fields, or they may help in the design of grassy areas along public highways.

One of the allied areas that turfgrass technicians may work in is the field of sod production; that is, preparing the ready-made squares of grass that are used in establishing new lawns and in renovating old ones. Other employment opportunities include producing or selling seeds, fertilizers, insecticides, fungicides, herbicides, and other equipment and supplies needed by contractors, public agencies, and homeowners. Finally, technicians may be employed by private firms or public agencies to carry out research related to turfgrass management.

The following paragraphs describe some of the specific jobs that turfgrass technicians may hold. Unless otherwise specified, these positions are appropriate for entry-level technicians.

Greenskeepers supervise and coordinate the activities of workers who are engaged in keeping the grounds and the turf of a golf course in good playing condition. They consult with the greens superintendent to plan and review work projects; they determine work assignments, such as fertilizing, irrigating, seeding, mowing, raking, and spraying; and they mix and prepare spraying and dusting solutions. They may also repair and maintain mechanical equipment.

Owners of turfgrass maintenance services are in business to provide services connected with the planning and maintaining of grounds and landscapes. Some technicians begin such a service before graduating from their post–high-school training program. This requires a little capital along with a knowledge of turfgrasses and the best methods of growing and maintaining them.

Turfgrass maintenance supervisors work for turfgrass maintenance services. They supervise workers, help plan all of the operations that go into building or maintaining grounds and landscapes, and deal directly with customers.

Sod salespeople recommend and sell various strains of sod to customers who are involved with planting, growing, or caring for sod. They give advice to customers on problems such as insects, diseases, and weeds.

Estimators estimate the amount of materials, the labor needed, and the costs of constructing a lawn or other sod job.

Turfgrass research and development technicians carry out turfgrass research and development activities for local, state, or federal government agencies or for privately owned turfgrass seed companies. They record data, write reports, and handle other details associated with scientific research projects.

Golf course construction supervisors or *contractors* are experienced technicians who construct golf courses from architects' designs. This highly specialized work calls for knowledge about earth moving, tree moving, and water diversion in addition to knowledge about turfgrass.

Commercial sod growers are experienced technicians who may be self-employed or who may grow sod for large individual growers or companies.

Greens superintendents are experienced turfgrass technicians who supervise and coordinate the activities of greenskeepers and other workers engaged in constructing new golf course areas and in preserving existing areas. They formulate work plans, applying their experience with turfgrass to the problems of maintaining and improving the turf and playing conditions of the course. They review test results of soil and turf samples, and they direct the application of fertilizer, lime, insecticide, or fungicide. Their other duties include touring the grounds to determine the need for supplemental irrigation or changes in mower height, keeping and reviewing all kinds of records, and interviewing and hiring workers.

Turfgrass consultants are experienced technicians who analyze turfgrass problems and recommend solutions, such as the type of turfgrass to use and the best schedule or techniques for mowing, and provide other advice about maintenance and growing procedures.

Ornamental horticulture technicians working in the field of arboriculture are generally employed in one of two broad areas: in the private sector, either with their own small business or working for a company; and in the public sector, working for a park system, a botanical garden or arboretum, or other county, state, or federal agency, such as those responsible for public highways, buildings, or monuments.

In general, *arboriculture technicians* plant, feed, prune, and provide pest control for trees. Some are called upon to diagnose the diseases infesting trees and to take corrective action. They must know about various tree species and where they thrive best. Arboriculture technicians need to know when and how trees should be removed, what trees to plant, and how to place them.

In the private sector, arboriculture technicians may work for or contract their services to large and small private businesses. Their duties may include planting, feeding, pruning, and spraying the trees that are found on the company grounds or in the landscaped areas of industrial parks. These technicians sometimes contract their services to a group of companies that are located in the same industrial park or neighborhood. Other private employers of arboriculture technicians include public utility companies, which hire technicians to keep trees healthy in order to prevent damage to power lines and to promote good public relations. Some arboriculture technicians working for utility companies write instructional materials for customers and for company work crews.

In the public sector, arboriculture technicians may be employed by local, state, or federal agencies. They decide when and how trees should be removed and where new trees should be placed on public property. They may also work for park and parkway systems, for public recreational agencies, and for public school systems.

The following paragraphs describe some of the specific jobs that arboriculture technicians may hold. The first four are appropriate for entry-level technicians, the second four for technicians who have gained additional experience and training.

Trees pruners and trimmers prune all kinds of trees to enhance their beauty, correct dangerous situations, or cure disease. They apply tar or other protective substances to cut surfaces to seal out insects.

Arboretum or botanical garden supervisors oversee the maintenance of grounds and tree areas. They supervise workers, plan work schedules, and carry out other duties related directly to planting and caring for trees.

Tree movers dig up, transport, and replant trees. They need to be able to determine when a move is possible and estimate how much it will cost.

Tree-supply salespeople sell trees, tools, fertilizers, peat moss, pesticides, and other kinds of equipment needed in planting and caring for trees. They work with customers, advising them about products and suggesting solutions to problems their trees may develop.

City foresters advise communities on the selection of trees, on planting schedules, and on the proper care of trees. They may also supervise or do the pruning, spraying, planting, or feeding of trees.

Tree surgeons prune and treat ornamental and shade trees to improve their health and appearance. They scrape decayed matter from cavities in the trees and fill the holes with cement to promote healing and to prevent further deterioration. They also spray trees with pesticides and fertilizers.

Tree-services proprietors own or are partners in businesses that perform all kinds of tree services from planting and removal to pest control and pruning. They may specialize in one service, but they usually work in all areas of arboriculture.

Arboretum or botanical garden superintendents supervise the entire operation of an arboretum or botanical garden. They decide what to plant, when to plant, and where to plant; and they determine the best methods for planting, spraying, and cultivating. They conduct or direct experiments, and they investigate new methods for improving various species of trees. They also hire, train, and supervise workers, plan work schedules, keep accounts, and buy equipment and materials.

Ornamental horticulture technicians working in the field of landscape development prepare sketches, develop planting plans, draw up lists of materials, and oversee or carry out the construction activities related to landscaping a piece of property.

Landscape-development technicians interested in landscape planning or design usually work for private companies that provide these services directly to customers. Alternatively, they may work for a city or county, doing landscape design for small parks, fire houses, play grounds, parking lots, or streets. They consult with local officials and select planting materials on the basis of appearance, required upkeep, and cost.

Some landscape-development technicians find employment on the staff of a landscape architect. They may perform or supervise landscape construction, including construction walks, pools, walls, or larger structures.

Landscape-development technicians often start their own businesses. The business usually requires only a small capital investment, and expansion can occur in many directions. Some technicians begin by taking on the job of grounds maintenance for one or more small industrial plants. Others start a small nursery on the side. This kind of beginning may lead to design work for customers, and the technician may be asked to do the construction of the approved plan and to carry out maintenance afterwards.

The following paragraphs describe some specific jobs that landscape-development technicians may hold. The first four of these are suitable for entry-level technicians; the remaining jobs are more appropriate for technicians who have additional experience or training.

Landscape gardeners care for hedges, lawns, gardens, and other landscaped areas. Depending on the setting, they may carry out or supervise the work activities. They are usually employed by an arboretum, botanical garden, a unit of government, or a private contractor; or they may own their own business.

Landscape-maintenance supervisors direct landscape-maintenance projects at private homes, industrial plants, government institutions, schools, arboretums, and botanical gardens. They are involved with purchasing materials and supplies, and with training, directing, and supervising employees.

Landscape-maintenance proprietors usually own their own small landscape maintenance firms. Generally they perform all kinds of landscape maintenance, including planting; insect, weed, and disease control; lawn maintenance and fertilization; and some tree work. Their usual customers include homeowners, industrial plants, schools, units of government, and utility companies.

Pest controllers do custom spraying for landscape maintenance businesses. They operate sprayers and trucks, mix and apply spray materials, and keep up-to-date on new insecticides and fungicides.

Landscape-construction supervisors read the plans for and then direct the construction of walls, walks, paths, pools, grassy areas, hedges, driveways, and small buildings. They generally work for landscape contractors, the landscape department of a general contracting company, or a local, state, or federal agency.

Landscape contractors perform landscape-construction work on a contract basis for homeowners, highway departments, and operators of industrial plants and other buildings with landscaping needs. They confer with pro-

Working in a botanical garden, an ornamental horticulture technician measures and records the growth of flowers.

spective clients and study the landscape design, drawings, and bills of material to determine the amount of landscape work required, such as the installation of lighting or sprinkler systems, erection of fences, and the types of trees, shrubs, or ornamental plants required. They inspect the grounds, and they calculate labor, equipment, and materials costs. They also prepare and submit bids, draw up contracts, and direct and coordinate, through middle-level supervisors, the activities of workers. They may also be involved with purchasing materials and with subcontracting certain kinds of tasks. In some states landscape contractors have to be licensed.

Supervisors of cemetery workers supervise and coordinate the activities of workers engaged in maintaining cemetery grounds and in related activities, such as grave digging and lining, grave-marker placement, and disinterments. They draw up plans and schedules for the work to be done, determine personnel and equip-

309

ment requirements for each task, and hire and train workers.

Supervisors of park workers direct and coordinate the activities of workers engaged in the maintenance of areas such as parks, playgrounds, and botanical gardens. They plan landscaping tasks and instruct workers in the planting, growing, pruning, and transplanting of flowers, shrubs, and trees. They also direct workers in the maintenance and repair of driveways, walks, hedges, swings, benches, and other park equipment.

Landscape consultants offer advice concerning landscape design or construction to private individuals, industrial companies, public utility companies, landscape contractors, builders, and government agencies.

Requirements

The most important quality that ornamental horticulture technicians can possess, regardless of their field of specialty, is the desire to cooperate with nature in creating a useful thing of beauty.

In high-school, prospective technicians should take courses in algebra, chemistry, biology, English, and geometry. If courses in horticulture, agriculture, or botany are available, they should also be included.

People who hire ornamental horticulture technicians usually prefer graduates from a two-year college or institute granting the associate in applied science degree. However, it is possible in most of these areas to obtain an entry-level job with a good high-school background coupled with practical experience.

Those who wish to become landscape architects must enroll in a four-year college and obtain a bachelor's degree with a major in landscape architecture. Advanced degrees are also required for individuals interested in the research or teaching of horticulture.

Special requirements

No special license or certification is needed to begin a career as an ornamental horticulture technician. Some advanced positions may require additional education, and some proprietors of businesses (such as nursery operators and landscape contractors) may require a license for their business.

Opportunities for experience and exploration

Those who enjoy mowing lawns, growing flowers, tending gardens, and as high-school students have worked part-time caring for home or commercial grounds have valuable experience to supplement their academic training. Many nurseries, flower shops, and public agencies use temporary summer employees to aid in various activities. Interested students can also join garden clubs, visit local flower shops, and attend botanical shows.

Methods of entering

Work experience obtained on a part-time basis or a summer job often leads to a full-time job with the same employer. Most institutes or colleges maintain a job placement service for their students. Faculty members will often be approached by prospective employers soliciting future graduates. Direct application to firms or governmental agencies is also an excellent means of obtaining employment.

Advancement

Floriculture technicians may advance to *garden center, greenhouse,* or *flower shop manager*. A nursery-operation technician can become a *horticultural inspector, a sales-yard manager,* or *proprietor of a nursery*. Arboriculture technicians find opportunities as *botanical garden superintendents, tree surgeons,* and *park supervisors*. Turfgrass technicians may advance to such positions as *grounds superintendent, commercial sod grower, consultant,* or *park, parkway,* or *golf course supervisor*. In the field of landscape development, technicians may become *landscape designers, consultants, contractors,* or *landscape-construction supervisors*. With further education, they can become landscape architects.

In general, ornamental horticulture technicians can expect to advance to more responsible and better-paying positions as they gain increased experience and additional education and training. To increase their chances for better positions, they should continue their education, not only by learning on the job, but also by taking short courses, attending seminars, and reading technical journals.

Many advancement opportunities in this field require technicians to start their own businesses. This requires some but not much money and the willingness to commit one's own financial resources to career development.

Employment outlook

The broad field of ornamental horticulture is currently growing at a healthy rate. An increasing population, a moderately prosperous economy, and the continuing development and redevelopment of urban, suburban, and rural areas for human needs have increased the demand for the services of ornamental horticulture technicians. Commercial establishments providing landscaped areas around their buildings, highways using more shrubs and bushes, and civic enthusiasm for parks and playgrounds all contribute and should continue to contribute to the need for trained people in this area.

Earnings

Graduates of two-year technical programs seeking employment can expect to receive starting salaries roughly in the $13,500 to $17,000 a year range. High-school graduates with no further education or training can expect to receive considerably less. Fringe benefits vary from employer to employer, but generally include hospitalization and other insurance coverage, retirement benefits, and educational assistance.

Conditions of work

Ornamental horticulture technicians generally work a forty-hour week. Whether working indoors in a greenhouse or florist shop, or outdoors in a park or on a golf course, they are often surrounded by the beauty of growing plants and a pleasant aroma. Arboriculture, landscape development, and turfgrass technicians spend a good deal of time out-of-doors, and occasionally must work under bad weather conditions. Those who work in parks are often required to work on weekends.

Social and psychological factors

As the population increases, and cities become more crowded, people are becoming tremendously aware of the need for flowers, parks, and gardens for aesthetic enjoyment and spiritual replenishment. Horticulture is an important part of urban beauty and city planners are cognizant of its values for the community in which they work. The young man or woman entering this field can find self-expression and satisfaction in a career that brings such pleasure and beauty.

GOE: 03.01.03, 03.01.04; SIC: 0783; SOC: 382, 5515, 5621

◇ **SOURCES OF ADDITIONAL INFORMATION**

American Institute of Biological Sciences
730 11th Street, NW
Washington, DC 20001

American Society for Horticultural Science
701 North Street Asaph Street
Alexandria, VA 22314

U.S. Department of Agriculture
Washington, DC 20250

◇ **RELATED ARTICLES**

Volume 1: Biological Sciences
Volume 2: Landscape architects
Volume 3: Agricultural scientists; Agricultural extension service workers; Farm operatives and managers; Soil scientists
Volume 4: Agribusiness technicians; Farm crop production technicians; Forestry technicians; Park technicians

Park technicians

Definition

Park technicians assist park rangers or park superintendents in the operation of state or national parks, monuments, historic sites, or recreational areas. They greet visitors and explain regulations, assign camping sites, collect fees, and monitor campgrounds, watching for possible infractions of rules. They replenish firewood and assist groundskeepers in maintaining camping and recreational areas in clean and orderly condition; conduct tours of premises and answer visitors' questions at historic sites, parks, and monuments; and operate projection and sound equipment to assist rangers in presentations and interpretive programs. They also provide simple first-aid treatment to visitors, participate in carrying out fire fighting or other conservation activities, and assist other workers in activities concerned with restoration of buildings and other facilities or excavation and preservation of artifacts at historic or archaeological sites.

History

The National Park System had its beginning in 1872, when President Ulysses S. Grant signed an act of Congress establishing the Yellowstone region as a "public park or pleasuring ground." This was the first national park in the world, and in the years that followed, many other areas were set aside for public enjoyment. The National Park Service was established in 1916 to manage the various national parks, monuments, and historic sites.

Many of these parks provided rustic picnic and camping areas, and for a long time it was possible for a family to pile into a car, drive for a couple of hours, pitch a tent by the seashore or in the woods by a stream, and spend a week or two in splendid isolation away from all the pressures of daily life. All of this began to change about thirty-five years ago. Now if you want to camp, you make reservations in a public or private camping ground a month or so in advance, and if you are lucky, you get to park trailer-to-trailer or tent-to-tent with thousands of other people seeking splendid isolation.

With urban sprawl gobbling up fields and forests, with water and air pollution becoming a major problem in village or city, with overcrowded parks and diminishing seashores, never has the need been so great for trained recreational management and planning specialists. Leisure, which was once considered sinful, is now a necessity; people have come to feel that they must have places to hike, picnic, bicycle, swim, and fish, to maintain their physical and emotional well-being. Thus, there is now a continuing demand for more parks and recreational lands and a corresponding demand for more park personnel, including park technicians, to build, maintain, and manage these areas.

Nature of the work

Technicians in the field of park and recreational land management are employed either by governmental agencies, or by private enterprise, and a number choose ownership and management of recreational facilities.

Technicians working for government agencies might find employment as assistants to a superintendent in a park, where they have charge of the day-to-day operations of maintaining the area. They make landscape plantings, maintain grounds, and direct people to various areas of interest in the park. They write some reports concerning conditions within the park and supervision of employees.

They may find employment at ski resorts or public golf courses. Here they are responsible for plantings to landscape the area and turf. If trees or turf are damaged by insects or diseases, it is one of their duties to find a remedy for the problem. They work with landscape architects in the planning of site development so they know the needed maintenance.

Technicians working in parks and recreation centers may act as guides. Guides must enjoy being with people and must be able to describe in some detail the points of interest of their tour. The tour may be an explanation of plant material, discussion of historical sites, nature trails, or some other facet of a recreational area.

Many private golf courses now exist and new ones are constantly being built. Technicians may find employment as assistant golf course superintendents or even as superintendents, the latter usually requiring two to five years of practical experience. Here, they manage maintenance crews, help develop the course, help plan budgetary needs, and work closely with members of the golf club.

Many resort hotels and large industrial centers are now hiring grounds superintendents. In this job, the technician is responsible for the old and new plantings, lawns, and development of the landscaping program of the entire layout of the enterprise.

Many technicians work for garden-supply stores where they sell horticultural supplies and advise customers concerning their needs. There are also large companies with recreational centers and camps for their employees, baseball fields, polo fields, playgrounds: all facilities that require technicians trained in park and recreational land management.

If the technician has the funds and ability, opportunities in ownership of recreational resources are unlimited. Even with a minimum budget, it is possible to develop a miniature golf course, or to develop riding trails. In addition, the stocking of ponds and small lakes for fishing is another enterprise that is successful in many areas and does not require a tremendous amount of capital.

Requirements

Park technicians need to have a combination of both theoretical and practical knowledge. For example, in taking measures to control weeds, they must know why they are using the methods they do. As they try to prevent widespread diseases of plants in the field, they must know what recent research has discovered that may help their work. As new methods, machinery, and facilities are developed, they must be able to use them to their best advantage.

Technicians should be able to meet and talk with all types of people. They should also like working outdoors, doing many kinds of work, including working with trees, shrubs, flowers, and grass.

Students preparing themselves to become park technicians must have a high-school diploma. While in high school, they should take at least two years of mathematics and two years of science. As they will be entering a biological field, earth science and biology are probably the best choices. If possible, they should also take a course in chemistry to become familiar with the chemical vocabulary and concepts they will meet in later courses and in the work itself.

High-school electives should be in a related field of interest such as conservation or ecology. Such courses are likely to be useful in a variety of technical careers whether or not the

A park technician leads a group of tourists through a forest preserve. She is able to identify many of the local plants and discuss their ecological role in the environment.

students remain specifically interested in park or recreational land management.

A high-school diploma is essential for continuing a technical education at the junior, community, or technical college level. In nearly all instances, a high-school diploma is required for employment and for acceptance to special training schools operated by industry.

Employers prefer park technicians who have trained in a two-year program at a junior, community, or technical college. The program at such an institution should include courses in soils and the basic concepts of soil texture, structure, and chemistry. Students should follow an academic program incorporating botany, nursery management, and other courses dealing with the growth and maintenance of plants. They should pursue opportunities for getting as much practical experience as possible with the growing of and caring for plants either during their school programs, through special

313

cooperative summer study programs, or through a combination of both.

Because much of the work in the field of park and recreational land management is mechanized, students should have a course in small engines and equipment. Also, they should have a course that introduces landscape design.

In addition, students should take at least one course in communication skills and one in report writing. Much of the park technician's daily work requires strong language—both oral and written—skills. They might also consider courses in economics and psychology to help them in working with people.

Typical first-year courses include communication skills, soil sciences, soil and water conservation, botany, nursery management, physical education, report writing, landscaping, plant physiology, and entomology.

Typical second-year courses in a postsecondary program may include U.S. history and politics, industrial psychology, plant pathology, surveying, wildlife management, recreational leadership, economics, turf grass management, grounds maintenance, outdoor education, and small business accounting.

Special requirements

No certification or license is required in this profession. There may be exceptions to this rule if one is involved in a specialty such as insect control, drawing landscape plans for sale, or land appraising. There may also be local licensing of commercial facilities. Employment by a governmental agency is often based on a competitive examination.

Opportunities for experience and exploration

Hiking, camping, gardening, and participating in nature study programs all provide opportunities for people to become acquainted with the work associated with managing and maintaining parks and recreational lands. State parks often hire high-school students in the summer to work as park assistants, performing many kinds of supervised chores. Technical colleges often have work programs that provide students with practical experience while they earn academic credit.

Methods of entering

Students completing courses of study leading to employment as park technicians are usually offered employment during their last semester in college. Representatives of state and federal agencies visit many college campuses and discuss employment opportunities with the students. The various park commissions often contact college campuses directly for possible employees. College placement offices and faculty members also can frequently direct students to potential job opportunities.

Students desiring to work in a specific geographical region should get in touch with the appropriate state and federal agencies that employ people for work in local parks. In addition, students may apply directly to the managers of facilities in areas where they hope to find employment. Many opportunities are listed in the classified section of the newspapers and in the "positions available" sections of magazines related to the field.

Work-study or cooperative education programs may be available. Students enrolled in such programs often find permanent jobs with or through their cooperative employers, or at least become familiar with opportunities in the field.

Advancement

Technicians advance because of their accomplishments and their abilities. As they gain experience and further their education by reading and attending night classes, they may assume supervisory or managerial positions. The following short paragraphs describe some of the jobs open to park technicians with some experience.

Recreational supply salespeople represent large firms and visit owners and operators of recreational facilities to suggest new and current varieties of planting materials and equipment. To do their job well, they must keep abreast of developments in the field of recreational land management.

Park supervisors draw up development plans for their parks, report on the condition and use of their parks to their supervisors, develop and present yearly budgets, determine personnel needs for the operation of the facilities, act as public relations representatives for their parks, inspect the parks for safety, usability, attractiveness, and consult with other park personnel concerning long-term planning and daily routine jobs.

Conservation planners consult with land owners and develop plans for conservation practices such as farm ponds, drainage systems, water control structures, wildlife sites and covers, and reforestation.

Recreational facility owners are responsible for the success of the total facility, whether it consists of a series of riding and snowmobile trails, a game farm, a hunting lodge, garden center, ski resort, golf course, or other type of recreational facility. They make the major decisions about spending available funds, about future and present development plans, as well as other facets of the business.

Landscape planners determine the costs and uses of planting materials for landscaping purposes. They supervise planting and make necessary changes in the landscape architect's plans.

Grounds superintendents determine the size of the labor force required to maintain a recreational facility. They select the employees, prepare budgets, plan for maintenance and development of old and new facilities, and are responsible for the complete care of the recreational facility.

Employment outlook

The public's total spending for recreational pursuits over the past forty years—including visits to parks and other recreational facilities—has increased much faster than the population. This rapid growth of the recreation business is a good indication of the future growth in the need for personnel to manage and maintain parks and recreational lands. It is important to note, however, that competition for jobs is strong in this area because so many people find park work attractive. Furthermore, levels of future employment will be significantly influenced by government spending, both by state and federal agencies. It is always difficult to predict future government policy; however, traditionally there has been strong public support for government action that preserves and makes available natural areas for the public.

Even with governmental action, local, state, and federal governments will be unable to meet all the demands of people looking for ways to enjoy the out-of-doors, so private enterprise may become a bigger employer in the field of outdoor recreation. Many marginally productive farms, for instance, could be converted to recreational facilities. In some places private ski resorts attract vacationers year-round.

As we approach the year 2000 the percentage of the population that is at retirement age

Many park technicians are involved with park maintenance and fire prevention. This technician is emptying garbage cans at a designated campground.

or beyond will become ever larger. Park and recreation areas that cater specifically to the people in this age group will probably be a good source of employment opportunities.

Earnings

Beginning technicians receive salaries approximately in the range of $15,000 to $18,000 a year. With additional experience they may move up to the $17,000 to $22,000 range. There is unlimited opportunity for those technicians who have demonstrate ability on the job and are willing to seek further training.

Most park technicians work for the federal government, and their salaries are determined by their Government Service rating. The salaries of technicians employed by state and local governments vary widely depending on the state or county they work for.

Fringe benefits vary with employer. Medical and hospitalization plans are usually paid by the employer. A life insurance plan of some type is often made available. Vacation allotments are normally from two to four weeks, but are usually restricted to periods when demands for the particular facility are light.

Conditions of work

Park technicians work outdoors. They must be very much at home in the outdoors, because they will probably have to work under all kinds of extreme conditions. Although they usually work a forty-hour week, their hours are often irregular during major tourist seasons.

Social and psychological factors

New methods, machinery, and facilities are constantly being developed for parks and other recreational lands, so a good park technician should be someone who is receptive to new ideas and willing to put them to good use. Good technicians must also be able to work with management, to direct other employees, and to assume the role of both employer and employee.

Park technicians must be people who can periodically respond to peak work loads and public demands without feeling undue stress. Constant contact with the public, not all of whom are pleasant, will require great reserves of tact and patience. Technicians must remain calm in times of crisis, because there may be times when people's property or even lives depend on their resourcefulness and flexibility.

People who love the outdoors and want to play a vital role in conserving, maintaining, and expanding the uses of our natural resources can find a unique satisfaction in being park technicians.

GOE: 07.04.03; SIC: 0851; SOC: 4645

⬦ **SOURCES OF ADDITIONAL INFORMATION**

National Parks and Conservation Association
1015 31st Street, NW
Washington, DC 20007

National Recreation and Park Association
3101 Park Center Drive, 12th Floor
Alexandria, VA 22302

U.S. Department of the Interior
National Park Service
PO Box 37126
Washington, DC 20013

⬦ **RELATED ARTICLES**

Soil conservation technicians

Definition

Soil conservation technicians help land users to develop plans for conservation practices, such as conservation cropping systems, woodlands management, and pasture planning. They often provide technical assistance based on their knowledge of agricultural and related sciences, such as agronomy, soil conservation, and hydrology. They also utilize basic engineering and surveying tools, instruments, and techniques. In doing this work, they take into account cost estimates of different practices, needs of land users, maintenance requirements, and life expectancy of various conservation practices. They compute design specifications for particular techniques to be adopted, using survey and field information, technical guides, and engineering field manuals. They submit their plans to land users for implementation, monitor projects during and after construction, and periodically revisit land users to review the land use practices and plans that have been adopted.

History

In 1908, President Theodore Roosevelt appointed a National Conservation Commission. As a result of the work of this commission, many state and local conservation organizations were formed, and Americans began to take a serious interest in preserving the natural resources of the land.

During World War I, farmers who wished to capitalize on the shortage of wheat planted many thousands of acres in wheat, mostly in Midwestern states. The crop was repeated year after year, until the soil was depleted. This depletion of the soil and the destruction of the natural cover of the land by too much plowing cultivation led to the disastrous dust storms of the mid-1930s.

In 1935, Congress established the Soil Conservation Service of the U.S. Department of Agriculture. Because more than 800 million tons of topsoil had already been blown away by the winds over the plains, the job of reclaiming the land through wise conservation practices was not an easy one. In addition to the large areas of the Middle West which had become desert land, there were other badly eroded lands throughout the country.

Fortunately, emergency planning came to the help of the newly established Soil Conservation Service. The Civilian Conservation Corps (C.C.C.), which had been created to help alleviate unemployment during the 1930s, established camps in rural areas and assigned people to aid in many different kinds of conservation. Soil conservationists directed those portions of the C.C.C. program designed to halt the loss of topsoil by wind and water action.

Much progress has been made since the Soil Conservation Service was established. Wasted land has been reclaimed and further loss has been prevented. Land-grant colleges have initiated programs to help farmers understand the principles and procedures of soil conservation. The Federal Extension Service (within the Department of Agriculture) provides personnel to work with these programs, some of whom are soil conservationists.

Today throughout the United States there are several thousand soil conservation districts whose employees demonstrate soil conservation. Generally speaking, the Soil Conservation Service assigns one or more professional soil conservationists and one or more soil conservation technicians to each district.

Nature of the work

Soil conservation technicians with the Soil Conservation Service act as assistants to scientists, engineers, and other professionals in obtaining preliminary data that is used in establishing and maintaining soil- and water-conservation plans. They also work closely with landowners and operators to establish and maintain sound conservation practices in land management and use.

Some of the specific duties of soil conservation technicians include the following: assisting with preliminary engineering surveys; laying out contours, terraces, tile drainage systems, and irrigation systems; planting grasses and trees; collecting soil samples and gathering information from field notes; improving woodlands; assisting in farm pond design and management; making maps from aerial photographs; and inspecting specific areas to determine conservation needs.

The Bureau of Land Management oversees the hundreds of millions of acres of public domain. Technicians in this federal agency assist professionals in surveying publicly owned areas, determining boundaries and pinpointing land features to determine the best use of public lands. They may be called upon to supervise a surveying party of four to six workers in carrying out the actual survey.

Technicians in the Bureau of Reclamation serve as assistants to civil, construction, materials, or general engineers. Their job is to oversee certain phases of construction on dams, irrigation projects, and the like. The ultimate goal is the control of water and soil resources for the benefit of farm, home, and city.

The following short paragraphs describe some positions typically held by entry-level soil conservation technicians.

Range technicians work closely with range conservationists helping to manage rangeland, most of which is in the western part of the United States. They determine the value of

Soil conservation technicians
Agriculture, Forestry, and Conservation Technician Occupations

A soil conservation technician and his assistant identify the various types of soils in a forest preserve. The data will be used in a report concerning soil conservation.

rangeland, its grazing capabilities, erosion hazards, and livestock potential.

Physical science technician aides gather data in the field, studying the physical characteristics of the soil, mapping land, and producing aerial survey maps for use by soil conservationists.

Engineering technician aides conduct field tests and oversee some phases of construction on dams and irrigation projects. They manage water resources and perform soil-conservation services. They also assist in determining quantities of earth in cuts and fills, measuring acreage, placing property boundaries, and defining drainage areas on maps.

Cartographic survey technician aides work with cartographers in surveying the public domain, setting its boundaries, pinpointing its land features, and determining its most beneficial public use.

The following short paragraphs describe some of the positions held by more experienced soil conservation technicians.

Cartographic technicians perform technical work in mapping or charting the earth or graphically representing geographical information.

Geodetic technicians perform nonprofessional work in the analysis, evaluation, processing, computation, and selection of geodetic survey data. (Geodesy is the science of determining the size and shape of the earth, the intensity and direction of the force of gravity, and the elevation of points on or near the earth's surface.)

Meteorological technicians analyze or predict weather elements and their effect upon the earth's surface and human activities.

Physical science technicians assist professional scientists in calibrating and operating measur-

ing instruments, mixing solutions, making routine chemical analyses, and setting up and operating test apparatus.

Surveying technicians survey for the purpose of field measurement and mapping or for other more immediate practical purposes, such as the laying out of construction, the checking of accuracy of dredging operations, or the provision of reference points and lines for related work. They gather data for the design of highways and dams or the construction of topographic maps or nautical and aeronautical charts.

Range conservationists administer and operate range conservation programs designed to conserve, develop, and utilize ranges and rangeland properly; to provide for the conservation management and utilization of related resources; and to stabilize the livestock industry, which is dependent upon the range for its existence.

Requirements

Soil conservation technicians must be able to apply practical as well as theoretical knowledge. They need to have a working knowledge of soil and water characteristics; they need to be skilled in management of woodlands, wildlife areas, and recreation areas; and they need to have a knowledge of surveying instruments and practices, mapping, and the procedures used for interpreting aerial photographs.

Soil conservation technicians should also be able to write clear, concise reports to demonstrate and explain the results of their tests, studies, and recommendations. A love for the outdoors and an appreciation for all natural resources are also essential for success and personal fulfillment in this job.

Opportunities for advancement in this field depend largely on specialized training. Employers of soil conservation technicians prefer to hire those who have completed two years of post–high-school training, such as is offered in a two-year technical institute program leading to an associate degree. A high-school diploma is an absolute necessity for admission to a technical institute or college.

While in high school, prospective technicians should take at least one year of algebra, enough English to be articulate and convincing in speech and writing, and one year of biology. For technicians who anticipate that they may work in areas of soil conservation involving contact with farmers and ranchers, high school courses in vocational agriculture are strongly recommended.

Once enrolled in a two-year post–high-school program, students can expect to take courses such as the following during their first year: psychology of human relations, applied mathematics, communication skills, basic soils, botany, chemistry, zoology, and introduction to range management. Typical second-year courses include the following: American government, surveying, forestry, game management, soil and water conservation, economics, problems in conservation, fish management, and soil and water conservation engineering.

Technicians must have some practical experience in the use of soil conservation techniques before they enter the field. Therefore, a good part of their post–high-school education will probably be taken up with application of techniques and theories to work situations.

Special requirements

No certification or license is required of soil conservation technicians. Employment by governmental agencies is usually based on a competitive examination.

Opportunities for experience and exploration

One of the best ways for students to become acquainted with the problems and opportunities connected with soil conservation technology is through summer or part-time work on a farm. Other ways to explore this career area include joining a 4-H Club or the Future Farmers of America. Science courses that include lab sections and mathematics courses that focus on practical problem-solving will also help give prospective technicians a feel for the kind of work they might do in the future.

Methods of entering

Most students in a two-year technical institute gain work experience during the summer between their first and second years by being employed at jobs in their specific areas of interest. Students are made aware of these summer positions by teachers or by the placement office of the technical institute. Often, contacts made during summer work lead to permanent employment after graduation. In addition, college placement officers and faculty members are of-

ten valuable sources of advice and information in finding employment.

Most soil conservation technicians find work with state, county, or federal agencies. The specific details of the application procedure will vary according to the level of government in which the technician is seeking work. In general, however, students should expect to begin the application procedure during the fourth semester of their program and should expect that some competitive examination may be part of the process. College placement personnel can help students find out about the details of application procedures. Often representatives of government agencies visit college campuses during the fourth semester to explain employment possibilities to students and sometimes to recruit for their agencies.

Advancement

Soil conservation technicians may continue their education while working, not only by learning on the job, but also by taking additional courses at night in a local college or at a technical institute. Federal agencies that employ technicians have a policy of "promotion from within." Because of this, there is a continuing opportunity for such technicians to advance through the ranks. The degree of advancement that all technicians can expect in their working careers is determined by their aptitudes, abilities, and their desire to advance.

Employment outlook

Most soil conservation technicians are employed by the federal government; therefore, employment opportunities will depend in large part on levels of government spending. It is always difficult to predict future government policies; however, this is an area where the need for government involvement is apparent and pressing. The vast majority of America's cropland has suffered from some sort of erosion, and only continued efforts by soil conservation professionals can prevent a dangerous depletion of our most valuable resource—fertile soil.

Some soil conservation technicians are employed by public utility companies, banks and loan agencies, state and local governments, and mining or steel companies. At present, a relatively small number of soil conservation technicians are employed by these firms or agencies; however, decreased levels of employment

Soil conservation technicians
Agriculture, Forestry, and Conservation Technician Occupations

by the federal government could lead to increased employment in these areas.

Earnings

Most soil-conservation technicians work for the federal government, and their salaries are determined by their Government Service rating. The salaries of technicians employed by state and local governments vary widely depending on the state or county they work for.

The salaries of technicians working for private firms or agencies will be roughly comparable to the earnings of other similarly trained agricultural technicians employed by private firms. In general, technicians in this area receive beginning salaries ranging roughly from $11,000 to $15,000 a year but may go as high as $18,000 a year or more.

Conditions of work

Soil conservation technicians usually work forty hours per week, except in unusual or emergency situations. They have opportunities to travel, and, in some positions with federal agencies, they may be away from home frequently.

Soil conservation is an outdoor job. Technicians usually travel by car, but often they must walk across country where cars cannot go. Although they sometimes work from aerial photographs and other on-site pictures, they cannot usually work from pictures alone. They must visit the spot that presents the problem in order to make appropriate recommendations.

Although soil conservation technicians spend much of their working time outdoors, it is necessary for them to make detailed reports of their work to agency offices. There is, in other words, some desk work associated with this job.

Social and psychological factors

In their role as assistants to professionals, soil conservation technicians often assume the role of public relations representatives of the gov-

ernment to landowners and land managers. They must be able to explain the underlying principles of the structures that they design and the surveys that they perform.

To meet these and other requirements of the job, technicians should be prepared to continue their education both formally and informally throughout their careers. They must stay aware of current periodicals and studies so that they can keep up to date in their area of specialization.

Soil conservation technicians gain satisfaction from knowing that theirs is a vitally important job to the economy of the nation. Without their work, large portions of land in the United States could become barren within a generation.

GOE: 02.02.02; SIC: 9512; SOC: 1852

◇ SOURCES OF ADDITIONAL INFORMATION

American Society of Agronomy
677 South Segoe Road
Madison,WI 53711

Soil and Water Conservation Society of America
7515 NE Ankeny Road
Ankeny, IA 50021

◇ RELATED ARTICLES

Volume 1: Agriculture; Civil Service; Physical Sciences
Volume 2: Geologists; Groundwater professionals; Surveyors
Volume 3: Agricultural scientists; Agricultural extension service workers; Foresters; Range managers; Soil scientists
Volume 4: Civil engineering technicians; Farm crop production technicians; Forestry technicians; Geological technicians; Hydrological technicians; Meterorological technicians; Surveying and mapping technicians

Broadcast, Media, and Arts Technician Occupations

The fields of broadcasting, media, and arts touch each of our lives every day. Radio and television are vital parts of American society. They exist not only as our greatest entertainment media but also as powerful forces for informing, educating, and influencing the public. With their great power to reach people and to affect them, radio and television help to shape our society and our culture. In similar, if sometimes less obvious ways, other media and arts constantly touch us and affect us—whether through music, drama, or the graphic arts. Much of the impact that we feel from all of these fields is made possible by technology that came about only during this century and that continues to develop rapidly. Broadcast, media, and arts technicians play a crucial role in making this changing array of methods and machines work on a day-to-day basis. They operate new and complex equipment, and they help solve the problems that inevitably arise as new generations of technology are introduced.

Broadcast, media, and arts technicians operate, maintain and repair, set up and monitor, and occasionally help design the electronic, electrical, and mechanical equipment used to help make possible a wide variety of kinds of entertainment and communication. Many of these technicians are involved with broadcasting live radio and television programs or with recording broadcasts for later transmission. These technicians work in studios with cameras, sound equipment, and lights; at transmitter sites with transmitters and microwave equipment; and at remote locations with portable cameras, microphones, lights, and communication links to the main station. Other media and arts technicians may be involved with educational efforts, helping to operate equipment or perform other technical services in schools, museums, or planetariums. Media and arts technicians may also be involved with the equipment and techniques required for printing books, developing photographs, or presenting live entertainment.

Much of the history of the technician occupations described in this section revolves around the history of broadcasting, which has its roots in the late 1800s, when scientists discovered methods by which they could use electromagnetic waves to send wireless messages. At first these transmissions covered short distances, but in 1901 Guglielmo Marconi received in Newfoundland a radio message transmitted from England, thus marking the birth of the broadcast industry.

Modern television is based on electronic theory that grew out of the experiments of Heinrich Geissler in 1857, in which he discharged electricity in a vacuum tube, causing rare gases in it to glow. Other scientists immediately began to experiment with vacuum tubes, and in 1898 Karl Braun made the first cathode-ray tube in which he could control the flow of electrons being released. These developments, along with the discovery of radio tubes that could detect and amplify electromagnetic radio waves, set the stage for the development of modern television. The only element missing by 1907 was a device for scanning and transmitting a picture—a camera.

It was not until 1927 that the first workable cathode-ray-tube camera was invented by a sixteen-year-old boy named Philo T. Farnsworth. Improvements by Vladimir Zworykin made the system practical. It was demonstrated in 1929, and regular television programming began at the World's Fair of 1939, although it was later interrupted by World War II.

Meanwhile, radio had been used for communications between ships at sea and from ships to shore receivers. In 1920, however, two commercial radio stations went on the air: KDKA in Pittsburgh and WWJ in Detroit. They were followed by stations in all parts of the United States. The first network broadcast (more than one station sharing a broadcast) was the World Series broadcast of 1922. The period from these early years through the early 1950s has been called the Golden Age of radio, because radio programming dominated home entertainment and information. With the rapid growth of television in the 1950s, radio lost its place as prime home entertainer, but it remained a vital source of entertainment, news, sports, and other information in American life.

In 1946, with World War II over, the interest and energy that had been diverted from television returned. The first commercial broadcasts began to be beamed along the East Coast (all early broadcasts originated in New York City) and gradually made their way to cities farther west, until by 1951 broadcasts were reaching coast-to-coast. In 1950 there were 6 million television sets in the United States; by 1960 there were 60 million.

Color programs began to be broadcast regularly in 1953, and the use of video recording tape was introduced in the 1950s as a major production technique. *Early Bird*, the first commercial communications satellite, was launched in 1965 and was followed by many more in the ensuing years.

Two additional developments greatly affected the broadcast industry: the use of tape recording (both video and audio) and growth of cable television transmission systems.

The first phonograph, invented by Thomas A. Edison in 1877, utilized a needle moved by a sound-activated diaphragm to record sound waves on a cylinder wrapped with tin foil. By the late 1800s recordings were being made by magnetizing steel wire. During the 1930s German scientists found plastic tape coated with metallic oxide to be a much more flexible and efficient substitute for wire. With many subsequent improvements, this is still the tape used in multi-track, stereophonic tape recordings.

By the end of the 1940s engineers were able to record light as well as sound waves as electromagnetic impulses. By the mid-1950s, it had become a regular practice of the television networks to videotape programs for presentation at a later time. This allowed them to improve the quality, continuity, and flexibility of programming by allowing editing and re-shooting of scenes. Previously programs had been presented live or on motion-picture film which did not transmit well. Today news, sports, and special events are nearly the only live broadcasts on television, and even these include inserted videotaped material and instant replays. Videotape cassettes are widely available and are played through television receivers in schools, industry training centers, and at home as conveniently as audio tapes and phonograph records.

The history of cable television can be traced to the development of coaxial cable (copper wire inside a copper tube, both with the same axis), which was invented in the 1930s in the Bell Telephone Laboratories, primarily to improve telephone transmission. It was soon found that a coaxial cable could also carry television transmissions very efficiently. One coaxial cable can carry sixty television signals, enabling a cable system to offer a wide variety of programming and still reserve channels for public-service use.

At first cable television transmission was used to carry television signals to areas where conventional transmission could not reach: valleys, extremely hilly regions, and large cities where buildings interfered with radio waves. By the late 1970s, however, cable television systems in the United States numbered about 3,500, and they were competing with conventional networks in areas that both could serve. Going into the 1990s, more than half of the households in the U.S. were served by cable.

Today radio and television continue to be major forces in American life, in entertainment, education, public affairs, and advertising. Virtually every American home has at least one radio, and 98 percent have at least one television set. Surveys show the average American views more than thirty hours of television per week and that 85 percent of all Americans listen to a radio at least once every day.

In the mid-1980s there were approximately 27,000 broadcast technicians employed in radio and television stations across the United States. There are technicians employed in every state, but the greatest concentrations are in the areas supporting the largest radio and television stations: New York, Chicago, Los Angeles, and Washington, D.C.

Several of the technician occupations described in this section are involved with photography. Some of the principles of photography can be traced back to the sixteenth century; however, the first real photographic camera was not developed until 1816. The nineteenth century saw several other important inventions relating to photography. These include the development by Louis J.M. Daguerre of the daguerreotype process, in which photographic images are recorded on a silver-coated copper plate; the first demonstration of motion pictures by Eadweard Muybridge in 1873; and the development of large-scale commercial film development by George Eastman in 1888.

During the twentieth century, further improvement in photographic equipment—such as the Leica 35-millimeter camera, introduced in 1924, and film to make color slides and prints, introduced in the 1930s and 1940s—

helped make still and motion picture photography a popular hobby. Photography also became an important art form and a powerful, ever-present force in advertising and journalism.

The growing use of cameras has been accompanied by an increased sophistication in the workings of cameras and of the equipment used to develop film. Today, photographic equipment must be serviced by trained technicians. Likewise, laboratories that develop film rely more and more on sophisticated equipment and skilled technicians to operate the equipment and oversee photofinishing processes.

Most of the remaining technicians described in this section work in a broad area sometimes referred to as craft technology. They are workers who have combined a craft working skill with some form of specialized training. In many ways, these workers are the descendants of traditional craft workers who used methods handed down from generation to generation or through apprenticeships organized by craft guilds. With the coming of the Industrial Revolution, the pace of change began to accelerate in all of the craft professions, so that the knowledge of one generation was no longer guaranteed to be sufficient for the next generation. Throughout the nineteenth century, to be sure, and even into the twentieth, individual craft workers still used handcrafting techniques in a wider range of activities. But the move towards increasing complexity and sophistication in all areas of human activities was, by the early nineteenth century, well established, steadily progressing, and virtually unstoppable.

The nineteenth century was a great period for inventions, and all of these inventions brought opportunities to and increased the need for workers who possessed the craft skills necessary to build, repair, and maintain these new devices. Throughout the twentieth century, the pace of change has not slackened. The space program, the development of computers, and improved means of communication have all produced innovations and applications of technology to new areas. These developments, especially since the end of World War II, have led to the need for specially trained craft workers, often with two-year degrees from community, technical, and vocational colleges.

Most of the technicians described in this section are broadcast technicians. They work in a wide variety of settings, including the broadcast studio itself. There they may set up lights, microphones, and cameras, or they may operate a control-room console, selecting the pictures and sound that go on the air, switching from camera to camera, from the studio to recorded video or audio material, or from the studio to remote location transmissions.

Broadcast technicians working at remote sites, broadcasting a sports event or a live interview or news event, unload and set up their equipment, locate a telephone transmission link to the studio or set up a microwave transmitter, and test their equipment and transmission link before broadcasting. They may go on location with only a reporter, and in this situation, they have to perform all technical functions of the broadcast.

Broadcast technicians working in large urban stations will generally find that their work is specialized; however, they may also find that they move from area to area frequently as the station rotates responsibilities, varying work tasks and ensuring the widest possible experience within the technical staff. In smaller stations technicians often perform many technical functions within one day's shift, from maintaining equipment to cueing and playing recordings or films.

Probably the most demanding technical work broadcast technicians have to perform is the installation and the maintenance of the complex electronic equipment that is the heart of a broadcasting facility. And because the technology of broadcasting is constantly changing, this occupies a considerable part of their off-the-air working time.

Several of the other technicians described in this volume are involved with photography. Some are involved with the maintenance and repair of cameras; others with developing film in film laboratories; and some with the maintenance and repair of equipment used in film laboratories.

The rest of the technicians in this volume work in a wide variety of jobs. Audiovisual technicians operate and repair audiovisual equipment used for instructional, informational, or educational programs. Electronic organ technicians install and service electronic organs. Exhibit technicians build and assemble various kinds of museum displays. Graphic arts technicians in all phases of printing and the graphic arts, including typographical layout, composition, press work, and binding. Museum technicians clean, repair, or help preserve art objects, such as pottery, statues, and paintings, and specimens of natural objects, such as fossils. Piano technicians tune and repair pianos. Pipe organ technicians install, repair, and tune pipe organs. Planetarium technicians install, operate, maintain, and modify the sound and light equipment used for planetarium shows. Sound technicians work on sound systems and internal communications equipment, usually in business settings such as offices and factories. Stage technicians build stages and install stage equipment in theaters and at other locations where entertainment productions will be performed.

People who are interested in becoming broadcast technicians should have a sincere interest in electronic devices, be above average in intelligence, and capable of learning radio repairing and radio communication. They should be in good health, have sound vision and hearing, and have good touch discrimination. They must also be able to make correct decisions quickly and handle many details speedily, without becoming confused or distracted by what is going on around them.

Although there are some technicians currently at work in broadcasting who have not received any post–high-school training, most technicians entering this field should plan on receiving some training beyond high school. Because of the ways in which broadcasting is expanding into more different kinds of activities and areas and because of the increasing complexity of most of the equipment used, specialized technical training is more important today than ever before.

People interested in becoming broadcast technicians should begin their preparation in high school. Students should plan their high-school studies to ensure that they will meet the entrance requirements of whatever post–high-school training program is most appropriate for them. They should plan on taking courses in algebra, geometry, physics, and trigonometry, as well as basic sciences and shop courses, such as electricity, mechanical drawing, radio and television repair, and beginning electronics.

Most technicians entering this field are graduates of two-year, post–high-school training programs. The curriculum in these programs usually includes such courses as direct and alternating current fundamentals, technical drafting, mathematics, electronics principles and circuitry, trigonometry, calculus, transmitters, television broadcast theory and practice, television workshops, and work in communications skills, psychology of human relations, and computer programming for technicians.

Almost all of the other occupations described in this section require that technicians have completed some specialized training beyond high school. Therefore prospective technicians in these field too should plan on earning a high-school diploma or its equivalent, and they should investigate early in their high-school years the entrance requirements of any school or program in which they might want to enroll following graduation from high school. By investigating early, they can ensure that they will be able to meet all requirements having to do with courses and standardized tests that need to be taken.

In several cases, the post–high-school training requirements for prospective technicians consist of completing a two-year courses of study offered in a junior, community, technical, or vocational college. These programs usually combine classroom teaching with practical or even on-the-job experience, and they usually lead to an associate degree.

Some of the jobs described in this section do not require a full two years of formal instruction. Some require only one year or so; some rely on employer-conducted training. Even if formal training in a two-year institution is not required, however, many technicians will find that their chances for employment and advancement are much enhanced by earning an associate degree.

There are numerous ways for students interested in careers as broadcast technicians to gain some experience and learn more about the work. Many high schools, community colleges, and technical institutes have radio and television stations of their own where students can experience the actual production of a broadcast program. Many schools also have clubs for persons interested in broadcasting that sponsor trips to broadcasting facilities, schedule lectures, and provide a place where students can meet others with an interest in broadcasting.

Local radio and television station technicians are usually willing to share their experience with interested young people. They can be a helpful source of informal career guidance. Summer employment may also be available to students.

For people interested in learning more about the nonbroadcasting jobs described in this section, there are also a number of opportunities for personal experience and exploration. Visits to places of employment are one of the most vivid means of learning about a career. Visits can often be arranged by a teacher or guidance counselor or through a personal call to someone in a position of responsibility at the place of employment. Through such visits, a student can see technicians involved in their work and perhaps to speak with them about their activities.

Students should also consider finding part-time or summer employment in a company or other organization that employs technicians. Even the simplest tasks can offer opportunities to learn more about the field and will demonstrate interest to future employers.

Broadcast technicians looking for their first job should apply directly to the chief engineer or the personnel manager of the station where they wish to work. Help in arranging interviews or career counseling in general can be obtained from the placement office of the applicant's school.

New technicians at a station, even those with formal training and experience, normally begin employment with a period of instruction from the chief engineer or a senior engineer. Each station has its own procedures that technicians must learn and follow carefully.

Most technicians begin their careers in small stations where their responsibilities are varied. As they gain experience and skill they work into more responsible positions and may move to larger stations. Those who exhibit above-average abilities may move into supervisory positions. A college engineering degree, however, is becoming increasingly necessary for advancement to higher technical positions.

The number of noncommercial, educational radio and television stations is increasing. They offer another opportunity for entry into the field.

The best method for entering the other technician occupations described in this section varies depending on the particular field. One of the most reliable and accepted methods, however, is for technicians to seek employment opportunities through the school where they were trained. Most of these institutions have student placement services and are in contact with employers in need of technicians.

Another method of entering some fields is through the on-the-job training programs offered by various companies. People who successfully complete such programs are usually assured of finding employment with the company that trained them.

Work-study programs offer another excellent method of getting started in a career field. These programs are run by schools in cooperation with local employers and offer students the opportunity to have part-time or summer employment in jobs related to the student's studies. Very often, the part-time or summer employer becomes the student's full-time employer after graduation.

Advancement in the broadcast industry is usually from a trainee position to one of independent responsibility and then to a supervisory position. The path of the successful technician often leads from a small station, where the opportunity to perform a wide variety of duties provides excellent experience, to larger stations, where there are more supervisory positions to aim for and where the financial rewards are potentially greater.

Higher technical positions, such as chief engineer, are increasingly open only to graduate electrical or electronics engineers.

Broadcast engineering is a competitive field. Some technicians turn to teaching (in technical schools or in high schools that have radio stations) as a means of advancement. High-school teaching requires a college degree and certification.

The opportunities for advancement for other technicians described in this section vary widely depending on the nature of the skills required in their occupational areas. In some fields, there may be opportunities to advance to supervisory, trainer, or administrative positions. In some fields there are also opportunities for technicians to become technical writers. In some fields, significant advancement is only possible for technicians who return to school for more education.

The employment outlook for broadcast technicians is influenced by the fact that competition is always extremely keen for positions in large metropolitan stations. Those technicians who are best prepared in electronics will have an advantage. However, there are usually good prospects for entry-level positions in smaller stations and in smaller cities.

Overall, the need for broadcast technicians is expected to grow about as fast as the average for all other occupations through the year 2000. New openings will appear as new stations open and as currently employed technicians retire or advance to higher positions. The growth of cable television systems is expected to create openings in various related fields. This increased need may be offset by the increasing use of computerized automatic switching devices and other new labor-saving technology. These new kinds of equipment, however, do require maintenance work, which is often performed by qualified broadcast technicians.

The employment outlook for other technicians described in this section is generally good. The need for technicians who can combine specialized technical training with a craft skill should remain strong as more and more occupational fields develop tasks that require specially trained workers.

Broadcast technicians entering this field can expect a starting salary of about $17,000 a year if they begin work with a radio station. Television technicians can expect somewhat higher salaries, about $18,000 to $19,000 a year. These averages are based on a regular forty-hour week which is standard in the industry. Overtime is fairly common, especially in smaller stations, and is usually paid at time-and-a-half.

The average salary for all radio broadcasting technicians, including those with considerable experience, is approximately $20,000 a year. The average for television technicians is approximately $22,000 a year. Highly accomplished senior broadcast technicians may earn as much as $50,000 a year or more.

Technicians in the largest urban stations earn, as a rule, two-thirds more than those in the smallest rural stations. Technicians employed by educational broadcasting stations generally earn less than those employed by commercial stations.

Salaries for technicians described in this section who are not in broadcasting depend in large part on the type of employer. Technicians who find jobs with commercial employers usually do better than those who work for schools, museums, or other institutions that command fewer financial resources.

Salaries also vary according to the person's education, experience, and the geographical location of the job. In general, however, technicians who are graduates of two-year post–high-school training programs can expect to receive starting salaries averaging around $14,000 to $17,000 a year. With increased experience, their earnings rise, usually up to $24,000 a year and often more.

Broadcast technicians in studios work in air-conditioned, soundproofed surroundings. They wear headphones much the time, and they work with numerous dials and switches that they must adjust as necessary. Timing is critical in the broadcasting industry. Technicians must make many split-second decisions and adjustments for which they alone are responsible.

When working in remote setups, technicians are required to work in all kinds of weather and sometimes in uncomfortable locations. They must be able to set up and adjust their equipment on the spot to carry out their part of a broadcast.

Most radio and television stations operate twenty-four hours a day, seven days a week. Shift work may be necessary, especially for new employees. The work of broadcast technicians is not physically strenuous, although it may involve standing for long periods while adjusting or repairing equipment.

On the positive side, technicians can take pride in their ability to master the complex, and sometimes hectic, operations necessary to maintain a radio or television station on the air. Their work also offers constantly varying subject matter and opportunities for meeting new challenges.

Working conditions for other technicians described in this section vary according to the type of work they are engaged in and the settings in which the work is done. Most, however, can expect to work indoors in clean, well-lighted surroundings that are generally safe and comfortable.

Broadcast technicians usually work behind the scenes with little public contact. They work closely with their equipment and as members of a small crew of experts whose closely coordinated efforts produce smooth-running programs. Constant close attention to detail and to making split-second decisions can cause tension. In emergency situations, especially in small stations, long hours and high pressures may result. When equipment fails, pressure to return it to service is great. Persons who enjoy meeting challenges will find satisfaction in coping with these emergencies.

The work of nearly all of the technicians described in this section will range from uncomplicated and routine tasks to challenging and complex tasks. Technicians who are most successful in their careers are usually those who have a good tolerance for both creative problem-solving and for careful meticulous work.

The work also often requires technicians to take full responsibility for some aspect of a project. This may involve supervising other workers, designing procedures, and foreseeing results. This kind of responsibility usually carries with it some mental and social pressures that technicians need to be able to meet.

Audio control technicians

Definition

Audio control technicians set up, operate, and maintain the equipment regulating volume and quality of sound during radio and television broadcasts. Technicians direct the placement of microphones to pick up best sound and adjust acoustical curtains or blinds within the studio to control reverberation. During broadcasts they switch on appropriate microphones, balance sound from different microphones using volume, fader, and mixer controls, and monitor audio signals by listening through headphones and watching control-panel dials. Technicians play taped and recorded music and sounds as part of programs, blending sound levels and coordinating sounds with televised pictures where necessary.

In smaller stations in particular, audio control technicians will also be called on to maintain sound transmission equipment and controls, and to function as field technicians during remote transmissions.

Nature of the work

Audio control technicians work with microphones and sound transmitting and recording equipment. In the studio, they operate equipment that regulates the quality of the sound that is being transmitted or recorded. They also operate controls that switch broadcasts from one microphone to another, or from one studio to another; switch transmission from live broadcasting to records or tapes, interviews, or other recorded material; or switch from the studio to remote broadcasting locations.

For both radio and television programs, audio operations can be very complex and must be precisely timed. Broadcasts of live musical performances, for instance, may involve dozens of microphones, placed so that individual instruments or singers can be highlighted.

Audio control technicians also give instructions to studio personnel about sound quality and other technical matters relating to sound transmission. At remote locations, they set up, adjust, and operate equipment used to broadcast or record on-the-spot interviews, sports events, or news reports.

In smaller radio and television stations, audio control technicians may also perform a wide variety of related duties. For disk-jockey programs, for instance, they might operate the record turntables. When more experienced, they might assume some of the duties of the technical director. In larger stations, duties are more specialized.

Audio control technicians work in support of technical engineering and supervisory personnel who specify, install, and maintain the sound recording and transmitting equipment of the station. Engineering and supervisory personnel are responsible for the most demanding technical work of broadcasting. They usually have baccalaureate or master's degrees in electrical or electronics engineering.

An audio control technician in a television studio maintains the sound quality and enhances the program by adding recorded music in the background.

Requirements

Persons interested in a career as an audio control technician should study high-school mathematics at least through solid geometry, as well as physics and any other available physical science courses. They should be prepared to take at least two years of technical training beyond high school at a community college or technical institute. Those persons who hope to rise to an administrative technical level, such as chief engineer, should aim toward a bachelor's degree in electrical or electronics engineering. Courses in a two-year technical program are likely to include basic and advanced electronics, communication theory, high-frequency receiver theory, as well as engineering mathematics, drawing, and technical writing.

On-the-job training, once the accepted road to a career as a broadcast technician, has been virtually done away with as a means of obtaining basic electronics training. Stations prefer applicants with advanced technical training and have no trouble finding such applicants. All new technicians receive training in station procedures, but they are expected to be thoroughly grounded in the fundamentals of broadcast technology.

Persons interested in careers in this field should have a strong interest in working with electronic equipment. They should have sound hearing and good visual acuity. They must be able to make decisions quickly and reliably in sometimes distracting surroundings.

GOE: 05.10.05; SIC: 483; SOC: 393

◇ **SOURCES OF ADDITIONAL INFORMATION**

Society of Broadcast Engineers
7002 Graham Road, Suite 118
Indianapolis, IN 46220

Audiovisual technicians

Definition

Audiovisual technicians, also called *educational media technicians*, are involved in a variety of activities related to producing educational audiovisual materials and operating and repairing equipment used to show the materials to their intended audience. Some technicians have charge of making films in an audiovisual department of an educational institution or other organization. Other technicians operate, adjust, make minor repairs on, and diagnose major difficulties in audiovisual systems that include such equipment as loudspeakers; video monitors; slide, movie film, or overhead projection equipment; and tape recorders. Audiovisual technicians may also handle acquiring, storing, and packaging for shipment audiovisual materials and equipment.

History

The equipment used by audiovisual technicians developed from a series of nineteenth century inventions, including the carbon-arc-lighted projector for slides or photographs, motion picture photography, and the phonograph. In the twentieth century developments in electronics led to radio, television, videotape, and modern microphone systems that amplify and modify sounds. The result of these technological advances is the large variety of complex equipment that is available today in learning situations from classrooms to conventions. Political, scientific, and business meetings utilize microphone systems to amplify speakers' voices. While they listen, audiences can watch graphic representations along with hearing the speaker.

Large screens are available to project videos, charts, graphs, slide illustrations, films, and overhead images to audiences. Even small conferences and discussion groups in schools, government, industry, and churches employ up-to-date media technologies.

Traditionally, people who are trying to impart information have depended on lecturing and have expected little or no response from the listener. While this is a widespread form of teaching, many studies have shown that, in terms of the learner's understanding and remembering, it is not a very effective method. Research conducted over the past forty years has demonstrated that if students can hear, see, feel, even interact with the subject that is being taught, they can learn faster, understand better, and retain the material much longer than through the traditional lecture approach. The need to present material so that a learner can understand it quickly and remember it becomes even more important as our society grows more and more complex.

Nature of the work

Audiovisual materials present informational, educational, or advertising ideas in films, videos, programmed learning materials, photos, tape recordings, television programs, or a combination of various media.

In the educational field, many different people are involved in preparing audiovisual materials for students to use. Behavioral psychologists work with teachers and curriculum groups to decide which knowledge and skills should be taught. Teachers and curriculum groups work with media specialists who translate the learning objectives into plans for audiovisual materials. Other specialists evaluate the effectiveness of the materials and measure how well they work as teaching tools.

Audiovisual technicians who produce audiovisual materials begin their work once the script or storyboard has been established. Working from their understanding of the overall goals of the project and the specific information to be presented, they select the scenes and locations for shooting motion pictures and still photographs. They set up equipment such as cameras, microphones, and lights, and they acquire any necessary props. They shoot the tape or film and later edit and splice it into a finished product that conforms to the original specifications. Before releasing the finished item, they operate projectors, tape players, and other equipment to show it to the people who requested that it be made. In some projects technicians may be involved in ordering or preparing simpler materials, such as transparencies for overhead projection, charts, posters, or displays.

Many technicians are employed mainly to operate audiovisual or sound-reproduction equipment. They may work for institutions such as museums, zoos, or libraries that offer educational or public service shows to entertain or enlighten their visitors. Technicians may operate motion picture projectors in auditoriums or lecture halls. In a more complicated program, a speaker's presentation is complemented with audiovisual materials that illustrate, clarify, or enhance the impact of the talk. Technicians operate various slide, video, audio tape, and turntable equipment to produce pictures, background music, oral commentary, and sound effects. They may have to coordinate their part of the presentation with the material being presented by the speaker by following notations on a script or other instructions.

Technicians in this type of position are also usually responsible for maintaining the equipment and materials in good working condition. They make minor adjustments and routine repairs and notify the appropriate personnel when a major repair is needed. Before a presentation, technicians must position, install, and connect all the necessary equipment such as microphones, amplifiers, and lights. They test the setup to make sure that it functions correctly and that it is completely ready to go. After the presentation, they may have to put equipment back into storage, prepare for the next presentation, or pack up rented or borrowed program materials so that they can be sent somewhere else.

Some audiovisual technicians who operate equipment travel to different locations to help present programs. For example, technicians who work for large companies may set up and operate equipment at conventions, trade shows, and employee training sessions held in various plants. In some school districts, or regional networks of school districts, technicians transport shared equipment and materials to different locations where they are to be used.

Audiovisual technicians are likely to be responsible for keeping records on program materials, whether they are part of a permanent media library in their department or rented or borrowed from outside sources. This can involve cataloging, duplicating, labeling, and repairing materials, and recording every time they are used. Materials from outside sources also require record-keeping. They must be requested in advance of when they are needed, orders must be confirmed, and materials checked in and returned on time.

Some audiovisual technicians specialize in installing and repairing audiovisual equipment. Using their knowledge of electronics, they inspect the equipment for defects and repair or replace parts. They use hand tools, soldering irons, and electronic testing devices. Some audiovisual equipment is quite sophisticated and expensive, and technicians must know when it is more appropriate to return equipment to the manufacturer or to a specialty repair shop instead of attempting repairs themselves.

Audiovisual technicians are employed by local school systems, college and university media centers, industrial training centers, marketing education centers, advertising agencies, government agencies, and the armed forces. Some work in businesses that provides audiovisual equipment and services to hotels or convention centers. Other technicians work for regional boards of cooperative education services. These are organizations formed by several school districts to provide specialized services to all the districts. Usually such a board has regional film and video libraries and traveling library, television, and media services.

Requirements

Audiovisual technicians need to have up to two years of postsecondary school technical training. Technicians who install, operate, adjust, and service audiovisual equipment need to learn some electronics and mechanical skills, while technicians who transform ideas and concepts into tangible media forms need to develop their artistic abilities as well as learn about techniques for using materials and equipment. In addition, audiovisual technicians need

Many audiovisual technicians are employed by educational institutions to maintain the equipment and provide services such as recording important lectures and symposiums.

Second-year courses may include audio materials production, television production, technical aspects of television, advanced graphics, advanced photography, internship in audiovisual technology, audiovisual office management, psychology, sales techniques, and technical writing.

There are other ways of preparing for the career. Sometimes people already working in related areas such as public relations or industrial training, or electronics or mechanical technicians with a special interest in the visual arts or audiovisual materials and equipment can get on-the-job training or study part-time to move into the field.

Technical training programs in the military can provide part of the necessary skills for this field. Such training, however, does not always provide a thorough enough understanding of the processes and equipment that technicians will encounter, so some additional study may be required.

Most employers provide an organized orientation period for new employees, during which they must learn the products or services of the employer's organization.

Special requirements

A license or certificate is not normally required for audiovisual technicians. Some employers have special requirements, such as security clearances in the military or in some industrial training situations. To work for some government agencies, technicians must pass civil service examinations.

Although not a requirement, audiovisual technicians may find it useful to become certified by the Institute for the Certification of Engineering Technicians. Affiliations with photographic, electronics, technical communications, or technical media associations keep technicians in touch with new developments and give them access to a wider range of people who are working in the same field.

Opportunities for experience and exploration

Students may be able to get valuable insight and information about this career field in a vocational program taught in their school or from teachers of drafting and electrical shop courses. Through a ham radio or photography hobby

certain personal qualities, such as creativity and the ability to communicate easily with others.

In high school, prospective audiovisual technicians should take courses that teach language skills (reading, writing, speaking, and listening), and also two years of mathematics and one year of physics or chemistry with laboratory. Elementary drafting and drawing and courses that introduce electronics are also a good idea.

Many public and private technical institutes, community colleges, and some divisions of four-year colleges offer programs to prepare audiovisual technicians. These programs are usually the quickest and best way to prepare for the career. They may have various names such as audiovisual technology, media technology, or audiovisual library technology.

Audiovisual technicians need a general preparation in the media and media equipment field. Typical first-year courses in technical training programs include graphic design, audiovisual history, basic learning theory, equipment operation and maintenance, duplicating processes, basic photography, basic electronics, English, mathematics, and science.

they can directly experience activities similar to those of audiovisual technicians.

Interested students may be able to find opportunities for involvement as amateur audiovisual technicians. School programs may need to be recorded or may utilize visual aids. Public address systems may be used to amplify speeches, plays, or concerts. Working as an audiovisual aide or volunteer can help the prospective technician become familiar with the equipment, methods, and tasks involved in audiovisual work. There are opportunities for the same type of involvement at a community college, technical institute, or four-year college.

Getting to know some of the people at local companies that supply audiovisual equipment and services is another way to learn firsthand about the career. Such contacts may lead to part-time work.

Methods of entering

Graduates of audiovisual programs are often helped in finding employment by the placement office at their school. In addition, many school districts, colleges, universities, businesses, and industries advertise in newspapers for audiovisual technicians.

In some states technicians who wish to work for public schools and universities or government agencies are required to take competitive civil service exams. There is usually a probationary period of from three months to a year for new employees. During the probationary period, newly employed technicians may receive training or orientation on the job. After this, they usually assume full responsibility for all duties.

Advancement

Advancement is usually within the department or area where the audiovisual technician works. Technicians may advance to positions as supervisors or senior technicians.

Attending a baccalaureate program in audiovisual technology can open up more supervisory and administrative job possibilities for ambitious technicians. The emphasis in these programs is on in-depth expertise in both conventional and rapidly changing technologies, as well as management and supervisory techniques and skills.

There are increasing opportunities for experienced audiovisual technicians to move into sales, demonstration, and service jobs for dis-tributors of audiovisual equipment. Experienced technicians also have opportunities to start or join a company that provides audiovisual equipment and service to hotels, conference centers, large corporations, and government agencies.

Employment outlook

The increasing use of films, records, videotapes, audio tapes, overhead transparencies, and related teaching tools in today's schools, libraries, and workplaces suggests that trained audiovisual technicians will continue to be needed to prepare and present these materials, to operate all types of projectors, language laboratory equipment, tape recorders, microphones and sound systems, and to ensure that all equipment is in good working order. In general, audiovisual technicians appear to have a good future because the number of job openings exceeds the number of well-qualified technicians. In business and industry, company educational centers need media support staff for training company personnel. The increasing complexity of industrial jobs is forcing more employers to provide organized education and training programs for their employees. Audiovisual methods of presenting technical information at these training programs have proven to be very effective.

The outlook for jobs in the public sector, however, may not be as good. Because of a continuing general emphasis on cost-cutting in government, at some point technicians who work for public schools or government agencies may find that funds are reduced for audiovisual programs and personnel.

Earnings

Starting salaries for audiovisual technicians vary depending on the requirements of the job, the technician's training, the type of employer, and other factors. Beginners may receive $13,000 to $16,500 a year, although some technicians make more and a few make less. Experienced technicians may grow into advanced positions that pay salaries of $20,000 to $27,000 per year or more. Benefits may include sick leave, paid holidays and vacation time, health insurance, and a pension plan. Technicians who succeed at starting their own company have the highest potential earnings.

Conditions of work

Working conditions for audiovisual technicians are usually pleasant, attractive, clean, and not hazardous. Technicians are almost always provided with all the tools and materials they need.

Audiovisual technicians usually work thirty-five to forty hours a week. Some employers operate on Saturday mornings as well as Mondays through Fridays. Some technicians in larger institutions may work a split shift or an evening shift. Technicians who provide the equipment and audiovisual services for hotels, conference centers, or major corporate training centers often must work long hours and during weekends. Some programs might start almost as soon as the previous ones are finished. To provide the equipment and service for a conference with more than one hundred separate sessions can be a collective task for several technicians, and many hours of exacting work may be required. The financial rewards for this work are naturally greater than for some less demanding jobs.

Social and psychological factors

Audiovisual technicians must keep up-to-date with the rapid changes that occur in the materials, methods, and equipment in this field. They will find that basic scientific principles do not change rapidly, but details of equipment and processes do change.

Audiovisual technicians should know how to work well under pressure, to coordinate simultaneous requests, and to maintain the discipline necessary for teamwork. They must be able to accept constructive criticism. A sense of humor and a pleasant disposition are valuable personal qualities. The ever-changing challenge of providing information to people can be one of the major satisfactions of this career.

GOE: 01.03.01, 05.05.10, 05.10.05; **SIC:** 8231; **SOC:** 399, 6151, 7479

◇ **SOURCES OF ADDITIONAL INFORMATION**

Association of Audio-Visual Technicians
3333C Veterans Memorial Highway
Ronkonkoma, NY 11779

Association for Educational Communications and Technology
1126 16th Street, NW
Washington, DC 20036

Electronics Industries Association
1722 I Street, NW, Suite 300
Washington, DC 20006

Institute of Electrical and Electronics Engineers
345 East 47th Street
New York, NY 10017

National Electronic Sales and Service Dealers Association
2708 West Berry Street
Fort Worth, TX 76109

Society for Technical Communication
815 15th Street, NW
Washington, DC 20005

Cable television technicians

Definition

Cable television technicians inspect, maintain, and repair antennas, cables, and amplifying equipment used in cable television transmission systems.

Nature of the work

Cable television technicians work in a variety of settings and perform a wide range of activities. Television cables usually follow the routes of telephone cables, running along poles in rural and suburban areas and through tunnels in cities. Working in tunnels and underground cable passageways, technicians inspect cables for evidence of damage and corrosion. Using schematic diagrams and blueprints, they trace cables to locate sites of signal breakdown. They may also work at pole-mounted amplifiers, where they analyze the strength of incoming television signals, using field-strength meters and miniature television receivers to evaluate reception. At customers' terminal boxes, they explain the workings of the cable system, answer customers' questions, and respond to complaints that may indicate cable or equipment problems. When major problems arise, they repair or replace damaged or faulty cable systems.

Cable television technicians use various electrical measuring instruments (voltmeters, ohmmeters, capacity meters) to diagnose causes of transmission problems. They also use electricians' hand tools (including screwdrivers, pliers, and so forth) to dismantle, repair, or replace faulty sections of cable or disabled equipment, such as amplifying equipment used to boost the signal at intervals along the cable system.

An important aspect of the work of cable television technicians involves implementing regular programs of preventive maintenance on the cable system. Technicians inspect connections, insulation, and the performance of amplifying equipment, using measuring instruments and viewing the transmitted signals on television monitors.

A large part of the cable television technician's time is spent on ladders or in confined spaces. As with all electrical maintenance work, there is some danger of electrical shock. The coaxial cables used to transmit television sig-

A cable television technician adjusts a transmission line. Thousands of people rely on his expertise to ensure quality cable reception.

nals are from two to three inches in diameter. Because of their tough shielding and thick insulation, they are heavy and awkward to handle. When a section of cable is replaced, heavy-duty lifting and pulling equipment is put to use. Cables still have to be manipulated into position for splicing, which involves medium to heavy physical work.

Cable television technicians must be able to deal with people, to analyze clients' descriptions of reception problems, and to explain cable system costs and operations when necessary. Because of the extensive public service that this work requires, strong interpersonal skills are a plus.

Requirements

Persons interested in careers as cable television technicians should take high-school mathematics courses at least through plane geometry and have a solid knowledge of shop math. They should have language skills sufficient to enable them to read technical manuals and instructions and to follow detailed maintenance procedures. They should also be prepared to follow a one- or two-year technical training program such as those offered at a community college or technical institute. Their courses should include the basics of electrical wiring and electronics, broadcasting theory and practice, blueprint and schematic diagram reading, and physics.

Acute vision, with no color-perception deficiency, is essential for analyzing cable reception. Technicians must be physically able to bend and stretch and to work in confined spaces easily. They should feel comfortable working with electrical equipment and with electricians' tools.

Conditions of work

The activities of these technicians require care and precision. The work is moderately heavy, involving occasional lifting of up to fifty pounds. Cable television technicians work both indoors and outdoors and must be able to climb utility poles and work at heights comfortably.

GOE: 05.05.05; SIC: 483; SOC: 6151

◇ **SOURCES OF ADDITIONAL INFORMATION**

Society of Cable Television Engineers
669 Exton Commons
Exton, PA 19341

◇ **RELATED ARTICLES**

Volume 1: Broadcasting; Telecommunications
Volume 3: Commercial and industrial electronic equipment repairers; Communications equipment mechanics; Electrical repairers; Electricians; Line installers and cable splicers; Telephone and PBX installers and repairers; Transmission and distribution occupations
Volume 4: Electrical technicians; Electronics technicians; Telecommunications technicians

---

Darkroom technicians

Definition

Darkroom technicians perform all functions necessary to develop exposed photographic film and to produce photographic prints or slides from the developed negatives.

They use various chemical solutions and procedures according to the type of film being developed: black-and-white negative, color negative, or color positive (reversal) film. Because of the complexity of the color developing process, some darkroom technicians are designated *color laboratory technicians* and specialize in this work.

Darkroom technicians most often work very closely with photographers to produce special photographic effects through the developing process.

History

The first permanent photographs were made in the 1820s by exposing light-sensitive plates for very long periods of time. Through the nineteenth century, advances in photography gradually made the exposure process and development time shorter, and photographic equipment became less cumbersome. The greatest leap forward came in 1888, when George Eastman introduced his Kodak camera: a hand-held, roll-film camera that brought photography within the reach of the amateur. The owner snapped the pictures, then sent the entire camera, film inside, to Eastman Kodak for development.

The Leica "miniature" 35-millimeter camera was introduced in 1924, and its convenient size and removable roll-film feature helped create a whole new hobby in amateur home photography with its enthusiasm for candid (unposed) photographs and home development of film.

Further developments in photographic technology soon followed, including the invention of light-sensitive photographic papers for printing enlargements, more sensitive films, and the development of color films and papers. Eastman Kodak introduced Kodachrome, the first widely distributed color slide film, in 1935. Color negative film, used to produce color prints, became available in the early 1940s.

Since photography became practicable for amateurs, the public's enthusiasm for it as a hobby has never lessened. Almost every household in the United States has at least one camera today. Photographs record family history and the family's travels; photos sent between separated family members and friends provide communication links; and hobbyists spend pleasant hours with their cameras and in the darkroom.

Professionally, photography has become a major art form and a powerful force in advertising and journalism in the twentieth century. National newspapers and magazines and local newspapers alike use photographs extensively in their reporting of events, to illustrate interviews and feature articles, and in their advertising. Each maintains a darkroom of its own or has an agreement with a professional photographic laboratory that serves its needs.

The great majority of amateur photographers do not develop and print their own photos. Camera stores, drug stores, and film convenience centers accept film for development and send it out to development laboratories specializing in large-volume, quick-turnaround development. More and more of the equipment in these laboratories is automated. Automation speeds the development and printing processes while ensuring that a consistently acceptable level of quality is maintained in the finished photographs.

Laboratories servicing professional photographers make use of the latest developments in photographic processing methods to analyze and control the quality of their product, but much of their work is still done by hand by highly skilled, experienced, and well-trained technicians who need to observe the film or photographic print they are working with as it develops. Fewer than half of the workers engaged in photographic processing work as darkroom technicians, with the remainder being employed as semiskilled workers operating equipment that prints photos, cuts and mounts slides, and packages photos for return to the customer.

Nature of the work

To develop black-and-white film, darkroom technicians take the exposed film from its protective cassette (for roll film) or film holder (for sheet film) in darkness or under "safe" lights that will not affect the film, and they place it in a chemical bath that will bring out the image the photographer has captured. The chemical action is stopped by a water bath when the negative has developed sufficiently, then "fixed" (made permanent) by immersion in a second chemical bath. The negatives are dried thoroughly with a sponge and a stream of warm air, then inspected by the technician for physical defects and to determine the best way to print them.

Color laboratory technicians work with two kinds of film: negative film from which color prints are made, and positive (or reversal) film which after development is mounted as slides. Color film processing is complex, and these technicians are particularly skilled at controlling the time and chemicals in the process to make prints and slides that reproduce faithfully the colors of the photographer's original subject.

Color film consists of three layers of chemical emulsion mounted on a plastic backing. Each layer of emulsion is sensitive to one of the three primary colors of light: blue, green, or red.

During development, the chemical developer affects each emulsion to develop and fix the image it has been exposed to, and binds it with a chemical "coupler" to color the image. The color laboratory technician regulates the conditions of development (time, temperature, and chemical strength) to produce the most accurate negatives or slides, and to produce special color effects when wanted.

Darkroom technicians also make photographic prints. Photographic prints are made by passing light through black-and-white or color negatives onto photosensitive paper (paper coated with chemicals similar to those forming the emulsion on photographic film). The paper is then developed in much the same way as film. Skilled technicians are better able to control the development of prints, because prints are larger and easier to view as they develop. An experienced darkroom technician can vary the light and time of development of various parts of a print to create special effects or to compensate for weaknesses in the original negative.

Darkroom technicians working in large-volume operations developing the photographs of amateur photographers are most likely to be in supervisory positions. In these laboratories, both black-and-white and color film are devel-

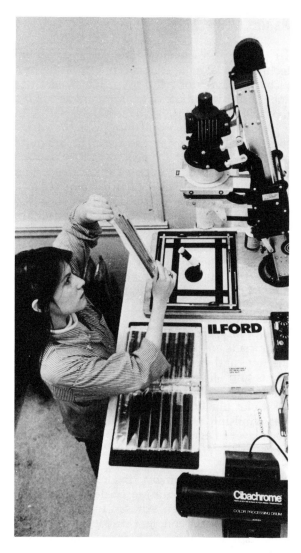

A darkroom technician inspects color negatives before making prints. She must look for scratches and remove bits of dust from the negative.

oped in machines that control and replenish their chemical supplies automatically, guided by timers and sensing devices. Operators of photographic laboratory equipment call on darkroom technicians for help with unusual developing problems, or when machine problems arise.

Darkroom technicians work with a variety of chemicals that can irritate the skin. They also work with magnifying glasses when inspecting negatives and prints and when using cutting and mounting equipment to ready final prints for return to the photographic studio. This close work can be tiring and produce eye strain. They mark each roll of negatives and each batch of prints with codes that ensure each photographer, professional or amateur, receives the correct film and prints back.

Requirements

People who are interested in this field should try to get at least six months of specialized training to qualify for jobs that involve more than the most routine tasks. Community colleges and technical institutes offer a variety of courses and short training programs that include practical, hands-on experience. A good high-school preparation for prospective darkroom technicians would include courses in photography, mathematics, and chemistry with laboratory instruction.

Programs that train people to be darkroom technicians vary in length from about three months to two years. The shortest courses provide only basic instruction in a few selected areas of photographic processing. A few community and junior colleges offer two-year courses leading to an associate degree in photographic technology. These programs provide a much broader grounding for the whole range of darkroom work. Such training is very desirable for anyone who hopes to advance to supervisory or management positions.

Some film laboratories provide on-the-job technical training for employees who start with little or no experience in the photographic processing field. People who take this approach, however, may need at least three or four years to become familiar with the different aspects of darkroom work.

There is little opportunity for on-the-job training for darkroom technicians working with professional photographers. Persons applying for such work need to have solid basic training in laboratory developing procedures.

Darkroom technicians should have mechanical aptitude and manual dexterity. They also must have good eyesight and unimpaired color perception.

Special requirements

There are no special requirements for a career as a darkroom technician.

Opportunities for experience and exploration

Many schools and social-activity centers sponsor photography clubs that offer excellent opportunities for interested persons to become experienced in photography, darkroom techniques, and the appreciation of good photographs. Such groups often arrange tours of photographic exhibits, laboratory facilities, and studios, and sponsor lectures by experienced professionals. They also organize exhibits by group members, where aspiring darkroom technicians can show the results of their experiments with printing techniques and special effects.

Methods of entering

Large bulk-processing photographic laboratories are best approached through their personnel manager or through the placement officer of a school. To apply for work at a laboratory servicing professional photographers, the prospective technician should contact the director of the laboratory or the senior technician. Here again, the placement officer of a school can be very helpful in arranging an interview.

At job interviews applicants should be prepared to show a portfolio of prints and negatives developed in school or hobby laboratory work, to give the prospective employer an idea of the range of experience gained.

Advancement

In a large-volume processing lab, advancement is usually from helper to independent worker to supervisor. In a laboratory servicing professional photographers the apprenticeship is usually longer, because of the variety and complexity of skills to be mastered. Experienced technicians often work alone with little supervision; as a result, there are fewer supervisory positions available than in other industries.

Advancement may also take the form of becoming a sales or customer representative for the laboratory. Some technicians prefer to open their own laboratories after they feel they are sufficiently experienced.

Employment outlook

Employment through the 1990s for darkroom technicians is expected to increase more quickly than the rate of growth for all other occupations. Increased use of photography—and especially color photography—in audiovisual sales presentations, educational programs, medical and technological research and development activities, and expanded interest in amateur photography is expected to lead to a

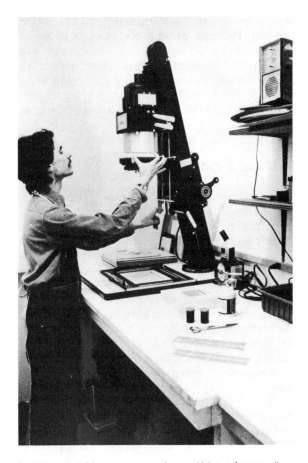

A darkroom technician operates an enlarger, which transforms small negatives into large prints.

greater demand for photo processing services. This demand will be partially offset, however, by advances in the development of automated processing equipment. To some degree, the level of activity in this field is influenced by the overall economy. In the event of an economic downturn, some technicians may be subject to layoffs.

Earnings

Earnings of darkroom technicians vary greatly, depending on experience and training, the employer's type of operation, and geographical location. Technicians in laboratories servicing professional photographers often earn as much as, or more than, beginning professional photographers.

Technicians who are graduates of two-year programs in photographic laboratory technology start at around $20,000 per year. On the other hand, technicians with only a small amount of training in photographic processing may begin at salaries in the range of $11,000 to $13,000. Technicians who become specialists in a particular aspect of darkroom processing—in developing color film, for instance—have higher earnings that all-around darkroom technicians. Highly skilled and experienced technicians make $25,000 to $30,000 a year or more.

Conditions of work

Photographic laboratories are clean, air-conditioned places in which to work. Physical work is light. The developing chemicals technicians work with are irritating to the skin and eyes, and have strong, pungent odors. Eyestrain can be a hazard because of the frequent close examination of small images on negatives.

A forty-hour week is normal in the industry, but technicians working with newspaper photographers may occasionally be involved in an emergency and have to work overtime to meet a deadline. Laboratories serving amateur photographers place great emphasis on the speed with which they can return finished photos to the customer. Employment with such a laboratory may mean considerable overtime, especially during holiday and vacation periods. These laboratories often work two or three shifts each day.

Social and psychological factors

Whether attending to a machine or developing negatives or prints by hand, darkroom technicians must concentrate on what they are doing at all times. Time factors are critical in film development, and only complete attention to detail will produce successful photographs. In high-volume operations there are likely to be pressures on the worker to produce as many finished photos as possible during a shift.

The pleasure a technician feels at producing the best possible photograph from the film exposed by the photographer—amateur or professional—can be a source of great job satisfaction.

GOE: 05.10.05; SIC: 7384; SOC: 6863

 SOURCES OF ADDITIONAL INFORMATION

Society of Photo-Technologists
PO Box 9634
Denver, CO 80209

Photo Marketing Association International
3000 Picture Place
Jackson, MI 49201

Professional Photographers of America
1090 Executive Way
Des Plaines, IL 60018

 RELATED ARTICLES

Electronic organ technicians

Definition

Electronic organ technicians install, service, test, and adjust electronic organs. They also may work with electronic pianos or other electronic musical instruments. Utilizing standard electronic testing equipment, following manufacturer's manuals and wiring diagrams, and using electrician's hand tools, electronic organ technicians make repairs and adjustments as necessary. In addition to servicing the console itself, technicians also place and connect speakers and maintain amplifying equipment. Some technicians may also be employed by manufacturers to assist in the design and quality-control testing of instruments.

History

The history of the ancestor of the electronic organ—the pipe organ—dates back more than 2,000 years. It was in 1934 that Laurens Hammond, an American inventor, patented the first practical electronic organ, an instrument that imitates the sound of the pipe organ but which requires much less space and is more economical and practical to own and operate.

The electronic organ has no pipes. It produces tones through the operation of electronic oscillators as current passes through them. These tones are then amplified, combined, and otherwise manipulated electronically to produce music. The electronic organ cannot match the richness and volume of sound that a pipe organ can produce, but electronic organs have become very popular because of their economy and because of their compact size, which makes them very convenient for home use. Their portability also makes them practical for bands and small musical groups. As a result, they greatly outnumber pipe organs in use today.

The development and increasing popularity of the electronic organ created a need for service that could not be met by existing pipe organ technicians. The electronic organ technician's career arose and has grown with the growth in popularity of the electronic organ.

Today thousands of people work as electronic organ technicians. The exact number is difficult to discover, because in many smaller communities much of the work of servicing and repairing electronic organs is done by other electronics technicians, such as radio and television service technicians.

Nature of the work

Although the electronic organ imitates the sound of the pipe organ, the workings of the two instruments have very little in common. The electronic organ consists of electrical and electronic components and circuits that channel electrical current through various oscillators and amplifiers to produce sound when each key is pressed. It is rare for an oscillator or other component to need adjustment in the way an organ pipe needs to be adjusted to tune it. An electronic organ is tuned by testing it for electronic malfunction and replacing or repair-

ing the component, circuit board, or wire involved.

The work of the electronic organ technician is closer to that of the television repair technician than it is to that of the pipe organ technician. The technician often begins looking for the source of a problem by checking for loose wires and solder connections. After making routine checks, technicians consult wiring diagrams that enable them to trace and test the circuits of the entire instrument to find malfunctions. An unusual or irregular voltage in a circuit may indicate a problem, for instance. Once the problem has been located, the technician often solves it by replacing a malfunctioning part, such as a circuit board.

The technicians work with common electrician's tools: pliers, wire cutters, screwdriver, and soldering iron, as well as testing equipment. Most repairs and adjustments can be made in the customer's home. Because different manufacturers' instruments are arranged differently, technicians follow manufacturers' wiring diagrams and service manuals to locate trouble spots and make repairs. In larger and more complex instruments, such as those in churches and theaters, this may require a day or more of searching and testing.

Requirements

Persons interested in pursuing a career as an electronic organ technician should take high-school mathematics courses at least through geometry and should acquire a good working knowledge of shop math. They should have language skills developed sufficiently to enable them to read technical instruction manuals. Because technicians work on-site, they meet and deal with customers in person. An ability to meet and talk with strangers comfortably and to extract information about problems they are having with their instruments is very useful.

Although most electronic organ technicians learn some of their skills on the job, at least one year of electronics technical training is necessary as a basis for learning organ repair skills. Training is available from community colleges, technical training schools, and private vocational schools. The armed forces also offer excellent training in electronics.

As a part of their on-the-job training, and to keep abreast of new developments, electronic organ technicians may also attend training courses offered by organ manufacturers.

Persons interested in becoming electronic organ technicians should have excellent hearing, manual dexterity, and the ability to work

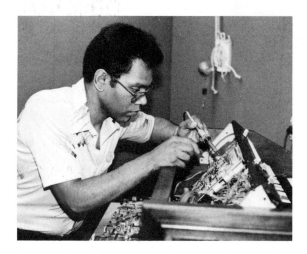

With the use of soldering equipment, a technician repairs an electronic organ.

with small components and to make precise adjustments. The ability to play an instrument is useful but not absolutely essential.

Special requirements

There are no special requirements for a career as an electronic organ technician.

Opportunities for experience and exploration

Details about the work of electronic organ technicians and about the availability of jobs can be best obtained from local technicians and from the owners of local music stores that sell organs. Spending some time in a shop or accompanying a technician on a call to a customer will provide excellent insight into the day-to-day work of a technician.

Methods of entering

Electronic organ technicians usually begin their careers as trainees in the repair shop of a large music store or organ sales facility. Interested persons should approach the shop manager directly for an interview, or they should use the services of the placement office of the school where they received electronics training.

Advancement

Electronic organ technicians may advance from trainee to qualified technician status immediately after finishing training. Once a technician is trained and able to work without supervision there is usually no further advancement. Some technicians choose to go into business for themselves, as the investment required to start such a business is usually relatively modest. Competition is keen, however, and less skilled or less businesslike electronic organ technicians often fail.

Technicians who work for manufacturers may advance to supervisory positions.

Employment outlook

There are millions of electronic organs in use, and the number is expected to continue to increase. Even in churches, where pipe organs have been traditional for many years, electronic organs are gaining popularity. But because electronic organ technicians comprise such a small field of employment, increased demand for their services is not expected to create many new job opportunities during the early 1990s. As currently active technicians retire they will have to be replaced. Offsetting these needs is the fact that organ repairs and adjustments are viewed as luxuries by most household consumers, and this field is therefore very sensitive to downturns in the economy.

Earnings

Beginning trainees or helpers earn an average of approximately $13,000 a year—although some trainees worked for no pay for the opportunity to receive training. Experienced workers earn roughly $16,000 to as much as $27,000 a year. Wages vary from one area of the country to another.

Self-employed electronic organ technicians may earn $15,000 a year or more. It should be pointed out that earnings for a self-employed technician depend to a large extent on the technician's skill, ability to attract new customers and keep them satisfied, and the competition from other technicians. Technicians in or near large cities where there are more instruments to be serviced fare better than those in smaller communities.

Conditions of work

Electronic organ technicians' work is seldom strenuous, but it often involves much bending, reaching, and sometimes working in cramped conditions. Work is usually performed under pleasant conditions, either in a shop or in customers' homes. There is some chance of electrical shock. Technicians employed by organ manufacturers work in well-lighted factory workshop conditions.

Electronic organs receive more use in the winter months, when customers spend more hours indoors and tend to play more. During this season self-employed technicians may expect a heavier volume of work. They should also expect to work at least part of their week during times most convenient to their customers, which means evening and weekend hours.

Social and psychological factors

Electronic organ technicians often work alone. The step-by-step search for problems in the many circuits and components of an organ may take considerable time and become tedious. Technicians, especially those who are self-employed, must be able to meet and deal with the public comfortably.

GOE: 05.05.12; SIC: 506; SOC: 6155

◇ **SOURCES OF ADDITIONAL INFORMATION**

Electronic Industries Association
1722 I Street, NW, Suite 300
Washington, DC 20006

Electronics Technicians Association, International
604 North Jackson
Greencastle, IN 46135

National Association of Electronic Keyboard Manufacturers
c/o Lowell Simpson
Baldwin Piano and Organ Co.
422 Ward's Corner Road
Loveland, OH 45140

◇ **RELATED ARTICLES**

Volume 1: Electronics
Volume 2: Musical occupations
Volume 3: Commercial and industrial electronic equipment repairers; Musical instrument repairers and tuners
Volume 4: Electromechanical technicians; Electronics sales and service technicians; Electronics technicians; Electronics test technicians; Mechanical technicians; Piano technicians; Pipe organ technicians

Exhibit technicians

Definition

Exhibit technicians are skilled craft workers who, using detailed plans supplied by designers and architects, build and set up various kinds of museum displays and fixtures.

Nature of the work

In the course of their work, exhibit technicians use carpenter's and electrician's hand and power tools on such materials as plywood, wood, fiberglass, and metal to build structures

An exhibit technician at Chicago's Field Museum removes the dust from the mouth of a mastodon. Permanent display pieces at museums must be cleaned regularly.

and displays and to assemble them in place. They often begin a project by consulting with museum scientists or curators to gather information about a new exhibit, or by studying sketches or engineering drawings to gain an idea of what is to be displayed, then suggesting display layouts. When the exhibit format has been decided, technicians cut and fit parts of the display structure—which may range from a cabinet to a rearrangement of an entire museum wing—and add fittings, lighting fixtures and wiring, plumbing when necessary, and audiovisual equipment or sound speakers if called for. They test and adjust components when the exhibit has been assembled. They may also help arrange pieces to be exhibited in the cases they have constructed. If they specialize in certain areas, technicians may be designated as exhibit carpenters or electricians, or as planetar-

ium sky-show technicians or science-center display builders.

Requirements

In high school, persons interested in this career should prepare by taking mathematics courses at least through solid geometry, and if possible, electronics, as well as shop math and shop practice. They should have sufficient language skills to read instructions, and they should be able to read blueprints and wiring diagrams. They should have at least two years of technical training beyond high school, taking courses in electrical and mechanical construction techniques, cabinet-making, and interior design or architectural design. They should become familiar with tools as well as plans.

Conditions of work

These technicians are likely to receive more specific, museum-oriented training on the job. The work is not physically strenuous, but requires moderate lifting and carrying (up to fifty pounds) and bending, stretching, standing on ladders, and working in tight spaces. Work is performed indoors in pleasant circumstances and the constant variety of assignments makes the work challenging.

GOE: 01.06.02; SIC: 7999; SOC: 6862

◇ **RELATED ARTICLES**

Volume 2: Architects; Interior designers and decorators; Museum occupations
Volume 3: Carpenters; Display workers; Electricians; Plumbers
Volume 4: Architectural and building construction technicians; Electrical technicians; Museum technicians; Planetarium technicians

Film laboratory technicians

Definition

Film laboratory technicians work in laboratories that process motion picture film. They carry out various tasks related to inspecting, developing, splicing, and otherwise preparing film for final printing.

Nature of the work

The duties of film laboratory technicians include testing exposed film that is to be processed for its sensitivity to light and other factors that will affect processing techniques. Technicians use densitometers, sensitometers, and timed-light readings to evaluate film. They record readings and expose test strips of film to guide film developers. The technicians who do these jobs may be designated as *densitometrists* or *sensitometrists.*

Technicians also operate machines that develop and dry motion picture film. They number film for identification purposes, tend machines that apply wax to splices and sprocket holes to allow film to run through projectors more smoothly, and rewind film when it has been processed and treated. They may also repair or remove damaged sections of film that is being processed. The technicians who specialize in these tasks may be designated as *developing-machine tenders, drying-machine tenders, rewinders, film numberers,* or *waxer tenders* according to their specific duties.

Another duty of film laboratory technicians is to mix chemicals to be used in processing film, following specified formulas. Technicians cut and splice strips of processed film, following written instructions or an edited test print, and compare the finished film with the edited print for differences in color and other details. They project the film to examine it for scratches, blurs, or other physical defects. They approve film for release, reject it, or route it to another department of the laboratory for further work. Technicians who do these jobs may be designated as *film inspectors* or *film splicers.*

Requirements

Persons interested in careers in film laboratory work should have a high-school diploma, and

A film laboratory technician inspects the quality of the film after he has processed it. On a motion picture screen, even the smallest scratches and specks of dust can be visible.

have mathematical skills that enable them to work arithmetical problems. They should be able to read operating instruction manuals and guidelines, and be able to communicate instructions to other workers.

Film laboratory technicians should have a minimum of three months of additional vocational training after they complete high school. Technicians will find that their advancement to more responsible and demanding laboratory duties will be directly tied to their vocational training. Those technicians who are assigned to testing and analyzing film to be processed and inspecting finished prints need two years of vocational training at a technical school or community college with emphasis on film laboratory techniques to prepare them for this important and demanding work.

Conditions of work

Film laboratory technicians work in pleasant, air-conditioned surroundings. Their work is not strenuous, but demands long hours of standing, precise and accurate attention to procedures, and good vision.

GOE: 02.04.01, 05.10.05, 05.12.14; SIC: 7819; SOC: 6868, 7671

◇ **SOURCES OF ADDITIONAL INFORMATION**

Society of Motion Picture and Television Engineers
595 West Hartsdale Avenue
White Plains, NY 10607

Professional Film and Video Equipment Association
PO Box 9436
Silver Springs, MD 20906

Field technicians

Definition

Field technicians set up and operate portable radio and television transmitting equipment in locations remote from the main station. They obtain a link with the station by locating telephone wires that can carry transmissions, then connecting microphones, amplifiers, and power supply to the lines. Where no wires are available, technicians set up, test, and operate microwave transmitters to broadcast to the station control center.

During remote broadcasts they monitor sound and video transmissions, controlling volume and picture quality, and maintaining the link with the station. Field technicians may occasionally be called on to perform announcing duties in the field. Technicians who are restricted to working with microwave transmitting equipment are usually designated as *microwave technicians*.

Nature of the work

Technicians usually travel to the site of a remote broadcast in a truck or van carrying their equipment and any tools and parts they may need to make emergency repairs. The van is usually also equipped with a microwave transmitter. At the remote site, technicians set up and test their equipment, locate and test telephone links for transmission to the main station control room, and make any other arrangements required for the successful transmission of the broadcast.

As the only technician in the crew, the field technician is responsible for the testing, replacement, or repair of microphones, amplifiers, auxiliary power supply, and wire connections. Technicians must be able to make emergency repairs using electricians' hand tools such as screwdrivers, pliers, and soldering irons, and be able to test for malfunctions using electrical test meters. The mobile units of larger stations are usually equipped with spare microphones, cameras, and parts, but the technicians of smaller stations have to be able to make repairs very quickly.

When the transmitting equipment is ready, the technicians switch cameras and microphones on and off and direct transmissions to the main station control room where they are broadcast live or recorded for use in a later broadcast.

Requirements

Persons interested in careers as field technicians should take high-school mathematics courses at least through solid geometry as well as physics, electrical shop, and electronics, if possible. Because field technicians also act as announcers on occasion, speech courses and experience in a school radio station as an announcer can be helpful. The ability to read and understand technical information is useful, since field technicians must face technical repair problems on location with only technical manuals to assist them.

Like other technicians in the broadcast industry, field technicians should expect to follow at least a two-year program of training beyond high school, concentrating on courses in electronics and radio and television theory. They should also continue to gain experience as announcers.

Field technicians need to have manual dexterity and to feel comfortable working with electronic equipment. More important, they need to be able to work independently without much support and to solve problems involving both equipment and people quickly and effectively.

According to federal law, anyone who generates microwave or certain other radio communications equipment must have a general radio telephone operator license issued by the FCC after the applicant has passed a series of written tests. Counselors can provide more information about agencies to contact regarding current licensing requirements and procedures.

Before broadcasting a live interview outdoors, field technicians adjust their equipment to ensure adequate lighting and sound.

Conditions of work

The work of field technicians is not strenuous, although it does involve carrying equipment from the truck to the remote site and setting it up. Persons in this career must be able to meet and deal with the public easily, since they will be working in many different kinds of settings and must secure the cooperation of the people who live or work on the location to be able to function.

GOE: 05.03.05; SIC: 483; SOC: 393

◇ **RELATED ARTICLES**

Volume 1: Broadcasting; Electronics; Telecommunications
Volume 2: Photographers and camera operators; Radio and television announcers and newscasters
Volume 4: Audio control technicians; Electronics technicians; Sound-recording technicians; Studio technicians; Video technicians

Graphic arts technicians

Definition

Graphic arts technicians work in all phases of printing and graphic arts, including typographical layout, composition, press work, binding, lithography, photoengraving, and other graphic reproduction. Some are knowledgeable in drawing and lettering and in the techniques of photography.

Graphic arts technicians may work in four-color process and printing; printing press operation, servicing, and elementary maintenance; cost estimation and the production,

inspection, quality control, handling, binding, packaging, and storage of printed materials.

History

For centuries people have been using the graphic arts to express their thoughts in writing and to complement the simple written word with illustration. No definite date can be assigned to many examples of early printing. It

345

has been established that by the end of the second century A.D. the Chinese had the means to print texts. They knew how to make paper and ink, and they knew how to make surfaces bearing texts carved in relief.

Early woodblocks for printing were made in Japan about A.D. 764–770. In the eleventh century, a Chinese alchemist named Pi Sheng invented movable type made of clay and glue hardened by baking. By A.D. 1400 the Chinese and the Koreans were extensively using movable type made from wood and bronze.

Papermaking techniques were introduced to the Europeans during the thirteenth century. Typography did not reach Europe from China, however. The first known book printed in Europe using movable type was an edition of the Bible in Latin, printed about A.D. 1450, which most historians credit to Johannes Gutenberg. From that time, printing spread rapidly to other parts of the world.

Other important developments followed with machines that could perform a wider variety of printing methods. Photography was invented around 1830, and it challenged inventors to learn how to transfer pictures as well as print or geometric lines to paper and other materials. The lithographic process, invented in Prague in 1796 by Aloys Senefelder, was successfully used in a mechanized printing press by 1850. An English scientist named Fox Talbot learned how to make photoengraved prints in 1852 when he found that designs etched in plates covered with ink held ink in the etched cavities when the ink was wiped off. The ink in the etched parts was picked up by paper, thus making a printed image. Further innovations proceeded steadily into the twentieth century, expanding the flexibility and efficiency of printing for many purposes.

New developments continue to be made. Within the last two decades, computer typesetting has been perfected. This innovation has brought a great improvement in the speed and cost of setting type.

Nature of the work

The graphic arts industry is really made up of several different industries and in each of these industries many different careers are found. A partial list of these industries includes book publishing, job shop printing, magazine and newspaper publishing, paper and paper-product processing, advertising, packaging, photography, printing machinery, manufacturing and service, general printing supplies, and printing inks and coatings.

The printing industry uses a number of different processes to produce today's vast quantities of printed products as rapidly as possible and at the least cost. The existing processes are constantly being modified and new processes introduced as new technology becomes available. Some of the major processes involved in today's printing include the following: letterpress, offset, gravure, and screen printing, half-tone photography, and line photography.

Letterpress printing, also known as relief printing, is the familiar process of transferring a thin film of ink from the printing surface of the type form to the surface of the paper by pressing the two together.

Offset printing, or lithography, is also known by several other names: planographic printing, offset-lithography, photolithography, photo-offset lithography, or just photo-offset. In a growing number of plants computer-aided machines are used that carry out this process automatically. In the offset process, the materials to be printed are photographed or electronic scanners are used to make a photographic film. The image on film is transferred to a printing plate by a process similar to developing a photograph. The plate is then inked and pressed against a rubber blanket. The blanket in turn carries the ink onto the paper. Rotary presses can print thousands of impressions per hour using this type of process.

Except in special cases, the printing industry has moved away from letterpress or relief printing and toward offset printing. As a result, electronic phototypesetting has overtaken mechanical typesetting as a method of generating images.

In the gravure process, the ink image is printed on paper from shallow ink-filled cavities engraved on the surface of a metal plate. These cavities are etched into the plate through a chemical process. There are thousands of these cavities, or dots, per square inch. When the printing is done from an etched metal cylinder instead of a flat plate, the process is called rotogravure. The major uses of gravure printing are high-quality magazines, and some specialty printing jobs such as packages, wood grain, and floor covering.

Screen printing, or heat-transfer printing, is very different from letterpress, gravure, and offset methods. Screen printing makes an image by forcing ink through a finely woven cloth or metal screen that is stretched tightly over a frame. The image to be printed is cut into a stencil which is fastened to the frame. Heat is used to transfer some special inks onto the fabric. This process is widely used in the textile industry. The process may be used to print on flat, irregular, or cylindrical surfaces. Common applications are printing on paper, cardboard, glass, metal, textiles, and plastic.

Half-tone photography, or picture reproduction, is both an image-generation method and a production process. It generates images on light-sensitive film placed in a camera. Transferring these images onto a film negative that can be used to produce photographic pictures is a production process. Photographs that contain varying degrees of tone from light to dark are reproduced by the half-tone process.

Related to the half-tone process is line photography. This process photographs typed copy, straight-line drawings, or pictures with no graduated or shaded tones.

The printing and graphic arts industry employs more than a million workers in commercial printing places, including those in newspaper and magazine publishing, in government, schools, libraries, and private businesses. Some printing operations employ hundreds of workers, but many employ only a few. Many printing operations need highly qualified, broadly prepared technicians, especially the small printing and reproduction operations where a few workers must understand and do all of the work.

Book publishing and printing represents just one field where graphic arts technicians may be employed. The entire process can involve many steps and may different kinds of skilled workers.

The first phase in printing a book is preparation of the copy and illustrations. This involves *writers, editors, artists, photographers,* and *designers.* They write and edit the text, make drawings, take photographs, decide on layout and design, and fit copy to the page in the proper order.

The second phase is composing the text. In offset printing this involves *cold-type machine operators, photocomposition machine operators, darkroom staff, typists,* and *proofreaders.*

The third phase in printing is converting picture images to relief carriers. This is done by *electroplaters, engraving machine operators, platemakers, photoengravers,* and *stereotypers,* all of whom produce relief plates. In offset printing this process is called art and photo conversion. *Camera operators, color separators, color correctors,* and *darkroom workers* produce photographic negatives, positives, or transparencies on film to make the image.

The fourth phase in offset printing is stripping. *Layout workers* and *strippers* assemble photographic negatives and positives into a flat, so they may be exposed to the image carrier. In letterpress printing this is called assembling the relief image carriers. *Lockup workers, press oper-*

Using advanced equipment, a graphic arts technician enhances a photograph.

ators, and *stone workers* assemble the hot type and relief images into forms for printing.

The fifth and final phase in letterpress printing is making duplicate plates if needed. The *letterpress workers* involved are *electrotypers, stereotypers,* and *platemakers.* In the offset process, the final step is to expose the flat to a metal plate with a photosensitive coating, develop the plate, and finish it for use on the press.

Relatively few people enter graphic arts as broadly trained technicians. There may be thousands of technicians in the industry, but in most cases workers reach the technician level after a period of advancing from one specialized position to another. This provides an understanding of all levels of work in printing and production.

About a third of the workers in graphic reproduction work in the skilled crafts. Typical job titles are *compositor, press operator, camera operator, scanner operator, etcher, platemaker, stripper,* and *bookbinder.* The machinists and the electricians who maintain the printing equipment are also included in this classification.

347

A second major group of workers are the technically trained specialists such as *estimators, process and quality controllers, color-laboratory technicians, darkroom technicians,* and *technical illustrators.*

A third major group of workers are those who create the messages and images for newspapers, books, and magazines. This group includes *editors, reporters, artists, technical illustrators, graphic designers,* and *advertising staff.* In this group, some workers are classified as technicians. In addition there are many workers in the industry who work in sales and marketing. Supervising all of these workers are the management personnel who are responsible for the operation and financial success of the industry. Technicians often find that their knowledge and experience qualify them to grow into excellent careers in sales and management.

Requirements

While formal education beyond high school is not always a requirement for employment, prospective graphic arts technicians who graduate from strong postsecondary programs find that their training make getting a good job easier. The requirements for a broad preparation in the sciences that support graphic arts technology make it increasingly important for prospective technicians to complete a formal program after high school before seeking a position in the industry.

Graphic arts technology programs are being offered in some high schools and in many vocational schools, technical institutions, and two-year and four-year colleges. Such programs generally include courses in English, mathematics, photography, printing, chemistry, physics, data processing, mechanical drawing, and art. Graphic arts programs also provide up-to-date equipment and laboratories to facilitate hands-on instruction.

While in high school, a student planning to enter a graphic arts technology program should complete four years of English, at least two years of mathematics, and one year of chemistry or physics with laboratory work. In addition, mechanical drawing, basic electronics, and any courses that develop computer skills are desirable.

A typical graphic arts training curriculum at a postsecondary school includes first-year courses in typography and copy preparation, English composition, photography, printing methods, keyboarding, lithography, technical writing, mathematics, psychology, and accounting.

The second year includes advertising, managerial techniques, printing management, lithography laboratory, printing production, printing estimating, layout and design, computer concepts, color reproduction processes, and screen printing.

Workers in the printing and publishing industry must be accurate and patient yet able to work fast under time pressure. They need good eyesight, physical coordination, hand-eye coordination, normal dexterity, and ability to distinguish colors. The ability to work with others is also important.

A graphic arts technician must master the details of procedures in a large variety of operations and processes used in the industry. Like all applied science technicians, they must understand the underlying principles of each process so that they can interpret results and adjust processes to get the best quality results. Some artistic ability in order to sense good proportion, perspective, and balance in the design of printed products is very useful in this career.

Special requirements

No special licenses or certificates are required in this career. A physical examination is often required for prospective employees in certain job areas. Union membership may be required for some employment. Several different unions represent graphic arts workers.

Opportunities for experience and exploration

While in high school, interested students should ask their guidance counselors and teachers to provide all the information they can about printing and the graphic arts industry. Field trips often are made by students and their guidance counselors to printing businesses or manufacturing operations that use lithography or other printing processes for packaging, labeling, and the like.

Visits to printing establishments can be made by individual students; and best of all, summer jobs can sometimes be found in such businesses. These jobs provide valuable information and experience that help a person decide to enter a graphic arts career.

Methods of entering

Students in postsecondary school graphic arts technician programs usually find employment before they graduate. Employers send recruiters to the schools or the schools let potential employers know about graduating students. Arrangements are then made for new graphic arts technicians to enter jobs after interviews and graduation.

Students who have participated in work-study programs often can arrange full-time employment with one of the employers for whom they have worked as a cooperative student. Some students contact employers directly and find work that way.

On-the-job experience and study is another way of entering the career of graphic arts technician, especially in nonapprentice and non-union employment. This method of entering is most often possible in small- to medium-size operations. This way of entering is longer and more difficult because it is harder to learn on the job all of the material that is taught in postsecondary programs.

Graduates of postsecondary programs can also enter the industry as photographic technicians, color technicians, or quality-control technicians.

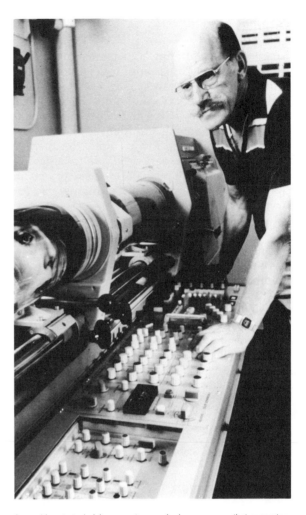

A graphic arts technician operates a color laser scanner that separates color photographs into four pieces of monochromatic film: cyan, magenta, yellow, and black.

Advancement

As stated earlier, many technicians in the printing industry start in a craft job and move from one craft job to another as they acquire work experience.

Courses in high school or in a two- or four-year postsecondary institution that is directly related to graphic arts serve two main purposes. First, they help secure entry-level jobs in the industry. Secondly, they help the worker move more rapidly to advanced jobs.

Skilled craft workers can become technicians, and technicians can become special researchers, product or process developers, control technicians, supervisors, or sales and service representatives. In some cases, technicians can start and operate their own businesses.

Management and supervisory positions in the industry are most frequently occupied by graduates of two- and four-year colleges. These graphic arts technicians are graduates who have usually completed a comprehensive printing technology, printing management, or journalism curriculum.

Employment outlook

Technician jobs in certain rapidly growing areas of the industry, such as lithography, are expected to increase faster than the average for all occupations through the 1990s. The total amount of printed materials produced is expected to continue growing. Labor-saving developments will probably cause a net reduction in semiskilled and some skilled jobs, but the increasing technological complexity of the industry suggests there will be excellent opportunities for graphic arts technicians who have comprehensive training. Some of the best opportunities should be in small- to medium-size commercial printing concerns that produce a wide variety of printed materials, such as brochures, direct mail advertising, and newspaper inserts.

Earnings

Salaries in the printing and publishing industries vary widely according to geographical location, type of employer, skills and experience required for the job, and other factors. The earnings of some skilled craft workers in printing plants are among the highest in the manufacturing industries. For example, the average yearly salary for experienced photoengraving workers is roughly $32,000. Some workers in the printing industry receive additional pay for overtime and night shifts. Apprentices start at about 60 percent of the rates paid to experienced workers and receive regular pay raises during their training period.

Graphic arts technicians who are recent graduates of two-year postsecondary programs may start at around $20,000 to $25,000 a year, and sometimes much less if they are working in a small shop. Salaries for experienced technicians working for large employers can range between $28,000 and $35,000 a year. Experienced salespeople usually work on a commission and may make well over $30,000.

Conditions of work

Workers in the printing and publishing industries usually work from thirty-five to forty hours a week. Some firms work around the clock, six or seven days a week, and pay a premium for the night shift. Workers are usually paid time-and-a-half or double-time for Sundays and holidays. Newspapers pay overtime rates for these days only when they are not a part of the regular shift of the employee.

In printing and publishing, most of the work is performed indoors. However, press rooms are noisy environments, and workers are required to wear ear plugs or headphones. Much of the work in printing plants requires standing for long periods of time.

Conditions vary from one printing plant to another, but most are clean, well-lighted, and air-conditioned.

Some chemicals in platemaking and other operations may be irritating to the skin, so workers must be careful to expose themselves as little as possible to the chemicals and to wash them off after exposure.

Social and psychological factors

The graphic arts technician must have the ability to understand how details affect the quality of the work and should enjoy the thrill and challenge of producing a product that is beautiful and perfect. The work of these technicians often involves the pressures of deadlines and satisfying the needs of customers. Graphic arts technicians can feel a deep sense of satisfaction in being a part of an essential industry that is growing more important and more complicated in this age of information transmission, processing, and recording.

GOE: 01.06.01; SIC: 7336; SOC: 7449

◇ **SOURCES OF ADDITIONAL INFORMATION**

Graphic Arts Technical Foundation
4615 Forbes Avenue
Pittsburgh, PA 15213

International Prepress Association
720 France Avenue, South, Suite 327
Edina, MN 55435

National Association of Printers and Lithographers
780 Palisade Avenue
Teaneck, NJ 07666

Printing Industries of America
1730 North Lynn Street
Arlington, VA 22209

◇ **RELATED ARTICLES**

Light technicians

Definition

Light technicians set up and control lighting equipment for television broadcasts, taped television shows, motion pictures, and video productions. They begin by conferring with the production director and technical director to establish lighting needs and special effects required. Working with spot and flood lights, mercury-vapor lamps, white and colored lights, reflectors (mainly employed out-of-doors), and a large array of dimming, masking, and switching controls, they light scenes to be broadcast or recorded.

During scenes, technicians follow scripts or the director's instructions and create lighting effects as called for. They make minor equipment repairs when necessary. On a large set they may direct the activities of assistants.

Nature of the work

Light technicians consult with the director of a production to determine the lighting effects that will be needed. They then arrange the lighting equipment and plan the light-switching sequence that will achieve the desired effects. For a television series program following a similar format for each broadcast, the lights are often already in position. For a one-time production, such as scene in a movie, the lights have to be physically set up.

During each scene, the technicians follow a script that they have marked, or they follow instructions from the technical director. They watch a monitor screen to check the lighting effects. If necessary they may alter the lighting as the scene progresses. In studios this is done by adjusting controls in the control room.

Remote broadcasts from indoor settings require carrying and setting up portable lights. In small television stations this work may be done by the camera operator or an assistant. In a large station or in any big movie or television production, a light technician may supervise several assistants in the setting up of lights.

Outdoor scenes often require lighting, especially to remove shadows from people's faces. For outdoor scenes in bad weather or on rough terrain, it may be a difficult task to secure the lighting apparatus firmly so that it is out of the way, protected, and cannot blow over.

During a scene, whether broadcast live or recorded on film, technicians must be able to concentrate on the lighting of the scene and must be able to make quick, sure decisions about lighting changes.

Light technicians employed by a television station or network normally work a forty-hour week and change jobs only as their experience makes advancement possible. Technicians employed in the motion picture industry are often employed for one production at a time and thus may work less regularly and under a more challenging variety of conditions than light technicians in television.

Requirements

People who are interested in careers in the technical side of television or the movies, including lighting careers, should learn as much as possible about electronics while in high school. Physics, mathematics, courses in using computers, and any shop courses that introduce electronics equipment provide a good background. Other valuable learning experiences might be building a radio from a kit, a summer job in a TV or appliance repair shop, and working on the lighting for a school stage production.

There is strong competition for broadcast and motion picture technician positions, and in general only well-prepared technicians get good jobs. Interested persons should attend a two-year postsecondary training program in electronics and broadcast technology, especially if they hope to advance to a supervisory position. For a position as a chief engineer, a bachelor's degree is usually required.

In small television stations, where much of the programming consists of network productions, light technicians may combine lighting with some other aspect of television production to keep staff size down.

Setting up lights can be heavy work, especially when lighting a large movie set. Technicians should be able to handle heavy lights on stands and work with suspended lights while on a ladder.

Repairs such as replacing light bulbs or replacing worn wires are sometimes necessary. Light technicians should be able to work with electricians' hand tools (screwdrivers, pliers,

A light technician prepares to operate a large stage light before the performance begins.

and so forth) and be comfortable working with electricity.

Communications skills, including both listening and speaking, are necessary when working with a director and with assistant light technicians.

GOE: 05.10.03; SIC: 483; SOC: 399

Museum technicians

Definition

Museum technicians help clean, repair, and prepare for exhibit the objects displayed in museums. They work both with art objects created by people, such as pottery, statuary, tapestries, etchings, medieval arms, and armor, and with natural objects, such as fossils or skeletons.

Nature of the work

Museum technicians who work with art objects are sometimes called *conservation technicians.* They are involved with restoring art objects to their original or natural appearance. To do this, they study descriptions and information about the object, and they perform chemical and physical tests to determine the age, physical composition, and original appearance of the object. Based on this information they develop a plan for cleaning and restoring the object. If the object is metal they may clean it by scraping it or applying chemical solvents. Statues can sometimes by washed with soap solutions, and furniture and silver can often be polished.

When a repair is necessary, technicians reassemble the broken pieces using glue or solder, then buff the object when the repair is complete. They may repaint objects where the original paint is faded or missing, using paint of the same chemical composition and color as the original. If the restoration work required is particularly difficult, they request help from outside experts. They may also make and repair picture frames and mount paintings in frames.

Museum technicians who work with natural objects, which are often called *specimens,* are mostly involved with preparing the specimens for collections and exhibits. One type of task they do is cleaning bits of rock off of fossils by using small electric drills, awls, dental picks, chisels, and mallets. Once a specimen is cleaned, they apply preservatives such as shellac. They may recreate and restore missing parts, using modeling clay and special molding and casting techniques. Technicians may make duplicate specimens of entire fossils or skeletons by using plaster, glue, latex, and other molding materials. They may help assemble newly acquired specimens that have arrived at the museum in pieces, fabricating substitutes for missing fragments as necessary. They may also construct mounts to hold fossil skeletons, using hand and power tools such as carpenter's tools, drill presses, welding and soldering equipment, and pipe threaders.

Museum technicians help maintain museum files. They catalog, label, and store materials, and help install and arrange exhibits.

Requirements

Museum technicians need to have completed at least high school. For most jobs in this field applicants are required to have completed from two to four years of post–high-school training.

While in high school, students interested in this career should take courses in chemistry, English, and other college-preparatory subjects, including algebra and geometry.

There are training programs in the conservation and restoration of art objects that last from six months to two years available at a number of colleges. The classroom training is usually followed by a year or two of on-the-job training, working under the direction of a skilled supervisor in a museum or laboratory.

Museum technicians who work with fossils and other natural specimens are often required to be graduates of four-year colleges. They may be introduced to the necessary skills by courses in geology, archaeology, or paleontology.

GOE: 01.06.02; SIC: 3412; SOC: 252

A museum technician restores a small cannon carriage to its original condition. Such work requires the historical knowledge of artillery.

◇ **RELATED ARTICLES**

Volume 2: Anthropologists and archaeologists; Archivists and curators; Geologists; Historians; Museum occupations
Volume 3: Display workers
Volume 4: Exhibit technicians; Library technicians

Photofinishing equipment technicians

Definition

Photofinishing equipment technicians test, analyze, repair, and maintain the equipment used in the developing and printing of photographic film.

Nature of the work

Some photofinishing equipment technicians are responsible for repairing and maintaining all kinds of photofinishing equipment, such as photographic printers, print washers, drier,

straighteners, and mounting presses. In doing their work, they examine the equipment, replace defective parts that they locate, and make minor repairs, such as cleaning and tightening connections, soldering and welding broken metal parts, and bending and installing piping and tubing.

Other photofinishing equipment technicians specialize in the computerized electromechanical equipment used in the automated processing of photographic film. When problems occur with this kind of equipment, these technicians consult with the equipment operating personnel to gather information about malfunctions. They examine the equipment visually, looking for loose connections or broken components, then make more detailed examinations using electrical testing equipment such as voltmeters and ohmmeters. They refer to technical manuals, equipment specifications, and schematic diagrams and blueprints. When the problem has been located, they make the necessary electrical or electronic repairs such as soldering loose wires; tightening connections; replacing worn switches, thermostats, and sensors; and replacing printed circuit boards. They also service the mechanical and plumbing parts of machines. This may involve repairing or replacing motors, pumps, heaters, piping and valves, and gears and drive chains. Because of the need to return the machinery to operation quickly, repair often means replacing parts rather than rebuilding or dismantling and reassembling a component.

Requirements

Persons interested in becoming technicians who work with photofinishing equipment should take at least one year of training beyond high school, concentrating on electronics and mechanical systems and on the basic servicing of computers. Technical schools offer such training, as well as manufacturers of the equipment. On-the-job training is unusual, because the experienced personnel who could offer training are needed to keep the photofinishing equipment functioning.

Conditions of work

The work of these technicians involves moderate physical demands, requiring the occasional lifting of weights of up to fifty pounds. It requires excellent manual dexterity, visual acuity, hand-eye coordination, and the ability to use electrician's hand tools and be comfortable working with electricity. Work is performed indoors, usually under air-conditioned, pleasant working conditions.

GOE: 05.05.09, 05.05.11; SIC: 7384; SOC: 6171

◇ RELATED ARTICLES

Volume 1: Electronics
Volume 3: Commercial and industrial electronic equipment repairers; Electrical repairers; Industrial machinery mechanics; Office-machine servicers; Photographic laboratory occupations
Volume 4: Computer-service technicians; Darkroom technicians; Electromechanical technicians; Electronics technicians; Mechanical technicians; Photofinishing equipment technicians

---

Photographic equipment technicians

Definition

Photographic equipment technicians, sometimes called *camera technicians*, maintain, test, disassemble, and repair cameras and other equipment used in the taking of still and motion pictures. They maintain the equipment in working order.

Photographic equipment technicians use a variety of hand tools (such as screwdrivers, pliers, wire cutters, etc.) in the maintainance and repair of the complex cameras employed both by motion picture and still photographers.

History

The first permanent photographs were made in the 1820s, but it was with the introduction of the Kodak camera in 1888 that photography came within the reach of the amateur. This hand-held, roll-film camera developed by George Eastman replaced the earlier bulky cameras and complicated dry-plate developing processes that had restricted photography to professionals. The Leica camera, the first 35-millimeter "miniature" camera, was introduced in 1924 and immediately created an interest in candid photography that had a great impact on both everyday American life and on the use of photography as an art form, as an entertainment medium, and as an influential tool in advertising.

The early development of motion pictures was also tied to a series of inventions—flexible celluloid film, Thomas Edison's kinetoscope (in which motion pictures were viewed by looking through a peephole at revolving reels of film), and his later projecting kinetoscope, the immediate ancestor of the modern film projector. In 1876, Edison presented the first public exhibition of motion pictures projected on a screen.

Further improvements in cameras, projectors, lighting equipment, films, and prints have contributed to making still and motion picture photography one of the most popular hobbies.

As hobbyists' cameras and equipment became more convenient to use, they became more complicated to maintain and repair. Professionals' cameras as well—especially those of filmmakers—became increasingly more complicated and expensive. In both cases, photographic equipment became too valuable to entrust to the care of anyone but a trained photographic equipment technician. Today there are thousands of these technicians working in the United States, providing services that range from quick and simple adjustments to complicated repairs requiring specialized equipment.

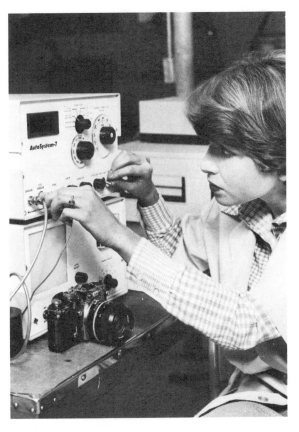

A photographic equipment technician uses several electronic devices to test the exposure gauge on a camera.

Nature of the work

Many photographic equipment technicians work in shops that specialize in camera adjustment and repair or in the service departments of large camera stores. Quite a few technicians also work for camera manufacturers, repairing cameras and photographic equipment that customers have returned to the factory. Some camera dealers have their own in-house repair departments, and technicians are sometimes hired by these dealers to adjust cameras on-site. Technicians specializing in motion picture cameras and equipment may work for motion picture or television studios, or for companies renting such equipment to studios.

Technicians diagnose a camera's problem by analyzing the camera's shutter speed and accuracy of focus through the use of sophisticated electronic test equipment. Once the problem is diagnosed, the camera is opened and checked for worn, misaligned, or defective parts. At least half of all repairs are done without replacing parts. All tests and adjustments are done to manufacturer's specifications, using blueprints, specification lists, and repair manuals.

Most repairs and adjustments can be made using small hand tools. A jeweler's loupe (magnifying glass) is used to examine small parts for wear or damage. Electronic and optical measuring instruments are needed to check and adjust focus, shutter speed, operating speed of motion picture cameras, and light readings of light meters.

Many modern cameras designed for amateur use include built-in light meters, automatic focusing, and aperture (lens opening) settings. These features are convenient for the user, but the mechanisms require careful adjustment by a skilled technician when they malfunction.

Cameras must be clean and well lubricated to operate properly. Photographic equipment technicians use vacuum and air pressure devices to remove tiny dust particles, and ultrasonic cleaning equipment to dislodge and remove hardened dirt and lubricant. Lens are cleaned with a chemical solvent and soft tissue paper. Very fine lubricants are applied, often using a syringe or fine cotton swab.

Occasionally technicians, especially those employed by manufacturers or shops servicing

355

Precision instruments make it possible for photographic equipment technicians to locate and handle the intricate parts of a camera.

professional studios, must fabricate replacement parts. They employ small instrument-makers' lathes, milling machines, grinders, and other tools.

Technicians must be able to discuss a camera's working problems with a customer to carefully extract information that will be useful in diagnosing the problem.

Requirements

Photographic equipment technicians perform highly technical work and need specialized training. This training is available through either classroom instruction or a correspondence course. The training provides basic technical background information for working with cameras as well as a thorough understanding and working knowledge of electronics. Not all camera models can be covered in the training course. More specialized training on additional models is obtained on the job or through specialized seminars.

Camera manufacturers and importers provide training for their technicians. This training usually covers the technical aspects of the manufacturer's own product only.

Photographic equipment technicians need excellent vision, manual dexterity, and mechanical aptitude. Those who work with the public directly must be able to communicate readily and clearly with other people.

Special requirements

There are no special requirements for a career as a photographic equipment technician.

Opportunities for experience and exploration

Larger camera stores often have an employee who does limited adjustment and repairing of cameras. This person can be a good source of information about opportunities in the field of camera repair. Information may also be obtained from technical schools and institutes offering courses for photographic equipment technicians. Many schools and community centers have photography clubs, some with their own darkrooms, that offer an excellent chance to explore the general field of photography.

Methods of entering

Individual shops looking for technicians usually notify the schools in their area or advertise through national photographic service publications. Manufacturers hire their technicians through their personnel departments. The placement counselor of a student's training institute can be of help in locating openings for graduates.

Advancement

Advancement in a photographic equipment repair facility is usually from trainee to experienced worker to a supervisory position. Many manufacturer's technicians also open their own shops, perhaps starting part-time on weekends and evenings. Although technicians who have worked for a manufacturer usually know only one line of cameras well, they can learn other manufacturers' models on their own.

Independent technicians advance as they establish a reputation for doing quality work. They must become familiar with all the major brands and models of camera equipment. In recent years, major camera manufacturers have begun to offer more training courses and seminars to inform independent technicians about their newer models, particularly what repairs can be done efficiently in their shops, and what repairs ought to be handled back at the factory. Because of this increased cooperation, technicians who decide to open independent businesses are now much better able to provide good quality services for the camera problems they do handle.

Some independent technicians expand their activities into selling small "add-ons" such as film, accessories, and used equipment. Some photographic equipment technicians are also professional photographers in their off-hours.

Employment outlook

In spite of the increasing popularity of photography as a hobby, the number of technicians required to service photographic equipment is not expected to increase greatly through the 1990s. In recent years, however, there have been some geographical areas where the demand for well-qualified technicians has greatly exceeded the supply. This suggests that technicians who are flexible about location will probably have the best job opportunities.

In general, the low price of many of today's point-and-shoot cameras and the high cost of labor often make it uneconomical to do extensive service on these cameras. As cameras incorporate more and more sophisticated electronics, a greater knowledge of this field as well as more extensive training and equipment is needed to analyze some models. Because independent shops often do only minor adjustments on the models they are not specifically equipped to service, only moderate numbers of new technicians may be needed to work in these settings. Technicians whose training has covered a wide variety of equipment brands and models will be in greatest demand.

Earnings

Photographic equipment technicians employed by camera and equipment manufacturers and repair shops can usually expect to earn starting salaries in the range of $13,000 to $15,000 a year. The average salary for an experienced technician working for a manufacturer is often between $19,000 and $26,000 a year. A skilled and experienced technician working on commission in a busy repair shop can make over $30,000 a year. Self-employed technicians have

earnings that vary widely. In the right location, independent technicians can build up businesses that give them earnings higher than those of technicians who work for manufacturers or shops.

Conditions of work

Photographic equipment technicians work in clean, well-lighted shop conditions. They are usually seated at a bench for much of the time, working with hand tools. Eyestrain and stiffness from long hours of sitting are common physical complaints. Tedium can be a problem for some technicians.

Social and psychological factors

Photographic equipment technicians work alone most of the time, concentrating on their work. Patience and steadiness are required to work successfully with the small mechanisms of modern camera equipment.

GOE: 05.05.11; SIC: 3861; SOC: 6171

◇ **SOURCES OF ADDITIONAL INFORMATION**

Society of Photo-Technologists
PO Box 9634
Denver, CO 80209

National Association of Photo Equipment Technicians
3000 Picture Place
Jackson, MI 49201

◇ **RELATED ARTICLES**

Volume 2: Photographers and camera operators
Volume 3: Photographic laboratory occupations
Volume 4: Darkroom technicians; Electronics test technicians; Photofinishing equipment technicians

Piano technicians

Definition

Piano technicians locate, identify, and correct problems in the operating mechanism of pianos. They adjust keys and hammers so they align properly with strings. They remove the action (that is, the operating mechanism) from the body of the piano and inspect it for wear or broken parts, replacing parts as necessary. They inspect strings and replace those that are broken or worn. Technicians also tune pianos, using a tuning fork or electronic tuning device.

Some technicians are also involved in the rebuilding of pianos. They completely disassemble the instruments, replace worn parts, install new strings, felts, and in many cases refinish the exterior of the piano.

History

The modern piano is the end product of a gradual evolution from plucked string instruments, such as the harp, to instruments employing hammers of one kind or another to produce notes by striking the strings. By the late 1700s the immediate ancestor of the modern piano had been developed. Improvements and modifications (most involving new materials or manufacturing processes) took place throughout the nineteenth century, resulting in today's piano.

The standard piano is a complex instrument containing 88 keys; about 230 strings, depending on the model and size; and more than 4,000 working parts (most of them made of wood) in its action. The shortest string is approximately two inches long, and the longest about eighty inches long in the largest concert grand piano. These strings are tightly stretched, and exert a combined pull of more than 35,000 pounds on the cast iron frame (or harp) to which they are attached.

There are two basic kinds of pianos: the grand and the vertical, or upright. The grand piano has strings that are stretched horizontally on its frame. The largest concert grand pianos are approximately nine feet long and extremely heavy because of their large cast iron harp. Vertical pianos have their strings stretched vertically, and consequently require much less floor space than a grand. Modern, more compact, vertical pianos became very popular soon after they were introduced in the mid-1930s. Today,

about 97 out of every 100 new pianos are vertical pianos.

Nature of the work

To perform well, a piano must be in tune—adjusted so that striking any key will produce one correctly pitched note of the musical scale. A piano may go out of tune for a variety of reasons. If its strings have stretched or tightened because of age, temperature change, having been moved, or through use, it can usually be tuned by using a special wrench to adjust the pins that control the tension on the strings. This adjustment is usually done by piano tuners who are specially trained for such work, but also may be done by piano technicians in connection with a more thorough inspection or overhaul of an instrument.

The performance of a piano is also affected by problems in any of the thousands of moving parts of the action or by problems in the sounding board or the frame holding the strings. These are problems that the technician is trained to analyze and correct. They may involve replacing or repairing parts or making adjustments that will enable the existing parts to function more smoothly.

Some piano technicians work in factories where pianos are made. Their work may consist of assembling and adjusting pianos or of inspecting the finished instruments. Some technicians work in shops that rebuild pianos. The life of a piano—the period of time before it can no longer be properly tuned or adjusted to correct operational problems—is usually estimated at twenty years. Because the harp and strong outer wooden frame are seldom damaged, pianos are often rebuilt by replacing the sounding board and strings, refurbishing and replacing parts where necessary and refinishing the outer case.

In all their work, from tuning to rebuilding, piano technicians get an idea of what a piano's problems are by talking to the owner and by playing the instrument themselves. They may partially dismantle a piano on-site to get an idea of the amount of wear to its parts and to look for broken parts. To do so they can use common hand tools such as screwdrivers, pliers, and hammer. To repair and rebuild pianos, they use a variety of tools, including some specialized ones for stringing and setting pins.

Requirements

Persons interested in careers as piano technicians should be high-school graduates and should have an additional one to two years of specialized training. A small number of technical and vocational schools and community colleges offer courses for piano technicians. There are also correspondence courses available, usually covering tuning and basic piano repairs; these courses will not be very useful unless backed up with some sort of hands-on experience.

Most piano technicians, however, obtain their in-depth experience through on-the-job training in a repair shop, music store, or factory, working alongside experienced technicians. Piano technicians often begin work as helpers, moving pianos, holding tools, and cleaning up the shop. They may also tune and repair pianos under the supervision of an experienced technician. Four or five years of such training are usually required to become a competent piano technician.

Courses in woodworking and wood refinishing are also helpful to the technician, because most of the moving parts of the piano's action are made of wood. Piano technicians sometimes are called on to refinish pianos, so a thorough knowledge of wood and furniture repair and restoration will be most helpful.

The Piano Technicians Guild helps its members improve their skills and keep up with developments in piano technology. Refresher courses and seminars in new developments are offered by local chapters, and courses offered by manufacturers are publicized in Guild publications. The Guild also administers a series of tests that can lead to certification as a Registered Tuner-Technician.

Good hearing is essential to a technician, and the ability to distinguish musical pitch very helpful. Musical interest, if not formal training in music, is also useful. Manual dexterity and mechanical aptitude are important.

In spite of the bulk and great weight of pianos, the technician's work is moderate in its physical demands. Pianos are almost always equipped with wheels for ease of moving; shops engaged in heavy work such as rebuilding will be equipped with lifting equipment.

The majority of piano technicians work in customers' homes. They should be able to communicate clearly when talking about a piano's problems and when advising a customer. A pleasant manner and good appearance are important to instill confidence.

A piano technician must have keen hearing, including perfect pitch, in order to locate the problems of a piano.

Special requirements

There are no special requirements for a career as a piano technician.

Opportunities for experience and exploration

Almost every school has a piano and retains someone to tune and inspect it regularly. That person may be willing to talk with interested students about career opportunities for piano technicians. Music teachers and owners or managers of music stores can also be good sources of information.

Methods of entering

The placement office of a high school, or the local public library, will have a list of schools that offer training courses for piano technicians. The best way to enter the field directly is to contact the owner or manager of a store that sells or services pianos or a self-employed piano technician who might be willing to take on a helper. A music teacher may be helpful in setting up an interview.

Advancement

Advancement in a music store or repair shop is usually from apprentice to helper to worker,

Piano technicians use special wrenches to adjust the tension of the strings. Temperature and normal use of a piano over a period of time often cause the strings to stretch or tighten.

to $19,000 a year. Experienced piano technicians make from $20,000 to $40,000 a year or more. Wages vary according to geographic area, and from rural to urban locations. Earnings of self-employed persons depend on their ability to attract customers, which in turn is influenced by local factors, such as population and the amount of competition.

Conditions of work

The work of piano technicians is usually performed in homes, schools, churches, or in small repair shops where conditions are comfortable. The work involves physical activities such as bending, stretching, and using tools requiring leverage, but little heavy lifting.

Social and psychological factors

Piano technicians who are self-employed work alone most of the time. Their contact with customers is usually limited to finding out what problems they are having with the instrument. Technicians working in shops also work individually, unless they are training new employees.

GOE: 05.05.12; SIC: 7699; SOC: 6172

and then to a supervisory position. Many piano technicians, however, go into business for themselves. Only a small investment is needed for tools, and self-employed technicians usually operate out of their own homes, using their private cars for transportation. It should be noted, however, that competition among self-employed technicians is very keen and even highly skilled technicians can fail if they cannot attract enough customers.

Employment outlook

There were about 8,000 persons employed as piano tuners and technicians in the early 1990s, and most of these were tuners. As more pianos are sold, the demand for service personnel should increase, but the field is so small that no substantial number of jobs will be created.

Most owners of pianos view tuning and repairing them as a luxury that can be dispensed with in difficult economic times. This field is closely tied, therefore, to downturns in the economy.

Earnings

Limited information suggests that beginning technicians earn salaries in the range of $13,000

◇ **SOURCES OF ADDITIONAL INFORMATION**

Piano Technicians Guild
4510 Belleview, Suite 100
Kansas City, MO 64111

◇ **RELATED ARTICLES**

Volume 1: Performing Arts
Volume 2: Musical occupations
Volume 3: Musical instrument repairers and tuners
Volume 4: Pipe organ technicians

Pipe organ technicians

Definition

Pipe organ technicians install, repair, and tune organs that produce musical notes by directing a stream of air through wooden or metal pipes of various lengths.

History

The history of the pipe organ stretches back more than 2,000 years. In the third century B.C., in Alexandria, Egypt, an organ was developed that used water power to produce a stream of air. A few centuries later organs appeared in Byzantium that used bellows to send air through the organ pipes. From that time until about A.D. 1500 all the features of the modern pipe organ were developed.

A pipe organ consists of three major parts: a source of a stream of air (in modern organs, usually an electric motor and fan or compressor), a keyboard to regulate the flow of air into the various pipes, and the pipes themselves, arranged in ranks (rows).

A large modern pipe organ may contain as many as 5,000 separate pipes; a small organ usually has about 200 pipes. These pipes range in size from seven inches in length and a quarter inch in diameter to thirty feet in length and more than one foot in diameter. The largest organs may have as many as six keyboards to enable the organist to combine the sounds of as many of the pipes as possible.

There are two types of organ pipes: the flue pipe and the reed pipe. The flue pipe produces its note by passing air through a pipe that has an opening in one side, much like a toy whistle. The note is determined by the length of the pipe. A reed pipe sounds its note by passing air over a slender brass reed, which vibrates inside the pipe. The length of the reed determines the note, along with the size and length of the pipe.

As the organist plays, air is directed into the various ranks of pipes, and from there into individual pipes. The combination of the various sounds of different pipes blends in the final musical effect. A pipe organ can produce a very delicate sound from one pipe, or music as complex and as loud (especially in the very largest organs) as that of a symphony orchestra.

The operation of the pipe organ has changed very little since 1500, except for the addition of electric power to produce the air stream, and improvements in the materials from which pipes and other moving parts are made. Pipes were originally carved from wood, but now are metal, usually some alloy containing lead.

Today the majority of pipe organs are found in churches, concert halls, and theaters. The largest are planned as part of the building in which they are to be played, because their vibrations can damage the structure severely if not taken into account by the architect.

Nature of the work

The largest part of the work of pipe organ technicians is repairing and maintaining existing organs. This primarily involves tuning the pipes; even in a moderate-sized organ, this can be a very time-consuming process.

To tune a flue pipe, the technician moves a slide that increases or decreases the length of the "speaking" (note-producing) part of the pipe, varying its pitch. A reed pipe is tuned by varying the length of the brass reed inside the pipe.

To tune an organ, the technician tunes either the "A" or "C" pipes by matching their notes with those of a tuning fork or electronic note-producing device. The other pipes are then tuned in harmony with the "A" or "C" notes. This may require a day or more for a moderate-sized organ, and much longer for a giant concert organ.

Pipe organ technicians also diagnose, locate, and correct problems in the operating parts of the organ and perform preventive maintenance on a regular basis. This involves working with the electric wind-generating equipment and with the slides, valves, keys, air channels, and other equipment that enables the organist to produce the desired music.

Occasionally a new organ is installed in a new or existing structure. The largest organs are designed and installed by the manufacturer. Each is unique, and its construction and installation are carefully supervised by the designer. Moderate-sized organs, usually installed in churches, are also often individually designed for the structure in which they will be played. Technicians follow the designer's blueprints closely during installation. The work involves assembling and connecting pre-

Pipe organ technicians test each metal pipe for flaws that may alter the sound quality.

manufactured components, using a variety of hand and power tools. Technicians may work in teams, especially when installing the largest pipes of the organ.

Most of the few hundred pipe organ technicians in the United States are self-employed. These pipe organ technicians are primarily engaged in repairing and tuning existing organs. A small number are employed by organ manufacturers and are engaged in testing and installing new instruments. The great expense involved in manufacturing and installing a completely new pipe organ makes this type of work scarce, however.

Requirements

Persons interested in careers as pipe organ technicians should have good hearing, manual dexterity and mechanical aptitude, and the ability to follow blueprints and printed instructions in planning and executing repair or installation work. Interest and training in music, although not absolutely necessary, can be extremely helpful in this career.

Special requirements

There are no special requirements for a career in pipe organ technology.

Opportunities for experience and exploration

The organist of a local church that has a pipe organ can explain the workings of the organ and can also direct you to the person who maintains that instrument. Most craft workers are willing to share an hour or so of conversation about their craft, and usually they can in a short time acquaint an interested person with the essential nature of the work they do.

The music departments of schools or nearby colleges can provide information about a career working with musical instruments and with musicians.

Methods of entering

Almost all pipe organ technicians enter the field by undergoing on-the-job training, working beside an established technician. This usually means such tasks as handing the experienced worker the correct tools and paying careful attention to the work being done. Some manufacturers of organs may offer training or refresher courses. Usually a period of four to five years is required to train a competent pipe organ technician.

Advancement

Because most pipe organ technicians are self-employed, the most likely opportunities for advancement are to open a shop or to take over the business of someone who is retiring. The few technicians employed by manufacturers or by large music stores usually remain technicians throughout their careers, unless they acquire some special additional training that will enable them to move into management or instrument design.

Employment outlook

Employment opportunities in the field of pipe organ technology are not expected to increase. As experienced technicians retire, they will need to be replaced. This is a small occupational area, however, and the opportunities will be few. Because most pipe organs are owned by churches and musical organizations, which are less easily affected by the economy's changes than individuals are, the field is not as sensitive to economic downturns as are some others that are more consumer-oriented.

Earnings

Self-employed pipe organ technicians—which includes most of the profession—earn about $16,000 to $25,000 a year. Earnings are quite variable and depend on the size of the community and its geographical location, with technicians in urban areas able to command higher earnings.

Conditions of work

The installation of a pipe organ involves considerable physical work. It also means working with tools and metal pipes that may cause small cuts or bruises. Tuning and repairing existing organs usually involves little physical strength, but it may require working in cramped locations for some length of time. Some work can be done in the technician's shop.

Most organs are in churches or concert halls, which are generally quiet, clean, pleasant places to work.

Social and psychological factors

Pipe organ technicians often work alone. Tuning an organ can often take more than a day, and it can become tedious and tiring. Because most technicians work for themselves, they must present themselves to their potential clients as being competent and pleasant, which involves being able to meet and work with others.

GOE: 05.05.12; SIC: 7699; SOC: 6172

◇ **SOURCES OF ADDITIONAL INFORMATION**

American Guild of Organists
475 Riverside Drive, Suite 1260
New York, NY 10115

Piano Technicians Guild
4510 Belleview, Suite 100
Kansas City, MO 64111

◇ **RELATED ARTICLES**

Volume 1: Performing Arts
Volume 2: Musical occupations
Volume 3: Electrical repairers; Musical instrument repairers and tuners
Volume 4: Electronic organ technicians; Piano technicians

Planetarium technicians

Definition

Planetarium technicians install, operate, maintain, and modify when necessary the complex sound and projection equipment used in the presentation of planetarium shows or demonstrations. These shows are performed in special museums devoted to study of the universe or they may be presented in planetariums that are part of natural history or other science museums. The work performed is similar, however, regardless of the type of planetarium.

Nature of the work

Technicians begin by consulting with the teacher of a class or the lecturer giving a public talk to determine what optical and audio effects are needed, and how they can best be produced. They then adjust the projectors, audio equipment, and controls to produce the effects required. They program the projector's computer, if it is automated, or operate the controls while following a script if it is not. Technicians select tapes from an audiovisual library, then

A planetarium technician performs a routine inspection of projection equipment. Such equipment is very complex, often requiring the services of engineers.

and language skills. They should study high-school mathematics through solid geometry at least and take English courses to a point that they can easily read technical manuals and articles, follow manufacturers' maintenance procedures, and read and follow scientific scripts. They should have at least two years of advanced specialized technical training, especially electronics and computer programming, and basic astronomy courses.

Conditions of work

The work is moderately heavy in physical requirements, and requires excellent hearing, visual acuity, and color perception. The working conditions in planetariums are similar to those in other museums or in schools: clean, quiet, and orderly.

GOE: 05.10.05; SIC: 8412; SOC: 615

combine them to produce a sound-effects and background music tape for the presentation. They maintain their equipment, following a schedule of inspections and service operations recommended by the manufacturer of each piece of equipment. They perform some repairs, applying a knowledge of electronic circuitry and optics, and contact engineers to perform the most serious repairs and adjustments.

Requirements

Persons interested in becoming planetarium technicians should have excellent mathematics

◇ **RELATED ARTICLES**

Volume 1: Physical Sciences
Volume 2: Astronomers; Engineers; Museum occupations
Volume 4: Audio control technicians; Audiovisual technicians; Electromechanical technicians; Electronics technicians; Light technicians; Mechanical technicians; Optics technicians; Sound-effects technicians; Stage technicians; Studio technicians

Sound technicians

Definition

Sound technicians install, maintain, and repair sound and internal communication systems that are used in business, offices, stores, and factories. These systems may be designed to play music, announce messages, monitor activities in remote areas, or provide the sound por-

tion of live or recorded lectures, performances or entertainment. Many of the systems are tailored to specific businesses. It is a sound technician's responsibility to ensure that the communications systems are installed properly and functioning according to the specifications of the business. Sound technicians must often readjust newly installed systems.

Nature of the work

Sound technicians usually work under the direction of a sound technician supervisor who has instructions about what kinds of equipment and connections are required for a job. After receiving instructions from the supervisor, sound technicians put the sound equipment into position and secure it in place with brackets, clamps, or screws. They install and attach the wires and cables that connect the various parts of the system, such as speakers, amplifier, microphones, and tape players. They also test the various parts of the system to see that they are functioning properly.

Not all sound systems work the same way. For example, the sound system in a dentist's office will play mostly soothing music at a low volume. The sound system in an airport or factory, on the other hand, is used to broadcast announcements and must be loud enough to be heard over the noise of engines, machines, and people's conversations. Sound technicians test the systems they install to be sure they work properly for the purpose and setting where they are located. They turn volume and control knobs to adjust sound levels to suit the size of the room, the level of other noises, and the uses to which the system is being put.

After the installation, sound technicians test, troubleshoot, repair, and maintain the sound equipment as necessary. Sound technicians may also install, maintain, and service closed-circuit TV systems and associated apparatus.

Sound technicians recently installed a sound system in a new mall in Boise, Idaho. The system projects pleasant music and special announcements.

Requirements

Sound technicians need to have at least a high-school education. In addition, many employers prefer to hire applicants who have completed one or two years of post–high-school training at a trade or vocational school or at a junior or community college.

While in high school, students interested in this kind of work should take courses in shop procedures, mathematics, physical sciences, and any other courses that include instruction in electricity, electronics, and how sound travels. The mathematics courses should include algebra and geometry. Students should also take English and courses that develop their reading and writing skills. They should be able to read safety rules, equipment and technical manuals, and other kinds of written instructions. They should be able to write reports with proper spelling, grammar, and punctuation.

GOE: 05.05.05; SIC: 483; SOC: 6151

◇ **RELATED ARTICLES**

Volume 1: Electronics
Volume 3: Electrical repairers; Electricians; Telephone and PBX installers and repairers
Volume 4: Audio control technicians; Audiovisual technicians; Electrical technicians; Electronics technicians

Sound-effects technicians

With the script as a guide, a sound-effects technician plays the necessary sounds during a television broadcast.

Definition

Sound-effects technicians produce artificial sounds that are used in dramatic, documentary, or other kinds of live or taped television or radio programs. The artificial sounds are used by the technicians to help give the impression that some action, either seen or unseen, is actually taking place.

Nature of the work

Sound-effects technicians set up and operate the equipment used to record and later play back recordings of sounds introduced during broadcasts. They prepare for a broadcast or taping session by consulting with the director of the program about what sound effects will be needed and where they will be inserted. If the program will be partly or wholly spontaneous, the director and the sound-effects technician discuss the range of sound effects that might be needed and the kinds of effects that the director will be looking for at various points in the program.

Most of the sound effects that technicians have to work with have been prerecorded on audiotape or records. When it comes time to do a program, technicians assemble the sound effects they need from a sound-effects library. The technicians add those that have been newly created in the studio and arrange the final tape with the effects in the order in which they will be needed. For a spontaneous program, the effects may be separately recorded on small cassette tapes and played as cued by the director.

As part of their duties, sound-effects technicians are usually in charge of the sound-effects library. They have to refile tapes after they have been used, add new tapes to the library, and replace all tapes and records that are not in good condition. They review catalogs of new tapes and records available and recommend purchases.

In most studios and broadcasting stations the duties of sound-effects technicians have been incorporated into those of sound-recording technicians. Few radio and television stations can afford to keep one technician occupied solely with the creation and reproduction of sound effects.

Requirements

Sound-effects technicians should plan on receiving one to two years of technical training beyond high school. They should develop their reading abilities to the point where they can read with ease professional journals, technical manuals, and standard reference books. They should be able to write letters and reports with correct punctuation, grammar, spelling, and diction. They should be able to express themselves well orally in both formal and informal settings. They also need to have taken mathematics courses at least through algebra and plane geometry.

GOE: 01.06.02; SIC: 483; SOC: 399

⬦ **SOURCES OF ADDITIONAL INFORMATION**

Society of Broadcast Engineers
Information Office
7002 Graham Road
Suite 118
Indianapolis, IN 46220

Sound-recording technicians

Definition

Sound-recording technicians, also known as *recording engineers*, operate recording equipment to record radio broadcasts, the sound portions of television programs, and studio recording sessions to make musical, dramatic, and spoken phonograph records, cassette tapes, and compact discs. They also operate equipment that transfers recorded sound from one recording medium to another, such as tape to tape or tape to disc. Sound-recording technicians in broadcasting usually work in studios on programs that are taped or filmed well before they are aired; however, sound-recording technicians are sometimes also involved with the broadcasting of live programs. These technicians adjust as needed the sound quality of the broadcast as they monitor the recording of the broadcast.

Nature of the work

Sound-recording technicians are responsible for preparing to record by loading tapes into recorders; adjusting volume, tone, and speed controls to proper levels; and switching on correct microphone connections. During recording, they monitor sound-level indicator dials and adjust volume accordingly. They listen through earphones to be sure the necessary sound is picked up adequately by the equipment and to detect equipment failures or tape defects that will affect the finished recording. They may switch microphone controls as different microphones are used.

When cutting a disk recording from a tape recording, a process used in making phono-graph records, technicians thread tape into their equipment, check recording heads and the cutting stylus, regulate operating speeds of the equipment, and adjust the cutting stylus to properly cut grooves in the record blank. During both the recording of live sound and the rerecording to create a finished product, technicians monitor sound levels and quality through earphones and watch recording dials on their equipment. Technicians may be designated *disk-recording machine operators* or *tape-recording machine operators* according to the equipment they specialize in. When transcribing sound from tape to disk for use in making phonograph records, they may be designated dubbing-machine operators.

After recording sessions, technicians label, file, and log tapes and records for ready reference when they are needed.

In large broadcasting stations there may be repair technicians to maintain recording equipment, but in most stations this is the job of the recording technician. Recording heads must be cleaned, tape drives lubricated, and other routine but essential maintenance carried out. Technicians must also be able to perform minor repairs, sometimes in emergency situations.

Sound-recording technicians work with common electricians' hand tools (screwdriver, pliers, and so forth) to perform small repairs. The work is physically light, and the material to be recorded is often interesting. In many cases technicians must be quick to switch to the proper microphone, and they must be constantly alert for sound defects or volume changes. This is particularly true in music-recording sessions, because a defective passage must be recorded again with the same musicians in the same positions for the sound to be identical when spliced into the master tape.

A sound-recording technician prepares to play a recently recorded album. She will check for any flaws before the album is released to the public.

With experience and talent, sound-recording technicians may eventually specialize in the rerecording of different sound tracks to mix them into one final sound track such as is produced to go with major television productions or motion pictures. Such work requires extensive training.

Requirements

In high school, students interested in a career as a sound-recording technician should take as many mathematics courses as possible, physics, and shop courses that introduce electronic equipment. After high school they need to receive training in basic electronics at a community college or technical institute. Correspondence courses are available but are usually impractical without hands-on experience to support them. The advanced training should cover basic electronic theory, theory and practice of broadcasting, physics, and technical writing.

According to federal law, anyone who operates broadcast transmitters in radio or television stations must have a restricted radiotelephone operator license. No examination is required to get such a permit. Counselors can provide more information about agencies to contact regarding current licensing requirements and procedures.

The work of sound-recording technicians is light, requiring little or no heavy lifting. It does require excellent hearing and visual acuity, as well as manual dexterity.

GOE: 05.10.05; SIC: 483; SOC: 3719

◇ **RELATED ARTICLES**

Volume 1: Broadcasting; Electronics; Performing Arts; Recording
Volume 2: Recording industry workers
Volume 4: Audio control technicians; Electronics technicians; Sound-effects technicians; Studio technicians

Stage technicians

Definition

Stage technicians install lights, rigging, sound equipment, and scenery for entertainment productions on stages. Sometimes they also build stages for special theatrical and musical events in parks, stadiums, arenas, and other places. These technicians work in close cooperation with the stage director, the lighting director, the actors, and the various prop people. In addition, stage technicians work directly with theater shops in the construction of sets.

Nature of the work

In installing stage equipment, stage technicians begin with blueprints, diagrams, and specifications concerning the stage area. They confer with the stage manager to establish what kinds of sets, scenery, props, lighting, and sound equipment are required for the event or show, and where they should be put.

Then the technicians gather together props provided by the production company and build other props or scenery, using hammers, saws, and other hand tools and power tools. If they are working in a theater, they climb ladders or scaffolding to the gridwork at the ceiling and use cables to attach curtains, scenery, and other equipment that need to be moved, raised, and lowered during performances. They may need to balance on and crawl along beams near the ceiling in order to connect the cables.

Stage technicians also position lights and sound equipment on or around the stage. They clamp light fixtures to supports and connect electrical wiring from the fixtures to power sources and control panels.

The sound equipment used on and around stages usually includes microphones, speakers, and amplifiers. Technicians position this equipment and attach the wires that connect it to power sources and to the sound-mixing equipment that controls the volume and quality of the sound.

During rehearsals and performances, stage technicians in some theaters may follow cues and pull cables that raise and lower curtains and other equipment. Sometimes they also operate the lighting and sound equipment.

A stage technician checks the sound and lighting controls several hours before the presentation is to begin. She must know how to operate all of the computerized electronic equipment.

Requirements

Stage technicians need to combine a working knowledge of theater operations with the skills of a carpenter and electrician. Most employers prefer to hire stage technicians who have at least two years of training beyond high school, such as that available in programs offered at junior and community colleges. Students should plan to take courses in theater arts and related subjects, including courses that introduce lighting and sound systems, and also carpentry and electronics. While in high school, people interested in this career should take college-preparatory courses, including mathematics through algebra and plane geometry and English courses that develop good reading and writing skills.

Stage technicians have to be reasonably strong and in good physical condition. They must be able to climb, balance, and lift heavy weights of up to one hundred pounds, and they must have good manual dexterity, vision, and hearing.

GOE: 05.10.04; SIC: 483; SOC: 399

◇ **RELATED ARTICLES**

Volume 1: Performing Arts
Volume 3: Carpenters; Construction workers; Electricians; Stage production workers
Volume 4: Electrical technicians; Light technicians; Sound technicians

Studio technicians

Definition

Studio technicians, also called *sound mixers*, are concerned with volume levels and the quality of sound in recording studios during the production of radio and television programs and motion pictures and in sound recording sessions for phonograph records, tapes, and compact discs. They operate complete electronic consoles to regulate the volume and quality of

A studio technician regulates the sound quality of a prerecorded program. This task is performed before the program is broadcasted.

sound as it is being recorded onto audiotape that will later be edited.

Nature of the work

Studio technicians control a range of variable factors that influence the acoustical conditions inside a recording studio. They set up different combinations and arrangements of equipment in the studio to best achieve the desired sound for the production. They direct the installation of microphones and amplifiers, and they operate controls to cut microphones in and out to blend the output so that a balance is obtained between music, dialogue, and sound effects. They instruct performers about which microphones to play to and how loud or soft their voices ought to be. They test machines and equipment, using electronic testing equipment, such as ohm and voltage meters, to detect defects. They may also copy and edit recordings and repair and replace audio amplifier parts.

Requirements

Studio technicians should plan on taking two to four years of technical training beyond the high-school level. They should develop their language skills to the point where they can read with ease instructional materials relating to electronic equipment as well as standard reference books. They should be able to write reports with proper punctuation, spelling, and grammar and be able to speak comfortably before small groups. They should take courses in mathematics including algebra, geometry, and courses dealing with practical applications of fractions, percentages, ratios and proportions, logarithms, and the basic principles of trigonometry. They should also receive training in mechanical drawing and layout work.

GOE: 05.10.05; SIC: 483; SOC: 3719

◇ **RELATED ARTICLES**

Volume 1: Broadcasting; Electronics; Motion Pictures; Recording
Volume 2: Recording industry workers
Volume 4: Audio control technicians; Electronics technicians; Field technicians; Sound-effects technicians; Sound- recording technicians; Video technicians

Transmitter technicians

Definition

Transmitter technicians, also known as *transmitter operators*, operate and maintain transmitters used in the broadcasting of radio and television programs. They switch power to units and stages of the transmitter as needed, monitor indicator lights to ensure operational status, and adjust the transmitter to its assigned frequency.

Throughout the broadcast day, technicians maintain a log of broadcasts and their times. They diagnose transmitter problems, using oscilloscopes, ammeters, and voltmeters, then disassemble and repair problem components. They may also operate microwave transmitters or receivers to send signals to or receive signals from other broadcast stations or remote field locations.

Nature of the work

Television cameras and microphones convert sound and light waves into electronic impulses. These electronic impulses are modified in a broadcasting station's control room and sent to the transmitter, where they are converted to radio or television signals and sent out into the air. The power of the transmitter and the height of its antenna determine how far the broadcast will be received.

Transmitter technicians operate switches that turn on the various stages of the transmitter and adjust the frequency of the AM or FM radio or television signal being transmitted. The exact frequency at which a station may broadcast is assigned to the station by the Federal Communications Commission (FCC). Technicians monitor broadcasts to ensure that the signal holds its assigned frequency and does not interfere with other assigned frequencies or with local transmitting or receiving equipment. They adjust the signal as necessary to maintain frequency and keep the signal clear and sharp. Technicians also maintain a log of programs transmitted, recording exact times of transmission, as required by the FCC.

Transmitter technicians maintain the transmitter and antenna in top working order. Most stations shut down their transmitters or shift to a backup transmitter once a week to enable technicians to dismantle and service their equipment. During the broadcast week, emergency shutdowns for repairs may be necessary. They must be kept to a minimum.

Transmitter technicians use standard electricians' hand tools (screwdrivers, pliers, soldering guns) to dismantle equipment and make minor repairs. They use electrical meters and measuring devices such as oscilloscopes to diagnose problems.

Smaller stations in suburban or rural communities have their transmitters in or near their station buildings. Large urban stations may have their transmitters located miles away in open land beyond the structural interferences of the city. Others transmit from antennas placed on the highest buildings of the city. Technicians in remote transmitter sites may also operate microwave equipment to receive signals from the main control room.

Requirements

Competition for positions as transmitter technicians, especially in larger stations, is strong. Even at smaller stations, training in electronics and broadcasting principles is essential. Many

A transmitter technician relays a live news broadcast onto television. At the same time, he monitors the frequency of the stations signals.

technical schools and community colleges offer two-year programs that would provide an adequate background for entering this field.

Persons interested in careers in this field should take as much mathematics as possible (through calculus if possible) in high school, along with physics and any electronics training offered. They will also profit from participating in a radio club or from assembling radio kits. Technicians in local radio and television stations are a good source of career information.

It is important for transmitter technicians to have strong language skills, to enable them to read technical manuals and instructions that they must use in maintaining and repairing their equipment.

Little heavy physical work is involved in maintaining and operating transmitters. Technicians should have excellent mechanical skills and the ability to work confidently with electrical equipment. Color perception is important, because wires are color-coded. Good hearing is especially important, as is the ability to make critical adjustments in controls and instruments.

According to federal law, anyone who operates broadcast transmitters in radio or television stations must have a restricted radiotelephone operator permit. No examination is required to get such a permit. Anyone who works with microwave communications equipment, however, must have a general radiotelephone operator license, issued after the applicant passes several written tests. Counselors can provide more information about agencies to contact regarding current licensing requirements and procedures.

GOE: 05.03.05; SIC: 483; SOC: 393

Video technicians

Definition

Video technicians usually work in television stations. They are involved in several different aspects of broadcasting and videotaping television programs. Technicians who are mostly involved with broadcasting programs are often called *video-control technicians.* In live broadcasts where more than one camera is in use they operate electronic equipment that selects which picture goes to the transmitter for broadcast. They also monitor on-air programs to ensure good picture quality and they make adjustments to the picture as necessary. Technicians who are mostly involved with taping programs are often called *videotape-recording technicians.* They record live performances on videotape using video cameras and tape-recording equipment. They also copy from one tape to another to splice together separate scenes into a finished program, and they sometimes create special effects by manipulating recording and rerecording equipment.

Nature of the work

Video-control technicians usually work at control consoles in control rooms of television stations. As a studio program is being televised or videotaped, the picture produced by each camera appears on a monitor in the control room. The video-control technician, operating electronic switches that adjust picture quality, corrects the color balance, brightness, framing, contrast, and other factors. As the director indicates which camera picture should be used, the technician (or, in larger stations, the technical director of the program) switches that camera's picture to the videotape machine (or, for a live broadcast, to the master control for transmission).

Some programs require that live action be combined with filmed or videotaped material. This is done by the video-control technician. The instant replay common in sports broadcasts today in controlled by the video-control technician who replays videotape recorded by one or more of the cameras being used, often replaying the scene in slow motion and from different angles. Because most studio-produced programs are videotaped before being broadcast, technicians are able to add slow- and fast-motion effects much like those used in motion pictures.

In addition to monitoring quality of programs as they are being produced, video-control technicians preview taped programs before they are broadcast and monitor them while they are on the air to ensure that the technical quality of the broadcast does not change.

The equipment used by video-control technicians is complex and sensitive. Technicians must perform many switching operations and monitor many different controls during a broadcast or taping session. Switching must be done smoothly and with split-second timing.

Videotape-recording technicians are in charge of the equipment that rolls tape to record productions. Technicians prepare for recording by checking their equipment, mounting an adequate supply of fresh tape, and making sure they are familiar with any adjustments they will have to make during the taping session. During the session, they operate the controls of the recording machine. They watch a television monitor that shows the picture being recorded, and they listen to the audio position through earphones and adjust sound levels as necessary. They may have to switch microphones if several are in use. As they listen, they also monitor the quality of the tape. A tape or equipment defect or malfunction necessitates a re-recording.

Technicians may work with producers, directors, and reporters in putting together videotaped material from various sources, such as networks, mobile camera units, and studio productions. Depending on their employer, technicians may be involved in a narrow or wide range of activities related to editing videotapes into a complete program.

Videotape-recording technicians are usually responsible for logging, labeling, and filing the finished tapes. Using electricians' hand tools, they perform routine maintenance tasks such as lubricating, adjusting, and inspecting equipment. In some stations they may perform minor repairs. There is little heavy physical work.

A video technician edits a prerecorded presentation before it is broadcast. He must shorten it to the designated length of the scheduled program.

ditional training or experience beyond the basics will give an applicant an advantage.

Video technicians must have excellent hearing and vision, including color perception. They must have good hand-eye coordination and must be able to react quickly to instructions and to correct technical problems as they arise. They should be able to work comfortably in stressful situations.

GOE: 05.03.05, 05.10.05; SIC: 483; SOC: 393, 3719

Requirements

In high school, students interested in careers as video technicians should take as many courses as they can in mathematics and physical science, as well as any courses that introduce broadcasting or electronics. After high school they should take a technician training course in radio and television broadcasting and electronics at a technical institute, college, or community college.

Any practical experience an aspiring technician can acquire, whether as a hobby, at a school, commercial station, or elsewhere, will be very useful. Because competition for broadcast technician positions is very strong, any ad-

◇ **RELATED ARTICLES**

Volume 1: Broadcasting; Recording
Volume 2: Photographers and camera operators; Radio and television program directors; Recording industry workers
Volume 4: Audio control technicians; Sound-recording technicians; Studio technicians; Transmitter technicians

Medical and Health Technician Occupations

The health-care system touches each of us personally from time to time, occasionally making a vital and dramatic difference in our lives. Yet most of the time we tend to forget that the medicine and health field is also big business, and that it plays an increasingly important role in our everyday economic existence. Approaching twelve percent of the gross national product is devoted to health, and the percentage grows every year. Health care is a very labor-intensive industry. This means, in effect, that a large part of its cost goes to paying all the people who are involved, directly and indirectly, in providing it. In fact, the health field is one of the biggest employers in the United States, employing more than six million people.

Not so long ago, most health-care personnel were either physicians, dentists, or nurses. Very few other kinds of workers existed, and very few were needed. Around the turn of the century about half of all health workers were physicians; now physicians are outnumbered fifteen or so times by a wide array of other workers.

Many of the new job categories in this complex field have come into being because of technological advances. As biomedical knowledge expands and skills become sophisticated enough to be applied to practical problems, a division of labor occurs. Specialists arise specifically to meet newly created needs. In other words, once a type of equipment or a technique is devised and determined to be useful, someone is needed to manage the new process safely and correctly on a moment-by-moment basis, and this person is often a technician.

This change in the makeup of the health labor force is also related to the increasing cost of health care. Because technological innovations tend to cost more money, the total cost of care can often be minimized by assigning appropriate routine tasks to less expensive personnel, such as technicians. Another reason for the proliferation of occupations is that as technologies and equipment become more complicated, human limitations become a greater factor. Technicians and other specialists can become quite expert at their relatively narrow range of duties, while physicians and other professionals have too little contact with the specifics to hone their skills to a comparable degree in all the necessary areas. Finally, an important reason for the delegation of some activities to new occupations has been simply the growing size of the workload.

Technicians, then, are middle-level members of a health team responsible for carrying out tasks that require skillful attention to detail. They work according to established methods and standards. Although they sometimes encounter problematic situations that require intelligence and ingenuity to resolve, much of their work consists of doing very well a number of recognized procedures.

In the health field, technicians have traditionally been distinguished from technologists, assistants, and a number of other categories of specialist workers. The general pattern has been that technologists assume more responsibility than technicians, and their knowledge and training combine the theoretical with the practical. In contrast, technicians have been oriented more toward the practical aspects of their field. In terms of education, technologists have usually had to undergo four years of post–high-school formal training leading to a baccalaureate degree, whereas most entry-level technician positions have required completion of one- to two-year programs, often leading to an associate degree. People in many jobs designated as assistant level have been concerned with carrying out routine procedures under the immediate direction of a professional (someone with extensive knowledge and training who does the most complex tasks). Assistants have generally had less education in their specialty than technicians—a year or even less—and they have been the most focused on applications, rather than theory, of these three levels of workers.

In many health-related occupational fields, these distinctions still hold; however, in other fields the labels of technician, technologist, and assistant are in great flux and are assigned a range of different meanings in different contexts. Depending on the area of health care, the generally accepted meanings may vary; and even within a given area, there is variation in what is meant by a given title. In the field of electroencephalography, for example, the terms "technician" and "technologist" are often used interchangeably. Emergency medical technicians are designated as "technicians," although they are usually not graduates of two-year programs. On the other hand, physical therapist assistants almost always are. And radiological technologists may be graduates of one-, two-, or four-year programs. The probable trend in future years is that more technically trained health-care workers in more fields will come to call themselves "technologists" rather than "technicians" because of the greater prestige that has traditionally been associated with the term "technologist."

As the technology of the medicine and health field has become more complicated and sophisticated, so have the education and training of technical personnel. Around the early 1960s, a series of changes started in the approach to technical education. Although the length and type of career preparation still vary considerably depending on the field, training is now much more formal and academically based than it was prior to that time. This transition has been related to several factors, including changing concepts of professional status and the value of education, government regulation, and concerns within the health-care industry for quality of care.

As a rule, a high-school diploma or its equivalent is now required for entrance into technical training, even for hospital programs that do not grant a degree. The most desirable courses in high school vary somewhat according to field, but normally include several science and health courses, as well as courses that help students to develop written and oral communications skills. In some areas, courses designed to provide general or specialized training for health occupations are presented in public high schools.

When a technological innovation is very new, the first people to be trained in its use are those already skilled in related areas. When the techniques and equipment have become a little more widely known and accepted, training programs are likely to be informal, conducted differently at each training site, and located in hospital settings. More formal, uniform training programs spring up in colleges, universities, and technical institutes, and educational standards and requirements tend to rise, when the technology has become well established and the field clearly demands a pool of trained personnel. Even in fields that have reached this stage of development, the overall trend is to upgrade the education of technicians, in order for them to keep up with the on-going evolution of technology. Technicians already employed in such fields may need to take continuing education courses during their careers.

In addition to undergoing the training process, both initially and perhaps continuing later, various combinations of personal characteristics may be necessary for success. For example, some technicians, such as dental laboratory, ophthalmic laboratory, and orthotic and prosthetic technicians, should be good at delicate tasks involving manual dexterity and patience, because they are in many ways skilled craft workers. Other technicians may need physical strength, good vision, an inclination toward mathematics or mechanics, or other special qualities and talents. Because technicians often act as intermediate links in a team, they must be able to get along with a variety of other personnel, even when working under pressure.

Many technical jobs in the health-care field involve little or no contact with patients, because the technicians are engaged instead in laboratory services, record-keeping, or other support activities. Prospective technicians contemplating a career that involves a lot of patient contact, however, have to assess carefully their interest in people and their ability to handle the special problems of direct-care jobs. Because physically and emotionally dependent people can be irritable and demanding, such technicians have to have a mature and understanding outlook. They may have to deal with patients in grim and hopeless situations. To remain efficient and effective, technicians in direct-care positions need self-control in times of stress and the ability to be caring without becoming emotionally ensnared. It should be noted that for technicians who can cope with these kinds of problems, patient-contact work can be especially rewarding.

Students who think they may want to pursue a career as a technician in the medicine and health-care field can benefit from some related practical experience before embarking on training. Often the best way to obtain this is through a part-time or summer job or volunteer work in a hospital, nursing home, laboratory, or other organization that is concerned with the field of interest. If this is not possible, an effort should be made to visit an appropriate facility to observe technicians on the job or to talk to them about their careers. This kind of exposure to a real work environment helps students to analyze realistically their own aptitudes and capacities before making any commitment. It is also a good idea to visit schools that offer post–high-school training for health occupations, not only to learn about the prospective field of study, but also to get specific recommendations and advice on courses that ought to be included in the remaining high-school curriculum.

Financial assistance is frequently available for students who meet certain criteria. Loans from various governmental agencies, a limited number of scholarships (some provided by national health professional organizations or local auxiliaries and service organizations), and often work-study or cooperative employment programs (in which the student works part-time while going to school) can ease the financial burden. For information about financial assistance, students should contact a guidance counselor, state or local health agencies, or the admissions offices of schools offering technical training as early as possible in their career explorations.

In selecting a training program students should be aware of the importance of accreditation. Accreditation is the method by which an agency or organization evaluates and recognizes a specialized program of study or a total institution as meeting predetermined standards for competence. In most but not all technical fields described in this book, this credentialing is available. Accreditation of a whole institution may not have the same meaning as accreditation of parts, because different agencies may be responsible for the different programs within the institution, and thus apply varying criteria. Graduation from an accredited program is normally a significant advantage for technicians, enabling them to get the best jobs and to receive better advancement opportunities. Graduation from an accredited program is often a requirement for individual certification or registration, or for admission to educational programs leading to a baccalaureate degree in the same area. Information on the current accreditation status of particular programs can be obtained from the schools offering the programs, high-school guidance counselors, or the professional association or societies granting the accreditation.

Certification and registration are the methods by which the competence of individuals to carry out certain activities is recognized. Certification is the granting of recognition by a government or nongovernment agency, based on predetermined standards; while registration involves listing individuals on an official roster maintained by a government or non-government agency. Persons who have met the requirements of education, experience, and competency are eligible for these designations in some fields. Certification and registration are not available in all fields, but where they are they usually are highly desirable and may even be required for certain positions. In general the trend is toward more fields introducing these credentials, so that technicians may voluntarily demonstrate the adequacy of their skills in relation to an accepted standard. In some fields several types of certification are available.

Licensure is the process by which a governmental agency, usually at the state level, grants permission to perform specified functions to persons who meet predetermined qualifications. Not many technical occupations discussed in this section require licensure at this time.

Once students have secured the appropriate education and met any basic credentialing requirements, their best method of obtaining a job is often through the institution that provided their training or through contacts formed during the supervised clinical or practical experience that is part of many programs. In some parts of the country there may be a local oversupply of some kinds of technicians, so new graduates may have to widen their search area and use a variety of traditional job hunting methods such as checking ads in newspapers and professional journals, private and public employment agencies, and so forth.

Job advancement possibilities vary. In some fields, technicians with experience can gain additional responsibilities and suitably higher pay, particularly if they earn whatever voluntary credentials are available. In many fields, however, advancement possibilities are limited unless technicians pursue additional education and obtain a baccalaureate degree. Earnings, too, vary greatly, depending on the individual's education, experience, field of activity, type of employer, geographical location, and sometimes other factors. Accurate specific salary data is very hard to come by for technicians, and figures presented in the articles in this book should be taken only as general indicators. On the whole, pay is better in urban than in rural areas and slightly lower in federally operated than in nonfederal organizations.

Hospitals employ a large number of technicians, but there are many other possible work settings that should not be overlooked. Depending on their field, technicians may be employed in nursing homes, medical and dental laboratories, public health departments, clinics, private practitioners' offices, rehabilitation centers, social service agencies, industrial plants, home-health agencies, ambulatory care centers, and other organizations. In most fields, working environments are clean, bright, and comfortable. Because the ill and injured need around-the-clock attention, many jobs include weekend and night hours or overtime. The necessity for total coverage also opens the possibility of part-time jobs for some technicians.

Employment prospects for technicians in the health-care field are generally good for the foreseeable future. Overall population growth and an increase in the proportion of elderly people in the population are expected to increase the demand for health services. In addition, advances in medical knowledge and technology will result in more kinds of treatment being available for more kinds of ailments. This will mean that many patients with these ailments who might have gone untreated in the past will be treated in the future.

The only real limit on the growth of employment in this field is the nation's ability to pay for more and more health services. In the future, cost-containment measures will affect, and to some extent have already affected, the way health care is delivered in this country. This cost-containment effort may cause employment dislocations for some individual technicians, but overall it seems unlikely that efforts at cost-containment will have serious adverse effects on the employment prospects for any whole group of technicians described in this section.

The tendency to shift more routine but important responsibilities and duties from higher-level professionals to technical occupations has, to this point, generally encouraged a sense of professionalism and an acceptance of accountability in these occupations, as exemplified by the credentialing procedures introduced from inside many fields. On the other hand, the same shift, which is still under way, has tended to fragment the health-care work force into increasing numbers of specialist groups. From the point of view of people trying to understand and plan for the future of the health-care industry, this fragmentation presents a dilemma: It sometimes makes efficient, cost-effective use of labor resources more difficult, while nonetheless enhancing the delivery of specific highly technical services. Prospective technicians can expect that sooner or later changing technology may play a part in reshaping their career fields, although a variety of sometimes contradictory currents may influence any such reshaping.

This overview has sought to describe generally some of the prevailing factors at work in the technical occupations of the medicine and health field, especially as they might concern students considering a career in one of those occupations. The articles that follow treat specific occupations and small clusters of occupations in greater detail.

Animal health technicians

Definition

Animal health technicians, also called *veterinary science technicians,* assist veterinarians and other members of a veterinary staff in diagnosing and treating animals for injuries, illness, and routine veterinary needs, such as standard inoculations and periodic checkups.

Working under the supervision of veterinarians, animal health technicians perform a wide variety of tasks ranging from soothing and quieting animals under treatment to drawing blood, inserting catheters, and conducting laboratory tests. Often times animal health technicians are the veterinary workers with the closest contact to the clinic's animal population.

History

The history of veterinary medicine goes back as much as 4,000 years. Throughout large parts of Africa and Asia in that period, people were developing an understanding of the health needs of sheep, goats, cows, and other animals kept for agricultural purposes. The ancient Egyptians wrote books on the subject of diseases of animals, as did the early Greek scholars Hippocrates and Aristotle.

The first modern veterinary hospital was founded in 1762 in Lyon, France, and was called the Ecole Nationale Veterinaire. In the United States, schools of veterinary medicine began to come into existence around the middle

377

of the nineteenth century, and in 1863 an organization was founded that later became the American Veterinary Medical Association.

As this field has grown and become more sophisticated during the twentieth century, the need has developed not only for more assistants to aid veterinarians in their work but also for better-trained assistants. Now referred to as technicians, the assistants are familiar with all aspects of animal care technology and are thus able to deliver care in a knowledgeable and professional fashion.

Nature of the work

Animal health technicians assist veterinarians in much the same way that medical assistants assist physicians. Working always under the supervision of a veterinarian, they perform many routine duties such as measuring and recording animal temperatures, pulse rates, and respiration. They also gather and record information about cases; apply bandages, dressings, and splints; draw blood and collect specimens; administer oxygen; and give pills and injections. There are also some kinds of special treatments that animal health technicians may administer under the general supervision of a veterinarian. These include cleaning teeth, removing sutures, and inserting catheters, endotracheal tubes, and related devices.

Animal health technicians involved with veterinary surgery gather and position surgical kits and related instruments and materials for use by the veterinary surgeon during surgery. They also wash, shave, and apply antiseptic solutions to the area of the animal about to be operated on. During and after the operation they assist with monitoring the patient's vital signs and reflexes, and they report any unanticipated changes to the veterinarian.

Other duties of animal health technicians working in a veterinary practice include observing animals in hospitals to monitor eating and elimination; detecting abnormal conditions, by conducting tests and microscopic examinations of specimens; dispensing drugs; maintaining prescription records; and keeping records of inventories and supplies. They also clean and sterilize instruments, maintain equipment and machines, and set up and operate X-ray equipment.

Animal health technicians usually work in veterinary clinics or in animal research laboratories where they help care for the animals who are being used as the subjects of experiments. They also work, however, in many other settings. They may be employed by laboratories doing biological research, companies producing drugs or animal feeds, breeders of laboratory animals, large corporate farms, zoos, meat packing companies, and local, state, and federal public health agencies. Their duties in such settings include record keeping, animal care and feeding, laboratory procedures, equipment maintenance, and any of the tasks performed by animal health technicians working for a veterinarian.

Requirements

Successful animal health technicians combine a love for animals, good manual dexterity, and an aptitude for recordkeeping, writing reports, and speaking effectively.

To become an animal health technician, students need to complete a two-year program leading to an associate degree from a community or technical college whose program has been accredited by the American Veterinary Medical Association. A high-school diploma is an essential requirement for admission to such a program. In most cases a student's high-school record must be above average because of the competition for admission to these programs. Courses in algebra, chemistry, biology, and English are essential.

During a two-year program, students can expect to take one or two introductory courses such as introduction to animal technology and animal science for the animal technician. In each semester of the program, they will take some general education courses, such as biology, chemistry, communications, mathematics, economics, and business management. In addition, students take courses directly aimed at the work they will do following graduation. These include courses in physiology, animal care, laboratory procedures, clinical techniques, radiology, ethics, and client relations.

Most programs also offer students practical experience with live animals and field experience under actual working conditions.

Special requirements

Many states require animal technicians to be registered or even licensed. Specific registration or licensure requirements vary from state to state, and students should consult their guidance counselors for sources of information about requirements in their state. In most cases it is either a state veterinary medical examining board or state veterinary medical association that is responsible for licensing or certification.

One national professional society that provides for voluntary certification of animal health technicians is the Animal Technicians Certification Board, which is sponsored by the American Association of Laboratory Animal Science. This organization actually provides for a number of different certification classifications that technicians can earn depending on their level of competence. Assistant Laboratory Animal Technician is the first level of certification, requiring one full year of experience; Laboratory Animal Technician is the second level, requiring three years of experience; Laboratory Animal Technologist is the highest level and requires six years of experience.

Opportunities for experience and exploration

Finding out whether they have the necessary interest and ability to work in this field is easy for most people. Any young person who has raised, cared for, and even bred and sold animals has a basic knowledge of what is involved, and whether or not he or she wants to pursue it further. For example, many young people raise hamsters, maintain and clean several cages, mate pairs, provide special diets for the nursing mother, separate and keep records of litters, and sell them.

In addition, veterinarians often hire high-school students for summer or part-time work to help with cleaning cages, feeding animals, and performing other simple tasks under supervision.

Methods of entering

Students attending two-year colleges can rely on their placement offices to provide information about job offerings. Technicians interested in working for large institutional employers can meet company or institutional recruitment officers who often visit college campuses to talk with interested students during their second year of instruction. Students interested in employment in a veterinarian's private practice or in a small clinic may have to rely on instructors or other people who may know about job openings or on contacts they make through their supervised experience or work-study programs.

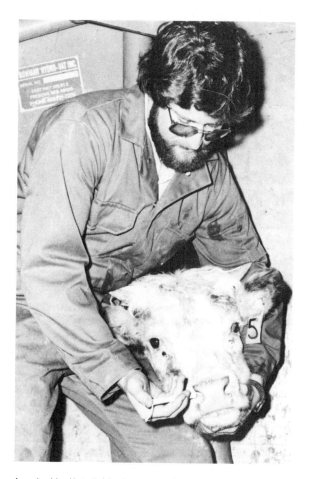

An animal health technician keeps a cow in a stable position as he injects a substance in the cow's nose. Working with farm animals requires strength.

Advancement

With experience and continuing education, animal health technicians can expect to advance to greater levels of responsibility. In some settings, this simply means that they can perform more difficult or sophisticated procedures. In other settings it may mean that the technicians take on supervisory or other administrative responsibilities.

Employment outlook

The employment outlook for animal health technicians should be good through the 1990s. Factors contributing to this favorable outlook include the growth in interest in companion and recreational animals (such as dogs, cats, and horses), emphasis on scientific methods of raising and breeding livestock, and the fact that more veterinarians are recognizing the value of qualified technicians in their practices. In addi-

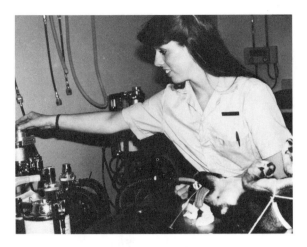

One of the many responsibilities of an animal health technician involves monitoring the effects of anesthesia during surgery.

tion, more animal health technicians are employed in recreational settings, such as resorts, riding stables, and race tracks.

Prospective animal health technicians should keep in mind, however, that the field of animal care and veterinary medicine is a very attractive one, and in recent years enrollments in various kinds of veterinary-medicine educational programs have increased. Because of this animal health technicians may find that they face stiff competition for good jobs.

Earnings

Animal health technicians can expect to receive starting salaries in the range of $14,000 to $17,000 a year. With several years of experience and increased responsibilities, they can expect salary increases up to $20,000 or more a year.

Fringe benefits vary considerably. Some jobs, especially those on farms, include housing in addition to salary. Many large companies offer free tuition for further education.

Conditions of work

Animal health technicians generally work a forty-hour week. Technicians employed in small practices, however, often have to work longer, more irregular hours and do some night work. The work of animal health technicians is usually conducted in clean, well-lighted facilities; however, there are odors that some people find unpleasant. It is also important to note that animal health technicians run the risk of being injured by some animals. They are also exposed to animal diseases that may be communicable to humans.

Animal health technicians who work with wild animals, such as zoo technicians, have several additional concerns. The first is that the information on behaviors and treatments for rare and endangered animals may be quite limited. Health care may be difficult to provide. With endangered species, proper treatment is essential since every animal is important to the genetic pool of the species. Another concern is in animal handling. Handling an injured dog is difficult; handling an injured tiger is life-threatening.

Social and psychological factors

People entering the career of animal health technician generally love working with and caring for animals, and the technicians employed by a veterinarian probably have the most satisfying job of all. There they can be actively engaged in the healing of sick or injured animals; and when treatment is successful, the pleasure of seeing the animal healthy once again is enormous.

For the large number of technicians who work in research laboratories, however, there can be a great conflict of feeling. It is imperative that the laboratory technician be able to realize the vital role these animals play in the discovery of medical knowledge that can aid all of humanity. Without the total acceptance of this fact, though, the killing of these animals in the experimental process can be extremely disturbing. For those who feel that they cannot realistically accept such aspects of the job as injecting parasitic agents into an animal, or deliberately causing tumors, it would be better to specialize in one of the many other areas of this profession.

GOE: 02.03.03; SIC: 0741, 0742; SOC: 369

◇ SOURCES OF ADDITIONAL INFORMATION

United States Animal Health Association
PO Box 28176
6924 Lakeside Avenue
Suite 205
Richmond, VA 23228

American Association for Laboratory
Animal Science
70 Timber Creek
Suite 5
Cordova, TN 38018

American Veterinary Medical Association
930 North Meacham Road
Schaumburg, IL 60196

United States Department of Agriculture
Washington, DC 20250

◇ **RELATED ARTICLES**

Volume 1: Agriculture; Health Care
Volume 2: Biologists; Medical technologists;
Physician assistants; Veterinarians
Volume 3: Agricultural scientists; Agricultural
extension workers; Dairy farmers; Dental assistants; Medical assistants
Volume 4: Animal production technicians; Biological technicians; Medical laboratory technicians; Surgical technicians

Cardiac monitor technicians

Definition

Cardiac monitor technicians operate and watch
the display screens of electronic machines
called cardiac monitors that record and show
graphically the heartbeat of patients in
intensive-care and cardiac-care units in hospitals. Cardiac monitors usually have a video
screen and wires that attach to the patient's
chest to detect each beat of the heart. By watching the screen, the cardiac monitor technician
can observe the person's heartbeat and detect
any abnormal rhythms. Cardiac monitor technicians are similar to and sometimes perform
some of the same duties as electrocardiograph
technicians. For more information about electrocardiograph technicians, readers should see
the article about them in this section of Volume
4.

Nature of the work

Cardiac monitor technicians usually work in
hospitals in intensive-care units or cardiac-care
units. The responsibility of a cardiac monitor
technician in such a unit is to watch all of the
screens that are monitoring the patients and to
be alert for any sign that a patient's heart is not
beating as it should. To do this correctly, cardiac monitor technicians must begin by reviewing each patient's records to determine what
that patient's normal heart-rhythms are like,
what the current pattern has been like, and

what kinds of deviations from the current pattern have been observed. Equipped with this
knowledge, the technician can know what
kinds of rhythms are to be expected from the
patients and what kinds require prompt medical attention. If medical attention is required,
the cardiac monitor technician is to notify immediately a nurse or doctor so that appropriate
care can be given.

Other duties of cardiac monitor technicians
who work in hospitals include measuring the
length and height of patients' heartbeat patterns as recorded on paper printouts and entering that information in the patients' medical
records. Cardiac monitor technician also give
help to patients when they ask for it and provide information about patients to doctors and
nurses.

Requirements

Cardiac monitor technicians need a high-school
education. In addition, they must receive on-
the-training that lasts from six months to two
years. In some settings technicians are generally expected to have taken courses relating to
cardiac monitoring in a two-year community or
technical college.

Cardiac monitor technicians need to have
training in mathematics, including algebra and
geometry, and be able to solve problems having
to do with ratios, proportions, and percentages. They should have good enough reading

A cardiac monitor technician views the monitors that display the heart rate of intensive care patients. If she notices a problem, she will contact a physician immediately.

skills that they can comfortably read equipment and training manuals and other written instructions. They should also be able to write reports with proper spelling, punctuation, and grammar, and they should be able to speak clearly and easily.

In addition to these educational requirements, cardiac monitor technicians should enjoy helping people and be able to deal with the sick and elderly. They should also be able to understand and follow instructions exactly when carrying out their duties.

GOE: 10.03.01; SIC: 806; SOC: 369

◇ **RELATED ARTICLES**

Volume 1: Health Care
Volume 2: Licensed practical nurses; Medical technologists; Physician assistants; Registered nurses
Volume 3: Medical assistants; Nursing and psychiatric aides
Volume 4: Biomedical equipment technicians; Electrocardiograph technicians; Electroencephalograph technicians; Medical laboratory technicians

Dental laboratory technicians

Definition

Dental laboratory technicians are skilled craft workers who work according to the written prescriptions of dentists or dental specialists to make and repair dental appliances such as dentures, inlays, bridges, crowns, and braces. Dental laboratory technicians work with plastics, ceramics, and metals, using models made from impressions taken by the dentist of a patient's mouth or teeth.

Some dental laboratory technicians perform the whole range of laboratory activities, while many others specialize in a particular activity. Dental laboratory technicians may specialize, for instance, in making orthodontic appliances such as braces for straightening teeth; in applying layers of porcelain paste or acrylic resin over a metal framework to form crowns, bridges, and tooth facings; in making and repairing wire frames and retainers for teeth used in partial dentures; and in making and repairing full and partial dentures.

History

Dental laboratory technicians are little known to most people who visit dentists, yet many dental patients today benefit from their skills. For centuries people have utilized various kinds of false teeth, with varying success. Thanks to sophisticated techniques and to materials such as acrylics and plastics, efficient, comfortable, cosmetically acceptable aids can now be supplied when natural teeth or tissue are unsatisfactory or missing. Technicians, usually employed in commercial dental laboratories, do much of the work to produce these aids.

Today nearly all dental practitioners make use of services provided by dental laboratories. Most of these services are from commercial laboratories, each of which may handle tasks for a number of practitioners. This was not always the pattern, however.

Until the last years of the nineteenth century, dentists performed all their own laboratory work. The first successful commercial dental laboratory was established in 1887 by a partnership of a dentist and a machinist. The idea of delegating work to such laboratories was slow to catch on among dentists before World War II, when many dental technicians were trained to provide services at scattered military bases and on ships. About 2,700 commercial dental laboratories in the United States in 1940 have grown to several times that number today. The average size of dental laboratories has remained small—only about half a dozen full-time workers per laboratory.

A growing number of technicians are employed by dentists, notably specialists in prosthodontics and orthodontics, to staff private dental laboratories. A recent estimate suggests that about one technician in five works in this type of private setting.

At first, dental laboratory technicians were trained on the job, but formal training programs are now the predominant approach to preparing for a career. In 1951, the American Dental Association began to accredit two-year postsecondary programs in dental technology. By the mid-1980s, fifty-nine institutions offered such training.

Nature of the work

Dental laboratory technicians often find that their talents and preferences lead them toward one phase of their field. The broad areas of specialization open to them include full and partial dentures, crowns and bridges, ceramics, and orthodontics.

Complete dentures, also called false teeth or plates, are worn by people who have had all their teeth removed on the upper or lower jaw, or both jaws. Applying their knowledge of oral anatomy and restoration, technicians who specialize in making dentures carefully position teeth in a wax model for the best occlusion (the relationship between tooth surfaces with the jaws closed), then build up wax over the denture setup. After the denture is cast in place, they clean and buff the product, using a bench lathe equipped with polishing wheels. When repairing dentures they may cast plaster models of replacement parts and match teeth for color and shape to the natural or adjacent teeth. They cast reproductions of gums, fill cracks in dentures, and rebuild linings using acrylics and plastics. They may also bend and solder wire made of gold, platinum, and other metals and sometimes fabricate wire using a centrifugal casting machine.

Partial dentures, often called partials, restore missing teeth for patients who have some

teeth remaining on the jaw. The materials and techniques in their manufacture are similar to those in full dentures. In addition, wire clasps are mounted to anchor the partial to the remaining teeth yet allow it to be removed for cleaning.

Crown and bridge specialists restore the missing parts of a natural tooth so that it is recreated in its original form. These appliances, made of plastics and metal, are sometimes called fixed bridgework because they are permanently cemented to the natural part of the tooth and are not removable. Technicians in this area are skilled at melting and casting metals. Waxing (building up wax around the setup before casting) and polishing the finished appliance are also usually among their responsibilities.

Some dental laboratory technicians are specialists in porcelain. They are often referred to as dental ceramists, and they fabricate natural-looking teeth to replace missing ones or to fit over natural teeth. Many patients concerned with personal appearance seek porcelain crowns, especially on front teeth. The ability to match color exactly and delicately shape teeth is thus crucial for these technicians. To create crowns, bridges, and tooth facings, dental ceramists apply multiple layers of mineral powders or acrylic resins to a metal base and fuse the materials in an oven. The process is repeated until the result conforms exactly to specifications. Ceramists have to know and understand all the phases of dental technology and have natural creative abilities. Because they must possess the highest level of knowledge and talent, ceramists are generally the best paid of dental technicians.

Orthodontics, the final area of specialization for dental laboratory technicians, involves bending wire into intricate shapes and soldering wires into complex positions. Technicians in this area, usually referred to as orthodontic technicians, shape, grind, polish, carve, and assemble metal and plastic appliances. Orthodontic devices such as retainers, positioners, and tooth bands are used in tooth-straightening and are thus not considered permanent, although they may have to stay in place for long periods of time.

Dental laboratory technicians may work in a general or full-service laboratory, a category that includes nearly half of all dental laboratories. Or they may find employment with a laboratory that performs specialized services. Most laboratories that specialize are concerned with the various uses of particular material. For example, one specializing in acrylics is likely to make complete and partial dentures; another

A dental laboratory technician chips off the plastic impression of a mouth to reveal the positive plaster mold below. The plaster mold will then be sent to an orthodontist for analysis.

laboratory that does gold work will make gold inlays and bridges.

The size of the laboratory may be related to the kinds of tasks its technical employees perform. Some large commercial laboratories may have staffs of 200 or more, allowing for a high degree of specialization. On the other hand, technicians working in one- or two-person private laboratories may be called on to do a wide range of jobs.

Requirements

Dental laboratory technicians who do best in their field combine the precision, patience, and dexterity of a skilled craft worker with a generous amount of artistic talent. They must be able to carry out written and sometimes verbal instructions exactly, because each dental fixture has to be constructed according to very specific designs provided by the dentist. Good eyesight and color discrimination and the ability to do delicate work with one's fingers are very important. Although it is by no means a requirement, prospective technicians will profit from having had hobbies involving mixing and

molding things or from having built models of airplanes or cars.

The basic educational requirement is a high-school diploma. Useful high-school courses include chemistry, shop, mechanical drawing, art, and ceramics. Any other course or activity that allows the student to learn about metallurgy or the chemistry of plastics would be very helpful.

Inevitably, these technicians must learn much of their job by working under the supervision of experienced technicians. Three to four years of on-the-job training in a dental laboratory is the method of career entry used by some technicians. They start as trainees doing simple jobs such as mixing plaster and pouring it into molds. As they gradually gain experience, they are assigned more complex tasks.

Another way to prepare for the career is to enroll in a formal training program that leads to an associate degree in applied science. A typical two-year curriculum might include courses in denture construction, processing and repairing dentures, tooth construction, waxing and casting inlays, and crowns. In addition, the student may be expected to take courses such as biochemistry, English, business mathematics, and American government.

After graduating from one of these programs that combines academic courses with laboratory instruction, new technicians still need several years of further experience to refine their practical skills. However, the broad exposure to the wide range of skills and materials that a degree program provides pays off for most graduates, and this approach to a career is becoming the norm.

Special requirements

Technicians with appropriate training and experience can become Certified Dental Technicians, thus earning the right to place the initials C.D.T. after their names. Certification is not mandatory for employment, but many employers regard it as the best evidence of competence.

Certification is conducted by the National Board for Certification in Dental Laboratory Technology. For initial certification, candidates must pass a basic written and practical examination in at least one of the five laboratory specialties: complete dentures, partial dentures, crown and bridge, ceramics, and orthodontics.

The requirements for certification also include five years' experience in the field. Time spent in an approved dental laboratory technology training program may be counted toward the total.

Every year Certified Dental Technicians must meet specific continuing education requirements in order to maintain certification status.

Although membership is not required, dental laboratory technicians may choose to belong to various professional organizations. The most prominent among these are the National Association of Dental Laboratories and the American Dental Association. Local meetings bring together technicians and laboratory owners to share ideas of common interest and information about job opportunities.

Opportunities for experience and exploration

While in high school, students with an interest in this area can seek out courses and activities that allow exploration of ceramics, metal casting and soldering, molding, and the related skills practiced by dental laboratory technicians. A local dentist or school guidance counselor may be able to suggest a technician or laboratory in the area that the student might visit in order to get a first-hand idea of the work involved.

Part-time or summer jobs as laboratory helpers may be available. Such positions usually consist of picking up and delivering work to dentists' offices, but they may provide a chance to observe and assist practicing technicians. Students in dental laboratory technology training programs often have part-time jobs like these that develop into full-time technician positions after graduation.

Methods of entering

Newly graduated dental laboratory technicians who are seeking job openings can apply directly to dentists' offices and laboratories as well as to private and state employment agencies. Often the best way to locate vacancies is through the placement office at the school that administered the training program.

Another source of information and contacts may be at the local chapter of various professional associations. Sometimes more experienced dental technicians can get leads by inquiring at dental supply houses. Their sales workers are in constant contact with dentists and laboratories in the area and therefore know something about staffing needs.

In general, initial jobs in this field are likely to involve training and routine tasks that allow the technician to become familiar with the lab-

oratory's operations. In a very large commercial laboratory, for instance, newcomers may be assigned to various departments. At the plaster bench they may make and trim models; some may do routine minor repairs of dentures and other appliances; others may polish dentures. As their skills become more evident, more complicated tasks may be added.

Advancement

The development of individual skills is the key to advancement for dental laboratory technicians. In general, they can expect advancement as they become expert in a specialized kind of work. Depending on skill, experience, and education, some technicians become supervisors or managers in commercial laboratories. The prospect of such promotions is one reason why many technicians whose careers have begun with on-the-job training in a commercial laboratory later find it desirable to attend an accredited school program to obtain an associate degree.

Technicians interested in advancing can often find out about new methods and update their skills in other ways. Local, state, and national organizations provide a variety of learning opportunities. Manufacturers of the materials that dental technicians use also offer courses, often free, in the use of their products. Outstanding technicians may be hired as instructors in these courses.

Some dental laboratory technicians, who are seeking variety and new outlets for their creativity, develop sideline activities that require similar skills and materials. Fine jewelry making, for example, is a natural career development for some technicians. Some technicians become teachers in training programs; others, sales representatives for manufacturers of dental products.

The goal some technicians aspire to is owning and operating an independent laboratory. This requires a broad understanding of dental laboratory work, a well-developed business sense, and a considerable investment. Nonetheless, most of today's commercial laboratory owners have come up "from the bench."

Employment outlook

There are good reasons to expect that the demand for dental laboratory technicians will continue to grow fairly rapidly at least through the decade of the 1990s. The level of public awareness of dental health and appearance has increased substantially in recent years. At the same time, the number of people covered by dental insurance plans is going up. People in older age groups, who utilize a large share of dental appliances, are becoming an ever-greater segment of the population. The outlook is therefore an optimistic one for dental laboratory technicians, particularly those with exceptional ability and experience. In addition, the climate in future years should be good for entrepreneurial technicians setting out to establish new commercial laboratories, because more dentists will probably send work out instead of doing it themselves.

Earnings

There is limited information available relating to salaries of dental laboratory technicians. According to data collected by the federal government, the overall average salary for dental laboratory technicians is probably around $20,000 a year. Technicians at the beginning of their careers can expect to make a good deal less than that, while experienced technicians with proven abilities and special skills earn more.

Generally technicians specializing in ceramics or gold make the most money, often over $30,000 a year. Managers and supervisors in large laboratories and self-employed technicians also exceed the average earnings.

Conditions of work

Most dental laboratory technicians work in well-lighted, calm, pleasant, and quiet surroundings. Usually technicians have their own workbenches and equipment.

The normal workweek is forty hours for technicians employed in commercial laboratories. Sometimes technicians face the pressure of deadlines, although dentists' requirements are usually flexible enough to allow for special problems or difficult jobs. Many laboratories must operate on weekends, and in areas where there is a shortage of technicians, it may be necessary to work overtime, with wages adjusted accordingly. Self-employed technicians or those in very small laboratories may have irregular or longer hours.

Technicians usually work by themselves, concentrating on details of the pieces they are making or repairing. While the work does not demand great physical strength, it does require constant carefulness and deft handling of materials and tools. Technicians usually have little contact with people other than their immediate coworkers and the dentists whose instructions they follow. Work is often brought in and out by messenger or by mail.

Social and psychological factors

Dental laboratory technicians should be people who enjoy detailed work, are good at following instructions, and take pride in perfection. A strong artistic inclination is a trait of many successful technicians. They should be comfortable working with many small hand tools, electric drills, lathes, and furnaces, as well as a wide range of materials including wax, plaster, plastics, porcelain, gold, silver, and other metals. They should be able to function independently but still be able to coordinate their activities with other workers in the same laboratory when necessary.

GOE: 05.05.11; SIC: 8072; SOC: 6865

◇ **SOURCES OF ADDITIONAL INFORMATION**

American Dental Association
211 East Chicago Avenue
Chicago, IL 60611

National Association of Dental Laboratories
3801 Mount Vernon Avenue
Alexandria, VA 22305

National Board for Certification of Dental Laboratories Technology
3801 Mount Vernon Avenue
Alexandria, VA 22305

◇ **RELATED ARTICLES**

Volume 1: Health Care
Volume 2: Dental hygienists; Dentists
Volume 3: Dental assistants; Jewelers and jewelry repairers
Volume 4: Biological specimen technicians; Museum technicians; Optics technicians; Orthotic and prosthetic technicians

Dialysis technicians

Definition

Dialysis technicians, also called *kidney machine operators* or *renal dialysis technicians*, assist in the care of patients with kidney conditions that require hemodialysis. Hemodialysis is a technique used to wash or cleanse normal waste products from the blood of a patient whose kidneys have lost their ability to remove these wastes. Technicians are responsible for maintaining and repairing dialysis equipment, providing support services such as recording patient data, and monitoring dialysis equipment and patient's vital signs during dialysis. They assist in educating the patient and family about dialysis, and they perform activities that protect against health hazards that might occur during dialysis.

History

Dialysis was first described in 1854 by a Scottish chemist, Thomas Graham. In his early experiments, Graham separated crystalloids from colloids. Crystalloids are chemical salts that dissolve, and colloids are jelly-like materials that remain uniformly suspended in a solvent and that will not dissolve. In the experiments, the crystalloids in the solution passed through a membrane into another solution. They were then recovered by evaporating the solution. Graham predicted possible medical uses for the discovery, but he did not do any experiments involving animals or humans.

In 1913, John J. Abel and Leonard G. Rowntree utilized the principle of dialysis in laboratory experiments using animals. Because the dialysis technique involved removing chemicals from the blood of animals, researchers called the process "hemodialysis." *Hemo* comes from a Greek word *haima*, which means "blood." In the process, blood is taken from the body and passed through membranous tubes. The surfaces of the membranes are bathed with solutions, and normal body waste chemicals that are usually removed by the kidneys pass through the membranes into the chemical solutions. The blood cells and other proteins act as colloids, which means that they do not pass through the membranes. They return to the body with the blood but without the harmful waste chemicals. The waste materials are soluble, so they act as crystalloids and are removed.

The rate of the waste removal depends on the amount of the waste products in the blood and the nature and strength of the solutions used to bathe the membranes through which the blood is flowing.

Improvements in equipment and the development of heparin, a drug that prevents clotting, made hemodialysis practical in humans in the early 1940s. Since then, further advances have made the process more efficient. By the late 1950s dialysis was available in health-care facilities throughout the United States. During the 1960s it became apparent that self-care dialysis could be successfully carried out in homes of patients more economically than in hospitals. This was an important development because dialysis is an expensive process.

Since 1973, Medicare funds have paid for dialysis carried out in health facilities. More recently, Medicare began to pay for the equipment patients need for home dialysis.

While most dialysis is still carried out in hospitals or special dialysis facilities, about one third of the patients can, after extensive education, participate in self-care programs in their homes. Many patients have difficulty coping with the emotional, intellectual, psychological, and physical problems involved in a self-care program. Special techniques and equipment have been devised for home dialysis, which patients administer to themselves several times a day. Even at home, patients must be monitored carefully by members of the dialysis team.

Nature of the work

The responsibilities, activities, and duties of the dialysis technician vary from one dialysis unit to another and sometimes within the unit. Responsibilities may be limited to technical procedures and direct patient care, or they may be expanded to include biochemical analyses, observations, and conducting research studies to improve equipment. The role of the dialysis technician is determined by a number of factors. Some of them include the management plan of the dialysis facility, the leadership and staff of the facility, the skills and background of the technician, the equipment and facilities of the unit, other activities conducted by the staff of the unit, the equipment available, and the long-term care plans for the patients.

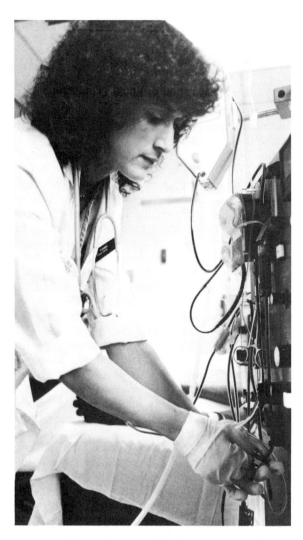

A dialysis technician prepares equipment that will be used to filter blood and remove excess fluid from a diabetic patient.

check alarms, set monitors, and test the dialyzer if necessary.

They prepare the patients for the dialysis first by weighing them and recording vital signs, including blood pressure, pulse, temperature, and rate of breathing. They also inspect and evaluate access sites, which are places to insert tubes to remove and return blood in the process, and obtain blood samples and culture specimens as ordered. Dialysis technicians begin the dialysis procedure using established access routes through veins or a catheter into the body cavity and adjust the heparin dosage according to a procedure prescribed by the patient's supervising physician.

During the dialysis, they measure and adjust blood-flow rates; measure, observe, and record dialysis treatment measurements and factors such as vital signs and weight changes; observe the fluid-delivery unit to be sure it is working properly; and respond to alarms and make appropriate adjustments.

Following the procedure, dialysis technicians clean and dress the access sites, clean and sterilize the equipment, dispose of used supplies, and perform routine maintenance tasks on the equipment. At any time during the procedure, they may be called upon to administer oxygen or to apply basic cardiopulmonary resuscitation measures in the event of a cardiac emergency.

The tasks performed by the dialysis technician may be carried out in a hospital, nursing home, dialysis center, or in a patient's home. To perform the tasks described, the technician must know and understand the dialysis equipment, design characteristics, and the principles of the operation of the dialysis system in order to obtain the best possible results safely and efficiently.

In the performance of dialysis treatment, technicians must understand the details of the standardized procedures and how important it is to follow them exactly. They must also master the standardized techniques that avoid potential dangers such as reaction to bacterial infections and to chemical substances.

In the self-care programs, the dialysis technician teaches the patient about the principles of dialysis and the tasks that patients must perform. Common problems are usually caused by poor technique, contamination of equipment or supplies, and failure of the equipment or supplies to work properly. Bacterial infections are of special concern. Patients must be able to reduce these risks to the very minimum, and must be able to recognize early symptoms if they occur.

Renal dialysis is one of the newer allied health technician careers, and it is still developing. For this reason, in most states, the duties of technicians are determined within the individual dialysis facilities; however, there are some aspects of the work of dialysis technicians that are common to all workplaces. For instance, dialysis technicians always work under the supervision of professional nurses and physicians. Some tasks that may be performed by dialysis technicians are described in the following paragraphs.

Prior to the actual dialysis treatment, technicians prepare the dialyzer by positioning the machine, attaching and installing all required tubing, preparing the fluid-delivery system, connecting the dialyzer and all its pumps, and assembling all necessary supplies and equipment at the patient's bedside. Dialysis technicians may also be called upon to calibrate and

Requirements

The career of renal dialysis technician is still evolving. When dialysis was a new technique, health workers with little training but some aptitude and interest in the field learned dialysis treatment procedures on the job. Today, training in basic patient-care skills and in responding to emergency situations that can arise during dialysis have become additional requirements.

High-school students who are interested in this field should study biology, chemistry, science, mathematics, communications, and health-related subjects. They should also learn to use a typewriter or word processor for preparation of reports. The ability to talk comfortably to patients and other team members is necessary. Dialysis technicians must be careful observers. They must be able to communicate with other team members. Verbal information and descriptions of procedures and techniques must be clearly conveyed to patients and to members of their families. In addition, technicians must be able to read scientific textbooks, manuals, and journals. Consequently, good language skills are essential.

The formal preparation for this career generally takes place in programs conducted by renal units of hospitals or in free-standing dialysis centers. Only a few dialysis preparatory programs may be found in two-year colleges or in technical schools. At present there is no accrediting body or officially prepared list of requirements for training programs, but such requirements may be developed in the future.

For dialysis technicians, the skills and knowledge are acquired through a systematic but loosely structured program of on-the-job supervised training in hospitals or health-care units that provide dialysis services. Technicians are taught by the staff of the unit, according to an organized plan drawn up by the physicians, nurses, and experienced dialysis technicians. Classroom instruction, demonstrations, and independent study comprise the formal instruction of the program. Observation and supervised practice on the job provide the necessary clinical experience. As students acquire more knowledge and become proficient, more responsibility and different tasks are introduced by the instructors. The rate of progress and the total content of the program depend upon the philosophy and staff of the particular training facility and on the ability and performance of the trainees.

More complete preparatory programs are based on a general medicine core of courses. It includes human anatomy, physiology, characteristics and nature of kidney disease, medical terminology, concepts of infectious diseases, microbiology, professional relationships, medications, medical record keeping, patient-care skills, vital signs, and emergency care procedures.

The specialized dialysis portion of the curriculum includes the history and principles of dialysis therapy, dialysis systems and components, technical dialysis procedures, equipment repair and maintenance, dietary considerations, drug therapy and potential complications in use of medicines, and basic biochemical principles and factors in dialysis treatments. It also may include a study of nephrology, the characteristics of normal and abnormal kidneys, kidney transplantation, appropriate responses to behavior, ethical issues, and other studies.

Special requirements

In most states, dialysis technicians are not required to be registered, certified, or licensed; however, in some states dialysis technicians are required to pass a test before they can work with patients. A voluntary program for certification is offered by the Board of Nephrology Examiners (Nursing and Technology). The program is open to nurses and technicians. The purpose of the program is to identify safe and competent practitioners, to promote quality care of the nephrology patient, and to encourage the study of nursing and technological fields in nephrology.

Technicians who apply for the certification examination must be high-school graduates. They must have at least one year of experience in the care of nephrology patients who have serious renal disease requiring dialysis. The applicants must be performing the functions described in the position paper published by the American Nephrology Nurses' Association, and they must be actively working in the care of nephrology patients on a regular and continuing basis in a federally recognized end-stage renal disease (ESRD) facility or Veterans Administration renal program.

The certification examination contains questions related to anatomy, normal and abnormal physiology, principles of dialysis, treatment and technology related to the care of patients with renal failure, and general medical knowledge. Certified technicians must be recertified every six years. To be recertified, technicians must continue working in the field and present evidence of having completed continuing education units related to the career.

389

Opportunities for experience and exploration

Persons considering entry into this career may obtain information from the Board of Nephrology Examiners (Nursing and Technology). Until there are organized and accredited dialysis technician programs, those who are interested in the career must obtain information from local sources.

Sources of information include high-school guidance centers, public libraries, and occupational counselors at technical or community colleges. Specific information is best obtained from dialysis centers, dialysis units of local hospitals, home-health-care agencies, medical societies, schools of nursing, and physicians who specialize in nephrology.

Opportunities for experience and exploration will be most likely available in hospitals, dialysis centers, or physician's offices. Most hospitals have volunteer programs open to high-school students. Although these programs may not provide opportunities to participate directly in patient care, they do provide opportunities to observe various members of the health-care team in action.

Training as a nursing assistant or as an emergency medical technician will provide the opportunity for students to learn some of the skills required of renal dialysis technicians. The skills will also be marketable in various health-care agencies.

Methods of entering

The best way to enter this field is through a formal training program in a hospital or other training facility. In the absence of formal training, a well-qualified high-school graduate may contact the local hospital and dialysis center to determine the possibility of on-the-job training. Some hospitals provide training opportunities in work-study programs; the trainees are paid while they learn.

The Department of Veterans Affairs renal programs accept applications from employees of the Veterans Administration medical facility. Trainees in this program are paid and receive benefits while learning.

Other avenues of entry are through schools of nurse assisting, practical nursing or nursing, and programs for emergency medical technicians. In these programs, students learn basic health care and elementary nursing. After that, they must gain the specific knowledge, skills, and experience required for the renal dialysis career. The length of time required for people to progress through the dialysis program and advance to higher levels of responsibility should be shorter if they first complete a nursing or related training program.

Advancement

Dialysis technicians who have gained knowledge, skills, and experience advance to positions of greater responsibility and can work more independently. The experienced technician can advance to supervisory positions, assuming responsibility for managing the work of others. The necessary skills can be acquired on the job, in the classroom, or through independent study. Technicians may also advance to positions in which they teach new techniques to student technicians, patients, and families of patients.

Further education opens other opportunities for career advancement. For the dialysis technician who wishes to become a nurse, both part-time and full-time training programs are available in public and private schools and in hospitals throughout the country. The length of the programs ranges from one to two years. Nurses have more independence and advancement opportunities. They can administer drugs, perform additional procedures, and carry out other duties cited in nursing practice acts.

Dialysis technicians who complete a baccalaureate degree in nursing have wider avenues for advancement. Completion of these programs increases the variety and importance of the duties the technician can assume, and therefore increases the certainty of an interesting and rewarding career. Opportunities to study nursing are widely available. There is a national shortage of registered nurses, and the health-care industry is responding to this shortage by improving working conditions, salaries, and benefits.

A third area of advancement is counseling. The social and psychological services required by the patients and their families could provide an expanded role for technicians. The insights the technician/counselor brings to the dialysis team can be a valuable contribution.

Employment outlook

Because of dialysis, more patients are living longer. In 1988, there were nearly 90,000 people in the United States receiving dialysis treatment, more than double he number in 1978. The survival of these patients depends on the continuation of dialysis programs. This means that dialysis technicians will continue to be needed to provide treatment and related services.

Although the staffing pattern for dialysis treatment facilities and units varies, technicians make up a large percentage of the team that provides the treatments, up to as much as 80 percent in some centers. These facts indicate the demand for technicians will remain strong through the 1990s.

A negative factor that may develop in the future is a possible decrease in Medicare funding for end-stage renal disease (ESRD) programs involving dialysis treatments. If this occurs, it may slow down the rate at which patients enter dialysis programs; therefore, it may affect the need for technical personnel.

Another negative factor is the advancement in procedures that may remove the need for dialysis treatments in health-care facilities. For instance, should the percentage and number of individuals able to participate in home dialysis increase, the staffing requirements and numbers of dialysis facilities would be affected. Similarly, if more and more kidney transplants are done, the number of people needing dialysis will decrease and with it the demand for dialysis technicians. The number of kidney transplants increased nearly fourfold between 1978 and 1988, and this trend may continue, as it costs much less to treat a patient with a kidney transplant than with dialysis. For the foreseeable future, however, there will be a continuing need for dialysis technicians.

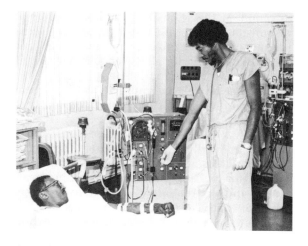
As a patient undergoes dialysis treatment, a dialysis technician monitors and adjusts the equipment.

scheduled for these times. Patients who work full-time or part-time often arrange to take their dialysis treatments at times that least interfere with their normal activities, and this may result in unusual working schedules for technicians. The work environment is usually a clean and comfortable patient-care setting.

The job may require some travel. Patients who use machine dialysis at home need assistance while being dialyzed. Although family members or friends are taught to assist the patient, technicians may have to stop in during any absence.

Earnings

Dialysis technicians earn salaries ranging from $14,000 to $25,000 per year, with entry-level personnel and trainees receiving the lowest rates of pay.

In addition to their salaries, technicians receive the customary benefits of sick leave, vacation, holiday leave, and health insurance. Also, as an incentive to further self-development, many hospitals or health-care centers pay for tuition and other education costs.

Social and psychological factors

Dialysis technicians have mastered a complex body of knowledge and have developed technical skills. The lives of the individuals they treat depend on their ability to practice these skills confidently and with a high degree of perfection. They must be able to keep up with a changing field and incorporate new technology as it becomes available.

Because of the nature of the treatment, technicians must make careful observations. Some observations require action; others require that the technician relate accurate and complete details to others on the dialysis team so they can take appropriate steps for the patient's care.

Dialysis technicians must be patient, attentive, systematic, and accurate in their work. The ability to work with patients, coworkers, and supervisors is an essential requirement for success in the career.

Technicians must remember that the complete management of the patient is under the

Conditions of work

Dialysis technicians customarily work forty hours per week. Some evening and weekend shifts may be required if dialysis treatments are direction of the team professionals, and final responsibility lies with the team leader. Technicians must recognize their limitations and should communicate all potentially important matters to the appropriate supervisor. This means that technicians must be able to accept their subordinate roles and realize that the care and safety of the patient come first. It also means that technicians have responsibilities that are both critical and rewarding. They must have good observation skills so that they can know how patients are reacting to the treatments and so that they can judge correctly when to report to other team members.

The satisfaction of being a dialysis technician comes from being part of a professional team that enables critically ill patients to function, even though their lives depend on dialysis treatments. Some patients are carried through a temporary crisis by dialysis treatments and return to normal after a period of time. Other patients may be best treated by kidney transplants. But while they wait for a suitable donated kidney, their lives depend on dialysis treatments.

GOE: 10.02.02; SIC: 8092; SOC: 369

◇ **SOURCES OF ADDITIONAL INFORMATION**

American Nephrology Nurses' Association
Box 56
North Woodbury Road
Pitman, NJ 08071

Board of Nephrology Examiners—Nursing and Technology
PO Box 4085
Madison, WI 53719

National Kidney Foundation
2 Park Avenue
New York, NY 10016

◇ **RELATED ARTICLES**

Volume 1: Health Care
Volume 2: Physician assistants; Licensed practical nurses; Registered nurses
Volume 3: Medical assistants; Nursing and psychiatric aides
Volume 4: Biomedical equipment technicians; Cardiac monitor technicians; Emergency medical technicians; Pulmonary function technicians

Dietetic technicians

Definition

Dietetic technicians are concerned with food-service management and nutritional-care services. Normally they work as members of a health team, under the direction of a dietitian, and in an institutional setting. In food-service management, dietetic technicians assist in planning menus that conform to established guidelines and supervise the food production operation on a day-to-day basis. They may act as administrative assistants to dietitians, doing such tasks as setting up work schedules, helping to implement cost-control measures, developing job specifications and job descriptions for food-service workers, and preparing and presenting orientation and education programs for workers. In the area of nutritional care services, dietetic technicians provide dietary counseling and instruction in basic principles of nutrition to individual patients and their families. They talk to these people to obtain dietary histories, assess the information they receive, and suggest improvements in selecting food, planning menus, and preparing food to best meet nutritional needs. They may help set up referrals for patients who will be in need of continued counseling and care in nutrition after leaving the institutional setting.

History

Dietetics is the study of food preparation, diet planning, and the resultant impact on health and well-being. In one way or another, dietetics has been an important concern throughout much of human history. Religious dietary laws, folk tradition, and medical lore have provided guidance about foods for thousands of years, although in an unscientific way. The Greek physician Hippocrates, recognized as the father of medicine, is one of the earliest names associated with a scientific understanding of the importance of diet in physiological processes. Hippocrates' observations and experimentation in the fourth and fifth centuries B.C. led him to some rather sound conclusions. A Roman cookbook from a few centuries later suggests that its author knew something about the importance of conserving certain constituents of food through proper preparation.

While the growth of scientific knowledge about food was slow until the eighteenth century, dietetics was always a central concern, as evidenced by medical writings from earliest times. Philosophy, superstition, social customs, and religion are among the many influences through the centuries. A few physicians in the late Middle Ages, notably Paracelsus, thought that properly chosen foods could help the body to heal itself. Despite the correct premise, however, the treatments they chose were often ineffective.

Perhaps the first discovery leading to the modern understanding of the real role of nutrition in our lives occurred about 1780. Antoine Lavoisier, sometimes called the father of nutrition, and Pierre-Simon LaPlace realized that metabolism, the physiological process in which food is broken down and used, is a form of combustion. This discovery, and Lavoisier's other work in the field, opened the way to much fruitful research, at first mostly by chemists, into how and why fats, carbohydrates, and proteins affect health.

By the late nineteenth century, a great deal was known about the benefits of good nutrition and proper food handling. Public interest in these subjects was substantial. Cooking schools that emphasized a scientific approach to food and health prospered in several large cities.

Around the turn of the century, several hospitals began to teach dietetics to nurses, stressing cookery as a means of therapy for the sick. Other workers were hired as specialists to prepare food for hospital patients in accordance with the most advanced knowledge of the day. The modern field of dietetics grew out of such early hospital work.

The importance of various minerals in diet emerged during the nineteenth century, but it was 1911 before vitamins were recognized by Casimir Funk as a category of substances needed in metabolic processes. Knowledge has accumulated fairly rapidly throughout this century on specific factors contained in food and the biochemical mechanisms through which they are utilized. With this growing knowledge, workers in the field of dietetics have been increasingly able to contribute to activities aimed at health maintenance, disease prevention, and restoration of health. In 1917, the American Dietetic Association was formed with thirty-nine charter members to promote and disseminate educational materials in order to improve the dietary habits of individuals and groups. It still serves as the principal professional organization for advancing the fields of dietetics and nutrition.

As dietetics developed and the field grew to encompass a wider range of activities, several separate categories of workers evolved, differentiated by the amount of their training and their type of activity. Two important levels of workers now are dietitians and dietetic technicians. Dietetic technicians are a relatively recent innovation designed to free the more highly trained dietitians to be more effective by allowing them to concentrate on work that only they are prepared to do. The separate status of dietetic technicians was given a boost in 1972 by a report of the Study Commission on Dietetics, an affiliate of the American Dietetic Association that urged various changes in the field and greater coordination of dietetics with other allied health professions.

Although the demand for dietetic technicians was uneven during the 1970s, and their eventual role in the field is still not clear, they are now considered a great asset in many settings. There are now about seventy-two approved dietetic technician training programs and about 115,000 people working as dietetic technicians in the early 1990s. As employers realize even more clearly the advantages of hiring technicians, the field is expected to continue to expand, at least for the foreseeable future.

At a health fair, a dietetic technician introduces a nutritional food program to an elderly woman.

Nature of the work

Dietetic technicians serve in two basic areas: as service personnel in food-service administration and as assistants in the nutrition care of individuals. Some dietetic technicians are involved in both kinds of activities. Most work in health-care facilities such as hospitals and nursing homes, although some dietetic technicians are employed in health agencies such as public health departments, neighborhood health centers, or home health agencies. Their specific duties and responsibilities vary widely, depending on the place of employment and on which of the two basic areas of the field they are working in.

In a medical center, where the food service prepares thousands of meals daily for patients and staff, there may be a staff of dietetic technicians, as well as dietetic aides and assistants and other food-service workers, all working under a staff of dietitians. In such cases, each of the dietetic technicians may specialize in a few activities out of the whole range of work. On the other hand, in a small organization, such as some nursing facilities, Head-Start programs, or geriatric care programs, there may be just one dietetic technician who is responsible for the overall management of the work done by the food-service staff and also for some nutrition counseling. The technician in a small facility may be supervised only by a consultant dietitian and probably reports directly to the administrator or director of the institution. Such a technician is apt to be involved in every phase of supervising and coordinating other workers.

Dietetic technicians are generally distinguished from dietetic assistants, who are food-service staff with less training than the technicians and who concentrate on supervising the details of the daily operations of the food service. In contrast, dietetic technicians are more management-oriented and generally have broader responsibilities. The range of activities of both categories of workers depends on the type of employer, however.

Dietetic technicians working in food-service administration may be involved in various phases of planning and preparation, perhaps spending a substantial part of their time on the phone or doing paperwork. They may set up the work and time schedules for other employees, based on their knowledge and experience of the time required for different production activities, and post updated schedules and other information at designated times during each day. Later they may follow up by helping to prepare evaluations of the food program and assessments of the efficiency of employees or particular production processes. They may help to develop standardized recipes, adapting them to the particular needs and circumstances of their institution. They may write modified diet plans for patients, using an approved diet manual, and incorporating the patients' preferences or physicians' orders. They may process regular meal orders received from patients or from medical staff members who choose patients' food, and they sometimes help patients select their menus. They may be responsible for keeping track of food items on hand, processing routine orders to the suppliers, and ordering miscellaneous supplies as needed, as well as supervising food storage. They may be involved with budget-control measures in the department and may participate in dietary department conferences. They may regularly serve as administrative assistants for dietitians, or substitute for dietitians on an occasional basis, and thereby become somewhat involved with various other office activities normally left to dietitians, such as basic meal planning.

At other times, dietetic technicians work more directly in the kitchen, overseeing and coordinating actual food production activities, including the making of special therapeutic food items as well as more routine fare. They may even participate in the preparation of meals; more usually, however, they monitor the preparations. They may supervise dietetic aides, who distribute food in the cafeteria and assemble and serve meals to patients in their rooms. Dietetic technicians may be responsible for maintaining and improving the overall standards of the food-service operation, or they may be charged specifically with supervising and upholding high standards in such areas as sanitation, housekeeping, safety in equipment operation, and security procedures.

In some large health-care facilities, the cafeteria is a big operation that dietetic technicians may manage. The running of the cafeteria and the patient food service generally overlap somewhat, but each requires separate attention in planning and many production activities.

Another area of dietetic technician responsibility in a food-service setting may be training other personnel. When they are first hired, food-service workers (who are the most directly involved with food production), dietetic aides and assistants, and other dietetic technicians must be instructed in methods, procedures, and equipment operation and maintenance. Dietetic technicians may present training sessions that introduce employees to such routine aspects of the operation.

Dietetic technicians who specialize in nutrition care and counseling work under the direction of a clinical or community dietitian. They may work in a health-care facility, where their duties include observing and interviewing patients about their eating habits and food preferences. Dietetic technicians report these diet histories, the progress that patients are making, and other such information they have gathered to dietitians. They or the dietitians utilize the information in outlining any desired modifications to basic diet plans and menus. They may supervise the serving of food to be sure that meals are nutritionally adequate and are in conformance with the physician's prescription.

Dietetic technicians teach the basic principles of sound nutrition, food selection and preparation, and good eating habits to patients and their families, so that after leaving the health-care facility the patients may continue to benefit. Later the technicians may contact those patients to see how well they are staying on the modified diets and to help them make any further adjustments in accordance with their preferences, habits at home, and the physician's prescription. Dietetic technicians may also be involved in instructing employees in the policies and procedures for nutrition care of patients.

Dietetic technicians specializing in nutrition care may work in community programs rather than inside a hospital or other inpatient health-care facility. Employed by a public health department, clinic, youth center, visiting nurse association, home health agency, or similar organization, dietetic technicians have many of the same counseling duties as they would in an inpatient institutional setting. They may work with low-income families, especially in inner cities, teaching the economics of food purchasing, preparation, and nutrition. They may assist people who have recently arrived from other countries to adapt their accustomed menu patterns to available food items and to purchase and prepare nutritious foods. Or they may help the elderly, parents of small children, or other special groups who develop characteristic dietary questions and problems.

Dietetic technicians may make follow-up home visits to check on menu plans, food buying, and cooking skills of people whom they have previously counseled. In some cases technicians may assist in establishing a permanent arrangement for continuing nutrition care and assistance for the needy, either in the home or at central locations, such as hot meals for the elderly or school lunch programs.

As part of a broad educational effort in the community, dietetic technicians may help prepare brochures, visual aids, and other teaching materials. Making healthy people aware of nutritional issues and of what they should change in their diets is a particularly important kind of work, because it may prevent the future development of many major health problems, such as heart disease, hypertension, diabetes, obesity, and other chronic conditions. Technicians may also contact and work with other community groups to promote interest in nutrition.

Some dietetic technicians work in other settings—in schools, colleges, industrial food-service establishments, and other organizations where large quantities of food are regularly prepared. These positions require technicians with some of the same administrative skills but do not emphasize meeting special dietary needs of individuals or the educational and counseling aspect of nutrition-care work. Other dietetic technicians are employed in research kitchens, working under the supervision of a dietitian, and taking care of such support activities as inventorying and ordering stocks of ingredients, inspecting equipment for proper functioning, weighing and packaging food items, checking for inaccuracies in precise procedures, and maintaining records.

Requirements

Anyone considering becoming a dietetic technician should appreciate good food and have a flair for making it attractive and tasty. Equally important are a genuine interest in people and in performing services for them and the ability to follow orders combined with a good potential for developing basic management skills.

Dietetic technicians must be in sound mental and physical health and should have reserves of patience and understanding, not only for their coworkers but also for patients who are ill or uncooperative. They must be able to

A dietetic technician discusses the weeklong menu with the cook of a soup kitchen. The technician must ensure that the cook is complying with government nutritional standards.

In post–high-school training programs, students can expect to take a mix of general education courses, such as English, biological sciences, humanities, social science, business mathematics, and technical courses. The technical instruction is likely to be in such subjects as normal nutrition and menu planning; nutrition related to disease and modified diets; interviewing techniques; food science; food purchasing, storage, preparation, and service; quantity food production; organization and management of food-service systems; sanitation and safety; laboratory work; and introduction to the organization of patient-care facilities and community agencies.

The period of supervised clinical experience, sometimes called a practicum, may last anywhere from a few weeks to a whole semester, depending on the school. It is intended to give the student a close look at the work of a dietetic technician, as well as provide experience that can be valuable during permanent employment.

Students may be assigned for the practicum to a patient-care facility, where they help with preparing schedules, ordering food, cooking, or instructing patients. If they are assigned to a health agency, they might accompany a nutritionist on home visits, help with teaching individuals, assist in demonstrating cooking techniques to groups, or observe and analyze information on the types of food people purchase at local grocery stores.

Special requirements

There are no general licensure requirements in this field. Technicians who have completed an approved education program, however, may take an examination to determine their credentials, given by the Commission on Dietetic Registration, and upon successful completion be designated a Dietetic Technician, Registered (DTR). Continuing education requirements are maintained by the Commission on Dietetic Registration. More than 2,200 dietetic technicians are members of the American Dietetic Association.

Opportunities for experience and exploration

High-school students interested in dietetics should try to find a part-time, summer, or even volunteer job in a food service of a hospital or

communicate well, both orally and on paper, and have a knack for planning and good organization. Dietetic technicians must be adaptable and ready to explore new ideas and methods, because there is a steady flow of changes in food products, equipment, and administrative practices.

The educational preparation required for this career includes a high-school diploma or its equivalent plus completion of a two-year, American Dietetic Association–approved program leading to an associate degree. This vocational preparation is available in junior and community colleges, and combines classroom studies with practical instruction and experience in the field under real working conditions.

During high school, prospective technicians should take courses in biology, chemistry, business mathematics, typing, and English and other courses that improve communications skills.

other health-care organization. This kind of position allows them to observe the work of the dietary department and to ask questions of people involved in the field. If such a job isn't possible, students should consider a job in another area of the hospital, which could provide first-hand contact with the general environment that dietetic technicians work in. A job in a non-hospital food service, even a restaurant kitchen, could also be of value. With the help of teachers or counselors, students may arrange to meet with and talk to a dietitian or dietetic technician. Extracurricular activities such as service clubs might help students to judge their organizational and administrative abilities and their interest in helping people as individuals.

Methods of entering

Contacts gained during the clinical experience part of their training program are usually the best sources of first jobs for dietetic technicians. Applying to the personnel offices of potential employers can be another productive approach. Other good places to check are the placement office at the college conducting the training program, the job listings in health-care journals, newspaper classified ads, and private and public employment agencies.

In some areas close to schools that have dietetic technician training programs, the local labor market is oversupplied, so that new graduates may have better results if they extend their job search to other areas where competition is less intense.

Advancement

Beginning jobs are usually rather closely supervised, because there is so much that the dietetic technicians must learn about the operations of their new employer. After a time, however, the technicians are often able to take on greater responsibilities and earn higher pay while still staying with the same employer, either keeping the same title but expanding the range of activities, or officially changing positions — for example, from dietetic technician to the position of kitchen manager. Experience and proven ability allow such advancement inside many organizations.

Some dietetic technicians return to school on a full- or part-time basis to complete a baccalaureate degree program in a related field such as dietetics, nutrition, food science, or food-service management. To become a dietitian, a year of internship is necessary after the baccalaureate degree is completed.

Employment outlook

The outlook for dietetic technicians, particularly those with certification, is generally very good for the foreseeable future. This is partly because of the strong emphasis on nutrition and health in this country and the fact that more health services will be used in future years. The population is growing, and the percentage of older people, who need the most health services, is increasing even faster.

Another reason for the positive outlook for dietetic technicians is that health-care organizations now realize the advantages of utilizing them for many jobs. Many tasks dietitians used to perform can be done well by dietetic technicians, while dietitians continue to be in short supply and are more expensive to hire.

Earnings

Earnings vary widely depending on the employer, the education and experience of the dietetic technician, the region of the country, and the nature of the technician's responsibilities. Information on earnings is sketchy. In general, however, beginning technicians can expect to receive salaries of about $14,000 a year. Technicians with several years' experience can make between $14,000 and $20,000 a year. Fringe benefits usually include paid vacations and holidays, health insurance plans, and meals during working hours.

Conditions of work

Dietary departments in health-care facilities are generally clean, well lighted, well ventilated, and near to the kitchen area. Kitchens and serving areas may be intensely active at peak hours, often very hot, steamy, and noisy. Modern equipment, when correctly used, has eliminated most of the accident hazards that used to be associated with a food-service operation.

Most dietetic technicians in food-service administration jobs work forty-hour weeks, in eight-hour shifts, and may be required to work some nights, weekends, or on an irregular schedule, depending on the type of employer. Shifts usually are divided into three eight-hour periods, with each shift responsible for preparing one major meal.

Much of the time dietetic technicians may be on their feet. Periodically there may be intense pressure to work quickly and accurately. At such times, technicians must be able to give full attention to the details of their own job while coordinating the work of other employees.

Dietetic technicians employed in health agencies or research organizations are likely to have more normal hours and a smoother pace of work. Working in nutrition care may involve local traveling to visit patients.

Social and psychological factors

For someone who enjoys food, helping people, and the rewards of seeing a planned and organized effort worked out to its conclusion at every meal, this field can be very satisfying. Sometimes, however, one confronts failure in the kitchen; the work may seem to be endless and very routine; and it is necessary to face the fact that good nutrition cannot solve all health problems. Nonetheless, many dietetic technicians find the sense of contributing and achievement outweighs such negatives.

Dietetic technicians working in nutrition care may have a more personal sense of reward because they often have more contact with individuals who need their services.

Dietetic technicians should be able to work well in groups and to tolerate the stress of responding to emergency situations. Because technicians are a middle link connecting the dietitians with dietetic assistants and other food-service workers, technicians may feel the pressure from both sides. A stable personality and a sense of perspective will make it easier to do the job well on such occasions.

GOE: 05.05.17; SIC: 8049; SOC: 302

◇ **SOURCES OF ADDITIONAL INFORMATION**

American Dietetic Association
216 West Jackson Boulevard, Suite 800
Chicago, IL 60606

National Health Council
350 Fifth Avenue, Suite 1118
New York, NY 10118

◇ **RELATED ARTICLES**

Volume 1: Food Service; Health Care
Volume 2: Dietitians; Food technologists; Health service administrators; Restaurant and food service managers
Volume 3: Cooks, chefs, and bakers; Food service workers; Homemaker-home health aides
Volume 4: Home-health technicians

Electrocardiograph technicians

Definition

Electrocardiograph technicians, sometimes called *EKG technicians,* operate electronic instruments called electrocardiograph machines. These machines detect the electronic impulses that come from a patient's heart during a heartbeat and record that information in the form of a paper graph called an electrocardiogram. By recording these impulses, the machines can provide physicians with information about the action of the heart during individual heartbeats. To operate these machines, electrocardiograph technicians attach electrodes to specified areas of the patient's body, move the chest electrodes to different positions on the chest, and operate controls on the paper that record information about the positions of the electrodes. After the test, they remove the paper from the machine and forward the paper record to the physician for interpretation and analysis. Electrocardiograph technicians sometimes conduct other tests, such as vectorcardiograms and phonocardiograms.

History

The historical roots of electrocardiography can be traced back 300 years to the work of the Dutch anatomist and physiologist Jan Swammerdam who demonstrated in 1678 that a frog's leg will contract when stimulated with an electrical current. It was not until 1856, however, that two German anatomists, Albert von Kolliker and Heinrich M. Mueller, showed that when the frog's heart contracted, it produced a small electric current. In succeeding years the electrical behavior of beating hearts was extensively studied but always with the chest open and the heart exposed.

In 1887, Augustus Desire Waller discovered that the electrical current of the human heart could be measured with the chest closed. He was able to do this by placing one electrode on a person's chest and another on the person's back and connecting them to a monitoring device. In 1903, a professor of physiology in Germany, Willem Einthoven, perfected the monitoring device involved so that even the faintest currents from the heart could be detected and recorded graphically.

Throughout the rest of this century, medical researchers have made further advancements and refinements on this machine. By the 1940s, for instance, portable electrocardiographs were in use, allowing electrocardiograms to be made in a physician's office or at a patient's bedside. During the 1960s, computerized electrocardiographs were developed to aid physicians in the interpretation of test results. Today, electrocardiographs are widely used in routine physicals, in presurgical physicals, in diagnosing disease, and in monitoring the effects of drug therapy. The continued wide use of these devices ensures a continuing need for trained personnel to operate them.

Nature of the work

Electrocardiograph technicians are responsible for preparing the patient and the machine before the procedure begins, for monitoring the patient and the machine during the procedure, and for various other duties related to the operation of the machine.

In preparing patients for the electrocardiography, technicians first explain the procedure to the patient. They then attach the electrodes, anywhere from three to twelve in number, to the chest, arms, and legs of the patient. In many cases, they apply an electrolyte gel between the electrodes and the skin to help the monitor pick up the signals more easily.

During the test, technicians move the chest electrodes to different positions on the chest to get multiple tracings of the electrical activity occurring in various parts of the heart muscle. Meanwhile a stylus records the tracings on a long roll of graph paper. The test may be given while the patient is resting or while doing exercise.

While the machine is in operation, technicians must be sure that the machine is not recording stray electrical impulses, such as those coming from tremors in other muscles or from electrical vibrations of nearby equipment. They should also be able to detect other kinds of false readings and to take necessary corrective actions.

To do this work correctly, technicians must know about the anatomy and the function of the heart and chest. Only by knowing anatomy well can they avoid placing the electrodes incorrectly. They must also know all about the machine so that they can spot malfunctions or other machine-related problems quickly.

After the electrocardiogram has been made, technicians remove the paper, edit or annotate the tracing as necessary, and forward it to the physician. Technicians must keep the machine supplied with paper and know generally how well the machine is operating; however, they are usually not responsible for repairing the machine.

Electrocardiograph technicians sometimes help to conduct other tests, such as vectorcardiographs, which produce multiple tracings of different aspects of the heart's electrical activity; phonocardiographs, which are sound recordings of the heart's valves and of the blood passing through them; stress testing, which records the heart's activity during physical activity; and echocardiographs, which use ultrasound to produce images of the heart's chambers and valves.

Another kind of test that electrocardiograph technicians are sometimes involved with is Holter monitoring. Holter monitoring involves the patient wearing a small monitor device strapped to the body, often for twenty-four hours, while going about normal daily activities. Technicians who do this kind of testing are often called Holter scanning technicians. Their duties include attaching and strapping the test equipment to the patient, checking to be sure that equipment is operating correctly, and reviewing and analyzing the information that comes from the monitor.

In addition to these duties, electrocardiograph technicians may also schedule appointments, write and type reports, and maintain patients' files.

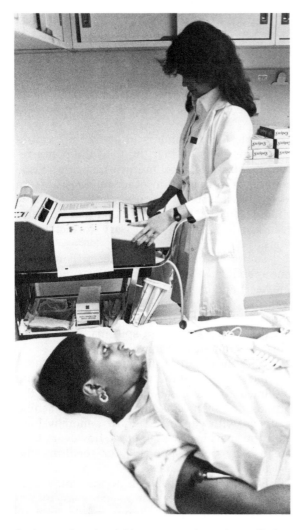

An electrocardiograph technician operates equipment that graphically records the electrical currents generated by a patient's heart.

Most electrocardiograph technicians work in hospitals, but other possible job locations include clinics, physicians' offices, or medical schools.

Requirements

Electrocardiograph technicians need to have good mechanical aptitude and the ability to follow directions. They should also have personalities that allow them to perform well under pressure, including medical emergencies, and to treat sick or nervous patients in a pleasant and reassuring manner.

Most electrocardiograph technicians are trained on the job in hospitals or in companies that manufacture the electrocardiograph equipment. These training programs, lasting from one month for basic electrocardiograph tests to up to one year for more advanced tests, teach the technicians how to operate the machines and read the tracings.

The basic requirement for receiving this kind of on-the-job training is a high-school diploma or its equivalent. During high school, students should take courses in English, health, biology, and typing. In addition, students might consider courses in the social sciences, if they are available, to help them understand their patients' social and psychological needs.

In recent years, some vocational, technical, and junior colleges have begun to offer one- and two-year training programs in electrocardiography. These programs give technicians more extensive preparation in the subject and allow them to earn certificates for the one-year program and associate degrees for the two-year program. These programs are still rather new, and only a few of them have received full accreditation.

Special requirements

At the present time, electrocardiograph technicians are not required to be licensed; however, there is credentialing available on a voluntary basis from the National Board of Cardiovascular Testing. These credentials may help them in advancement and in obtaining better salaries. In some cases, hospitals may require that electrocardiograph technicians have received these credentials.

Opportunities for experience and exploration

Prospective electrocardiograph technicians will find it difficult to gain any direct experience on a part-time basis in electrocardiography. Their first direct experience with the work generally comes during their on-the-job training sessions. They may, however, be able to gain some exposure to patient-care activities in general by signing up for volunteer work at a local hospital. In addition, they could arrange to visit a hospital, clinic, or physician's office where electrocardiographs are taken. In this way they might be able to watch a technician at work or at least talk to a technician about what the work is like.

Methods of entering

Because most electrocardiograph technicians receive their initial training on their first job, great care should be taken in finding this first employer. Attention should be paid not only to the pay and working conditions but also to the kind of on-the-job training that is provided. In many cases, hospitals will earn reputations for their training programs, and high-school guidance counselors may be the best source of information about those reputations. Additional information can be gained from classified ads in the newspaper, from friends and relatives who may work in hospitals, and from contacting local hospitals directly.

For students who graduate from one- to two-year training programs, finding a first job should be easier. First, employers are always eager to hire people who are already trained. Second, these graduates can be less concerned about the training programs offered by their employers. Third, they should find that their teachers and guidance counselors can be excellent sources of information about job possibilities in the area. If the training program includes any practical experience, graduates may find that the hospital in which they trained or worked before graduation would be willing to hire them after graduation.

Advancement

Opportunities for advancement are best for electrocardiograph technicians who learn to do or assist with more complex procedure, such as stress testing, Holter monitoring, echocardiography, and cardiac catheterization. With proper training and experience, they may eventually become cardiovascular technicians, cardiopulmonary technicians, cardiology technologists, or other specialty technicians or technologists.

In addition to these kinds of specialty positions, experienced technicians may also advance to supervisory and training posts.

Employment outlook

The total number of people employed as electrocardiograph technicians is expected to grow about as fast as the average for all occupations through the 1990s. This growth will be caused by a number of factors, most notable among them being the increased use by physicians of electrocardiographs during routine physical examinations, examinations prior to surgery, and in other specialized diagnostic situations. Another factor contributing to the increased demand for electrocardiograph technicians is the growth in the population in general, and, more importantly, a growth in the percentage of the population represented by older people, who are the most frequent users of electrocardiograph testing.

Not all of this growth in the use of electrocardiograph testing, however, will translate to growth in the number of people hired as electrocardiograph technicians. The reason for this is that electrocardiograph equipment and procedures are now much more efficient than they used to be. This means that one technician can perform many more tests each day than was previously possible, and, because of this, fewer technicians are required. In addition, the newer equipment is easier to use, which has allowed some hospitals to train personnel other than electrocardiograph technicians in the operation of the equipment, thus further reducing the demand for electrocardiograph technicians.

Earnings

Beginning electrocardiograph technicians can expect to receive starting salaries of approximately $14,000 a year. Experienced technicians can expect to earn considerably more, in some settings more than $25,000 a year.

Electrocardiograph technicians with formal training earn more money than those who trained on the job, and those who are able to perform more sophisticated tests are paid more than those who perform only the basic ones.

Electrocardiograph technicians working in hospitals receive the same fringe benefits as other hospital workers. These benefits usually include hospitalization insurance, paid vacations, and sick leave. In some cases they also include educational assistance, pension benefits, and uniform allowances.

Conditions of work

Electrocardiograph technicians should be able to adapt well to changing situations, as each patient presents a different personality and a different medical task. Technicians should also be able to work under pressure and to remain calm in emergencies, as pressure and emergencies are often a part of providing care to patients.

Electrocardiograph technicians usually work in clean, quiet, well-lighted surroundings. They should expect to do a good deal of standing and to move equipment frequently. They generally work five-day, forty-hour weeks, although technicians working in small hospitals may be on twenty-four-hour call for emergencies, and all technicians in hospitals, large or small, can expect to do occasional evening or weekend work. With the growing emphasis in health care on cost containment, more jobs are likely to develop in various outpatient settings, so that in the future it is likely that electrocardiograph technicians will work more often in clinics, offices of cardiologists, HMOs, and other nonhospital locations.

Social and psychological factors

Electrocardiograph technicians do most of their work with patients who either are ill or who have reason to fear they might be ill. As such, there are opportunities for the technicians to do these people some good or some harm. A well-conducted test can reduce anxieties or make a physician's job easier; a misplaced electrode or an error in record keeping could cause an incorrect diagnosis. Electrocardiograph technicians need to be able to cope with that responsibility and to conduct themselves consistently in the best interests of their patients.

Part of the technician's job includes putting patients at ease about the procedure they are to undergo. Towards that end, technicians should be pleasant, patient, alert, and able to understand and sympathize with the feelings of others. In explaining the nature of the procedure to patients, they should be able to do so in a calm, reassuring, and confident manner.

Inevitably, some patients will try to get information about their medical situation from the technician. In cases like this, technicians need to be both tactful and firm in explaining that they are only making the electrocardiogram; the interpretation is for the physician to make.

Another large part of a technician's job involves getting along well with other members of the hospital staff. This task is sometimes made more difficult by the fact that in most hospitals there is a formal, often rigid, status structure, and electrocardiograph technicians may find themselves in a relatively low position in that structure. In emergency situations or at other moments of frustration, electrocardiograph technicians may find themselves dealt with brusquely or angrily. Technicians should not take outbursts or rude treatment personally, but instead should respond with stability and maturity.

GOE: 10.03.01; SIC: 801, 806; SOC: 369

◇ SOURCES OF ADDITIONAL INFORMATION

American Cardiology Technologists Association
1980 Isaac Newton Square, South
Reston, VA 22090

National Alliance of Cardiovascular Technologists
1133 15th Street, NW, Suite 1000
Washington, DC 20005

National Society for Cardiovascular and Cardiopulmonary Technology
1133 15th Street, NW, Suite 1000
Washington, DC 20005

◇ RELATED ARTICLES

Volume 1: Health Care
Volume 2: Licensed practical nurses; Medical technologists; Physician assistants; Registered nurses
Volume 3: Medical assistants; Nursing and psychiatric aides
Volume 4: Biomedical equipment technicians; Cardiac monitor technicians; Electroencephalographic technicians; Medical laboratory technicians

Electroencephalographic technicians

Definition

Electroencephalographic technicians, sometimes called *EEG technicians,* operate electronic instruments called electroencephalographs. These instruments measure and record the brain's electrical activity. The information gathered in this way is used by physicians (usually neurologists) to diagnose and determine the effects of certain diseases and injuries. Brain tumors, cerebral vascular strokes, epilepsy, some metabolic disorders, and brain injuries caused by accidents or by infectious diseases are among the problems that electroencephalographs can help neurologists to investigate. With the information gathered by the electroencephalographic technician, physicians are able to prescribe medications or perform surgeries to correct the diagnosed problems.

Electroencephalographic technicians prepare patients for this procedure by first taking a medical history from the patient, then explaining the procedure to the patient, and finally fastening electrodes to the patient's head. They attach the terminals of the electrodes to monitoring devices and then carefully watch both the patient and the machine. Electroencephalographic technicians observe the patient's behavior, make notes on the graph for later reference by the physician, and perform minor adjustments and repairs to the machine as necessary.

Electroencephalographic technicians may also monitor other kinds of tracings of the patient's electrical activity, such as electromyograms (recordings of the electrical activity associated with the skeletal muscles), electrocardiograms (recordings of the activity associated with the heart), and electrooculograms (recordings of the electrical activity associated with the eye).

Young people interested in a career in this medical field should realize that the terms "electroencephalographic technician" and "electroencephalographic technologist" are sometimes used interchangeably and do not necessarily indicate any different level of skills or training.

In this article, the term "technician" is used, except to refer to those people who have received certification as Certified/Registered Electroencephalographic Technologists or as Registered Electroencephalographic Technologists; however, it is possible that in coming years the term "technologist" will come to replace "technician" as the job designation for this career.

History

The living brain is constantly discharging small electrical impulses that can be picked up from the surface of the head, amplified, and then recorded on paper. These currents were first detected in England in 1875 by Richard Caton. He reported having placed electrodes on the exposed brains of rabbits and monkeys. The picture, usually called a tracing, of this electrical brain activity is known as an electroencephalogram, or by its abbreviated term, EEG.

Other researchers independently discovered this phenomenon of brain activity in the late 1800s and early 1900s. In 1929, the first practical electroencephalograph for use on human beings was developed in Germany by Hans Berger. Berger's work also included extensive testing of both diseased and healthy brains.

In the mid-1930s, the use of electroencephalograms to diagnose epilepsy was developed. Shortly afterward, they were used to locate brain tumors. Thus, by the end of the 1930s, a new field had opened up through which doctors and technicians could improve the diagnosis and treatment of neurological diseases.

Nature of the work

The basic principle behind all of the diagnostic uses of electroencephalography is that the electrical impulses given off by the brain, often thought of as brain waves, vary according to the age, activity, and condition of the brain. Specifically, it is known that certain troubling conditions of the brain are accompanied by characteristic kinds of brain waves. Therefore, a neurologist (a physician specially trained in the study of the brain) can study a patient's electroencephalogram, the graphic representation of these brain waves, and be aided in making a diagnosis of the person's illness or injury. In some complex medical cases, electroencephalograms are also used as an aid in determining whether or not death has occurred in a patient.

The main responsibility of the electroencephalographic technician in this endeavor is to produce the electroencephalograms under the supervision of an electroencephalographic technologist or a physician specializing in electroencephalography. The first step with a new patient is always to take a simplified medical

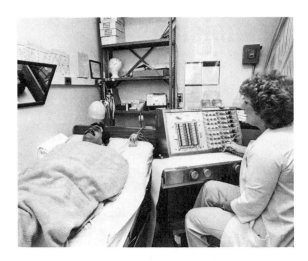

Before conducting any tests, an electroencephalographic technician ask the patient a few questions concerning his medical history and discusses the testing procedure.

history of the patient. This entails asking questions and recording answers about the person's family and personal history and specifically about his or her past health and present illness. This provides the technician with needed information about the patient's condition. It also provides an opportunity to help the patient relax before the test.

The technician then applies electrodes to the patient's head according to a prearranged plan. The electrodes are held in place by various methods, depending on the hospital, including adhesive paste, glue, and, rarely, needles. Often, the technician must choose the best combination of instrument controls and placement of electrodes to produce the kind of tracing that has been requested. In some cases, the technician will be given special instructions by the electroencephalographic technologist or the physician concerning where to place the electrodes.

Once the electrodes are in place on the patient's head, the examination can begin. The electrodes are connected to the recording equipment, which includes a bank of extremely sensitive electronic amplifiers. Tracings from each electrode are made as a row of pens move up and down on a moving strip of paper in response to the amplified impulses coming from the brain. The resulting graph is a recording of the waves of the patient's brain during the test.

Electroencephalographic technicians are not responsible for interpreting the tracings (that is the job of the neurologist); however, they must be able to recognize any readings on the tracing that are coming from somewhere other than from the brain, such as from eye

movement or from nearby electrical equipment. These stray readings are known as artifacts, and technicians must be able to determine which kinds of artifacts should be expected for an individual patient on the basis of his or her medical history or present illness. They should also be able to conduct their procedures so that any of these artifacts can be readily identified if they occur.

Faulty recordings may also be caused by faulty techniques on the part of the technician or by malfunctions in the machine. Technicians must be able to detect false readings of these sorts also. In the case of mechanical problems, technicians notify their supervisors so that the machine can be repaired by trained equipment repairers.

Throughout the procedure, electroencephalographic technicians observe the patient's behavior and make detailed notes about any aspect of the behavior that might be of use to the physician later in interpreting the tracing. They also keep watch on the patient's brain, heart, and breathing functions during the procedure. They must be able to recognize any change in the status of any of these functions that might indicate that the patient is in any kind of danger.

During the testing, the patient may be either asleep or awake and alert. In some cases, the physician may want recordings taken in both states. Sometimes drugs or special procedures are required to create in the patient a specific kind of condition that the physician has requested. Seeing that the drugs or procedures are properly administered is frequently a responsibility of the technician.

Electroencephalographic technicians need a basic understanding of the kinds of medical emergencies that can occur during this procedure. By being prepared in this way, they can react properly if one of these emergencies should arise. For instance, if a patient suffers an epileptic seizure, technicians must know what to do.

Electroencephalographic technicians may be involved with taking other special kinds of electroencephalograms. For example, in a procedure called ambulatory monitoring, activity of the heart as well as the brain is tracked over a twenty-four-hour period by a small recording device on the patient's side. In evoked potential testing, a special machine is used to measure the brain's response to specific types of stimulus. An area where electroencephalograms are increasingly used on a routine basis is in the operating room to monitor patients during major surgery.

Besides conducting various kind of electroencephalograms, other duties of electroencephalographic technicians may include keeping the machine in good working order, performing minor repairs to the machine (major repairs require specially trained repairers), scheduling appointments, and ordering supplies. In some cases they may have some supervisory responsibilities; however, most supervision is done by electroencephalographic technologists.

Requirements

Electroencephalographic technicians need good vision and manual dexterity, an aptitude for working with mechanical and electronic equipment, and the ability to get along well with patients, their families, and with members of the hospital staff.

Prospective electroencephalographic technicians should plan on getting a high-school diploma, as it is usually a requirement for entry into any kind of training program for electroencephalographic technicians, whether in a school or on the job. Specific course requirements, if any, will vary from program to program, and early in their high-school career students should investigate entrance requirements of programs they might be interested in to make sure that they can meet all of the requirements. In general, students will find it helpful to have had three years of mathematics, including algebra, and three years of science, including biology, chemistry, and physics. In addition, students should take courses in English, especially those that help them improve their reading, writing, and speaking skills, and in social sciences so that they can better understand the social and psychological needs of their patients.

There are two main types of post–high-school training available for electroencephalographic technicians: on-the-job training and formal classroom training. Many electroencephalographic technicians currently working received on-the-job training; however, electroencephalographic equipment is becoming so sophisticated that many employers are now especially interested in hiring technicians who have received prior formal training.

On-the-job training generally lasts from a few months to one year, depending on the special requirements of the employer. Trainees learn how to handle electroencephalographic equipment and how to carry out procedures by observing and receiving instruction from senior electroencephalographic technicians or technologists.

Formal training for electroencephalographic technicians consists of both practice in the clinical laboratory and instruction in the classroom. The classroom instruction usually focuses on basic subjects such as human anatomy, physiology, neuroanatomy, clinical neurology, neuropsychiatry, clinical and internal medicine, psychology, and electronics and instrumentation. The postsecondary programs usually last from one to two years and are offered by hospitals, medical centers, and community or technical colleges.

Special requirements

Students who have completed one year of on-the-job training or who have graduated from a formal training program in electroencephalography may apply for certification and/or registration. There are two separate boards of certification and registration for electroencephalographic technicians in the United States: the American Board of Certified and Registered Electroencephalographic Technicians and Technologists (ABCRETT) and the American Board of Registration of Electroencephalographic Technologists (ABRET).

The American Board of Certified and Registered Electroencephalographic Technicians and Technologists offers the opportunity for certification at three levels: as a Certified Medical Electroencephalographic Technician (C.M.E.T.), as a Certified/Registered Electroencephalographic Technologist (C.R.E.T.), and as a Certified/Registered Neurodiagnostic Technologist (C.R.N.T.).

The American Board of Registration of Electroencephalographic Technologists registers electroencephalographic technologists at one level of experience and education, that is, as a Registered Electroencephalographic Technologist (R/EEGT). Technicians who have been in the field for at least one year and who have completed a required number of electroencephalographic recordings can earn this registration by passing an examination.

Those certified/registered technologists who have been on the job for five years or more and who have taken on more responsibilities and other electrophysiological testing should consider advanced levels of certification and registration.

Although none of these forms of registration or certification are requirements for employment, they are acknowledgments of the technician's training and do make advancement easier. They may also provide increases in salary ranges.

Electroencephalographic technicians
Medical and Health Technician Occupations

Opportunities for experience and exploration

Prospective electroencephalographic technicians will find it difficult to gain any direct experience on a part-time basis in electroencephalography. Their first direct experience with the work will generally come during their on-the-job training sessions or in the practical-experience portion of their formal training. They may, however, be able to gain some exposure to patient-care activities in general by signing up for volunteer work at a local hospital. In addition, they could arrange to visit a hospital, clinic, or doctor's office where electroencephalograms are taken. In this way, they might be able to watch a technician at work or at least talk to a technician about what the work is like.

Methods of entering

Technicians who receive their training in a hospital or in a junior, community, or technical college or other one- or two-year institution affiliated with a hospital can often obtain permanent employment in the hospital where they receive their training.

Prospective technicians can also find employment through classified ads in newspapers and through contacting the personnel offices of hospitals, medical centers, clinics, and government agencies employing electroencephalographic technicians.

Advancement

Opportunities for advancement for electroencephalographic technicians are good if they become certified/registered electroencephalographic technologists. Electroencephalographic technicians who do not take this step will find their opportunities for advancement severely limited.

Electroencephalographic technologists are usually assigned to conducting more difficult or specialized electroencephalograms. They also supervise other electroencephalographic technicians, arrange work schedules, and teach techniques to new trainees. They may have other administrative duties, such as managing a laboratory, keeping records, scheduling appointments, ordering supplies, and establishing procedures.

Electroencephalographic technologists may advance to chief electroencephalographic technologist and thus take on even more responsibilities in laboratory management and in teaching new personnel and students from electroencephalographic training programs. Chief electroencephalographic technologists generally work under the direction of an electroencephalographer, neurologist, or neurosurgeon.

Employment outlook

The total number of people employed as electroencephalographic technicians is expected to grow much faster than the average for all occupations at least through the year 2000. This growth will be caused by a number of factors, most notable among them being the increased use of electroencephalographs in surgery, in diagnosing and monitoring patients, and in research on the human brain. Electroencephalographic technicians will be used to conduct new forms of electrophysiological examinations that are being developed by researchers in clinical neurophysiology.

Another factor contributing to the increased demand for electroencephalographic technicians is the growth in the population in general, and, more importantly, a growth in the percentage of the population represented by older people, who are the most frequent users of health-care services.

Earnings

Electroencephalographic technicians receive starting salaries that average approximately $15,000 a year. Experienced electroencephalographic technicians earn salaries averaging approximately $22,000 a year but sometimes ranging as high as $30,000 a year. Salaries for certified/registered electroencephalographic technologists tend to be $1,000 to $4,000 a year higher for equivalent experience.

The highest salaries for electroencephalographic technicians tend to go to those who work as laboratory supervisors, teachers in training programs, and program directors in schools of electroencephalographic technology.

Electroencephalographic technicians working in hospitals receive the same fringe benefits as other hospital workers. These benefits usually include hospitalization insurance, paid vacations, and sick leave. In some cases the benefits also include educational assistance, pension plans, and uniform allowances.

Conditions of work

Electroencephalographic technicians usually work five-day, forty-hour workweeks, with only occasional overtime required. Some hospitals require electroencephalographic technicians to be on call for emergencies during weekends, evenings, and holidays. Technicians involved in doing sleep studies may work most of their hours at night.

Electroencephalographic technicians work in clean, well-lighted surroundings; however, they often have to spend long periods standing and bending.

Social and psychological factors

Electroencephalographic technicians generally work with people who are ill and may be frightened or perhaps emotionally disturbed. The technicians who do best at this job are the ones who like people, who can quickly recognize what another person may be feeling, and who have a pleasing and reassuring manner. At the same time, they need to be reconciled to the fact that some of the patients that they work with will be very ill; others may be in the process of dying. Technicians need to be able to carry out their responsibilities accurately and efficiently even in the face of case histories that may be quite tragic.

Most electroencephalographic technicians work in hospitals, where it is very important that they get along well with other staff members. This task is sometimes made more difficult by the fact that in most hospitals there is a formal, often rigid, status structure, and electroencephalographic technicians often find themselves in a relatively low position in that structure. In emergency situations or at other moments of frustration, electroencephalographic technicians may find themselves dealt with brusquely or angrily. Technicians should not take these outbursts or rude treatment personally, but instead should respond with stability and maturity.

GOE: 10.03.01; SIC: 801, 806; SOC: 369

◇ SOURCES OF ADDITIONAL INFORMATION

American Electroencephalographic Society
2579 Melinda Drive
Atlanta, GA 30345

American Board of Registration of Electroencephalographic Technologists
Davis Medical Center, EEG Lab
2315 Stockton Boulevard
Sacramento, CA 95817

American Medical Electroencephalographic Association
850 Elm Grove Road
Elm Grove, WI 53122

American Society of Electroneurodiagnostic Technologists
Sixth at Quint
Carrol, IA 51401

◇ RELATED ARTICLES

Volume 1: Health Care
Volume 2: Licensed practical nurses; Medical technologists; Physician assistants; Registered nurses
Volume 3: Medical assistants; Nursing and psychiatric aides
Volume 4: Biomedical equipment technicians; Cardiac monitor technicians; Electrocardiograph technicians; Medical laboratory technicians

Emergency medical technicians

Definition

Emergency medical technicians, often called *EMTs,* respond to medical emergencies, providing immediate treatment for ill or injured persons both on the scene and during transport to a medical facility. They function as part of an emergency medical team, and the range of medical services they perform varies according to their level of training. EMTs drive specially equipped emergency vehicles, responding to instructions of an emergency medical dispatcher and maintaining two-way radio contact with the dispatcher. At the site of the emergency, EMTs free trapped victims from the accident or catastrophe, if necessary, and determine the nature and extent of the illness or injury. Relying on their knowledge and their examination of the victims, the EMTs perform certain first-aid procedures and determine the need for additional assistance. Using the communications equipment in the vehicle, EMTs obtain instructions for any further on-site treatment from medical personnel at the base facility and arrange for bringing the victims to the facility. After transferring victims to the facility, they help the admitting staff to obtain and record necessary information regarding the victims and the circumstances of the emergency. EMTs must also see that the emergency vehicles and communications equipment are maintained in good operating condition and that the vehicles are adequately stocked with the required medical supplies.

History

The systems for providing emergency medical services and transport to hospitals for the American public did not receive much attention until the 1960s. Prior to that time, ambulance drivers and attendants were often volunteers who had undergone some first-aid training, but the quality and quantity of their instruction and experience varied widely, as did the equipment they had available in their vehicles. By current-day standards, much of the nation's ambulance service was deplorable.

The changes in emergency services were related to advances in medical practice and medical technology that began to make it possible to save certain very sick and badly injured victims, provided they were reached by skilled care providers within a very short time. In particular, during the 1950s and 1960s Americans began to drive more and more, and they became involved in more and more automobile accidents. Growing public awareness of the desirability of better emergency medical services for victims of these accidents was a major impetus behind the effort to upgrade public emergency services.

A major milestone in this movement was the federal Highway Safety Act of 1966 which included, for the first time, uniform standards for emergency medical services. Another important piece of federal legislation was the Emergency Medical Services System Act of 1973, which authorized funds for research and training and also made money available for organizing regional emergency medical systems.

In the late 1960s the emergency medical technician's fledgling vocation was finally beginning to receive careful study and consideration. Beginning in 1968, the Committee on Emergency Medical Services of the National Academy of Sciences and the National Research Council published a series of recommendations and guidelines on the training of ambulance personnel. Working with the Committee on Highway Safety established by President Lyndon Johnson, the American Medical Association's Commission on Emergency Medical Services studied the feasibility of a national certification organization for EMTs.

In response to these various directives, the National Registry of Emergency Medical Technicians (NREMT) was formed in 1970. Today NREMT is an independent agency that has assumed the responsibility for establishing levels of qualifications for EMTs, determining by examination the competency of working EMTs, and promoting the improved delivery of emergency medical services through educational and training programs. NREMT provides uniform national certification for qualified EMTs who wish to be included in the National Registry.

In 1971 the U.S. Department of Transportation published a national standard basic training course to increase the competence of ambulance personnel. By 1977 all the states had adopted the Department of Transportation course or a close equivalent as the basis for state certification. By the early 1990s more than 300,000 persons have taken this basic training course.

Nature of the work

EMTs work in fire departments, private ambulance services, police departments, volunteer community first-aid squads, hospitals, or other local organizations that provide pre-hospital emergency care. This care is directed at rapidly identifying the nature of the emergency, stabilizing the patient's condition, and initiating proper procedures at the scene and en route to a hospital. Unfortunately, even well-intentioned emergency help from persons who are not trained in the best methods for achieving these goals can be disastrous, especially in the case of automobile accident victims. Communities often take great pride in their emergency medical services, knowing that they are as well prepared as possible and that they can minimize the tragic consequences of mishandling emergencies.

EMTs are sent out in an ambulance to the scene of an emergency by a dispatcher who acts as a communication channel for all aspects of emergency medical services. The dispatcher may also be trained as an EMT. It is normally the dispatcher who receives the call for help, sends out the appropriate medical resource, serves as the continuing link between the emergency vehicle and the medical facility throughout the situation, and relays any requests for special assistance at the scene.

EMTs, who often work in two-person teams, must be able to proceed safely yet quickly to an emergency scene in any part of the geographical area they serve. For the protection of the public and themselves, they must obey the traffic laws that apply to emergency vehicles. They must be familiar with the roads and any special conditions affecting the choice of route, such as traffic, weather-related problems, and road construction.

Once at the scene, they must cope immediately and effectively with whatever awaits them. They may find victims who appear to have had heart attacks, who are burned, trapped under fallen objects, lacerated, in childbirth, poisoned, emotionally disturbed—in short, people with any urgent problem for which medical assistance is needed. If no police are available, the EMTs may have to get bystanders to help with the rescue effort by directing traffic, moving debris, or providing other assistance. Because people who have been involved with an emergency directly or indirectly are sometimes very upset, EMTs often have to exercise skill in calming both victims and bystanders. They must do their work efficiently and in a reassuring manner.

EMTs are often the first qualified personnel to arrive on the scene, so they must make the

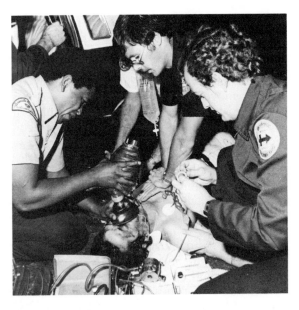

Emergency medical technicians are the first to arrive at the scene of an accident. Their assessment of treatment is crucial to the life of an accident victim.

initial evaluation of the nature and extent of the medical problem. The accuracy of this early assessment can be crucial. EMTs must be on the lookout for any clues, such as medical identification emblems, indicating the victim has significant allergies, diabetes, epilepsy, or other conditions that may affect the choice of emergency treatment. The EMTs must know what questions to ask bystanders or family members if there is a chance they need more information before proceeding.

On the basis of such information and their own observations, EMTs establish the priorities of required care and administer specified diagnostic procedures and emergency treatment under standing orders or in accordance with specific instructions received over the radio from a physician. For example, they may have to control bleeding, open breathing passages, perform cardiac resuscitation, immobilize fractures, treat shock, or restrain emotionally disturbed patients.

The particular procedures and treatments that EMTs may carry out depend partly on the level of certification they have achieved. A majority of EMTs have only basic certification. A small but growing number of EMTs have attained the highest level of certification as Registered EMT-Paramedics and are authorized to administer drugs intravenously or to operate complicated life-support equipment in an advanced life-support ambulance—for example, an electric device (defibrillator) to shock a stopped heart into action.

In the case of victims who are trapped, the EMTs must first assess the medical problem and take appropriate steps to manage it before extricating them. After the victims have received suitable medical care and protection, the EMTs remove the victims, using special equipment and techniques. The EMTs may have to radio requests for special assistance in freeing victims. During a longer extrication process, it may be necessary for EMTs to help police with crowd control and protecting valuables. Sometimes freeing victims involves lifting and carrying them, climbing to high places, or dealing with other difficult or physically demanding situations.

Victims who must be transported to the hospital are put on stretchers, lifted into the ambulance, and secured in place for the ride. The choice of facilities is not always up to the EMTs, but when it is they must base the decision on their knowledge of the equipment and staffing needed by the patients. The receiving hospital's emergency room must be informed by radio, either directly or through the dispatcher, of details such as the number of persons being transported and the nature of their medical problems, so that they may be prepared for the arrival. Meanwhile the EMTs must continue to monitor the patients and administer care as directed by the medical professional with whom they are maintaining radio contact. When necessary the EMTs also try to be sure that contact has been initiated with any utility companies, municipal repair crews, or other services that should be called to correct dangerous problems at the emergency scene.

Once at the hospital, EMTs help the staff to bring the victims into the emergency department, and they may help the staff with the first steps of in-hospital care. They supply whatever information they can, verbally and in writing, for the hospital's records on the patients. In the case of a victim's death, they notify the proper authorities and complete the necessary procedures to ensure that the deceased's property is safeguarded.

After the patient has been delivered to the hospital, the EMTs must check in with their dispatchers and then make the vehicle ready for another emergency call. This includes replacing used linens and blankets; replenishing supplies of drugs, oxygen, and so forth; sending out some equipment to be sterilized; and inventorying the contents of the vehicle to assure completeness. In the case of any special kind of contamination, such as certain contagious diseases or radioactivity, the EMTs report the situation to the proper authorities and follow procedures for decontamination.

In addition to maintaining the medical facility part of the vehicle, the EMTs must see to it that the ambulance is clean and in good running condition. At least once during the shift, they must check the gas, oil, battery, siren, brakes, radio, and other systems.

Requirements

Anyone contemplating a career as an EMT should possess a combination of personal characteristics including an orientation toward serving people, a strong interest in the health field, a stable and adaptable personality, and good physical health. Other requirements are good manual dexterity and motor coordination; the ability to lift and carry up to one hundred pounds; good visual acuity, with lenses for correction permitted; accurate color vision, enabling safe driving and immediate detection of diagnostic signs; and competence in giving and receiving verbal and written communication.

While still in high school, students interested in becoming EMTs should take courses in health and science, driver education, and English. To be admitted to a basic training program, applicants usually must have a high-school diploma, a valid driver's license, and be at least eighteen years old. Exact requirements vary slightly in different states and in different training courses. Another good form of preparation, although by no means required, is training as a medic in the armed forces.

The standard basic training program for EMTs was designed by the U.S. Department of Transportation. It is taught in many hospitals, community colleges, and police, fire, and health departments across the country. It is approximately 110 hours in length and constitutes the minimum mandatory requirement for an EMT. In this course, students learn to manage common emergencies such as bleeding, cardiac arrest, fractures, and airway obstruction; and how to handle equipment such as stretchers, backboards, fracture kits, and oxygen delivery systems.

Successful completion of the basic course opens several training opportunities for EMTs. Among these are a two-day course on removing trapped victims and a five-day course on driving emergency vehicles. Another course lasting several days trains dispatchers. Completion of these recognized training courses may be required for EMTs to be eligible for certain jobs in some areas. In addition, EMTs who have graduated from the basic program may work toward meeting further requirements to become registered at one of several levels recognized by the National Registry of Emergency Medical Technicians.

All fifty states have some certification requirement. Certification is only open to those who have completed the standard basic training course. In some states, EMTs meet the certification requirement by meeting the requirements for basic registration with the National Registry of Emergency Medical Technicians. Some states offer new EMTs the choice of the National Registry examination or the state's own certification examination. A majority of states accept national registration in place of their own examination for EMTs who move into the state.

Special requirements

At present, the National Registry of Emergency Medical Technicians (NREMT) recognizes three levels of competency. While it is not always essential for EMTs to become registered with one of these three ratings, EMTs can expect better prospects for good jobs as they attain higher levels of registration. As time passes, requirements for registration may increase, and a larger proportion of EMTs are expected to become registered voluntarily.

Candidates for the basic level of registration, known as Registered EMT-Ambulance (or EMT-A), must have completed the standard Department of Transportation training program (or their state's equivalent), have six months' experience, and pass both a state-approved EMT-A practical examination and a written examination.

Since 1980, the National Registry has recognized the EMT-Intermediate level of competency. This registration requires all candidates to have current registration at the basic EMT level. They must also have experience and pass a written and a practical examination that together demonstrate knowledge and skills above those of EMT-As, but below those of the highest-rated registrants.

EMT-Paramedics (or EMT-Ps), the EMTs with the highest of the levels of registration, must be already registered at least at the EMT-A level. They must have completed a special EMT-Paramedic training program, have six months' experience as an EMT-Paramedic, and must pass both a written and a practical examination. Because their training is so much more comprehensive and specialized than other EMTs, EMT-Ps are prepared to make more physician-like observations and judgments.

The training programs for EMT-Paramedics are now accredited by the Committee on Allied

After an immediate examination, two emergency medical technicians take the accident victim to the hospital for further tests.

Health Education and Accreditation of the American Medical Association. In 1987 there were about 450 such accredited programs in the United States. They are roughly nine months in duration. Course length depends largely on the availability of actual emergency care incidents in which students can gain supervised practical experience. The course is very broad in scope, and includes classroom instruction and exposure to in-hospital clinical practice in addition to the field internship.

Once they have attained registration, EMTs must re-register every two years. To re-register, they must meet certain experience and continuing education requirements. Refresher courses that help EMTs keep current on new techniques and equipment are available.

Opportunities for experience and exploration

Students in high school have little opportunity for direct experience with this field. However, they can probably arrange to talk with EMTs who work for a local fire or police department or for a voluntary agency that provides emergency ambulance service to the community. It may be possible to learn a great deal about the health-services field through a part-time, summer, or volunteer job in a hospital or clinic. Service jobs can provide students a chance to observe and to talk to staff members concerned with emergency medical services.

411

Health courses in high school are a useful introduction to some of the concepts and terminology that EMTs use. Students may be able to take a first-aid course or training in cardiopulmonary resuscitation. Local organizations such as the Red Cross can provide details on training available in the area.

Many EMTs first become interested in the field while in the armed forces, where they receive training as medics.

Methods of entering

A good source of employment leads for a recent EMT graduate of the basic minimum training program is the school or agency that provided the training. EMTs can also apply directly to local ambulance services, hospitals, other potential employers, and to private and public employment agencies. However, new EMT graduates can face stiff competition in many areas if they are seeking full-time paid employment. While these EMTs may sometimes qualify to apply for positions with fire and police departments, they are generally more likely to be successful in pursuing positions with private companies. Volunteer EMTs, who are likely to average eight to twelve hours of work per week, do not face the same competition. Beginning EMTs without prior work experience in the health field may therefore find it advantageous to start their careers as part-time volunteers. As they gain training and experience, these EMTs can work toward registration, thus opening for themselves many new job opportunities.

Flexibility about location may help EMTs in getting a foothold on the career ladder. In some areas, salaried positions are hard to find because of a strong tradition of volunteer ambulance services. In other areas, however, the demand for EMTs is much greater, although the greatest demand is likely to be for EMT-Paramedics.

Advancement

With experience, EMTs can gain more responsibility while holding the same essential job. But more significant advancement becomes possible with moving up through the progression of ratings recognized by the NREMT. These ratings acknowledge increasing qualifications, making higher paying jobs and more responsibility easier to obtain. In general, public EMT jobs, such as those with public hospitals, police, and fire departments, offer the best salaries and fringe benefits and are thus the most sought-after by EMTs with good experience and training.

Another avenue of advancement for some EMTs leads to becoming an EMT administrator. For others, experience as an EMT prompts further training in another area of the health-care field.

Employment outlook

The employment outlook for paid EMTs will depend on the community in which they are seeking employment. In many communities, especially those in which the public and the health-care planners perceive the advantages of high-quality emergency medical services and are willing to raise tax dollars to support them, the employment outlook should remain favorable. Volunteer services are being phased out in these areas, and well-equipped emergency services operated by salaried EMTs are replacing them. In a growing number of municipalities, private ambulance companies contract to provide emergency medical services to the community. If this trend continues, job opportunities with these private companies should be good.

Another important factor affecting the outlook for EMTs is that the proportion of older people, who use most emergency medical services, is growing in many communities, placing more demands on the emergency medical services delivery system and increasing the need for EMTs.

In some communities, however, the employment outlook is not so favorable. Maintaining a high-quality emergency medical services delivery system can be expensive, and financial strains on some local governments could inhibit the growth of these services. In addition, cutbacks in federal aid to local communities and an overall national effort to contain medical expenditures may lead health-care planners to look for ways that growth in community-based health-related costs may be controlled or reduced. Under economic conditions such as these, communities may not be able to support the level of emergency medical services that they would otherwise like to, and the employment prospects for EMTs may remain limited.

Earnings

Earnings of EMTs are dependent on the type of employer, geographic location, and individual training and experience. Those working for police and fire departments usually receive the same salaries as other department members.

The salaries of EMTs who are graduates of basic training programs average approximately $19,500. EMT-Intermediates earn about the same, while EMT-Paramedics earn salaries that average approximately $25,500 a year. Benefits available to all levels of EMTs vary widely depending on employer, but generally include paid holidays and vacations, health insurance, and pension plans.

Conditions of work

EMTs must work under all kinds of conditions, both indoors and outdoors, and sometimes in very trying circumstances. They must do their work regardless of weather and are often called on to do fairly strenuous physical tasks such as lifting, climbing, and kneeling while dealing with life and death matters. Usually they must work irregular hours including some nights, weekends, and holidays. Those working for fire departments often put in fifty-six-hour weeks, while EMTs employed in hospitals, private firms, and police departments often work forty hours a week. Volunteer EMTs work much shorter hours. Many EMTs find that their working conditions are such that they must have a high degree of commitment to the job.

Social and psychological factors

It is important that EMTs project an impression of confidence and efficiency to both victims and bystanders. They have to exhibit leadership qualities, acting firm but pleasant and courteous. Their appearance should be neat and clean.

Moreover, EMTs must back up the impression of competence with genuine levelheadedness and sufficient calmness to let them consistently exercise good judgment in times of stress. They must be efficient, neither wasting time nor working too fast to do a good job. EMTs should have stable personalities yet remain flexible in their approach to problems. A strong desire to help people, even when that involves difficult work, is essential.

One additional stress factor that EMTs now face is concern over contracting AIDS from bleeding patients. The actual risk of exposure is quite small, and most emergency medical programs have procedures in place to protect EMTs from exposure to the greatest possible degree; however, some risk of exposure does exist, and prospective EMTs should be aware of this factor as they consider the career.

In spite of the intensity of their often-demanding job, EMTs can derive enormous satisfaction from knowing that they are able to render a unique and vital service to the victims of sudden illness or injury.

GOE: 10.03.02; SIC: 8049; SOC: 369

◇ **SOURCES OF ADDITIONAL INFORMATION**

National Registry of Emergency Medical Technicians
PO Box 29233
Columbus, OH 43229

National Association of Emergency Medical Technicians
9140 Ward Parkway
Kansas City, MO 64114

American Ambulance Association
3814 Auburn Boulevard, Suite 70
Sacramento, CA 95821

◇ **RELATED ARTICLES**

Volume 1: Health Care
Volume 2: Licensed practical nurses; Physicians; Physician assistants; Registered nurses
Volume 3: Fire fighters; Medical assistants; Nursing and psychiatric aides; Police officers
Volume 4: Home health technicians; Surgical technicians

Home health technicians

Definition

Home health technicians work with elderly, handicapped, and convalescent patients and their families in their homes. With appropriate help from these technicians, elderly or disabled people may be able to continue living at home instead of going to a nursing home, and the sick may return home from the hospital sooner. The technicians are part of a health-care team and work under the direction of a medical professional such as a physician or registered nurse.

Nature of the work

The duties of home health technicians fall into three main areas: personal services, medical services, and instruction. When providing personal services, they aid patients, some of whom are bedridden, with routine personal activities (dressing, eating, bathing, exercising, for example). The technicians may transfer patients to and from wheelchairs, and they may help them walk to and from the bathroom.

In providing routine medical services, the technicians must utilize their knowledge of proper techniques and of the structure and function of body systems. This care may include changing surgical dressings, caring for wounds, and administering massages, hot and cold applications, enemas, and oral and injected medications. The technicians periodically gather basic information on the patients' progress and make observations such as blood pressure, pulse, temperature, respiration rate, and fluid intake and output, for reporting to the supervising medical professionals.

Instructional activities include teaching patients and families skills and techniques that are useful in coping with illness and disability at home. At the same time they also provide encouragement and the stability needed to help patients make the best possible adjustment to their situation. They instruct patients in how to use such devices as walkers and wheelchairs. They suggest and demonstrate methods of housekeeping and meal planning and preparation that are adapted to the patients' physical and economic needs and limitations.

Requirements

People interested in becoming home health technicians can expect to undergo one to two years of post–high-school training. They should be good at following written and oral instructions, interested in attending to the specific needs of individuals, and in good physical and emotional health.

GOE: 10.03.02; SIC: 8082; SOC: 369

◇ **RELATED ARTICLES**

Volume 1: Health Care
Volume 2: Human services workers; Licensed practical nurses; Physician assistants; Registered nurses
Volume 3: Homemakers-home health aides; Medical assistants; Nursing and psychiatric aides
Volume 4: Emergency medical technicians; Psychiatric technicians

---

Medical laboratory technicians

Definition

Medical laboratory technicians perform routine tests in medical laboratories in order to assist physicians, surgeons, pathologists, and other professional medical personnel in the diagnosis and treatment of disease. They prepare samples of patients' tissues; execute laboratory tests, such as urinalysis and blood counts; and make quantitative and qualitative chemical and biological analyses of samples of cells, tissues, blood, or other body specimens. They usually work under the supervision of a medical technologist or a laboratory director. Medical laboratory technicians may work in many fields, or they may specialize in one area of medical laboratory work, such as cytology, hematology, serology, or histology.

History

The history of medical laboratory technology shares many of its important historical milestones with the history of medicine itself. For instance, both medicine in general and medical laboratory technology can claim as their founder Aristotle, who has often been called the father of biology and physiology. Some significant achievements shared by both medicine and medical laboratory technology include Jan Swammerdam's discovery of red blood corpuscles in 1658; Antonie van Leeuwenhoek's many observations of microorganisms through the microscope during the latter part of the seventeenth century; and the discoveries of Robert Koch and Louis Pasteur in bacteriology in the 1870s. Through these efforts and others like them, medical professionals became aware by the end of the nineteenth century of much valuable information and many possibilities for therapy available in the medical specialties of bacteriology (the study of microorganisms in the human body), cytology (the study of human cells), histology (the study of human tissue), and hematology (the study of human blood). The growth of these medical specialties created a steadily increasing need for laboratory personnel.

During the twentieth century, further great advances have taken place in the field of medicine, making physicians even more dependent on laboratory procedures and personnel for assistance in diagnosing and treating disease. In the early part of this century, individual physicians often taught their assistants how to perform some of the laboratory procedures frequently employed in their practice. Because the quality of work done by these technicians varied considerably, many physicians and medical educators became concerned with the problem of assuring that assistants did the highest-quality work possible. In 1936, one of the first attempts was made to standardize the training programs that were then available for the preparation of skilled assistants, in that case, the training of medical technologists. Since then, the National Accrediting Agency for Clinical Laboratory Sciences (NAACLS), in association with the Committee on Allied Health Education and Accreditation of the American Medical Association (CAHEA), has instituted standards of training for medical laboratory technicians. CAHEA has accredited more than one hundred educational programs offered in community, junior, and technical colleges for the training of medical laboratory technicians, and other accrediting agencies have also entered the field. For example, the Accrediting Bureau of Health Education Schools (ABHES) accredits education programs for medical laboratory technicians and medical assistants. In addition, CAHEA and other agencies have accredited dozens of additional programs for students willing to concentrate their studies in a medical laboratory specialty such as cytology, histology, or blood bank technology.

Nature of the work

Medical laboratory technicians may be generalists in the field of laboratory technology; that is, they may be trained to carry out many different kinds of medical laboratory work. Alternatively, they may specialize in one type of medical laboratory work, such as cytology, hematology, blood bank technology, serology, or histology. This article will describe first the work of medical laboratory technicians who are employed as generalists. Then it will describe three of the specialty fields: cytology, histology, and blood bank technology.

Medical laboratory technicians who work as generalists perform a wide variety of tests and laboratory procedures in chemistry, hematology (the study of blood, especially on the cellular level), urinalysis, blood banking, serology

415

A medical laboratory technician tests blood samples from a routine physical examination. Among other things, she is testing for the cholesterol level, iron level, and white blood cell count.

correct their own errors by means of established strategies; and they must be able to monitor on-going quality control measures. To carry out these responsibilities, medical laboratory technicians must have a sound knowledge of specific techniques and instruments, and they must be able to recognize factors that potentially influence both the procedures they use and the results they get.

As part of this work, medical laboratory technicians frequently utilize precision equipment, such as microscopes and automated blood analyzers, which determine levels of certain components of the blood, such as cholesterol, sugar, and hemoglobin.

Medical laboratory technicians who specialize in cytology are usually referred to as cytotechnicians. Cytotechnicians prepare and stain body cell samplings using special dyes that accentuate the delicate patterns of the cytoplasm and subcellular structures such as the nucleus. Mounted on slides, the various features of the specimen then stand out brightly under a microscope. Using a microscope that magnifies cells perhaps 1,000 times, the cytotechnician screens out normal samplings and sets aside those with minute irregularities in cell size, shape, and color that may signal disease, for further study by a pathologist.

It is important to point out that most trained laboratory workers in the field of cytology are designated cytotechnologists. Cytotechnologists differ from cytotechnicians in that they are trained to examine slides under a microscope to determine whether the cells are normal or show signs of disease. They decide whether the cells have undergone any changes and, if so, whether the change is cancerous or the result of other disease processes.

Cytotechnologists also differ from cytotechnicians in that they are required to have completed college-level academic work in addition to their training program in cytotechnology. Since 1988, cytotechnologists have been required to have completed a bachelor's degree program in order to earn certification.

Without going through this process, cytotechnicians cannot expect to handle much more than the most routine work in laboratory cytology. They may, for instance, be able to work as diagnostic screeners, assisting the pathologist in processing material submitted to the laboratory. With the additional education and certification, however, they may be able to work without close supervision, handle more sophisticated screening assignments, and eventually be given supervisory responsibilities.

Medical laboratory technicians specializing in histology are usually referred to as histologic technicians or tissue technicians. Histology is

(the study and identification of antibodies found in the blood), and microbiology. By performing these tests and procedures, they help to develop vital data on the blood, tissues, and fluids of the human body. This data is then used by physicians, surgeons, pathologists, and other medical personnel in diagnosing and treating patients.

The tests and procedures that these technicians perform are more complex than the routine duties assigned to laboratory assistants, but they do not require specialized knowledge like that of the more highly trained medical technologists. In general, this means that medical laboratory technicians work with only limited supervision. It also means that while the tests they perform may have well-established procedures, the technicians themselves must exercise independent judgment. For instance, they must be able to discriminate among very similar colors or shapes; they must be able to the study of the structure and chemical composition of the tissues, while histologic technology, an important offshoot of this science, is mainly concerned with detecting tissue abnormalities and determining appropriate treatments for the disease conditions associated with the abnormalities.

The main responsibility of histologic technicians is to prepare sections of body tissues for examination by pathologists, who are medical specialists skilled in interpreting the changes brought on by disease. The technicians freeze and cut tissue samples, mount them on slides, and stain them with special dye so that the parts of the cells and the tissue structure stand out clearly under a microscope. Sometimes they use alternative methods for processing the tissue samples—for example, dehydration (drying out the specimen), embedding the tissue in some other material to facilitate sectioning, or microincineration (in which very high temperatures are employed for driving off organic constituents of cells or tissue fragments, leaving the inorganic matter for chemical identification).

A large fraction of the histologic technician's job is likely to be the preparation of frozen sections of tissue for immediate analysis while a patient is on the operating table. A surgical team frequently removes a possibly malignant growth and gives it to a pathologist for gross examination. The pathologist, in turn, often selects a suspicious portion and passes it on to the histologic technician, who flash-freezes it by putting it under liquid nitrogen or by some other method and then places it on a cutting instrument called a microtome. With the microtome, the technician can cut an extremely thin sliver of tissue. This minute wafer is mounted on a slide and stained so that the cell and tissue structures will show up. Based on the microscopic appearance of the stained tissue, the pathologist reports to the waiting surgeon whether a body malfunction or malignancy is present, and the operation proceeds accordingly.

Histologic technicians work with sophisticated and delicate instruments and equipment such as high-power microscopes, chemical analyzers, and, in some cases, electron microscopes.

Medical laboratory technicians who specialize in blood bank technology perform a wide variety of routine tests related to running blood banks, offering transfusion services, and investigating blood diseases and reactions to transfusions. Examples of tasks frequently performed by medical laboratory technicians specializing in this field include donor screening, determining blood types, performing tests of patients' blood counts, and assisting physicians in the care of patients with blood-related problems.

As with cytotechnicians, the advancement possibilities of medical laboratory technicians specializing in blood bank technology are limited unless they get additional education and further certification. Most positions of responsibility in blood bank technology are held by certified Specialists in Blood Bank Technology. To become certified in this field, a person needs to have earned a baccalaureate degree and to have completed an additional year of training. With this additional training and certification, specialists in this field may become involved with research projects, with teaching other health-care workers, and with employee supervision.

Requirements

Medical laboratory technicians must have good manual dexterity, normal color vision, the ability to follow orders, and a tolerance for working under pressure.

To be hired as a medical laboratory technician, one must have a high-school diploma and have completed one or two years of post–high-school training. No specific kind of high-school training is required; however, students must be able to meet the admissions requirements of institutions offering post–high-school training. Prospective technicians should investigate these requirements early in their high-school careers to ensure that these requirements can be met. In general, courses in biology, chemistry, mathematics, and English are the ones that will be most helpful in a career as a medical laboratory technician.

After high school, prospective technicians enroll in one- or two-year training programs accredited by the American Medical Association's Committee on Allied Health Education and Accreditation or the Accrediting Bureau of Health Education Schools. One-year programs include both classroom teaching and practical laboratory training and focus on areas such as medical ethics and conduct, medical terminology, basic laboratory solutions and media, manipulation of cytological and histological specimens, blood collecting techniques, as well as introductions to basic hematology, serology, blood banking, and urinalysis.

To earn an associate degree, students need to complete a two-year post–high-school program. Like certificate programs, associate degree programs include classroom instruction and practical training. Courses are taught both on campus and in local hospitals. On-campus courses focus on general knowledge and basic skills in laboratory testing associated with hematology, serology, chemistry, microbiology, and other pertinent biological and medical areas. The clinical training program focuses on basic principles and skills required in medical diagnostic laboratory testing.

Students completing such a two-year program are eligible for certification from several different agencies. They may become certified by the Board of Registry of the American Society of Clinical Pathologists as a certified Medical Laboratory Technician, MLT (ASCP); by the National Certification Agency for Medical Laboratory Personnel as a Clinical Laboratory Technician, CLT; or by the American Medical Technologists as a Medical Laboratory Technician, MLT (AMT).

Prospective medical laboratory technicians who think they might want to specialize in cytology or blood bank technology should definitely consider the two-year program, as this will best prepare them for the additional education they may later decide they need.

Prospective technicians who think they might want to specialize in histological technology can consider a one-year post–high-school program, especially if the program is designed to prepare students for meeting certifying requirements of the Board of Registry of the American Society of Clinical Pathologists. Such a program is essentially the same as the one-year certificate program for medical laboratory technicians, but it includes as well instruction in microscopy, preparing museum specimens, and in records administration.

Typical courses in a one-year program include the following: orientation to the laboratory, use and care of the microscope, microtomes and other instruments, medical terminology, laboratory mathematics, histology, instrumentation, processing techniques, mounting procedures, and staining and impregnation methods. If certified in this field, medical laboratory technicians are designated as certified Histological Technicians, HT (ASCP).

Even if a one-year program in histological technology does lead to certification, students should remember it does not lead to an associate degree, which is often necessary for advancement. Associate degrees are only awarded at the end of a two-year program. For students who have earned an associate degree in medical laboratory technology in general, specialized training leading to certification as a histologic technician can usually be completed with six months of additional study.

Special requirements

In addition to completing the educational programs described above, prospective technicians need to pass an examination after graduation to receive certification. In some states, this certificate is all that is required for employment. In other states, state licensure is also required. School officials are the best source of information regarding state requirements.

Opportunities for experience and exploration

It is difficult for people interested in a career in medical laboratory technology to gain any direct experience through part-time employment. There are some other ways, however, to learn more about this career on a first-hand basis. Perhaps the best way is to arrange a visit to a hospital, blood bank, or commercial medical laboratory to see technicians at work at their jobs. Another way to learn about this kind of work in general, and about the training required in particular, is to visit a CAHEA- or ABHES-accredited school of medical laboratory technology to discuss career plans with the admissions counselor at the school. Prospective technicians can also write to the sources listed at the end of this article for more reading material on medical laboratory technology. Finally, students should remember that science courses in high school that have laboratory sections will give them exposure to some of the kinds of work they might do later in their careers.

Methods of entering

Graduates of schools of medical laboratory technology usually receive assistance from faculty and school placement services in finding their first jobs. Hospitals, laboratories, and other concerns employing medical laboratory technicians often get in touch with local schools and notify them of job openings. Often the hospital or laboratory at which students receive their practical training will offer them full-time employment after graduation. Positions may also be secured with the assistance of the various registries of certified medical laboratory workers. Newspaper job advertisements and commercial placement agencies are other sources of help in locating employment.

Advancement

Medical laboratory technicians often gain advancement by returning to school to earn a baccalaureate degree. In this way they can advance to positions as medical technologists, histological technologists, cytotechnologists, or specialists in blood bank technology.

Other technicians advance by taking on more responsibility while retaining the title of technician. For instance, with experience, they can advance to some supervisory positions, such as those overseeing certain facets of medical laboratory work, or other positions assigning work to be done by other medical laboratory workers. Some experienced medical laboratory technicians may also advance by training to do very specialized or complex laboratory or research work.

Employment outlook

There was tremendous growth during the mid-1980s in the number of people employed as medical laboratory personnel. This growth is expected to continue for the foreseeable future, although at a much slower pace. Federal government sources project that employment of medical laboratory workers will grow about as fast as the average for all other occupations through the 1990s.

One of the most important factors that may slow the growth of employment in this field is the overall national effort to control health-care costs. Hospitals, where most medical-laboratory technicians are employed, will seek to control costs in part through cutting down on the amount of laboratory testing they do and, consequently, the personnel they require.

Despite these forces, the overall amount of medical laboratory testing will probably increase, as much of medical practice today relies on high-quality laboratory testing. However, because of the increased use of automation, this increase in laboratory testing will probably not lead to an equivalent growth in employment.

One other technological factor that will influence employment in this field is the development of laboratory-testing equipment that is easier to use. This means that some testing that formerly had to be done in hospitals or commercial laboratories can now be done in physicians' offices. This development may serve to slow growth in medical laboratory employment; however, it may increase the number of technicians hired by medical groups and clinics. In addition, equipment that is easier to use may also lead to technicians being able to do more kinds of testing, including some tests that used to be done only by medical technologists.

Despite these projections for only moderate growth in this field, prospective technicians should keep in mind that medical laboratory testing is an absolutely essential element in today's medicine. For well-trained technicians who are flexible in accepting responsibilities and willing to continue their education throughout their careers, employment opportunities should remain good.

Earnings

Salaries of medical laboratory technicians vary according to employer and geographical area. In general, medical laboratory technicians working in large cities receive the highest salaries. Overall, people seeking employment as medical laboratory technicians can expect starting salaries averaging approximately $17,000 a year. As medical laboratory technicians gain experience, their salaries will increase, rising to an average of approximately $22,000 a year.

Cytotechnicians who take the additional year of training and become certified cytotechnologists can expect starting salaries around $20,000 a year. Other medical laboratory technicians who return to school to earn their baccalaureate degrees and certification as medical technologists can expect starting salaries, after certification and depending on prior experience, of around $21,000 a year.

Most medical laboratory technicians receive paid vacations and holidays, sick leave, hospitalization and accident insurance, and retirement benefits.

Conditions of work

Medical laboratory technicians work in clean, well-lighted, and usually air-conditioned settings. There may, however, be unpleasant odors and some infectious materials involved in the work. In general, there are few hazards associated with these odors and materials as long as proper methods of sterilization and handling of specimens, materials, and equipment are used.

Medical laboratory technicians often spend much of their days standing or sitting on stools. A forty-hour, five-day week is normal, although those working in hospitals can expect some evening and weekend work.

Social and psychological factors

Medical laboratory technicians have the satisfaction of knowing that they are working in a field that is very important to the patients and physicians who rely on the results of their labors. The work carries with it a great deal of responsibility and often requires individual judgment and great personal care; however, it also involves some very repetitive tasks that some people may find annoying. The work must often be done under time pressure, even though it is often very painstaking.

Another factor that medical laboratory technicians should keep in mind is that advancement opportunities, although they do exist for medical laboratory technicians, are limited. If they want to maximize their chances for advancement they must consider receiving additional training. If they are reluctant to undertake additional training, they must realize that they may face the frustration of limited advancement opportunities.

GOE: 02.04.02; SIC: 8071; SOC: 369

◇ **SOURCES OF ADDITIONAL INFORMATION**

American Medical Technologists
710 Higgins Road
Park Ridge, IL 60068

American Medical Association
535 North Dearborn Street
Chicago, IL 60610

American Society for Medical Technology
2021 L Street, NW
Suite 400
Washington, DC 20036

National Certification Agency for Medical Lab Personnel
1101 Connecticut Avenue, NW
Suite 700
Washington, DC 20036

◇ **RELATED ARTICLES**

Volume 1: Health Care
Volume 2: Biochemists; Crime laboratory technologists; Medical technologists; Nuclear medicine technologists; Physicians
Volume 3: Medical assistants
Volume 4: Biological technicians; Biological specimen technicians; Electrocardiograph technicians; Electroencephalographic technicians; Pharmacy technicians; Radiological technologists

Medical record technicians

Definition

In any hospital, clinic, or other health-care agency or institution, permanent records are created and maintained for all the patients treated by the staff. *Medical record technicians* help perform the technical tasks associated with compiling, maintaining, and using these records.

Each patient's individual medical record describes in detail his or her condition over time, including any illness and injuries, operations, treatments, outpatient visits, and the progress of hospital stays. Medical record technicians review records for completeness and accuracy; assign codes to the diseases, operations, diagnoses, and treatments according to detailed standardized classification systems; and post the codes on the medical record, thus making the information on the record easier to retrieve and analyze. They transcribe medical reports; maintain indices of patients, diseases, operations, and other categories of information; compile patient census data; and file records or supervise other personnel who do so. In addition, they may direct the day-to-day operations of the medical records department. They maintain the flow of records and reports to and from other departments, and sometimes assist medical staff in special studies or research that draws on information in the records.

History

Medical practitioners have been writing down information about their patients' illnesses and treatments for hundreds of years. Before the twentieth century, such records were kept mostly to help the practitioners learn as much as possible from their own experience. There was little centralization or standardization of this information, so it was difficult to organize it and share the knowledge that can result from studying many instances of similar successes and failures.

By the early 1900s, medical record-keeping was changing, along with many other aspects of medicine. Medicine was more sophisticated, more scientific, and more successful in helping patients. Hospitals were increasingly accepted as the conventional place for middle-class patients to go for care. As a consequence, hospitals became more numerous and better organized. With medical-record keeping becoming more important and time consuming, it seemed most efficient and natural to centralize it in the hospital. Recommendations by distinguished committees representing the medical profession helped to encourage standardized record-keeping procedures.

By the 1920s, there were many hospitals in the United States with central libraries of patient information, and there were employees specifically charged with keeping these records in good order. As time passed, these tasks became more complicated. The personnel responsible for this work, who used to be called medical record librarians, eventually became differentiated into two basic professional categories. These two professional categories are now designated medical record administrators and medical record technicians. Formal training programs specifically for medical record technicians have been operated in hospital schools and junior colleges since 1953. Medical record clerks, the third main category of medical record personnel, carry out the most routine tasks in a records department and require comparatively little specialized training.

In recent years the move to computerization of records, the growing importance of privacy and freedom of information issues, and the changing requirements of third-party reimbursement organizations have all had major impacts on the field of medical records technol-ogy. These areas can be expected to continue to reshape the field in future years.

Nature of the work

The individual medical record consists of all relevant observations and findings of the physicians and other members of the health team who deal with the patient. It may contain, for example, several diagnoses, X-ray and laboratory reports, electrocardiogram tracings, test results, and drugs prescribed. This summary of past events and experience is very important as an aid to the physician in making speedy and correct decisions about care. Later, information from the record is often needed in authenticating legal forms and insurance claims. The medical record documents the adequacy and appropriateness of the care received by the patient. It is the basis of any investigation when the care seems to have been questionable in any way.

Confidentiality and privacy laws have a major bearing on the medical records field. These laws require that individual records be in secure storage but also be available for retrieval and specified kinds of properly authorized use. The laws vary in different states for different types of data, and can be expected to change as time goes on. Maintaining the confidentiality of individual records, however, will continue to be a concern to medical records workers.

Patterns and trends can be discerned when data from many records are considered together. This type of statistical information is relied on by hospital administrators, scientists, public health agencies, accrediting and licensing bodies, people who evaluate the effectiveness of current programs or plan future ones, medical reimbursement organizations, and others. Medical records can provide, for example, the data to show whether a new treatment or medication really works or the relative effectiveness of alternative treatments or medications. Other groupings of data might be used to uncover important clues about the causes of or methods of preventing certain kinds of disease.

Medical record technicians are involved with routine preparing, handling, and safeguarding of individual records as well as the statistical information extracted from groups of records. The specific tasks and the scope of responsibilities of medical record technicians depend a great deal on the size and type of the employing institution. In large organizations, there may be a number of technicians and also other levels of workers all working with medical records. The technicians may serve as assistants to the medical record administrator as

Medical records technicians enter diagnosis and procedure codes in a hospital's computer system. The computers enable the hospital to process information quickly and efficiently.

needed, or may regularly specialize in some particular phase of the work done by the department. In small facilities, however, technicians may carry out the whole range of activities and may function fairly independently, perhaps bearing the full responsibility for all day-to-day operations of the department. A technician may even be department director. Sometimes technicians in small facilities take care of medical records and also spend part of their time helping out in the business or admitting office.

The majority of medical record technicians are employed in hospitals. But many work in other health-care settings, including health maintenance organizations (HMOs), industrial clinics, skilled nursing facilities, rehabilitation centers, large group medical practices, ambulatory care centers, and state and local government health agencies. Records must be maintained in any of these facilities, although record-keeping procedures vary.

Whether they work in hospitals or other settings, medical record technicians are concerned with organizing, transferring from one form to another, analyzing, preserving, and locating when necessary vast quantities of detailed information. The sources of this information may be physicians, nurses, laboratory workers, and other members of the health team.

In a hospital, a patient's cumulative record goes to the medical record department at the end of the hospital stay. A technician checks over the information in the file to be sure that all the essential reports and data are included and apparently accurate. Certain specific items must be supplied in any record, such as signatures, dates, the patient's physical and social history, the results of physical examinations, provisional and final diagnoses, periodic progress notes on the patient's condition during the hospital stay, the medications prescribed and administered, therapeutic treatments, surgical procedures, and an assessment of the outcome or the condition at the time of discharge. If any item is missing, the technician refers the record back to the person responsible for the information. After this review, the record is considered the official document describing the patient's case.

When it has been determined as far as possible that all the required information is present, the medical record technician codes the record. Most hospitals in the United States use a nationally accepted system for coding. Every diagnosis and procedure and many conditions can be assigned a numerical code. The lists of diseases, procedures, and conditions are published in classification manuals that medical records personnel refer to frequently. By reducing information in disparate forms to a single consistent coding system, the data contained in the record is rendered much easier to handle, tabulate, and analyze. It can be indexed under any suitable heading; for example, under patient, disease, type of surgery, physician attending the case, and so forth. Creating multiple cross-indexes is likely to be an important part of the medical record technician's job. Because the same code systems are used nearly everywhere, the data may be used not only by people working inside the hospital, but may also be submitted to one of the various programs that pool information obtained from many institutions.

After the information on the medical record has been coded, technicians may use a packaged computer program to assign the patient to one of several hundred "diagnosis-related groupings" or DRGs. The DRG for the patient's stay determines the amount of money the hospital will receive if the patient is covered by Medicare or one of the other insurance programs that based their reimbursement on DRGs.

All records and reports produced in the medical records department must be easy to read. In health-care facilities where paper records are used, it often falls to medical records technicians to type these documents or enter them into a computer.

Another vital part of the job concerns filing. Regardless of how accurately and completely information is gathered and stored, it is worthless unless it can be retrieved promptly. If paper records are kept, technicians are usually responsible for preparing records for storage, filing them, and getting them back from storage. In some organizations, technicians supervise other personnel who carry out these tasks.

In many health care facilities, computers, not paper, are used for nearly all the medical record-keeping. Medical and nursing staff make notes on an electronic "chart." They enter the same kinds of patient-care information on computers, and medical record technicians access the information using their own terminals. Computers have greatly simplified many traditional routine tasks of the medical records department, such as generating the daily hospital census figures, tabulating data for research purposes, and updating special registries of certain types of diseases such as cancer and stroke.

Some older medical records that were originally on paper were later photographed and stored on microfilm, particularly after they were a year or two old. Technicians may be responsible for retrieving and maintaining the films in good order. It is not unusual for a health-care institution to have a combination of paper and microfilm files, as well as computerized record storage, reflecting the evolution over time of the technology available for storing information.

Because information in medical records is used to determine how much hospitals are paid for caring for insured patients, the accuracy of the work done by medical records personnel is vital. A coding error could cause the hospital to lose money.

Medical record technicians may also be involved in the medicolegal aspect of record keeping. They may prepare records to be released in response to a patient's written authorization, a subpoena, or court order. This requires special knowledge of legal statutes and often requires consultation with attorneys, judges, insurance agents, and other parties with legitimate rights to the patient's health information.

Medical record technicians may participate in the quality-assurance, risk-management, and utilization-review activities of a health-care facility. The technician may serve as a data abstractor and analyst, reviewing records against established standards to assure quality of care. Technicians may also prepare statistical reports for the medical or administrative staff concerned with reviewing appropriateness of care.

Medical record technicians may participate in medical research activities by maintaining special records, called registries, in such areas as cancer, heart disease, transplants, or adverse outcomes of pregnancies. Medical record technicians are required to abstract and code very detailed information from records of patients with conditions of interest to medical researchers. Once again, technicians may also prepare statistical reports and trend analyses of their findings.

Not all medical record technicians are employed in a single health-care facility; some serve as consultants to several small facilities. Other medical record technicians do not work in health-care delivery settings at all. They may be employed by health and property-liability insurance companies collecting and reviewing information to help settle medical claims. Government agencies also hire some medical record technicians, as do manufacturers of medical records systems and equipment. A few medical record technicians are self-employed providing medical transcription services.

Requirements

Medical records is a field where slipshod work could have serious consequences for patients, physicians, and the hospital. Therefore a prospective technician must have the capacity to do consistently reliable and accurate routine work. Records must be completed and maintained with care and attention to detail. The medical record technician may be the only person to check through the whole record, and he or she must understand and accept the responsibility that goes with this fact.

Good keyboard skills are needed, and some experience in transcribing dictated reports may be useful.

Most employers prefer to hire medical record technicians who have completed a two-year associate degree program accredited by the American Medical Association's Committee on Allied Health Education and Accreditation (CAHEA) and the American Medical Record Association (AMRA). In 1986, there were about eighty-eight accredited programs available. These degree programs, mostly offered in junior and community colleges, usually include classroom instruction in such subjects as anatomy, physiology, medical terminology, medical record science, word processing, medical aspects of record keeping, statistics, computers in health care, personnel supervision, business management, English, and office skills.

In addition to classroom instruction, the student is given supervised clinical experience in medical record departments in local health-care institutions. This provides the student with practical experience in performing many of the medical record functions learned in the classroom and with the opportunity to interact with health-care professionals.

An alternative method of becoming a medical record technician is open to individuals who have experience with certain related activities. It requires completion of the American

Medical Record Association's Independent Study Program in Medical Record Technology. Students in this program must successfully complete a lesson series and a period of clinical experience in a health-care institution, and they must also earn thirty semester hours of credits in prescribed fields at a college or university.

For either of these approaches to training to become a medical record technician, a high-school diploma is required. A high-school student contemplating a career in medical records should take as much English as possible in high school, because technicians on the job are constantly working with words, writing reports, and communicating verbally with various other health-care personnel. Basic mathematics, which can be business mathematics, is very desirable. Biology courses will familiarize the student with the kind of terminology that medical record technicians use. Other science courses, computer training, typing, and office procedures are also good subjects to have in the high-school curriculum.

Special requirements

Medical record technicians who have completed an accredited training program are eligible to take the national qualifying examination to earn the credential of an Accredited Record Technician (ART). Most health-care institutions prefer to hire individuals with an ART credential, because it signifies that he or she has met the standards set by the American Medical Records Association as the mark of a qualified health professional.

Technicians who have achieved the ART credential are required to obtain twenty hours of continuing education credits every two years in order to retain their ART status. The continuing education credits may be obtained by attending educational programs, by participating in further academic study, or pursuing other independent-study activities approved by the American Medical Records Association.

There is no state licensure for medical record technicians at the present time.

Opportunities for experience and exploration

A high-school student interested in a career in medical records may be able to find summer, part-time, or volunteer work in a hospital or other health-care facility. Sometimes such jobs are available in the medical records area of the organization. This experience would provide the student an ideal chance to measure his or her aptitude and interests against those of people already employed in the medical records field.

If a job experience that allows contact with the field is not possible, the student may still be able to arrange to talk with someone working as a medical record technician or administrator. Faculty and counselors at area schools that offer medical record technician training programs may be very helpful sources of information. The student should also try to seek out and read available literature on the profession.

Methods of entering

Most successful medical record technicians are graduates of two-year accredited programs, and those who have become ARTs stand the best chance of getting the most desirable positions. Help in finding jobs is available through the American Medical Record Association and through school placement offices. Individuals may also apply directly to the personnel departments of hospitals. Many openings are listed in the classified advertising sections of local newspapers and in private and public employment agencies.

Advancement

Medical record technicians can often achieve some advancement and salary increase without additional training simply by taking on greater responsibility in the same health-care facility. With experience, they may move to supervisory or department head positions, depending on the type and structure of the employing organization. Some technicians with broad experience may be able to establish themselves as independent consultants. Technicians who have an associate degree and who have the ART designation are generally most likely to advance satisfactorily. Those working in government agencies move up by the traditional methods of civil service.

More assured job advancement and salary increases come with completing the academic training leading to a baccalaureate degree in medical record administration. Among the intentions guiding accredited associate degree programs is the idea that the educational programs for medical record technicians and medical record administrators should be coordinated to allow ease of progression, avoid subject matter duplication, and minimize loss of academic credit. Because of a general shortage of medical record administrators, hospitals often try to make it easy for technicians to obtain the baccalaureate degree by giving them work time off for classes and providing financial aid. The American Medical Record Association has a student loan program for individuals who need tuition assistance to move up the career ladder.

Employment outlook

The prospect through the 1990s is that the demand for well-trained medical record technicians will grow rapidly and will continue to exceed the supply. This expectation is related to the health-care needs of a population that is both growing and aging, to the trend toward more technologically sophisticated medicine and greater use of diagnostic procedures, and to increased pressure on health providers by regulatory bodies that scrutinize both costs and quality of care.

Technicians with two-year associate degrees and ART status will have the best prospects. The importance of such qualifications is likely to increase.

Most opportunities for employment will be found in hospitals; however, opportunities will also be found in extended-care facilities, ambulatory-care facilities, HMOs, medical group practices, nursing homes, and home-health agencies. Technicians are also finding opportunities with computer firms, consulting firms, and government agencies. The importance of complete and well-organized medical records for financial management of health-care institutions is especially likely to lead to increased demand for medical record technicians in almost all types of facilities.

Earnings

The salaries of medical record technicians are greatly influenced by the location, the size, and the type of employing institution, as well as the technician's training and experience. The salaries of entry-level technicians average approximately $16,000 a year. Experienced technicians in managerial positions can earn into the range of $20,000 to $30,000 a year. By earning a bachelor's degree or advanced degree, the technician becomes more valuable to an employer and can expect higher wages.

In general, medical record technicians in large cities working in large hospitals make the most money, and those in rural areas make the least. Like most hospital employees, medical record technicians usually receive paid vacations and holidays, life and health insurance, and retirement benefits.

Conditions of work

Medical records departments are usually pleasantly clean, well-lighted, and air-conditioned areas. Sometimes, however, records are kept in cramped, out-of-the-way quarters. Although the work requires thoroughness and careful attention to many details, the work area may be busy with a constant bustle of activity, some of which interrupts the technician's work. The job is likely to involve frequent routine contact with nurses, physicians, and other staff of the health-care facility. Sometimes technicians have to walk to various other departments to gather missing information and paperwork.

A forty-hour workweek is the norm, but because hospitals must operate on a twenty-four-hour basis, the job may regularly include night or weekend hours. Part-time work is sometimes available.

Social and psychological factors

People who work in the medical records field must have an inclination to be very precise and a high tolerance for detail work. Medical record technicians must also feel comfortable about dealing with a variety of people, including medical staff members, hospital administrators, other health-care professionals, attorneys, and insurance agents.

In many hospital settings, the medical record technician is under pressure caused by a heavy work load. As health-care institutions come under increasing demands for cost containment and productivity, medical record technicians will be required to produce a significant volume of high-quality work in short periods of time.

Nonetheless, the knowledge that their work is significant for patients and for medical research can be personally very satisfying for medical record technicians.

GOE: 07.05.03; SIC: 806; SOC: 364

Ophthalmic laboratory technicians

Definition

Ophthalmic laboratory technicians perform a variety of duties related to making prescription eyeglasses and contact lenses. In general, they grind, polish, measure, surface, finish, inspect, and mount the lenses according to established specifications or according to the specifications of opticians, optometrists, or ophthalmologists. These technicians need not work only on eyeglasses; many of their skills and activities are equally applicable to the manufacture of optical instruments such as telescopes, microscopes, and aerial cameras. However, this article concentrates on lens-related activities as they apply to eyeglasses and contact lenses. Those interested in the building of optical instruments other than strictly ophthalmic products (eyeglasses and contact lenses) should see the article on optics technicians in the Engineering and Science section. There they will find discussed the careers of optomechanical technicians, photo-optic technicians, precision-lens technicians, and precision-lens grinders, sometimes called optical technicians. Some of the jobs described in this article are not, strictly speaking, technician jobs; that is, they require more of the manual skills of a craft worker than the academic training of a technician. However, in many smaller ophthalmic laboratories or retail outlets, technicians are sometimes required to handle the entire range of lens-preparation activities. Technicians, then, would not specialize in any of the activities described below but would instead be prepared to perform many of them.

History

Humans have been using simple lenses for magnification for more than 1,000 years, and eyeglasses have been in use since the fourteenth century. In Europe, eyeglasses first appeared in Italy and then spread to the various royal courts until eventually there were trained lens grinders in all European countries. By the seventeenth century, these craft workers had banded together into an association called a guild.

The first eyeglass lenses were convex (that is, they were thicker in the middle than at the edges) which is the shape used to correct farsightedness. There is no evidence of concave lenses (thicker at the edges than in the middle) for nearsightedness until the sixteenth century. Further development of eyeglasses was made by Benjamin Franklin, who invented the bifocal lens in the eighteenth century. Thomas Young discovered the eye condition called astigmatism in 1801, and cylindrical and compound lenses to correct this condition were developed about twenty-five years later.

In 1887 a Swiss physician, A. E. Fick, made the first contact lens. These first lenses were made of heavy glass, exerted an uncomfortable pressure on the eyeball, and were difficult to fit. In the late 1930s a light plastic was developed that could be easily molded to shape. In 1950, a lens that floated on the wearer's tears was introduced; and today, an even smaller corneal lens, covering only the cornea, is in widespread use.

By the mid-1980s there were approximately 50,000 dispensing opticians (many of whom were technicians) and 24,000 ophthalmic laboratory technicians employed in this field.

Nature of the work

There are two major aspects of ophthalmic laboratory work: lens grinding and lens finishing. The work of the *lens grinder* begins with a standard-size lens blank, which is usually mass-produced by an optics company and sold to the ophthalmic laboratory. Following the specifications included in a patient's prescription, lens grinders pick the proper lens blank for the job, measure and mark the lens for grinding and polishing according to specification, and set up and operate the machines that grind and polish the lenses. They then measure the lens with precision instruments, such as lensometers and objective lens analyzers, to make sure that the prescribed specifications have been met.

Lens finishers make and cut the lenses and shape, smooth, and bevel the edges. They then assemble lens and frame parts into finished glasses, using special tools such as lens cutters and glass drills. Finally, they use precision instruments to detect imperfections in the completed product.

In some small laboratories, technicians may have to perform all of these tasks; in large laboratories they may specialize in one phase of the work. The following paragraphs describe some of the specific jobs included in this field.

Glass cutters lay out and cut glass to specified sizes and weights for molding into lens blanks. They examine the glass stock for defects, trace outlines onto the glass using templates, and grind rough edges from the blank using a grindstone.

Sizers set up the machines that grind and polish the edges and surfaces of lens blanks. They select the specified grinding and polishing tools, adjust the machines according to the size of the lens holders, and set time cycles which automatically stop the machine after a specified amount of grinding or polishing.

Hand grinders tend the machines that grind the approximate curve onto lens blanks in preparation for the fine grinding. Working from a production order, they choose a lens blank, put

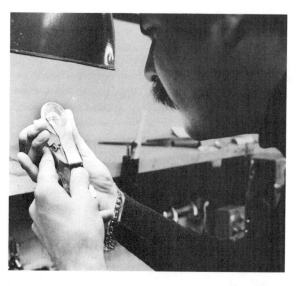

An ophthalmic laboratory technician uses a precision instrument to measure and mark a lens for grinding. He follows the specifications of each patient's prescription.

the blank in a holder that holds it during grinding, and position the blank and holder on the grinding machine. They move the control arm of the machine back and forth or they hold the blank against a grinding wheel in order to grind the blank to the specified curvature.

Precision-lens generators operate and sometimes set up the lens-generating machines that grind the ophthalmic blanks to specified curvature and thickness. They read work orders to learn the specifications, then pick out specified holders and diamond grinding wheels to do the grinding. They adjust the grinding machine for speed, rate of feed, angle of arc, and depth of cut. After a specified length of time, they stop the machine and measure the curvature and thickness of the glass.

Precision-lens polishers operate the machines that polish the lenses. They mount lenses into holders that hold the lens during the polishing operation, apply abrasives, and stop the machine periodically to rinse off the abrasive and to measure the lens for conformance to specifications.

Eyeglass-lens cutters set up and operate bench-mounted cutting machines to cut eyeglass lenses to specified sizes and shapes. They select the metal cutting pattern according to specifications, mount the pattern in the cutting machine, and press the cutting arm down to cut the lens. They then remove the cut lens, chip away the excess material from the edges, and send the lens on to the people who do the edging.

Precision-lens centerers and edgers operate grinders to edge and bevel lenses according to work orders. Their work involves using a variety of machines, such as truing machines and edge-grinding machines, and being able to center lenses precisely in these machines using beams of light and other techniques. They start, stop, and adjust the machines, and they measure the lens edges using micrometers and calipers.

Layout technicians draw reference lines and write specifications onto lens blanks to guide workers who surface or finish lenses. To guide the workers, they locate and mark centers, axis points, and terminal points on lens blanks, using precision instruments, such as optical-centering and lens-power-determining instruments that have dials and built-in marking devices. They also examine lens blanks to ensure conformance to work orders and absence of defects.

Lens mounters mount prescription lenses into metal or plastic frames. They inspect lenses for flaws such as pits, chips, and scratches; remove flaws, when possible, using a grinding wheel; and assemble eyeglass frame, attaching ornaments, nose pads, and temple pieces.

Contact lens blockers and cutters and *contact lens lathe operators* operate jeweler's lathes and hand tools to cut inside or outside curvature in contact lenses. This job involves using a variety of different kinds of instruments and lens materials because more and more different kinds of contact lenses are being developed.

Multifocal-lens assemblers fit and secure lens parts together for bifocals and trifocals. They clean the surfaces carefully, apply cement, and inspect for any imperfections.

Requirements

Ophthalmic laboratory technicians need to have good vision and well-developed eye-hand coordination. In addition, they should have mechanical aptitude, an interest in mathematics and science, and a tolerance for doing work that requires close attention to detail.

Ophthalmic laboratory technicians need to have a high-school diploma. While in high school they should take courses in physics, algebra, geometry, and mechanical drawing.

Most technicians receive their training on the job, in formal apprenticeship programs, or in vocational or technical school. Technicians who train on the job usually begin by performing simple tasks, such as simple lens-grinding operations. As they gain experience, they progress to more difficult operations, such as lens cutting or eyeglass assembly. It usually takes about three years to reach the highest level of skills. Some technicians specialize in one type of job, and their training usually takes less time.

Formal apprenticeship programs in this field usually take about three to four years to complete; however, some technicians manage to complete the programs sooner. Requirements for entry into these programs vary from program to program, but a high-school diploma is almost always required. The programs provide extensive training, and the technicians who complete them generally have much better job opportunities than do technicians who trained on the job. Apprentices generally train to be either ophthalmic surfacers or finishers. Ophthalmic surfacers train in lens grinding and related activities. Ophthalmic finishers concentrate on assembling eyeglasses and doing frame repairs.

The number of formal apprenticeship programs is decreasing, and the percentage of technicians learning their trade in vocational, technical, or community colleges is increasing. These programs usually last from one to two years and graduates may receive certificates or associate degrees. However, they will still require some on-the-job training in addition to their formal instruction.

Special requirements

Licensing requirements for ophthalmic laboratory technicians vary from state to state. In those states where licensing is required, technicians must meet certain standards of education and training and pass a written examination. Students considering a career in this field should consult with their guidance counselors or contact directly their state's licensing board to find out about licensing requirements.

Opportunities for experience and exploration

People who are considering a career in ophthalmic laboratory technology can explore this field by visiting the shops and laboratories where ophthalmic laboratory technicians work. Part-time or summer employment in an ophthalmic laboratory or a retail optical shop in any kind of position, even as a messenger or stock clerk, may give the interested person an opportunity to observe first-hand the skills needed in this operation.

Methods of entering

The easiest method of entering this field is probably through a formal technical training program. Such a program provides students with skills that employers seek and puts them in touch with faculty and placement officers who can provide good assistance in finding a first job. However, the method of entering most frequently used is an on-the-job training program. High-school graduates can apply for such training directly at the personnel offices of ophthalmic laboratories or retail outlets known to hire ophthalmic laboratory technicians. State and private employment agencies and sometimes classified ads in newspapers are good sources of information about employers seeking interested people in this field.

Advancement

Ophthalmic laboratory technicians can expect advancement as they gain experience and increased skills. They may become supervisors or managers or assist in the training of newer technicians. With additional training and education many technicians become dispensing opticians. As dispensing opticians, they measure and fit customers with eyeglass frames and contact lenses, read customers' prescriptions for lenses, and prepare work orders for the ophthalmic laboratory technicians who will fabricate the lenses.

Some technicians who gain extensive experience in laboratory dispensing and managerial aspects of ophthalmic laboratory work begin businesses of their own.

Employment outlook

The total number of people employed as ophthalmic laboratory technicians is expected to grow faster than the average of all other occupations through the year 2000. There will be some increase in the number of ophthalmic laboratories and the number of technicians needed because of rising demand for corrective lenses and because of increased customer demand for faster service in delivering finished eyeglasses. This demand will be related to overall population growth and especially the growth in the percentage of the population represented by older people, who require the most vision care.

All of these factors tending to increase demand will be offset in part by the technological innovations that are being introduced into oph-

Ophthalmic laboratory technicians often use computerized lens analyzers to measure the preciseness of newly ground contact lenses.

thalmic laboratories, especially larger laboratories. Machines used to grind and polish lenses are becoming increasingly sophisticated, often computer-aided. They are increasing technicians' productivity and eliminating some tasks wholly. However, the demand for prescription glasses is expected to be so strong that job opportunities for ophthalmic laboratory technicians should remain very good.

Most of the new job opportunities will be in retail stores that increasingly are making prescription glasses on their own premises rather than relying on large outside ophthalmic laboratories as suppliers. Nonetheless, opportunities in large ophthalmic laboratories should also remain good.

Earnings

Ophthalmic laboratory technicians can expect to receive starting salaries that average approximately $15,000 a year after they have completed their training. These salaries, however, vary greatly by geographical area. During their training period, they may start out at approximately 60 percent of the skilled worker's wage rate. Throughout the course of their training, they receive wage increases, so that by the time they finish their training, they are receiving the beginning rate for experienced workers.

Experienced technicians can earn $25,000 a year or more. Those who work as nonmanagement supervisors usually earn about 20 percent more than nonsupervisory technicians.

Some ophthalmic workers are members of unions, and their wages and benefits are determined by negotiation.

Ophthalmic laboratory technicians who develop their own businesses have earnings depending on the success of their business, but generally they make much more than technicians who are strictly employees.

Conditions of work

Ophthalmic laboratory technicians usually work in well-lighted, well-ventilated surroundings. However, they also usually have to work with machines that are noisy; and the equipment used for coating, dyeing, and some other processes generates noxious fumes. Safety measures, such as wearing goggles and using exhaust hoods to remove fumes, have eliminated many of the hazards encountered in ophthalmic laboratories, but technicians are still subject to some accidents while using hand tools or operating lathes or grinding machines.

Most ophthalmic laboratory technicians work five-day, forty-hour weeks and spend most of their days standing. In retail outlets where lenses are guaranteed in an hour, ophthalmic laboratory technicians may be required to work under time restraints.

Social and psychological factors

Ophthalmic laboratory work involves performing precision tasks using precision instruments such as small hand tools, lens cutters, chippers, optical pliers, files, protractors, and diamond-point glass drills. These tasks also involve superior dexterity and eye-hand coordination, and they can become extremely tedious or frustrating to someone who lacks the interest in or the ability to do this kind of work.

GOE: 06.01.04, 06.02.08; SIC: 8011; SOC: 6864

◇ **SOURCES OF ADDITIONAL INFORMATION**

American Academy of Ophthalmology
655 Beach Street
San Francisco, CA 94109

Joint Commission on Allied Health Personnel in Ophthalmology
2025 Woodland Drive
St. Paul, MN 55125

◇ **RELATED ARTICLES**

Optometric technicians

Definition

Optometric technicians, sometimes called *paraoptometrics*, assist optometrists in a wide range of diagnostic, therapeutic, and general office responsibilities. Optometrists are vision-care specialists who measure and treat problems of vision through the use of corrective lenses and exercises but without using drugs or surgery. Optometric technicians assist the optometrist by performing preliminary tests, such as having patients read eye charts, giving peripheral vision tests, taking blood pressure readings and readings of the pressure within the eye, and determining the power of patients' old lenses. In addition they may instruct patients in the care of glasses or contact lenses and help in therapeutic programs or post-surgical treatment.

History

Although eyeglasses have been in use in Europe since the fourteenth century, the modern science of optometry dates from the nineteenth century. By that time, research in physics, mathematics, and optics helped early practitioners in this field to develop methods for measuring the eye and instruments for testing sight. By 1897 a national association of optometrists had been formed, and in 1901 the state of Minnesota passed the first law regulating the practice of optometry.

During the twentieth century the practice of optometry has greatly expanded as more people have taken the opportunity to avail themselves of the benefits of eyeglasses and other forms of optometric vision care. This expanding demand for optometric services has led to the need for skilled assistants who can extend the capabilities of optometrists by assuming routine or repetitive tasks.

This need for assistants has developed further to the point that we have specialized forms of assistants. Optometric assistants concentrate on office duties such as scheduling appointments, maintaining files, and acting as receptionists, while optometric technicians concentrate on patient-care activities.

As the importance of these technicians has become increasingly recognized, specialized forms of post–high-school instruction have been developed for them; the American Optometric Association has recognized the career and now accredits qualifying schools; and a formal program for certifying technicians has been set up.

Nature of the work

Together, optometric assistants and optometric technicians accomplish two kinds of jobs: those related to general office procedures and those related to actual patient care. In general, assistants perform the general office work, while technicians provide the patient care; however, in some settings, especially those involving optometrists with small practices, assistants and technicians take on some of the responsibilities of the other.

Most of the duties of optometric technicians are complex in nature. They test patients for color perception, depth perception, peripheral vision, and other facets of vision; they administer visual acuity tests using standard eye charts; and they take measurements of the curvature of the patient's cornea and of the pressure inside the eyeball. They may also be responsible for determining the strength of the patient's present eyeglass or contact lens prescription. Following these tests and measurements, they record all of their results for the use of the optometrists in diagnosing and treating patients.

Some optometrists not only write prescriptions for eyeglasses but sell the eyeglasses as well. When working for an optometrist whose practice includes selling optical goods, technicians are often involved in preparing work orders for the ophthalmic laboratories that make the lenses and mount them in frames. They may also assist patients in choosing frames, take measurements of the patient's face and frames before sending out the work order, test the lenses when they come in to ensure they match the prescription, and adjust the frames to fit the patient's head comfortably.

In some cases, optometrists do not have lenses sent out to be made, but instead have them made in the office by an ophthalmic laboratory technician. In such cases, the optometric technician may also train as an ophthalmic laboratory technician. Technicians trained in this way begin with a lens blank that usually has been mass-produced by an optical company and sold to the optometrist. The technician then cuts it to conform to the prescription, polishes it, edges it (cuts a bevel or slanting surface around the edge of the lens), and fits it into a frame chosen by the patient.

In cases where optometrists prescribe visual training (eye exercises) for patients, optometric technicians frequently supervise the training. They do not choose the exercises or teach them—that is the optometrist's responsibility—but they do help the patient practice the exercises, offer some coaching, and report their observations to the optometrist to help in evaluating the patient's progress.

One of the most important aspects of the optometric technician's job is to make patients feel comfortable by developing good relationships with them. They inform patients about what is involved in an examination or procedure and try to reduce fears and build confidence in the treatment.

Optometric technicians frequently instruct patients in the insertion, removal, and care of contact lenses. They also perform a number of basic laboratory procedures, such as edging of

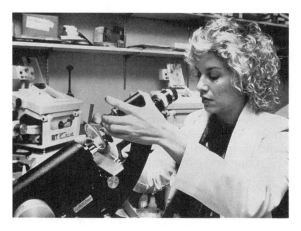

An optometric technician prepares some equipment before performing a routine visual exam on a patient.

contact lenses to make them comfortable to wear, polishing lenses to remove scratches, repairing spectacle frames and nose pads, and replacing hinges and temple pieces.

As already stated, in some settings, technicians must perform duties not directly involving patient care. They may have to maintain inventories of optometric materials, clean and care for instruments, schedule appointments, and perform other bookkeeping, secretarial, and office functions. If they are involved in scheduling appointments, they need to know the length of time required for each kind of service provided by the optometrist to schedule appointments properly. If they are involved with record-keeping they need to know how to route and maintain patients' records so that they are available when needed. They may also be responsible for a recall system to notify patients when it is time for their follow-up appointments.

The technician's bookkeeping responsibilities could include maintaining records of accounts receivable, accounts payable, payroll, bank account balances, and petty cash, as well as ordering office supplies and billing patients. Technicians might also be responsible for filing reports, tax forms and correspondence.

In some cases where optometric technicians are involved mostly or exclusively in patient-care activities, they may specialize in one form of care, such as ophthalmic laboratory work, filing contact lenses, visual training, or assisting optometrists in special procedures.

Requirements

Optometric technicians need to be neat, precise, and accurate in their work. They need good coordination, a pleasant personality, and the ability to communicate well with others.

Prospective optometric technicians need to have a high-school diploma or its equivalent to be admitted to a training program. In addition they need to be able to pass a college entrance examination for enrollment in a two-year program leading to an associate degree. While in high school, students should take courses that will help prepare them for their college-level optometric courses. In general, this means mathematics (especially algebra), English and other communications skills courses, and some secretarial courses such as typing, records management, and bookkeeping, if available.

A two-year associate degree program usually includes general academic courses, such as English, mathematics, history, and psychology. It will also include professional and technical courses in the terminology, history, and scope of services of optometry; vision care and treatment; examination procedures; a survey of vision disorders; eye exercises; laboratory procedures; and testing for vision abnormalities. The two-year program also provides technicians with practical clinical and laboratory training and experience in optometric clinics.

Most programs for optometric technicians are available in community, technical, and junior colleges, or in colleges of optometry. Students should consult their high-school guidance counselors to find out about specific programs that might fit their special needs.

Special requirements

Optometric technicians are not required to be licensed or certified. The American Optometric Association (AOA) does sponsor the National Paraoptometric Registry, which registers technicians who have achieved a recognized level of knowledge and skill in the paraoptometric field. Being registered with the AOA may help some technicians find employment, because it assures employers of the quality of the technician's preparation and training.

Opportunities for experience and exploration

It is unlikely that prospective technicians will be able to find any kind of part-time or summer employment that will give them direct experience with this kind of work. However, there are other ways in which they may find out more about the work of optometric technicians. Certainly one of the best ways is to arrange a visit to an optometrist's office where optometric technicians are employed. In this way, it is possible to observe technicians going about their work and to talk to them about what they do. Another good way for prospective technicians to find out about this career is to visit a school offering an accredited program for training optometric technicians. On such a visit they can talk to students and admissions personnel about the program and the requirements for entry. People interested in this career might also consider doing some volunteer work at a local clinic or hospital to give them a general introduction to providing patient-care services.

Methods of entering

Most graduates of two-year optometric training programs have no difficulty finding employment. Many students find and may even begin employment before graduation. School placement offices and faculty members often have requests from employers for graduate optometric technicians. Other sources of information about employment opportunities for optometric technicians include professional journals, classified ads in newspapers, and public and private employment agencies.

Advancement

As optometric technicians gain experience and are able to take on more responsibilities, they usually receive salary increases to match their increasing value to the optometrist or the optometric office in which they work.

Some technicians receive additional training in a specialty field and find advancement, usually in a larger office, as a specialist in their area of training. Also, in large offices, experienced technicians may be able to take on supervisory responsibilities. Some technicians move up to teaching positions in training programs for optometric technicians.

Employment outlook

Increased demand for eye-care services should ensure good employment opportunities for optometric technicians through the 1990s. Other factors contributing to the need for more optometric technicians include the increased inter-

est on the part of optometrists in employing technicians to increase office efficiency, growth in the general population, and specifically growth in the percentage of the population represented by older people, who are major consumers of vision-care services.

Earnings

Earnings for optometric technicians vary widely according to employer, geographical region, and level of training. In general, most optometric technicians receive starting salaries ranging from $13,000 to $20,000 a year. Benefits likewise vary with the employer. Larger optometric offices can usually offer better benefits.

Conditions of work

Most optometric technicians work a forty-hour week. Some optometrists' offices are open one or two evenings a week or on Saturday mornings. Usually optometric technicians and other staff members work out rotating schedules to meet the needs of both the office and the employees.

The physical surroundings are usually pleasant and attractive in an optometrist's office. In a laboratory, there are some fumes, a slight danger of accidents with machinery, and some noise from machines and equipment. In general, however, there are no serious health hazards or dangerous conditions.

Social and psychological factors

As in all health fields, the opportunity to help others is an important reward for some optometric technicians. Patients may experience discomfort with their progress in visual training or anxiety about some aspect of their visit to the office, and it is often the technician's job to give the patient the needed encouragement or reassurance. Technicians need to have a friendly and mature attitude, and they must be able to communicate with people of widely different ages and backgrounds.

An aptitude for precision and accuracy is important in many phases of the optometric technician's work. An error in the laboratory or in diagnosis may be critical, and technicians need to be able to accept that responsibility.

Most technicians work in private optometric offices, which usually employ only a limited

433

number of people. For some technicians the friendliness and closeness that is possible in such settings is attractive. Other technicians may miss the greater range of social and professional opportunities available when one is employed in a workplace with more people.

GOE: 10.03.02; SIC: 8042; SOC: 369

◇ **SOURCES OF ADDITIONAL INFORMATION**

American Optometric Association
243 North Lindberg Boulevard
St. Louis, MO 63141

American Academy of Optometry
5530 Wisconsin Avenue, NW, Suite 1149
Washington, DC 20815

◇ **RELATED ARTICLES**

Volume 1: Health Care
Volume 2: Dispensing opticians; Optometrists; Physician assistants
Volume 3: Dental assistants; Medical assistants; Opticians and optical mechanics
Volume 4: Ophthalmic laboratory technicians; Optics technicians

Orthotic and prosthetic technicians

Definition

Orthotic and prosthetic technicians make, fit, repair, and maintain orthotic and prosthetic devices according to specifications and under the guidance of orthotists and prosthetists. Orthotic devices, sometimes also referred to as orthopedic appliances, are braces that are used to support weak or ineffective joints or muscles or to correct physical defects, such as spinal deformities. Prosthetic devices are artificial limbs and plastic cosmetic devices. Prosthetists or orthotists are the people who actually design the devices, choose the materials, and fit the patient with the device. Orthotic and prosthetic technicians read the specifications prepared by orthotists and prosthetists to determine the type of device to be built and the materials and tools required. Part of their work involves making models of patients' torsos, limbs, or amputated areas. The models are usually made from impressions of the affected area made by the orthotist or prosthetist and are used to aid in the fitting of the device. Most of the efforts of orthotic and prosthetic technicians go into actually building the devices. Using drills, hammers, anvils, rotary saws, and other hand and machine tools, they cut, grind, carve, bend, rivet, and weld a variety of materials, including wood, plastic, metals, fabric, and leather, to build and finish the devices. Some technicians

specialize in either orthotics or prosthetics, while others work with both kinds of devices.

A technician whose work is closely related to that of the orthotic and prosthetic technician is the *arch-support technician*. Arch-support technicians make steel arch supports to fit a patient's foot according to prescriptions supplied by podiatrists, prosthetists, or orthotists.

History

Humans have sought ways to replace lost limbs artificially and to support or correct the function of weak body parts since the dawn of civilization. The ancient Egyptians, Greeks, and Romans studied and knew a great deal about dislocations, muscular paralysis, and other musculoskeletal disorders. The famous Greek physician Galen, who lived in the second century A.D., introduced some of the terms still used in designing orthotic devices and described therapies to accompany their use. The Egyptians began experimenting with splints around 5,000 years ago, and archaeologists have discovered evidence that even prehistoric people made use of crude braces and splints.

The modern origins of both orthotics and prosthetics are usually traced to the sixteenth century French surgeon Ambroise Pare. Some of the orthotic and prosthetic devices dating from that century include metal corsets, splints made out of leather and other materials for deformities of the hips and legs, special shoes, and solid metal hands.

During the seventeenth century, there was rapid progress in the field of orthotics spurred in England, at least in part, by the Poor Relief Act of 1601, which created certain kinds of government responsibility for the disabled. The introduction of splints and braces to treat the deformities arising from rickets dates from this century. It was also during this century that leather-covered wooden hands and single metal hooks were introduced to replace lost hands.

During more recent centuries, improvements in the design and materials used in prosthetics have generally come during or after major wars, such as World War I or World War II. Following World War II, for instance, prosthetic designers discovered new lightweight plastics to use in artificial arms and hands.

Prosthetic technicians and prosthetists also developed the process of cineplasty, whereby a part of the control mechanism inside a mechanical prosthesis could be attached to the end of a patient's biceps muscle, thus allowing for finer control over the moving parts of the prosthesis. All of these developments in prosthetics have led to more sophisticated, more useful, and more lifelike body parts.

Similar dramatic developments have occurred in the field of orthotics during the past two centuries. During the nineteenth century, some of the most famous practitioners in this field, such as Hugh Owen Thomas, Sir Robert Jones, and James Knight, developed many of the appliances and treatments we use today. Development in this field led to greater specialization wherein orthopedic surgeons came to write "prescriptions" for the kind of brace a patient needed, and orthotists would design and build it.

Continued growth during the twentieth century in the fields of both orthotics and prosthetics has been spurred by two world wars, the Korean war, and the Vietnam war; by injuries resulting from sports activities and from increased use of the automobile; and by new developments in both fields that allow more ailments to be successfully treated with orthotics and prosthetics. This continued growth in new and improved orthotics and prosthetics has led to yet further specialization and to the need for specially trained technicians to assist orthotists and prosthetists in their duties. Further advances will only improve employment opportunities for these technicians.

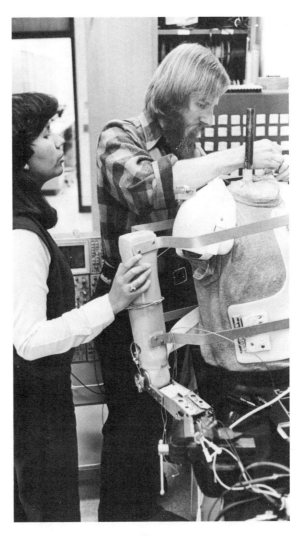

Two prosthetic technicians assemble and adjust false limbs on a cast model.

Nature of the work

The work of orthotic and prosthetic technicians is chiefly that of the skilled craft worker. They usually have no contact with patients and concentrate solely on building orthotic and prosthetic devices. Their job begins with reading the diagrams and specifications drawn up by the orthotist or prosthetist to determine the type of orthotic or prosthetic device to be built and the type of materials and tools that will be needed.

In building orthotic devices, technicians bend, weld, and cut pieces of metal or sometimes plastic in order to shape them into the structural components of the device. In doing this work they use hammers, anvils, welding equipment, and saws. They drill and tap holes into the components for rivets and then rivet the components together.

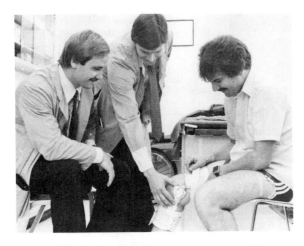

Orthotics technicians harness a knee device onto a patient and give instructions on its proper use.

To assure a proper fit of the device when finished, they often shape the plastic or metal parts around a cast model of the patient's torso or limbs. In many cases they are also responsible for making this cast model, which is usually made by pouring wet plaster or molten plastic into impressions of the patient's torso or limb made by the orthotist. When the basic structure of the device has been assembled, they cover and pad the structure, using layers of rubber, felt, plastic, and leather.

In building prosthetic devices, technicians cut, carve, and grind a variety of materials, including wood, plastic, metal, and fabric, to build the component parts of the prosthetic devices. In doing this work, they use rotary saws and cutting machines and hand cutting tools. They drill and tap holes for rivets and screws; glue, bolt, weld, sew, and rivet parts together; and assemble layers of padding and fit covers of leather, plastic, or fiberglass over the prosthesis.

Like orthotic technicians, prosthetic technicians sometimes build and often rely on models of patients' features to build their devices. They rely on these models especially when making plastic cosmetic replacements, such as ears, noses, or hands. To build these models, the prosthetist makes a wax or plastic impression of the patient's amputated area. Then the prosthetic technician makes a mold from the impression and pours molten plastic into the mold to make the cosmetic appliance.

When prosthetic technicians finish building the basic device, they fit it with an outer covering and any necessary padding, using sewing machines, riveting guns, and hand tools. Where necessary, they mix pigments to duplicate the skin coloring of the patients, and they apply the pigments to the outer coverings of the prosthesis.

Orthotic and prosthetic technicians are responsible for testing their devices for freedom of movement, alignment of parts, and functional stability. They are also responsible for repairing and maintaining orthotic and prosthetic devices as directed by the orthotist or prosthetist.

Arch-support technicians build steel arch supports to fit patients' feet inside their shoes according to medical prescriptions. Like orthotic and prosthetic technicians, arch-support technicians work with plaster casts which, in the case of arch supports, are supplied by podiatrists, orthotists, and prosthetists. Working from these models, they determine the shape and size of the support to be built. They select stainless steel sheets of prescribed thickness and cut the sheets to the necessary size. They hammer the steel in prescribed contours to form the support and check the accuracy of the fit against the model. They also polish the support with abrasive polishing wheels, glue protective leather pieces to the support, and rivet additional leather pieces to the support for additional patient comfort.

Requirements

The minimum educational requirement for orthotic and prosthetic technicians is a high-school diploma or its equivalent.

Following high school, prospective orthotic and prosthetic technicians must either enroll in a two-year program of supervised clinical experience and training, or enroll in a one- or two-year program of formal instruction leading to a certificate or associate degree in orthotics-prosthetics technology. The program of clinical experience and training must be under the close supervision of a Certified Orthotist (CO), Certified Prosthetist (CP), or Certified Prosthetist-Orthotist (CPO).

The one- or two-year programs of formal instruction are usually offered in hospitals, vocational or technical schools, or universities. They usually include courses in anatomy, psychology, use of materials, building appliances, and supervised clinical experience.

Special requirements

There are no licensing requirements for orthotic and prosthetic technicians. There is a program for the voluntary registration of orthotic and prosthetic technicians conducted by the American Board for Certification in Orthotics and Prosthetics. Candidates must have a minimum of a high-school diploma and have completed two years of work experience supervised by a Certified Orthotist, Certified Prosthetist, or Certified Prosthetist-Orthotist. The work requirement is waived for students who have completed a one- or two-year program of formal instruction in an institution accredited by the board. In addition, all candidates must pass an examination administered by the board. Depending on their area of concentration, technicians who pass the examination are designated as Registered Technician (Orthotics), RT(O); Registered Technician (Prosthetics), RT(P); or Registered Technician (Orthotics-Prosthetics), RT(OP).

Opportunities for experience and exploration

There are very few opportunities for people without training to get any part-time or summer work in the field. The prospective technician's first actual exposure to the work will probably be as part of a supervised training program or a clinical experience in a formal degree program. There are, however, some ways in which interested people can find out more about this kind of work. Teachers or guidance counselors can arrange a visit to a rehabilitation center or hospital with a department of orthotics or prosthetics. On such a visit, students can see technicians at work and perhaps speak with them about their activities.

As stated earlier, the work of orthotic and prosthetic technicians is principally that of the skilled craft worker. Therefore, courses in wood shop, metal shop, or plastic shop will give students valuable experience and will help them gauge their aptitude for this kind of work.

Orthotic and prosthetic technicians usually have no contact with patients as part of their work; however, prospective technicians might consider doing some volunteer work in a hospital. Such work may allow students to see patients in various stages of being fitted for an appliance, and it will demonstrate interest in the field to future employers.

Methods of entering

Graduates of one- or two-year programs of formal instruction usually have the easiest time

finding a first job. Teachers and placement officers will have valuable advice and information about local employers that they can share with students about to graduate.

Students looking for supervised training programs should write directly to hospitals and rehabilitation centers and inquire about programs that they have to offer or that they might recommend.

Advancement

In some large departments of orthotics and prosthetics in hospitals or rehabilitation centers, technicians may advance to supervisory, training, or other specialized positions. However, in general, significant advancement is only open to those who pursue additional training and education. By getting their additional education and by meeting prescribed training requirements, technicians can advance to the positions of Certified Orthotist, Certified Prosthetist, or Certified Prosthetist-Orthotist.

Technicians working for the Veterans Administration or other state or federal agencies will find that advancement is conducted according to civil service rules and procedures.

Employment outlook

The employment outlook for orthotic and prosthetic technicians is generally good. Among the factors contributing to the favorable outlook are the general growth of the population and the fact that more people have access to medical and rehabilitation care through private and public insurance programs. Also, continuing developments in this field will mean that more people with more different kinds of disabilities will be candidates for new or improved orthotic or prosthetic devices.

Earnings

There is limited information available relating to salaries of orthotic and prosthetic technicians. Technicians in supervised training programs may earn no more than minimum wage, or less than $10,000 a year. Technicians who have gained training and experience earn more. In some parts of the country they may make as much as $14,000 a year for a starting salary after completing their training and as much as $18,000 after they have gained more years of on-the-job experience. Technicians who return to school to earn their bachelor's degree and acquire the additional training necessary to become an orthotist or prosthetist can earn about $18,000 in their first job as an orthotist or prosthetist and about $30,000 a year or more after they have more experience.

Technicians working for the Veterans Administration or other federal agencies will find that their salaries are determined by their Government Service rating. Government Service ratings are determined by a number of factors including level of training, area of expertise, and performance on standardized tests. Most graduates of two-year post–high-school training programs begin at least at a GS-4 level.

Conditions of work

Working conditions for orthotic and prosthetic technicians are generally good. Offices, fitting rooms, workshops, storage rooms, and other patient and employee areas are kept clean, well lighted, and well ventilated. Technicians do work with power tools and sharp hand tools, so that there is some danger of injury. However, careful adherence to safety procedures greatly reduces this risk.

Orthotic and prosthetic technicians usually work five-day, forty-hour weeks. There is usually little need for overtime or weekend and evening work.

Social and psychological factors

Orthotics and prosthetics technicians usually have no contact with patients, as most of the work requiring direct contact with patients is handled by the orthotist or prosthetist. This may be a relief to some people for whom direct contact with patients might be upsetting; however, for some other technicians this distance from the people they are trying to help may be a source of frustration.

Orthotic and prosthetic technicians need also to face the fact that any meaningful advancement in their careers will probably require their returning to school.

The satisfactions of this job are in many ways similar to that of other skilled craft workers: the sense of pride that comes from a job well done. In addition, orthotic and prosthetic technicians have the satisfaction of knowing that their work is a direct source of help to people in need.

GOE: 05.05.11; SIC: 8049; SOC: 6869

◇ **SOURCES OF ADDITIONAL INFORMATION**

American Board for Certification in Orthotics and Prosthetics
717 Pendleton Street
Alexandria, VA 22314

American Academy of Orthotists and Prosthetists
717 Pendleton Street
Alexandria, VA 22314

◇ **RELATED ARTICLES**

Volume 1: Health Care
Volume 2: Kinesiotherapists; Physical therapists; Prosthetists and orthotists; Rehabilitation counselors
Volume 3: Furniture upholsterers; Shoe leather workers and repairers
Volume 4: Dental laboratory technicians; Ophthalmic laboratory technicians; Physical therapist assistants

Pharmacy technicians

Definition

Pharmacy technicians, also called *medication aides*, usually work in hospitals or similar facilities under the supervision of a nurse, pharmacist, or other health-care professional. They perform specific routine tasks related to record keeping and the preparation and distribution of drugs.

Nature of the work

Activities relating to the preparation and distribution of drugs include assembling the requested substances when an order to administer medication is received, making sure that each patient receives the correct medication, and administering the medications to patients, using established procedures.

Activities related to record keeping include recording the drug, dosage, and time of administration on specified records or forms. Pharmacy technicians also observe and note on records the patient's vital signs and response to the drug. If the reaction is unusual, they notify appropriate medical personnel. If for some reason it is not possible to administer the drug that has been prescribed, the technicians see that the record contains an explanation of this fact.

Depending on their experience and their employer, technicians may have other clerical duties pertaining to taking inventories and restocking supplies of pharmaceuticals. They may also be involved in patient-care activities such as bathing, dressing, feeding, and assisting with treatments and examinations.

Requirements

Prospective pharmacy technicians should be alert, observant, attentive to details, and able to follow written and oral instructions exactly. They may have as little as three to six months of post–high-school training on the job. However, two-year associate-degree programs are now offered in junior colleges, and in the future this type of training will probably be increasingly the norm for pharmacy technicians employed in institutional settings.

GOE: 10.03.02; SIC: 806; SOC: 5233

A pharmacy technician at a university hospital packages an ointment for a patient.

Physical therapist assistants

Definition

Physical therapist assistants are skilled health-care workers who assist physical therapists in a variety of techniques (such as exercise, massage, heat, and water) to help restore physical function in patients with impaired use of their muscles, nerves, joints, and bones.

Physical therapist assistants work directly under the supervision of physical therapists, instructing and assisting patients to learn and to improve functional activities required in their daily lives, such as walking, climbing, and moving from one place to another. The assistants observe patients during treatments, record the patients' responses and progress, and report these to the physical therapist, either orally or in writing. They fit patients for and help them learn to use braces, artificial limbs, crutches, canes, walkers, wheelchairs, and other devices. They may make physical measurements to assess the effects of treatments or to use in patient evaluations, determining the patients' range of motion, length and girth of body parts, and vital signs. Physical therapist assistants act as members of a team, and regularly confer with other members of the physical therapy staff. They may also perform various clerical tasks in the department, such as ordering supplies, taking inventories, and answering telephones.

History

The treatment of ailments by application of agents such as heat and exercises is very old. For many centuries people have known of the therapeutic value of hot baths, sunlight, and massage. The ancient Greeks and the Romans used these methods, and there is a long tradition of them in the far northern part of Europe.

Since its beginnings in the eighteenth century, the modern medical specialty of orthopedics (which is the treatment of diseases, deformities, and injuries of bones, joints, and muscles) has made use of the techniques of physical therapy to aid in treatment programs. In addition, other medical specialties have come to rely on physical therapy techniques to meet certain patient needs. For example, the emotionally disturbed have long been treated with hydrotherapy.

By the nineteenth century, orthopedic physicians were using hydrotherapy and manipulations to treat the disabled. It became fashionable, especially in Europe, for the rich to vacation at resorts featuring hot springs and baths, heat applications, and massage to relieve rheumatism, arthritis, paralysis, and other disabling ailments, as well as minor aches and pains.

Two factors spurred the development of physical therapy techniques during this century: the world wars and epidemic poliomyelitis. These catastrophes created large numbers of young but seriously disabled patients.

World War I helped to bring about great strides in medicine and in our understanding of how the human body functions. Among these advances was the realization that physical therapy could help decrease the convalescence time of the wounded. A Reconstruction Aide Corps in the U.S. Army was organized to perform physical therapy in military hospitals, and the Army's Walter Reed Hospital organized the first department of physical therapy in 1916. Training programs were hastily started to teach physiotherapy, as physical therapy used to be called, to those administering services.

Prior to World War I, very few people knew any physical therapy techniques, and the few who did had learned them during an apprenticeship period with an orthopedic surgeon. However, after the war, with the value of physical therapy better appreciated, civilian demand for trained workers and for training programs increased. The American Physical Therapy Association was organized in 1921, thus establishing physical therapy's professional stature. In 1925 the association took on the responsibility of identifying approved training programs for physical therapy personnel.

During World War II the real worth of physical therapy was recognized. Medical teams in the armed forces were able to rehabilitate seriously injured patients and thereby contributed much toward the medical acceptance of this field.

Between the wars, polio grew to be a major health problem, especially because it left many of its victims paralyzed. In 1944 the United States suffered the worst polio epidemic in its history. Public demand for improved physical therapy services focused further efforts on training more therapists and improving techniques. As knowledge grew and the number of people in the field grew, physical therapy services were redefined and expanded in scope. Physical therapy is now available in many settings outside the hospital. Currently there is preventive musculoskeletal screening for children in pediatric clinics and public schools, therapy in industrial settings for workers recovering from injuries on the job, therapy for the elderly in nursing homes and in community health agencies, and therapy for people with athletic injuries in sports medicine clinics.

The physical therapist assistant's occupation is rather new. It was developed in 1967 to help meet this greatly expanded interest in physical therapy services. Physical therapist assistants and physical therapy aides (another new occupational category, requiring less education than the assistants) specialize in some of the less complex treatments that were formerly the physical therapists' to administer.

Nature of the work

Physical therapy personnel are concerned with prevention, diagnosis, and rehabilitation. Their objective is to restore physical function and to prevent permanent disability as much as possible, and to assist people toward maximum attainable performance. For many patients this objective is expressed in terms of activities involved in daily living, such as eating, grooming, dressing, bathing, and the other basic movements that unimpaired people can do without thinking.

There are many disorders that cause conditions that physical therapy may alleviate, including fractures, burns, amputations, arthritis, nerve or muscular injuries, trauma, birth defects, stroke, multiple sclerosis, and cerebral palsy. Responding to physical therapy are such symptoms as muscular pain, spasm, and weakness; joint pain and stiffness; and neuromuscular incoordination. Patients needing physical therapy services may be any age; they may be severely disabled, or they may need only minimal therapeutic intervention.

Many kinds of equipment may be used in physical therapy. Mechanical devices, such as parallel bars, stationary bicycles, pulleys and weights, and dumbbells, are common. Heat may be applied to the body using a whirlpool bath, paraffin bath, infrared lamp, heating pad, or diathermy, which is a technique for generating heat inside body tissue using a carefully controlled small electrical current. Other equipment is needed to produce ultrasound, which is sound vibrations of extremely high frequency that acts to heat body tissue. Swimming pools are often found in physical therapy depart-

ments. Therapy may involve teaching patients how to use corrective and helpful equipment, such as wheelchairs, canes, crutches, orthotic devices (orthopedic braces and splints), and prosthetic devices (artificial limbs and other body parts).

Often physical therapy personnel must work on improving the emotional state of patients, preparing them psychologically for treatments. The overwhelming sense of hopelessness and lack of confidence that afflict many disabled patients can reduce the patients' success in achieving improved functioning. The health team must be attuned to both the physical and the nonphysical aspects of patients to assure that physical therapy treatments are most beneficial. Sometimes physical therapy personnel work with patients' families, so that the families will be aware of how to provide simple physical treatments and psychological support in the home environment.

Physical therapist assistants always work under the direction of a qualified physical therapist. Other members of the health team may be a physician or surgeon, a nurse, an occupational therapist, a psychologist, and a vocational counselor. Each of these practitioners contributes to establishing and achieving goals that are realistic and consistent with the patient's individual needs. Physical therapist assistants help the physical therapist to perform tests to evaluate disabilities and to determine the most suitable treatment for the patient; then as the treatment progresses, they routinely report the patient's state of health to the physical therapist. If they observe a patient having serious problems during treatment, the assistants notify the therapist as soon as possible. Physical therapist assistants normally help carry out complicated therapeutic procedures that the physical therapist has decided on; however, assistants may perform routine procedures alone.

These procedures may include exercises, which are the most varied and widely used physical treatments. Exercises may be simple or complicated, easy or strenuous, active or passive. Active motions are performed by the patient alone and strengthen or train muscles. Passive exercises involve the assistant moving the body part through the motion, which improves mobility of the joint but does not strengthen muscle. For example, for a patient with a fractured arm, both active and passive exercise may be appropriate. The passive exercises would probably be designed to maintain or increase the range of motion in the shoulder, elbow, wrist, and finger joints, while active resistive exercises would strengthen muscles weakened by disuse. An elderly patient who has suffered a stroke may need guided exer-

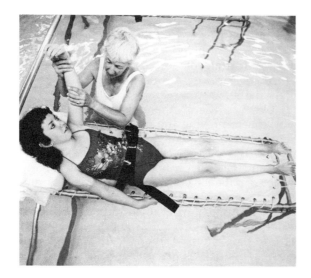

A physical therapist assistant uses water therapy to help a patient suffering from severe arthritis.

cises aimed at keeping the joints mobile, regaining the function of a limb, walking, or climbing stairs. A child with cerebral palsy who would otherwise never walk may be helped to learn coordination exercises that will enable crawling, sitting balance, standing balance, and, finally, walking.

Exercises are sometimes performed with the patient in bed or immersed in warm water. Besides being used for alleviating stiffness or paralysis, exercise is also useful in improving circulation, improving breathing of patients with lung problems, relaxing tense muscles, and correcting posture.

Other treatments that physical therapist assistants may administer include massages, traction for patients with neck or back pain, ultrasound, and various kinds of heat treatment for diseases such as arthritis that inflame joints or nerves, cold applications to reduce swelling, pain, or hemorrhaging, and ultraviolet light.

Physical therapist assistants train patients to manage devices and equipment that they will need temporarily or permanently. For instance, assistants instruct patients how to walk with canes or crutches using proper gait and how to manoeuver well in a wheelchair. They also instruct patients in how to apply, remove, care for, and cope with splints, braces, and artificial body parts.

In addition, physical therapist assistants may have office duties such as scheduling patients, keeping records, and handling inventorying and ordering of supplies.

Requirements

Physical therapist assistants must have large amounts of stamina, patience, and determination, but at the same time they must be able to establish personal relationships quickly and successfully. They should genuinely like and understand people, both under normal conditions and under the stress of illness. An outgoing personality is highly desirable, as is the ability to instill confidence and enthusiasm in patients. Much of the work of physical retraining and restoring is very repetitive, and assistants may not perceive any progress during long periods of time. At times, patients may seem unable or unwilling to cooperate. In such cases, assistants have to have boundless patience, to appreciate small gains, and to build on them. When restoration to good health is not attainable, physical therapist assistants must help the patient to adjust to a different way of life and to find ways to make the most of their situation. A creative imagination is an asset in devising methods that enable the disabled person to achieve maximum possible self-sufficiency. Assistants should also be flexible and open to suggestions offered by their co-workers, and they should be willing and able to follow directions closely.

Because the job can be physically quite demanding, physical therapist assistants must be reasonably strong and should enjoy physical activity. Manual dexterity and good coordination are needed in adjusting equipment and assisting patients. Assistants should be able to lift, climb, stoop, and kneel.

The educational requirement for becoming a physical therapist assistant is completion of high school followed by a two-year training program that awards an associate degree in physical therapy. Programs are offered in community and junior colleges, vocation-technical schools, and universities. These programs combine academic instruction with a period of supervised clinical practice in a hospital physical therapy department.

Enrolling in a program accredited by the American Physical Therapy Association is a good idea, partly because graduation from such a program is usually required by state licensing bodies. It can also help assure better advancement opportunities on the job. In recent years admission to accredited programs has sometimes been fairly competitive, with three to five applications for each available opening.

While still in high school, prospective physical therapist assistants should take courses in health, biology, mathematics, psychology, social science, physical education, computer data entry, English, and other courses that develop communications skills. In the physical therapist assistant training program, students can expect to study general education, plus anatomy, physiology, biology, history and philosophy of rehabilitation, human growth and development, psychology, and physical therapist assistant procedures such as massage, therapeutic exercise, and heat and cold therapy. Other courses in mathematics and applied physical sciences aid students in understanding the physical therapy apparatus and the scientific principles on which therapeutic procedures operate.

Special requirements

The credential requirements for physical therapist assistants vary, with licensure currently mandatory in about half the states. The requirements for licensure are graduation from an American Physical Therapy Association–accredited two-year associate degree program and passing a written examination administered by the state. Conditions for renewing the license also vary by state. For information about licensing requirements, candidates should consult their school's career guidance office or the state licensure board.

Opportunities for experience and exploration

While still in high school, students can get experience by working in the summer or on a part-time or volunteer basis in the physical therapy department of a hospital or clinic. Also many schools, both public and private, have volunteer assistance programs for work with their disabled student population. These opportunities provide prospective physical therapy workers with direct contact with the activities of the job and, more importantly, helps them determine whether they have the personal qualities necessary for this career.

Another excellent way to gain useful direct experience is to work with disabled children in a summer camp. Students who have not had such direct experience should make an effort to talk to a physical therapist or a physical therapist assistant at a high-school Career Day, for example. It may be possible to arrange to visit a physical therapy department, watch the staff at work, and ask questions.

Some physical therapist assistants first became interested in their careers while in the

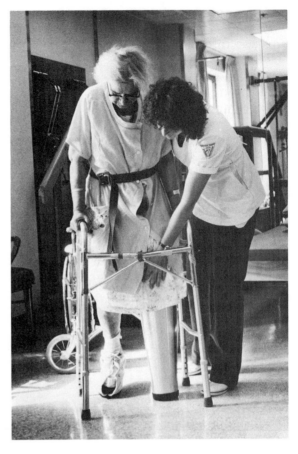

An amputee patient is aided by a physical therapy assistant. The patient is learning to use a walker and an airboot, a device that prepares the limb for a prosthetic.

armed forces, which operate training programs. These programs are not sufficient for state licensure and they do not award degrees, but they can serve as an excellent introduction to the field for students who later enter more complete training programs.

Methods of entering

The placement office at the school offering the training program is probably the best place for a newly graduated physical therapist assistant to find a job. Alternatively, assistants can apply to the physical therapy departments of local hospitals, rehabilitation centers, extended-care facilities, and other potential employers. Openings are also listed in the classified ads of newspapers, in professional journals, and with private and public employment agencies. In locales where training programs have produced many physical therapist assistants, competition for jobs may be keen. In such cases, assistants

443

may want to widen their search to other areas where there is less competition, especially suburbs and rural areas.

Advancement

With experience, physical therapist assistants are often given greater responsibility and better pay. In large health-care facilities, supervisory possibilities may open up. Especially in small institutions, where there is only one physical therapist, the physical therapist assistant may eventually be able to take care of all the technical tasks that go on in the department, within the limitations of his or her training and education.

Physical therapist assistants with degrees from accredited programs are generally in the best position to gain advancement in any setting. They sometimes decide to earn a bachelor's degree in physical therapy and move up by becoming fully qualified therapists.

Employment outlook

The job prospects are very good for physical therapy technicians who have graduated from accredited programs. Demand for people who can provide rehabilitation services is expected to continue to grow much more rapidly than the average for all occupations, and the rate of turnover among workers is relatively high. Many new positions for physical therapist assistants will be created as hospital programs for aiding the disabled expand and as long-term facilities seek to offer residents more adequate services.

A major contributing factor in this trend is the aging of the U.S. population. People over age sixty-five tend to suffer a disproportionate amount of the accidents and chronic illnesses that necessitate physical therapy services. Legislation requiring appropriate public education for all disabled children may also serve to increase the demand for physical therapy services. As more adults engage in strenuous physical exercise, more musculoskeletal injuries will result, also increasing demand for services.

Other factors may negatively affect the employment picture, however. Among these are the decreased availability of funds to pay for such services through private and public insurance programs and changes in the degree to which health-care providers encourage this intense level of care for elderly patients.

Earnings

Salaries for physical therapist assistants vary considerably depending on geographical location, the employer, and the technician's level of experience. Information is sketchy, but the yearly income for a recently graduated assistant is usually between $15,000 and $20,000 a year, while experienced physical therapist assistants usually earn between $18,000 and $26,000 a year. Fringe benefits also vary, although they usually include paid holidays and vacations, health insurance, and pension plans.

Conditions of work

Physical therapy is usually administered in pleasant, clean, well-lighted, and well-ventilated surroundings, most often located in a physical therapy department of a hospital, but also in rehabilitation centers, schools for the disabled, nursing homes, community and government health agencies, physicians' or physical therapists' offices, and facilities for the mentally handicapped. The area devoted to physical therapy services is often large, in order to accommodate activities such as gait training and exercises and procedures requiring equipment. Some procedures are given at patients' bedsides.

In the physical therapy department, patients come and go all day, usually on an appointment basis, many in wheelchairs, on walkers, canes, crutches, or stretchers. The staff tries to maintain a purposeful, harmonious, congenial atmosphere as they and the patients work toward the common goal of restoring physical efficiency.

The work can be exhausting. Physical therapist assistants may be on their feet for hours at a time, and they may have to move heavy equipment, lift patients, and assist them in standing and walking. Most assistants work only normal daytime hours, five days a week, although in some positions night or weekend work may be required. Some assistants work on a part-time basis.

Social and psychological factors

Physical therapist assistants have to try to be patient, cheerful, and encouraging to their patients, even in the face of problems that sometimes appear insolvable. The combined physical and emotional demands of the job can exert a considerable strain. Prospective assistants would be wise to seek out some job experience related to physical therapy, so that they have a practical understanding of their psychological and physical capacities. If they know they really can do the work, they can make a better commitment to the training program.

Job satisfaction can be great for physical therapist assistants, because they can see how their efforts help to make people's lives much more rewarding.

GOE: 10.02.02; SIC: 80; SOC: 5233

◇ **SOURCES OF ADDITIONAL INFORMATION**

American Physical Therapy Association
1111 North Fairfax Street
Alexandria, VA 22314

U.S Physical Therapy Association
1803 Avon Lane
Arlington Heights, IL 60004

American Association for Rehabilitation Therapy
Information Officer
PO Box 93
North Little Rock, AR 72116

National Rehabilitation Association
633 South Washington Street
Alexandria, VA 22314

◇ **RELATED ARTICLES**

Volume 1: Health Care; Sports
Volume 2: Human services workers; Kinesiotherapists; Physical therapists; Rehabilitation counselors
Volume 3: Medical assistants; Nursing and psychiatric aides
Volume 4: Home health technicians; Orthotic and prosthetic technicians

Psychiatric technicians

Definition

Psychiatric technicians provide nursing care and participate in treatment programs for mentally ill, emotionally disturbed, or mentally retarded patients in psychiatric hospitals or mental health clinics. The psychiatric technician's nursing duties often include helping patients with bathing and with keeping their beds, clothing, and living areas clean; administering oral medications and hypodermic injections according to physicians' prescriptions and hospital procedures; and taking and recording readings of patients' pulse, temperature, and respiration rate. Psychiatric technicians participate in treatment programs by leading individual or group therapy sessions in a prescribed manner as part of a specific therapeutic procedure. Another important aspect of the psychiatric technician's work is to observe the behavior patterns of patients and to report their observations to members of the medical and psychiatric staff. In addition to these duties, psychiatric technicians may also complete initial admitting forms for new patients, contact patients' families to arrange conferences, issue medications from the dispensary, and maintain records in accordance with specified procedures.

History

Although some mentally ill people were treated as early as the fifteenth century in institutions like Saint Mary's of Bethlehem hospital in London (whose name was often shortened to Bedlam, from which we get our word "bedlam"), the general practice of institutionalizing people with mental disorders did not become common until the seventeenth century.

During the seventeenth, eighteenth, and even into the nineteenth century, the treatment of mentally ill patients was quite crude and often simply barbarous. This state of affairs began to change in the late eighteenth century as

A psychiatric technician conducts a group therapy session for college students.

medical practitioners such as Benjamin Rush of Philadelphia, often called the father of American psychiatry, began to see mental illness as a medical problem. During the late eighteenth and early nineteenth centuries, hospitals began to stop treating mental illness as the product of possession, demonology, and witchcraft, and began concentrating instead on keeping patients clean and comfortable, building their self-respect, and treating them with friendliness and encouragement. This new conception of mental illness led, in the early nineteenth century, to the establishment of specially designed institutions for the care of mental patients, such as the McLean Asylum in Boston, the Morningside Heights branch of the New York Hospital, the Hartford Retreat, and the Institute of the Pennsylvania Hospital.

During the late nineteenth and early twentieth centuries, medical researchers made important discoveries relating to the anatomical, chemical, and physical aspects of mental illness. During the first half of the twentieth century, much of the care of mentally ill patients focused on physical aspects of their disease and was provided by means of long-term confinement in an institution designed exclusively for mentally ill patients.

This picture of the mental health field began to change in the 1940s, as mental health institutions tried to find more effective therapeutic services for their patients, including more kinds of social activities for their residents and other innovative treatment programs. There was also a shift towards providing more treatment services in community and general hospitals and community mental health centers, rather than relying solely on state mental hospitals.

These changes were undertaken to shorten periods of hospitalization and to decrease the stigma and dislocation associated with treatment in mental hospitals. However, these changes also created sharply increased personnel needs. One strategy for dealing with this increased need for trained personnel has been to train more professionals—psychiatrists, psychologists, social workers, nurses, and others. Another strategy has focused on training more nonprofessionals—aides, attendants, orderlies, and others.

Beginning in the 1960s the drive to develop new therapies and the trend towards de-institutionalizing patients led to the creation of a new category of mental health worker with a level of training between that of the professional and the nonprofessional. Workers with this level of training are usually referred to as paraprofessionals, and in the mental health field they are known as psychiatric technicians or mental health technicians. These people are graduates of two-year post–high-school programs, and in most cases they are employed not only to take over for or assist professionals in traditional treatment activities, but also to provide new services in innovative ways. The treatments and services they provide are the kind that require they be skilled and specially trained but not necessarily that they have all of the academic preparation of nurses or physicians.

Nature of the work

Psychiatric technicians work in a wide variety of settings, including mental hospitals, community general hospitals, community mental health centers, psychiatric clinics, schools for the mentally retarded, social service agencies, and other residential and nonresidential facilities that provide psychiatric services such as geriatric nursing homes, child or adolescent development centers, and halfway houses. The patients that they work with may include alcohol and drug abusers, psychotic or emotionally disturbed children and adults, mentally retarded people, and the aged.

Psychiatric technicians work under the supervision of mental health professionals, such as psychiatrists, psychologists, registered nurses, or in some cases, senior psychiatric technicians. Psychiatric technicians work with these and other mental health–care workers as part of a team in which their special responsibility is to provide physical and mental rehabilitation for patients through recreational, occupational, and psychological readjustment programs.

In general, psychiatric technicians participate in both the planning of individual treatment plans and in the implementing of these plans. Their specific activities will vary according to the setting in which they work, but they may include any, or sometimes nearly all of the following: interviewing and information gathering; working in a unit of a hospital where they are responsible for admitting, screening, evaluating, or discharging patients; record keeping; making referrals to community agencies; working for patients' needs and rights; visiting patients at home after their release from a hospital; and participating in individual and group counseling and therapy programs. These programs may include behavior modification, activities designed to build social skills, and certain forms of psychotherapy, such as rational emotive therapy, Gestalt transactional analysis, and reality therapy. In all of these activities, they endeavor to work with patients in a broad, comprehensive manner, seeing each patient as a person whose peculiar or abnormal behavior is the result of an illness or disability and taking as their main responsibility the assistance of each patient in achieving his or her maximum level of functioning. This means helping them to strengthen their social and mental skills, to accept greater responsibility for themselves and for others, and to develop the confidence to enter into social, educational, or vocational activities.

In addition to the activities already mentioned, psychiatric technicians working in hospitals handle a certain number of nursing responsibilities. They may take temperatures, count pulses and respiration rates, measure blood pressures, and assist in the administration of medications and physical treatments. In many cases, technicians working in hospitals will find themselves concerned with all aspects of the lives of their patients—from eating, sleeping, and personal hygiene to helping them develop social skills and an improved self-image.

Technicians working in clinics, community mental health centers, halfway houses, day hospitals, or other noninstitutional settings perform many of the activities already mentioned in addition to some that are special to their situation. They interview newly registered patients and their relatives, make visits to patients

and their families at home, administer psychological tests, participate in group activities, write reports about their observations to supervising psychiatrists or other mental health professionals, and try to ease the transition of patients leaving hospitals and returning to their communities. They may arrange for consultations with mental health specialists, and they may refer patients to these specialists. They may also help patients resolve their employment, housing, and personal finance problems. In this and in other respects, psychiatric technicians act as aides to their patients, helping them through the maze of services, agencies, and professionals that are available for them but that have their own separate and often varying sets of rules, regulations, policies, and procedures.

Although most psychiatric technicians are trained as generalists in providing mental health services, there are some opportunities for technicians to specialize in a particular aspect of mental health care. For example, some technicians work as specialists in the problems of mentally disturbed children. Others specialize in working as counselors in drug and alcohol abuse programs or as members of psychiatric emergency or crisis-intervention teams.

Another area of specialization is working in community mental health. Technicians employed in this area are sometimes known as human-services technicians, and they specialize in using rehabilitation techniques that do not involve hospitalization for patients who have problems in adjusting to their social environment. These technicians may be primarily concerned with drug and alcohol abuse, parental effectiveness, the elderly, or problems dealing with interpersonal relationships. Human-services technicians work in social welfare departments, child-care centers, preschool nurseries, vocational rehabilitation workshops, and schools for the learning disabled, emotionally disturbed, and mentally handicapped.

With slightly different training, psychiatric technicians may specialize in the treatment of mentally retarded people. Known as mental-retardation technicians, these technicians assist in the rehabilitation of patients through teaching recreational activities. Mental-retardation technicians generally work in halfway houses, state hospitals, training centers for the retarded, or for state and local service agencies.

Other places of employment for psychiatric technicians include correctional programs and juvenile courts, public school counseling or psychology services, nursing homes, senior citizen centers, schools for the blind and deaf, community action programs, family service centers, and public housing programs.

Requirements

Psychiatric technicians need to have stable personalities; the ability to relate well to people, including patients, their families, and fellow staff members; and the motivation to help others. This does not mean that psychiatric technicians desire to do everything for other people; rather, it means that they respect the worth of each person and that they have a desire to help people function at their highest potential.

Because psychiatric technicians will be interacting with people, they must be sensitive to the needs and feelings of others. Some aspects of sensitivity can be learned. However, the learning process requires not only a willingness to listen and be extremely observant but also to risk involvement in situations which at first may seem ambiguous and confusing. In addition, psychiatric technicians need to be willing to look at themselves, their attitudes, and how they function, and be flexible and open about effecting changes in themselves. The more they know of themselves, the more effective they will be in helping others.

Patience and understanding are required in working with people who may be disagreeable and unpleasant because of their illness. A sense of responsibility and the ability to remain calm in emergencies are also essential characteristics for psychiatric technicians to have.

Psychiatric technicians must have two years of training beyond high school. Each college has somewhat different entrance requirements. Technicians should find out as early as possible in the high-school years about the requirements of schools they might want to attend, in order that they are assured of meeting all the relevant requirements. In general, students in high school should take courses in English, biology, and, if available, psychology and sociology.

The two-year post–high-school training programs usually lead to an associate of arts or associate of science degree. In general, the programs include study in human development, personality structure, the nature of mental illness, and, to a limited extent, anatomy, physiology, basic nursing, and medical science. Other subjects usually encountered in two-year programs include some introduction to basic social sciences, so that technicians can better understand relevant family and community structures; some overview of the structure and functions of the institutions that treat patients; and, most importantly, some practical instruction in doing the essential work that psychiatric technicians are called upon to do.

On the average, programs include about one-fourth general study, such as English, psychology, and sociology; about one-fourth mental health-related courses, such as early childhood development, general and abnormal psychology, the family, and social welfare institutions; about one-fourth mental health courses that deal with specific topics related to psychopathology, concepts and techniques of its prevention, forms of therapy, rehabilitation, general and psychiatric nursing, and community mental health; and about one-fourth practical and field learning. The practical and field learning is essential in giving students a personal and realistic orientation to the problems they will face, and in terms of actual hours spent, may equal about one-half of the total program.

Most mental health technology programs emphasize interviewing skills. This training guides technicians in correctly reading the tones of voice and shades of meaning of what people say and do, so that they are well equipped to observe and record the behavior that people exhibit. Some programs also teach the administration of selected psychological tests. Students may also gain knowledge and training in crisis intervention techniques, child guidance, group counseling, family therapy, behavior modification, and skills in consultation, such as with small local agencies about mental health problems and with other workers about individual patients.

Special requirements

Some states require that psychiatric technicians be licensed. Prospective technicians and technicians-in-training should consult their guidance or placement counselors for information about requirements in their state.

Opportunities for experience and exploration

There are a number of ways in which prospective psychiatric technicians can gather some personal experience in this field. If they can manage to take on the responsibility of a full-time job they can apply for a position as a nurse's aide at a local general hospital. In this way they gain direct personal contact with providing care to patients. If such a job requires too much of a time commitment, students might consider volunteering their time to the hospital on a part-time basis or during summer months. Other relevant job experiences include playground and summer camp counseling.

These positions will give prospective technicians an idea about how well they do in getting along with people, supervising group activities, and taking responsibility for the behavior of others.

People interested in this career might also consider offering their help to their local mental health association or a local social welfare agency. Most of the opportunities for experience that these agencies will have entail work as an unpaid volunteer; however, they may provide a good chance for becoming acquainted with the nature of the work in this field. In some cases, the mental health association can arrange opportunities for people to do volunteer work inside a mental hospital or mental health clinic. Finally, students, or their teachers, can arrange a visit to a mental health clinic. If permission has been received ahead of time, students may be able to talk with staff members and to observe first-hand how these people do their jobs.

Methods of entering

Graduates from mental health and human services technology programs can usually choose from a variety of job possibilities. College placement officers can be extremely helpful in locating employment. Students can follow want ads or apply directly to clinics, agencies, or hospitals of their choice. Job information can also be obtained from the department of mental health in each state.

Advancement

Working as a psychiatric technician is still a relatively new occupation, and there are not yet any clearly defined sequences of promotions. Advancement normally takes the form of being given greater responsibilities with less supervision. It usually results from gaining experience, developing competence and leadership abilities, and continuing formal and practical education. In some cases, promotions are governed by civil service regulations, and in these cases, advancement is based on experience and on test scores on promotion examinations.

As more technicians come to be employed in a given setting, needs inevitably arise for additional supervisory personnel. This growth will provide advancement opportunities, because many supervisors will probably be picked from the ranks of senior psychiatric technicians.

Some psychiatric technicians specialize in problems of mentally or emotionally disturbed children. This technician works with an autistic child.

In large part, advancement is linked to gaining further education. Thus, after working a few years, technicians may decide to obtain a baccalaureate degree in psychology. Advanced education, coupled with previous training and work experience, should greatly enhance advancement potential. For instance, with a baccalaureate degree, experienced technicians may be able to find rewarding positions as instructors in one of the new programs or in an older expanded program for training future mental health workers.

Employment outlook

The total number of people employed as psychiatric technicians is expected to rise because of, in large part, a well-established trend of returning hospitalized patients to their communities after shorter and shorter periods of hospitalization. The trend has encouraged the development of comprehensive community mental health centers and has led to an increased need for psychiatric technicians to staff these facilities.

In addition, as more legislation is enacted requiring public schools to offer classes to neurologically impaired, educable mentally retarded, and emotionally handicapped students, the need for psychiatric technicians in schools will increase further.

Finally, concerns over rising costs of health care should increase employment levels for technicians, because technicians and other paraprofessionals can take over some functions of higher-paid professions. This kind of substitution has been demonstrated to be an effective way of reducing costs without reducing the quality of care.

Earnings

Salaries for psychiatric technicians vary according to the geographical area in which they are employed and the setting in which they work, with technicians in community settings generally receiving higher salaries than those in institutional settings. In general, psychiatric technicians receive starting salaries ranging anywhere from the minimum wage, or less than $10,000 a year, to as much as $20,000 a year, or more. With increased experience technicians can expect at least modest increases in their salaries each year. Some senior psychiatric technicians earn as much as $27,000 a year, or more.

Most psychiatric technicians receive fringe benefits including hospitalization insurance, sick leave, and paid vacations. Technicians working for state institutions or agencies will probably also be eligible for financial assistance for further education.

Conditions of work

Psychiatric technicians work in a variety of settings and their working conditions vary accordingly. Typically they work forty-hour workweeks and five days a week, although one of those days may be a weekend day. Some psychiatric technicians work evening or night shifts, and all technicians may be asked to work holidays.

For the most part, the physical surroundings are pleasant. Most institutions, clinics, mental health centers, and agency offices are kept clean and are comfortably furnished. Technicians who work with the mentally ill must nonetheless be adjusted to an environment that is often chaotic and sometimes upsetting. Some patients are acutely depressed and withdrawn or excessively agitated and excited. Some patients may become unexpectedly violent and verbally abusive. However, institutions treating these kinds of patients always have enough staff on hand to maintain order and to protect workers from any physical harm. Psychiatric technicians who make home visits may sometimes confront rather unpleasant conditions.

Social and psychological factors

Work with mentally ill people demands a high degree of emotional stability. Psychiatric technicians may work with patients who are acutely ill and who have lost contact with reality. Some patients may be suicidal. Technicians must have the ability to be absolutely honest, yet compassionate. Most importantly, they must maintain their perspective and not permit a patient's problems to become their own. They should not take occasional insults to heart. They also need to realize that many of the patients they work with will never be restored to good health.

To help patients most effectively, technicians must learn to understand themselves and the effect their own behavior and attitudes have on others. They must be willing to become involved with the people they treat, and they must be able to communicate an optimistic attitude towards their patients. Successful psychiatric technicians realize that their own optimistic expectations for their patients are crucial and integral to the kind of recovery the patients can make.

Finally, psychiatric technicians work not only with individuals but often with the community. In that role these technicians can be called upon to take advocacy positions for their patients, such as motivating community agencies to provide services, obtaining exceptions to rules when needed for individual patients, and bringing about changes in rules when needed for groups of patients. Successful psychiatric technicians develop competence in working with community and neighborhood groups and in dealing with their various decision-making processes.

GOE: 10.02.02; SIC: 8063; SOC: 366

◇ **SOURCES OF ADDITIONAL INFORMATION**

American Psychiatric Association
Information Officer
1400 K Street, NW
Washington, DC 20005

National Mental Health Association
1021 Prince Street
Arlington, VA 22314

Pulmonary function technicians

Definition

Pulmonary function technicians perform tests on patients to gather data that will be used in medical evaluations of the patients' respiratory functions. They work under a physician's direction, and they are primarily concerned with diagnosis, not therapy. Many of the tests they conduct involve the patient breathing into equipment that measures various factors, but some blood analysis is also involved.

Nature of the work

Some of the tests performed by pulmonary function technicians are quite simple, while others require complex electronic machinery. Among the different types of tests that they perform are tests of lung efficiency and function and tests of lung capacity. Spirometers, which are devices for measuring amounts of air breathed in and out, are used in several of these tests, such as those for vital capacity (total lung volume) and maximum breathing capacity (the quantity of air that can be breathed in one minute).

Other kinds of equipment used by pulmonary function technicians include co-oximeters, which are machines for determining the red blood cell count, the amount of oxygen in the blood, and other factors, and oxygen analyzers, which technicians use to collect and analyze expired air from patients. This test is used to de-

Two pulmonary function technicians measure the breathing capacity of a patient. The machine measures the lung efficiency and total lung volume.

termine the amounts of oxygen and carbon dioxide eliminated.

Before conducting any of these procedures, the technician explains to the patient what is about to happen. This is very important, because the patient's total cooperation is often required if the test results are to be meaningful. As technicians operate the equipment, they observe the patient for signs of trouble or anything that could affect the accuracy of test results, record test results, and report their findings to a supervising professional for further analysis.

Requirements

In general, pulmonary function technicians should have communication skills that enable them to gain the confidence and cooperation of patients quickly. They should be good at carrying out procedures and recording results with precision. Prospective technicians ought to have an inclination toward mathematics and science. They can expect to study for one to two years in a post–high-school training program to prepare for this career.

GOE: 10.03.01; SIC: 806; SOC: 369

◇ **RELATED ARTICLES**

Volume 1: Health Care
Volume 2: Licensed practical nurses; Physicians; Physician assistants; Medical record administrators; Registered nurses; Respiratory therapists
Volume 3: Medical assistants; Nursing and psychiatric aides
Volume 4: Electrocardiograph technicians; Electroencephalographic technicians; Radiological (X-ray) technologists

Radiological (X-ray) technologists

Definition

Radiological technologists, sometimes called *radiographers* or *X-ray technicians*, operate various kinds of equipment that use X rays and radioactive materials for medical diagnostic and therapeutic purposes. They work under the direction of a physician. If they are making X-ray photographs, radiological technologists may administer drugs or chemical mixtures to the patient to make internal organs opaque to X rays. They put the patient in the correct position between the X-ray source and the film, and they make sure that body areas, which are not to be exposed, are protected from radiation. After determining the proper duration and intensity of the exposure, they operate the controls to beam X rays through the patient and expose the photographic film. They may operate computer-aided imaging equipment that does not involve X rays. They also help to treat diseased or affected areas of the body by exposing the patient to specified concentrations of radiation for prescribed times.

History

Radiography is the process of creating an image, usually on a photographic film or plate, by means of a form of electromagnetic radiation. Unlike photography, however, in which the film or plate is exposed to the most familiar kind of electromagnetic radiation, ordinary light rays, in radiography the film or plate is exposed to X rays, which have shorter wave lengths and different energy levels.

X rays were discovered by Wilhelm Conrad Roentgen in 1895. X rays, or roentgen rays, are generated in a glass vacuum tube (an X-ray tube) that contains two differently charged electrodes, one of which gives off electrons. When the electrons travel from one electrode to the other, some of the energy they emit is X-radiation. X rays have the property of being able to pass through skin and muscle and other soft body tissue. Bones and denser objects show up as shadows on the photographic emulsion when film is exposed to X rays, and a picture can thus be developed of the inside of the body.

In fluoroscopy, a beam of X rays passes through the body and onto a fluorescent screen, enabling the physician to see the internal organs in motion. Sometimes the patient is given a dense fluid to drink, such as a mixture containing barium sulfate. That increases the contrast between the digestive tract and the surrounding organs, making the picture clearer.

In nuclear medicine an image of internal organs is produced using radioactive materials, and it enables the physician to diagnose diseased tissue and functional disorders. Unlike X-ray radiography, where the radiation from the X-ray source passes through the body to expose the photographic film, nuclear medicine views the radiation from radioactive isotopes inside the body. A substance is made radioactive and then is injected into or swallowed by the patient. For example, to investigate thyroid function, radioactive iodine is given to the patient because it accumulates in the thyroid gland. The radiation, or gamma rays, given off by the patient is recorded and amplified into in image on a television-type screen that can be photographed. There are a variety of radioactive compounds that are used to study different body organs and functions.

All forms of radiation are potentially harmful. Exposure to ultraviolet radiation may tan the skin but it can also result in burning and other damage to tissue, including the development of cancer cells. Low-level infrared radiation can warm tissues, but, at higher levels it cooks them like microwaves do; the process can destroy cells. Protective measures to avoid all unnecessary exposure to radiation must be taken whenever X rays are being used, because they can have both short and long term harmful effects.

Radiation therapy uses radiation's ability to destroy diseased tissue in a way that is beneficial. Carefully controlled and precisely directed doses of radiation are used to treat certain tumors. Radiological equipment may be used to bombard the tumor or a radioactive substance may be implanted in the affected area. Great skill is needed to ensure that healthy tissue is protected insofar as possible from the effects of the radiation therapy.

Other forms of diagnostic imaging do not expose patients to any potentially harmful radiation. Sound waves are used in ultrasound technology, or sonography, to obtain a scanner picture of internal organs. High frequency sound waves beamed into the patient's body bounce back and create echoes which can be recorded on a paper strip or photograph. The sound waves are harmless; ultrasound is very frequently employed to determine the size and development of a human fetus. Magnetic resonance imaging involves magnetic fields instead of sound waves but works in very much the same fashion. Positron emission scanners, which use electrons to create images, are another type of equipment used in diagnostic imaging without radiation.

The use of imaging techniques that do not involve radiation has grown rapidly during the 1980s and 1990s because of their safety and because of great improvements in computer technology. Computers can now handle a vast quantity of data much more rapidly, making it possible to enhance images to great clarity and sharpness.

Nature of the work

All radiological work is done at the request of and under the supervision of a physician. Just as a prescription is required for some kinds of drugs to be dispensed or administered, so also must a physician's request be issued before a patient can receive any kind of radiologic treatment.

There are four principle specializations in which radiological technologists may work: radiography, which is taking X-ray pictures or radiographs; nuclear medicine; radiation therapy; and sonography. In each of these the technologist often works under the direction of a radiologist, who is a physician who specializes in interpreting the pictures produced by X rays and other imaging techniques. Technologists can work in more than one of these areas. Some technologists specialize in a particular part of the body or a specific condition.

X-ray pictures or radiographs represent the most familiar use of radiologic technology. They are used to diagnose and determine treatment for a wide variety of afflictions, including ulcers, tumors, and bone fractures. X-ray pictures of the chest can determine whether a person has a lung disease. To do their job, radiological technologists who operate X-ray equipment first help the patient prepare for the radiologic examination. They may administer a substance to make the part of the body to be seen clearly visible on the film. They make sure that the patient is not wearing any jewelry or other metal that would obstruct the X rays. They position the person sitting, standing, or lying down so that the correct view of the body can be radiographed and they cover adjacent areas with lead shielding.

The technologist positions the X-ray equipment at the proper angle and distance from the part to be radiographed and determines exposure time based on the location of the particular organ or bone and the thickness of the body in that area. The controls of the X-ray machine must be set to produce pictures of the correct density, contrast, and detail. Placing the photographic film on the far side of the patient's body, the technologist makes as many exposures as the physician has requested, repositioning the patient as needed. The film is then developed for the radiologist or other physician to interpret.

For a fluoroscopic examination the technologist first prepares a solution of barium sulfate for the patient to drink. The technologist assists the physician by positioning the patient, determining the correct exposure, operating the machine, and preparing follow-up radiographs as needed.

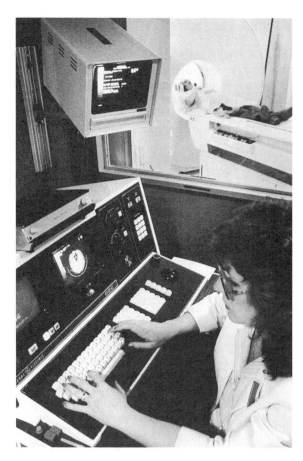

A radiological (X-ray) technologist operates the controls via a computer, which directs the rays and regulates the duration of the patient's exposure.

A nuclear medicine technologist prepares radioactive materials that are used for diagnosing certain conditions and for therapy in some forms of cancer. Substances containing radioactive isotopes are injected into or swallowed by the patient. The radioactivity of the tissues or organ where the isotope material concentrates can be measured over a period of time with special cameras or scanners. The technologist operates these and other instruments to trace the radioactivity. A nuclear medicine technologist also performs laboratory tests of blood volume, red cell survival, and fat absorption to determine any effect of the radioactive substances. (For more about this kind of work, see the article entitled "Nuclear medicine technologists" in Volume 2.)

Radiation therapy is used mainly for certain cancers. Radiological technologists who work in this field expose patients to the prescribed amounts of radiation at carefully specified body sites. They use many kinds of sophisticated equipment, such as high-energy linear accelerators. They may also administer radioactive substances to patients. In contrast to most other radiological technologists, radiation therapy technologists tend to work repeatedly with the same patients, returning for multiple treatments.

Sonography, or ultrasound, is one of the more recent technologies used to monitor and diagnose a variety of conditions, including abdominal tumors, cysts, fetal abnormalities, impaired function of the heart valves and the blood vessels, and intracranial bleeding in newborns. Ultrasound technologists, or sonographers, are the specialists who select and operate the appropriate equipment. Using a device called a transducer, the technologist directs high-frequency sound waves into the affected part of the patient's body. The sound waves, similar to sonar in a submarine, create an echo when reflected from body tissues. The echoes are displayed on a video monitor as two-dimensional gray moving images, which the technologist then records on film or videotape. These patterns and pictures are reviewed by a physician who specializes in interpreting images created using ultrasound.

Many radiological technologists perform a range of duties, beginning with greeting patients and trying to make them feel comfortable and at ease through developing the finished film. Some technologists specialize in radiography of joints and bones, while others may be involved in such areas as angiocardiography (visualization of the heart and large blood vessels) or neuroradiology (the use of radiation in diagnosing and treating diseases of the nervous system).

In addition to operating radiologic equipment and assisting physicians working with patients, radiological technologists often have routine administrative tasks. Patients' records must be maintained and records of the use and maintenance of equipment must also be kept. Senior staff, often with titles like "chief radiological technologist" or "chief nuclear medicine technologist," may organize work schedules and generally manage a radiologist's large practice or a department of radiology. Some radiological technologists teach in programs to train other technologists.

Requirements

People who wish to become radiological technologists must complete a training program in radiography, radiation therapy technology, nuclear medicine technology, or diagnostic medical sonography. Programs range in length from one to four years, although most are two years long. Depending on length, the programs award a certificate, an associate degree, or a bachelor's degree. One-year programs, however, are mostly intended for people who are already working in health care and who wish to change careers.

Training programs are available in hospitals, medical centers, colleges and universities, and vocational and technical institutes. In the late 1980s there were nearly 850 programs accredited by the Committee on Allied Health Education and Accreditation (CAHEA) of the American Medical Association. It is also possible to get an education in radiological technology in the armed forces.

All of the accredited programs require that applicants be high-school graduates, and some may require one or two years of higher education. High-school courses in mathematics, physics, chemistry, and biology are useful background preparation. The courses that are taught in radiological technology training programs include anatomy, physiology, patient care, physics, radiation protection, medical ethics, principles of imaging, medical terminology, radiobiology, and pathology.

For some supervisory or administrative jobs in this field, a bachelor's or master's degree is required.

Special requirements

Radiological technologists may register with the American Registry of Radiologic Technologists after graduating from an accredited program in radiography, radiation therapy, or nuclear medicine. Nuclear medicine technologists also may earn credentials from the Nuclear Medicine Technology Certification Board, and ultrasound technologists may be certified by the American Registry of Diagnostic Medical Sonographers. Although registration and certification are voluntary, many jobs are open only to technologists who have acquired these credentials. As the work of radiological technologists grows increasingly complex and as the employment opportunities within this field become more competitive, the desirability of registration and certification will also grow.

An increasing number of states have licensing requirements. In the late 1980s, licenses were needed by radiographers in sixteen states, by radiation therapy technologists in eleven states, and by nuclear medicine technologists in seven states.

Opportunities for experience and exploration

There is no way to get direct experience in this field without the appropriate qualifications. However, it is possible to learn about the duties of radiological technologists by talking with them and by seeing the facilities and equipment they use. It is also possible to have interviews with teachers of radiological technology. Prospective technologists should contact local hospitals or schools with radiography training programs to locate technologists who would be able to talk to interested students.

Methods of entering

With more states regulating the practice of radiologic technology, completion of a accredited formal training program is fast becoming a necessity for employment. Persons who acquire training in schools that have not been accredited by the American Medical Association, or who learn on the job, may have difficulty in qualifying for many positions, especially those with a wide range of assignments. Graduates of AMA-accredited schools usually receive a great deal of assistance from placement services at their schools in securing their first jobs. People who are trained in programs offered by hospitals often take jobs in the same institution after completing their training.

Advancement

About three-quarters of all radiological technologists are employed in hospitals, where there are opportunities for advancement to administrative and supervisory positions such as chief technologist or technical administrator. Other technologists develop special clinical skills in advanced procedures such as CT scanning or magnetic resonance imaging. Some radiological technologists qualify as instructors. There is more chance of advancement for persons who hold a bachelor's degree. For teaching and administration a master's degree and considerable experience are necessary.

Employment outlook

The number of people working in the field of radiological technology is expected to grow much faster than the average for occupations through the 1990s. Although enrollments in accredited schools have increased in recent years, the demand for qualified people in some areas of the country far exceeds the supply. The shortage of trained technologists is particularly acute in rural areas and small towns.

In the years to come, increasing numbers of radiological technologists will be employed in nonhospital settings, such as physicians' offices, clinics, health maintenance organizations, laboratories, and government agencies. This pattern will be part of the overall trend toward holding down costs by delivering more health care outside of hospitals. Nevertheless, hospitals will remain the major employers of radiological technicians for the foreseeable future. Because of the increasing importance of radiological technology in the diagnosis and treatment of disease, it is unlikely that hospitals will do any fewer radiological procedures than in the past. Instead, they will probably try to do more on an outpatient basis and on weekends and evenings. This should increase the demand for part-time technologists and should open more opportunities for flexible work schedules.

At present, most of the nation's radiological technologists are radiographers, and that is the field that will continue to employ most technologists. Although they are presently quite small, the fields of radiation therapy technology and diagnostic ultrasound offer excellent prospects. Radiation, either alone or in combination with surgery and chemotherapy, will continue in the foreseeable future to be an important weapon against cancer and certain other diseases. More widespread use of ultrasound testing, especially in cardiology and obstetrics/gynecology, will have a positive effect on the hiring of technologists trained in that specialty.

Earnings

Salaries for radiological technologists compare favorably with those of similar health care professions. The starting salary in a hospital or medical center averages about $18,400 a year for radiological technologists. With experience technologists earn average salaries of about $24,100 a year.

Technologists with specialized skills make larger salaries. Radiation therapy technologists earn about $24,000 to start and the average salary for experienced workers is about $27,000. In ultrasound technology, the average pay is $19,000 for beginning technologists and about $26,300 for those with experience.

Conditions of work

Full-time technologists generally work eight hours a day, forty hours a week, and may be on call for some night emergency duty for which they receive equal time off or additional compensation. Most are covered by the same vacation and sick leave provisions as other workers in the organizations which employ them, and some receive free medical care and pension benefits.

In diagnostic radiologic work, technologists perform most of their tasks while on their feet. They move around a lot and often are called upon to lift patients who need help in moving. Radiation therapy technologists do not have quite as physically demanding a job, but they still must frequently assist in handling patients who are too ill to help themselves very much.

Great care is exercised to protect technologists from radiation exposure. Each technologist wears a badge that measures radiation exposure, and records are kept of total exposure accumulated over time. Routine precautions include the use of safety devices such as individual instruments that measure radiation, lead aprons, rubber gloves, and other shielding. Careful attention to safety procedures has greatly reduced or eliminated radiation hazards for the technologist.

Social and psychological factors

Radiological technology is dedicated to conserving life and health and to preventing or arresting disease. Technologists can feel great personal gratification from helping to promote health and alleviate human suffering. Those who specialize in radiation therapy technology need to be able the handle the close relationships they inevitably develop while working with very sick or dying people over a period of time.

GOE: 02.03.04, 02.04.01, 10.02.02; SIC: 80; SOC: 362, 365

◇ SOURCES OF ADDITIONAL INFORMATION

American Registry of Radiologic Technologists
2600 Wayzata Boulevard
Minneapolis, MN 55405

American Society of Radiologic Technologists
15000 Central Avenue, SE
Albuquerque, NM 87123

Society of Diagnostic Medical Sonographers
12225 Greenville Avenue, Suite 434
Dallas, TX 75243

American Cancer Society
1599 Clifton Road
Atlanta, GA 30329

◇ **RELATED ARTICLES**

Volume 1: Biological Sciences; Health Care; Nuclear Sciences
Volume 2: Biomedical engineers; Medical technologists; Nuclear medicine technologists; Physicians
Volume 3: Dental assistants, Medical assistants
Volume 4: Chemical-radiation technicians; Industrial radiological technicians

Surgical technicians

Definition

Surgical technicians, also called *operating room technicians* or *surgical technologists*, assist surgeons, nurses, anesthesiologists, and other operating room personnel before, during, and after surgery. Before an operation, they may wash, shave, and disinfect the area of the patient in which the incision will be made. They arrange the equipment, instruments, and supplies in the operating room according to the preference of the surgeons and nurses. During the operation, they adjust lights and other equipment as needed. They also assist by counting sponges, needles, and other instruments used during the operation, by handing instruments and supplies to the surgeon, and by holding retractors and cutting sutures, as directed. They maintain specified supplies of fluids such as saline, plasma, blood, and glucose and may assist in administering these fluids. Following the operation, they clean may the operating room and wash and sterilize the used equipment using germicides, autoclaves, and sterilizers, although in most larger hospitals these tasks are done by housekeepers and other central service personnel.

History

The origins of surgery go back to prehistoric time. Ancient people all over the world probably used sharpened flints and other sharp-edged devices as their first surgical instruments. With these instruments, they attempted primitive operations such as trephination (removing circular pieces of the skull to treat epilepsy and other brain disorders), draining abscesses, bloodletting, and removing cataracts. As people learned to make tools of bronze and iron, newer and better instruments (such as needles and scissors) were developed, and more difficult operations were attempted.

The art of surgery was further refined by the ancient Greeks and Romans who practiced surgery with such skill and cleanliness that infections following surgery were relatively uncommon.

During the Middle Ages in Europe, many of the surgical and sanitary techniques of the Greeks and Romans were lost, and surgical practice fell into the hands of usually uneducated barber-surgeons. It was not until the eighteenth century that surgery began to regain its professional and scientific level.

Two scientific developments made modern surgery possible. The first was the discovery of anesthesia in the mid-nineteenth century. With anesthesia, surgeons were able to take their time at operations and therefore to be more careful and to try more complex procedures.

The second important discovery was that of the causes of infection. Until Louis Pasteur's discovery of germs and Joseph Lister's development of aseptic surgery in the nineteenth century, so many people died of infection after operations that the value of surgery was limited.

During the twentieth century, surgeons have developed techniques for operating on every part of the body, including the heart, brain, and eye. Technology has greatly aided the development of surgery in this century. Electrically powered surgical instruments and X-ray techniques have made new procedures possible, as have new drugs, new monitoring devices, and new machines, such as the heart-lung machine.

From its earliest days, surgery has required more than a single surgeon to accomplish a successful operation. However, throughout the twentieth century, the nature of most surgical procedures, with all of their sophisticated techniques for monitoring and safeguarding the patient's condition, has become so complex that more and more people are required to assist the surgeon or surgeons. While many of the tasks that are performed during the operation require highly trained professionals with many years of education, there are also simpler, more standardized tasks that require people with less complex training and skills. Over the years such tasks have been taken care of by people referred to as orderlies, scrub nurses, and surgical orderlies.

Today, such people are referred to as operating room technicians, surgical technicians, or surgical technologists. For the most part, these are people who have received specialized training in a community college, vocational or technical school, or a hospital-sponsored program. They are eligible to earn certificates of competence, and, in general, enjoy a higher degree of professional status and recognition than did their predecessors of earlier years.

Nature of the work

The responsibilities and activities of surgical technicians vary considerably from one part of the country to another, from one hospital to another, and even from one part of the hospital to another, depending on whether the technician works in an operating room, an emergency room, or a hospital delivery room. Surgical technicians usually work under the supervision of a registered nurse or a senior surgical technologist.

In general, the work responsibilities of surgical technicians may be divided into three areas: preoperative (before surgery), operative or intraoperative (during surgery), and postoperative (after surgery).

In the preoperative period, surgical technicians prepare the operating room for any situation that might take place during the operation. They set out the sterile instruments in the operating room according to the surgeon's instructions and prepare other operating room equipment and supplies according to established procedures. It is the responsibility of the surgical technician to maintain a specified supply of sterile linens and of such fluids as glucose, blood, saline, and plasma for use during the operation. Technicians lay out the sterile linens and surgical drapes and assist the surgeons and other personnel in putting on their sterile gowns and gloves.

The surgical technician is usually the first person to scrub in for a surgical procedure. The term "scrub" comes from the first activity of surgical teams in which they literally scrub their hands and arms before putting on their sterilized gowns and gloves.

Sometimes surgical technicians are required to position the patient on the operating table and to wash, shave, and disinfect the surgical area of the patient.

During surgery, the technician assists the surgical team by passing instruments and supplies to the surgeon as requested, holding retractors, and cutting sutures. Technicians adjust lights and other equipment as directed. They may assist in administering blood plasma or other kinds of injections and transfusions.

Sometimes the surgical technician is given other responsibilities. During surgical procedures, someone in the operating room must serve as a circulator. This person, although appropriately capped and masked, is not scrubbed to assist at the table. However, when supplies or additional equipment are needed, the circulator is the person who supplies them. When the anesthesiologist needs assistance or supplies, the circulating technician is there to render this assistance also.

Surgical technicians also help prepare, care for, and dispose of specimens (including samples of tissues and organs) taken during the operation and help apply dressings. They may operate sterilizers, lights, suction machines, diagnostic equipment, and other operating room machines.

Another responsibility of surgical technicians may be to weigh blood-soaked sponges to determine the amount of blood a patient has lost.

Immediately following surgery, the surgical technician is sometimes asked to assist with the application of postoperative dressings and to help the team transfer the patient from the table to a stretcher and from the stretcher to a bed in the recovery room. When the transfer is completed, the technician takes all of the equipment, instruments, and linen to the clean-up area of the operating room suite.

In some hospitals, surgical technicians wash and sterilize used equipment, using germicides, autoclaves, and sterilizers. It may also be their responsibility to clean the operating room, repack the instruments into sets, and generally to make the area ready for the next surgical procedure. However, in most hospitals these tasks are done by other personnel.

Requirements

Surgical technicians should possess good manual dexterity, as they are frequently required to handle awkward surgical instruments with speed and agility. In addition, they should have good physical stamina so that they are able to stand throughout long surgical procedures.

Most surgical technicians receive their training either through a hospital or through post–high-school training programs lasting from nine months to two years and conducted by a vocational, technical, community, or junior college. A high-school diploma is usually a requirement for entry into any of these programs. During their high-school years, prospective technicians should take courses developing their basic skills in mathematics, science, and language. In addition, they should take whatever courses are available to them in health and biology.

Students who attend a post–high-school training program receive classroom instruction as well as some supervised operating room experience in hospitals. They should expect to take courses in anatomy, medical terminology, operating room instruments and equipment, medical ethics and legal responsibilities, psychology, biology, microbiology, operating room procedures, operating room assisting, chemistry, and English. Some of the specific areas in which they receive instruction include the care and safety of patients during surgery, use of anesthesia, and some nursing procedures. They also learn how to sterilize instruments; to prevent and control infection; and to handle special drugs, supplies, and equipment.

Special requirements

No special license is required for surgical technicians; however, most hospitals prefer, and some require, that surgical technicians be certified by Liaison Counsel on Certification, which is part of the Association of Surgical Technologists. Technicians who pass the com-

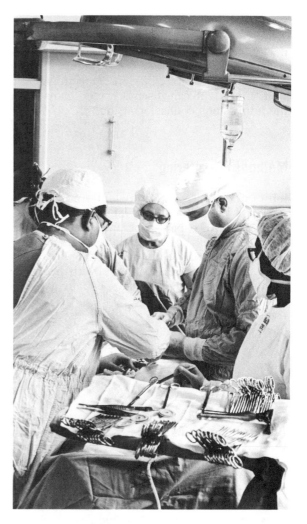

Surgical technicians serve as general assistants to the surgical team during medical operations.

prehensive examination conducted by this organization become certified surgical technologists (CSTs).

Opportunities for experience and exploration

It is difficult for interested students to gain any direct experience on a part-time basis in surgical technology. The first opportunities for direct experience afforded to students generally come in the clinical and laboratory phases of their training program. However, interested students can explore some aspects of this career in several ways. They can write to the sources listed at the end of this article for more reading material on surgical care. They or their teachers can arrange a visit to a hospital, clinic, or other surgical setting in order to learn about the work. It would also be desirable for an interested student to visit a school of surgical technology accredited by the American Medical Association's Committee on Allied Health Education and Accreditation. During such a visit, a student can discuss career plans with the admissions counselor at the school.

Methods of entering

Job opportunities for competent surgical technicians exceed the supply of such personnel. Graduates of hospital programs often work in the same hospital after graduation. Community colleges that offer a surgical technology program usually cooperate closely with hospitals in the area. These hospitals are usually eager to employ technicians trained by the local schools. Available positions are also advertised in the newspaper.

Advancement

Surgical technicians usually begin work as assistants in operating rooms and delivery rooms. With increased experience, they can advance to positions as assistant operating room administrators or assistant operating room supervisors. Assistant operating room administrators assist with administrative tasks such as ordering supplies and arranging work schedules. Assistant operating room supervisors direct other surgical technicians in the operating room.

Many surgical technicians advance by taking jobs outside the operating room setting. They can put their experience to use in sales and management positions with companies that sell sterile supplies or operating room equipment to hospitals. Others go to work for insurance companies. Another avenue for advancement for some technicians is to become an instructor in a surgical technology training program.

Employment outlook

Population growth, longevity, and improvement in medical and surgical procedures have all contributed to a growing demand for surgical services and hence for surgical technicians. As long as the rate at which people undergo surgery continues to grow, there will continue to be a need for more surgical technicians. And as surgical methods become increasingly complex, more and more trained personnel will probably be needed. General economic conditions and changes in levels of government assistance could affect this growth pattern; however, the present trend will probably continue at least through the 1990s.

Other factors may weigh against the general trend. Patterns are shifting in surgical practice. The need to control health-care costs is stimulating a shift toward performing minor surgery more often on an ambulatory or outpatient basis. If more and more minor surgical procedures are performed in hospital outpatient departments, then the demand for surgical technicians will remain strong. But if a significant amount of surgery is done in nonhospital settings—in such places as clinics and surgeons' offices—the total demand for surgical technicians will drop, because fewer technicians are used in such settings.

Staffing patterns are also changing in response to the need to control costs. In the future some hospitals may be inclined to employ staff members who can do a wider range of tasks than surgical technicians are trained to do. On the other hand, the shortage of some kinds of staff, especially surgical nurses, is presently making it desirable to assign more tasks to surgical technicians. As more tasks become appropriate for surgical technicians to perform, more technicians are needed to perform them.

All of these factors taken together suggest that overall employment in this field should grow faster than the average of all other occupations through the 1990s, but that future opportunities may vary from one community to another depending on local practice and availability of staff.

Earnings

Most surgery is performed in hospitals, and salaries vary greatly in different institutions and localities. According to one survey conducted by the University of Texas, however, the average starting salary for surgical technicians is in the range of $16,000 to $17,000 a year. Graduates of accredited training programs receive salaries higher than technicians without such training. In general, technicians working on the East and West Coasts earned more than surgical technicians in other parts of the country. Also, surgical technicians employed directly by surgeons tend to earn more than surgical technicians employed by hospitals.

Experienced surgical technicians earn salaries that average approximately $20,800 a year;

however, many experienced surgical technicians, especially those in major cities on the East and West coasts, earn significantly more than that.

Conditions of work

Surgical technicians naturally spend most of their time in the operating room. Operating rooms are cool, well lighted, orderly, and extremely clean. Technicians are often required to be on their feet for long intervals.

Members of the surgical team, including surgical technicians, wear sterilized gowns, sterilized rubber gloves, and caps to cover their hair. They also wear masks of gauze or other material to cover their mouths and noses so they will not breathe germs into the area.

Surgery is usually performed during the day; however, hospitals, clinics, and other facilities performing emergency surgery require twenty-four-hour-a-day coverage. Most surgical technicians work regular forty-hour weeks, although many are periodically required to be available to work on short notice on weekends and at night.

Social and psychological factors

Surgical technicians sometimes work under great pressure and tension. The need for surgery is often a matter of life and death, and one can never assume that procedures will go as planned. If operations do not seem to be going well, nerves may fray and tempers flare. Technicians must understand that this is the result of stressful conditions and that therefore they should not take this anger personally.

In addition, surgical technicians should have a strong desire to help others. Surgery is performed on people, not machines. Patients literally trust their lives to the surgical team, and they trust that they will be treated in a dignified and professional manner.

GOE: 10.03.02; SIC: 806; SOC: 369

◇ **SOURCES OF ADDITIONAL INFORMATION**

American Hospital Association
840 North Lake Shore Drive
Chicago, IL 60611

American Medical Association
535 North Dearborn Street
Chicago, IL 60610

Association of Surgical Technologists
8307 Shaffer Parkway
Littleton, CO 80127

◇ **RELATED ARTICLES**

Volume 1: Health Care
Volume 2: Licensed practical nurses; Physicians; Physician assistants; Registered nurses
Volume 3: Medical assistants; Nursing and psychiatric aides
Volume 4: Emergency medical technicians

Technician Occupations in Other Fields

Technicians described in this section are those whose work falls outside of the broad categories established in the other four sections. Technicians involved in engineering and science, medicine and health, agriculture, or in broadcasting and media are the ones most familiar to the general public; however, today there are technicians working in a broad range of activities and settings, including in schools and libraries, in factories and boat yards, and in police stations and government installations. They conduct psychological and vocational testing, inspect products, keep records, and operate office equipment. They are almost all in what is known as the service sector of our economy, and their common trait is they have combined a service skill with some form of specialized training. They are representative of a kind of employee who is in more and more demand today and who will continue to be in demand in the future. As our society becomes increasingly complex, more and more of its activities will require these kinds of people who have developed their skills and expertise in a specialized area.

The history of most of the technician occupations described in this section can be traced back to a profound change in the American economy. For much of this country's history, most people were employed either in agriculture or in manufacturing. In either case, they were employed in what economists now refer to as the goods-production sector of the economy. However, just as the Industrial Revolution of the nineteenth century drew people off of farms and into factory jobs, so has the increasing sophistication of our society during the twentieth century drawn people out of manufacturing and into service-producing jobs, which include transportation and public utilities; retail and wholesale trade; finance, insurance, and real estate; services (which includes a variety of industries, such as barber shops, repair shops, business services, and hospitals);

and government. By 1950, approximately 60 percent of all nonagricultural jobs were in the service-producing sector; by 1980, more than 70 percent; and it is estimated that in the year 2000, 80 percent of all nonagricultural jobs will be in the service-producing sector.

In the first half of this century, service-producing employers tended mostly to hire two kinds of workers: managers, who usually had a college education, and clerical workers, who usually had no formal education beyond high school and may not have finished high school. However, as this sector of the economy has grown, so too has its need for more people with specialized training. With the growth of two-year community, technical, and vocational colleges following World War II, there developed an excellent way for providing the additional training that service workers were coming to need.

Increasingly, employers have come to rely on these two-year colleges as the source of the skilled service workers they need. And it is this combination of practical skills and classroom training that has come to be the hallmark of today's technicians. Today there are technicians working in schools, libraries, and police stations, performing a wide range of activities from helping to administer tests to guarding government installations. Technicians even help maintain collections of career guidance information.

The tasks that each of these technicians does varies widely depending on the area of activity. The range of activities is, in fact, so broad that it is impossible to summarize them in any meaningful way in this introduction. All this introduction can do is to describe briefly some of the broad areas in which technicians are employed—namely, in administrative support services and in educational and library services—and to mention some of the technicians employed in those areas whose jobs are not described in this section. Beyond that, readers are encouraged to browse through the individual articles that follow this introduction.

Jobs in the area of administrative support usually involve performing clerical work which requires special skills and knowledge. Technicians may perform management-related activities according to established instructions and procedures. They may also work in records processing, where they prepare, review, maintain, and distribute information. They may even be involved in some specialized aspects of business-machine operations. Jobs like this are usually found in businesses and government agencies, but they can sometimes also be found in doctors' and lawyers' offices. Technicians described in this volume who work in administrative support jobs include cryptographic technicians, who operate very specialized kinds of office equipment; identification technicians, who work in police departments and are very involved with records processing; and testing technicians, who administer psychological, vocational, and educational tests. Other technicians working in this area might help oversee clerical operations in a business office, help search public records for a title insurance company, or be involved with special aspects of processing insurance policy applications.

Jobs in the area of educational and library services usually involve specialized teaching, vocational training, or library work of various kinds. Jobs in this field are usually found in schools, colleges, and libraries, but they may occasionally be found in businesses and government agencies. Technicians described in this volume who work in this area include career-guidance technicians and library technicians. Other technicians involved in this area might assist teachers in some special aspect of an instructional program. Audiovisual technicians, described in another section of this volume, provide a good example of this kind of work. Or they might be involved with presenting information to groups of people. Energy-conservation technicians and many of the agricultural, forestry, and conservation technicians described in this volume provide example of this kind of work.

As the proceeding paragraphs have indicated, not all service-producing technicians are described in this section. Some service-producing technicians working in the area of public utilities are described in the Emerging Fields Technicians section, especially in the articles about nuclear power and telecommunications technicians, or in the Engineering and Science Technicians section, especially in the article about electrical technicians. And the health-care occupations in this volume are described in the Medicine and Health Technicians section.

More importantly, many jobs in this area are so new that there is little reliable information available about them beyond a commonly used job title and a very general description of what they do. In the area of finance, insurance, and real estate, for instance, there are people who are sometimes called financial technicians. They mostly work in banks, and their jobs often involve helping to reconcile discrepancies among financial accounting statements coming from various sources.

Within the public sector, there are social service technicians and human service technicians. The duties of these technicians vary, but in general they help people such as the elderly, unemployed, or handicapped to get the assistance they need from government agencies or private institutions. Some may work in offices where they assist social workers or other government agency personnel. Others may have jobs in day-care centers, halfway houses, or other settings where they work directly with people in need.

In the service area of the private sector, there are people working as fitness technicians. They work in settings like health clubs and gyms and they use their knowledge of body mechanics, anatomy and physiology, and the operation of exercise equipment to assist people in identifying and pursuing their own fitness goals. They help people to outline a personalized program for reducing stress, strengthening, slimming, body-building, or achieving some other fitness objective, and they teach exercise techniques that will promote the desired results.

Another service field is that of building maintenance technicians, who keep buildings clean and in good condition. These technicians often are employed by building management firms. They must know how to operate cleaning equipment, make proper use of chemical cleaners and pest control methods and materials, and take care of problems with heating and ventilating systems, plumbing, and electricity.

Almost all of the occupations described in this section require technicians who have completed some specialized training beyond the high-school level. Prospective technicians therefore should plan on earning a high-school diploma or its equivalent. They should also investigate early in their high-school years the entrance requirements of any school or program in which they might want to enroll following graduation from high school. By investigating these requirements early they can ensure that they will be able to meet all requirements having to do with courses and standardized tests that need to be taken.

In many cases, the post–high-school training requirements for prospective technicians consist of completion of a two-year course of study offered in a junior, community, technical, or vocational college. These programs usually combine classroom teaching with practical or even on-the-job experience. The programs usually lead to the granting of an associate degree.

Some of the jobs described in this section do not require a full two years of formal instruction. Some require only a year or so; some rely heavily on employer-conducted training programs. However, even if formal training in a two-year institution is not required, technicians will find that their chances for employment and for advancement are enhanced by earning an associate degree.

Once prospective technicians have secured their required training, their best method of entering a technical occupation will vary depending on the particular field they wish to enter.

One of the most reliable and accepted methods, however, is for technicians to seek employment opportunities through the institutions that gave them their training. Most of these institutions have student placement services and are in constant contact with industries and agencies in need of technicians.

Another method of entering is through the on-the-job training programs offered by various companies. Those people who successfully complete such training programs are usually assured of finding employment with the company that gave them their training.

Work-study programs offer another excellent method of entering a career. Such programs are run by schools in cooperation with local agencies, institutions, and businesses and offer students the opportunity to find part-time or summer employment in jobs related to the student's studies. Very often the part-time or summer employer will become the student's full-time employer following graduation.

The opportunities for advancement for technicians described in this section vary widely depending on the complexity of the skills required in their occupational areas. In some areas there may be opportunities to advance to supervisory or trainer positions after technicians have gained sufficient experience and skills. For almost any kind of technician there may be opportunities for advancement into administrative responsibilities, such as planning projects, ordering supplies, and keeping records. In some fields there are also opportunities for technicians to become technical writers. It is important to point out, however,

that in some fields, significant advancement is only possible for technicians who return to school for more education.

Salaries for technicians in this section will depend in large part on the type of activity in which they are employed. Technicians who find jobs in manufacturing industries will do better than those technicians who work for schools, museums, or libraries that command fewer financial resources.

Salaries also vary according to an individual's education, experience, and the geographical location of the job. In general, however, technicians who are graduates of two-year post–high-school training programs can expect to receive starting salaries averaging around $13,000 to $17,000 a year. With increased experience they will earn more, usually up to $25,000 a year and sometimes more.

Technicians working in the federal government's civilian work force or for the armed forces will find their salaries determined by their rank or grade level. Technicians who work for local and state government agencies will also find their salaries determined by government rules. Their salaries will also vary from town to town and from state to state.

Working conditions for technicians vary according to the type of work they are engaged in and the setting in which the work is done. Some of the technicians described in this section, such as library technicians or testing technicians, can expect to work indoors in clean, well-lighted surroundings. Other technicians, such as marine services technicians, can expect to work outdoors in all kinds of weather. And obviously the working conditions of a security technician are much different from those of a career-guidance technician. However, most technicians can expect to work in safe surroundings that are generally comfortable.

The work of nearly all of the technicians described in this section will range from uncomplicated, routine tasks to highly challenging and complex tasks. Technicians who are most successful in their careers are usually those who have a good tolerance for both creative problem-solving and for careful meticulous work.

The work also often requires technicians to take full responsibility for some aspect of a project. This may involve supervising other workers, designing procedures, and foreseeing results. This kind of responsibility usually carries with it some mental and social pressures that technicians need to be able to meet.

The employment outlook for technicians described in this section is generally good. The need for technicians who use specialized technical training in a service activity should remain strong as more and more occupational fields develop tasks that require specially trained workers. Whether it is in the factory, the classroom, the library, or the repair shop, our society is daily becoming more mechanized, more automated, and more computerized; and more trained workers will be needed to carry out new procedures and to operate, build, assemble, repair, and help design new kinds of equipment.

Some specific areas of employment may experience temporary or even sustained lack of growth. Employment of all technicians is dependent to some degree on the general level of economic activity. In particular, people who work for local, state, or federal government in education-related or law enforcement- related jobs could face difficult times as public sector spending is more tightly constrained during economic downturns. However, many economists foresee slow but steady growth in the economy through most of the 1990s. Unlike some industries, where machines are replacing people, in many service fields personal contact is essential, making it less likely that workers will be squeezed out by technological advances. In addition, most technicians, given their skills and training, are usually able to find similar work in a related field if some particular prob-

lem arises concerning employment in their area of primary interest.

For students interested in learning more about any of the occupations described in this section, there are a number of opportunities for personal experience and exploration. Visits to places of employment are one of the most vivid means of exploration and can often be arranged by a teacher or guidance counselor, or through a personal call to someone in a position of responsibility at the place of employment. Through such visits, one is able to witness technicians actually involved in their work. It may also be possible to speak with several of these people about their work or with their employer about opportunities for technicians in that organization.

Interested students should consider the possibilities for finding part-time or summer employment in a company or other organization that employs technicians. Even the simplest tasks will offer opportunities to learn more about the field and will demonstrate interest to future employers.

Another way to learn more about a career field is to put together a list of schools offering technical training and write to a selected group of them requesting catalogs and other information regarding their programs.

Career guidance technicians

Definition

Career guidance technicians collect and organize information about careers and occupations for school career information centers. They usually work under the direction of a librarian or career guidance counselor.

Nature of the work

The principal duty of career guidance technicians is to help with the ordering, cataloging, and filing of materials having to do with job opportunities, careers, technical schools, scholarships, careers in the armed forces, and other programs. They also help students and teachers find materials relating to a student's interests and aptitudes. These various materials

may be in the form of books, pamphlets, magazine articles, microfiche, videos, computer software, or other media.

Often career guidance technicians help students take and score self-administered tests that determine their aptitude and interest in different career fields or kinds of job-related activities. If the career guidance center has audiovisual equipment, such as VCRs or film or slide projectors, career guidance technicians are usually the ones responsible for keeping the equipment in good condition and for helping people to operate it.

To assist the counseling and guidance staff, career guidance technicians may sometimes schedule students' appointments with the school guidance counselors, and they may give talks to parents, students, or other groups about the activities and services of the career guidance center. They may also help keep

465

A career guidance technician at a college operates a computer software program that lists all of the events of the day including the scheduled interviews for recruiting companies.

records of students enrolled in work-study or other vocational programs. If they are aware of a student's interest, they make contact with the student when a job is posted.

Requirements

Career guidance technicians need to be high-school graduates. In addition, most employers look for applicants who have completed two years of training beyond high school, usually at a junior, community, or technical college. These two-year programs, which usually lead to an associate degree, may combine classroom instruction with practical or sometimes even on-the-job experience.

Career guidance technicians need good reading and writing skills. They should be able to read and understand newspapers, magazine articles, dictionaries, instruction manuals, and encyclopedias. They should be able to write letters and reports with proper spelling, punctuation, and grammar and be able to speak clearly and easily in front of a group of people. They also need to have had some training in mathematics, including algebra and geometry.

In addition to meeting these educational requirements, career guidance technicians should enjoy helping and working with other people. They also need to be well organized and to feel comfortable using organized systems for finding and storing information.

GOE: 11.02.04; SIC: 8211; SOC: 4632

◇ **RELATED ARTICLES**

Volume 1: Education; Human Resources; Library and Information Science
Volume 2: Career counselors; College career planning and placement counselors; Employment counselors; Guidance counselors; Librarians
Volume 3: File clerks; General office clerks; Teacher aides
Volume 4: Library technicians

Cryptographic technicians

Definition

Cryptographic technicians operate cryptographic equipment used for coding, decoding, and sending secret messages.

Nature of the work

In order to code and send secret messages, cryptographic technicians first select the partic-

ular code that they should use for the message. Then they set up their machine to translate the message into that code, and they type the message into the machine. The machine converts the message into code form in a process known as encryption. After the message is encrypted, the technicians send the message to a receiver via telephone lines, satellites, or other kinds of communication links.

When receiving a coded message, cryptographic technicians feed the incoming transmission into a decoding machine and take the resulting message to its intended receiver. If a message appears to have been improperly coded, technicians may try to straighten out the message using special decoding procedures and equipment, or they may request that the message be sent again.

In sending and receiving coded messages, cryptographic technicians may operate teletype machines or radio transmitters and receivers.

Requirements

Cryptographic technicians need to be high-school graduates. In addition, they need to receive special training that lasts from six months to a year. This kind of training is offered by branches of the armed forces and government agencies that employ cryptographic technicians, and occasionally by other organizations.

While in high school, students interested in becoming cryptographic technicians should take courses in mathematics and English. They should be able to add, subtract, multiply, and divide with ease and be able to compute ratios and percentages. They should be able to read equipment and instruction manuals and be able to write reports with proper grammar, spelling, and punctuation. Students should also look for courses that train them in typing and operating computers and business machines. These courses can be taken in high school, but training after high school in a business school will also be helpful.

Due to the secret nature of their work, cryptographic technicians often need govern-

A cryptographic technician uses a computer to help him decipher a coded message.

ment clearance. Employers seek those can be trusted to maintain confidentiality.

GOE: 07.06.02; SIC: 9711; SOC: 4793

◇ **RELATED ARTICLES**

Volume 1: Civil Service; Military Service
Volume 2: Security consultants
Volume 3: Computer and peripheral equipment operators; Data entry clerks; FBI agents; Fingerprint classifiers
Volume 4: Identification technicians; Transmitter technicians

Fish-production technicians

Definition

Fish-production technicians work in fish hatcheries and fish farms helping to raise young fish through part or all of their life cycle. Several familiar kinds of fish can be successfully raised in captivity, among them trout, catfish, and salmon. The fish-production technicians are responsible for record-keeping activities and for the day-to-day care of the fish.

Nature of the work

The duties of fish-production technicians vary depending on the type of hatchery or fish farm where they are employed. Some technicians work in hatcheries run by federal, state, or county governments to produce fish for release in open bodies of water. These fish are intended to be caught later by sport fishers. Other technicians work for privately owned

These fish production technicians are preparing fish for frozen packaging.

commercial fish farms that raise fish to be sold for food for people or for animals.

In either of these settings, fish-production technicians may carry out various activities related to the day-to-day operation of the hatchery. For example, they may monitor and record conditions in the tanks or ponds, feed the fish, keep the water clear of sick and dead fish, and maintain equipment such as the machinery that circulates water, aerates it, and regulates its temperature.

Some fish-production technicians work in laboratories at fish farms or hatcheries. They assist biologists in studying methods of increasing the production of healthy fish. For some types of fish, regulating factors such as the feed, the size and depth of the fish pond or other enclosure, the oxygen level in the water, and the temperature can make a big difference in how fast the fish grow. In the laboratory, fish-production technicians may be involved in tests of such factors. They operate equipment such as microscopes and measuring devices and keep records of results of experiments.

Another duty of technicians is to attach small tags to individual fish before letting them go in lakes or rivers. Then, when a fish is caught, the tag can be returned to the hatchery.

Technicians record information from the fisher about the fish's size, condition, and location when caught. This information helps in the study of factors that affect the health and survival of fish. Technicians sometimes catch wild fish for use in laboratory research.

Fish that are being raised for sport fishing must be moved from the hatchery to lakes or rivers when they are large enough. Usually the fish are transported in tank trucks. The loading and unloading of the fish in the trucks is often done by fish-production technicians.

Requirements

A high-school diploma is normally required for fish-production technicians. For many jobs, especially those involved with laboratory work, employers look for applicants with some post–high-school training. Only a few community colleges and technical institutes offer two-year post–high-school programs concerned with fish production. However, a program that includes courses in biology, chemistry, and mathematics should provide suitable preparation for many technician jobs in fish hatcheries and farms.

While still in high school, students interested in this field should take courses in science, mathematics, and environmental studies.

GOE: 03.01.02, 03.04.03; SIC: 0912, 0913; SOC: 5524, 5618

◇ **RELATED ARTICLES**

Volume 1: Agriculture; Biological Sciences
Volume 2: Biologists
Volume 3: Fishers, commercial
Volume 4: Animal production technicians; Biological technicians

Identification technicians

Definition

Identification technicians work in police departments. They work at various jobs that are related to maintaining police records. An important part of their work has to do with handling fingerprint records; however, they also work with other kinds of records, such as reports and information about crimes and accidents.

Nature of the work

Identification technicians who work with fingerprint records usually do so in police identification-and-records departments. Their principal duties are to classify and match fingerprints taken from a crime scene with those taken from people arrested for crimes or from unidentified bodies. They may also assist in taking fingerprints from applicants for licenses and for civil-service positions.

Some identification technicians also operate equipment used to microfilm police records, such as reports and information about crimes and accidents. These technicians are responsible for storing the microfilmed records and for getting the filmed records out of storage or making copies of them upon request from police officers or other public officials. They may also operate fax machines that transmit and receive photographs, fingerprints, and other information to and from other police departments.

Some identification technicians are required to compile and submit periodic reports about their department's activities to supervisory personnel.

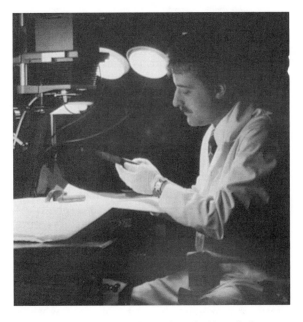

An identification technician examines a piece of evidence for fingerprints. If he finds some, he will try to match them with those that are on file.

and English. Identification technicians need to be able to handle with ease computations involving fractions, ratios, rates, and percentages. They need language skills to read instruction manuals and to write reports with proper spelling, grammar, and punctuation.

GOE: 07.05.03; SIC: 9211; SOC: 4799

Requirements

It is usually necessary to be a high-school graduate to become an identification technician. Some police departments prefer workers who have completed post–high-school training programs in general business or a related area. In addition, beginning identification technicians can expect to receive from three to six months of specialized on-the-job training after they are hired.

While in high school, students interested in this career should take courses in mathematics

◇ **RELATED ARTICLES**

Volume 1: Civil Service
Volume 2: Crime laboratory technologists; Polygraph examiners; Security consultants
Volume 3: FBI agents; Fingerprint classifiers; Police officers; Private investigators; State police officers
Volume 4: Cryptographic technicians; Security technicians

Library technicians

Definition

Library technicians, sometimes called *library technical assistants,* support professional librarians in a wide variety of ways. They help order and catalog books; assist library patrons in locating books, periodicals, and reference materials; and help make the various services and facilities of the library available to the public.

Technicians help library users locate materials through the card catalog and the Library of Congress catalog, or through the library's interlibrary loan system. They answer routine questions about library services, and refer questions requiring professional help to librarians. They verify bibliographic information on order requests before ordering books and perform routine cataloging of books received.

Library technicians also help with desk operations in the circulation department of the library and oversee the work of stack workers and catalog-card typists. They also often circulate audiovisual equipment and materials, and inspect the materials when they are returned.

History

The earliest libraries referred to in Egyptian manuscripts date from the fourteenth century B.C. and the first public library is believed to have been established in Athens in 537 B.C. The centuries since have seen great changes in libraries and their place in society. In the Middle Ages, books were so rare that they were often chained to their shelves to prevent their loss. The inventions of the printing press and movable type, increases in the literacy rate, and the increasing availability of books and periodicals all contributed to the growth of libraries.

The growth of public education in the 1800s was accompanied by a rapid growth of public libraries across the United States, greatly aided in the latter part of the century by the generosity of such philanthropists as Andrew Carnegie. Aids to locating information were developed, such as *Poole's Index to Periodical Literature* in 1882 and the Dewey Decimal System in 1876, that made libraries much more convenient for users. The American Library Association was founded in 1876, an event that is usually regarded as marking the birth of librarianship as a profession.

The great increase in the amount of recorded information in this century (the "information explosion") has led to a steady increase of library facilities and expansion of services. It is estimated that the amount of information published on almost every general subject doubles every ten to twenty years. Libraries need to be able to keep informed about what new information is available, to be selective in what they purchase, and to share materials with other libraries as an extension of their own resources.

As the responsibilities of librarians became more complex, the need for technically trained assistants to support them became evident. During the 1940s many libraries began training their own support staffs. In-service training programs proved costly, however, and since 1965 the bulk of the training of library technicians has been assumed by community colleges.

An estimated 51,000 library technicians work in libraries of every kind in the United States. Approximately 3,600 of these work for the federal government.

Nature of the work

Work in libraries falls into two general categories: user services (assisting patrons in using the library's facilities) and technical services (maintaining the library's collections and making them most conveniently available to users). Library technicians work in both areas.

Working with librarians in user services, technicians direct library patrons to the card catalog in response to inquiries, and answer questions about how the catalog works. They describe the general arrangement of the library for new patrons and answer basic questions about the library's collections. They may also help patrons use microfiche and microfilm machines or assist them in using computer terminals to locate materials in an interlibrary system's computerized listing of holdings.

Working in technical services, technicians work with order requests, verifying bibliographic information and preparing order forms for the materials. They perform routine cataloging of new materials and file new cards in catalog drawers. They direct the workers shelving books and periodicals. They often operate audiovisual equipment for library and school programs and maintain the equipment in working order.

Whatever their duties, library technicians refer questions or problems requiring professional experience and judgment to librarians. In this way, they relieve the professional library staff of many routine chores, freeing them to respond to situations for which they have been trained.

A library technician assists children with tape recorder to make sure that they are using it properly.

Requirements

The technical nature of the work performed by library technicians, especially when working in technical services, is prompting more and more libraries to hire only graduates of two-year programs in library technology. The typical program leads to an associate of arts degree and includes courses in the basic purpose and functions of libraries, as well as technical courses in processing materials, cataloging acquisitions, library services, and one year of liberal arts studies.

Persons entering such programs should understand that the library-related courses they take will not apply toward a professional degree in library science.

After employment, technicians may be encouraged to take more courses, to obtain training in special areas, and to keep abreast of new technical advances in library functions.

Some smaller libraries, especially in rural communities, may hire persons with high-school education as library technicians. Whatever their background, library technicians should demonstrate aptitude for careful, detailed work and should enjoy working with the public as well as with books.

Special requirements

There are no special requirements for a career as a library technician.

Opportunities for experience and exploration

Persons interested in careers as library technicians can explore the career by talking with their school and community librarians and library technicians, and by working in the school library. A visit to a large or specialized library will also be helpful. Library personnel are usually agreeable to discussing career possibilities with interested young people.

Methods of entering

Libraries may be approached directly for employment—usually by contacting the head librarian—or through the placement office of a community college offering training for library technicians. Civil service examination notices, for those interested in government service, are usually posted in these schools as well as in government buildings.

Applicants interested in school libraries should remember that most openings occur at the end of the school year and are filled for the following year.

Advancement

The trend toward requiring more formal training for library technicians suggests that advancement opportunities will be limited for those lacking such training. In smaller libraries and less populous communities the shortage of trained personnel may lessen this limitation. Nonetheless, those with adequate or above-average training will perform the more interesting tasks.

Persons interested in library work will find generally that any continuing education courses they take will enhance their chances for advancement.

Library technicians
Technician Occupations in Other Fields

Employment outlook

The number of persons working in library technician careers is expected to grow more slowly than the average growth rate for all occupations. Slow growth is expected in public and school libraries as the school-age population increases. Growth is expected to continue in specialized medical, business, and law libraries.

Earnings

Earnings for library technicians vary widely. Public library salaries vary according to the size and location of the community and usually fall somewhere between $11,000 to $18,000 a year; however, in some communities, especially those where library jobs are not full-time, salaries may be lower. Salaries for library technicians in the federal government average approximately $18,000 a year. Salaries in specialized libraries depend on the size of the library and of the parent institution.

Conditions of work

Libraries are usually clean, well-lighted places in which to work. The work is not strenuous, although it does occasionally require bending and stretching to find or shelve books. Hours are regular in company and school libraries, but university, public, and some specialized libraries are open during longer hours. These libraries may require evening and weekend work, usually on a rotating basis.

Social and psychological factors

Tasks performed by library technicians are sometimes repetitive and may become tedious, but there is a sufficient variety of overall assignments to offset this. Heavy public contact requires tact and patience, and the ability to communicate clearly. In general, the library atmosphere is relaxed, genial, and interesting.

GOE: 10.02.04; SIC: 8231; SOC: 399

◇ SOURCES OF ADDITIONAL INFORMATION

Council on Library-Media Technical-Assistants
Library/Media Technology Department, SC126
2900 Community College
Cuyahoga Community College
Cleveland, OH 44115

American Library Association
50 East Huron Street
Chicago, IL 60611

Association for Library Information Science Education
5623 Palm Aire Drive
Sarasota, FL 34243

American Society for Information Science
1424 16th Street, NW, Suite 404
Washington, DC 20036

◇ RELATED ARTICLES

Volume 1: Library and Information Science
Volume 2: Archivists and curators; Librarians
Volume 3: Audiovisual technicians; Career-guidance technicians; Medical record technicians

---

Marine services technicians

Definition

Marine services technicians inspect, maintain, and repair boats and marine vessels of all kinds, including their hulls, propulsion systems, rigging, and navigational equipment.

Nature of the work

Marine services technicians usually begin a project by inspecting the boat to be worked on and consulting with supervisors about how they will proceed with repairs and installation of new parts and how long the work will take. Technicians remove the boat from the water, using a crane or a combination of railway tracks and winches. They then block the boat into a good working position using carpenter's hand and power tools and wooden blocks and timbers. When working on hulls, technicians clean the boats' bottoms and remove marine growth. They also scrape loose paint and remove and replace the rotten or damaged sections of the hull. Wooden hulls are repaired by cutting and shaping replacement wooden sections; fiberglass hulls are repaired by removing damaged sections and replacing them with resin-impregnated fiberglass cloth. Replaced sections are smoothed with sanding equipment and the finished repair is painted.

Some marine services technicians test and repair boat engines, transmissions, and propellers; rigging, masts, and sails; and navigational equipment and steering gear. They repair or replace defective parts and sometimes make new parts to meet special needs. They may also inspect and replace when necessary internal cabinets, refrigeration systems, electrical systems and equipment, sanitation facilities, and hardware and trim.

Requirements

In preparation for a career as marine services technicians, interested persons should take as many shop courses as possible in high school, as well as basic mathematics and language courses. They need at least two years of training beyond high school, primarily in blueprint reading, machine repair, woodworking, sailing, and boat handling. Specific training in boat repair and rebuilding is usually obtained on the job in a boat yard or boat manufacturer's facility. Familiarity and experience with boats of all kinds is an asset in this field.

Conditions of work

Marine services technicians perform heavy physical work, frequently lifting weights of fifty pounds and sometimes up to one hundred pounds. They work in both indoor and outdoor situations, under generally pleasant conditions.

GOE: 05.05.02; SIC: 4499; SOC: 6179

◇ **RELATED ARTICLES**

Volume 1: Military Services; Transportation
Volume 2: Merchant marine occupations
Volume 3: Diesel mechanics; Fishers, commercial; General maintenance mechanics; Motorboat mechanics; Stevedoring occupations

Security technicians

At an airport, a security technician must be alert at all times.

Definition

Security technicians guard government installations, materials, and documents against illegal acts, such sabotage, espionage, and riots.

Nature of the work

Security technicians work for government agencies, and their task is usually to guard secret or restricted installations. They spend much of their time patrolling areas, which they may do on foot, on horseback, or in automobiles or aircraft. They may also monitor activities in an area through the use of surveillance cameras and video screens. Their assignments usually include detecting and preventing unauthorized activities, searching for explosive devices, standing watch during secret and hazardous experiments, and other routine police duties within government installations.

Security technicians are usually armed and may be required to use their weapons or other kinds of physical force to prevent some kinds of activities. They are usually not, however, required to remove explosive devices from an installation. When they find such devices, they notify a bomb disposal unit, which is responsible for removing and then defusing or detonating the device.

Security technicians may be assigned to installations in this country or in foreign countries.

Requirements

Security technicians are required to be high-school graduates. In addition, they should expect to receive from three to six months of specialized training in security procedures and technology. While in high school, they should take mathematics courses that ensure that they can perform basic arithmetic operations with different units of measure, that they can compute ratios, rates, and percentages, and that they can interpret charts and graphs. They should also take English courses and should develop their reading and writing skills. They should be able to read manuals, memos, textbooks, and other instructional materials and to write reports with correct spelling, grammar, and punctuation. They should also be able to speak to small groups with poise and confidence.

Security technicians need to have good vision and be in good physical shape. They should be able to lift at least fifty pounds; climb ladders, stairs, poles, and ropes; and maintain their balance on narrow, slippery, or moving surfaces. They should also be able to stoop, crawl, crouch, and kneel with ease.

GOE: 04.02.02; SIC: 7381; SOC: 5132

◇ **RELATED ARTICLES**

Volume 1: Civil Service
Volume 2: Security consultants
Volume 3: Correction officers; FBI agents; Police officers; Security guards; State police officers
Volume 4: Cryptographic technicians; Identification technicians

Testing technicians

Definition

Testing technicians give tests to people. The tests they give are usually the kind that are designed to measure a person's educational level, psychological condition, or vocational interests and talents. They may work in the guidance or counseling offices of schools, personnel departments of companies, social service agencies, employment agencies, and other settings.

Nature of the work

When they are giving a test, testing technicians give out blank test papers or other testing equipment and materials to the people being tested. They provide directions to the people and sometimes lead them through practice exercises. If testing equipment is involved, they demonstrate how to use it.

While the test is in progress they watch the people who are taking the test to be sure that they follow all of the rules and directions of the test. Technicians also time the test, using stop watch or electric timer, and they tell people when the time is up for the test.

After the test is over, technicians score the tests using a test-scoring key or answer sheet or sometimes a test-scoring machine. They record the results on the test papers, work applications, or test-profile forms.

Requirements

Testing technicians need to be at least high-school graduates. Once they are hired, technicians can expect to receive from three to six months of training that introduces them to the kinds of tests that they will be giving and the procedures for giving them.

While they are in high school, students who are interested in this field should be sure to take courses in mathematics and English. Their mathematics courses should cover such

A test technician administers a standardized test to a young student. The technician must time each section and make sure that the student stops working when instructed.

topics as handling fractions, computing ratios and percentages, and drawing and interpreting bar charts. A course that introduces basic concepts in statistics would also be desirable. Their English courses should prepare them to write reports with proper spelling, grammar, and punctuation. Testing technicians are often required to perform general clerical tasks, so students should also try to take courses that help to develop office skills. Other courses that will be of value include those that familiarize the student with computers and those that concern the social sciences, such psychology, sociology, or economics.

GOE: 07.01.07; SIC: 8211; SOC: 4756

◇ **RELATED ARTICLES**

Tire technicians

A tire technician tightens bolts on a truck tire that has been installed on a testing machine. He is preparing it for a wear test that will last for hundreds of hours.

Definition

Tire technicians work for tire companies, testing tires to find out how strong the tires are, how long they will last, and whether or not there are any flaws in their construction.

Nature of the work

Most tire technicians work either with experimental models of tires that are not yet ready for manufacturing, or they test samples of production tires as they come out of the factory. Technicians who are involved mostly with testing tires from the factory are called "quality-control technicians."

To do testing, tire technicians inflate the tires and mount them on testing machines that recreate the stresses of actual road conditions, such as traveling at high speeds, carrying heavy load, or going over bumpy roads. The technicians can adjust the machines to change the speed or the weight of the load or the bumpiness of the road surface. Then, either while the tire is on the machine or after it is taken off, they use pressure gauges and other devices to detect whether any parts of the tire are damaged and to evaluate tire uniformity, quality, and durability. They continue testing the tire until it fails or until it has lasted for some specified period of time.

Another kind of testing that tire technicians do involves cutting cross-sections from brand-new or road-tested tires. Technicians use power saws to cut up tires and then inspect the pieces to assess the condition of the cords, plies (which are rubbery sheets of material inside the tire), and the tread.

Throughout the testing, tire technicians keep careful records of all test results. Later they prepare reports which sometimes include charts, tables, and graphs to help describe and explain the results of the tests.

Requirements

Tire technicians need to be high-school graduates. For some jobs, employers prefer applicants who have post–high-school training in a field related to manufacturing or product-testing. This kind of training may be received at a vocational school or a community or junior college.

While in high school, students interested in this career should take courses in science and mathematics, including algebra and geometry, and English courses that improve their reading and writing skills. They should also take shop or laboratory science courses that introduce them to measuring devices, electrical machinery, and electronic testing equipment.

GOE: 06.03.01; SIC: 3011; SOC: 783

◇ **RELATED ARTICLES**

Volume 1: Rubber
Volume 2: Industrial designers
Volume 3: Rubber goods production workers
Volume 4: Product test technicians; Quality-control technicians

Appendix 1:
Resources and Associations for Individuals with Disabilities

Federal agencies

The recently-enacted Americans with Disabilities Act of 1990 (ADA) will have a profound effect on the employment of the disabled. In general, the new law states that all businesses, with the exception of ones that employ less than 15 people, must have facilities that accommodate disabled employees. This ranges from handicap access to office equipment. The ADA proclaims that businesses may not discriminate on the basis of a person's physical disability. In addition, all new public transportation facilities must be accessible to the disabled. There is no doubt that this law will extend the rights of the disabled and allow them to gain employment in nearly all vocational areas.

The addresses listed in this appendix serve as general sources. They will lead a disabled person to the related agencies at the state and local levels. In general, the federal government allocates funds to programs in states and cities. Each state determines the distribution of the funds and sponsors its own programs. For this reason, it is important to consult state and local agencies for specific information.

There are several programs and agencies that are sponsored by the federal government. Some deal with specific disabilities, such as deafness, while others simply disseminate information. Most federally-sponsored programs for the disabled are run through the U.S. Department of Education. This department focuses on vocational rehabilitation, education, financial and medical assistance, civil rights, housing, tax benefits, and public transportation. The Department can direct a disabled person to any relevant program.

A particularly useful program, the Job Training Partnership Program (JTPA), prepares unskilled youth and adults for entry into the labor force. Many disabled people are eligible to join the program. Contact your State Employ-ment Security Service or Mayor's Office for more information.

To learn more about government-sponsored agencies for the disabled, the rights of disabled individuals, and other problems or questions that need guidance, contact:

Clearinghouse on Disability Information
U.S. Department of Education
Switzer Building, Room 3132
Washington, DC 20202-2524

The Clearinghouse on Disability Information issues a booklet titled *Pocket Guide to Federal Help for Individuals with Disabilities* that may provide some helpful advice and information.

The federal government offers several programs for those with specific disabilities. Again, many of these programs have state and local offices all over the country. A selection of the programs is listed below.

For those with hearing disabilities, contact:

Deafness and Communicative Disorders Branch
Switzer Building, M/S 2736
Washington, DC 20202
Voice telephone: 202-732-1401
TDD telephone: 202-732-1298

The federal government offers a variety of programs for the developmentally disabled. Many of the programs are sponsored through the individual states. Contact:

Administration on Developmental Disabilities
Department of Health and Human Services
Humphrey Building, Room 329B
Washington, DC 20201

Among the many job-related programs, the government offers financial assistance to disabled citizens who would like to start their own small businesses. These people are eligible for low-cost loans. For more information, contact:

Small Business Administration
1441 L Street, NW
Washington, DC 20416

National organizations

There are many associations and programs in the private sector that rehabilitate individuals with disabilities and train them for professional occupations. Listed below are a selection of the associations available.

General vocational associations:

American Vocational Association
1410 King Street
Alexandria, VA 22314

Center on Education and Training for Employment
1960 Kenny Road
Ohio State University
Columbus, OH 43210

National Career Development Association
5999 Stevenson Avenue
Alexandria, VA 22304

General associations for those with disabilities:

Center on Human Policy
724 Comstock Avenue
Syracuse University
Syracuse, NY 13244

Human Resources Center
I.U. Willets Road
Albertson, NY 11507

ICD—International Center for the Disabled
340 East 24th Street
New York, NY 10010

Job Accommodation Network
809 Allen
PO Box 6122
West Virginia University
Morgantown, WV 26500

Learning How
PO Box 35481
Charlotte, NC 28235

Mainstream
1030 15th Street, NW
Suite 1010
Washington, DC 20005

National Industries for the Severely Handicapped
2235 Cedar Lane
Vienna, VA 22180

Vocational Evaluation and Work Adjustment Association
PO Box 31
Anderson, IN 46015

Associations for the hearing impaired:

American Professional Society of the Deaf
35 Rainbow Trail
Mountain Lakes, NJ 07045

Hellen Keller Center for Deaf-Blind Youths and Adults
111 Middle Neck Road
Sands Point, NY 11050

National Association of the Deaf
814 Thayer Avenue
Silver Spring, MD 20910

National Center on Employment of the Deaf
One Lomb Memorial Drive
Rochester, NY 14623

Associations for the visually impaired:

American Council of the Blind
1010 Vermont Avenue, NW
Suite 1100
Washington, DC 20005

American Foundation for the Blind
15 West 16th Street
New York, NY 10011

Associated Services for the Blind
919 Walnut Street
Philadelphia, PA 19107

Association for Education and Rehabilitation of the Blind and Visually Impaired
206 North Washington Street
Suite 320
Alexandria, VA 22314

Council of Citizens with Low Vision
1400 North Drake Road
Suite 218
Kalamazoo, MI 49007

National Federation of the Blind
1800 Johnson Street
Baltimore, MD 21230

National Industries for the Blind
524 Hamburg Turnpike, CN 969
Wayne, NJ 07474

Association for the speech impaired:

American Speech-Language-Hearing Association
10801 Rockville Pike
Rockville, MD 20852

Association for people with spinal injuries:

National Spinal Cord Injury Association
600 West Cummings Park, Suite 2000
Woburn, MA 01801

Association for amputees:

American Amputee Foundation
Box 55218, Hillcrest Station
Little Rock, AR 72225

Associations for the mentally disabled:

Association for Children and Adults with Learning Disabilities
4156 Library Road
Pittsburgh, PA 15234

Young Adult Institute and Workshop
460 West 34th Street
New York, NY 10001

Appendix 2:
Internships, Apprenticeships, and Training Programs

Internships

Internships are usually short-term (one semester or trimester) programs where the student works at the company in some beginning level capacity in the field he or she is studying. Programs are frequently done for college credit, although some programs will accept students who are not receiving college credit. Internships are rarely with pay. Stipends may be offered to students for living expenses. The college or university may provide funding for students to cover some expenses. It is unusual for the company providing the internship to make housing arrangements. Internships in the arts and journalism are among the most competitive, and the most influential in providing an edge to graduating students looking for work.

Internships with major organizations and companies have an effect because of the name of the organization, but may not provide the most educational experience. Because of union restrictions or departmentalization of the company, the intern may be limited in the capacity that he or she can work. Smaller companies may allow the intern a larger role in the company during the student's stay.

Internships are available to college students, routinely offered to students in their junior and senior years. Graduate internship programs are also widely available. High school internships are not as common. The most widely known is the page program in the United States Congress. See addresses for more information.

Information on internships is customarily available through school placement offices and advisorial staff at high-schools and colleges. However, internships may be available with companies that do not regularly contact schools. It is worth while for the student to contact companies that are of interest, for information on internship programs.

Apprenticeships

Apprenticeships are offered to trainees in an occupational field. An apprenticeship differs from an internship in that it is almost always a paid position, that the education and training elements are combined under one program, and the apprenticeship is usually offered directly by the company and not through a school. Required educational courses in the apprenticeship program may be offered through a local educational facility, but usually the sponsor arranges those courses. There are more than 800 apprenticeship programs currently recognized by the Department of Labor's Bureau of Apprenticeship and Training. Of those programs, the majority are in the manufacturing and construction industries.

Apprentices are paid wages lower than experienced personnel. They may maintain the apprentice wage throughout their training, or they may receive raises that put them at regular salary rates by the end of the program. The average apprenticeship lasts between three and four years.

Information on specific apprenticeships is available through the local and regional offices of the Department of Labor's Bureau of Apprenticeship and Training. Contacting relevant unions is also helpful, as is contacting a company directly to see if a program is in place.

Co-operative training programs involve a combined effort between a school and a sponsoring company. The programs vary, but tend to involve one portion of the school year being spent at the company in a training program and the rest of the year in school. The student is paid for the work period (a trimester or semester, usually) and then attends school for the rest of the year in regular school programs. The co-op program routinely lasts three or four years during college. Some programs involve extending the undergraduate program to a five year period because of the training periods.

Training programs

Training programs done through private enterprises consist of the regular application procedure to work at the company. The applicant is hired into the program directly, or in some instances applies to the program after working at the company for some time. The trainees are paid regular wages throughout the training program, which may last from two weeks to two or three years.

The programs vary widely. They may involve training in several departments or training only in one area. Training may include classroom experience. Trainees are almost always guaranteed positions with the company after completion of the training.

Some companies require management staff to participate in the training program. Others may only train employees new to the management level. Training programs also may be ongoing for the duration of employment with the company. There may be annual or bi-annual classes to improve and retrain staff.

Information on training programs is obtained by contacting companies with which one wishes to work. Specifics about the availability of training programs will be provided by the personnel or human relations office. Some companies recruit from school placement offices, so students should remain in contact with placement officers on which companies will be interviewing on campus, and which have listed openings with the school.

General information is available through local unions, local government offices, and school guidance counselors. Information on training programs is also listed in Volumes 2, 3, and 4 in the "Requirements" and "Methods of Entering" sections. Other sources of information follow.

Sources of additional information

Department of Labor
Bureau of Apprenticeship and Training
Room N–4649
Frances Perkins Building
Third Street and Constitution Avenue
Washington, DC 20210

Association for Experiential Education
Internships and Apprenticeships
Box 249-CU
Boulder, CO 80309

Department of Labor
Employment and Training Programs
Room N–4469
Frances Perkins Building
Third Street and Constitution Avenue
Washington, DC 20210

National Society for Internships and Experiential Education
3509 Hayworth Drive
Suite 207
Raleigh, NC 27609

For internships for academic administration positions in postsecondary education, contact:

ACE Fellows Program
American Council on Education
1 DuPont Circle, NW
8th Floor
Washington, DC 20036

For information on postsecondary scholarship programs for study and training abroad, please write:

Institute of International Education
Fulbright Scholarship Programs
809 United Nations Plaza
New York, NY 10017

Rotary International
Rotary Foundation Scholarships
1 Rotary Center
1560 Sherman Avenue
Evanston, IL 60201

For high-school foreign study programs, write:

AFS Intercultural Programs
313 East 43rd Street
New York, NY 10017

Youth For Understanding
3501 Newark Street, NW
Washington, DC 20016

For information on the Congressional page program, write:

Office of the Doorkeeper
Page Program Information
U.S. House of Representatives
Washington, DC 20515

DOT Index

This list of job titles and occupational classification numbers is provided so users can explore the occupational description further after reading the material in this encyclopedia. The classified numbers refer to those used in the Dictionary of Occupational Titles (Government Printing Office. U.S. Department of Labor, 1977). If you wish to know more about a particular job or occupation described, look up the occupational title in this list and copy the nine digit number. Use this number to look up the occupation in the Dictionary of Occupational Titles. In that book, job descriptions are presented by DOT numbers according to occupational categories. This standard reference tool is found in the reference collection of most public libraries. If you are uncertain about how to locate a copy, ask the librarian.

Calibration laboratory technicians, **019.281–010**
Camera operators, **971.382–014**
Camp counselors, **159.124–010**
Camp directors, **195.167–018**
Cancellation clerks, **203.382–014**
Candy spreaders, **520.687–022**
Candy–maker helpers, **520.685–050**
Canning and preserving industry workers, **529.686–014**
Capsule–filling–machine operators, **559.682–010**
Captain, **197.167–010**
Car rental agents, **295.477–010**
Carcass splitters, **525.684–018**
Cardiac monitor technicians, **078.367–010**
Cardiologists, **070.101–014**
Cardiopulmonary technologists, **078.362–030**
Career planning and placement counselors, **166.167–014**
Career–guidance technicians, **249.367–014**
Caretakers, **301.687–010**
Carpenters, **860.381–022**
Carpet cutters, **929.381–010**
Carpet layers, **864.381–010**
Cartographers, **018.**
Cartographic drafters, **018.261–010**
Cartographic technicians, **018.261–026**
Cartography supervisors, **018.131–010**
Cartoonists, **141.061–010**
Case aides, **195.367–010**
Casework supervisors, **195.137–010**
Caseworkers, **195.107–010**
Cash grain farmers, **401.161–010**
Cashier–checkers, **211.482–014**
Cashiers, **211.362–010**
Cashiers, courtesy booth, **211.467–010**
Cashiers, tube room, **211.482–010**
Casting directors, **159.267–010**
Casting drafters, **007.261–014**
Catalog librarians, **100.387–010**

Catalytic converter operators, **558.362–010**
Caterer helpers, **319.677–010**
Caterers, **187.167–106**
Cathode makers, **554.585–010**
Cement masons, **844.364–010**
Cement mixers, **550.685–026**
Central office equipment installers, **822.361–014**
Central office facilities planning, **003.061–050**
Central office operators, **235.462–010**
Central office repairers, **822.281–014**
Central supply workers, **381.687–010**
Central–office equipment engineers, **003.187–010**
Central–office operators, **235.462–010**
Centrifuge operators, **551.685–026; 551.685–034; 599.685–018**
Ceramic engineers, **006.061–014**
Ceramic engineers—design, **006.061–010**
Ceramic engineers—product sales, **006.151–010**
Ceramic engineers—research, **006.061–018**
Ceramic engineers—test, **006.061–022**
Ceramic restorers, **102.361–014**
Chart calculators, **214.487–010**
Chart clerks, **221.584–010**
Chasers, **921.667–014**
Check pilots, **196.263–022**
Checkers, **017.261–010**
Cheesemakers, **529.361–018**
Chefs, **313.131–014**
Chemical design engineers, processes, **008.061–014**
Chemical engineers, **008.061–018**
Chemical engineering technicians, **008.261–010**
Chemical engineers—equipment sales, **008.151–010**
Chemical engineers—research, **008.061–022**
Chemical engineers—test, **008.061–026**
Chemical laboratory chiefs, **022.161–010**
Chemical laboratory technicians, **022.261–010**
Chemical processing supervisors, **559.130–010**

Chemicals and plastic materials lab technicians, **559.382–046**
Chemistry technologists, **078.261–010**
Chemists, **022.061–010**
Chief bank examiners, **160.167–046**
Chief controller, **193.167–010**
Chief cook, **315.131–010**
Chief design drafter, **017.161–010**
Chief drafter, **007.261–010**
Chief engineer, **197.131–010**
Chief engineers, **010.167–010**
Chief engineers for research, **010.161–010**
Chief librarians, **100.127–010**
Chief mate, **197.133–022**
Chief medical technologists, **078.161–010**
Chief petroleum engineers, **010.161–014**
Chief pilot, **196.167–010**
Chief projectionists, **960.132–010**
Chief psychologists, **045.107–046**
Chief steward, **350.137–014**
Child care workers, **313.361–014**
Child monitors, **301.667–010**
Child welfare caseworkers, **195.107–014**
Children's librarians, **100.167–018**
Chippers, **564.685–014**
Chiropractors, **079.101–010**
Chocolate temperers, **523.682–010**
Choke setters, **921.687–014**
Choral directors, **152.047–010**
Choreographers, **151.027–010**
Cigar banders, **920.685–046**
Cigar packers, **790.687–014**
Cigarette packing machine operators, **920.665–010**
City editors, **132.037–014**
City managers, **188.117–114**
Civil drafters, **005.281–010**
Civil engineers, **005.061–014**
Claim examiners, **168.267–014**
Claims clerks, **205.367–018**
Claims supervisor, **241.137–018**
Classified ad clerks, **247.367–010**
Classifiers, **100.367–014**

Classroom teacher aides, **099.327–010**
Clay–structure builders and servicers, **579.665–010**
Clean–rice brokers, **162.167–018**
Clerk–typists, **203.362–010**
Clinical dietitian, **077.127–014**
Clinical psychologists, **045.107–022**
Clinical sociologists, **054.107–010**
Cloth designers, **142.061–014**
Cloth testers, **689.384–010**
Clowns, **159.047–010**
Coding clerks, **203.582–026**
Collection workers, **241.357–010**
College and university faculty, **090.227–010**
College financial aid administrators, **090.117–030**
College placement service managers, **166.167–014**
Color matchers, **550.381–010**
Color–printer operators, **976.382–014**
Colorists, **022.161–014**
Columnists, **131.067–010**
Combination welders, **819.384–010**
Comedians, **159.047–014**
Commentators, **131.067–010**
Commercial airline pilots, **196.263–014**
Commercial artists, **141.061–022**
Commercial decorators, **298.381–010**
Commercial drafters, **017.261–026**
Commercial engineers, **003.187–014**
Commercial or institutional cleaners, **381.687–014**
Commodities brokers, **162.157–042**
Communication center operators, **235.662–014**
Communications consultants, **253.157–010**
Communications technicians, **962.362–010**
Community dietitian, **077.127–010**
Community health nurses, **075.124–014**
Community organization workers, **195.167–010**
Community outreach librarians, **100.167–014**

Community relations lieutenants, 375.137–018

Community workers, 195.367–018

Community–antenna–television line technicians, 821.261–010

Companions, 309.677–010

Compensation managers, 166.167–022

Composers, 152.067–014

Compositors and typesetters, 973.381–010

Compounders, 540.382–010

Computer operating personnel, 213.362–010

Computer operations supervisors, 213.132–010

Computer operators, 213.362–010

Computer–application engineers, 020.062–010

Computer–assisted drafters, 017.261–042

Computerized photofinishing equipment service technicians, 714.281–030

Concrete products dispatcher, 579.137–030

Condominium managers, 186.167–062

Confectionery cookers, 526.328–014

Confectionery industry workers, 527.361–014

Congressional–district aides, 209.362–030

Conservation technicians, 012.261–010

Console operators, 213.362–010

Construction inspectors, 168.167; 182.267–010

Construction workers, 869.664–014

Consultant dietitians, 077.127–018

Continuity editors, 132.037–010

Continuity writers, 131.087–010

Continuous mining machine operators, 930.683–010

Controller, 186.117–014

Convention managers, 187.167–078

Conveyor operators, 921.382–010

Cookroom supervisors, 529.132–038

Cooks, 313.361–014; 526.685–010

Copyists, 152.267–010

Copywriters, 131.067–014

Coremakers, 518.381–014

Corporation lawyers, 110.117–022

Correction officers, 372.137–010

Correctional–treatment specialists, 195.107–042

Correspondence–school instructors, 099.227–014

Cosmetologists, 332.271–010

Cost accountants, 160.167–018

Cost estimators, 160.267–018

Costume designers, 142.061–018

Cottage cheese makers, 522.382–010

Counseling psychologists, 045.107–026

Counselors, 045.107–010

County–agricultural agents, 096.127–010

County–home demonstration agents, 096.121–010

Court reporters, 202.362–010

Creative directors, 141.067–010

Credit analysts in banking, 191.267–014

Credit card operations manager, 186.167–022

Credit union manager, 186.167–026

Crime laboratory technologists, 029.281–010

Criminal lawyers, 110.107014

Critics, 131.067–018

Cruiser, 459.387–010

Cryptographic technicians, 203.582–018

Cullet crushers and washers, 570.685–026

Cultural anthropologists, 055.067–022

Curators, 102.017–010

Currency exchange cashiers, 211.462–026

Customer–equipment engineers, 003.187–018

Customer–service representative instructors, 239.227–010

Customs import specialists, 168.267–018

Customs inspectors, 168.267–022

Customs patrol officers, 168.167–010

Customs–house brokers, 186.117–018

Cut–file clerks, 222.367–014

Cut–out–and–marking machine operators, 690.685–110

Cylinder press operators, 651.362–010

Cytologists, 041.061–042

Cytotechnologists, 078.281–010

Dairy farm managers, 180.167–026

Dairy farm supervisors, 410.131–018

Dairy farmworkers, 410.684–010

Dairy helpers, 529.686–026

Dairy products manufacturing workers, 529.382–018

Dairy scientists, 040.061–018

Dairy–processing equipment operators, 529.382–018

Dance instructors, 151.027–014

Dance therapists, 076.127–018

Dancers, 151.047–010

Data base managers, 169.167–030

Data entry clerks, 203.582–030

Data typists, 203.582–022

Data–coder operators, 203.582–026

Day workers, 301.687–014

Dean of students, 090.117–018; 091.107–010

Dehydrator tenders, 523.685–054

Delinquency prevention social workers, 195.107–026

Demographers, 054.

Dental assistants, 079.371–010

Dental hygienists, 078.361–010

Dental service directors, 072.117–010

Dental–laboratory technicians, 712.381–018

Dentists, 072.101–010

Department editors, 132.037–018

Department head, 090.167–010

Deposit–refund clerks, 214.482–014

Dermatologists, 070.101–018

Derrick workers, 930.683–018

Designers, 142.

Detailers, 017.261–018

Developers, 976.681–010

Developmental psychologists, 045.061–010

Diagrammers and seamers, 789.484–010

Dialysis technicians, 078.362–014

Dictionary editors, 132.067–018

Die makers, 601.280–010

Die setters, 612.360–010

Die sinkers, 601.280–022

Diesel engine pipefitters, 862.361–018

Diesel mechanics, 625.281–010

Diesel–engine erectors, 625.361–010

Diesel–engine testers, 625.261–010

Dietetic technicians, 077.121–010

Dietician, 077.127–014

Digester operators, 532.362–010

Directional survey drafters, 010.281–010

Director of admissions, 090.167–014

Director of counseling, 045.107–018

Director of placement, 166.167–014

Director of religious activities, 129.107–018

Director of student affairs, 090.167–022

Directors of photography, 143.062–010

Directory assistance operators, 235.662–018

Disc jockeys, 159.147–014

Dispatchers, 193.262–014

Dispensing opticians, 299.474–010

Display designers, 142.051–010

Display managers, 142.031–014

Distribution field engineers, 003.167–014

District attorneys, 110.117–010

Diversified crop farmers, 407.161–010

Dividing–machine operators, 520.685–086

Dock workers, 911.364–014

Doctor of osteopathy, 071.101–010

Dog bathers, 418.677–010

Dog groomers, 418.674–010

Domestic laundry workers, 302.685–010

Door–to–door sales workers, 291.357–010

Doorkeepers, 324.677–010; 324.677–014
Dough mixers, 520.582–010
Dough–brake–machine operators, 520.685–090
Dough–mixer operators, 520.462–010
Drafter, 007.261–010
Drama teachers, 150.027–014
Dramatic coaches, 150.027–010
Drier operators, 523.362–014
Driving instructors, 099.263–010
Drug and alcohol counselors, 195.267–014
Drug preparation lab technicians, 559.382–042
Dry cleaning workers, 362.382–014
Drywall finishers, 842.664–010
Drywall installers, 842.381–010
Dumping–machine operators, 529.685–102
Dye–lab technicians, 582.384–010
Dye–range operators, 582.582–010

Economists, 050.067–010
Editorial assistants, 132.267–014
Editorial directors, 132.037–022
Editorial writers, 131.067–022
Editors of technical and scientific publications, 132.017–018
Editors–in–chief, 132.017–014
Education and training managers, 166.167–126
Education directors, 099.117–030
Educational directors, 075.117–018
Educational psychologists, 045.067–010
Educational resource coordinators, 099.167–030
Educational secretaries, 201.362–022
Educational therapists, 094.227–010
Effervescent–salts compounders, 559.685–058
Electric–distribution checkers, 824.281–014

Electric–sign repairers, 824.281–018
Electrical drafters, 003.281–014
Electrical engineers, 002.061–010
Electrical engineers—design, 003.061–018
Electrical engineers—product sales, 003.151–010
Electrical engineers—research, 003.061–026
Electrical engineers—test, 003.061–014
Electrical inspectors, 168.167–034
Electrical repairers, 829.281–014
Electrical technicians, 003.161–010
Electricians, 824.261–010; 825.381–030
Electro–optical engineers, 023.061–010
Electrocardiography technicians, 078.362–018
Electroencephalographic technicians, 078.362–022
Electroformers, 500.684–010
Electrologists, 339.371–010
Electrolysis and corrosion control engineers, 003.167–022
Electromechanical drafters, 003.281–018
Electromechanical inspectors, 710.381–014
Electromechanical technicians, 710.281–018
Electromechanisms design drafters, 017.261–014
Electronic data–processing systems, 003.167–062
Electronic intelligence operations specialists, 193.383–010
Electronic sales–and–service technicians, 828.251–010
Electronic–organ technicians, 828.261–010
Electronics drafters, 003.281–014
Electronics engineers, 003.061–030
Electronics engineers—design, 003.061–034
Electronics engineers—product and system sales, 003.151–014
Electronics engineers—research, 003.061–038
Electronics engineers—testing, 003.061–042
Electronics technicians, 003.161–014
Electroplaters, 500.380–010

Electrotypers, 974.381–010
Elementary school teachers, 092.227–010
Elevator constructors, 825.361–010
Elevator inspectors, 168.167–038
Embalmer, 338.371–014
Embossers, 690.682–030
Emergency medical technicians, 079.374–010
Employee relations representatives, 166.257–010
Employee–health maintenance program specialists, 166.167–050
Employee–welfare managers, 166.117–014
Employment agency managers, 187.167–098
Employment clerks, 205.362–014
Employment consultants, 166.
Employment counselors, 045.107–010
Employment interviewers, 166.267–010
Employment managers, 166.167–030
Endodontists, 072.101–014
Engineering analysts, 020.067–010
Engineering psychologists, 045.061–014
Engineering technicians, 005.261–010
Engineers of system development, 003.167–026
Enologists, 183.161–014
Entomologists, 041.061–046
Environmental health inspectors, 079.117–018
Equipment design marine engineers, 014.061–010
Estimators, 620.261–014
Estimators and drafters, 019.261–014
Etymologists, 059.067–010
Eviscerators, 525.687–010
Executive housekeepers, 187.167–046
Executive pilots, 196.262–030
Exhibit artists, 149.261–010
Exhibit designers, 142.061–058; 142.061–560
Exhibit technicians, 739.261–010
Experimental psychologists, 045.061–018
Exploration geophysicists, 024.061–026
Export managers, 163.117–014

Extension service specialists, 096.127–014
Extension work instructors, 090.227–018
Exterminators, 389.684–010
Extractive metallurgists, 011.061–018
Extractor operators, 552.682–018
Extras, 159.647–014
Extruder operators, 557.382–010
Extruder tenders, 557.685–014
Eyeglass lens cutters, 716.682–010

Factory layout engineers, 012.167–018
Factory or mill maintenance repairers, 899.281–014
Fallers, 454.384–010
Family caseworkers, 195.107–018
Family practitioners, 070.101–026
Farm general managers, 180.167–014
Farm–equipment mechanics, 624.281–010
Farriers, 418.381–010
Fashion designers, 142.061–018
Fashion illustrators, 141.061–014
Fast food workers, 311.472010
FBI special agents, 375.167–042
Fee clerks, 214.362–018
Felling–bucking supervisors, 454.134–010
Fermenter operators, 559.685–070
Fiberglass dowel drawing machine operators, 575.682–010
Field contractors, 162.117–022
Field crops farmers, 404.161–010
Field service respresentatives, 621.221–010
Field service technicians, 638.261–026
Field technicians, 193.262–018
Field–contact technicians (dairy), 162.117–026
File clerks, 206.
Filler–shredder feeders, 529.687–182
Film laboratory technicians, 976.381–010

Film processing utility workers, **976.685–030**
Film rental clerks, **295.367–018**
Filter–press operators, **551.685–082**
Financial aid counselors, **169.267–018**
Financial aid officer, **090.117–030**
Financial analysts, **020.167–014**
Financial institution manager, **186.117–038**
Financial institution president, **186.117–054**
Financial institution treasurer, **186.117–070**
Financial institution vice–president, **186.117–078**
Fine arts packers, **102.367–010**
Fingerprint classifiers, **375.387–010**
Finish photographers, **143.382–014**
Finished stock inspectors, **763.687–026**
Fire captains, **373.134–010**
Fire chiefs, **373.117–010**
Fire fighters, **373.364–010**
Fire inspectors, **367–010**
Fire investigation lieutenants, **373.267–018**
Fire marshalls, **373.267–014; 373.267–018**
Fire prevention bureau captains, **373.167–014**
Fire–prevention research engineers, **012.167–022**
Fire–protection engineering technicians, **019.261–026**
Fire–protection engineers, **012.167–026**
Firers, **951.685–018**
First–aid attendants, **354.677–010**
Fish cleaners, **525.684–030**
Fish farmers, **446.161–010**
Fishing–rod markers, **732.684–070**
Fitters, **805.361–014**
Flame–hardening machine operators, **504.685–014**
Flatware makers, **700.682–010**
Flight attendants, **352.367–010**
Flight engineers, **621.261–018**
Flight surgeon, **070.101–030**
Flight–test shop, **621.381–010**
Floral designers, **142.061–030**
Flying instructors, **097.227–010; 196.223–010**

Foam dispensers, **554.684–014**
Foam rubber mixers, **550.685–086**
Foam–gun operators, **741.684–014**
Foam–rubber molders, **556.685–046**
Folding machine operators, **653.382–010**
Food and drug inspectors, **168.267–042**
Food checkers, **211.482–014**
Food chemists, **022.061–014**
Food preparation quality control technicians, **529.387–030**
Food service managers, **187.167–106**
Food tabulator, **211.582–010**
Food technologists, **041.081–010**
Food–management aides, **195.367–022**
Foreign clerks, **214.476–010**
Foreign–exchange position clerks, **210.367–014**
Foreign–exchange trader, **186.167–014**
Foreign–Service officers, **188.117–106**
Foreign–student advisors, **090,107–010**
Forest civil engineers, **005.167–018**
Forest ecologists, **040.061–030**
Forest engineers, **005.167–018**
Foresters, **040.061–034**
Forestry technicians, **452.364–010**
Forming machine workers, **575.382–014**
Formula figurers, **216.482–022**
Foundry metallurgists, **011.061–010**
Four–H Club agents, **096.127–022**
Frame spinners, **682.685–010**
Frame wirers, **822.684–010**
Freezer operators, **529.482–010**
Front office managers, **187.167–110**
Front–end mechanics, **620.281–038**
Fruit–press operators, **521.685–146**
Fumigators, **383.361–010**
Fund–raising directors, **165.117–010**
Fundraisers, **165.117–010**

Funeral directors, **187.167–030**
Fur designers, **142.081–014**
Fur farmers, **410.161–014**
Furnace installers, **862.361–010**
Furnace operators, **512.362–010; 542.562–010**
Furnace–combustion analysts, **572.382–010**
Furniture and bedding inspectors, **168.267–046**
Furniture designers, **142.061–014**
Furniture finishers, **763.381–010**
Furniture movers, **905.**
Furniture upholsterer, **780.381–018**

Gambling dealers, **343.467–018**
Gambrelers, **525.687–030**
Garde managers, **313.361–034**
Gas engine engineers, **950.382–018**
Gas welders, **811.684–014**
Gas–appliance repairers, **637.261–018**
Gas–burner mechanics, **637.261–018**
Gas–regulator repairers, **710.381–026**
Gasoline service station attendants, **915.467–010**
Gate agents, **238.367–010**
Gem cutters, **770.281–014**
Gemnologists, **199.281–010**
Genealogists, **052.067–018**
General duty nurses, **075.374–010**
General farmers, **421.161–010**
General house workers, **301.474–010**
General maintenance mechanics, **899.**
General practitioners, **070.101–022**
Geneticists, **041.061–050**
Geodetic surveyors, **018.167–014**
Geodesists, **024.061–014**
Geographers, **029.067–010**
Geological drafters, **010.281–014**
Geologists, **024.061–018**
Geophysical drafters, **010.281–018**
Geophysical prospecting surveyors, **018.167–042**
Geophysical prospectors, **024.061–026**
Geophysicists, **024.061–030**

Geriatric nursing aides, **355.674–026**
Glass decorators, **775.381–014**
Glass manufacturing lab technicians, **579.384–014**
Glass manufacturing quality control technicians, **579.367–014**
Glass manufacturing workers, **772.687–010**
Glaziers, **865.381–010**
Golf–club assemblers, **732.684–078**
Government property inspectors, **168.267–050**
Graduate assistants, **090.227–014**
Grain broker and market operators, **162.157–010**
Grain buyers, **162.157–018; 162.167–010**
Grain elevator managers, **162.167–010**
Grain merchants, **162.157–010**
Granulator–machine operators, **559.382–026**
Graphic arts technicians, **979.382–018**
Graphic designers, **141.161–018**
Graphic programmers, **020.**
Greens superintendents, **406.137–014**
Greenskeepers I, **406.137–010**
Greenskeepers II, **406.683–010**
Greeting card editors, **132.067–010**
Grinders, **705.484–010**
Grinding–machine operators, **555.685–026**
Ground helpers, **821.684–014**
Ground services instructors, **099.227–018**
Groundwater professionals, **024.**
Group sales representatives, **259.357–010**
Group workers, **195.107–022; 195.164–010**
Group–sales representatives, **259.357–010**
Guidance counselors, **045.107–010**
Gunsmiths, **632.281–010**
Gynecologists, **070.101–034**

Hairstylists, **332.271–018**
Hammer operators, **610.462–010**

Laboratory animal care
veterinarians,
073.061–010

Laboratory equipment
cleaners, **381.687–022**

Laboratory supervisors,
022.137–010

Lace and textile restorers,
102.361–010

Lacquer makers,
559.682–030

Laminated plastics
assemblers and gluers,
754.684–014

Land development
managers, **186.117–042**

Land leases and rental
managers, **186.167–038**

Land surveying managers,
018.167–022

Land surveyors,
018.167–018

Landscape architects,
001.061–018

Landscape contractors,
182.167–014

Landscape drafters,
001.261–014

Landscape gardeners,
408.161–010

Landscape laborers,
408.687–014

Laser technicians,
019.181–010

Laser test technicians,
019.161–014

Laser–beam–color–scanner
operators, **972.282–014**

Lathers, **842.361–010**

Laundry workers,
361.684–014

Lawn and tree service
spray supervisors,
408.131–010

Lawn–service workers,
408.684–010

Lawyers, **110.107–010**

Lay–out technicians,
716.381–014

Layout workers,
809.281–010; 809.381–010

Lead recovers, **541.685–014**

Lease buyers, **191.117–030**

Leather coaters,
584.687–010

Legal secretaries,
201.362–010

Letter of credit negotiator,
186.117–050

Librarians, **100.127–014**

Library directors,
100.117–010

Library technicians,
100.367–018

Librettists, **131.067–030**

License inspectors,
168.267–066

Licensed practical nurses,
079–374–014

Light technicians,
962.362–014

Light, heat and power lab
technicians, **029.361–018**

Line fishers, **442.684–010**

Line installers,
821.361–018; 822.381–014

Line maintainers,
821.261–014

Line repairers, **821.361–026**

Linen–room attendants,
222.387–030

Linen–room supervisors,
222.137–014

Linguists, **059.**

Linkers, **529.687–150**

Linotype operators,
650.582–010

Liquor establishment
managers, **187.167–126**

Literary and talent agents,
191.117–010

Lithographic artists,
972.281–010

Lithographic press
operators, **651.382–014**

Livestock inspectors,
073.161–010

Livestock ranchers,
410.161–018

Load dispatchers,
952.167–014

Loan collection supervisors,
241.137–010

Loan counselors,
186.267–014

Loan officers, **186.267–018**

Lobbyists, **165.017–010**

Local truck drivers,
906.683–022

Locksmiths, **709.281–010**

Locomotive engineers,
910.363–014

Log graders, **455.367–010**

Log loaders, **921.683–058**

Logging industry workers,
454.684–018

Logging markers,
454.687–018

Logging superintendents,
183.167–038

Logging supervisors,
459.133–010

Logging-operations
inspectors, **168.267–070**

Logging-tractor operators,
929.683–010

Logistics engineers,
019.167–010

Long haulers, **904.383–010**

Lunchroom counter
attendants, **311.477–014**

Lyricists, **131.067–034**

Machine coremakers,
518.685–014

Machine drillers,
930.382–010

Machine milkers,
410.685–010

Machine molders,
518.682–010

Machine operators,
600.380–018

Machine tool operators,
601.280–054

Machine–records unit
supervisors,
213.132–014

Machinery erectors,
638.261–014

Machinists, **600.280–022**

Magazine keepers,
222.367–038

Magicians, **159.041–010**

Magistrates, **111.107–014**

Magnetic–tape composer
operators, **203.382–018**

Mail carrier supervisors,
230.137–018

Mail carriers, **230.367–010**

Mail clerks, **209.587–026**

Maintainability engineers,
019.081–010

Maintenance supervisors,
382.137–010

Management aides,
195.367–014

Management analysts and
consultants, **161.167–010**

Management trainees,
189.167–018

Managing editors,
132.017–010

Manicurists, **331.674–010**

Manual–arts therapists,
076.124–010

Manufacturer's sales
respresentatives,
279.157–010

Manufacturing engineers,
012.167–042; 189.117–014

Marble setters, **861.381–030**

Marine architects,
001.061–014

Marine drafters,
014.281–010

Marine engineers,
014.061–014

Marine engineers—research,
014.061–018

Marine engineers—sales,
014.151–010

Marine engineers—testing,
014.061–022

Marine surveyors,
018.167–046

Marine–cargo surveyors,
168.267–094

Marine–service technicians,
806.261–026

Maritime lawyers,
110.117–018

Market managers,
186.167–042

Market research analysts,
050.067–014

Market research managers,
050.067–014

Marketing managers,
164.117–010

Mat punchers, **690.685–286**

Material clerks,
222.387–034

Materials engineers,
019.061–014

Mathematical statisticians,
020.067–022

Mathematical technicians,
020.162–010

Mathematician,
020.067–014

Meat boners, **525.684–010**

Meatcutters, **316.684–018**

Mechanical design
engineers of facilities,
007.061–018

Mechanical design
engineers of products,
007.061–022

Mechanical drafters,
007.281–010

Mechanical engineers,
007.061–014

Mechanical equipment
testing engineers,
007.151–010

Mechanical laboratory
technicians, **715.261–010**

Mechanical research
engineers, **007.161–022**

Mechanical technician,
007.161–026

Mechanical technicians,
007.161–026

Mechanical test technicians,
869.261–014

Mechanics, **805.361–010**

Media assistants,
247.383–010

Media planners,
164.117–018

Mediators, **169.207–010**

Medical and scientific
illustrators, **141.061–014**

Medical assistants,
079.367–010

Medical caseworkers,
195.107–030

Medical laboratory
technicians, **078.381–014**

Medical officers,
070.101–046

Medical physicists,
079.021–014

Medical record
administrators,
079.167–014

Packaging technicians, 739.361–010
Paint–sample clerks, 206.367–014
Painters, 144.061–010; 840.381–010
Paintings restorers, 102.261–014
Paleontologists, 024.061–042
Paper–and–prints restorers, 109.361–010
Paper–machine operators, 539.362–014
Paperboard box estimators, 221.362–018
Paperhangers, 841.381–010
Paraffin–plant operators, 541.682–010
Paralegal assistant, 119.267–026
Parasitologists, 041.061–070
Park rangers, 169.167–042
Park technicians, 249.367–082
Parking enforcement officers, 375.263–010
Parking engineering technicians, 199.261–014
Parks and grounds groundskeepers, 406.687–010
Parole officers, 195.167–030
Parts clerks, 222.367–042
Parts–order–and–stock clerks, 249.367–058
Passenger car conductors, 198.167–010
Passenger rate clerks, 214.362–030
Passport–application examiners, 169.267–030
Pastry cooks, 313.381–026
Patent drafters, 007.261–018
Patent lawyers, 110.117–026
Pathologists, 070.061–010
Patrol conductors, 372.677–010
Pattern assemblers, 685.685–014
Patternmakers, 600.280–050
Payroll cashiers, 219.137–010
PBX operators, 235.662–022
Pediatricians, 070.101–066
Pedodontists, 072.101–026
Pelting room workers, 589.137–010
Perfumers, 022.161–018
Perfusionists, 078.362–034
Periodontists, 072.101–030
Peripheral equipment operators, 213.382–010

Personal attendants, 309.674–014
Personnel managers, 166.117–018
Personnel recruiters, 166.267–010; 166.267–038
Personnel service representatives, 236252.010
Pesticide control inspectors, 168.267–098
Petrol refining lab technicians, 029.261–022
Petroleum engineers, 010.061–018
Petroleum engineers—sales of equipment and services, 010.151–010
Petroleum engineers-design, 010.061–010
Petroleum laboratory technicians, 029.261–022
Petroleum prospecting engineers, 003.061–022
Petrologists, 024.061–046
Pharmaceutical compounding supervisors, 559.131–010
Pharmaceutical industry workers, 559.382–042
Pharmacists, 074.161–010
Pharmacologists, 041.061–074
Pharmacy technicians, 355.374–014
Philologists, 059.067–101
Photo checkers and assemblers, 976.687–014
Photo–optics technicians, 029.280–010
Photoengravers, 971.381–022
Photofinishing quality control technicians, 976.276–010
Photogrammetric engineers, 018.167–026
Photogrammetrists, 018.261–026
Photograph finishers, 976.487–010
Photographic darkroom technicians, 976.681–010
Photographic engineers, 019.081–014
Photographic equipment maintenance technicians, 714.281–026
Photographic equipment technicians, 714.281–022
Photographers, 971.382–014
Photojournalists, 143.062–034
Photolithographic strippers, 972.381–022

Phototypesetting equipment monitors, 650.682–010
Phototypesetting operators, 650.582–022
Physiatrists, 070.101–070
Physical anthropologists, 055.067–014
Physical education teachers, 099.224–010
Physical metallurgists, 011.061–022
Physical therapists, 076.121–014
Physical therapy assistants, 076.224–010
Physical–education instructors, 153.227–014
Physician assistants, 079.364–018
Physicians, 070.; 071.
Physicists, 023.061–014
Physiologist, 041.061–078
Piano technicians, 730.281–038
Piano tuners, 730.361–010
Picklers, 522.687–034
Pie makers, 313.361–038
Pier superintendents, 911.137–022
Pig–machine operators, 514.362–010
Pigment processors, 559.685–130
Pilot instructors, 196.223–014
Pilots, 196.
Pinsetter mechanics, 638.261–022
Pipe cutters, 862.682–010
Pipe fitters, 862.381–018
Pipe organ installers, 730.381–046
Pipe organ technicians, 730.361–014
Pipe testers, 930.382–014
Pipe–organ tuners and repairers 730.361–014
Pipefitters, 862.381–018
Placement directors, 166.167–014
Planetarium technicians, 962.261–010
Planimeter operators, 219.387–022
Plant breeders, 041.061–082
Plant engineers, 007.167–014
Plant maintenance technicians, 822.281–030
Plant managers, 183.167–026
Plant pathologists, 041.061–086
Plant propagators, 405.361–010
Plasterers, 842.361–018

Plastics pattern makers, 754.381–014
Platemakers, 972.381–010
Platen press operators, 651.362–108
Plater, 500.380–010
Plater supervisors, 500.131–010
Playwrights, 131.067–038
Plumbers, 862.381–030
Plumbing drafters, 017.261–038
Plumbing inspectors, 168.167–050
Podiatrists, 079.101–022
Poets, 131.067–042
Police clerks, 375.362–010
Police district switchboard operators, 235.562–014
Police officers, 375.263–018
Police officers, 375.367–010
Police–academy instructors, 375.227–010
Policy–change clerks, 219.362–042
Political scientists, 051.067–010
Pollution–control engineers, 019.081–018
Pollution–control technicians, 029.261–014
Polygraph examiners, 199.265–826
Polystyrene–bead molders, 556.382–018
Port engineers, 014.167–014
Postal clerks, 243.367–014
Pot fishers, 441.684–014
Pottery–and–porcelain-decorating instructors, 240.221–010
Poultice–machine operators, 692.685–134
Poultry boners, 525.687–066
Poultry dressers, 525.687–070
Poultry farmers, 411.161–018
Poultry field service technicians, 411.267–010
Poultry hangers, 525.687–078
Poultry killers, 525.684–042
Poultry scientists, 040.061–042
Poultry veterinarians, 073.101–014
Poured–concrete–wall technicians, 869.261–018
Power plant operators, 952.382–018
Power system engineers, 003.167–108
Power–distribution engineers, 003.167–046

Power–reactor operators, 952.362–022

Practical nurses, 354.374–010

Precision–lens technicians, 716.280–008

Prefab plumbers, 862.681–010

Preparole counseling aides, 195.367–026

Preschool teachers, 092.227–018

Prescription clerks, 222.367–050

Press operators, 611.482–010

Pressers, 575.685–074

Print controllers, 976.360–010

Print shop stenographers, 202.362–018

Printing press operators, 651.482–010

Private branch exchange advisers, 235.222–010

Private duty nurses, 057.374–018

Private investigators, 376.267–018

Probate clerks, 216.362–030

Probate lawyers, 110.1117–030

Probation officers, 195.167–034

Probation–and–parole officers, 195.107–046

Process control programmers, 020.187–014

Proctologists, 070.101–086

Procurement engineers, 162.157–034

Producers, 159.117–010

Product test technicians, 019.161–014

Product–safety engineers, 012.061–010

Production engineers, 012.167–046

Production managers, 652.137–010

Production proofreaders, 247.667–010

Professional athletes, 153.341–010

Professional athletes coaches, 153.227–010

Professional conciliators, 169.207–010

Professional sports scouts, 153.117–018

Profile–grinder technicians, 601.482–010

Project engineers, 019.167–014

Projection printers, 976.381–018

Promotion managers, 163.117–018

Prompters, 152.367–010

Proof technicians, 199.171–010

Proofreaders, 209.387–030

Property accountants, 160.167–022

Property and casualty insurance agents and brokers, 250.257–010

Property and real estate managers, 186.

Property custodians, 222.387–042

Prose writers, 131.067–046

Prospecting operators, 930.382–018

Prosthetics assistants, 078.361–026

Prosthetics technicians, 712.381–038

Prosthetists, 078.261–022

Prosthodontists, 072.101–034

Protection engineers, 003.167–054

Protestant ministers, 120.007–010

Psychiatric aide instructors, 075.127–010

Psychiatric aides, 355.377–014

Psychiatric technicians, 079.374–026

Psychiatric–aide instructors, 075.127–010

Psychologists, 045.

Psychometrists, 045.067–018

Public events facilities rental managers, 186.117–062

Public housing community–relations–and–service workers, 195.167–014

Public relations managaers, 165.067–010

Public relations representatives, 165.067–010

Public relations specialists, 165.067–010

Public–health dentists, 072.101–038

Public–health microbiologists, 041.261–010

Pullman (sleeping car) conductors, 198.167–014

Pulmonary function technicians, 078.262–010

Pulp and paper testers, 539.364–010

Puppeteers, 159.041–014

Purchase–price analysts, 162.167–030

Purchasing agents, 162.157–038

Purser, 197.167–014

Pyschiatric caseworkers, 195.107–034

Pyschiatrists, 070.107–014

Quality assurance inspectors, 168.287–014

Quality control engineers, 012.167–054

Quality control technicians, 012.261–014

Quality–control engineers, 012.167–054

Quartermaster, 911.363–014

Rabbis, 120.007–010

Radiation protection engineers, 015.137–010

Radiation–therapy technologists, 078.361–034

Radio and television announcers, 159.147–010

Radio and television time salespeople, 259.357–018

Radio communications superintendents, 193.167–018

Radio directors, 159.067–010

Radio officer, 193.262–022

Radio officers, 193.262–022

Radio operators, 193.

Radio station operators, 193.262–026

Radio–intelligence operators, 193.362–014

Radio–telegraph operators, 193.262–030

Radioactive materials waste management engineers, 005.061–042

Radiologic technologist, 078.362–026

Radiologists, 070.101–090

Radiology directors, 070.117–014

Radiopharmacists, 074.161–014

Radiotelephone operators, 193.262–034

Rail–tractor operators, 919.683–018

Railroad civil engineers, 005.061–026

Railroad conductors, 198.167

Railroad inspectors, 168.287–018

Railroad maintenance clerks, 221.362–026

Range managers, 040.061–046

Rate reviewers, 214.387–014

Raters, 214.482–022

Real estate agents, 186.117–058

Real estate brokers, 250.357–018

Real estate firm managers, 186.167–066

Real estate lawyers, 110.117–034

Receiving and processing supervisors, 579.137–026

Receptionists, 237.367–038

Record clerks, 206.387–022

Record custodians, 206.387–026

Recording engineers, 194.362–010

Recording industry workers, 194.

Recreation aides, 195.367–030

Recreation center directors, 195.167–026

Recreation leaders, 195.227–014

Recreation supervisors, 187.137–010

Recruiters, 166.267–038

Redrying–machine operators, 522.622–014

Refinery laborers, 549.687–018

Refrigerating engineers, 950.362–014

Refuse collectors, 909.687–010

Registrars, 090.167–030

Rehabilitation counselors. 045.107–042

Relay technicians, 821.261–018

Reliability engineers, 019.081–022

Reporters and correspondants, 131.267–018

Repossessors, 241.367–022

Reproduction technicians, 976.361–010

Reptile farmers, 413.161–014

Rescue workers, 373.167–018; 373.663–010

Research and development directors, 189.117–014

Research associate‑ 109.067–014

Research dietitians, 077.061–010

Reservation agents, 238.137–014

Reservations clerks, 238.367–014

Unleavended dough mixers,
520.685–226
Upper–leather sorters,
788.387–010
Upsetters, 611.462–010
Urban and regional
planners, 199.167–014
Urologists, 070.101–098
Used–car renovators,
620.684–010
Ushers, 3444.677–014
Utilization engineers,
007.061–034

Van drivers, 905.663–018
Van–driver helpers,
905.687–014
Varnish makers,
553.382–022
Vegetable farmers,
402.161–010
Vending–machine
mechanics, 639.281–014
Ventriloquists, 159.044–010
Verifier and sorting–
machine operators,
203.582–070; 208.685–030
Verifier operators,
203.582–070
Veterans' coordinators,
169.267–026
Veterinarians, 073.101–010
Veterinary anatomists,
073.061–014
Veterinary bacteriologists,
073.061–018

Veterinary epidemiologists,
073.061–022
Veterinary lab technicians,
073.361–010
Veterinary meat–inpsectors,
073.264–010
Veterinary parasitologists,
073.061–026
Veterinary pathologists,
073.061–030
Veterinary pharmacologists,
073.061–034
Veterinary virologists,
073.061–042
Veterinary virus–serum
inspectors, 073.261–010
Veterninary physiologists,
073.061–038
Violin repairers,
730.281–050
Vocational–rehabilitation
counselors, 045.107–042
Vocational–training
instructors, 097.227–014
Voltage testers,
821.381–014

Wage and salary
administrators,
166.167–022
Waiters and waitresses,
311.477–026
Wall cleaners, 381.687–026
Wastewater–treatmaent
plant chemists,
022.261–022

Wastewater–treatment–plant
operators, 955.362–010
Watch repairers and
watchmakers,
715.281–010
Watch–assembly instructors,
715.221–010
Water tenders, 599.685–122
Water–pollution control
inspectors, 168.267–090
Water–purification chemists,
022.281–014
Water–treatment plant
operators, 954.382–014
Waterworks engineers,
005.167–010
Waterworks pump–station,
954.382–010
Weavers or loom operators,
683.682–038
Weaving instructors,
683.222–010
Weed inspectors,
408.381–014
Weight analysts,
020.187–018
Weir fishers, 441.684–022
Welders, 805.381–010
Welding engineers,
011.061–026
Welding machine operators,
810.382–010
Welding technicians,
011.261–014
Well pullers, 930.382–030
Wholesale trade sales
workers,
260. to 279.357

Wholesalers, 185.157–018
Wind–instrument repairers,
730.281–054
Window unit air–
conditioning installer
servicers, 637.261–010
Wipers, 699.687–014
Wire editors, 132.267–010
Wood patternmakers,
661.281–022
Woods bosses, 459.137–010
Wool pullers, 589.687–050
Word–processing operators,
203.362–022
Worm growers,
413.161–018

X–ray technicians,
199.361–010

Yard clerks, 209.367–054
Yard couplers, 910.664–010
Yard workers, 301.687–018
Yarding engineers,
921.663–066
Young–adult librarians,
100.167–034

Zoo veterinarians,
073.101–018
Zookeeper, 412.674–010
Zoologists, 041.061–090

Photographic Credits

497

Index

500

501

506

512

520